Training Manual on International Environmental Law

FOREWORD

Today's world is facing an unprecedented environmental crisis. Deterioration of the Earth's environment increasingly threatens the natural resource base and processes upon which all life on Earth depends. Without strong and multifaceted action by all of us, the biosphere may become unable to sustain human life and future generations will suffer deprivation and hardship unless current patterns of production, consumption and waste management dramatically change. The urgency of balancing development with the Earth's life support systems is being finally recognized and understood. Now it is time to act upon this understanding.

It is widely recognized that most environmental problems, challenges and solutions are transboundary, regional or global in scope. The environment is an area where states and stakeholders are cooperating extensively and progressively. Although environmental degradation and competition for scarce resources are potential sources for conflict, history has repeatedly shown that they are more often catalysts for cooperation. Problems of shared resources regularly produce shared solutions. The environment can make its full and rightful contribution to peace and stability in the world.

Worldwide commitments are necessary to protect environmental features such as the biosphere including the ozone layer, migratory species, habitats and ecosystems. Control of movement of wastes, environmentally harmful activities and installations can only be achieved by common and widely applied standards. Environmental law is recognized as an effective tool for catalyzing national and international action to achieve such protection and control. As one of UNEP's priority areas, environmental law has expanded rapidly over the last decades and today comprises hundreds of global and regional norms that aim to protect our Earth.

Without analyzing each of the hundreds of agreements and instruments in the field, this Training Manual seeks to provide a comprehensive overview of the current body of environmental law. It is aimed at legal stakeholders from all backgrounds including government representatives, judges, university professors and students from both developed and developing countries, to enable them to more effectively participate in the global, regional and national efforts to preserve our Earth for future generations.

Specific topics are first presented at the international level and then followed by extracts of national legislation showcasing real life examples of how national law today reflects developments in the international arena.

Klaus Töpfer
Executive Director
United Nations Environment Programme

ACKNOWLEDGEMENTS

Writing this book was a collaborative effort and the editors are indebted to many people. First and foremost we like to express our gratitude to all internationally acclaimed authors for contributing their expertise to the different chapters of this Training Manual. The editors further thank Donald Kaniaru for using his scrutinizing eyes and boundless knowledge in the final stages of this publication, as well as Melis Lucas Korlaar, Pieter Thomaes, Justin Wolst, Paul Awi and especially María Elena García Mora for their advice and assistance.

We are grateful also to the Pace University School of Law Center for Environmental Legal Studies, including the Law School's Dean, Prof. Stephen Friedman, the Center's Co-Director, Prof. Richard L. Ottinger, and the Director of the Pace Law School's Environmental Law Programs, Prof. LeRoy Paddock, and the environmental law interns at the Center: Deepa Bandrinaraya, Laura Bucher, Erin Flanagan, Megan Kelly, Susan Marriott, and Janice Woods Weber. The contributions of Leslie Crincoli and Mary Stagliano are gratefully acknowledged also.

The editors wish to furthermore thank the visionary frontrunners who pioneered the development of UNEP's first Environmental Law Training Manual, in particular Professor Ben Boer. Last but not least the editors are indebted to the many legal experts who participated in UNEP training courses useful suggestions and comments on this editions predecessor. In the same spirit comments of those who come to use this edition are most welcome to further enrich future editions of this Training Manual.

Lal Kurukulasuriya
Chief, Environmental Law Branch (retired)
Division of Environmental Policy & Law
United Nations Environment Programme

and

Nicholas A. Robinson
Gilbert & Sarah Kerlin Distinguished Professor
of Environmental Law
Pace University School of Law (New York)
On behalf of the IUCN Academy of Environmental Law

TABLE OF CONTENTS

Foreword iii
Acknowledgements v

Chapter 1: Multilateral environmental agreements 1
    I.   Introduction 1
    II.   Sources of international environmental law 1
        1. Law of treaties 2
        2. Customary international law 7
        3. General principles of law 8
        4. Judicial decisions and qualified teachings 9
    III. Negotiating multilateral environmental agreements 9
    IV. Administering treaties 11

Chapter 2: The role of national environmental law 15
    I.   Introduction 15
    II.   Foundations of national environmental law 15
        1. Environmental law and sustainable development 17
        2. The prerequisites for effective national environmental law 17
            a) Adequate regulation and institutional regimes 17
            b) The role of case law 18
            c) Implementation, enforcement and compliance of national laws 18
        3. Template for elements of comprehensive national legal regimes for
            environmentally managing of different sectors 19
        4. Implementation of international environmental law at the national level 20
        5. UNEP's capacity building programme on environmental law 20

Chapter 3: Principles and concepts of international environmental law 23
    I.   Introduction 23
    II.   Overview of international environmental law principles and concepts 23
    III. Emerging principles and concepts 24
        1. Sustainable development, integration and interdependence 25
        2. Inter-generational and intra-generational equity 26
        3. Responsibility for transboundary harm 27
        4. Transparency, public participation and access to information and remedies ... 28
        5. Cooperation, and common but differentiated responsibilities 29
        6. Precaution 30
        7. Prevention 32
        8. "Polluter Pays Principle" 33
        9. Access and benefit sharing regarding natural resources 35
        10. Common heritage and common concern of humankind 36
        11. Good governance 36

Chapter 4: Compliance and enforcement of multilateral environmental agreements 39
    I.   Introduction 39
    II.   International framework 39
        1. The importance of compliance and enforcement 40
        2. Institutional arrangements for the implementation of MEAs 41
            a) Conferences/meetings of the Parties of a MEA 41
            b) Convention secretariats 41
            c) Advisory bodies 41
            d) Reporting mechanisms to track progress in the implementation of treaties ... 42
            e) Financial mechanisms 42
            f) Non-compliance procedures/mechanisms 43
        3. Effectiveness of the non-compliance procedure 44
        4. Capacity building programmes: the role of international organizations and
            compliance and enforcement networks 45

	5.		Compliance and enforcement opportunities	46
	III.		National implementation	47

Chapter 5: Liability and compensation regimes related to environmental damage — 51
	I.	Introduction	51
	II.	International framework	51
		1. *Rationale* for introducing liability regimes for environmental damage	51
		2. Liability for environmental damage versus traditional liability systems	52
		3. State responsibility and liability versus civil liability	52
		4. State responsibility and liability for environmental harm	53
		a) Transboundary environmental damage	53
		b) State responsibility and state liability	53
		c) State responsibility for wrongful acts	53
		d) State liability for lawful acts	55
		e) Civil liability regimes for environmental damage	57
		f) Types of civil liability for environmental damage	57
		g) Scope and threshold of environmental damage	58
		5. Who is liable?	58
		6. Forms of compensation	58
		7. International civil liability	59

Chapter 6: The Global Environment Facility — 65
	I.	Introduction	65
	II.	GEF structure	65
	III.	National participation, eligibility and coordination	66
	IV.	GEF projects	66
	V.	Project eligibility and basic principles of the GEF	67
	VI.	GEF programming framework: focal areas, operational programmes and strategic	68
		1. Focal areas	68
		2. Operational programmes	68
		3. Strategic priorities in the current phase of the GEF	68
	VII.	The GEF project cycle	69
		1. Full size projects	70
		2. Medium-sized projects	70
		3. Enabling activities	70
		4. Small grant projects	70
	VIII.	The GEF project portfolio scope and division of responsibility among GEF agencies	70
	IX.	UNEP as an implementing agency of the Global Environment Facility	71
	X.	The scientific and technical advisory panel of the GEF	71
	XI.	UNEP/GEF projects	72
		1. Regional environmental frameworks and programmes of action	72
		a) Africa	72
		b) Central Asia	73
		c) Asia	73
		d) Latin America	73
		(i) Formulation of a water resources management framework for the Plata river basin	73
		(ii) Supporting stakeholder participation in international environmental legal processes	74
		(iii) Fostering active and effective civil society participation in preparations for implementation of the Stockholm Convention	74
		(iv) The global biodiversity forum: multistakeholder support for the implementation of the Convention on Biological Diversity	74
		(v) The indigenous peoples' network for change	74
		(vi) Providing environmental information for policy making	74

(vii) Building national capacity to implement global environmental agreements		75
a) Biodiversity		75
b) Biosafety – the safe use of biotechnology		75
c) Climate change		75
d) Climate change national adaptation programme of action		76
e) Persistent organic pollutants		76
f) National capacity needs self-assessment for global environmental management		76
(xii) Current developments within the GEF		76

Chapter 7: Information, public participation, and access to justice in environmental matters — 79
I. Introduction — 79
II. International framework — 80
  1. Global principles — 80
  2. Global conventions — 82
  3. Regional conventions — 85
  4. Non-binding international legal instruments — 85
III. National implementation — 86

Chapter 8: Transboundary air pollution — 91
I. Introduction — 91
II. International framework — 91
  1. Long-range transboundary air pollution — 91
    a) The problem — 91
    b) Smog — 91
    c) The Geneva Convention on Long-Range Transboundary Air Pollution — 92
    d) LRTAP's general rules — 92
    e) Protocols to 1979 LRTAP — 92
    f) LRTAP compliance and supervision — 94
  2. Haze pollution — 95
    a) The problem — 95
    b) Negotiation history — 95
III. National implementation — 96
  1. Europe — 96
    a) Austria — 96
    b) Poland — 96
  2. Asia — 97
IV. The 2002 ASEAN Agreement — 98

Chapter 9: Ozone depletion — 101
I. Introduction — 101
II. International framework — 102
  1. The Vienna Convention for the Protection of the Ozone Layer — 102
  2. The 1987 Montreal Protocol on Substances that Deplete the Ozone Layer — 102
    a) Institutions — 103
    b) The Multilateral Fund, its executive committee and secretariat — 104
    c) Non-compliance procedure — 105
III. National implementation — 106
  1. Malaysia — 106
  2. Canada — 107
  3. South Africa — 109

Chapter 10: Global climate change — 111
I. Introduction — 111
II. International framework — 111
  1. The climate change convention regime — 111
  2. The United Nations Framework Convention on Climate Change — 113
    a) Capacity building and financial mechanism — 114

		b)	Compliance and dispute settlement	114
	3.	The Kyoto Protocol to the United Nations Framework Convention on Climate Change		115
		a)	The negotiations	115
		b)	Commitments	115
		c)	The flexible mechanisms	116
	4.	Compliance mechanism – compliance committee		118
III.	National implementation			119
	1.	Europe		119
	2.	Japan		120
	3.	China		121

Chapter 11: Hazardous wastes — **125**

I.	Introduction			125
II.	Institutional framework			126
	1.	Multilateral instruments on hazardous wastes		126
		a)	Basel Convention on the Control of Transboundary Movements of Hazardous Wastes and their Disposal	126
			i. Background and contents of the convention	126
			ii. Strict control of transboundary movement of hazardous wastes	127
			iii. Environmentally sound management of hazardous wastes	129
			iv. Enforcement of provisions for strict control of transboundary movements and for environmentally sound management of hazardous wastes	130
			v. Dispute settlement mechanisms	131
			vi. Institutional framework for implementation	131
			vii. Developments since the adoption of the convention	
		b)	Marine environment compensation and liability agreements and marine pollution prevention agreements	132
			i. Marine environmental compensation and liability agreements	132
			ii. Marine pollution prevention agreements	133
		c)	Convention for Prevention of Marine Pollution by Dumping of Wastes and Other Matter	134
	2.	Regional instruments on hazardous wastes		134
		a)	Bamako Convention on the Ban of Imports into Africa and the Control of Transboundary Movement and Management of Hazardous Wastes within Africa	134
		b)	Regional sea agreements	135
			i. Convention for the Protection and Development of Marine Environment of the Wider Caribbean Region	135
			ii. Kuwait region.	135
			ii.a. Kuwait Regional Convention on the Protection of the Marine Environment from Pollution	136
			ii.b. Kuwait Regional Protocol on the Control of Marine Transboundary Movements and Disposal of Hazardous Wastes and other Wastes	137
			iii. Convention to Ban the Importation into the Forum Island Countries of Hazardous and Radioactive Wastes and to Control the Transboundary Movement and Management of Hazardous Wastes within the South Pacific Region	138
	3.	Bilateral instruments on hazardous wastes		139
	4.	Non-legally binding instruments on hazardous wastes		139
III.	National implementation			139
	1.	Japan		140
	2.	Kenya		141

Chapter 12: Chemicals   **145**
   I.   Introduction   145
   II.   The international framework   145
        1.   Rotterdam Convention on the Prior Informed Consent procedure for
            certain hazardous chemicals and pesticides in international trade   147
               a)   Institutions   148
               b)   PIC procedure   148
               c)   Information exchange   148
               d)   Core PIC procedure   148
               e)   PIC listing   149
               f)   Import decisions   149
               g)   General obligations   149
               h)   Technical assistance   149
               i)   Non-compliance   150
        2.   Stockholm Convention on Persistent Organic Pollutants   150
               a)   Intentionally produced POPs   150
               b)   Unintentionally produced POPs   151
               c)   Stockpiles   151
               d)   General obligations   151
               e)   Institutions   152
               f)   Addition of new POPs   152
               g)   Financial and technical assistance   152
               h)   Non-compliance   152
        3.   Clustering of related agreements   152
   III.   National implementation   153
        1.   The European Union – PIC procedure   153
        2.   Ghana – PIC and POPs   153

Chapter 13: Marine pollution   **157**
   I.   Introduction   157
   II.   International framework   157
        1.   The problem   157
        2.   The law of the sea process   158
        3.   The law of the sea and the marine environment   159
        4.   Land-based sources of marine pollution   160
        5.   Vessel-based sources of marine pollution   161
        6.   Dumping of wastes at sea   164
        7.   Offshore hydrocarbon and mineral recovery   165
        8   Regional sea agreements   165
               a)   Convention for the Protection of the Marine Environment and
                   the Coastal Region of the Mediterranean   166
               b)   Convention for the Protection and Development of the Marine
                   Environment of the Wider Caribbean Region   167
               c)   Convention for the Protection of the Marine Environment of
                   the North-East Atlantic   167
   III.   National implementation   168
        1.   Romania   168
        2.   South Africa   168
        3.   Australia   168

**Chapter 14: Conservation of species and habitats, including trade in and sustainable use of
              endangered species**   **171**
   I.   Introduction   171
   II.   International framework   171
        1.   The 1979 Convention on the Conservation of Migratory Species of Wild Animals   171
               a)   Obligations and Instruments   172

	b)	Appendix I species	173
	c)	Appendix II species and other species	173
	d)	National implementation	173
	e)	Relationship and cooperation with other biodiversity related MEAs	174
	f)	Agreements concluded under the CMS	174
		i. Agreement on the conservation of seals in the Wadden Sea	174
		ii. Agreement on the conservation of small cetaceans of the Baltic and North Seas	174
		iii. Agreement on the conservation of populations of European bats	174
		iv. Agreement in the conservation of African-Eurasian migratory waterbirds	175
		v. Agreement on the conservation of cetaceans of the Black Sea, Mediterranean Sea and contiguous Atlantic area	175
		vi. Memorandum of understanding concerning conservation measures for the Siberian crane	175
		vii. Memorandum of understanding concerning conservation for the slender-billed curlew	175
		viii. Agreement on the conservation of albatrosses and petrels	176
		ix. Memorandum of understanding on the conservation and management of marine turtles and their habitats of the Indian Ocean and South East Asia	176
		x. Memorandum of understanding concerning conservation measures for marine turtles of the Atlantic coast of Africa	176
		xi. Memorandum of understanding on the conservation and management of the Middle-European population of the great bustard	177
		xii. Memorandum of understanding concerning conservation and restoration of the Bukhara deer	177
		xiii. Memorandum of understanding and action plan concerning measures for the aquatic warbler	177
2.		The 1971 Ramsar Convention on Wetlands of International Importance especially as Waterfowl Habitat	177
	a)	Obligations	178
	b)	National implementation	179
	c)	Institutions	179
	d)	Relationship and cooperation with other biodiversity related MEAs	179
3.		The 1973 Convention on International Trade in Endangered Species of Wild Flora and Fauna ("CITES")	179
	a)	Definitions	180
	b)	Obligations and structure	180
		i. Trade in appendix I specimens (article III)	180
		ii. Trade in appendix II specimens (article IV)	181
		iii. Trade in appendix III specimens (article V)	181
		iv. Compliance and enforcement	181
	c)	National implementation	181
	d)	Institutions	182
	e)	Relationship and cooperation with other biodiversity-related MEAs	182
4.		The 1994 Lusaka Agreement on Cooperative Enforcement Operations Directed at Illegal Trade in Wild Flora and Fauna	182
	a)	Obligations of the parties	183
	b)	National implementation	183
	c)	Institutions	183
	d)	Relationship and cooperation with other biodiversity-related MEAs	183
5.		The 1972 Convention Concerning the Protection of the World Cultural and Natural Heritage	184
	a)	World Heritage Committee	185
	b)	World Heritage List	185

		c)	List of World Heritage in Danger	185
		d)	International assistance	186
		e)	World Heritage Fund	186
		f)	Advisory bodies	186
		g)	Secretariat	186
		h)	National implementation, supervision and compliance	187
		i)	Relationship with other biodiversity-related MEAs	187
III.	National implementation			187
	1.	Uganda: implementing the Ramsar convention		187
	2.	Singapore: implementing CITES		189
	3.	South Africa: implementing the World Heritage Convention		189

Chapter 15: Biological diversity — **193**

I.	Introduction			193
II.	International framework			193
1.	The Convention on Biological Diversity			194
		a)	General principles and concepts	195
		b)	Measures for the conservation and sustainable use	196
		c)	Access to genetic resources and benefit sharing	197
		d)	Access to and transfer of technology	199
		e)	The role of indigenous and local communities	201
		f)	International cooperation and the financial mechanism	202
		g)	Institutional arrangements	203
		h)	Compliance, liability and dispute settlement	203
		i)	Relationship with other international agreements	203
	2.	Intellectual property rights and biological diversity		204
	3.	International convention for the protection of new varieties of plants		207
		a)	Agenda 21	208
		b)	FAO global system for the conservation and sustainable use of plant genetic resources	208
III.	National implementation			211
	1.	Costa Rica		211
	2.	India		212
	3.	China		213

Chapter 16: Biosafety — **217**

I.	Introduction			217
II.	International framework			218
1.	General			219
2.	Some of the specific requirements of the Cartagena Protocol on Biosafety			219
		a)	Advance informed agreement procedure	219
		b)	LMOs intended for direct use of food, feed or for processing	220
		c)	Risk assessment and risk management	221
		d)	Information sharing	221
		e)	Unintentional transboundary movement of LMOs (article 17)	222
		f)	Identification of LMOs	222
		g)	Confidential information (article 21)	222
		h)	Capacity building (article 22)	222
		i)	Public awareness and participation (article 23)	222
		j)	Compliance procedure and mechanisms (article 34)	222
		k)	Liability and redress (article 27)	223
		l)	Transboundary movement of LMOs with non-parties	223
		m)	Administration of the Biosafety Protocol	223
	3.	Relationship of the Cartagena Protocol with other agreements		223
III.	National Implementation			224
	1.	Indonesia		224

| | | 2. | Australia | 225 |
| | | 3. | Cuba | 225 |

Chapter 17: Protecting and preserving marine biodiversity, including through sustainable fisheries   **229**

I.	Introduction			229
II.	International framework			232
	1.	Global legally binding instruments		232
		a)	United Nations Convention on the Law of the Sea	232
		b)	Fish Stocks Agreement and other developments	235
		c)	Convention on Biological Diversity	236
		d)	Global conventions on marine pollution	238
		e)	International Convention for the Regulation of Whaling	239
	2.	Regional legally binding instruments		241
		a)	Regional fisheries management organizations	241
			i. International Convention for the Conservation of Atlantic Tunas	241
			ii. Convention on the Conservation of Antarctic Marine Living Resources	242
		b)	Regional sea agreements	243
			i. Convention for the Protection and Development of the Marine Environment of the Wider Caribbean Region (Cartagena Convention)	243
			ii. OSPAR convention	244
	3.	Global non-legally binding instruments		245
		a)	Rio Declaration and Agenda 21	245
		b)	FAO Code of Conduct for Responsible Fisheries	245
		c)	Johannesburg Plan of Implementation	246
III.	National implementation			246
		a)	China: implementation of UNCLOS	246
		b)	Belize: implementation of UNCLOS	247
		c)	Australia: implementation of the Convention on Biological Diversity	248

Chapter 18: Freshwater resources   **253**

I.	Introduction			253
	1.	The hydrological cycle		253
	2.	Water scarcity		255
	3.	Water pollution		255
	4.	Water uses		255
II.	International framework			256
	1.	Major developments in the field of cooperation on freshwater		256
	2.	Freshwater regulation at the international level		257
		a)	The 1997 United Nations Convention on the Law of Non-navigational Uses of International Watercourses	258
	3.	Freshwater regulation at the regional and subregional level		260
		a)	The 1992 UNECE Convention on the Protection and Use of Transboundary Watercourses and International Lakes	260
		b)	Protocol on Shared Watercourse Systems in the Southern African Development Community	261
		c)	Agreements concerning specific watercourses	262
III.	National implementation			263
	1.	Major trends in national legislation		263
	2.	Lessons learned		264

Chapter 19: Desertification   **269**

I.	Introduction			269
II.	International context			269
	1.	The problem		269
	2.	Causes and consequences		270
	3.	Scope and magnitude of the problem		270

III.   National/regional examples   271
   1.   Chile   271
   2.   China   271
   3.   Africa   271
IV.   The international legal regime   272
   1.   Committee on science and technology   274
   2.   Resolution of disputes   275
   3.   Developments since adoption   275
V.   National Implementation   276
   1.   China   276
   2.   Malawi   277
   3.   Cameroon   278

Chapter 20: Mountain, forest and polar ecosystems   **281**
I.   Introduction   281
II.   Mountain ecosystems   281
   1.   Ecosystem characteristics and vulnerabilities   281
   2.   International environmental regime relating to mountain ecosystems   282
      a)   Convention on the Protection of the Alps   282
      b)   Framework Convention on the Protection and Sustainable Development of the Carpathians   283
      c)   Non-legally binding instruments   284
   3.   National and local initiatives relating to mountain ecosystems   285
III.   Forest ecosystems   286
   1.   Ecosystem characteristics and vulnerabilities   286
   2.   International environmental regime relating to forest ecosystems   287
      a)   The Ramsar Convention on Wetlands of International Importance, especially as Waterfowls Habitat   287
      b)   The Convention Concerning the Protection of the World Cultural and Natural Heritage   288
      c)   The Convention on International Trade in Endangered Species of Wild Flora and Fauna   288
      d)   The Rio Conference instruments   288
      e)   The International Tropical Timber Agreement   289
      f)   The Rio Forest Principles   290
   3.   National initiatives relating to forest ecosystems   291
      a)   United States   291
      b)   Japan   292
IV.   Polar ecosystems   293
   1.   Ecosystem characteristics and vulnerabilities   293
   2.   International environmental regime relating to Antarctica   296
      a)   The Antarctic Treaty   296
      b)   Convention for the Conservation of Antarctic Seals   297
      c)   Convention on the Conservation of Antarctic Marine Living Resources   297
      d)   Protocol on Environmental Protection to the Antarctic Treaty   299
   3.   International environmental regime relating to the Arctic   300
      a)   Declaration on the Protection of the Arctic Environment   300
      b)   The Arctic Council   300
      c)   The Barrow Declaration   300
      d)   Regional programme of action for the protection of Arctic marine environment from land-based activities   301
      e)   Sub-regional regimes   301
      f)   Legally binding instruments   301
   4.   National and local initiatives relating to the polar regions' ecosystems   301
      a)   United States   302
      b)   Australia   303

Chapter 21: Environmental impact assessment — 307
   I.   Introduction — 307
   II. International framework — 308
      1. Convention on Environmental Impact Assessment in a Transboudary Context — 308
      2. Protocol on Strategic Environmental Assessment — 309
   III. National implementation — 310
      1. Brazil — 310
      2. Uganda — 310
      3. Kiribati — 311

Chapter 22: Human rights and the environment — 313
   I.   Introduction — 313
      1. General — 313
      2. The relationship between human rights and environmental law — 313
      3. Human rights relevant to the environment — 314
   II. International framework — 314
      1. Human rights instruments — 314
      2. Environmental law instruments — 316
      3. The international framework from an indigenous peoples' perspective — 317
   III. Regional human rights systems — 318
      1. The European Convention on Human Rights — 318
      2. The Inter-American human rights system — 319
      3. The African human rights system — 321
   IV. National implementation: national legislation/judicial decisions — 321
      1. Philippines — 322
      2. India — 322
         a) The right to life — 322
         b) Equality before the law — 322
         c) The right to property — 323
         d) Environmental laws and policies — 323
         e) Procedural right — 323
         f) Right to remedy — 323
      3. South Africa — 323
         a) Right to life — 323
         b) Equality before the law — 324
         c) The right to property — 324

Chapter 23: International labour, health and the environment — 327
   I.   Introduction — 327
   II. International framework — 327
      1. The problem — 327
      2. International regulatory bodies — 328
      3. Selected ILO conventions relating to the workplace environment — 328
      4. The WHO and "environmental health" — 329
   III. National implementation — 330
      1. China — 330
      2. South Africa — 331
      3. Kenya — 331

Chapter 24: Trade and environment — 333
   I.   Introduction — 333
   II. International framework: the pillars of the World Trade Organization system - the agreements and the dispute settlement understanding — 335
      1. The agreements of the World Trade Organization — 335
      2. 1994 General Agreement on Tariffs and Trade — 335

3. General Agreement on Trade in Services ... 337
4. Agreement on Trade-Related Investment Measures ... 338
5. Agreement on Technical Barriers to Trade ... 339
6. Agreement on the Application of Sanitary and Phytosanitary Measures ... 339
7. Agreement on Trade-related Aspects of Intellectual Property Rights ... 340
8. Dispute Settlement Understanding ... 340
9. Institutional structure of the World Trade Organization ... 341
10. Examples of cases dealt with by the dispute settlement system of the GATT/WTO concerning environmental issues ... 342
11. Trade and multilateral environmental agreements ... 345
12. Trade-restrictive measures in multilateral environmental agreements ... 345
13. Reconciling trade restrictive provisions with GATT 1994 ... 345
14. Regional trade agreements and the environment ... 346
    a) North American Free Trade Agreement ... 346
    b) Free Trade Agreement of the Americas ... 347
    c) Mercado Común del Sur ... 347
    d) European Union ... 348
III. National implementation ... 349

Chapter 25: Energy, renewable energy and nuclear energy ... 353
I. Introduction ... 353
1. Challenges of sustainable energy ... 353
2. Energy efficiency and renewable energies ... 354
3. Nuclear energy ... 356
II. International framework ... 356
1. International legal regimes: nuclear ... 356
    a) Convention on Early Notification of a Nuclear Accident ... 356
    b) Convention on Assistance an the Case of a Nuclear Accident Emergency or a Radiological Emergency ... 357
    c) Convention on the physical protection of nuclear material ... 357
    d) Joint Convention on the Safety of Spent Fuel Management and on the Safety of Radioactive Waste Management ... 357
    e) The Convention on Nuclear Safety ... 358
2. International cooperation on energy ... 358
    a) The Energy Charter Treaty ... 358
    b) The Energy Charter Protocol on Energy Efficiency and Related Environmental Aspects ... 359
III. National implementation ... 360
1. Republic of Korea ... 360
    a) Energy conservation policy ... 360
    b) Policy objectives ... 360
    c) Major energy efficiency and conservation programmes ... 360
    d) Energy audits and technical support ... 360
    e) Financial and taxation assistance to energy efficiency investments ... 361
    f) Regional energy planning ... 361
    g) Energy impacts assessments on energy-intensive projects ... 361
    h) Demand-side management ... 361
    i) Management and publication of energy statistics ... 361
    j) Public awareness programmes ... 361
    k) Energy equipment efficiency management: standards and labelling ... 361
    l) Inspection of heat-using equipment ... 362
    m) Promotion of research and development of energy technologies ... 362
2. Germany ... 362
3. Australia ... 363
    a) Regulatory framework for promotion of energy conservation and energy efficiency ... 363

			b)	Domestic appliances and equipment	363
			c)	Mandatory programmes	364
			d)	Voluntary programmes	364
			e)	Buildings	364
			f)	Electricity generation and distribution	365
			g)	Transport	365

Chapter 26: Corporations and the environment   **369**

I.	Introduction				369
II.	International framework				371
	1.	The international legal regime			371
		a)	United Nations Convention on the Law of the Sea and the Fish Stocks Agreement		371
		b)	Framework Convention on Tobacco Control		372
		c)	Ozone regime		372
		d)	Basel convention		373
		e)	Liability for oil pollution		374
	2.	International non-legally binding instruments			375
		a)	Agenda 21 and the Rio Declaration		375
		b)	Pesticides code		376
		c)	Fisheries code		377
		d)	OECD guidelines		377
		e)	International standards - ISO		378
		f)	Other instruments		379
	3.	Regional agreements			380
		a)	North Atlantic Free Trade Agreement		380
		b)	Association of South East Asian Nations		381
		c)	European Union		382
III.	National implementation: national legislation governing private businesses				382
	1.	The Oil Pollution Act of the United States of America			382
	2.	Philippine Fisheries Code of 1998			383
	3.	National Pollutant Inventory of Australia			384
	4.	Kenya and the Standards act (Chapter 496)			385

1. MULTILATERAL ENVIRONMENTAL AGREEMENTS

I. Introduction

1. Widespread concern about the need for global action for the protection of the natural environment is a relatively recent phenomenon. General public awareness of the problems relating to the global environment and the need for coordinated multilateral action to address these problems was not evident even a few decades ago. With the wider dissemination of information relating to the ever increasing environmental challenges, international concern has grown steadily over the years. Some inter-state efforts to address problems relating to the oceans, endangered species, and other natural resources, date back to the nineteenth century, but many problem areas relating to the environment remained to be addressed. These early international efforts were relatively uncoordinated. Modern international environmental law received a major boost with the 1972 United Nations Conference on the Human Environment held in Stockholm, Sweden, which brought much broader attention to the issues.

2. In order to understand international environmental law, it is necessary to have a basic grasp of general international law. International environmental law is a subset of international law; and international law has been developing over a long period of time. Since a significant part of international environmental law is incorporated in Multilateral Environmental Agreements ("MEAs"), an introduction to treaty law is essential for understanding the contents of this Manual. In addition to exploring the basic principles relating to treaty law, this chapter will also discuss certain aspects of the negotiation of MEAs.

3. While every effort will be made to provide factual guidance on the sources of international law in this chapter, due to obvious space constraints and the limited objectives of this publication, it will not be possible to make this a comprehensive work. Should further detail be required, the reader should consult one or more of the reference materials suggested at the end of the chapter.

II. Sources of International Law

4. The principal judicial organ of the United Nations ("UN") is the International Court of Justice ("ICJ").

The jurisdiction of the ICJ, specified in article 36(1) of its Statute, "...comprises all cases which the parties refer to it and all matters specially provided for in the Charter of the United Nations or in treaties and conventions in force..." The United Nations' Charter further stipulates that all members of the United Nations are *ipso facto* parties to the ICJ Statute (article 93). Besides decisions, the ICJ is authorized to render advisory opinions on any legal question, when requested by the General Assembly or the Security Council. Other organs of the United Nations and specialized agencies may also request advisory opinions of the ICJ on legal questions arising within the scope of their activities, when authorized by the United Nations General Assembly ("UNGA") (article 96). The ICJ, by the very nature of its functions, plays an important role in the development of international law. Accordingly, the sources of law relied upon by the ICJ are pertinent when examining the sources of international law and, consequently, international environmental law.

5. Article 38(1) of this Statute lists the four sources that the ICJ may rely upon to determine the law applicable to a case brought to its attention. The sources listed in article 38(1) are regarded as the authoritative sources of international law, and thus also of international environmental law.

Statute of the International Court of Justice (Article 38)

"1.The Court, whose function is to decide in accordance with international law such disputes as are submitted to it, shall apply:
a. international conventions, whether general or particular, establishing rules expressly recognised by the contesting states;
b. international custom, as evidence of a general practice accepted as law;
c. the general principles of law recognized by civilized nations;
d. subject to the provisions of Article 59, judicial decisions and the teachings of the most highly qualified publicists of the various nations, as subsidiary means for the determination of rules of law."

---

6. Article 38 establishes a practical hierarchy of sources of international law in settling of disputes. First, relevant treaty provisions applicable between the parties to the dispute must be employed. In the event that there are no applicable treaty provisions, rules of "customary international law" should be applied. If neither a treaty provision nor a customary rule of international law can be identified, then reliance should be placed on the

general principles of law recognized by civilized nations. Finally, judicial decisions and writings of highly qualified jurists may be utilized as a subsidiary means of determining the dispute. It is important to remember that in many cases, due to the absence of any unambiguous rules, the ICJ has had to rely on multiple sources.

7. Article 38(1)(a), (b) and (c) are the main sources of international law and international environmental law. However, given the uncertainties that prevail, article 38(1)(d) also becomes a significant source in this area of law.

1. Law of Treaties

8. Today, treaties are the major mechanism employed by states in the conduct of their relations with each other. They provide the framework for modern international relations and the main source of international law. The starting point for determining what constitutes a treaty is to be found in a treaty itself, the Vienna Convention on the Law of Treaties, a treaty on treaty law. It was concluded in 1969 and entered into force in 1980 ("1969 Vienna Convention"). Whilst the United Nations has 191 Member States, the 1969 Vienna Convention has only 105 parties (as of September 2005). A treaty is binding only among its parties. Although the 1969 Vienna Convention is not a treaty with global participation, it is widely acknowledged that many of its provisions have codified existing customary international law. Other provisions may have acquired customary international law status. Since customary international law and treaty law have the same status at international law, many provisions of the 1969 Vienna Convention are considered to be binding on all states.

9. A reliable source of practical information on treaty law and practice is the "Treaty Handbook", accessible through the internet at http://untreaty.un.org, prepared by the Treaty Section of the United Nations Office of Legal Affairs. Although mainly designed for the use of government officials and others involved in assisting governments on the technical aspects of participation in treaties deposited with the United Nations Secretary-General and the registration of treaties pursuant to article 102 of the Charter of the United Nations, it is of use to anyone interested in treaty law and practice. The "Handbook of Final Clauses of Multilateral Treaties", also produced by the Treaty Section of the United Nations Office of Legal Affairs, is available at the same web address.

10. Article 2(1)(a) of the 1969 Vienna Convention defines a treaty as "an international agreement concluded between states in written form and governed by international law, whether embodied in a single instrument or in two or more related instruments and whatever its particular designation." Accordingly, the designation employed in a document does not determine whether it is a treaty. Regardless of the designation, an international agreement falling under the above definition is considered to be a treaty. The term "treaty" is the generic name. The term "treaty" encompasses, among others, the terms convention, agreement, pact, protocol, charter, statute, covenant, engagement, accord, exchange of notes, *modus vivendi,* and Memorandum of Understanding. As long as an instrument falls under the above definition, it would be considered to be a treaty and, therefore, binding under international law. International organizations are also recognized as capable of concluding treaties, depending on their constituent instruments.

11. Occasionally, some of these terms employed by drafters and negotiators may suggest other meanings without much consideration for their traditionally accepted meanings; that is, they may also be used to mean something other than treaties, which, on occasion, makes treaty terminology confusing and interpretation a problem.

12. The terms vary because they are often employed to indicate differing degrees of political or practical significance. For example, a simple bilateral agreement on technical or administrative cooperation will rarely be designated to be a "covenant" or "charter", whereas an agreement establishing an international organization will usually not be given such labels as "agreed minutes" or "Memorandum of Understanding". So, the nature of the labelling used to describe an international agreement may say something about its content, although this is not always the case. The two principal categories of treaties are the bilateral and the multilateral agreements, the former having only two parties and the latter at least two, and often involving global participation.

13. The term "treaty" can be used as a generic term or as a specific term which indicates an instrument with certain characteristics. There are no consistent rules to determine when state practice employs the term "treaty" as a title for an international instrument. Although in the practice of certain countries, the term "treaty" indicates an agreement of a more solemn nature, and is usually reserved

for regulating matters of some gravity. In the case of bilateral agreements, affixed signatures are usually sealed. Typical examples of international instruments designated as "treaties" include Peace Treaties, Border Treaties, Delimitation Treaties, Extradition Treaties and Treaties of Friendship, Commerce and Cooperation. The designation "convention" and "agreement" appear to be more widely used today in the case of multilateral environmental instruments.

14. The term "agreement" can also have a generic and a specific meaning. The term "international agreement" in its generic sense embraces the widest range of international instruments. In the practice of certain countries, the term "agreement" invariably signifies a treaty. "Agreement" as a particular term usually signifies an instrument less formal than a "treaty" and deals with a narrower range of subject matter. There is a general tendency to apply the term "agreement" to bilateral or restricted multilateral treaties. It is employed especially for instruments of a technical or administrative character, which are signed by the representatives of government departments, and are not subject to ratification. Typical agreements deal with matters of economic, cultural, scientific and technical cooperation, and financial matters, such as avoidance of double taxation. Especially in international economic law, the term "agreement" is also used to describe broad multilateral agreements (e.g., the commodity agreements). Today, the majority of international environmental instruments are designated as agreements.

15. The term "convention" can also have both a generic and a specific meaning. The generic term "convention" is synonymous with the generic term "treaty." With regard to "convention" as a specific term, in the last century it was regularly employed for bilateral agreements but now it is generally used for formal multilateral treaties with a broad range of parties. Conventions are normally open for participation by the international community as a whole or by a large number of states. Usually, the instruments negotiated under the auspices of the United Nations are entitled conventions (e.g., the 1992 Convention on Biological Diversity and the 1982 United Nations Convention on the Law of the Sea). Because so many international instruments in the field of environment and sustainable development are negotiated under the auspices of the United Nations, many instruments in those areas are called "conventions," such as the 1994 United Nations Conventions to combat Desertification in Countries experiencing serious

Drought and/or Desertification, particularly in Africa, and the 2001 Convention on Persistent Organic Pollutants, among others.

16. The term "charter" is used for particularly formal and solemn instruments, such as the constituent treaty of an international organisation. The term itself has an emotive content that goes back to the Magna Carta of 1215. More recent examples include the 1945 Charter of the United Nations, the 1963 Charter of the Organization of African Unity and the 1981 African (Banjul) Charter on Human and Peoples' Rights. The 1982 World Charter for Nature is a resolution adopted by the General Assembly of the United Nations and is not a treaty.

17. The term "protocol" is used for agreements less formal than those entitled "treaty" or "convention", but they also possess the same legal force. A protocol signifies an instrument that creates legally binding obligations at international law. In most cases this term encompasses an instrument which is subsidiary to a treaty. The term is used to cover, among others, the following instruments:

• An optional protocol to a treaty is an instrument that establishes additional rights and obligations with regard to a treaty. Parties to the main treaty are not obliged to become party to an optional protocol. An optional protocol is sometimes adopted on the same day as the main treaty, but is of independent character and subject to independent signature and ratification. Such protocols enable certain parties of the treaty to establish among themselves a framework of obligations which reach further than the main treaty and to which not all parties of the main treaty consent, creating a "two-tier system." An example is found in the optional protocols to the 1966 International Covenant on Civil and Political Rights, the first optional protocol of which deals with direct access for individuals to the committee established under it.

• A protocol can be a supplementary treaty, in this case it is an instrument which contains supplementary provisions to a previous treaty (e.g., the 1966 Protocol relating to the Status of Refugees to the 1951 Convention relating to the Status of Refugees).

• A protocol can be based on and further elaborate a framework convention. The framework "umbrella convention," which sets general objectives, contains the most fundamental rules of a more general character, both procedural and substantive. These objectives are subsequently elaborated by a protocol, with specific substantive obligations, consistent with the rules agreed upon in the framework treaty. This structure is known as the so-called "framework-protocol approach." Examples include the 1985 Vienna Convention for the Protection of the Ozone Layer and its 1987 Montreal Protocol on Substances that deplete the Ozone Layer with its subsequent amendments, the 1992 United Nations Framework Convention on Climate Change with its 1997 Kyoto Protocol, and the 1992 Convention on the Protection and Use of Transboundary Watercourses and International Lakes with its 1999 Protocol on Water and Health and its 2003 (Kiev) Protocol on Civil Liability and Compensation for Damage caused by the Transboundary Effects of Industrial Accidents on Transboundary Waters. (See chapters 9 and 10 of this Manual).

- A protocol of signature is another instrument subsidiary to a main treaty, and is drawn up by the same parties. Such a protocol deals with additional matters such as the interpretation of particular clauses of the treaty. Ratification of the treaty will normally also involve ratification of such a protocol. The Protocol of Provisional Application of the General Agreement on Tariffs and Trade ("GATT") was concluded to bring the 1947 GATT quickly into force in view of the difficulties facing the ratification of the International Trade Organization.

18. The term "declaration" is used to describe various international instruments. However, in most cases declarations are not legally binding. The term is often deliberately chosen to indicate that the parties do not intend to create binding obligations but merely seek to declare certain aspirations. Examples include the 1992 Rio Declaration on Environment and Development, the 2000 United Nations Millennium Declaration and the 2002 Johannesburg Declaration on Sustainable Development. Exceptionally, declarations may sometimes be treaties in the generic sense intended to be binding at international law. An example is the 1984 Joint Declaration of the Government of the United Kingdom of Great Britain and Northern Ireland and the Government of the People's Republic of China on the Question of Hong Kong, which was registered as a treaty by both parties with the United Nations Secretariat, pursuant to article 102 of the United Nations Charter. It is therefore necessary to establish in each individual case whether the parties intended to create binding obligations, often a difficult task. Some instruments entitled "declarations" were not originally intended to have binding force but their

provisions may have reflected customary international law or may have gained binding character as customary international law at a later stage, as is the case with the 1948 Universal Declaration of Human Rights.

19. Once the text of a treaty is agreed upon, states indicate their intention to undertake measures to express their consent to be bound by the treaty. Signing the treaty usually achieves this purpose; and a state that signs a treaty is a signatory to the treaty. Signature also authenticates the text and is a voluntary act. Often major treaties are opened for signature amidst much pomp and ceremony. The United Nations Treaty Section organizes major theme based treaty events in conjunction with the annual General Assembly of the United Nations to encourage wider participation in the treaties deposited with the Secretary-General. The events tend to encourage states to undertake treaty actions in much larger numbers than usual. Once a treaty is signed, customary law, as well as the 1969 Vienna Convention, provides that a state must not act contrary to the object and purpose of the particular treaty, even if it has not entered into force yet.

1969 Vienna Convention on the Law of Treaties (Article 18)

"A State is obliged to refrain from acts which would defeat the object and purpose of a treaty when: (a) it has signed the treaty or has exchanged instruments constituting the treaty subject to ratification, acceptance or approval, until it shall have made its intention clear not to become a party to the treaty; or (b) it has expressed its consent to be bound by the treaty, pending the entry into force of the treaty and provided that such entry into force is not unduly delayed."

---

20. The next step is the ratification of the treaty. Bilateral treaties, often dealing with more routine and less politicised matters, do not normally require ratification and are brought into force by definitive signature, without recourse to the additional procedure of ratification.

1969 Vienna Convention on the Law of Treaties
(Article 12)

"The consent of a State to be bound by a treaty is expressed by the signature of its representative when: (a) the treaty provides that signature shall have that effect; (b) it is otherwise established that the negotiating States were agreed that signature should have that effect; or (c) the intention of the State to give that effect to the signature appears from the full powers of its representative or was expressed during the negotiation.
(...)"

---

21. In the first instance, the signatory state is required to comply with its constitutional and other domestic legal requirements in order to ratify the treaty. This act of ratification, depending on domestic legal provisions, may have to be approved by the legislature, parliament, the Head of State, or similar entity. It is important to distinguish between the act of domestic ratification and the act of international ratification. Once the domestic legal requirements are satisfied, in order to undertake the international act of ratification the state concerned must formally inform the other parties to the treaty of its commitment to undertake the binding obligations under the treaty. In the case of a multilateral treaty, this constitutes submitting a formal instrument signed by the Head of State or Government or the Minister of Foreign Affairs to the depositary who, in turn, informs the other parties. With ratification, a signatory state expresses its consent to be bound by the treaty. Instead of ratification, it can also use the mechanism of acceptance or approval, depending on its domestic legal or policy requirements. A non-signatory state, which wishes to join the treaty after its entry into force, usually does so by lodging an instrument of accession. Reflecting a recent development in international law, some modern treaties, such as the 1997 Convention on the Prohibition of the Use, Stockpiling, Production and Transfer of Anti-Personnel Mines and on their Destruction, make it possible for accession from the date of opening for signature.

22. Accordingly, the adoption of the treaty text does not, by itself, create any international obligations. Similarly, in the case of multilateral treaties, signature by a state normally does not create legally binding obligations. A state usually signs a treaty stipulating that it is subject to ratification, acceptance or approval. It is the action of ratification, accession, acceptance, approval, *et cetera*, which creates legally binding rights and obligations. However, the creation of binding rights and obligations is subject to the treaty's entry into force. A treaty does not enter into force and create legally binding rights and obligations until the necessary conditions stipulated by it are satisfied. For example, the expression of the parties' consent to be bound by a specified number of states. Sometimes, depending on the treaty provisions, it is possible for treaty parties to agree to apply a treaty provisionally until its entry into force.

23. One of the mechanisms used in treaty law to facilitate agreement on the text is to leave the possibility open for a state to make a reservation on becoming a party. A reservation modifies or excludes the application of a treaty provision. A state may use this option for joining a treaty even though it is concerned about certain provisions. A reservation must be lodged at the time of signature, or ratification, or acceptance, or approval, or accession. The 1969 Vienna Convention deals with reservations in its articles 19 through 23, including their formulation, their acceptance and the issue of objecting to reservations, the legal effects of reservations and of objections to reservations, the withdrawal of reservations and of objections to reservations, and the procedure regarding reservations. In general, reservations are permissible except when they are prohibited by the treaty, they are not expressly authorized reservations if the treaty provides only specified reservations, or they are otherwise incompatible with the object and purpose of the treaty.

24. The Secretary-General of the United Nations, in his capacity as depositary of multilateral treaties, entertains late reservations, i.e. reservations lodged after the act of ratification, acceptance, approval or accession. Late reservations are accepted in deposit only in the absence of any objection by a party to the treaty. Where a treaty is silent on reservations, it is possible to lodge reservations as long as they are not contrary to the object and purpose of the treaty. Other parties to a treaty can object to a reservation when it is contrary to the object and purpose of the treaty. An objecting party can even state that it does not want the treaty to enter into force between the state that made the reservation and itself but this happens very rarely and is unusual today. Recently, it has become more common for treaties, including most of the recently concluded environmental treaties, to include provisions that prohibit reservations. Examples are the 1985 Vienna Convention for the Protection of the Ozone Layer (article 18) and its 1987 Montreal Protocol on Substances that deplete the Ozone Layer (article 18), the 1992 Convention on Biological Diversity (article 37) and its 2000 Cartagena Protocol on Biosafety (article 38).

25. A state may also make a declaration to a treaty on becoming party to it. A declaration simply states the understanding of that state with regard to a treaty provision without excluding the application of or modifying a treaty provision. Some treaties provide for mandatory and/or optional declarations. These create binding obligations. Reservations are lodged by a state at signature or when expressing its consent to be bound by a treaty. Where a reservation is made on signature it must be confirmed on ratification. A declaration, in contrast, can be made at any time although normally they are deposited on signature or when the consent to be bound is expressed.

26. An important issue is how to make changes to an already agreed treaty text. The treaty itself normally provides for a procedure to change its provisions, usually by amending the specific provision. Depending on the provisions of the treaty, amendment of a treaty usually needs the consensus of all parties or a specified majority such as two-thirds of the parties, who must be present and voting. Besides amending, there is also the possibility of revising a treaty. The term "revision" is typically reserved for a more profound change of text.

**1969 Vienna Convention on the Law of Treaties
(Article 40)**

"1. Unless the treaty otherwise provides, the amendment of multilateral treaties shall be governed by the following paragraphs.

2. Any proposal to amend a multilateral treaty as between all the parties must be notified to all the contracting States, each one of which shall have the right to take part in:

    (a) the decision as to the action to be taken in regard to such proposal;

    (b) the negotiation and conclusion of any agreement for the amendment of the treaty.

3. Every State entitled to become a party to the treaty shall also be entitled to become a party to the treaty as amended.

4. The amending agreement does not bind any State already a party to the treaty which does not become a party to the amending agreement; Article 30, paragraph 4(b), applies in relation to such State.

5. Any State which becomes a party to the treaty after the entry into force of the amending agreement shall, failing an expression of a different intention by that State:

    (a) be considered as a party to the treaty as amended; and

    (b) be considered as a party to the unamended treaty in relation to any party to the treaty not bound by the amending agreement."

---

27. Another important term relating to treaty law is the depositary. A depositary is usually designated in the text of a multilateral treaty. The depositary is the custodian of the treaty and is entrusted with the functions specified in article 77 of the 1969 Vienna Convention.

**1969 Vienna Convention on the Law of Treaties
(Article 77)**

"1. The functions of a depositary, unless otherwise provided in the treaty or agreed by the contracting States, comprise in particular:

(a) keeping custody of the original text of the treaty and of any full powers delivered to the depositary;

(b) preparing certified copies of the original text and preparing any further text of the treaty in such additional languages as may be required by the treaty and transmitting them to the parties and to the States entitled to become parties to the treaty;

(c) receiving any signatures to the treaty and receiving and keeping custody of any instruments, notifications and communications relating to it;

(d) examining whether the signature or any instrument, notification or communication relating to the treaty is in due and proper form and, if need be, bringing the matter to the attention of the State in question;

(e) informing the parties and the States entitled to become parties to the treaty of acts, notifications and communications relating to the treaty;

(f) informing the States entitled to become parties to the treaty when the number of signatures or of instruments of ratification, acceptance, approval or accession required for the entry into force of the treaty has been received or deposited;

(g) registering the treaty with the Secretariat of the United Nations;

(h) performing the functions specified in other provisions of the present Convention.

(...)"

---

28. Among others, the depository acts as the "collection point." A state will transmit its instrument of ratification, acceptance, approval, accession, or its reservation or denunciation to the depositary, who notifies other states. Usually, the Chief Executive of an international organization is designated as the depositary. States deposit their treaty actions with the depositary instead of with all other states parties to the treaty. Often, the Secretary-General of the United Nations is designated as the depositary. The Secretary-General is at present the depositary for over 500 multilateral treaties, including over 55 Multilateral

Environmental Agreements. Individual states, and various international and regional organizations, are also designated as depositaries. There are over two thousand multilateral treaties at present. Bilateral treaties are deposited with the two states involved, since a bilateral treaty is usually signed in duplicate. A regional treaty is often deposited with a regional organization.

29. All treaties entered into by members of the United Nations must be registered with the United Nations Secretariat pursuant to article 102 of the Charter of the United Nations once they have entered into force. Registered treaties are published in the United Nations Treaty Series, the most authoritative collection of existing treaties. The United Nations Treaty Series contains over fifty thousand treaties and a similar number of related treaty actions. This is done to ensure transparency. The United Nations Treaty Series is available on the internet at http://untreaty.un.org.

30. Entry into force is the moment in time when a treaty becomes legally binding for the parties. The provisions of the treaty determine the moment upon which the treaty enters into force. If there is nothing governing the entry into force in the treaty, the general rule is that the treaty will enter into force when all the states participating in drafting the treaty have expressed their consent to be bound. It is possible for the treaty to stipulate a specific date, such as 1 January 2007, for its entry into force.

31. In most cases, the treaty enters into force when a specified number of states has ratified it. A provision in the treaty that governs its entry into force will stipulate that entry into force will occur after a certain time period has elapsed (such as 90 days) after the tenth (i.e., 1973 Convention on International Trade in Endangered Species of Wild Fauna and Flora), fifteenth (i.e., 1979 Convention on the Conservation of Migratory Species of Wild Animals), twentieth (i.e., 1985 Vienna Convention for the Protection of the Ozone Layer), thirtieth (1992 Convention on Biological Diversity) or fiftieth (i.e., 1992 United Nations Framework Convention on Climate Change, 1994 Desertification Convention ratification, accession, approval, acceptance, etc. A treaty enters into force only for the states that have ratified it. (See also chapter 14 of this Manual).

32. A treaty can also specify certain additional conditions regarding the states that have to ratify the treaty before it can enter into force. For example, the 1987 Montreal Protocol to the

Vienna Convention includes the provision that it would enter into force on 1 January 1989, provided that there were at least eleven ratifications of states which were responsible in 1986 for at least two-thirds of the estimated global consumption of the substances the protocol is covering (article 16). The entry into force of the 1997 Kyoto Protocol is also subjected to strict conditions- it will enter into force "on the ninetieth day after the date on which not less than fifty-five parties to the Convention, incorporating parties included in Annex I which accounted in total for at least 55% of the total carbon dioxide emissions for 1990 of the parties included in Annex I, have deposited their instruments of ratification, acceptance, approval or accession "(article 24).

2. Customary International Law

33. The second most important source of international law, and thus of international environmental law, is customary international law. Before treaties became as important as they are today, customary international law was the leading source of international law: the way things have always been done becomes the way things must be done.

34. Once a rule of customary law is recognized, it is binding on all states, because it is then assumed to be a binding rule of conduct. Initially, customary international law as we know it today developed in the context of the evolving interaction among European states. However, there is an increasingly prominent group of writers who suggest that other regions of the world also contributed to the evolution of customary international law.

35. There are two criteria for determining if a rule of international customary law exists: (1) the state practice should be consistent with the "rule of constant and uniform usage" (*inveterata consuetudo*) and (2) the state practice exists because of the belief that such practice is required by law (*opinio juris*). Both elements are complementary and compulsory for the creation of customary international law. Since customary law requires this rather heavy burden of proof and its existence is often surrounded by uncertainties, treaties have become increasingly important to regulate international relations among states.

36. Customary law was mentioned in relation to the 1948 Universal Declaration of Human Rights. Namely, the provisions of the declaration, although not specifically intended to be legally binding, are now generally accepted as constituting customary international law.

Customary international law is as legally binding as treaty law. It can be argued that customary international law has a wider scope: a treaty is applicable only to its parties and it does not create either rights or obligations for a third state without its consent, but customary law is applicable to *all* states (unless it constitutes regional custom).

37. Occasionally, it is difficult to distinguish clearly between treaty law and customary law. For example, the 1982 United Nations Convention on the Law of the Sea ("UNCLOS") comprises new international legal norms as well as codification of existing customary law. Between the date of its adoption in 1982 and the date it entered into force in 1994, non-parties to the treaty, in practice, followed many of the norms incorporated into the UNCLOS. It can therefore be said that UNCLOS largely represents customary law, which is binding on all states. (For a discussion on UNCLOS as well as Marine Living Resources see chapters 13 and 17 herein).

38. Two specific terms related to the concept of customary international law require further attention. The first one is "soft law." This term does not have a fixed legal meaning, but it usually refers to any international instrument, other than a treaty, containing principles, norms, standards or other statements of expected behaviour. Often, the term soft law is used as synonymous with non-legally binding instrument, but this is not correct. An agreement is legally binding or is not legally binding. A treaty that is legally binding can be considered to represent hard law; however, a non-legally binding instrument does not necessarily constitute soft law. The consequences of a non-legally binding instrument are not clear. Sometimes it is said that they contain political or moral obligations, but this is not the same as soft law. Non-legally binding agreements emerge when states agree on a specific issue, but they do not, or do not yet, wish to bind themselves legally; nevertheless they wish to adopt certain non-binding rules and principles before they become law. This approach often facilitates consensus, which is more difficult to achieve on binding instruments. There could also be an expectation that a rule or principle adopted by consensus, although not legally binding, will nevertheless be complied with. Often the existence of non-legally binding norms will fuel civil society activism to compel compliance. The Non-Legally Binding Authorative Statement of Principles for a Global Consensus on the Management, Conservation and Sustainable Development of all Type of Forests ("Forest Principles"), for example, are an illustration of this phenomenon. The relationship between the Forest Principles and a binding forest regime is that they are shaping or will shape consensus for a future multilateral convention, or are building upon a common legal position that will possibly come to constitute customary international law.

39. The second term is "peremptory norm" (*jus cogens*). This concept refers to norms in international law that cannot be overruled other than by a subsequent peremptory norm. They are of the highest order. *Jus cogens* has precedence over treaty law. Exactly which norms can be designated as *jus cogens* is still subject to some controversy. Examples are the ban on slavery, the prohibition of genocide or torture, or the prohibition on the use of force.

3. General Principles of Law

40. The third source of international law, as included in article 38(1)(c) of the Statute of the International Court of Justice, are general principles of law. The principles that are considered to be specifically relevant to international environmental law will be discussed in chapter 3. There is no universally agreed upon set of general principles and concepts. They usually include both principles of the international legal system as well as those common to the major national legal systems of the world. The ICJ will sometimes analyse principles of domestic law in order to develop an appropriate rule of international law.

41. The ICJ, in its 1996 Advisory Opinion on Legality of the Threat or Use of Nuclear Weapons, points to the Martens Clause as an affirmation that the principles and rules of humanitarian law apply to nuclear weapons. In his dissenting opinion, Judge Shahabuddeen cites the Martens Clause: "the inhabitants and the belligerents remain under the protection and the rule of the principles of the law of nations, as they result from the usages established among civilized peoples, from the laws of humanity, and the dictates of the public conscience". Judge Shahabuddeen states that the Martens Clause provided its own self-sufficient and conclusive authority for the proposition that there were already in existence principles of international law under which considerations of humanity could themselves exert legal force to govern military conduct in cases in which no relevant rule was provided by conventional law. It can be construed that some treaties reflect, codify or create general principles of law.

4. Judicial Decisions and Qualified Teachings

42. The fourth source enumerated in article 38(1)(d) of the Statute of the International Court of Justice, judicial decisions and the teachings of the most highly qualified publicists of the various nations, is qualified as an additional means for the determination of rules of law. Decisions of the ICJ itself or of other international tribunals, and writings of publicists are considered if: there is no treaty on a particular contentious issue in international law, no customary rule of international law and no applicable general principles of international law. Many international law journals publish articles by eminent lawyers addressing a great variety of issues pertaining to all aspects of international law.

43. Another source for the category "highly qualified publicists" is the International Law Commission ("ILC"), established by the United Nations General Assembly in 1947 to promote the progressive development of international law and its codification. The ILC, which meets annually, is composed of thirty-four members who are elected by the General Assembly for five year terms and who serve in their individual capacity, thus not as representatives of their governments. Most of the ILC's work involves the preparation of drafts on topics of international law. Some topics are chosen by the ILC and others referred to it by the General Assembly or the Economic and Social Council. When the ILC completes draft articles on a particular topic, the General Assembly usually convenes an international conference of plenipotentiaries to negotiate the articles of a convention, which is then open to states to become parties. Examples of topics on which the ILC has submitted final drafts or reports include issues pertaining to state succession, immunities and treaty law.

44. Article 38 is not intended to provide an exhaustive list of sources of international law. There are other possible sources which the ICJ might rely on to assist in its deliberations, such as acts of international or regional organizations, Resolutions of the United Nations Security Council and the United Nations General Assembly, and Regulations, Decisions and Directives of the European Union, among others.

45. Also, decisions of the Conference of the Parties to a MEA, and conference declarations or statements, may contribute to the development of international law.

III. Negotiating Multilateral Environmental Agreements

46. There is no definite procedure established on how to negotiate a Multilateral Environmental Agreement. Some common elements, however, may be derived from the practice of states over the last few decades.

47. The first step in the negotiation process is for an adequate number of countries to show interest in regulating a particular issue through a multilateral mechanism. The existence of a common challenge and the need for a solution is necessary. In certain cases, the number of acutely interested parties may be as few as two. For example, the draft Convention on Cloning was tabled in the Sixth Committee of the General Assembly by Germany and France. A counter proposal was advanced by the United States of America. In other cases, a larger number of countries need to demonstrate a clear desire for a new instrument. Once this stage of establishing a common interest in addressing a global problem is established, states need to agree on a forum for the negotiation of a multilateral instrument. Usually an existing international organization such as the United Nations or an entity such as the United Nations Environment Programme ("UNEP") will provide this forum. The United Nations has frequently established special fora for the negotiation of MEA through General Assembly resolutions. The 1992 United Nations Framework Convention on Climate Change ("UNFCCC") was negotiated by a specially established body - the Intergovernmental Negotiating Committee ("INC"). It is also possible to conduct the negotiations in a subsidiary body of the General Assembly such as the Sixth Committee, which is the Legal Committee. Treaty bodies could also provide the fora for such negotiations. For example, pursuant to article 19(3) of the 1992 Convention on Biological Diversity, the Conference of the Parties, by its decision II/5, established an Open-Ended Ad Hoc Working Group on Biosafety to develop the draft protocol on biosafety, which later resulted in an agreed text and subsequent adoption of the 2000 Cartagena Protocol on Biosafety.

48. The negotiating forum will start the negotiating process by establishing a committee or convening an international conference to consider the particular issue. This could take many forms, from an informal ad hoc group of governmental experts to a formal institutional structure as in the case of the INC for the negotiation of the 1992 UNFCCC. It is also possible for an international

organization to establish a subsidiary body to prepare a text for consideration and adoption by an Intergovernmental Diplomatic Conference. Certain treaties were first proposed by the International Law Commission and subsequently negotiated and adopted by intergovernmental bodies. Governments also often draft negotiating texts. During the negotiations, delegates generally remain in close contact with their governments; they have preliminary instructions which are usually not communicated to other parties. At any stage they may consult their governments and, if necessary, obtain fresh instructions. Governments could also change their positions depending on developments. Depending on the importance of the treaty under negotiation, governments may expend considerable resources in order to safeguard and advance their own national interests in the context of arriving at a global standard. In many cases this may require building numerous alliances and interest groups in order to advance national positions. The European Union usually operates as a block in MEA negotiations but often formed alliances with other like-minded countries The host organization will organize preparatory committees, working groups of technical and legal experts, scientific symposia and preliminary conferences. The host body will also provide technical back-up to the negotiators.

49. Increasingly, the need for universal participation in the negotiation of MEA has been acknowledged. Consequently, developing countries are often provided financial assistance to participate in environmental negotiations. Given this opportunity and the widely acknowledged need for developing countries to be closely engaged in these negotiations in view of the global nature of environmental challenges, they have the possibility to exert a greater influence on the future development of legal principles in the environmental field than was available to them in other treaty negotiating fora.

50. In the negotiating forum, states are the most important actors, since most treaties only carry direct obligations for states. However, the proper implementation of and compliance with a treaty cannot be achieved without involving a whole range of non-state actors, including civil society groups, Non-Governmental Organizations ("NGOs"), scientific groups, and business and industry, among others. Therefore the participation of these groups in the negotiating processes that lead to an MEA is now more readily facilitated. Some national delegations to

intergovernmental negotiations now contain NGO representatives while some smaller states might even rely on NGOs to represent them at such negotiations. In such situations, NGOs may have a notable influence on the outcomes of the negotiations.

51. The role of NGOs has often been significant in the treaty negotiating processes, as well as in stimulating subsequent developments within treaty regimes. An example is the influence of the International Council for Bird Preservation (now BirdLife International) and the International Waterfowl and Wetlands Research Bureau, two NGOs, in the conclusion and on the implementation of the 1971 Ramsar Convention on Wetlands. NGO influence is achieved in most cases through the mechanism of participation as observers, in international organizations, at treaty negotiations, and within treaty institutions. Some NGOs are well prepared with extensive briefs. Some national delegations rely on NGOs for background material. The inclusion of NGOs may be seen as representing a wider trend towards viewing international society in terms broader than a community of states alone and in the progressive democratization of international norm making processes. This might indicate a development in international law making and implementation with significant implications for the future.

52. In the Intergovernmental Negotiating Committee process, one ideally starts with the identification of needs and goals, before the political realities get in the way. Research must have been undertaken and show the need for a legally binding international instrument to address the perceived problem. This phase may sound logical, but as the negotiations surrounding climate change show, states can always invoke opinions of scientists, deviating from the majority, who argue more in line with their national interests. During treaty negotiations, states will often cite scientific evidence that justifies the general policies they prefer.

53. At the time the first formal discussions take place, information has been disseminated, the preliminary positions of states are established, and the initial scope of the agreement is further defined. It is also likely that interested states have made representations concerning their own interests to other states using diplomatic channels. Then the long process to international consensus-building begins, often lasting years and with many lengthy drafts, negotiated over and over again.

54. Negotiations may be open-ended in time or established for a limited period. For example, the United Nations Convention on the Law of the Sea negotiations took nearly ten years to complete, while the negotiations for the 1992 Convention on Biological Diversity were concluded in about fifteen months.

55. Once the draft text has been negotiated it needs to be adopted and "opened" for signature. The text itself is usually finalised by the negotiators and might even be initialled at a final meeting of plenipotentiaries. Most United Nations-sponsored treaties are adopted in the six official languages of the organization. If the negotiations had been conducted in one language (now, usually English) the text is formally translated into the other official languages. The mechanism of a final act might also be employed to adopt the text. For this purpose, a conference of plenipotentiaries might be convened. These are representatives of governments with the authority to approve the treaty. Subsequently, the adopted text will be opened for signature.

56. Where a treaty is to be deposited with the Secretary-General of the United Nations, it is necessary that the Treaty Section of the United Nations be consulted in advance, particularly with regard to the final clauses.

57. As mentioned above, international environmental treaty making may involve a two-step approach, the "Framework Convention-Protocol" style. In this event, the treaty itself contains only general requirements, directions and obligations. Subsequently the specific measures and details will be negotiated, as happened with the 2000 Cartagena Protocol on Biosafety with the 1992 Convention on Biological Diversity. Or, additional non-legally binding instruments can elaborate on these measures to be taken by the parties, as was the case with the 2002 Bonn Guidelines on Access to Genetic Resources and Fair and Equitable Sharing of the Benefits Arising out of their Utilization, with the same convention. The convention-protocol approach allows countries to "sign on" at the outset to an agreement even if there is no agreement on the specific actions that need to be taken under it subsequently. Among the major shortcomings of the convention-protocol approach is that it encourages a process that is often long and drawn out.

IV. Administering Treaties

58. Treaties do not only create rights and obligations for state parties, they often also create their own administrative structure to assist parties to comply with their provisions and to provide a forum for continued governance.

59. Environmental treaties usually rely on voluntary compliance with their obligations, rather than on coerced compliance. Accordingly, there is a tendency to develop non-compliance mechanisms designed to secure compliance by the parties with the terms of a treaty or decisions of the Conference of the Parties ("COP") through voluntary means. The emphasis in these non-compliance mechanisms is to assist parties to meet their obligations rather than identify guilt in non-compliers and impose punitive sanctions. Even in the absence of a formal procedure, non-compliance problems are likely to be handled in a similar way in many environmental regimes. Non-compliance procedures are best understood as a form of dispute avoidance or alternative dispute resolution, in the sense that resort to binding third party procedures is avoided. The treaty parties will instead seek to obtain compliance through voluntary means and in the process reinforce the stability of the regime as a whole.

60. An example is the non-compliance procedure adopted by the parties to the 1987 Montreal Protocol on Substances that Deplete the Ozone Layer. Whenever there are compliance problems, the matter is referred to an implementation committee consisting of ten parties, whose main task is to consider and examine the problem and then find an amicable solution based on the 1987 Montreal Protocol. It is possible for a party itself to draw the attention of the implementing committee to its inability to comply with the Protocol with a view to obtaining assistance with compliance measures.

61. Breach of an environmental treaty is unlikely to justify punitive action. Punitive action is generally avoided by states in favour of softer non-compliance procedures which rely on international supervisory institutions to bring about compliance through consultation and practical assistance. Effective supervision of the operation and implementation of treaty regimes often depends on the availability of adequate information.

62. Most environmental treaties establish a Conference of the Parties, a Secretariat, and subsidiary bodies.

63. The COP forms the primary policy-making organ of the treaty. All parties to a treaty meet, usually

annually or biannually, and survey the progress achieved by the treaty regime, the status of implementation, possibilities for amendments, revisions, and additional protocols. For example article 18 of the 1998 Convention on the Prior Informed Consent Procedure for Certain Hazardous Chemicals and Pesticides in International Trade ("PIC Convention") held in Rotterdam, the Netherlands.

1998 Convention on the Prior Informed Consent Procedure for Certain Hazardous Chemicals and Pesticides in International Trade
(Article 18)

"1. A Conference of the Parties is hereby established.
2. The first meeting of the Conference of the Parties shall be convened by the Executive Director of UNEP and the Director-General of FAO, acting jointly, no later than one year after the entry into force of this Convention. Thereafter, ordinary meetings of the Conference of the Parties shall be held at regular intervals to be determined by the Conference.
(…)
4. The Conference of the Parties shall by consensus agree upon and adopt at its first meeting rules of procedure and financial rules for itself and any subsidiary bodies, as well as financial provisions governing the functioning of the Secretariat.
5. The Conference of the Parties shall keep under continuous review and evaluation the implementation of this Convention. It shall perform the functions assigned to it by the Convention and, to this end, shall:
   a) Establish, further to the requirements of paragraph 6 below, such subsidiary bodies, as it considers necessary for the implementation of the Convention;
   b) Cooperate, where appropriate, with competent international organizations and intergovernmental and non-governmental bodies; and
   c) Consider and undertake any additional action that may be required for the achievement of the objectives of the Convention.
(…)"

---

64. The Secretariat of a convention is responsible for the daily operations. In general, it provides for communication among parties, organizes meetings and meeting documents in support of the COP, assists in implementation and it may assist in activities such as capacity building. The Secretariat gathers and distributes information and it increasingly coordinates with other legal environmental regimes and secretariats. UNEP is administering secretariat functions to the following MEAs which are addressed in this

Manual respectively in chapters 15 and 16, 14 in the case of Biodiversity Cluster, 11, 12 and 9 in the case of Chemicals and Hazardous Wastes Cluster:

• Biodiversity Cluster:

   a) 1992 Convention on Biological Diversity
   b) 2000 Cartagena Protocol on Biosafety
   c) 1979 (Bonn) Convention on the Conservation of Migratory Species of Wild Animals, Related Agreements and Memoranda of Understanding concerning Specific Species concluded under the Auspices of CMS
   d) 1973 Convention on International Trade in Endangered Species

• Chemicals and Hazardous Wastes Cluster:

   a) 1989 Basel Convention on the Control of Transboundary Movements of Hazardous Wastes and their Disposal
   b) 1999 Protocol on Liability and Compensation to the Basel Convention
   c) 2001 (Stockholm) Convention on Persistent Organic Pollutants
   d) 1998 (Rotterdam) Convention on the Prior Informed Consent Procedure for Certain Hazardous Chemicals and Pesticides in International Trade
   e) 1985 Vienna Convention for the Protection of the Ozone Layer
   f) 1987 Montreal Protocol on Substances that Deplete the Ozone Layer

In addition, UNEP has supported the negotiations of twelve conventions and action plans for the protection of the various regional seas. There are also stand-alone secretariats of MEAs under the United Nations umbrella such as the Desertification Convention Secretariat, and secretariats of regional agreements with regional organizations.

65. Many environmental regimes provide for a scientific commission or other technical committee, comprised of experts. In most cases, they include members designated by governments or by the COP, although they generally function independently. They can be included in the treaty or by a decision of the COP. For example, the 1992 Convention and Biological Diversity has a Subsidiary Body on Scientific, Technical and Technological Advice, the 1998 PIC Convention provides for a Chemical Review Committee, and the Committee for Environmental Protection was established by the 1991 Protocol on Environmental

Protection to the Antarctic Treaty. They can address recommendations or proposals to the COP or to other treaty bodies. They usually provide informative reports in the area of their specialization related to the convention and its implementation.

Dr. Palitha Kohona, Chief, Treaty Section, United Nations Office of Legal Affairs

Barbara Ruis, Legal Officer, Division of Policy Development and Law, UNEP

Resources

Internet Materials

HANDBOOK OF FINAL CLAUSES OF MULTILATERAL TREATIES: available at http://untreaty.un.org/English/TreatyHandbook/hbframeset.htm

INTERNATIONAL COURT OF JUSTICE: available at http://www.icj-cij.org/

TREATY HANDBOOK: available at http://untreaty.un.org/English/TreatyHandbook/hbframeset.htm

TREATY REFERENCE GUIDE: available at http://untreaty.un.org/ENGLISH/guide.asp#treaties

Text Materials

A. Aust, MODERN TREATY LAW AND PRACTICE (Cambridge University Press, 2000).

D. Shelton, *International Law and 'Relative Normativity'*, in INTERNATIONAL LAW, (M. Evans ed., 2003).

H. Thirlway, *The Sources of International Law*, in INTERNATIONAL LAW, (M. Evans ed., 2003).

J. DiMento, THE GLOBAL ENVIRONMENT AND INTERNATIONAL LAW (University of Texas Press, 2003).

J. Kaufmann, CONFERENCE DIPLOMACY (1970).

P. Birnie & A. Boyle, INTERNATIONAL LAW & THE ENVIRONMENT (Oxford University Press, 2002).

L. D. Guruswami, Sir G.W.R. Palmer, B. H. Weston & J. C. Carlson, INTERNATIONAL ENVIRONMENTAL LAW AND WORLD ORDER (Westgroup, 1999).

L. Susskind, ENVIRONMENTAL DIPLOMACY, NEGOTIATING MORE EFFECTIVE GLOBAL AGREEMENTS (1994).

M. Fitzmaurice, *The Practical Working of the Law of Treaties*, in INTERNATIONAL LAW (M. Evans ed., 2003).

Palitha T.B. Kohona, THE ROLE OF NON STATE ENTITIES IN THE MAKING OF INTERNATIONAL NORMS AND THEIR IMPLEMENTATION, IJWI (September 2001).

R.P. Arnand, *The Influence of History on the Literature of International Law*, in THE STRUCTURE AND PROCESS OF INTERNATIONAL LAW: ESSAYS IN LEGAL PHILOSOPHY, DOCTRINE AND THEORY (States, MacDonald & Johnston eds., 1983).

2. THE ROLE OF NATIONAL ENVIRONMENTAL LAW

I. Introduction

1. Environmental law is a broad category of laws that include laws that specifically address environmental issues and more general laws that have a direct impact on environmental issues. The definition of what constitutes an environmental law is as wide as the definition of environment itself. "Environment" in the modern context of sustainable development encompasses the physical and social factors of the surroundings of human beings and includes land, water, atmosphere, climate, sound, odour, taste, energy, waste management, coastal and marine pollution, the biological factors of animals and plants, as well as cultural values, historical sites, and monuments and aesthetics. Environmental law can be generally defined as the body of law that contains elements to control the human impact on the Earth and on public health.

2. Environmental law can be divided into two major categories namely, international environmental law and national environmental law. The relationship between international environmental law and national environmental law is mainly on the purposes for which each of the two categories of law were created as well as on the scope that each of the two types of law covers. International environmental law is a law developed between sovereign states to develop standards at the international level and provide obligations for states including regulating their behaviour in international relations in environmental related matters. (See chapters 1, 2, 3, 4, 5, 7, 8, 9, 10, 11, etc). National environmental law on the other hand applies within a state and regulates the relations of citizens among each other and with the executive within the state. International law can find its application in national law when a state takes measures to implement its international obligations through enactment and enforcement of national legislation. In most of the chapters of the manual, a section on National Implementation refers to national legislation, institutions and capacity building. All that helps build up this chapter. This chapter will focus on the role of national environmental law.

3. National environmental law includes rules at the national level that protect the environment. These consist of the legislation, standards, regulations, institutions and administrations adopted to control activities damaging to the environment within a state. This would include *inter alia* framework environmental legislation, sectoral legislation and incidental legislation, and regulations, depending on the culture of a given country.

II. Foundations of National Environmental Law

4. In any society, the role of law generally reflects and shapes a society's norms. Laws can change attitudes towards particular aspects of life, and control behaviour. Laws can be defined as codes of conduct appropriate to the values of the community drafting and enforcing them. There are, of course, many types and sources of law, such as common law, civil law, customary or traditional law, canon law, and islamic law. These may be written or unwritten, but all define acceptable behaviour within that society. Law is one of the key instruments of social regulation established through norms of conduct, and creation of the required machinery with their accompanying empowerment for ensuring compliance. Codes of conduct with regard to the environment are contained in all sources of law, some of which date back thousands of years.

5. There are several types of environmental laws and national legislative approaches to environmental management. These include, *inter alia*, the following:

   • Constitutions
   • Sectoral laws
   • Framework environmental laws
   • Comprehensive codification of environmental laws
   • Penal codes
   • Implementation of international environmental legal instruments

6. National constitutions provide a source of environmental law when they provide environmental rights for the citizens. In a number of countries the constitutional right to an environment not harmful to citizens' health have been interpreted in Court to provide redress where such an environment was lacking. This has further strengthened environmental law and enhanced access to justice by providing redress to the parties in a suit.

7. Sectoral legislation addresses specific aspects of the environment and human activity such as a law on water, land, energy, forest, wildlife, marine environment, or a law establishing a national park or legislation to control factories. The sectoral laws

are characterized by fragmented and uncoordinated sectoral legal regimes that were initially developed to facilitate resource allocation and to deal with the environmentally adverse effects of resource exploitation. Gradually, to supplement the existing sector laws, were anti-pollution laws, as the process of industrialization created new environmental risks. The main cause of the development of framework laws in recent years was the realization of synergies within the ecosystems and the linkages in environmental stresses that not even a combination of sector specific resource legislation and anti-pollution laws were sufficient to safeguard the quality of the environment or to guarantee sustainable development.

8. The framework environmental legislation is a single law that provides the legal and institutional framework for environmental management without seeking to legislate comprehensively. It was developed in response to the deficiencies inherent in the sectoral approach to environmental management. It represents an integrated, ecosystem-oriented legal regime that permits a holistic view of the ecosystem, the synergies and interactions within it, and the linkages in environmental stresses and administrative institutions. The flexibility is achieved through investing relevant authorities with wide regulatory powers to promulgate subsidiary legislation addressing specific environmental issues and completing the generality of the framework statute. In addition the framework law provides a basis and a reference point for coordination of sectoral activities and the rationalization and harmonization of sectoral legal regimes. This is the reason for referring to the framework law as the umbrella legislation to signify its overarching role as a framework environmental law which provides for the legal and institutional framework for environmental management, this underlining the need for regulations as necessary or as a state is able to manage and fund.

9. Although the framework laws address environmental problems that are unique to each country and reflect specific socio-economic situations and legal traditions, some common elements can be discerned. These may be referred to as the basic elements of a framework environmental statute and should be used as a general guide for purposes of legislative drafting. The framework legislation lays down the basic principles without any attempt at codification. It normally entails and covers cross sectoral issues such as indicated in the box below. The legislation may also establish links and hierarchy

with other laws impacting the environment. The framework environmental legislation may cover the following issues:

- Definitions;
- Declaration of general objectives and principles;
- Establishment of relevant environmental management institutions including streamlining institutional arrangements, and the definition of the common procedural principles for environmental decision-making applicable to all sectors;
- Environmental policy formulation and planning;
- Environmental impact assessment and audits;
- Environmental quality criteria and standards;
- Integrated pollution control;
- Environmental management;
- Public participation in decision-making and implementation;
- Environmental inspectorates;
- Dispute settlement procedures; and
- Establishes links and hierarchy with other laws impacting the environment.

10. This would include the institutional issues such as which government authority will be in charge of protecting the environment, controlling pollution and, enforcing the laws and the coordinating mechanisms.

11. Most countries have both sectoral legislation and a framework environmental legislation while other countries have one or the other or neither. There are countries that have consolidated all of their environmental laws in one single comprehensive statute or code. For example Sweden has consolidated some sixteen national legislations into a code.

12. Criminal laws in the form of penal codes and other incidental legislation establishing liability in tort law are legislation, which although not specifically intended to address environmental issues, contain some elements that have an impact on environmental issues by having environmental related laws defined as punishable offenses made against the state. This might include, for example, criminal legislation that contains a prohibition on polluting or more generally applicable nuisance crimes involving odour, noise or other noxious substances.

13. In some cases, these national laws are a reflection of international norms or commitments and are adopted with the intent of implementing

international environmental conventions. For example, legislation must be enacted at the national level to create a management authority to issue export permits for species protected under the 1973 Convention on the International Trade in Endangered Species of Wild Fauna and Flora. Further discussion on the implementation of Multilateral Environmental Agreements ("MEAs") at the national level is found below.

1. Environmental Law and Sustainable Development

Agenda 21 and World Summit on Sustainable Development Plan of Implementation

14. To provide an effective legal and regulatory framework for sustainable development the United Nations Conference on Environment and Development held in Rio de Janeiro, Brazil, in 1992 ("1992 UNCED"), declared as its basis for action in Chapter 8, para.13 of Agenda 21 that "laws and regulations suited to country-specific conditions are among the most important instruments for transforming environment and development policies into action, not only through "command and control" methods, but also as a normative framework for economic planning and market instruments".

15. In 1992 UNCED observed, however, that although the volume of legal texts in this field is steadily increasing, much of the law-making in many countries remains *ad hoc* and piecemeal, or has not been endowed with the necessary institutional machinery and authority for enforcement and timely adjustment. 1992 UNCED concluded that to effectively integrate environment and development in the policies and practices of each country, it is essential to develop and implement integrated, enforceable and effective laws and regulations that are based upon sound social, ecological, economic and scientific principles.

16. The 2002 World Summit on Sustainable Development ("WSSD") Plan of Implementation also calls upon countries to promote sustainable development at the national level by, *inter alia*, enacting and enforcing clear and effective laws that support sustainable development. As for the kind of institutions national environmental legislation should set up or strengthen, the WSSD Plan of Implementation, underlines the importance of national governments to strengthen institutional frameworks for sustainable development at the national level.

17. In Paragraph 162 of the WSSD Plan of Implementation, "States are required to promote coherent and coordinated approaches to institutional frameworks for sustainable development at all national levels, including through, as appropriate, the establishment or strengthening of existing authorities and mechanisms necessary for policy-making, coordination and implementation and enforcement of laws..." Paragraph 163 establishes that "... countries have a responsibility to strengthen governmental institutions, including by providing necessary infrastructure and by promoting transparency, accountability and fair administrative and judicial institutions." Paragraph 164 calls upon "all countries to promote public participation, including through measures that provide access to information regarding legislation, regulations, activities, policies and programmes..."

18. Among components listed in chapter 8 of Agenda 21, and the WSSD Plan of Implementation which stand out that concerning the effectiveness of laws are country specific national environmental laws; adequate laws; effective laws; compliance and enforcement of national environmental laws and strengthened institutions.

2. The Prerequisites for Effective National Environmental Law

a) Adequate Regulation and Institutional Regimes

19. In many countries the functions of environmental legislation include the following:

- Reflection of the particular policies and schemes considered by the Legislature to be most appropriate for achieving the desired goals;
- Establishment of the institutional machinery for giving effect to those principles and schemes;
- Empowering of the related institutions and partners to function efficiently within the framework of policy parameters;
- Establishment of legislative techniques and regulatory approaches, such as command and control regimes, economic incentives and land use planning and zoning; and
- Provision of adequate financial and human resources.

20. Command and control regulation emphasises deterrence and punishment. To illustrate this point when a government regulation establishes specific environment standards (the "command") and

when it establishes a detailed inspection and enforcement scheme (the "control"). To be effective the sanctions of the command and control regulation have to "deter" other violations to effectively protect the environment.

21. Governments also use economic instruments to control environmental behaviour. The main incentive or disincentives used for environmental management and regulation include pollution charges (including emission charges, user charges, product charges, administrative charges, and tax differentiation); user charges (fees for direct cost of collective or public treatment of pollution, paying for units discharged in surface water); product charges, administrative charges (paid to authorities for such fees as chemical use, or mining registration to finance the licensing and control activities), tax measures (charges used to encourage or discourage the use of environmental friendly products), market creation, tradable permits, environmental liability insurance; subsidies (tax incentives), environmental impact assessment fees, deposit refund systems and enforcement incentives.

22. Land use planning and zoning is another legislative approach to ensure that industries, airports, and other facilities in cities are located away from residential areas to avoid noise and air pollution and for waste management disposal. For example effective environmental management may require that forest reserves be located far from growing human settlements.

23. Strengthening institutional regimes for environmental management is equally important in terms of building capacity of human resources to be well informed when managing different aspects of the environment. It is also important to ensure that there is adequate coordination of different sectors or government ministries handling environmental issues in the planning and management of various environmental resources and national legislation can streamline this coordination, by a link with other players, e.g. NGOs and Civil Society.

b) The Role of Case Law

24. In addition to national legislation, countries with a "common law" tradition may rely on case law to protect the environment. In general, "common law" represents a body of law developed through judicial decisions, as distinguished from legislative enactments. A fundamental tenet of the common law is the doctrine of *stare decisis*. This doctrine states that when a point of law has been settled by Court Decisions, it establishes a precedent that is followed in later cases unless and until the

precedent is overturned in a subsequent case for very specific reasons. These reasons can vary, for example, for the interruption of a precedent is required to vindicate plain, obvious principles of law or to remedy continued injustice.

25. In countries that follow "civil law" traditions, the heart of the legal system is a set of codes. In civil law countries, the basis for a court's decision must be found in the country's codes. Nevertheless, many civil law jurisdictions examine decisions of leading judges as a source of valuable experience in formulating and applying norms. It is to be noted that fusion in environmental laws and regulations and directives blurs the differences between the two systems. E.g. in EU Directions, or in the legislation to implement international treaties and principles as recent examples of framework laws demonstrate.

c) Implementation, Enforcement and Compliance of National Laws

26. Implementation and enforcement is important for the effectiveness of national environmental legislation. Where national environmental legislation calls for further regulation it is important for the Government to enact the required regulations and to ensure enforcement mechanisms are in place. It is also expected that the Government would put in place the right structure, systems and tools, skills, incentives, strategies, coordination and partnerships for all stakeholders, and assign roles and responsibility to competent staff members to enforce laws and strengthen the legal and institutional framework for environmental management. It is equally important for the Government to promote and to monitor compliance, and to evaluate the effectiveness of national legislation to ensure that enforcement requirements are in place, laws are enforceable, and they do deter violations.

27. All stakeholders who have a role to play in the implementation and enforcement of national environmental laws need to understand clearly both the legal and technical issues associated with environmental programmes if they have to implement and enforce national environmental law. Chapter 8, para. 14 of Agenda 21 provides that "... it is equally critical to develop workable programmes to review and enforce compliance with the laws, regulations and standards that are adopted. Technical support may be needed for many countries to accomplish these goals. Technical cooperation requirements in this field include legal information, advisory services, specialized training and institutional capacity-building."

28. Agenda 21 recognizes the need for enhancing capacity building for implementation and enforcement of national environmental law. The activities envisaged include raising awareness of all stakeholders associated with this process and equipping them for their work. The raising of awareness of various stakeholders may include prosecutors, legal practitioners, members of the Judiciary, government officials at all levels, local authorities including municipalities, compliance officers in environmental agencies handling air quality issues, water quality regulators, waste regulators in local authorities, national park enforcement officers, customs officers, etc.

3. Template for Elements of Comprehensive National Legal Regimes for Environmentally Managing of Different Sectors

General Objective of the Legislation	Pollution prevention and control (reduce risk, improve maintain and restore environmental quality, prevent and control pollution, sustain environmental uses, clean up past pollution). Protection, conservation and sustainable use of resources. Integration of environment and development processes into the planning process.
Scope or Relevant areas of Regulation (examples)	• Air pollution (source: fuel, industry, ozone depleting substances, forest fire causing haze) • Noise ppllution (noise in residential areas causing nuisance and town planning for example near airports, industrial premises/occupational health regulating acceptable noise levels) • Freshwater pollution (pollution from sewage and or industrial effluent, standards of treating waste, pollution of rivers, lakes, dams and underground waters and other sources of drinking water) • Protection of the coastal and marine environment from pollution (from sewage disposal, from built structures around the coast including industrial effluent, from ships, and from dumping of wastes), protection from coastal erosion, destruction of habitats and breeding grounds. • Land degradation and soil pollution (caused by bad agricultural practices, unplanned towns and settlements, pollution from different sources, industry, dump sites, mining, etc.) • Sustainable use of environmental resources (manage and control use at a standard which can protect, conserve and sustain the resources). This can apply to energy use, water utilization, protection of species, including fish resources and other biological resources. • Framework environmental laws provide general principles of environmental regulation including providing for cross cutting issues and mechanisms.
Selection of Environmental Management Approaches	Command and control, the use of Economic and Market Based Instruments, Risk Based Instruments, Pollution Prevention (Regulatory, Voluntary, Liability). Standard Setting (ambient, technology, performance, economic and voluntary standards), permits/authorization, inspection and monitoring compliance, use of economic instruments such as the Polluter Pay Principle to internalize the cost, use of market based mechanisms to discourage or encourage behaviour with its incentives or disincentives, self regulation, Clean Development Mechanisms ("CDM"), land use planning and zoning, international cooperation, Environmental Impact Assessment ("EIA"), integrated resource management, training, education and public awareness, etc.
Types of National Actions and Laws	Legislation, regulations, permits and licences, court cases/precedents, taking administrative action, setting up compliance programmes.
Ensuring Compliance and Enforcement of Laws	Promoting and monitoring compliance, and reviewing and evaluating the effectiveness of national legislation to ensure adequate enforcement mechanisms are in place, institutions have capacity, laws are deterrent and are enforceable.

4. Implementation of International Environmental Law at the National Level

29. Agenda 21 underlines the importance of implementing international treaties through the enactment and enforcement of laws and regulations at the regional, national, state/provincial or local/municipal level because these laws and regulations are essential for the implementation of most international agreements in the field of environment and development, in fact, treaties often include obligations to report on legislative measures.

30. A survey of existing agreements has indicated that many countries have failed to enact appropriate national legislation; that states must improve national implementation if the international goals are to be achieved; and that technical assistance may be needed to assist some countries with the necessary implementing national legislation. In developing their national priorities, countries should take account of their international obligations. The adoption of a MEA is just the beginning of the process of implementation, full implementation of MEA's provisions is vital to ensure the effectiveness and full value of the MEA. Each party may be required to adopt policies, to develop and/or strengthen national legislation and institutions, and/or to take up administrative action such as preparation of action plans, designating sites, or appointing focal points as part of measures provided to implement MEAs. Depending on the MEA, other actions aimed at facilitating the process of implementation at the national level may include planning, capacity building, financial assistance, and technology transfer.

31. Application at the national level by domesticating MEAs may be through a "monist" or "dualist" approach. These approaches are meant to separate those countries that implement treaty obligations automatically upon ratification, from those that sought to conform these treaties to their domestic law/process first, before implementation. The first category of countries would be pursuing the monist tradition and the latter the dualist tradition. It is, however, clear from authoritative sources that the practice of states did not show such sharply contrasted notions. Even in countries associated with the monistic tradition, the ratification of a treaty is often followed by deliberate national law-making processes to set the stage for the implementation of the treaty. On the other hand in countries associated with the

dualistic tradition, in some cases, obligations emanating from international law have sometimes been applied as a matter of course under the judicial process.

32. It thus makes more practical sense to see treaty law, for purposes of implementation, as either self-executing or non-self-executing. Self-executing treaties require no special measures in domestic legislation for implementation, as they readily fit into the operative scheme of the national legal process. But non-self-executing treaties require deliberate legislative or other related decisions at the national level, as a basis for carrying out the required implementation.

33. Formal legislative adoption of treaty law may be regarded as the technical aspect of the broader process of domestication. The notion of domestication of treaty law essentially addresses the acceptance of such law and its principles within the policy, legal and administrative structure of a particular jurisdiction. It should be noted that in most chapters of this manual the section titled National Implementation provides examples of national effort to domesticate one multilateral treaty. These sections reinforce and strengthen this chapter. When the discrete elements of the treaty are implanted into the national governance apparatus and the routine motions of regular administration, they are then assured of application, in the same manner as the ordinary law of the land. The treaty law, in this respect, undergoes a process of transformation, and is assimilated into the domestic law. In this way, it is possible to achieve the most effective scheme of implementation for treaty law.

5. UNEP's Capacity Building Programme on Environmental Law

34. UNEP provides assistance to governments to translate sustainable development policies into action by developing and strengthening capacity to develop, strengthen and implement environmental laws. The capacity-building programme of UNEP on environmental law focuses on building capacity of legal stakeholders to develop, apply, strengthen and implement environmental law. The targeted groups are mainly decision-makers in the government, legal professionals such as members of the Judiciary, state attorneys and other prosecutors, and academicians (to enhance the teaching of environmental law in higher learning institutions).

Interventions include training programmes, advisory services and technical assistance in environmental law, and enhancing access to environmental law information. UNEP also provides its expertise and support in negotiation processes of international environmental instruments, as well as in other international processes.

35. UNEP has been receiving requests from developing countries and countries with economies in transition to assist them in developing and/or strengthening their environmental legislation and institutional regimes. The response to these requests have been through technical assistance programmes to developing countries in the field of environmental law and institutions which stems from the United Nations General Assembly Resolution 3436 (XXX) of 1975. This resolution required the UNEP Executive Director to take measures designed to provide technical assistance to developing countries for development of their national legislation. This mandate was subsequently reinforced by UNEP Governing Council decisions requesting UNEP to assist governments in the developing countries to strengthen the legal and institutional framework for environmental management, the UNCED Agenda 21, and the WSSD Plan of Implementation. These instruments recognize that the short-comings in existing environmental legislation and institutions affect the effective integration of environment and development policies and practices, particularly in the developing countries. Consequently, UNEP emphasizes the need for strengthening national legislative and institutional regimes for translating sustainable development policies and strategies into action, including effective implementation of international environmental legal instruments, particularly in developing countries and countries with economies in transition. An important decision adopted in the 7th Governing Council Special Session in Cartagena, Colombia, in February 2002 operationalizes UNEP at country level and hence can comfortably assist countries on request alone jointly with others.

36. UNEP's capacity building activities in the field of national environmental legislation and institutions are participatory in nature. The UNEP staff members work with government officials and local experts all through the programme to develop and/or strengthen national legislation. UNEP's work is guided by the Programme for the Development and Periodic Review of Environmental Law for the First Decade of the 21st Century ("Montevideo Programme III"), which is a ten-year environmental law programme that was adopted by the UNEP Governing Council under decision 21/23. The Montevideo Programme III is the third in a series of law programmes that UNEP is implementing since 1982 when Montevideo I was adopted. In decision 17/25, Montevideo II was adopted. Paragraph 2 of the programme addresses capacity-building and provides, as its objective, for strengthening the regulatory and institutional capacity of developing countries, in particular the Least Developed Countries, Small Island Developing States and countries with economies in transition, to develop and implement environmental law. The strategy is to provide appropriate technical assistance, education and training based on assessment of needs.

37. Under the framework of the Montevideo Programme, through its biennial programme of work, UNEP continues to assist governments to strengthen the legal and institutional framework for environmental management upon request. UNEP also prepares guide materials and publications to enhance access to environmental information. Global, Regional and National Training programmes are conducted to build capacity of decision-makers and other legal stakeholders to apply, interpret, enforce, strengthen, implement and to develop environmental law.

38. In addition to UNEP, various bodies of the United Nations are involved in specific environmental management such as the International Atomic Energy Agency ("IAEA"), the United Nations Development Programme ("UNDP"), the United Nations, Economic Commissions; the specialized agencies that include, World Health Organization ("WHO"), the World Meteorological Organization ("WMO"), the International Civil Aviation Organization ("ICAO"), the Food and Agriculture Organization ("FAO"), the United Nations Education, Science and Culture Organization ("UNESCO") and the International Maritime Organization ("IMO"); the World Bank and Regional Banks and other international organizations including the Organization for Economic Cooperation and Development ("OECD"), the North Atlantic Treaty Organization ("NATO"), the European Union ("EU"), the Council of Europe; the Organization of African

Unity, now African Union ("AU"), and such other international NGOs as the World Conservation Union/IUCN. These organizations have played a role in development of international environmental law as well as undertaking activities that can facilitate implementation of national environmental law. These organizations have been active in issues such as atmospheric pollution, marine environment, water pollution, land use and conservation of natural resources, urban environmental problems.

Sylvia Bankobeza, Legal Officer, Division of Policy Development and Law, UNEP

Resources

Internet Materials

AGENDA 21 AND THE WSSD PLAN OF IMPLEMENTATION available at http://www.un.org, http://www.un.org/esa/sustdev/documents/agenda21/index.htm, http://www.johannesburgsummit.org/ and http://www.un.org/esa/sustdev/documents/WSSD_POI_PD/English/POIToc.htm

GATEWAY SITE FOR ENVIRONMENTAL LAW INCLUDING TREATIES, NATIONAL LEGISLATION, COURT DECISIONS AND ENVIRONMENTAL LITERATURE available at http://www.ecolex.org/ecolex/index.php

UNITED NATIONS ENVIRONMENT PROGRAMME, DIVISION OF POLICY DEVELOPMENT AND LAW ("UNEP/DPDL") available at http://www.unep.org/DPDL/law/

Text Materials

Donald K. Anton, Jennifer Kohout & Nicola Pain, NATIONALIZING ENVIRONMENTAL PROTECTION IN AUSTRALIA: THE INTERNATIONAL DIMENSIONS, (23 Envtl. L. 763, 1993).

Durwood Zaelke, Donald Kaniaru & Eva Kruzikova, MAKING LAW WORK, ENVIRONMENTAL COMPLIANCE AND SUSTAINABLE DEVELOPMENT, (Cameroon, May, 2005).

J.H. Jans, EUROPEAN ENVIRONMENTAL LAW, (Kluwer Law International, 1995).

Jennifer M. Gleason & Bern A. Johnson, ENVIRONMENTAL LAW ACROSS BORDERS, (10 J. Envtl. L. & Litig. 67).

John Norton Moore, THE NATIONAL LAW OF TREATY IMPLEMENTATION, (Carolina Academic Press, 2001).

Jonathan B. Wiener, RESPONDING TO THE GLOBAL WARMING PROBLEM: SOMETHING BORROWED FOR SOMETHING BLUE: LEGAL TRANSPLANTS AND THE EVOLUTION OF GLOBAL ENVIRONMENTAL LAW, (27 Ecology L.Q. 1295, 2001).

Leah Sandbank, DIRTY LAUNDRY: WHY INTERNATIONAL MEASURES TO SAVE THE GLOBAL CLEAN WATER SUPPLY HAVE FAILED, (13 Fordham Envtl. L.J. 165, 2001).

Matthew R. Auer, GEOGRAPHY, DOMESTIC POLITICS AND ENVIRONMENTAL DIPLOMACY: A CASE FROM THE BALTIC SEA REGION, (11 Geo. Int'l Envtl. L. Rev. 77 -100, 1998).

Peter H. Sand, TRANSNATIONAL ENVIRONMENTAL LAW: LESSONS IN GLOBAL CHANGE, (Kluwer Law International, 1999).

Rudiger Wolfrum & Fred L. Morrison, INTERNATIONAL, REGIONAL AND NATIONAL ENVIRONMENTAL LAW, (Kluwer Law International, 2000).

3. PRINCIPLES AND CONCEPTS OF INTERNATIONAL ENVIRONMENTAL LAW

I. Introduction

1. This chapter provides an overview of the main principles (i.e. fundamental doctrines on which others are based, or rules of conduct) and concepts (i.e. central unifying ideas or themes) in international environmental law. It identifies important emerging principles and concepts, describes the roles they play, and provides examples to illustrate some of the ways in which they have been applied. In doing so, it provides a backdrop for the rest of this UNEP Training Manual and assists the user in better understanding why specific approaches to protecting the environment have come about and how they work. Understanding the basic principles and concepts will facilitate a sound appreciation of many of the treaties reviewed in this Manual, and in the development and consolidation of international environmental law. Comprehension of modern and evolving international environmental law and its different facts, needs not only knowledge of treaty law, but also the translation of principles and concepts into legally binding rules and instruments.

II. Overview of International Environmental Law Principles and Concepts

2. Principles and concepts embody a common ground in international environmental law; and they both reflect the past growth of international environmental law and affect its future evolution. Principles and concepts play important roles in international environmental law, which itself is one of the most rapidly evolving areas of public international law. They can indicate the essential characteristics of international environmental law and its institutions, provide guidance in interpreting legal norms, constitute fundamental norms, and fill in gaps in positive law. Principles and concepts also appear in national constitutions and laws; and they are referred to in, and influence, international and national jurisprudence. Today, almost all major binding and non-legally binding international environmental instruments contain or refer to principles or concepts and are engines in the evolving environmental law.

3. The development of environmental law during the past three decades has led to the emergence of an increasing number of concepts, principles and norms (i.e. binding rules of international law). The reason why principles and concepts play such important role is linked to the origin and development of international environmental law. Environmental law has developed mainly in a piecemeal fashion, not in a structured orderly way, as *ad hoc* responses to environmental threats and challenges. Indeed, in the case of UNEP, this was the way till 1982 when the first ten year programme of environmental law, often referred to as Montevideo Programme I, was agreed. Thereafter this has been prepared and approved by the Governing Council for each subsequent ten years: Montevideo Programme II in 1993 and Montevideo Programme III in 2001. There are many international arenas and many international instruments dealing with specific environmental problems. Not surprisingly, therefore, principles and concepts have been repeated or referred to in many different treaties or non-binding instruments. The frequent inclusion of these principles and concepts in international legal instruments reinforces them and, together with state practice, will continue to contribute to the creation of a global framework for international environmental law.

4. Of particular importance are the principles established at two important United Nations conferences, the 1972 Conference on the Human Environment ("Stockholm Conference") and the 1992 United Nations Conference on Environment and Development ("UNCED") in Rio de Janeiro. Both of these conferences produced declarations of principles (the "1972 Stockholm Declaration" and the "1992 Rio Declaration", respectively), which were adopted by the United Nations General Assembly. Together with the hundreds of international agreements that exist relating to protecting the environment (including human health), the principles in the 1972 Stockholm Declaration and 1992 Rio Declaration are widely-regarded as the underpinnings of international environmental law.

5. The Rio Declaration contains a preamble and twenty-seven international environmental law principles that guide the international community in its efforts to achieve sustainable development. Since the adoption of the Rio Declaration, major developments in international environmental law have taken place that affect the definition, status and impact of principles and concepts in international environmental law. These

developments include the negotiation and entry into force of several major multilateral agreements. (See chapters 1, 4, 7, 9, 10, 11, 12, 13, 14, 15 and 19 of this Manual).

6. A general characteristic of present international environmental law is the utilization of non-binding international instruments. Such texts are often easier to negotiate and amend in the light of new problems where scientific knowledge and public awareness can be the major factors pressing for international action. Principles in non-binding texts can help develop international environmental law and directly or indirectly give birth to new legal rules in conventions and/or customary law.

7. The legal status of international environmental law principles and concepts is varied and may be subject to disagreement among states. Some principles are firmly established in international law, while others are emerging and only in the process of gaining acceptance, representing more recent concepts. Some principles are more in the nature of guidelines or policy directives which do not necessarily give rise to specific legal rights and obligations. Principles have acquired recognition, among other means, through state practice, their incorporation in international legal instruments, their incorporation in national laws and regulations, and through judgements of courts of law and tribunals. Some principles are embodied or specifically expressed in global or regionally binding instruments, while others are predominantly based in customary law. In many cases it is difficult to establish the precise parameters or legal status of a particular principle. The manner in which each principle applies to a particular activity or incident typically must be considered in relation to the facts and circumstances of each case, taking into account of various factors including its sources and textual context, its language, the particular activity at issue, and the particular circumstances in which it occurs, including the actors and the geographical region, since the juridical effect of principles and concepts may change from one legal system to another.

8. For the reasons outlined in the preceding paragraph, this chapter does not address the question of whether a particular principle is, in fact, binding international law. In order to avoid confusion in this respect, part III, below, refers to principles and concepts jointly as "concepts" unless referring to a particular text, e.g. one of the Rio "Principles".

9. Some scholars believe the development of a single comprehensive treaty of fundamental environmental norms may be a future solution to counteract fragmentation and provide clarity about the legal status of various principles. Such an overarching agreement may provide the legal framework to support the further integration of various aspects of sustainable development, reinforcing the consensus on basic legal norms both nationally and internationally. It could thus create a single set of fundamental principles and concepts to guide states, international organizations, NGOs and individuals. It could consolidate and codify many widely accepted, but scattered, principles and concepts contained in non-binding texts on environment and sustainable development and fill in gaps in existing law. It could also facilitate institutional and other linkages among existing treaties and their implementation, and be taken into account in judicial and arbitral decisions, negotiations of new international legal instruments, and national law-making.

10. Finally, it is important to recognize that international environmental law is an inseparable part of public international law. Public international law principles such as the duty to negotiate in good faith, the principle of good neighbourliness and notification, and the duty to settle disputes peacefully, thus may pertain to a situation regardless of its designation as "environmental" and may affect the evolution of international environmental law principles more generally. At the same time, the development of international environmental law principles and concepts may affect the development of principles in other areas of international law. The application and, where relevant, consolidation and further development of the principles and concepts of international environmental law listed in this chapter, as well as of other principles of international law, will be instrumental in pursuing the objective of sustainable development.

III. Emerging Principles and Concepts

11. The principles and concepts discussed in this chapter are:

1. Sustainable Development, Integration and Interdependence
2. Inter-Generational and Intra-Generational Equity
3. Responsibility for Transboundary Harm
4. Transparency, Public Participation and Access to Information and Remedies
5. Cooperation, and Common but Differentiated Responsibilities
6. Precaution

7. Prevention
8. "Polluter Pays Principle"
9. Access and Benefit Sharing regarding Natural Resources
10. Common Heritage and Common Concern of Humankind
11. Good Governance

1. Sustainable Development, Integration and Interdependence

12. The international community recognized sustainable development as the overarching paradigm for improving quality of life in 1992, at UNCED. Although sustainable development is susceptible to somewhat different definitions, the most commonly accepted and cited definition is that of the Brundtland Commission on Environment and Development, which stated in its 1987 Report, Our Common Future, that sustainable development is "development that meets the needs of the present without compromising the ability of future generations to meet their own needs." The parameters of sustainable development are clarified in Agenda 21 and the Rio Declaration, both adopted at UNCED, and in subsequent international regional and national instruments.

13. Principle 4 of the Rio Declaration provides: "In order to achieve sustainable development, environmental protection shall constitute an integral part of the development process and cannot be considered in isolation from it." Principle 25 states that "Peace, development and environmental protection are interdependent and indivisible." Principles 4 and 25 make clear that policies and activities in various spheres, including environmental protection, must be integrated in order to achieve sustainable development. They also make clear that the efforts to improve society, including those to protect the environment, achieve peace, and accomplish economic development, are interdependent. Principles 4 and 25 thus embody the concepts of integration and interdependence.

14. The concepts of integration and interdependence are stated even more clearly in paragraph 6 of the 1995 Copenhagen Declaration on Social Development, which introduction states that "economic development, social development and environmental protection are interdependent and mutually reinforcing components of sustainable development, which is the framework for our efforts to achieve a higher quality of life for all people…". Paragraph 5 of the 2002 Johannesburg Declaration on Sustainable Development confirms

this, by stating that "we assume a collective responsibility to advance and strengthen the interdependent and mutually reinforcing pillars of sustainable development (economic development, social development and environmental protection) at the local, national, regional and global levels." Integration was one of the main themes discussed at the 2002 Johannesburg World Summit on Sustainable Development, with particular emphasis on eradicating poverty. One of the commitments of Millennium Development Goal number 7 ("Ensure environmental sustainability"), is to "Integrate the principles of sustainable development into country policies and programmes…" Paragraph 30 of the Millennium Declaration speaks of the need for greater policy coherence and increased cooperation among multilateral institutions, such as the United Nations, the World Bank, and the World Trade Organization. The definition of "sustainable development" from the Brundtland Commission's report, quoted above, indicates the interdependence of generations, as well. On the basis of these and other international instruments, it is clear that integration and interdependence are fundamental to sustainable development.

15. The concepts of integration and interdependence in international environmental law are wholly consistent with the nature of the biosphere, i.e. the concentric layers of air, water and land on which life on earth depends. Scientists increasingly understand the fundamental interdependence of the various elements of the biosphere, how changes in one aspect can affect others, and the essential roles that nature plays with respect to human activities and existence (e.g., purifying water, pollinating plants, providing food, providing recreation opportunities, and controlling erosion and floods). In this respect, international environmental law mirrors the most fundamental infrastructure of human society (i.e., the environment).

16. The concept of integration demonstrates a commitment to moving environmental considerations and objectives to the core of international relations. For example, environmental considerations are increasingly a feature of international economic policy and law: the Preamble to the 1994 World Trade Organization Agreement mentions both sustainable development and environmental protection, and there are numerous regional and global treaties supporting an approach that integrates environment and economic development, such as the 1992 Convention on

Biological Diversity ("CBD"), the 1994 United Nations Convention to combat Desertification in Countries Experiencing Serious Drought and/or Desertification, particularly in Africa and the 1997 Kyoto Protocol on Climate Change.

17. At the national level, the concept of integration of environmental concerns with all other policy areas is usually formulated as a procedural rule to be applied by legislative and administrative bodies. It is also a fundamental postulate of most of the national strategies for sustainable development. The future may well witness increased attention to "sustainable development law", in which the specific laws regarding all spheres of activity appropriately integrate environmental, economic and social considerations.

18. Environmental Impact Assessment ("EIA") has become one of the most effective and practical tools to support the implementation of sustainable development and its integrative aspects. The great majority of countries in the world have adopted informal guidelines or mandatory regulations, applicable not only to public projects but often also as a direct obligation of citizens. In addition, in many countries informal procedures of impact assessment for governmental activities have been developed. EIA is also widely accepted as a mechanism for public participation in planning processes and decision-making and a tool to provide information and data to the public regarding projects and other activities.

19. Also necessary are approaches that take into account long-term strategies and that include the use of environmental and social impact assessment, risk analysis, cost-benefit analysis and natural resources accounting. Some have proposed so-called sustainable development impact assessments, which take into account environmental social and economic aspects. The integration of environmental, social and economic policies also requires transparency and broad public participation in governmental decision-making, as discussed in part c below.

2. Inter-Generational and Intra-Generational Equity

20. Equity is central to the attainment of sustainable development. This is evident from many international instruments. For example, the 1992 United Nations Framework Convention on Climate Change ("UNFCC") refers in article 3.(1) to intergenerational equity, as do the last preambular paragraph of the 1992 CBD, the 1992 United Nations Economic Commission for Europe Convention on the Protection and Use of

Transboundary Watercourses and International Lakes, the 1994 Desertification Convention and the 2001 Stockholm Convention on Persistent Organic Pollutants ("POPs"), among others. As noted above, the Brundtland Commission's Report defined sustainable development as "development that meets the needs of the present without compromising the ability of future generations to meet their own needs"; and it goes on to identify two "key concepts" of sustainable development. The first of which is "the concept of 'needs,' in particular the essential needs of the world's poor, to which overriding priority should be given." Similarly, Principle 3 of the 1992 Rio Declaration states that "The right to development must be fulfilled so as to equitably meet developmental and environmental needs of present and future generations"; and Rio Principle 5 provides that "All States and all people shall cooperate in the essential task of eradicating poverty as an indispensable requirement for sustainable development, in order to decrease the disparities in standards of living and better meet the needs of the majority of the people of the world." Paragraph 6 of the Copenhagen Declaration, the first sentence of which is reproduced above, refers in subsequent sentences to "Equitable social development" and "social justice". The concept of equity is also embodied in the United Nations Millennium Goals (e.g. the Eradication of Poverty) and Millennium Declaration (e.g. paragraphs 6, 11 and 21).

21. Equity thus includes both "inter-generational equity" (i.e. the right of future generations to enjoy a fair level of the common patrimony) and "intra-generational equity" (i.e. the right of all people within the current generation to fair access to the current generation's entitlement to the Earth's natural resources).

22. The present generation has a right to use and enjoy the resources of the Earth but is under an obligation to take into account the long-term impact of its activities and to sustain the resource base and the global environment for the benefit of future generations of humankind. In this context, "benefit" is given its broadest meaning as including, inter alia, economic, environmental, social, and intrinsic gain.

23. Some national courts have referred to the right of future generations in cases before them. For example, the Supreme Court of the Republic of the Philippines decided, in the Minors Oposa case (Philippines - Oposa et. al. v. Fulgencio S. Factoran, Jr. et al. G.R. No. 101083), that the petitioners could file a class suit, for others of their generation and for the succeeding generations. The Court,

considering the concept of inter-generational responsibility, further stated that every generation has a responsibility to the next to preserve that rhythm and harmony necessary for the full enjoyment of a balanced and healthful ecology.

3. Responsibility for Transboundary Harm

24. Principle 21 of the Stockholm Declaration recognizes the sovereign right of each state upon its natural resources, emphasizing that it is limited by the responsibility for tranboundary harm.

**1972 Stockholm Declaration
Principle 21**

"States have, in accordance with the Charter of the United Nations and the principles of international law, the sovereign right to exploit their own resources pursuant to their own environmental policies, and the responsibility to ensure that activities within their jurisdiction or control do not cause damage to the environment of other States or of areas beyond the limits of national jurisdiction."

Twenty years later, Principle 21 was reiterated in Principle 2 of the Rio Declaration, with the sole change of adding the adjective "developmental" between the words "environmental" and "policies":

**1992 Rio Declaration
Principle 2**

"States have, in accordance with the Charter of the United Nations and the principles of international law, the sovereign right to exploit their own resources pursuant to their own environmental and developmental policies, and the responsibility to ensure that activities within their jurisdiction or control do not cause damage to the environment of other States or of areas beyond the limits of national jurisdiction."

---

25. Stockholm Principle 21/ Rio Principle 2, although part of non-binding texts, are nonetheless well-established, and are regarded by some as a rule of customary international law. Either or both of them have been reaffirmed in declarations adopted by the United Nations, including the Charter of Economic Rights and Duties of States, the World Charter for Nature, and the Declaration of the 2002 World Summit on Sustainable Development. Their contents are included in the United Nations Convention on the Law of the Sea ("UNCLOS") as well as in article 20 of the Association of South East Asian Nations ("ASEAN") Agreement on the Conservation of Nature and Natural Resources. The 1979 Convention on Long- Range Transboundary Air Pollution reproduces Principle

21, stating that it "expresses the common conviction that States have" on this matter. Principle 21 also appears in article 3 of the 1992 Convention on Biological Diversity, to which virtually all the states of the world are parties, and, as restated in the 1992 Rio Declaration, in the preamble of the 1992 UNFCCC, the 1999 Protocol on Water and Health to the Convention on the Protection and Use of Transboundary Watercourses and International Lakes, and the 2001 Stockholm Convention on Persistent Organic Pollutants ("POPs"). Also, the International Court of Justice ("ICJ") recognized in an advisory opinion that "The existence of the general obligation of states to ensure that activities within their jurisdiction and control respect the environment of other states or of areas beyond national control is now part of the corpus of international law relating to the environment." (See Legality of the Threat or Use of Nuclear Weapons, Advisory Opinion, ICJ Reports, pp. 241-42, 1996).

26. Stockholm Principle 21/Rio Principle 2 contain two elements which cannot be separated without fundamentally changing their sense and effect: (1) the sovereign right of states to exploit their own natural resources, and (2) the responsibility, or obligation, not to cause damage to the environment of other states or areas beyond the limits of national jurisdiction. It is a well-established practice that, within the limits stipulated by international law, every state has the right to manage and utilize natural resources within its jurisdiction and to formulate and pursue its own environmental and developmental policies. However, one of the limits imposed by international law on that right is that states have an obligation to protect their environment and prevent damage to neighbouring environments.

27. Stockholm Principle 21/Rio Principle 2 affirm the duty of states 'to ensure' that activities within their jurisdiction or control do not cause damage to the environment of other states. This means that states are responsible not only for their own activities, but also with respect to all public and private activities within their jurisdiction or control that could harm the environment of other states or areas outside the limits of their jurisdiction. The responsibility for damage to the environment exists not only with respect to the environment of other states, but also of areas beyond the limits of national jurisdiction, such as the high seas and the airspace above them, the deep seabed, outer space, the Moon and other celestial bodies, and Antarctica.

28. The exact scope and implications of Stockholm Principle 21/Rio Principle 2 are not clearly determined. It seems clear that not all instances of

transboundary damage resulting from activities within a state's territory or control can be prevented or are unlawful, though compensation may nevertheless be called for; but the circumstances in which those outcomes arise are not entirely clear.

4. Transparency, Public Participation and Access to Information and Remedies

29. Public participation and acces to information are recognized in Principle 10 of the Rio Declaration.

**1992 Rio Declaration
Principle 10**

"Environmental issues are best handled with the participation of all concerned citizens, at the relevant level. At the national level, each individual shall have appropriate access to information concerning the environment that is held by public authorities, including information on hazardous materials and activities in their communities, and the opportunity to participate in decision-making processes. States shall facilitate and encourage public awareness and participation by making information widely available. Effective access to judicial and administrative proceedings, including redress and remedy, shall be provided."

---

30. Transparency and access to information are essential to public participation and sustainable development, for example, in order to allow the public to know what the decision making processes are, what decisions are being contemplated, the alleged factual bases for proposed and accomplished governmental actions, and other aspects of governmental processes. Public participation is essential to sustainable development and good governance in that it is a condition for responsive, transparent and accountable governments. It is also a condition for the active engagement of equally responsive, transparent and accountable Civil Society organizations, including industrial concerns, trade unions, and Non Governmental Organizations ("NGOs"). Public participation in the context of sustainable development requires effective protection of the human right to hold and express opinions and to seek, receive and impart ideas. It also requires a right of access to appropriate, comprehensible and timely information held by governments and industrial concerns on economic and social policies regarding the sustainable use of natural resources and the protection of the environment, without imposing undue financial burdens upon the applicants and with adequate protection of privacy and business confidentiality.

31. The empowerment of people in the context of sustainable development also requires access to

effective judicial and administrative proceedings. For example, states should ensure that where transboundary harm has been or is likely to be caused, affected individuals and communities have non-discriminatory access to effective judicial and administrative processes.

32. Principle 10 combines public participation with public access to information and access to remedial procedures. According to chapter 23 of Agenda 21, one of the fundamental prerequisites for the achievement of sustainable development is broad public participation in decision-making. Agenda 21 (chapters 23-32, and 36) emphasises the importance of the participation of all Major Groups, and special emphasis has been given in Agenda 21, the Rio Declaration, and in legally binding international instruments to ensuring the participation in decision-making of those groups that are considered to be politically disadvantaged, such as indigenous peoples and women. Principle 10 also supports a role for individuals in enforcing national environmental laws and obligations before national courts and tribunals.

33. The 1992 United Nations Framework Convention on Climate Change, in article 4.(1)(i), obliges Parties to promote public awareness and participation in the process, including that of NGOs, though it does not create a public right of access to information. The 1994 Desertification Convention recognizes, in article 3(a)(c), the need to associate Civil Society with the action of the State. (See also article 12 of the 1995 United Nations Fish Stocks Agreement). The 1993 North American Agreement on Environmental Cooperation requires parties to publish their environmental laws, regulations, procedures and administrative rulings (article 4), to ensure that interested persons have access to judicial, quasi-judicial or administrative proceedings to force the government to enforce environmental law (article 6), and to ensure that their judicial, quasi-judicial and administrative proceedings are fair, open and equitable (article 7). More commonly, international legal instruments addressing access to information and public participation are confined to distinct contexts, such as Environmental Impact Assessment. For example, the 1992 CBD requires appropriate public participation in EIA procedures in article 14.(1)(a); article 13 addresses the need for public education and awareness.

34. These concepts mean that international institutions, such as international financial institutions, should also implement open and transparent decision-making procedures that are fully available to public participation. Examples of this include the World Bank Inspection Panel, which provides groups affected by World Bank projects the opportunity to

request an independent inspection into alleged violations of Bank policies and procedures. The petitioning process included in articles 14 and 15 of the 1993 North American Agreement on Environmental Cooperation also provides significant new rights for citizens to participate in monitoring domestic enforcement of environmental laws. These concepts also imply that NGOs should be provided at least observer status in international institutions and with respect to treaties, and should be appropriately relied upon for expertise, information and other purposes.

35. In many countries, public participation rights are granted through Environmental Impact Assessment procedures with broad public participation or in various sectoral laws adapted to the special circumstances of each sector. Consultation with, and dissemination of information to the public are important objectives of EIAs. For example, article 16(3) of the 1986 Convention for the Protection of the Natural Resources and Environment of the South Pacific Region requires that the information gathered in the assessment be shared with the public and affected parties. In Africa, the Memorandum of Understanding ("MOU") of October 22, 1998, between Kenya, Tanzania and Uganda contains the agreement of the three states to develop technical guides and regulations on EIA procedures, including enabling public participation at all stages of the process and to enact corresponding legislation (article 14). This provision was subsequently embodied in the Treaty for East African Community by the three states Kenya, Tanzania and Uganda. As noted above, the 1992 CBD also requires appropriate public participation in environmental assessment in article 14(1)(a); and it includes a notification and consultation requirement in article 14(1)(c).

5. Cooperation, and Common but Differentiated Responsibilities

36. Principle 7 of the Rio Declaration provides:

> **1992 Rio Declaration**
> **Principle 7**
>
> "States shall cooperate in a spirit of global partnership to conserve, protect and restore the health and integrity of the Earth's ecosystem. In view of the different contributions to global environmental degradation, States have common but differentiated responsibilities. The developed countries acknowledge the responsibility that they bear in the international pursuit of sustainable development in view of the pressures their societies place on the global environment and of the technologies and financial resources they command."

37. Principle 7 can be divided into two parts: (1) the duty to cooperate in a spirit of global partnership; and (2) common but differentiated responsibilities.

38. The duty to cooperate is well-established in international law, as exemplified in articles 55 and 56 of chapter IX of the Charter of the United Nations, to which all UN member states, at present 191, subscribe, and applies on the global, regional and bilateral levels. The goal of the Rio Declaration is, according to the fourth paragraph of its preamble, the establishment of a "...new and equitable global partnership..." The concept of global partnership can be seen as a more recent reformulation of the obligation to cooperate, and is becoming increasingly important. Principle 7 refers to states, but the concept of global partnership may also be extended to non-state entities. International organisations, business entities (including in particular transnational business entities), NGOs and Civil Society more generally should cooperate in and contribute to this global partnership. Polluters, regardless of their legal form, may also have also responsibilities pursuant to the "Polluter–Pays Principle", described in paragraph 62 and further.

39. Principle 7 also speaks of common but differentiated responsibilities. This element is a way to take account of differing circumstances, particularly in each state's contribution to the creation of environmental problems and in its ability to prevent, reduce and control them. States whose societies have in the past imposed, or currently impose, a disproportionate pressure on the global environment and which command relatively high levels of technological and financial resources bear a proportionally higher degree of responsibility in the international pursuit of sustainable development.

40. In practical terms, the concept of common but differentiated responsibilities is translated into the explicit recognition that different standards, delayed compliance timetables or less stringent commitments may be appropriate for different countries, to encourage universal participation and equity. This may result in differential legal norms, such as in the 1987 Montreal Protocol on Substances that deplete the Ozone Layer (See chapter 9 of this Training Manual). In designing specific differentiated regimes, the special needs and interests of developing countries and of countries with economies in transition, with particular regard to least developed countries and those affected adversely by environmental, social and developmental considerations, should be recognized.

41. According to the concept of common but differentiated responsibilities, developed countries bear a special burden of responsibility in reducing and eliminating unsustainable patterns of production and consumption and in contributing to capacity-building in developing countries, *inter alia* by providing financial assistance and access to environmentally sound technology. In particular, developed countries should play a leading role and assume primary responsibility in matters of relevance to sustainable development. A number of international agreements recognize a duty on the part of industrialized countries to contribute to the efforts of developing countries to pursue sustainable development and to assist developing countries in protecting the global environment. Such assistance may entail, apart from consultation and negotiation, financial aid, transfer of environmentally sound technology and cooperation through international organizations.

42. Article 4 of the 1992 Cimate Change Convention recognizes the special circumstances and needs of developing countries and then structures the duties and obligations to be undertaken by states accordingly. The idea of common but differentiated responsibilities and respective capabilities is stated in article 3 as the first principle to guide the parties in the implementation of the Convention. Article 12 allows for differences in reporting requirements. The provisions of the Convention on joint implementation (article 4.(2)(a), (b)) and guidance provided on the issue by its Conference of the Parties are also of relevance. The 1992 Convention on Biological Diversity states in article 20 (4) that implementation of obligations undertaken by developing countries will depend on the commitments of developed countries to provide new and additional financial resources and to provide access to and transfer of technology on fair and most favourable terms. Other parts of this Convention relate to the special interests and circumstances of developing countries (e.g., paragraphs 13-17, 19 and 21 of the Preamble and articles 16-21).

43. The 1994 Desertification Convention contains specific obligations for affected country parties (article 5) and recognizes additional responsibilities for developed country Parties (article 6). Article 26 of the 1996 Protocol to the Convention on the Prevention of Marine Pollution by Dumping of Wastes and other Matter of 1972 creates the opportunity for parties to adhere to an adjusted compliance time schedule for specific provisions. The idea of common but differentiated responsibilities can be seen as the main idea behind the Fourth APC-EEC Convention of Lome and is included in the fourth preambular paragraph of the 2001 Stockholm Convention on Persistent Organic Pollutants.

6. Precaution

44. Precaution (also referred to as the "precautionary principle," the "precautionary approach," and the "principle of the precautionary approach") is essential to protecting the environment (including human health) and is accordingly one of the most commonly encountered concepts of international environmental law. It is also one of the most controversial, however, because of disagreements over its precise meaning and legal status and because of concern that it may be misused for trade-protectionist purposes.

45. Probably the most widely accepted articulation of precaution is Principle 15 of the Rio Declaration.

**1992 Rio Declaration
Principle 15**

"In order to protect the environment, the precautionary approach shall be widely applied by States according to their capabilities. Where there are threats of serious or irreversible damage, lack of full scientific certainty shall not be used as a reason for postponing cost-effective measures to prevent environmental degradation."

---

46. Principle 15 was one of the first global codifications of the precautionary approach. Other formulations also adopted in 1992 at UNCED appear in the ninth preambular paragraph of the 1992 Convention on Biological Diversity and in article 3(3) of the 1992 Climate Change Convention. The 1992 CBD states: "..where there is a threat of significant reduction or loss of biological diversity, lack of full scientific uncertainty should not be used as a reason for postponing measures to avoid or minimize such a threat." This language is less restrictive than Principle 15, because "significant" is a lower threshold than "serious or irreversible" and the language does not limit permissible action to cost-effective measures. Article 3(3) of the 1992 Climate Change Convention appears to take a somewhat more action-oriented approach than Principle 15, stating: "The parties should take precautionary measures to anticipate, prevent or minimize the cause of climate change and mitigate its adverse effects..." The next sentence, however, repeats Principle 15 almost *verbatim*.

47. Other formulations also exist. One of the most forceful is that in article 4(3)(f) of the 1991 Bamako Convention on the Ban of the Import into Africa and the Control of their Transboundary Movement and Management of Hazardous Wastes within Africa, which requires parties to take action if there is scientific uncertainty. Another example can be found in the 1996 Protocol to the London Convention, which states in article 3(1): "In implementing this Protocol, Contracting parties shall apply a precautionary approach to environmental protection ... when there is reason to believe that wastes or other matter introduced in the marine environment are likely to cause harm even when there is no conclusive evidence to prove a causal relation between inputs and their effects". Its second preambular paragraph, emphasizes the achievements, within the framework of the London Convention, especially the evolution towards approaches based on precaution and prevention.

48. The 2000 Cartagena Biosafety Protocol to the 1992 CBD is based upon the precautionary approach. It is contained in article 1 on the objective of the Protocol which refers explicitly to Rio Principle 15. Articles 10 and 11 contain the key provisions regarding precaution. Article 10(6) provides that "lack of scientific certainty due to insufficient relevant information and knowledge regarding the extent of the potential adverse effects of Living Modified Organisms ("LMO") shall not prevent the Party from taking a decision, as appropriate with regard to the import of the LMO in question..., in order to avoid or minimize such potential adverse effects." Article 11 uses similar language. Thus, a country may reject an import even in the absence of scientific certainty that it will potentially cause harm. These provisions are broader than Rio Principle 15 because they do not refer to "serious or irreversible damage" or cost-effectiveness.

49. The 1995 Agreement on Fish Stocks adopts the precautionary approach in article 6; and its article 5(c) states that the application of the precautionary approach is one of the general principles of the Agreement. (See also Annex II to the Agreement, "Guidelines for Application of Precautionary Reference Points in Conservation and Management of Straddling Fish Stocks and Highly Migratory Fish Stocks"). The precautionary approach is also included in Annex II, article 3(3)(c), of the Convention for the Protection of the Marine Environment of the North-East Atlantic.

50. Other international agreements in which the precautionary approach appears include: Helsinki Convention on the Protection of the Marine Environment of the Baltic Sea, Area article 3(2)(1992); Amendments to the Protocol for the Protection of the Mediterranean Sea against Pollution from Land-Based Sources, Preamble (1996); Protocol to the 1979 Convention on Long-Range Transboundary Air Pollution to abate Acidification, Eutrophication and Ground-Level Ozone, Preamble (1999); the Cartagena Protocol on Biosafety, Preamble (2000); Convention on the Conservation and Management of Highly Migratory Fish Stocks in the Western and Central Pacific Ocean, Preamble (2000); Convention on the Conservation and Management of Fishery Resources in the South-East Atlantic Ocean, Preamble (2001); the Stockholm Convention on Persistent Organic Pollutants, Preamble (2001); the European Energy Charter Treaty, article 19(1) (1994); Agreement on the Conservation of Albatrosses and Petrels, article II(3) (2001); the Convention for Cooperation in the Protection and Sustainable Development of the Marine and Coastal Environment of the Northeast Pacific, article 5 (6)(a) (2002); and the ASEAN Agreement on Transboundary Haze Pollution, article 3.(3) (2002).

51. Concrete application of the precautionary approach can be found in treaties for the management of living resources, especially those concerning fishing. The 1995 United Nations Agreement for the Implementation of the Provisions of the United Nations Convention on the Law of the Sea of 10 December 1982, relating to the Conservation and Management of Straddling Fish Stocks and Highly Migratory Fish Stocks declares that states shall apply the precautionary approach (article 5(c)). Article 6 adds that such application includes taking a precautionary approach widely to conservation, management and exploitation of straddling fish stocks and highly migratory fish stocks, *inter alia,* by improving decision-making in this field, by taking into account uncertainties relating to the size and productivity of the stocks, by developing knowledge, by not exceeding reference points, by enhanced monitoring and by adopting, if necessary, emergency measures. Similarly, the 2000 Convention on the Conservation and Management of Highly Migratory Fish Stocks in the Western and Central Pacific Ocean provides that the Commission created by this instrument shall apply the precautionary approach (article 5(c)). EC Regulation 2371/2002 of December 2002 on the

Conservation and Sustainable Exploitation of Fisheries Resources under the Common Fisheries Policy also foresees that the Community "...shall apply the precautionary approach in taking measures designed to protect and conserve living aquatic resources, to provide for their sustainable exploitation and to minimize the impact of fishing activities on marine ecosystems..." (article 2(1)).

52. The precautionary principle has been invoked before the International Court of Justice. Judge Weeramantry in his opinion dissenting from the Order of the Court of 22 September 1995 concluded that the precautionary principle was gaining increasing support as part of the international law of the environment. Judge Weeramantry stated:

"The law cannot function in protection of the environment unless a legal principle is involved to meet this evidentiary difficulty, and environmental law has responded with what has come to be described as the precautionary principle – a principle which is gaining increasing support as part of the international law of the environment."

ICJ Order of 22 September 1995, at p. 342 (Weeramantry, J., dissenting). In the Gabčikovo Case, the International Court of Justice did not accept Hungary's argument that a state of necessity could arise from application of the precautionary principle.

53. The European Court of Justice ("ECJ") has adopted the precautionary approach, particularly in respect to environmental risks that pose dangers to human health. The Court held that the Commission had not committed manifest error when banning the export of beef during the "mad cow" crisis. The Court said: "At the time when the contested decision was adopted, there was great uncertainty as to the risks posed by live animals, bovine meat and derived products. Where there is uncertainty as to the existence or extent of risks to human health, the institutions may take protective measures without having to await the reality and seriousness of those risks to become fully apparent." Judgement of the ECJ in Cases C-157/96 (The Queen vs Ministry of Agriculture, Fisheries and Food) and C-180/96 (UK vs Commission of the EC).

54. In the Southern Bluefin Tuna Case, the International Tribunal on the Law of the Sea ("ITLOS") could not conclusively assess the scientific evidence regarding the provisional measures sought by New Zealand and indeed, the country requested the measures on the basis of the precautionary principle, pending a final settlement of the case. ITLOS found that in the face of scientific uncertainty regarding the measures, action should be taken as a measure of urgency to avert further deterioration of the tuna stock. In its decision-making, the tribunal said that in its view, "the Parties should in the circumstances act with prudence and caution to ensure that effective conservation measures are taken to prevent serious harm to the stock of southern bluefin tuna." See ITLOS, Southern Bluefin Tuna Case (Australia and New Zealand v. Japan), Order of August 27, 1999. The decision prescribed a limitation to experimental fishing to avoid possible damage to the stock.

55. Central to all of the preceding formulations is the element of anticipation, reflecting the need for effective environmental measures to be based upon actions which take a long-term approach and which anticipate possible revisions on the basis of changes in scientific knowledge. Also central to precaution is the reality that environmental decision makers seldom, if ever, have all the information they would like to have before making a decision.

56. The exercise of precaution with respect to risk management can take many forms, including most commonly taking pollution-prevention actions or placing the burden of proof safety on the person or persons carrying out or intending to carry out an activity that may cause harm, including using or importing a drug or other potentially dangerous substance. Another precautionary method is to provide additional margins of safety, beyond those that are directly verifiable by existing scientific information, for vulnerable groups such as children.

7. Prevention

57. Experience and scientific expertise demonstrate that prevention of environmental harm should be the "Golden Rule" for the environment, for both ecological and economic reasons. It is frequently impossible to remedy environmental injury: the extinction of a species of fauna or flora, erosion, loss of human life and the dumping of persistent pollutants into the sea, for example, create irreversible situations. Even when harm is remediable, the costs of rehabilitation are often prohibitive. An obligation of prevention also emerges from the international responsibility not to cause significant damage to the environment extra-

territorially, but the preventive approach seeks to avoid harm irrespective of whether or not there is transboundary impact or international responsibility.

58. The concept of prevention is complex, owing to the number and diversity of the legal instruments in which it occurs. It can perhaps better be considered an overarching aim that gives rise to a multitude of legal mechanisms, including prior assessment of environmental harm, licensing or authorization that set out the conditions for operation and the consequences for violation of the conditions, as well as the adoption of strategies and policies. Emission limits and other product or process standards, the use of best available techniques and similar techniques can all be seen as applications of the concept of prevention.

59. One obligation that flows from the concept of prevention is prior assessment of potentially harmful activities. Since the failure to exercise due diligence to prevent transboundary harm can lead to international responsibility, it may be considered that a properly conducted Environmental Impact Assessment might serve as a standard for determining whether or not due diligence was exercised. Preventive mechanisms also include monitoring, notification, and exchange of information, all of which are obligations in almost all recent environmental agreements. ITLOS, in its Order of 3 December 2001 in the MOX Plant Case, considered (para. 82) the duty to cooperate in exchanging information concerning environmental risks a "fundamental principle in the prevention of pollution of the marine environment" under the United Nations Convention on the Law of the Sea and general international law. Obligations to conduct EIAs are also found in the 1991 Espoo Convention on Environmental Impact Assessment in a Transboundary Context, the 1992 Convention on the Transboundary Effects of Industrial Accidents, and the 1993 North American Agreement on Environmental Cooperation. Principle 17 of the 1992 Rio Declaration, Agenda 21, principle 8(h) of the 1992 Non-Legally Binding Authorative Statement of Principles for a Global Consensus on the Management, Conservation and Sustainable Development of all Types of Forests ("Forests Principles, and article 14(1)(a) and (b) of the 1992 CBD treat both the national and international aspects of the issue. The concept is also contained in article 206 of UNCLOS.

60. The duty of prevention extends to combating the introduction of exogenous species into an ecosystem. Article V(4) of the 1976 Convention on Conservation of Nature in the South Pacific provides that the contracting parties must carefully examine the consequences of such introduction. More stringently, article 22 of the 1997 United Nations Convention on the Law of the Non-Navigational Uses of International Watercourses requires watercourse states to "...take all measures necessary to prevent the introduction of species, alien or new, into an international watercourse which may have effects detrimental to the ecosystem of the watercourse resulting in significant harm to other watercourse States."

61. In fact, the objective of most international environmental instruments is to prevent environmental harm, whether they concern pollution of the sea, inland waters, the atmosphere, soil or the protection of human life or living resources. Only a relatively few international agreements use other approaches, such as the traditional principle of state responsibility or direct compensation of the victims.

8. "Polluter Pays Principle"

62. Principle 16 of the Rio Declaration provides:

> **1992 Rio Declaration**
> **Principle 16**
>
> "National authorities should endeavour to promote the internalization of environmental costs and the use of economic instruments, taking into account the approach that the polluter should, in principle, bear the cost of pollution, with due regard to the public interest and without distorting international trade and investment."

63. Principle 16 on internalisation of costs includes what has become known as the "Polluter Pays Principle" or "PPP". According to the PPP, the environmental costs of economic activities, including the cost of preventing potential harm, should be internalized rather than imposed upon society at large. An early version of the PPP was developed by the Organization for Economic Co-operation and Development ("OECD") in the 1970s in an effort to ensure that companies would pay the full costs of complying with pollution-control laws and were not subsidised by the state. The PPP was adopted by the OECD as an economic principle and as the most efficient way of allocating costs of pollution-prevention-and-control measures introduced by public authorities in the member countries. It was intended to encourage rational use of scarce resources and to avoid distortions in international trade and investment. It was meant to apply within a state, not between states. As a goal of domestic policy, it has been realized only partially in practice. See also chapter 5 of this Manual.

64. Since 1972, the PPP has gained increasing acceptance, has expanded in its scope to include (at least in theory) all costs associated with pollution, and has moved beyond the developed-country context. Some recent international instruments that include it are: the 2003 Protocol on Civil Liability and Compensation for Damage caused by the Transboundary Effects of Industrial Accidents on Transboundary Waters to the 1992 Convention on the Protection and Use of Transboundary Watercourses and International Lakes and to the 1992 Convention on the Transboundary Effects of Industrial Accidents, Preamble, paragraphs two and three; and the 1996 Protocol to the London Convention, article 3.2. of which states that the polluter should, in principle, bear the cost of pollution.

65. Prior to UNCED, the polluter pays requirement was included in different European Community ("EC") documents such as the 1986 Single European Act, the 1992 Maastricht Treaty and in the successive Programs of Action on the Environment. An important application of the principle is found in article 9 of EC Directive 2000/60 on water, which requires member states to take account of the principle of recovery of the costs of water services, including environmental and resource costs. Water pricing policies by 2010 are to provide adequate incentives for the efficient use of water resources. The Treaty Establishing the European Community, Title XIX, sets out the principles meant to guide policy on the environment, principles that shape legislation in the EC. Article 174(2) provides that EC environmental policy "...shall be based on the precautionary principle and on the principles that preventive action should be taken, that environmental damage should as a priority be rectified at source and that the polluter should pay." In sum, the polluter pays principle has to be taken into account by all the EC institutions, and the European Court of Justice should ensure respect for the principle in the cases it decides.

66. The 1990 International Convention on Oil Pollution Preparedness, Response and Cooperation states in its preamble that the PPP is "a general principle of international environmental law" (para. 7). The 1992 Convention on the Protection of the Marine Environment of the Baltic Sea Area states in article 3(4) that the PPP is an obligatory norm, while the 1992 Helsinki Convention on the Protection and Use of Transboundary Watercourses and International Lakes includes it as a guiding principle in article 2(5)(b). More recent examples of reference to it are found in the 1996 Amendments to the 1980 Protocol for the Protection of the Mediterranean Sea against Pollution from Land-Based Sources (Preamble para. 5), and the 2001 Stockholm Convention on Persistent Organic Pollutants (Preamble, para. 17).

67. Issues relating to the content of the polluter pays principle are evident in the 1992 Convention for the Protection of the Marine Environment of the North-East Atlantic. According to article 2(2)(b), "The Contracting Parties shall apply: ...the polluter pays principle, by virtue of which the costs of pollution prevention, control and reduction measures are to be borne by the polluter." This can be interpreted in different ways depending upon the extent of prevention and control and whether compensation for damage is included in the definition of "reduction". Further, the very concept of the "polluter" can vary, from the producer of merchandise to the consumer who uses it and who pays the higher price resulting from anti-pollution production measures.

68. In fact, pollution costs can be borne either by the community, by those who pollute, or by consumers. Community assumption of the costs can be demonstrated using the example of an unregulated industry that discharges pollutants into a river. There are at least three possibilities:

(1) the river can remain polluted and rendered unsuitable for certain downstream activities, causing the downstream community to suffer an economic loss;
(2) the downstream community can build an adequate water treatment plant at its own cost;
(3) the polluter may receive public subsidies for controlling the pollution.

In all these possibilities, the affected community bears the cost of the pollution and of the measures designed to eliminate it or to mitigate its effects. The PPP avoids this result by obliging the polluter to bear the full costs of pollution, to "internalise" them. In most cases, presumably, the enterprise will in fact incorporate the costs into the price of its product(s) and thus pass the cost on to the consumer; but it need not do this for the PPP to have its intended effect.

69. Without elaboration, it should be noted that the PPP has also been increasingly accepted and applied at national level including in statutes in many countries in the developing world, and in their national supreme courts such as in South Asia, Africa and elsewhere in the world.

9. Access and Benefit Sharing regarding Natural Resources

70. Many indigenous and other local communities rely on natural resources such as forests, high deserts, wetlands, waterways, and fisheries for their livelihood or even existence. In addition, indigenous and other local communities often have unique cultures integrated with natural resources. These communities typically relate to these resources in a sustainable way, or else their livelihoods would disappear or their cultures would perish.

71. As a general matter, it is clear from Rio Principle 10 (quoted in paragraph 29 above) and international human rights norms that these communities and the individuals comprising them have the right to participate in decision-making processes with respect to those resources. They may also have substantive rights to those resources, the nature of which depends on both international and domestic law. See, e.g., Awas Tingni Mayagna (Sumo) Indigenous Community vs the Republic of Nicaragua, Inter-American Court of Human Rights (2001). In addition to international human rights law, an international law example is the 1995 United Nations Agreement on Fish Stocks, which in article 24(2)(b) requires states to take into account when establishing conservation and management measures the need to ensure access to fisheries by indigenous people of developing states, particularly Small Island Developing States. At the domestic level, in addition to standard legislation protecting property rights for everyone, several nation's constitutions, legislation or customary law recognizes property rights which indigenous or other local communities may exercise over their land and waterways or which enable indigenous or other local communities to take part in decision-making processes.

72. A related issue is the extent to which indigenous and other local communities have the right to participate in, or otherwise should be involved in, the management, development and preservation of the resources on which they rely. Principle 22 of the Rio Declaration provides:

**1992 Rio Declaration
Principle 22**

"Indigenous people and their communities and other local communities have a vital role in environmental management and development because of their knowledge and traditional practices. States should recognzse and duly support their identity, culture and interests and enable their effective participation in the achievement of sustainable development."

Principle 22 finds its further elaboration in chapter 26 of Agenda 21.

73. The 1993 Nuuk Declaration on Environment and Development in the Arctic States, in Principle 7, recognizes the vital role of indigenous peoples in managing natural resources.

**1993 Nuuk Declaration on Environment and
Development in the Arctic States
Principle 7**

"We recognize the special role of indigenous peoples in environmental management and development in the Arctic, and of the significance of their knowledge and traditional practices, and will promote their effective participation in the achievement of sustainable development in the Arctic."

---

74. With respect to biological diversity, the vital role of indigenous and other local communities is expressly recognized in preambular paragraph 12 of the 1992 Convention on Biological Diversity, and is further detailed in its articles 8(j), 10(c), and 17.2. Article 8(j) states that:

**1992 Convention on Biological Diversity
Article 8(j)**

Contracting Parties shall:
"subject to its national legislation, respect, preserve and maintain knowledge, innovations and practices of indigenous and local communities embodying traditional lifestyles...and promote their wider application with the approval and involvement of the holders of such knowledge, innovations and practices and encourage the equitable sharing of the benefits arising from the utilization of such knowledge, innovations and practices".

---

75. As a practical matter, the knowledge of indigenous and other local communities, their participation in decision-making and their involvement in management is often crucial for the protection of local ecosystems, for sound natural resource management, and for the broader effort to achieve sustainable development taking into account their traditional knowledge and cultural environment. Their involvement in EIA procedures is an example of their valuable participation in decision-making for sustainable development.

76. As a legal matter, the question has arisen whether indigenous and local communities have, in addition to the procedural and substantive rights identified above, the right to Prior Informed Consent ("PIC") (sometimes referred to as "free, prior and informed consent" or "FPIC") with respect to the use of their knowledge and the

genetic resources on which they rely. In the words of article 8(j) (quoted above), what does "with their approval" entail? Some believe that there is an absolute right to such prior informed consent; some believe that such a right exists but that it is subject to the proper exercise of eminent domain; and others believe that no such right exists unless embodied in domestic law. Similarly, questions exist regarding the terms on which such knowledge and genetic resources may be used or, in the words of article 8(j), what is "equitable sharing"? The analysis of these questions may differ depending on whether the local community is indigenous or not, to the extent indigenous people have different or additional rights under international or domestic law. For example, the International Labour Organization has adopted various conventions relating to indigenous people, starting in 1936 with the, now outdated, Recruiting of Indigenous Workers Convention, to the 1989 Indigenous and Tribal Peoples Convention; also the 1992 Forest Principles 2(d), 5(a) and 12(d) refer to the recognition of traditional or indigenous rights.

77. At the time of this writing (2005), these questions are being discussed in several international fora, including the Conference of the Parties to the 1992 Convention on Biological Diversity, the World Intellectual Property Organization, the World Trade Organization Agreement on Trade-Related Aspects of Intellectual Property Rights, the World Bank, the International Finance Corporation, and various regional development banks and export credit agencies. Some institutions already have processes in place that are similar to prior informed consent.

10. Common Heritage and Common Concern of Humankind

78. The concepts of "common heritage of humankind" and "common concern of humankind" reflect the growing awareness of the interdependence of the biosphere and the environmental problems besetting it, as well as of the global nature of many environmental problems and the critical importance of those problems. It is thus increasingly acknowledged that the international community has an interest in these issues.

79. The protection, preservation and enhancement of the natural environment, particularly the proper management of the climate system, biological diversity and fauna and flora of the Earth, are generally recognized as the common concern of humankind. Basic assumptions implicit in the common concern concept include that states and

other actors should not cause harm with regard to issues of common concern, and that states and other actors share responsibility for addressing common concerns.

80. The resources of outer space and celestial bodies and of the sea-bed, ocean floor and subsoil thereof beyond the limits of national jurisdiction are generally recognized as the common heritage of humankind. The international community's interest in these is probably stronger, generally speaking, than it is with respect to common concern, though the contours of that interest are not clearly defined.

11. Good Governance

81. The concept of good governance is relatively recent and reflects a growing awareness of the importance to sustainable development of transparent, accountable, honest governance, as well as a growing awareness of the corrosive effect of corruption on public morale, economic efficiency, political stability and sustainable development in general. The concept implies, among others, that states and international organizations should: (a) adopt democratic and transparent decision-making procedures and financial accountability; (b) take effective measures to combat official or other corruption; (c) respect due process in their procedures and observe the rule of law more generally; (d) protect human rights; and (e) conduct public procurement in a transparent, non-corrupt manner.

82. Good governance implies not only that Civil Society has a right to good governance by states and international organizations, but also that non-state actors, including business enterprises and NGOs, should be subject to internal democratic governance and effective accountability. In addition, good governance calls for corporate social responsibility and socially responsible investments as conditions for the existence of a sustainable global market that will achieve an equitable distribution of wealth among and within communities.

83. Good governance requires full respect for the principles of the 1992 Rio Declaration on Environment and Development, including the full participation of women in all levels of decision-making. Achieving good governance is essential to the progressive development, codification and implementation of international and domestic law relating to sustainable development. Also, Goal 8 of the Millennium Development Goals on developing a global partnership for development,

has as one of its targets (target 12) to "Develop further an open, rule-based, predictable, non-discriminatory trading and financial system. Includes a commitment to good governance, development, and poverty reduction - both nationally and internationally."

Dr. Daniel B. Magraw Jr., President, Center for International Environmental Law (CIEL)

Barbara Ruis, Legal Officer, Division of Policy Development and Law, UNEP

Resources

Text Materials

Afshin A-Khavari and Donald R. Rothwell, The ICJ and the Danube Dam Case: A Missed Opportunity for International Environmental Law?, (22 Melbourne U.L.R. 507, December, 1998).

John S. Applegate, The Taming of the Precautionary Principle, 27 Wm. & Mary Envtl. L. & Pol'y Rev. 13, (Fall 2002).

Patricia W. Birnie and Alan E. Boyle, International Law and the Environment, (Oxford: Clarendon Press; New York: Oxford University Press, 1992).

Alan Boyle and David Freestone (Eds.), International Law and Sustainable Development, (Oxford; New York: Oxford University Press, 1999).

Declaration of Principles of International Law relating to Sustainable Development, (United Nations General Assembly, Doc. A/57/329, 31 August 2002, International Law Association, New Delhi , adopted in New Dehli, 6 April 2002).

Nicolas De Sadeleer, Environmental Principles: from Political Slogans to Legal Rules, (Oxford University Press, 2002).

Joseph F. DiMento, The Global Environment and International Environmental Law, (1st Ed., Austin: University of Texas Press, 2003).

Draft International Covenant on Environment and Development, (elaborated by the Commission on Environmental Law of the IUCN/World Conservation Union, in cooperation with the International Council of Environmental Law) Launched at the United Nations Congress on Public International Law, (New York, 13-17 March 1995).

Final Report of the Expert Group Workshop on International Environmental Law aiming at Sustainable Development, (UNEP/IEL/WS/3/2).

David Freestone and Ellen Hey (Eds.), The Precautionary Principle and International Law: The Challenge of Implementation, (Boston: Kluwer Law International, 1996).

Anita Margrethe Halvorssen, Equality Among Unequals in International Environmental Law: Differential Treatment for Developing Countries, (Boulder; Westview Press, 1999).

David Hunter, James Salzman, Diuwood Zaelke, International Environmental Law and Policy, chapter 7, Casebook Series, (Foundation Press, 2002).

Alexandre Kiss and Dinah Shelton, INTERNATIONAL ENVIRONMENTAL LAW, (Transnational Publishers Incorporated, third edition 2004).

Graham Mayeda, Where Should Johannesburg Take Us? Ethical and Legal Approaches to Sustainable Development in the Context of International Environmental Law, 15 COLO. J. INT'L. L. & POL'Y 29, (Winter 2004).

Dr. Hans-Joachim Priess & Dr. Christian Pitschas, Protection of Public Health and the Role of Precautionary Principle under WTO Law: A Trojan Horse before Geneva's Walls?, 24 FORDHAM INT'L L. J. 519, (2000).

REPORT OF THE INTERNATIONAL ENVIRONMENTAL CONFERENCE ON CODIFYING THE RIO PRINCIPLES IN NATIONAL LEGISLATION, (The Hague, 22-24 May 1996, organized by the Netherlands Ministry of Housing, Spatial Planning and the Environment, Publikatiereeks milieubeheer, No. 1996/4).

RIO DECLARATION ON ENVIRONMENT AND DEVELOPMENT: APPLICATION AND IMPLEMENTATION, REPORT OF THE SECRETARY-GENERAL, (United Nations, Economic and Social Council, E/CN.17/1997/8, 10 February 1997).

Philippe Sands, PRINCIPLES OF INTERNATIONAL ENVIRONMENTAL LAW, (Cambridge University Press, second edition, 2003).

Nico Schrijver, SOVEREIGNTY OVER NATURAL RESOURCES, BALANCING RIGHTS AND DUTIES, (Cambridge University Press, 1997).

Maurice Sheridan and L. Lavrysen, ENVIRONMENTAL LAW PRINCIPLES IN PRACTISE, (Bruxelles: Bruylant, 2002).

Krista Singleton-Cambage, INTERNATIONAL LEGAL SOURCES AND GLOBAL ENVIRONMENTAL CRISES: THE INADEQUACY OF PRINCIPLES, TREATIES AND CUSTOM, (2 ILSA J Int'l & Comp L 171, Fall 1995).

Candice Stevens, Interpreting the Polluter Pays Principle in the Trade and Environment Context, 27 CORNELL INT'L L. J. 577 (Summer, 1994).

Arie Trouwborst, EVOLUTION AND STATUS OF THE PRECAUTIONARY PRINCIPLE IN INTERNATIONAL LAW, (Hague; London: Kluwer Law International, 2002).

C.G. Weeramantry, NAURU: ENVIRONMENTAL DAMAGE UNDER INTERNATIONAL TRUSTEESHIP, (Melbourne; New York: Oxford University Press, 1992).

World Commission on Environment and Development, OUR COMMON FUTURE, (Oxford Unversity Press, 1987).

4. COMPLIANCE AND ENFORCEMENT OF MULTILATERAL ENVIRONMENTAL AGREEMENTS

I. Introduction

1. Multilateral Environmental Agreements (MEAs) are a result of international action by governments to develop standards through treaties or through non-binding instruments, that come from intergovernmental fora and influential international declarations, resolutions, and conference documents. These treaties or non-binding instruments provide obligations for Governments to undertake either individual or joint action to implement international legal instruments. This chapter focuses on MEAs in the form of treaties, which follow the process of ratification, adhesion, or accession by governments who then assume the obligations as soon as the treaty enters into force. The ratification, accession or adherence of a treaty by a state is the beginning of the process of implementation of its provisions at the national level.

2. The process and required actions for implementation of MEAs normally depend upon the provisions of the treaty but in most cases the actions range from implementing national measures provided for in the environmental treaty such as adopting policies, developing and/or strengthening national legislation and institutions, and/or taking up administrative action to implement MEAs. Since parties to most MEAs are required to report on measures taken to implement treaties, a review process is vital as well as early determination of which entity, at national level, will handle reporting, or the focal point of the particular treaty.

3. For many years, issues of compliance with and enforcement of MEAs were considered as matters for a state to address when implementing any international environmental legal instrument. More recently, the negotiation of MEAs, decisions of the Conference of the Parties ("COP"), and the work of Convention Secretariats have established and/or provided for mechanisms to monitor compliance which have included, inter alia, reporting mechanisms and the development and implementation of non-compliance procedures for

some core MEAs. MEAs are normally negotiated under the framework of international organizations that parties also work with to facilitate the implementation of the conventions and intervene by providing technical assistance to governments in the implementation process. Institutional mechanisms established by MEAs such as Convention Secretariats and the main governing bodies of treaties (COP) also play a role in facilitating and overseeing implementation of MEAs. Compliance mechanisms are tools that have also been established by MEAs to ensure efficacy of environmental treaties and to keep track of the implementation of MEAs.

4. Under the auspices of the United Nations Environment Programme ("UNEP"), governments recently adopted global guidelines to assist and guide the process of implementation of MEAs. These guidelines were adopted in February 2002 by UNEP Governing Council decision SSVII/4 for the purpose of enhancing compliance with, and enforcement of environmental law, and are referred to as Guidelines for Compliance with and Enforcement of Multilateral Environmental Agreements.

5. Compliance efforts can take a wide variety of forms, including education, technical assistance, voluntary compliance programmes, subsidies and other forms of financial assistance, or incentives, administrative enforcement, civil judicial enforcement and criminal enforcement. This chapter focuses on implementation of MEAs and explores some of the issues and challenges that led governments to address issues of compliance and enforcement of MEAs at the international level in the past few years. This chapter also analyzes existing mechanisms developed to ensure compliance with and enforcement of MEAs as well as the opportunities brought by the adoption of the UNEP's Compliance and Enforcement Guidelines to enhance the implementation of MEAs.

II. International Framework

6. "Compliance" means the conformity with obligations, imposed by a state, its competent authorities and agencies on the regulated community, whether directly or through conditions and requirements, permits, licenses and authorizations, in implementing MEAs Compliance also means the fulfilment by the contracting parties of their obligations under a MEA.

7. "Environmental law violation" means the contravention of national environmental laws and

regulations implementing MEAs. "Environmental crime" means the violations or breaches of national environmental laws and regulations that a state determines to be subject to criminal penalties under its national laws and regulations.

8. "Enforcement" means the range of procedures and actions employed by a state, its competent authorities and agencies to ensure that organizations or persons, potentially failing to comply with environmental laws or regulations implementing MEAs, can be brought or returned compliance and/or punished through civil, administrative or criminal action.

1. The Importance of Compliance and Enforcement

9. The need to ensure implementation of MEAs, the proliferation of MEAs as well as the emergence of environmental violations or offenses (at times loosely referred to as crimes), crimes emanating from violations of existing environmental conventions are said to be the reason for the emphasis at the international level on issues relating to compliance and enforcement of environmental law.

10. With more than 500, or according to some almost 1000, MEAs in place around the globe and the realization that there is a need for the implementation of these MEAs, the attention is shifting from treaty-making which preoccupied the international community since the 1970s to compliance and enforcement and implementation of existing treaties.

11. Another issue of great concern, which also caused governments to focus on issues of compliance and enforcement was the emergence of criminal activity involving violations of existing MEAs (dealing with trade, chemicals, wastes) including illegal traffic and trade in banned products.

12. In response to concerns by governments on the increase of environmental crimes with transboundary effects, UNEP organized a workshop on MEAs Compliance and Enforcement, held in 1999 in Geneva, Switzerland. The workshop examined the implementation of three major MEAs, including the Convention on International Trade in Endangered Species of Wild Fauna and Flora ("CITES"), the Montreal Protocol on Substances that deplete the Ozone Layer ("Montreal Protocol"), and the Basel Convention on the Control of Transboundary Movements of Hazardous Wastes and their Disposal ("Basel Convention"). This workshop indicated there was

a significant increase in environmental crimes, including illegal traffic in banned chlorofluorocarbons and hazardous wastes, as well as illegal trade in wildlife species which were undermining the objectives of the three treaties. The serious global problem of environmental crimes was underscored, as well as the need to enhance the capacity of different actors who have a role in ensuring compliance with and enforcement of MEAs.

13. The participants and experts attending this workshop were drawn from different types of enforcement agencies from both developed and developing countries including the Convention Secretariats and other enforcement organizations like INTERPOL, the World Customs Organization, the International Network for Environmental Compliance and Enforcement ("INECE"), the European Union Network for the Implementation and Enforcement of Environmental Law ("IMPEL"), and the Commonwealth Secretariat.

14. CITES, the Montreal Protocol, and the Basel Convention have some form of compliance mechanisms. In comparing the reports and statistics on violations of the MEAs and the cost of the environmental damages caused by these violations, it was clear that there was a need to find ways to prevent environmental crimes by enhancing compliance with and enforcement of MEAs.

15. In assuming obligations in a MEA to be implemented at the national level, a state party to a treaty is expected to take measures to implement the MEA and to make use of the facilities provided for by environmental treaties that are aimed at facilitating the process of implementation at the national level, including *inter alia*:

- Provision of technical assistance in development and strengthening of legislation;
- Adoption of compliance and enforcement policies;
- Undertaking administrative action;
- Planning (action plans, inventories, strategies);
- Capacity building;
- Financial assistance; and
- Technology transfer.

16. In identifying some of the challenges parties face in the process of implementation, it is important to note, for example, that compliance requires identifying roles and responsibilities of the key players (depending on the MEA, the lead organization should be identified). It also requires effective coordination in the government structure

because, in almost all cases, implementation requires a multi-sectoral approach and must be organized to ensure that those responsible for implementation are involved and do take action. In ensuring compliance competency, expertise or equipment may also be required because some items that are being protected by MEAs are technical. Another challenge that state parties face is to promote, encourage and to monitor compliance. Most of these measures involve costs and require each party's ability and willingness to invest resources in these areas or to use facilities developed under the MEA to facilitate its implementation.

17. For the purpose of facilitating implementation, most MEAs establish institutions such as Secretariats, COPs and other technical bodies to oversee the implementation of the Convention, and to provide policy guidance. Other innovative ways to ensure the effectiveness of MEAs include a financial mechanism (project development) and reporting requirements aimed at verifying the implementation of the Convention. A number of international organizations responsible for overseeing the implementation of these international environmental legal instruments, however, have been providing some form of technical assistance, including capacity-building programmes to assist governments to implement or meet their international obligations.

2. Institutional Arrangements for the Implementation of MEAs

18. Apart from establishing various institutions such as the Conference of the Parties also referred to as the Meeting of the Parties, Convention Secretariats, and Advisory bodies, other innovative ways to ensure the effectiveness of MEAs include a reporting mechanism with monitoring facilities that are aimed at verifying the implementation of the convention and a financial mechanism that is intended to provide financial facilities to cover costs for implementation of activities. Compliance mechanisms have been equally developed to address issues of non-compliance with environmental conventions, including liability and compensation regimes.

a) Conferences/Meetings of the Parties of a MEA

19. Regarding compliance considerations in MEAs, the competent body of a MEA such as the COP could, where authorized to do so by the convention, regularly review the overall implementation of obligations under the MEA and examine specific difficulties of compliance and consider measures

aimed at improving it. This is not a model for all MEAs but parties through the MEA or the COP are best placed to choose the approaches and modalities that are useful and appropriate for enhancing compliance with MEAs. It is to be noted that older treaties did not provide for such approaches or modalities while recent environmental treaties do in almost all cases. A recent such treaty is the African Convention for Nature Protection, Algiers 1968 which was revised and adopted by the African Union in 2003; the new instrument has established a COP and regular mechanism for review.

b) Convention Secretariats

20. MEAs also establish or designate Convention Secretariats to carry out a number of functions such as to prepare and convene COPs and to undertake Secretariat functions on behalf of the parties. The Secretariat is also expected to transmit to the parties information, as well as to consider enquiries by, and information from, the parties and, among other functions, to consult with them on questions relating to the convention and its protocols, to coordinate the implementation of cooperative activities agreed upon by the Meetings of the Parties ("MOPs"), and to ensure the necessary coordination with other regional and international bodies that the parties consider competent. Parties are also expected to designate focal points or a relevant national authority to act as channels of communication with the Convention Secretariat.

c) Advisory bodies

21. Scientific advisory panels, technical groups, working groups, or various committees including implementation committees, are normally established for specific purposes. Scientific advisory panels are set up when the convention is dealing with technical matters that only a group of scientists can advise parties on managing the problem that the convention wishes to address. The COP is empowered by most MEAs to establish technical groups and working groups on an ad hoc basis, when need arises to address certain issues and to report back to the parties. A number of conventions have established financial mechanisms that have designated bodies to deal with financial aspects such as trust funds, multilateral funds or the Global Environmental Facility ("GEF"). Most MEAs also provide that the parties would establish compliance procedures where these procedures set up implementation committees comprising of various parties which look into claims of violations of the MEA.

d) Reporting Mechanisms to track Progress in the Implementation of Treaties

22. Most environmental conventions provide for contracting parties to transmit regularly to the Secretariat information on the measures adopted by them in the implementation of the convention to which they are parties. This information is transmitted in such form and at such intervals as the meetings of the contracting parties shall determine. The intention of this reporting is a way of monitoring implementation and a way of verifying if the MEA is being implemented. With the proliferation of MEAs there has been a concern raised by parties of the many requirements for reporting, and attempts are made to streamline the reporting process which, hitherto, has not been successful because different MEAs require different types of information.

23. MEAs often include provisions for reporting, monitoring and verification of the information obtained on compliance. These provisions can help promote compliance by, *inter alia*, potentially increasing public awareness. When data collection and reporting requirements are too onerous and are not coordinated or do not take into account synergies with similar MEAs, they can discourage and burden parties in complying with reporting requirements. MEAs can and do include such requirements as the following:

- Provisions in treaties that call for regular and timely reports on compliance, using an appropriate common format that is sent out by the Secretariat. Simple and brief formats could be designed to ensure consistency, efficiency and convenience in order to enable reporting on specific obligations. MEAs Secretariats can consolidate responses received to assist in the assessment of compliance. Reporting on non-compliance can also be considered, and the parties can provide for timely review of such reports;
- Provisions on monitoring requirements that involve the collection of data and in accordance with a MEA can be used to assess compliance with an agreement. As a country collects data, it is easy to identify compliance problems and indicate solutions. States that are negotiating provisions regarding monitoring in MEAs could consider the provisions in other MEAs related to monitoring; and
- Provisions on verification requirements that include checking the accuracy of data and technical information in order to assist in ascertaining whether a party is in compliance and, in the event of non-compliance, the degree, type and frequency of non-compliance. The principal source of verification might be national reports. Consistent with the provisions in the MEAs and in accordance with any modalities that might be set by the COP, technical verification could involve independent sources for corroborating national data and information.

24. At the receipt of such reports the Secretariats in most MEAs examine the national reports to determine if they have been presented in the right format, and circulate them to other parties. The Secretariats also bring to the attention of the parties any request for assistance in the implementation of the particular MEA.

e) Financial Mechanisms

25. A financial mechanism is important not only to support implementation efforts of the contracting parties but also to undertake projects that can enhance the implementation of MEAs. The realization over the years that some implementing measures can be costly and hence difficult for developing country contracting parties to undertake, resulted in parties including provisions of a financial mechanism within MEAs. Parties of some MEAs have also established financial rules by outlining rules that govern the different financial mechanisms. The financial mechanisms so far developed by MEAs have taken different forms, including the following:

- Trust Funds developed under the framework of Regional Seas Conventions that were negotiated under the auspices of UNEP, whose contribution comes from parties to those conventions. UNEP which provides Secretariat services for Regional Seas Conventions under its auspices, provides seed money to implement the work programme of the Regional Seas Programme with activities that are intended to enhance capacity of the parties to implement their Convention.
- The Convention on Biological Diversity ("CBD") and the United Nations Framework Convention on Climate Change ("UNFCCC") ,among other MEAs, designate the GEF as their financial mechanism. (See Chapter 6). Through GEF, parties from developing countries have received financial support to cover incremental costs that they would otherwise have incurred in the implementation of the pertinent MEA. GEF also supports projects in a number of focal areas, namely, ozone depletion, climate change, biodiversity, shared water resources, desertification and chemicals

to cover the incremental costs of member states in implementing these conventions at the national level and at the trans-boundary level.

- The parties to the UNFCCC also agreed to establish three new funds to promote compliance by developing countries. Two of these funds are under the UNFCCC and one under the Kyoto Protocol. The new funds, in addition to the GEF funding that is available to the parties, are also managed by GEF. COP-7 decided to create "a special climate change fund" complementary to GEF funding to provide finances for the adaptation to technology transfer, and the mitigation of greenhouse gases. In addition, countries that are heavily dependent on the export of fossil fuels are encouraged and assisted in diversifying their economies. The second fund, reserved for the Least Developed Countries ("LDC"), is intended to assist financially in the preparation of national programmes. The third is an adaptation fund under the Kyoto Protocol to be financed by voluntary contributions and by 2% of proceeds from certified emissions reductions generated by the Clean Development Mechanism ("CDM") under article 12 of the Kyoto Protocol. It marks the first time that a levy is anticipated on business transactions to finance environmental and developmental activities.

- The Multilateral Environment Fund of the Montreal Protocol, along with GEF funding which is also available to the parties of the United Nations' ozone conventions, was established to support implementation of the Vienna Convention on the Protection of the Ozone Layer and in particular to enable developing countries to meet the requirements of the Montreal Protocol, thereby addressing ozone depletion and related problems. The fund was also established to implement articles 5, paragraphs 2 and 3, in conjunction with articles 9 and 10 of the Montreal Protocol. A number of parties and organisations such as United Nations Development Programme ("UNDP"), United Nations Environment Programme ("UNEP"), World Bank, or other appropriate agencies depending on their respective areas of expertise are part of the Executive Committee of the Multilateral Fund for the Implementation of the Montreal Protocol. The role of the Executive Committee is to develop and monitor the implementation of specific operational policies, guidelines and administrative arrangements, including the disbursement of resources for the purpose of achieving the objectives of the Multilateral Fund. The COP reviews the work of the Multilateral Fund. For further information on the Multilateral Environment Fund of the Ozone Convention including its terms of reference, source of contributions, functions, and criteria for disbursing funds for incremental costs of implementation of the ozone conventions and the countries that have so far benefited from this facility, read the latest edition of the Handbook for the International Treaties for the Protection of the Ozone Layer.

f) Non-Compliance Procedures/Mechanisms

26. In the non-compliance procedure of the Montreal Protocol, a party that cannot meet its obligations may report its compliance problems to the Implementation Committee. In addition, any party or parties that have concerns about another party's implementation of its obligations under the Montreal Protocol may communicate the concerns in writing, supported by corroborating information, to the Secretariat. The Implementation Committee can request further information upon the invitation of the party concerned and can gather information. At the end of the procedure, the Implementation Committee reports to the meeting parties. Any recommendation it considers appropriate can be included in the report, which is made available to the parties six weeks before the meeting. The MOP may decide upon steps to bring about compliance with the Montreal Protocol. Any state involved in a matter under consideration by the Implementation Committee cannot take part in the elaboration and adoption of any recommendations concerning it. The parties subject to the procedure must subsequently inform the MOP of the measures they have taken in response to the report.

27. Annex V of Decision IV/18 contains an indicative list of measures that might be taken by the MOP in respect of non-compliance with the Montreal Protocol. The first consists of providing assistance, for example, the collection and reporting of data, technology transfer, financing, information transfer and training. At the second level, "cautions" are issued. The third level involves the suspension of specific rights and privileges under the Montreal Protocol. Such rights and privileges can concern industrial rationalization, production, consumption, trade, transfer of technology, financial mechanisms and industrial arrangements. A number of countries have been considered under the Montreal Protocol's non-compliance procedure.

28. The Kyoto Protocol compliance regime was developed pursuant to Article 17 of the Climate Change Convention by the Conference of the Parties serving as the MOP to the Kyoto Protocol.

A joint working group elaborated a draft regime on compliance that COP 7 approved in 2001 as part of the Marrakech Accords. The objective of the regime is to "facilitate, promote and enforce compliance with the commitments under the Protocol." The Marrakech Accords contain an innovative, unprecedented compliance mechanism. It foresees a compliance committee with two branches, a facilitative branch and an enforcement branch. The facilitative branch supports efforts by parties to comply. The enforcement branch monitors compliance with the most important obligations. The enforcement branch has several tools available to bring about compliance: a party may be prohibited from selling under the emissions trading regime and for every ton of emissions by which a party exceeds its target, 1.3 tons will be deducted from its assigned among for the subsequent commitment period. The party will be required to submit a compliance action plan for review by the committee. An appeals procedure provides for a review of decisions by the UNFCCC COP serving as the Kyoto Protocol's MOP. During the procedure, the decisions by the Compliance Committee remain in force. Overturning the decision requires a three-fourth's majority of the COP/MOP. Both branches of the committee are composed of ten members, one each from the five regions, one Small Island Developing State and two from Annex I and two from non-Annex I countries. A double majority vote is required for decisions: three-fourths of all members including a simple majority of Annex I and non-Annex I countries.

29. The compliance procedure was not adopted as an amendment to the Kyoto Protocol and thus is not legally binding as part of the treaty. However, upon adoption, it has the advantage of being applicable to all parties to the Kyoto Protocol.

3. Effectiveness of the Non-Compliance Procedure

30. Although a number of MEAs have adopted some form of non-compliance procedures, other procedures are still being developed. The compliance procedures are characterized by their cooperative, non-confrontational and non-judicial nature and in their aim of seeking amicable solutions to problems arising in connection with the application and implementation of environmental agreements. The trend is to move from the traditional confrontational mechanisms for enforcing MEAs to new mechanisms that can help parties better comply with their contractual obligations. Most procedures do not aim at compelling a party to comply with the obligations and requirements of the treaty but rather a party is assisted in its problems of compliance. The status

of these procedures is between dispute avoidance and dispute settlement. The very purpose of the non-compliance procedures is to encourage or enable states to avoid resorting to formal dispute settlement procedures that are also usually provided by international environmental agreements but, outside the WTO, are hardly used.

31. In fact, many compliance procedures combine elements of three distinct processes: (1) processes designed to clarify norms and standards employed by a treaty; (2) processes designed to further the evolution of these norms and standards; and (3) processes designed to resolve problems among parties. The effect on states or a proceeding before formally constituted bodies under a MEA such as the Implementation Committee or Compliance committee is mainly to provide assistance to the defaulting state and to assist parties having compliance problems and addressing individual cases of non-compliance. It does not have the effect of compelling the state to act as such. The long-standing procedure is the one that has been elaborated under article 8 of the Montreal Protocol.

32. To strengthen the effectiveness of implementation mechanisms developed by the convention, parties should place particular emphasis on the following aspects:

- Encourage parties to MEAs to develop and apply effective mechanisms for implementation of and compliance with those agreements;
- Promote the development and effective application of economic, legal and other incentives to enhance parties' implementation and compliance of their international obligations; and
- Promote greater use of civil liability approaches at the national level to enhance implementation of environmental law.

33. In principle, provisions for settlement of disputes complement the provisions aimed at compliance with MEAs. The appropriate form of dispute settlement mechanism can depend upon the specific provisions contained in a MEA and the nature of the dispute. A range of procedures could be considered, including good offices, mediation, conciliation, fact-finding commissions, dispute resolution panels, arbitration and other possible judicial arrangements that might be reached between parties to the dispute.

34. Developing effective national legal regimes should be considered including considering development of any further regulations if required as provided in chapter 8 of Agenda 21, and paragraphs 162

through 167 of the Plan of Implementation of the World Summit on Sustainable Development ("WSSD"). The "Polluter Pays Principle", the "Common but Differentiated Responsibility Principle" and other principles and concepts should be taken into account by decision-makers when considering measures and the timing for implementation of MEAs. The use of economic instruments is important in implementation of environmental law including in compliance and enforcement, not only for the purpose of financing environmental management, but particularly for encouraging environmentally responsible behaviour through the use of incentives or disincentives in environmental management. This can be a very effective choice in measures to be considered in implementation of MEAs.

35. Enforcement capacity and strengthening of compliance institutions are important if the enforcement is to be undertaken in an informed manner by the responsible authorities, especially when some of the environmental problems are very technical and sometimes hard for some people to understand. This situation points out the importance of training, public awareness and sensitization of all who are responsible for enforcement and compliance of MEAs. This capacity building can be undertaken in government as part of human resource development or in collaboration with Convention Secretariats. Access to information as well as access to justice, public awareness and participation are important in implementing MEAs. Consideration should also be given to liability issues.

36. Cooperation in trans-boundary matters to address issues that have a bearing in one country but are caused by issues beyond one country's jurisdiction is also important in implementation of MEAs. The Lusaka Agreement on Cooperative Enforcement of Wildlife is a good example of countries coming together to enhance enforcement efforts in a cooperative manner.

4. Capacity Building Programmes: The Role of International Organizations and Compliance and Enforcement Networks

37. Depending on the subject or issue, MEAs are normally negotiated under the framework of international organizations: global, regional and subregional. There are MEAs that are negotiated under the framework of different organizations, including, *inter alia*, the International Maritime Organization conventions, International Labour Organization conventions, World Health Organization conventions, United Nations conventions and United Nations Environment Programme conventions. At regional level regional economic commissions of the United Nations; regional intergovernmental organizations e.g. in Europe, the European Union; Council of Europe; in Africa, the Organization of Africa Unity now African Union; Southern Africa Development Community and similar regional bodies in Asia and Latin America. The role of these organizations is to facilitate the work of the Convention Secretariat and other bodies that are established by the MEA as well as to support their work especially as it relates to capacity building in the form of technical assistance for implementation related activities of the MEA.

38. Several specialized organizations, regional and international groups exist to support compliance and enforcement such as the European Union Network for the Implementation and Enforcement of Environmental Law ("IMPEL"), International Network for Environmental Compliance and Enforcement ("INECE"), the Commission for Environmental Cooperation under the North America Free Trade Area ("NAFTA"), INTERPOL, and the World Conservation Union/IUCN Specialist Group on Environmental Compliance.

39. IMPEL is an informal network of the environmental authorities of Norway, and the member states, future member states and candidate countries of the European Union. The network is commonly known as the IMPEL Network. The European Commission is also a member of IMPEL and shares the chairmanship of meetings. The IMPEL Cluster on Training and Exchange groups projects and activities on environmental inspection with a particular focus on training and exchange of experience, comparison and evaluation of different practices, and development of minimum criteria.

40. The IMPEL Cluster usually meets twice a year to discuss new project ideas and to review the progress of projects.

41. IMPEL-TFS is a network of representatives from enforcement authorities of the member states and some other European countries dealing with matters on Transfrontier Shipments of Waste. It is also a cluster of projects within IMPEL. The IMPEL-TFS network was established in 1992 in order to harmonize the enforcement of EU Regulation 259/93 (replacing EC Directive 84/631) on Transfrontier Shipments of Waste with regard to the supervision and control of waste shipments into, out of and through the European Union.

42. The aim of the IMPEL Cluster is to:

    • Promote compliance with the EU Regulation 259/93 through enforcement;
    • Carry out joint enforcement projects; and
    • Promote exchange of knowledge and experience with the enforcement of the EU Regulation 259/93.

43. Every year, the IMPEL-TFS Network has a plenary conference where the working programme for this cluster is discussed. The IMPEL Cluster group's projects and activities are tailored to the specific needs of the future member states and the candidate countries. Through consultants, the IMPEL Cluster undertakes the following activities:

    • Conducts studies, specific to the acceding/candidate countries, on enforcement of key directives are elaborated and discussed in workshops, including recommendations for follow-up;
    • Trains the trainers, seminars are held in the PHARE country inspectorates;
    • Carries out peer reviews of enforcement bodies ("PEEPs"); and
    • Organizes study tours and carries out comparative analysis of administrative, implementation and enforcement capacity in selected countries.

44. NAFTA has a citizen enforcement submission process under its Environmental Side Agreement. The "citizen submissions on enforcement matters" mechanism enables the public to play an active whistle-blower role when a government appears to be failing to enforce its environmental laws effectively. Members of the public trigger the process by submitting claims alleging such a failure on the part of any of the NAFTA partners to NAFTA's Citizen Enforcement Commission ("CEC"). Following a review of the submission, the CEC may investigate the matter and publish a factual record of its findings, subject to approval by the CEC.

45. INECE is a network of government and non-government enforcement and compliance practitioners from over 100 countries. INECE's goals are to raise awareness of compliance and enforcement, to develop networks for enforcement cooperation, and to strengthen capacity to implement and enforce environmental requirements. The Principles of Environmental Enforcement were developed under the auspices of INECE.

46. In 1993, INTERPOL established a working party on environmental crime, it now has subgroups on wildlife crime and hazardous waste, which recently has been extended to cover other forms of pollution such as ozone depleting substances.

47. IUCN's Commission on Environmental Law formed a Special Group on Enforcement and Compliance to assist IUCN member organizations and IUCN programs strengthen efforts in this area.

48. To further develop the area of implementation of environmental law as well as compliance with and enforcement of MEAs, it is important for UNEP, under the Montevideo Programme III, to find ways to further develop environmental law in this area. UNEP works with parties of different MEAs to enhance compliance and enforcement of MEAs through advisory services and technical assistance to governments, training programmes, promoting the UNEP Guidelines for Compliance with and Enforcement of MEAs, undertaking studies of the existing mechanisms and enforcement problems in different sectors of the environment, and through preparation and dissemination of information in both print and electronic format.

5. Compliance and Enforcement Opportunities

49. The UNEP Guidelines for Compliance with and Enforcement of MEAs are in the form of a non-binding legal instrument which was developed by governments through an inter-governmental consultative process organized under the auspices of UNEP and adopted by consensus. The guidelines have two parts: one on Compliance with and Enforcement of MEAs and the second for National Enforcement, and International Cooperation in Combating Violations of Laws that are implementing MEAs. The Guidelines, although not specific to any convention, are provided as a "tool box" of proposals, suggestions and potential measures that governments and stakeholders may consider taking to improve compliance with and enforcement of MEAs.

50. The Global Guidelines recognize the need for national enforcement of laws to implement MEAs. Enforcement is essential to secure the benefits of these laws, protect the environment, public health and safety, deter violations, and encourage improved performance. The Guidelines also recognize the need for international cooperation and coordination to facilitate and assist enforcement that arises from the implementation of MEAs, and to help establish an international level playing field.

III. National Implementation

51. The purpose of these Guidelines is to outline actions, initiatives and measures for states to consider in strengthening national enforcement and international cooperation to combat violations of laws implementing MEAs. The Guidelines can assist governments, their competent authorities, enforcement agencies, Secretariats of MEAs, where appropriate, and other relevant international and regional organizations in developing tools, mechanisms and techniques in this regard.

52. The scope of the Guidelines is to address enforcement of national laws and regulations implementing MEAs in a broad context, under which states, consistent with their obligations under such agreements, develop laws and institutions that support effective enforcement and pursue actions that deter and respond to environmental law violations and crimes. Approaches include the promotion of effective laws and regulations for responding appropriately to environmental law violations and crimes. The Guidelines accord significance to the development of institutional capacities through cooperation and coordination among international organizations for increasing the effectiveness of enforcement.

53. As a follow up to the adoption of the Guidelines and to facilitate the implementation thereof, a Draft Manual on Compliance with and Enforcement of MEAs was prepared. The Guidelines and the Manual were promoted and tested in five regional workshops in 2003 to 2005. Thereafter, further work on implementation and enforcement of MEAs is being undertaken at national levels with a few selected countries to ensure that, where necessary, countries develop national enforcement programmes in defined areas of the environment to enhance compliance with and enforcement of environmental law.

Prof. Kilaparti Ramakrishna, Deputy Director, Woods Hole Research Center

Sylvia Bankobeza, Legal Officer, Division of Policy Development and Law, UNEP

Resources

Internet Materials

CARNEGIE COUNCIL ON ETHICS AND INTERNATIONAL AFFAIRS, ENVIRONMENTAL RIGHTS ENFORCEMENT IN U.S. COURTS, Hari M. Osofsky available at http://www.carnegiecouncil.org/viewMedia.php/prmTemplateID/8/prmID/4462

INTERNATIONAL NETWORK FOR ENVIRONMENTAL COMPLIANCE AND ENFORCEMENT ("INECE") available at http://www.inece.org/

UNITED NATIONS ENVIRONMENT PROGRAMME, COMPLIANCE AND ENFORCEMENT available at http://www.unep.org/DPDL/law/Compliance_enforcement/index.asp

WORLD CONSERVATION UNION ("IUCN"), COMMISSION ON ENVIRONMENTAL LAW, SPECIALIST GROUP ON ENFORCEMENT AND COMPLIANCE available at http://www.iucn.org/themes/law/cel03A.html

YALE CENTER FOR ENVIRONMENTAL LAW AND POLICY available at http://www.yale.edu/envirocenter/clinic/cities.html

Text Materials

Brad L. Bacon, ENFORCEMENT MECHANISMS IN INTERNATIONAL WILDLIFE AGREEMENTS AND THE UNITED STATES: WADING THROUGH THE MURK, (12 Geo. Int'l Envtl. L. Rev. 331, Fall 1999).

Cesare P. Romano, THE PEACEFUL SETTLEMENT OF INTERNATIONAL ENVIRONMENTAL DISPUTES: A PRAGMATIC APPROACH, (Boston, Kluwer Law International, 2000).

Dinah Shelton, Alexandre Kiss & Ishibashi Kanami, ECONOMIC GLOBALIZATION AND COMPLIANCE WITH INTERNATIONAL ENVIRONMENTAL AGREEMENTS, (Kluwer Law International, New York, 2003).

Dinah Shelton, COMMITMENT AND COMPLIANCE: THE ROLE OF NON-BINDING NORMS IN THE INTERNATIONAL LEGAL SYSTEM, (Oxford University Press, 2000).

Durwood Zaelke, Donald Kaniaru & Eva Kruzikova, MAKING LAW WORK ENVIRONMENTAL COMPLIANCE AND SUSTAINABLE DEVELOPMENT, (Cameroon May, 2005).

Edith Brown Weiss & Harold K. Jacobson (Eds.), ENGAGING COUNTRIES: STRENGTHENING COMPLIANCE WITH INTERNATIONAL ACCORDS, (MIT Press, 1998).

Edward E. Shea, ENVIRONMENTAL LAW AND COMPLIANCE METHODS, (Oceana Publications, 2002).

Elia V. Pirozzi, COMPLIANCE THROUGH ALLIANCE: REGULATORY REFORM AND THE APPLICATION OF MARKET-BASED INCENTIVES TO THE UNITED STATES-MEXICO BORDER REGION HAZARDOUS WASTE PROBLEM, (12 J. Envtl. L. & Litig. 337, 1997).

ENFORCEMENT OF AND COMPLIANCE WITH MEAS: THE EXPERIENCES OF CITES, MONTREAL PROTOCOL AND BASEL CONVENTION, (Vols. I & II, UNEP, 1999).

Eugene Skolnikoff, Kal Raustiala & David Victor, THE IMPLEMENTATION AND EFFECTIVENESS OF INTERNATIONAL ENVIRONMENTAL COMMITMENTS: THEORY AND PRACTICE, (MIT Press, 1998).

James Cameron, Jacob Werksman & Peter Roderick, IMPROVING COMPLIANCE WITH INTERNATIONAL ENVIRONMENTAL LAW, (Earthscan Pub, 1996).

Johanna Rinceanu, ENFORCEMENT MECHANISMS IN INTERNATIONAL ENVIRONMENTAL LAW: QUO VADUNT? (15 J. Envtl. L. & Litig. 147, Fall 2000).

Joseph F.C. Dimento, PROCESS, NORMS, COMPLIANCE, AND INTERNATIONAL ENVIRONMENTAL LAW, (18 J. Envtl. L. & Litig. 251, Fall 2003).

Michael Anderson and Paolo Galizzi, INTERNATIONAL ENVIRONMENTAL LAW IN NATIONAL COURTS, (The British Institute of International and Comparative Law).

Neil Hawke, ENVIRONMENTAL POLICY: IMPLEMENTATION AND ENFORCEMENT, (Ashgate, 2002).

Roger Fisher, IMPROVING COMPLIANCE WITH INTERNATIONAL LAW, (University Press of Virginia, 1980).

Ronald B. Mitchell, INTERNATIONAL ENVIRONMENTAL AGREEMENTS: A SURVEY OF THEIR FEATURES, FORMATION AND EFFECTS, (Annual Reviews, 2003).

Rüdiger Wolfrum, ENFORCING ENVIRONMENTAL STANDARDS: ECONOMIC MECHANISMS AS VIABLE MEANS? (Springer, 1996).

Sevine Ercmann, ENFORCEMENT OF ENVIRONMENTAL LAW IN UNITED STATES AND EUROPEAN LAW: REALITIES AND EXPECTATIONS, (26 Envtl. L. 1213, Winter 1996).

William L. Thomas, Bertram C. Frey & Fern Fleischer Daves, CRAFTING SUPERIOR ENVIRONMENTAL ENFORCEMENT SOLUTIONS, ENVIRONMENTAL LAW REPORTER, (Environmental Law Institute, 2000).

Xiaoying Ma & Leonard Ortolano, ENVIRONMENTAL REGULATION IN CHINA: INSTITUTIONS, ENFORCEMENT, AND COMPLIANCE, (Rowman & Littlefield, 2000).

Zhenghua Tao & Rüdiger Wolfrum, IMPLEMENTING INTERNATIONAL ENVIRONMENTAL LAW IN GERMANY AND CHINA, (The Hague, Kluwer Law International, 2001).

5. LIABILITY AND COMPENSATION REGIMES RELATED TO ENVIRONMENTAL DAMAGE

I. Introduction

1. The numerous cases of severe damage to the environment that have affected the territory of countries all over the world, as well as global commons such as the oceans in the last decades, have awakened public consciousness to the serious consequences that human activities can have on the environment and human health. Unfortunately, examples of incidents resulting in serious environmental damage are numerous. Well-known illustrations include such events as: the 1984 Bhopal gas leak disaster, resulting almost immediately in more than 1,600 deaths and injuries to over 200,000 people; the 1986 Chernobyl nuclear power plant accident which caused radioactive contamination of the natural environment and very substantial damage to human health across the borders in Europe and Asia; the 1986 Basel chemical spill into the Rhine, rendering the river biologically dead and fouling municipal water systems in downstream countries; the cyanide spill in the year 2000 from the Baia Mare mine in northwestern Romania, resulting in toxic pollution of the Danube and its tributaries in downstream countries, killing hundreds of tons of fish in some sectors of the river; and the marine oil spill incidents that have caused massive damage to the coasts of a number of countries, especially in Europe.

2. While incidents such as these attract widespread attention, environmental damage occurs regularly at the regional, state and local level but are not always covered by the media. Common examples include land contamination as a consequence of industrial accidents and the improper handling and disposal of waste; water contamination as a result of various causes including discharge of untreated industrial effluents; and loss of biodiversity due to a wide variety of impacts including habitat loss and introduction of alien species.

3. These situations and others like them raise the question of who should be held responsible for environmental harm. Specifically, who should pay for the costs involved in pollution clean-up and restoration of the damaged environment, and what

should be the standards for acceptable cleanups? These questions are encompassed in the concept of liability for environmental harm. Legal liability is one way of forcing major polluters to repair the damage that they have caused, to pay for those repairs or to compensate someone for the damages if the damage cannot be repaired. Given the evolving nature of the topics covered in this chapter, only an international framework is embraced without a corresponding regime of national implementation.

4. Liability can be seen as a mechanism for implementing the "Polluter Pays Principle" ("PPP"). That principle, originally adopted by the Organization for Economic Cooperation and Development ("OECD") in 1972, contemplates the internalization of pollution-control costs. The principle was reaffirmed at the United Nations Conference on Environment and Development ("UNCED" or Earth Summit, 1992) in principle 16 of the Rio Declaration.

**1992 Rio Declaration
(Principle 16)**

"National authorities should endeavour to promote the internalization of environmental costs and the use of economic instruments, taking into account the approach that the polluter should, in principle, bear the cost of pollution, with due regard to the public interest and without distorting international trade and investment."

The "Polluter Pays Principle" has evolved to embrace liability as well as cost internalization. In either context, the Principle expresses a policy that the polluter should prevent or pay for environmental harm. (See the discussion of the "Polluter Pays Principle" in chapter 3 above).

II. International Framework

1. *Rationale* for introducing Liability Regimes for Environmental Damage

5. While environmental legislation and international instruments lay down norms and procedures aimed at preserving the environment, liability is a necessary complement to ensure that persons responsible for non-compliance resulting in environmental damage face the prospect of having to pay for restoration of the affected environment or compensating for the damage caused.

6. Liability regimes for environmental harm, therefore, serve different purposes:

- As economic instruments that provide incentives to comply with environmental obligations and to avoid damage;
- As means of penalizing wrongful conduct; and
- They deter environmentally harmful conduct and prevent environmental damage by encouraging the party responsible for activities that may have an adverse impact on the environment to exercise caution to avoid the harm.

7. Most existing environmental liability regimes cover activities with an inherent risk of causing damage. National systems of liability for environmental damage are normally linked to the existing programmes of environmental regulation, so if, for example, an industry fails to comply with the applicable environmental law, it will also be held liable for any damage to the environment that resulted from its non-compliance in addition to facing an administrative or penal sanction. Compliance with environmental requirements, on the other hand, may in certain cases prevent liability.

2. Liability for Environmental Damage versus Traditional Liability Systems

8. To serve as an effective vehicle for environmental protection, liability regimes must be expanded from traditionally recognized forms of compensable damage to cover harm to the environment itself. While traditional liability systems cover damage to persons and goods and contamination of privately (or sometimes publicly) owned sites, they usually don't cover damage to the environment as such. This is largely a consequence of the fact that the environment is seen as a "public good" which is freely accessible to every member of society and for which there are no private ownership interests, thus no one can be held responsible for damaging it. The challenge in developing environmental liability regimes is therefore to help people realize that they are "responsible" for consequences of their acts on the environment – a public good that constitutes the basis of the life-support system for humans and all other living things.

9. There is no commonly accepted definition of environmental damage; different legal regimes adopt different definitions. Neither is there a generally accepted definition to be found in international law. However, a working definition was proposed in 1998 by the UNEP Working Group of Experts on Liability and Compensation for Environmental Damage:

"Environmental damage is a change that has a measurable adverse impact on the quality of a particular environment or any of its components, including its use and non-use values, and its ability to support and sustain an acceptable quality of life and a viable ecological balance."

In this sense, environmental damage does not include damage to persons or property, although such damage could be consequential to the damage caused to the environment.

10. Many countries have recently enacted legislation dealing with some form of liability and compensation for environmental harm or "natural resource damage." It is important to note, however, that a number of countries have chosen not to introduce separate ad hoc liability regimes for environmental harm, instead relying on traditional liability standards or principles found in civil law codes and common law traditions applied in the environmental context.

3. State Responsibility and Liability versus Civil Liability

11. In general, concepts of liability and compensation stem from the principles of tort law in which a wrongful act causing injury permits the injured party to obtain compensation, usually in the form of money damages, through a private civil action against the person who caused the injury.

12. In this sense, civil "liability" differs from what is commonly referred to as state "responsibility." Civil liability operates on the level of national law, and creates a relationship between the person liable and the person injured by conduct for which he/she is held responsible. State responsibility, on the other hand, operates on the plane of public international law. It creates a relationship not between two or more individuals but between two or more states: the state where the harmful activities have taken place and the state or states where the harm has occurred. In other words, in the case of state responsibility it is the state, rather than a private individual, that must provide a remedy for damage that occurs as a consequence of a breach it committs of an international legal obligation established by treaty or rule of customary international law.

13. The concept of state liability, as it has been developed chiefly by the United Nations International Law Commission ("ILC"), usually refers to the responsibility that a state faces for harm occurring as a consequence of a lawful activity, independently of whether there was any violation of an international norm.

4. State Responsibility and Liability For Environmental Harm

a) Transboundary Environmental Damage

14. Environmental damage can affect the territory of the state where the activity causing the harm occurs, the territory of a different state, or the global commons (that is, territories that do not fall under the national jurisdiction of any state such as the high seas). For purposes of this discussion, pollution is of concern to the international community and thus potentially the object of international law in two cases:

    - In the case of transfrontier pollution, defined by OECD as "any intentional or unintentional pollution whose physical origin is subject to, and situated wholly or in part within the area under the national jurisdiction of one state and which has effects in the area under the national jurisdiction of another state". Transfrontier pollution can result from the violation of conventional or customary rules, and therefore impair the rights of the state in which the effects occur.
    - In the case of pollution affecting areas not subject to the jurisdiction of any state, commonly known as pollution of the "global commons". In this case no state is directly entitled to react, unless the state responsible for the pollution harm has violated an obligation *erga omnes*, that is, an obligation owed to all.

b) State Responsibility and State Liability

15. "State responsibility" may be subdivided into two categories or forms of responsibility:

    - "State responsibility" for internationally wrongful acts, that is for breach of international obligations, which can be fault responsibility, arising from violation of due diligence standards, and strict responsibility that occurs even if the state has not contravened due diligence standards, but has nevertheless breached an obligation resulting in damage; and
    - A much narrower and more recently recognized concept of "state liability" for the harmful consequences of lawful activities, i.e., for damage resulting from activities that are not prohibited by international law. An activity that is not prohibited by international law but whose consequences may nonetheless give rise to international liability would virtually always be a "hazardous" activity. The International Law

Commission has defined the term "hazardous activity" as "an activity which involves a risk of causing significant harm through its physical consequences". These activities – such as nuclear and chemical plants – are common in today's world, and international law is gradually adapting to this reality. This form of liability is similar to the common law concept of strict liability for abnormally dangerous activities.

c) State Responsibility for Wrongful Acts

16. State responsibility is a principle by which states may be held accountable for inter-state claims under international law. Such claims may be brought before the International Court of Justice ("ICJ") or other international tribunals. Alternatively, states may use diplomatic means to present claims and negotiate settlements. The foundation of "responsibility" lies in the breach of obligations under international agreements or customary international law. The existence of primary obligations of states in the field of environment is therefore the precondition for existence of State responsibility for environmental damage.

17. According to customary international law, states are not allowed to conduct or permit activities within their territories, or in common spaces, that adversely affect the rights of others states, including in the field of environment. This obligation is a concrete expression of the general principle of "good neighbourliness". More specifically, two general duties can be identified which may now have become customary international law:

    - The duty to prevent, reduce and control pollution and environmental harm; and
    - The duty to cooperate in mitigating environmental risks and emergencies, through notification, consultation, negotiation, and in appropriate cases, Environmental Impact Assessment ("EIA").

18. In addition to these general duties, a number of global and regional treaties establish much more detailed obligations for states whose breach could give rise to state responsibility.

19. While state responsibility is a general concept that applies to a wide range of actions such as violation of international humanitarian law, breaches of trade agreements, or mistreatment of foreign nationals, a limited number of cases exist in the environmental field that help define the concept of state responsibility for environmental harm.

20. The landmark Trail Smelter Arbitration involved a dispute between Canada and the United States over sulphur dioxide (SO_2) pollution from a Canadian smelter in the town of Trail, British Columbia. The smelter was located in the Columbia River Valley. The Columbia River flows from Canada across the border into the state of Washington. The SO_2 emissions were carried down the valley by the prevailing winds, damaging trees and crops on the American side of the border. The tribunal constituted by the two states to resolve the dispute declared that:

> "...under principles of international law, as well as the law of the United States, no state has the right to use or permit the use of its territory in such a manner as to cause injury by fumes in or to the territory of another or the properties or persons therein, when the case is of serious consequence and the injury is established by clear and convincing evidence..."

21. In the Lac Lanoux Arbitration, Spain alleged that French plans to construct and operate a hydroelectric facility would adversely affect Spanish rights and interests contrary to the Treaty of Bayonne, 1866, which permitted the joint use of the Carol River. Spain contended that France could proceed with the project only if a prior agreement had been concluded. The tribunal's decision, although generally based on interpretation of this specific treaty, is worth mentioning because it also relies on principles of general applicability. The tribunal stressed that the exclusive jurisdiction of a state over activities in its own territory finds its limit in the rights of other states. This was a clear repudiation of the theory of absolute sovereignty, known as the Harmon doctrine. At the same time, the tribunal held that while the two states had an obligation to negotiate in good faith concerning the project, and France had a duty to respect Spain's rights and take into account its interests, there was no requirement of a prior agreement.

22. The principle of prevention of transboundary harm was reaffirmed in general terms by the International Court of Justice in the Corfu Channel Case, where the Court declared that it was the obligation of every state "not to allow knowingly its territory to be used for acts contrary to the rights of other states". The ICJ also recognized in its Advisory Opinion on the Legality of the Threat or Use of Nuclear Weapons and in the Gabcikovo Case that "the existence of the general obligation of states to ensure that activities within their jurisdiction and control respect the environment of other states or of areas beyond national control is now part of the corpus of international law relating to the environment."

23. Principle 21 of the 1972 Stockholm Declaration affirms that states have, in addition to "...the sovereign right to exploit their own resources pursuant to their own environmental policies, and the responsibility to ensure that activities within their jurisdiction or control do not cause damage to the environment of other States or of areas beyond the limits of national jurisdiction". Principle 21 was repeated in Principle 2 of the 1992 Rio Declaration.

**1992 Rio Declaration
(Principle 2)**

"States have, in accordance with the Charter of the United Nations and the principles of international law, the sovereign right to exploit their own resources pursuant to their own environmental and developmental policies, and the responsibility to ensure that activities within their jurisdiction or control do not cause damage to the environment of other states or of areas beyond the limits of national jurisdiction."

---

24. Principle 22 of the Stockholm Declaration provides that states are to "...cooperate to develop further the international law regarding liability and compensation for the victims of pollution and other environmental damage caused by activities within the jurisdiction or control of such States to areas beyond their jurisdiction." Twenty years later, Principle 13 of the Rio Declaration called on States to develop national law regarding liability and compensation for victims of pollution and other environmental damage, and that

---

**1992 Rio Declaration
(Principle 13)**

States shall also cooperate in an expeditious and more determined manner to develop further international law regarding liability and compensation for adverse effects of environmental damage caused by activities within their jurisdiction or control to areas beyond their jurisdiction.

---

25. The principle of prevention of environmental harm to other states or areas beyond national jurisdiction has been widely reaffirmed in a number of instruments in the field of international environmental law. However, while a number of international agreements contain obligations to protect the environment, very few expressly refer to state responsibility or liability. One of the few examples is the 1982 Montego Bay Convention on the Law of the Sea, whose article 235 provides that: "...1. States are responsible for the fulfilment of their international obligations concerning the protection and preservation of the marine environment. They shall be liable in accordance

with international law..." Another example is the 1972 Convention on International Liability for Damage caused by Space Objects, whose objective is to establish rules and procedures for damage caused by space objects and to ensure the prompt payment of full and equitable compensation to victims of such damage. The Convention establishes a regime of absolute liability for the launching state for damage caused by its space object on the surface of the earth or to aircraft flight.

26. The concept of state responsibility only covers the case of breach of the states' own obligations owed to another state or states. These obligations extend to the duty to ensure that activities undertaken by private parties do not cause harm to the territory of other states, as indicated by the Trail Smelter Arbitration, but do not include the responsibility of the private parties themselves. The latter is the object of civil liability regimes, which are designed to allow private individuals or organizations causing transboundary environmental harm to be held responsible for such damage.

27. State responsibility for environmental harm is a highly complex and rather controversial issue that has been the subject of ongoing discussions reflected in the 2001 set of draft articles on "Responsibility of States for Internationally Wrongful Acts", developed by the UN International Law Commission, after decades of study. Although articles refer to state responsibility in general terms, the articles are applicable to cases of environmental harm.

d) State Liability for Lawful Acts

28. State liability for lawful activities may occur only if an international instrument specifically provides for liability. However, only very few international agreements do so. The Convention on International Liability for Damage caused by Space Objects provides for absolute liability without a wrongful act for damage caused on the surface of the Earth or to aircraft in flight (article II) and for fault responsibility for other kinds of damage (article III). There are also some bilateral agreements that establish liability resulting from lawful acts for damage suffered by a party and caused by any kind of activity carried out in the territory of the other party. An example is the 1964 Agreement between Finland and the Union of Soviet Socialist Republics ("USSR") on Common Waterways, which provides that a contracting party that causes damage in the territory of the other contracting party through activities carried out in its own territory shall be liable and pay compensation.

29. The International Law Commission has been working on the issue of "International Liability for Injurious Consequences arising out of Acts Not Prohibited by International Law (Prevention of Transboundary Damage from Hazardous Activities)" as a question of customary international law since 1977. At its forty-fourth session in 1992, however, the Commission decided to continue its work on this topic in stages. It would first complete work on prevention of transboundary harm and subsequently proceed with remedial measures. Work on prevention was completed by the Commission at its fifty-third session in 2001, when it adopted a set of 19 articles on prevention of transboundary harm from hazardous activities. The Commission later resumed its work on liability in a strict sense, and adopted a set of 8 Draft principles on the allocation of loss in the case of transboundary harm arising out of hazardous activities at its fifty-sixth session in 2004.

30. The Draft Articles on Prevention of Transboundary Harm from Hazardous Activities concern "activities not prohibited by international law which involve a risk of causing significant transboundary harm through their physical consequences", where "harm" includes harm caused to persons, property or the environment and "transboundary harm" means "harm caused in the territory of or in other places under the jurisdiction or control of a state other than the state of origin, whether or not the states concerned share a common border".

31. According to the draft articles, states should take all appropriate measures "to prevent significant transboundary harm or at any event to minimize the risk thereof", and states concerned "shall cooperate in good faith and, as necessary, seek the assistance of one or more competent international organizations in preventing significant transboundary harm or at any event in minimizing the risk thereof". The provisions of the articles must be implemented by states through the adoption of the necessary legislative, administrative or other measures, including the establishment of suitable monitoring mechanisms.

32. The articles establish an obligation for the state of origin to obtain a prior authorization, within the same state of origin, for:

"(a) Any activity within the scope of the present articles carried out in its territory or otherwise under its jurisdiction or control;
(b) Any major change in an activity referred to in subparagraph (a);
(c) Any plan to change an activity which may

transform it into one falling within the scope of the present articles".

Decisions on granting the authorization must be based on the assessment of the possible transboundary harm caused by that activity. If such assessment indicates a risk of causing significant transboundary harm, the state of origin shall provide the state likely to be affected with timely notification of the risk, and shall not take any decision on authorization of the activity pending the receipt, within a period not exceeding six months, of the response from the state likely to be affected.

33. The articles also provide for an obligation for the states concerned to "enter into consultations, at the request of any of them, with a view to achieving acceptable solutions regarding measures to be adopted in order to prevent significant transboundary harm or at any event to minimize the risk thereof "and "seek solutions based on an equitable balance of interests. If the consultations fail to produce an agreed solution, the state of origin shall nevertheless take into account the interests of the state likely to be affected in case it decides to authorize the activity to be pursued, without prejudice to the rights of any state likely to be affected". The articles also specify that all relevant factors and circumstances should be taken into account for achieving an "equitable balance of interests", and provides a non-exhaustive list of such factors and circumstances.

34. The articles also include norms on exchange of information among the states concerned while the activity is being carried out, information to the public likely to be affected, response to emergencies, settlement of disputes as well as a norm on non-discrimination, according to which "a state shall not discriminate on the basis of nationality or residence or place where the injury might occur, in granting to such persons, in accordance with its legal system, access to judicial or other procedures to seek protection or other appropriate redress".

35. The ILC recommended to the General Assembly the elaboration of a convention on the basis of these draft articles. So far, no action has been taken in this direction.

36. The International Law Commission adopted, at its 56th session in 2004, the Draft Principles on the Allocation of Loss in the Case of Transboundary Harm arising out of Hazardous Activities. This is a set of eight principles, meant to apply to transboundary damage caused by activities not prohibited by international law which involve a risk of causing significant transboundary harm through their physical consequences. Damage is defined, as significant damage caused to persons, property or the environment. In this case, though, the definition also lists different kinds of damage that fall under such definition. These include:

(i) Loss of life or personal injury;

(ii) Loss of, or damage to, property other than the property held by the person liable in accordance with these articles;

(iii) Loss of income from an economic interest directly deriving from an impairment of the use of property or natural resources or environment, taking into account savings and costs;

(iv) The costs of measures of reinstatement of the property, or natural resources or environment, limited to the costs of measures actually taken;

(v) The costs of response measures, including any loss or damage caused by such measures, to the extent of the damage that arises out of or results from the hazardous activity.

37. The draft principles also define "environment" as including: "natural resources both abiotic and biotic, such as air, water, soil, fauna ad flora and the interaction between the same factors; property which forms part of the cultural heritage; and the characteristic aspects of the landscape".

38. The main purpose of the draft principles is to ensure "prompt and adequate compensation to natural or legal persons, including states that are victims of transboundary damage, including damage to the environment". Each state must ensure that such compensation is available "for victims of transboundary damage caused by hazardous activities located within its territory or otherwise under its jurisdiction or control these measures should include the imposition of liability" (without proof fault). These measures should also include the requirement on the potential polluter "to establish and maintain financial security such as insurance, bonds or other financial guarantees to cover claims of compensation". National measures should also include, when appropriate, the establishment of funds.

39. The principles also address the issue of minimization of transboundary damage in case of incident and the establishment of national and international remedies for ensuring that the general principle of ensuring compensation is translated into action in practice. They also contain a provision on cooperation among states for the

development of specific international regimes, at the global, regional and bilateral level, regarding the prevention and response measures in respect of particular categories of hazardous activities.

40. These principles are very general, and it is not clear whether they will be translated into a legally-binding instrument, guidelines for negotiators, or other non-legally binding instruments.

41. While state responsibilities for environmental harm, as well as international liability for non wrongful acts are often discussed, states have seldom made recourse to either of them. This is due to a number of factors of a political and technical nature, including, among others:

- The difficulty of ascertaining the full extent of damages,
- The fact that often the damage to the environment cannot be fully remedied,
- The difficulty of establishing a causal link between the activity that allegedly caused the damage and the damage suffered due to such factors as the geographical distance between source and damage, the fact that multiple sources of pollution may exist, and the cumulative effect of different pollution sources,
- The rigidity of traditional forms of international responsibility and of dispute settlement mechanisms and therefore the preference for informal mechanisms for settling environmental disputes,
- The concern about establishing precedents in a very delicate field of international relations.

42. For these reasons, transboundary environmental cases are often resolved on an inter-personal level rather than among states, that is through recourse to private rather than public international law. This implies that the polluter and the victim appear directly before the competent domestic authorities. The transnational element present in these cases can, however, give rise to problems of jurisdiction, choice of the applicable law, and enforcement of judgments, leading states to enter into treaties regulating the liability of private individuals for environmental harm.

e) Civil Liability Regimes for Environmental Damage

43. Civil liability regimes for environmental damage can be only applied to situations in which (1) there are one or more identifiable actors (polluters), (2) the damage is concrete and quantifiable, and (3) it is possible to establish a causal link between the damage and the actions of the identified polluter(s).

As a result, it is much easier to establish personal liability for activities such as industrial accidents, hazardous waste disposal, or water pollution from distinct "point-sources" such as end of pipe discharge of pollutants than it is for diffuse sources of pollution such as agricultural or urban runoff ("non-point sources"), acid rain or automobile pollution where it is difficult or impossible to link the negative environmental effects with the activities of specific individual actors. Civil liability regimes can apply at the national and the international levels. International civil liability regimes are briefly dealt with in section f below.

f) Types of Civil Liability for Environmental Damage

44. There are basically three types of civil liability for environmental damage.

- Fault liability. If liability is based on "fault" (wrong doing) the plaintiff must prove that the perpetrator acted with intent or that he/she acted negligently or without due care. Fault may be difficult to establish, especially in environmental cases where legal rules may not be clearly established and evidence may be difficult to obtain.
- Strict liability. If liability is "strict", fault need not be established. No intention to violate a duty of care or a norm and no negligence need be shown in a case to prevail. In other words, it does not matter whether the perpetrator behaved correctly or incorrectly; the decisive factor is that the damage was caused by the defendant's conduct. The plaintiff need only prove the causal link between the action of the alleged perpetrator and the damage. However, strict liability regimes typically do provide for some defenses; a person may be exonerated from liability if the damage was caused by, for instance, an act of God (or natural disaster), an act of war, or by the interference of a third party. Strict liability has become an increasingly common form of liability for environmental harm. The rationale for strict liability is that an actor that profits from potentially harmful or inherently dangerous activities should be liable for damage that occurred as a result of the harmful activity, an application of the "Polluter Pays Principle". Strict liability shifts the burden for risk avoidance to the source of pollution by removing the need to establish intentional or negligent behaviour to recover damages.

The distinction between strict liability and fault liability is not always clearcut. For example, some strict liability systems allow defendants to avoid liability if they can demonstrate that they have used the best available technology to control pollution or that they have complied with their environmental permits. These rather generous defences make it more difficult to establish liability and reintroduce elements similar to fault in strict liability system.

- Absolute liability. Absolute liability differs from strict liability because it allows no defences to the perpetrator apart from an act of God. This type of liability is rarely imposed, and only for what are deemed ultra-hazardous activities, such as nuclear installations.

g) Scope and Threshold of Environmental Damage

45. In addition to traditional types of damage such as personal injury or property damage, environmental cases may result in damage to the environment itself (so-called pure environmental damage) where damage is measured by the costs of remediating or restoring the impaired environment. Examples of pure environmental damage are damage to biodiversity or natural resources as such (e.g. damage to habitats, water, wildlife or species of plants) and damage in the form of contamination of sites.

46. An example of regime that recognizes damage to natural resources as such is the USA Comprehensive Environmental Response, Compensation and Liability Act of 1980, which covers damage for injury or loss of natural resources. Other examples are to be found in Italy (Law N. 349/1986, art. 18) that establishes liability for "natural resource damages". The recent EU Directive 2004/35/EC on Environmental Liability is to date one of the few, if not the only regime, to include liability for damage to biodiversity. Contamination of sites can for instance take the form of contamination of soil, surface water or ground water, independent from whether or not human health or private property is affected.

47. A number of civil liability instruments establish a threshold, beyond which environmental damage is deemed significant and therefore justifies the imposition of liability, although this level may vary significantly from one country to another.

48. Liability regimes for environmental damage normally contain clean-up standards and clean-up objectives. Clean-up standards are used to evaluate whether clean-up of a contaminated site is necessary. The main criterion for this decision is usually whether the contamination leads to a

serious threat to human health or the environment. Clean-up objectives, in contrast, are usually set to identify the quality of soil and water that is acceptable for the type of economic activity that will be carried out at the particular location after clean up. Clean-up objectives may be established based on future land uses, the type of technology available to remedy the contamination and cost considerations.

5. Who is Liable?

49. The question of who is legally responsible for damage is the cornerstone of an effective liability regime. In most conventions, the "operator" or "owner", typically the person who exercises control over an activity, is liable. This is consistent with the Prevention and Polluter-Pays Principles, because it provides an incentive to the person who carries out the activity to take preventive steps to eliminate or reduce the risk of damage, and a compensation mechanism to pay for the costs of environmental harm caused by the activities.

50. In some cases it is difficult to determine which specific individual or organization caused environmental harm. For example, if several waste generators dispose of the same chemical in a landfill, it may be impossible to identify the particular portion of the contamination that can be attributed to a specific contributor to the overall problem. As a result, some liability regimes hold all of the parties that disposed of a particular contaminant liable for cleaning up the entire site. This form of liability is referred to as "joint and several" liability because each of the polluters can be held responsible for the cost of the entire cleanup. Joint and several liability gives the plaintiff the choice to pursue more than one actor and reduces some of the burden of establishing causation by the specific defendant, thereby affording the plaintiff a greater likelihood of obtaining compensation or remediation. The defendant(s) held liable for the entire cleanup under a joint and several liability regime are usually allowed to sue other parties who contributed to the contamination.

6. Forms of Compensation

51. In most cases of environmental damage, the victim is likely to seek financial reparation to cover the costs associated with material damage to environmental resources. Problems arise because environmental damage cannot be addressed with the traditional approach of civil liability, that is, to

compensate for the economic costs of the lost or damaged property. Pure environmental damage may be incapable of calculation in economic terms, such as in the case of loss of fauna and flora which is not commercially exploited and therefore has no market value and in the case of damage to ecosystems or landscapes, economic value cannot be assessed with and in traditional approaches. Therefore, the issue arises of how to calculate the economic value of purely environmental assets. A fairly widely accepted solution to this problem is to calculate the damage in the basis of the link between reasonable costs of restoration measures, reinstatement measures or preventative measures. Environmental liability regimes may also foresee compensation for further damages exceeding those related to the adoption of such restoration measures, when both restoration and comparable measures, are not technically feasible or not reasonable.

52. The fact that environmental damage is irreparable or unquantifiable should not result in an exemption from liability. Several criteria for the calculation of damage have been developed for this purpose and are used in different legal systems. These include, for instance, linking the damage to the market price of the environmental resource (such as in the Trail Smelter Case), or to the economic value attached to its use, for example, in terms of travel costs made by individuals to visit and enjoy an environmental resource amenity, of the extra market value of private property where certain environmental amenities are located, of the willingness of individuals to pay for the enjoyment of environmental goods, such as clean air or water or the preservation of endangered species (usually taken from public opinion surveys). Liability regimes normally require that the part of compensation paid for restoration or clean up be spent for that purpose and any additional compensation should be used for specific environmental purposes.

53. Most civil liability regimes require the operator to establish financial security, usually in the form of insurance, to ensure that the risk of liability is covered. Compulsory insurance is used as a means to secure that adequate payment of compensation is made and to avoid the bankruptcy of companies that have to compensate for severe damages. However, compulsory insurance systems could reduce the incentive for potential polluters to exercise caution and prevent damage. Another problem is that insurers may limit their coverage to certain types of damage only, considering the seriousness and unpredictability of the value of

potential harm. To address this problem and the need for a measure of legal certainty for economic actors, most regimes establish caps on the amount of compensation. These caps usually differ from sector to sector, in accordance with the level of risk and potential scale of damage.

54. Another mechanism utilized to ensure the coverage of damage is the creation of victim compensation funds, which are replenished by the operators of the specific sector for which the fund is established. These funds are intended to provide compensation for victims and paying for the remedying of damages in cases where, for different reasons, compensation cannot be provided by the operator. Such funds are, for example, very common in international regimes regulating oil pollution from ships.

7. International Civil Liability

55. When plaintiffs resort to private law to address transboundary environmental issues a number of unique issues are raised including which court in which country has jurisdiction over the matter, which country's laws apply, and where and how can the judgment of the court be enforced. States have sought to overcome these and other problems through treaties regulating the liability of private individuals for environmental harm.

56. Several treaties establish rules on civil liability for environmental or related damage, generally with respect to specific activities, such as nuclear installations, oil pollution and hazardous wastes. Recent regional agreements in Europe apply more generally to industrial operations (the Lugano Convention on Civil Liability for Damage resulting from Activities Dangerous to the Environment, adopted in 1993, but not yet in force).

57. Most of the treaty regimes listed above define the activities or substances and the harm covered, the criteria to establish who is liable, the standard of care that must be exercised to avoid liability and provide exceptions from liability. Most agreements set limitations on the amount of liability and provisions for enforcement of judgments. In addition, many of them include provisions on mandatory insurance or other financial guarantees and establish funds.

58. In the field of marine pollution, the International Convention on Civil Liability for Oil Pollution Damage ("CLC") was adopted in 1969 and amended by the Protocols of 1976 and 1992. It was adopted under the auspices of the

International Maritime Organization ("IMO") in response to the "Torrey Canyon" oil spill disaster of 1967, as a regime to guarantee the payment of compensation by shipowners for oil pollution damage. The objective of the Convention is not only to ensure that adequate compensation is available to persons who suffer damage caused by oil pollution, but also to standardize international rules and procedures for determining questions of liability and adequate compensation in such areas. The 1969 CLC places the liability for such damage on the owner of the ship from which the polluting oil escaped or was discharged. The shipowner is strictly liable unless the incident is caused by war, a natural phenomenon of exceptional character, a malicious act of a third party, or through the negligence of the government. It does not apply to warships or other vessels owned or operated by the state that are used for non-commercial purposes, but does apply to ships owned by a state and used for commercial purposes. The 1992 Protocol widens the scope of the convention to cover pollution damage in the Exclusive Economic Zone ("EEZ"), and extends the scope of the Convention to cover spills from sea-going vessels constructed or adapted to carry oil in bulk as cargo so that it applies to both laden and unladen tankers, and includes spills of bunker oil from such ships. The 1992 Protocol also further limits liability to costs incurred for reasonable measures to reinstate the environment.

59. The International Convention on the Establishment of an International Fund for Compensation for Oil Pollution Damage ("FUND") was adopted in 1971 and amended by the Protocols of 1976 hand 1992. It was adopted under the auspices of IMO to ensure that adequate compensation is available to persons suffering damage caused by oil pollution discharged from ships in cases where compensation under the 1969 CLC was inadequate or could not be obtained.

60. The 1996 International Convention on Liability and Compensation for Damage in connection with the Carriage of Hazardous and Noxious Substances by Sea ("HNS") was adopted to regulate compensation for victims of accidents involving the transport of hazardous and noxious substances. Damage, as defined in the 1996 HNS includes loss of life, personal injury, loss of or damage to property outside the ship, loss or damage by contamination of the environment, and the costs of preventative measures. This Convention excludes pollution damage as defined in the 1969 CLC and the 1971 FUND to avoid overlap with these conventions. It also does not apply to damage caused by radioactive material or to warships or

other ships owned by the state used for non-commercial service. Under the 1996 HNS the shipowner is strictly liable for damage and is required to have insurance and insurance certificates. The Convention is not yet in force.

61. The International Convention on Civil Liability for Bunker Oil Pollution Damage ("Bunker Oil Pollution") was adopted in 2001 and is not yet in force (as of September 2005). Its objective is to ensure that adequate, prompt, and effective compensation is paid to persons who suffer damage caused by oil spills when carried as fuel in ships' bunkers. It applies to damage caused in the territory of the Contracting Party, including the territorial sea and the EEZ. Pollution damage includes loss or damage caused outside the ship by contamination resulting from the escape or discharge of bunker oil from the ship, and the costs of preventive measures. The Convention requires ships over 1,000 gross tonnage to maintain insurance or other financial security to cover the liability of the registered owner for pollution damage in an amount equal to the limits of liability under the applicable national or international limitation regime. In addition, this Convention also allows for direct action against the insurer.

62. The Convention on Civil Liability for Oil Pollution Damage resulting from Exploration for and Exploitation of Seabed Mineral Resources ("Seabed Mineral Resources") was adopted in 1977 with the objective to ensure adequate compensation is available to victims of pollution damage from offshore activities by means of the adoption of uniform rules and procedures for determining questions of liability and for providing such compensation. The operator is liable for damage originating from the installation, and liability extends for five years after abandonment of the installation. The operator will be exonerated if he/she can prove that the damage resulted from a war, a natural disaster, an act or omission by the victim with the intent to cause damage, or the negligence of the victim. The Convention is not in force (as of September 2005).

63. In the field of nuclear installations, a comprehensive liability regime was established through the OECD Convention on Third Party Liability in the Field of Nuclear Energy ("Paris Convention"), concluded in 1960, the International Atomic Energy Agency's Convention on Civil Liability for Nuclear Damage ("Vienna Convention") concluded in 1963 and their Joint Protocol relating to the Application of the Vienna Convention and the Paris Convention ("Joint Protocol") was adopted in 1988. The objective of

the 1960 Paris Convention is to ensure adequate and equitable compensation for persons who suffer damage caused by "nuclear incidents," which covers cases of gradual radioactive contamination, but not normal or controlled releases of radiation. The 1960 Paris Convention establishes a regime of absolute liability for the operator of a nuclear installation for damage including loss of life, and damage or loss to property other than the nuclear installation itself. The limitation period to bring forth a claim is ten years, although nations may shorten this time to a period of not less than two years from the date the claimant knew or ought to have known of the damage and the identity of the operator liable. The 1960 Paris Convention was supplemented by the Convention of 31st January 1963 Supplementary to the Paris Convention of 29th July 1960 ("Brussels Supplementary Convention"). With the coming into force of the 1988 Joint Protocol most features of the 1960 Paris Convention have been harmonized with the 1963 Vienna Convention.

64. The latter was adopted under the aegis of the IAEA and provides financial protection against damage resulting from the peaceful uses of nuclear energy. The 1963 Vienna Convention is unique in that it defines "persons" to include both individuals and states. Nuclear damage includes the loss of life, personal injury, and damage to property. Under the 1963 Vienna Convention, the operator of the nuclear installation is absolutely liable for damage caused by a nuclear incident, and is required to maintain insurance. Liability is channeled to the operator although direct action may also lie with the insurer. The operator will be exonerated from liability if the nuclear incident was due to an act of armed conflict or war, by the gross negligence of the person suffering the damage, or from an act or omission of such person done with the intent to cause damage. The time limit to bring forth a claim of compensation is also limited. The 1988 Joint Protocol established a link between the 1963 Vienna Convention and the 1960 Paris Convention combining them into one expanded liability regime. Parties to the Joint Protocol are treated as though they were parties to both Conventions and a choice of law is provided to determine which of the two Conventions should apply to the exclusion of the other in respect of the same incident.

65. The Convention relating to Civil Liability in the Field of Maritime Carriage of Nuclear Material ("NUCLEAR Convention"), was adopted in 1971 with the purpose of resolving difficulties and conflicts which arise from the simultaneous application to nuclear damage of certain maritime conventions dealing with shipowners' liability. A person otherwise liable for damage caused in a nuclear incident shall be exonerated for liability if the operator of the nuclear installation is also liable for such damage by virtue of the 1960 Paris Convention or the 1963 Vienna Convention, or national law of similar scope of protection.

66. The Convention on Supplementary Compensation for Nuclear Damage ("CSC") was adopted in 1997 with the purpose to provide a second tier of compensation for damage resulting from a nuclear incident. The convention is not yet in force (as of September 2005).

67. The Protocol to amend the Vienna Convention on Civil Liability for Nuclear Damage ("Vienna Protocol"), adopted in 1997, extends the possible limit of the operator's liability and the geographical scope of the 1963 Vienna Convention to include the territory of non-contracting states, established maritime zones, and EEZs. It also provides for jurisdiction of coastal states over actions incurring nuclear damage during transport. Furthermore, this Protocol includes a better definition of nuclear damage that addresses the concept of environmental damage, the costs of reinstatement, preventive measures and any other economic loss. It also extends the period during which claims may be brought for loss of life and personal injury with respect to the Vienna Convention.

68. In the field of hazardous wastes, the Basel Protocol on Liability and Compensation for Damage resulting from Transboundary Movements of Hazardous Wastes and their Disposal ("Basel Protocol") was adopted in 1999 as a Protocol to the 1989 Basel Convention on the Control of Transboundary Movements of Hazardous Wastes and their Disposal ("Basel Convention"). The Basel Protocol establishes a comprehensive regime for assigning liability in the event of an accident involving hazardous wastes as well as adequate and prompt compensation for damage resulting from its transboundary movement, including incidents occurring because of illegal traffic in such materials.

69. Damage, as defined in the Basel Protocol, includes traditional damage (loss of life, personal injury or damage to property), economic loss, and the costs of reinstatement and preventive measures (environmental damage). Liability is strict and the notifier or exporter is liable for damage until the disposer has taken possession of the wastes. However, fault-based liability can be imposed for intentional, reckless or negligent acts or omissions. The notifier is exonerated from liability if he/she proves that damage was the result of an armed

conflict or war, a natural phenomenon of exceptional character, compliance with state law, or the intentional conduct of a third party. In any case, all transboundary hazardous waste movements must be covered by insurance.

70. The Basel Protocol applies to the territories under jurisdiction of the state parties, including any land, marine area or airspace within which a state exercises administrative and regulatory responsibility in accordance with international law in regard to the protection of human health or the environment. It applies only to damage suffered in an area under the national jurisdiction of a state party arising from an incident as defined, as well as to areas beyond national jurisdiction and non-contracting states of transit, provided those states afford reciprocal benefits on the basis of international agreements.

71. The Basel Protocol places a cap on financial liability and the limits correspond to the units of shipment in tonnes (listed in the Annex B). A working group is currently in the process of drafting financial limits of the liability under the Protocol. There is also a limit on the time period in which claims for compensation may be brought forward. Claims must be brought within ten years from the date of the incident and within five years from the date the claimant knew or ought reasonably to have known of the damage. Claims may be brought in the courts where the damage was suffered, the incident occurred, or the residence or place of business of the defendant. The Protocol is not yet in force (as of September 2005).

72. Another important instrument in the field of international civil liability for environmental damage is the Protocol on Civil Liability and Compensation for Damage caused by the Transboundary Effects of Industrial Accidents on Transboundary Waters to the 1992 Convention on the Protection and Use of Transboundary Watercourses and International Lakes and to the 1992 Convention on the Transboundary Effects of Industrial Accidents ("Civil Liability Protocol") adopted in 2003 but not yet in force (as of September 2005). The 2003 Civil Liability Protocol provides individuals affected by the transboundary impact of industrial accidents on international watercourses (e.g. fishermen or operators of downstream waterworks) a legal claim for adequate and prompt compensation.

73. According to the Civil Liability Protocol, companies will be liable for accidents at industrial installations, including tailing dams, as well as during transport via pipelines. Damage covered by the Protocol includes physical damage, damage to property, loss of income, the cost of reinstatement and response measures will be covered by the Protocol. The Protocol sets financial limits of liability depending on the risk of the activity, based on the quantities of the hazardous substances that are or may be present and their toxicity or the risk they pose to the environment and requires companies to establish financial securities, such as insurance or other guarantees. It also contains a non-discrimination provision, according to which victims of the transboundary effects cannot be treated less favourably than victims from the country where the accident has occurred.

74. A general instrument in the field of civil liability for environmental harm, although adopted at the regional level, is the 1993 Lugano Convention on Civil Liability for Damage resulting from Activities Dangerous to the Environment ("Lugano Convention"), not yet in force (as of September 2005). The 1993 Lugano Convention aims at ensuring adequate compensation for damage resulting from activities dangerous to the environment and also provides for means of prevention and reinstatement. It only applies to dangerous activities, defined as an open-ended category that includes but is not limited to: hazardous substances specified in Annex I, genetically modified organisms, micro-organisms and waste. It covers all types of damage including loss of life, personal injury, damage to property, loss or damage by impairment to the environment, and the costs of preventive measures (both traditional damage and environmental damage) when caused by a dangerous activity.

75. The Convention applies whether the incident occurs inside or outside the territory of a party, but does not apply to damage arising from carriage, or to nuclear substances. The extension of the territorial application of the Convention is based on rules of reciprocity. The operator is strictly liable for damage caused during the period when he/she exercises control over that activity, and is required to maintain insurance. The operator may be exonerated from liability for damage if he/she proves that the damage was caused by an act of war, a natural phenomenon of exceptional

character, an act done with the intent to cause damage by a third party, or resulted from compliance with a specific order from a public authority. Contributory fault on the part of the victim may also reduce the amount received in compensation. Actions for compensation must be brought within three years from the date on which the claimant knew or ought reasonably to have known of the damage and of the identity of the operator. In no case shall actions be brought after thirty years from the date of the incident which caused the damage.

Stephen C. McCaffrey, Distinguished Professor and Scholar, University of the Pacific, McGeorge School of Law

Maria Cristina Zucca, Assiociate Legal Officer, Division of Policy and Development and Law, UNEP

Resources

Internet Materials

INTERNATIONAL LAW COMMISSION ("ILC") available at http://www.un.org/law/ilc/

INTERNATIONAL MARITIME ORGANIZATION ("IMO") available at http://www.imo.org

UNITED NATIONS ECONOMIC COMMISSION FOR EUROPE ("UNECE") available at http://www.unece.org/env/civil-liability/welcome.html

UNITED NATIONS TREATY DATABASE available at http://untreaty.un.org/

Text Materials

Birnie, P. and Boyle, A., INTERNATIONAL LAW AND THE ENVIRONMENT, (second edition, 2002).

Boisson de Chazournes, L., *La Mise en Oeuvre du Droit International dans le Domaine de la Protection de l'Environnement: Enjeux et Defis,* in REVUE GENERALE DE DROIT INTERNATIONAL PUBLIC, (Vol. 55, 1995).

Brownlie I., *State Responsibility and International Pollution: a Practical Perspective,* in Magraw, D., INTERNATIONAL LAW AND POLLUTION, (University of Pennsylvania Press, Philadelphia, 1991).

Conforti B., *Do States really accept Responsibility for Environmental Damage?* in Francioni, F., and Scovazzi. T., INTERNATIONAL RESPONSIBILITY FOR ENVIRONMENTAL HARM, (Graham & Trotman, 1991).

Dupuy P.M., *Overview of the Existing Customary Legal Regime regarding International Pollution,* in Magraw, D., INTERNATIONAL LAW AND POLLUTION, (University of Pennsylvania Press, Philadelphia, 1991).

Durwood Zaelke, Donald Kaniaru & Eva Kruzikova, MAKING LAW WORK, ENVIRONMENTAL COMPLIANCE AND SUSTAINABLE DEVELOPMENT, (Cameroon, May, 2005).

European Union, WHITE PAPER ON ENVIRONMENTAL LIABILITY, (COM(2000) 66 final, 9 February 2000).

Francioni, F. and Scovazzim, T., eds., INTERNATIONAL RESPONSIBILITY FOR ENVIRONMENTAL HARM, (Graham & Trotman, 1991).

Kiss A. and Shelton D., INTERNATIONAL ENVIRONMENTAL LAW, (third edition, 2004).

Kiss A., *Present Limits to the Enforcement of State Responsibility for Environmental Damage*, in , Francioni, F. and Scovazzim, T., eds., INTERNATIONAL RESPONSIBILITY FOR ENVIRONMENTAL HARM, (Graham & Trotman, 1991).

Magraw, D., INTERNATIONAL LAW AND POLLUTION, (University of Pennsylvania Press, Philadelphia, 1991).

McCaffrey S., *Private Remedies for Transfrontier Environmental Disturbances*, in IUCN ENVIRONMENTAL POLICY & LAW, (Paper No. 8, World Conservation Union "IUCN", 1975).

McCaffrey S., THE LAW OF INTERNATIONAL WATERCOURSES: NON-NAVIGATIONAL USES, (Oxford University Press, 2001).

Organization for Economic Cooperation and Development ("OECD"), GUIDING PRINCIPLES CONCERNING ECONOMIC ASPECTS OF ENVIRONMENTAL POLICIES, (May 1972).

Pisillo-Mazzeschi R., *Forms of International Responsibility for Environmental Harm*, in , Francioni, F., and Scovazzi. T., INTERNATIONAL RESPONSIBILITY FOR ENVIRONMENTAL HARM, (Graham & Trotman, 1991).

Rosas A., ISSUES OF STATE LIABILITY FOR TRANSBOUNDARY ENVIRONMENTAL DAMAGE, (Nordic Journal of International Law, Vol. 60, 1991).
Schwartz, M. L., INTERNATIONAL LEGAL PROTECTION FOR VICTIMS OF ENVIRONMENTAL ABUSE, (18 Yale Law J. Int'l Law 355, 1993).

Shaw Malcolm N., INTERNATIONAL LAW, (Cambridge, 1997).

Spinedi M., *Les Conséquences Juridiques d'un Fait Internationalement Illicite causant un Dommage à l'Environnement* in Francioni, F., and Scovazzi. T., INTERNATIONAL RESPONSIBILITY FOR ENVIRONMENTAL HARM, (Graham & Trotman, 1991).

United Nations Environment Programme ("UNEP"), GLOBAL ENVIRONMENT OUTLOOK 3, (UNEP, 2002).

United Nations Environment Programme ("UNEP"), LIABILITY AND COMPENSATION FOR ENVIRONMENTAL DAMAGE: COMPILATION OF DOCUMENTS, (UNEP, 1998).

Weiss, E. B., INTERNATIONAL ENVIRONMENTAL LAW: CONTEMPORARY ISSUES AND THE EMERGENCE OF A NEW WORLD ORDER, (Vol. 81, Georgetown Law Journal, 1993).

World Commission on Environment and Development ("WCED"), Experts Group on Environmental Law, *Legal Principles for Environmental Protection and Sustainable Development*, in ENVIRONMENTAL PROTECTION AND SUSTAINABLE DEVELOPMENT, (Graham & Trotman Martinus Nijhoff Publishers, 1987).

6. THE GLOBAL ENVIRONMENT FACILITY

I. Introduction

1. The Global Environment Facility (GEF) is an international financing facility that provides grant funding to developing countries, and countries with economies in transition, for projects that generate global environmental benefits within the context of sustainable development.

2. Following a three year pilot phase financed by donors with a capital of $1.1 billion, the GEF was restructured and formalized in 1994 with a first replenishment of US$2 billion to promote global environmental benefits in four focal areas addressing biological diversity, climate change, international waters and ozone layer depletion.

3. In 1998, 36 donor states agreed to a second replenishment, comprising new pledges totaling US$2 billion. A third replenishment in 2002, comprising new funding of US$2.2 billion, was associated with a broadening of the GEF mandate to include two new focal areas addressing land degradation and Persistent Organic Pollutants (POPs).

4. The operation and structure of the GEF are defined by the Instrument for the Establishment of the Restructured Global Environment Facility adopted in 1994 and amended in 2003 subsequent to agreements of the second GEF Assembly held in 2002 (GEF, 1994 and 2004).

5. The GEF serves as the financial mechanism of the Convention on Biological Diversity ("CBD"), the United Nations Framework Convention on Climate Change ("UNFCCC") and the (Stockholm) Convention on Persistent Organic Pollutants ("POPs"). Articles 21 and 39 of the CBD, articles 11 and 21 of the UNFCCC and articles 13 and 14 of the Stockholm Convention outline the establishment of a financial mechanism for each of the Conventions and the designation of GEF to serve in this capacity. This designation is reflected in paragraph 6 of the GEF Instrument.

6. The GEF supports actions in eligible countries that contribute to achieving the objectives of these three Conventions and supports countries to meet their direct obligations under the Conventions, such as preparation of National Communications.

7. The GEF also serves as a financial mechanism to the United Nations Convention to combat Desertification in Countries experiencing Serious Drought and/or Desertification, particularly in Africa ("UNCCD") and funds actions that support the objectives of the Montreal Protocol on Substances that deplete the Ozone Layer and the objectives of the Regional Seas Agreements.

8. In determining its operational programming and priorities, the GEF responds to guidance provided by the Conferences of the Parties ("COP") of the Conventions to which it relates.

9. In accordance with chapter 33 of Agenda 21, article 20 of the CBD, article 4.3 of the UNFCCC, and article 13 of the Stockholm Convention, the purpose of the GEF is to provide funding for measures to achieve global environmental benefits that is "new and additional".

II. GEF Structure

10. The GEF is founded and operates on the basis of collaboration and partnership among three Implementing Agencies: The United Nations Development Programme ("UNDP"), the United Nations Environment Programme ("UNEP") and the World Bank, responsible for the operation of the facility by supporting development and implementation of projects, providing administrative support, and providing corporate services to the GEF. Such services include implementation of corporate programmes, support to the development of operational policies and joint outreach.

11. Seven other organizations – the GEF Executing Agencies operating under a GEF policy of expanded opportunities – contribute to the development and implementation of GEF projects within areas of their comparative advantage. These agencies are the Food and Agriculture Organization of the United Nations, the International Fund for Agricultural Development, the United Nations Industrial Development Organization, and the four regional development banks : the Inter-American Development Bank, the European Bank for Reconstruction and Development, the Asian Development Bank and the African Development Bank.

12. Governance of the Facility is provided by a Council and an Assembly. The GEF Council, comprising 32 members made up of constituency groupings of GEF participant countries and meeting twice per year, is responsible for developing,

adopting and evaluating the operational policies and programmes for GEF-financed activities. To provide balanced and equitable representation of all participating countries, giving due weight to the funding efforts of all donors, sixteen members are from developing countries, two from the countries with economies in transition and fourteen from developed countries.

13. A GEF Assembly of all participating countries has convened every four years to review policy and operations and to consider, for approval by consensus, amendments to the Instrument recommended by the Council.

14. Support to the development of policy and programmes, and coordination of their implementation, is provided by the GEF Secretariat under the direction of its Chief Executive Officer, appointed by the Council, who also serves as the Chairperson of the GEF. The Secretariat serves and reports to the Council and the Assembly, ensuring that their decisions are translated into effective actions. The Secretariat coordinates preparation of new GEF policy papers for review by Council, formulation of the four GEF work programmes prepared annually, monitors implementation of the GEF portfolio, and ensures that the GEF operational strategy and policies are followed. Functionally independent, the Secretariat is supported administratively by the World Bank.

15. The Scientific and Technical Advisory Panel (STAP) of the GEF provides scientific and technical guidance to the Facility. The GEF Office of Monitoring and Evaluation is responsible to the GEF Council for monitoring and evaluating, on a continuing basis, the effectiveness of GEF programmes and resource allocations on project, country, portfolio and institutional bases. The World Bank, acting in a fiduciary and administrative capacity, serves as the Trustee of the GEF Trust Fund.

III. National Participation, Eligibility and Coordination

16. 176 countries are participants in the GEF. Any member state of the United Nations or of any of its specialized agencies may become a participant in the GEF by depositing with the Secretariat an instrument of participation. In the case of a state contributing to the GEF Trust Fund, an instrument of commitment is deemed to serve as an instrument of participation.

17. A country is an eligible recipient of GEF grants if it is eligible to borrow from the World Bank (IBRD and/or IDA) or if it is an eligible recipient of UNDP technical assistance through its country Indicative

Planning Figure ("IPF"). GEF grants for activities within a focal area addressed by a convention referred to in paragraph 6 of the GEF Instrument but outside the framework of the financial mechanism of the convention, may only be made available to eligible recipient countries that are party to the convention concerned.

18. Relations of recipient countries within the GEF and policy and operations at national level are coordinated by government designated GEF focal points. An Operational Focal Point ("OFP") is responsible for operational, project and portfolio related, issues and a Political Focal Point is responsible for policy issues. In some cases the functions are combined under a single office or individual.

IV. GEF Projects

19. Projects may be proposed, designed and executed by a broad range of proponents. These include government agencies and other national institutions, international organizations, academic and research institutions, private sector entities, and national and international Non Governmental Organizations ("NGOs"). These bodies are responsible for managing the projects, on the ground, and are referred to as project executing agencies.

20. Proponents access GEF funding through one or more of the GEF Implementing Agencies and GEF Executing Agencies who provide technical and administrative support throughout the project cycle, from conception to final evaluation and closure. This support ensures that projects address GEF priorities, are designed and executed cost-effectively, provide maximum impact, and are executed in conformance with GEF policy and requirements.

21. GEF provides support to eligible countries through three main categories of projects: (i) full size projects, (ii) medium-sized projects and (iii) "enabling activities".

22. Full size projects and medium-sized projects (the latter requiring no more than $1 million GEF funding) are designed within the framework and according to the criteria of fifteen Operational Programmes (Section 6). Project Preparation and Development Facility ("PDF") grants may be provided to assist in the preparation of projects.

23. PDF Block B grants ("PDF-B") of up to $350,000 are available for activities needed to prepare full size projects involving a single country and up to $700,000 for those involving more than one

country. PDF Block A grants ("PDF-A") of up to $25,000 may also be provided for initial activities needed to prepare full size projects. PDF-A grants of up to $50,000 are available to support the preparation of medium-sized projects.

24. Enabling activities support countries - and build their capacity - to meet the obligations of being Party to the CBD, the UNFCCC, and the Stockholm Convention. Such direct obligations include the preparation of national reports to the CBD and UNFCCC and a National Implementation Plan for the management of POPs. Funding of up to $500,000 is provided for enabling activities through expedited procedures. (Section 7).

25. In addition, a GEF Small Grants Programme ("SGP"), administered by UNDP on behalf of the GEF partners, provides grants of up to $50,000 to community groups to carry out small-sized projects.

26. With the exception of enabling activities, GEF only part-finances projects, specifically co-financing the incremental cost of measures designed to generate global environmental benefits. Co-financing from other sources is required, and considered to be funding committed for the GEF project as part of the initial financing package without which the GEF objectives could not be met. Required co-financing for medium-sized and full size projects varies, depending on the nature of the project and focal area, roughly from 1:1 to 1:7 (GEF : other sources).

27. Co-financing may comprise cash - provided for example by the recipient governments, organizations involved in the project execution, or other donors - and "in-kind" contributions dedicated to the project including staff, office space, services, utilities and equipment. Co-financing expands the resources available to finance environmental objectives; is a key indicator of the commitment of the counterparts, beneficiaries, and Implementing and Executing Agencies; and helps ensure success and local acceptance of projects by linking them to sustainable development, and thereby maximizes and sustains their impacts.

V. Project Eligibility and Basic Principles of the GEF

28. Projects must support the objectives and conform to the criteria established within one or more of the fifteen Operational Programmes of the GEF. In addition projects must contribute to the attainment of one or more of twenty five Strategic Priorities

(Section 6) and their associated measurable objectives, defined and adopted for the third phase of the GEF (GEF-3, 2002-2006).

29. In the case of those focal areas related to a global environmental convention for which GEF serves as a financial mechanism or whose objectives it supports, projects must support the objective of the convention, responding to relevant COP programme priorities. To ensure that projects are based on sound science and technology, all full size project proposals are subject to an independent review by an expert drawn from the STAP Roster.

30. Projects must be "country-driven", based upon and addressing national priorities. In demonstration of this, it is required that projects are officially endorsed by the GEF Operational Focal Point of the beneficiary country or countries. Projects must involve all relevant stakeholders in their development and implementation, and demonstrate consultation with and participation of affected people.

31. Projects must generate global environmental benefits. The GEF covers the difference (or "increment") between the costs of a project undertaken with global environmental objectives in mind, and the costs of an alternative project that the country would have imple-mented in the absence of global environmental concerns. This difference is referred to as the "incremental costs." With the exception of Enabling Activities, which are considered fully incremental, project proposals must include an analysis of the incremental costs.

32. Projects must demonstrate cost-effectiveness in realizing their objectives, and provide evidence of the sustainability of objectives beyond the life of the project and the potential for replication of methodology in other areas or countries. Projects must include a rigorous monitoring & evaluation plan, including objectively verifiable indicators of the attainment of project objectives and impacts. Letters of commitment of co-financing are required prior to final approval.

33. Initial screening of project ideas for their conformance with GEF criteria and eligibility is provided by the Implementing Agencies. Once project proposals have been finalized, they are reviewed by the GEF Secretariat prior to approval by the Council or CEO (Section VII).

VI. GEF Programming Framework: Focal Areas, Operational Programmes and Strategic

Priorities of the GEF

1. Focal Areas

34. The Instrument for the Establishment of the Restructured Global Environment Facility adopted in 1994, established the GEF as "a mechanism for international cooperation for the purpose of providing new and additional grant and concessional funding to meet the agreed incremental costs of measures to achieve agreed global environmental benefits" in four focal areas: climate change, biological diversity, international waters and ozone layer depletion. Following decision at the second GEF Assembly held in

Beijing in October 2002, the GEF Instrument was amended to include two new focal areas in land degradation and persistent organic pollutants.

2. Operational Programmes

35. In October 1995 the GEF Council adopted an operational strategy to guide the preparation of country-driven initiatives in the GEF focal areas (GEF, 1996). Consistent with outlines provided in the strategy, ten operational programmes were subsequently developed that define eligibility and specific objectives to be addressed in each of the four existing focal areas (GEF, 1997). Subsequently five additional operational programmes have been defined to address emerging priorities and new focal areas. The fifteen operational programmes of the GEF are shown in table 1.

Table 1. Operational Programmes of the GEF

Biodiversity	
OP1	Arid and Semi-Arid Zone Ecosystems
OP2	Coastal, Marine and Freshwater Ecosystems
OP3	Forest Ecosystems
OP4	Mountain Ecosystems
OP13	Conservation and Sustainable Use of Biological Diversity Important to Agriculture
Climate Change	
OP5	Removal of Barriers to Energy Efficiency and Energy Conservation
OP6	Promoting the Adoption of Renewable Energy by removing Barriers and reducing Implementation Costs
OP7	Reducing the Long-Term Costs of Low Greenhouse Gas Emitting Energy Technologies
OP11	Promoting Environmentally Sustainable Transport
International Waters	
OP8	Waterbody-based Operational Programme
OP9	Integrated Land and Water Multiple Focal Area Operational Programme
OP10	Contaminant-based Operational Programme
Multifocal Area	
OP12	Integrated Ecosystem Management
Persistent Organic Pollutants	
OP14	Draft Operational Programme on Persistent Organic Pollutants
Land Degradation	
OP15	Operational Programme on Sustainable Land Management

3. Strategic Priorities in the Current Phase of the GEF

36. For the operation of its third phase (GEF-3) the GEF adopted 25 Strategic Priorities ("SPs"), summarized in table 2. These reflect the major

themes or approaches under which resources would be programmed within each of the focal areas.

Table 2. Strategic Priorities in GEF-3

Capacity Building	
CB-1	Enabling Activities (climate change and biodiversity)
CB-2	Crosscutting Capacity Building
Biodiversity	
BD-1	Catalyzing the Sustainability of Protected Areas
BD-2	Mainstreaming Biodiversity in Production Landscapes and Sectors
BD-3	Capacity Building for the Implementation of the Cartagena Protocol on Biosafety
BD-4	Generation and Dissemination of Best Practices for Addressing Current and Emerging Biodiversity Issues

Climate Change	
CC-1	Transformation of Markets for High Volume Products and Processes
CC-2	Increased Access to Local Sources of Financing for Renewable Energy and Energy Efficiency
CC-3	Power Sector Policy Frameworks Supportive of Renewable Energy and Energy Efficiency
CC-4	Productive Uses of Renewable Energy
CC-5	Global Market Aggregation and National Innovation for Emerging Technologies
CC-6	Modal Shifts in Urban Transport and Clean Vehicle/Fuel Technologies
CC-7	Short Term Measures
CC-A	Strategic Priority on Adaptation to Climate Change
International Waters	
IW-1	Catalyze Financial Resources for Implementation of Agreed Actions
IW-2	Expand Global Coverage with Capacity Building Foundational Work
IW-3	Undertake Innovative Demonstrations for Reducing Contaminants and Addressing Water Scarcity
Ozone Depletion	
OZ-1	Methyl Bromide Reduction
Persistent Organic Pollutants	
POP-1	Targeted Capacity Building
POP-2	Implementation of Policy/Regulatory Reforms and Investments
POP-3	Demonstration of Innovative and Cost-Effective Technologies
Land Degradation OP on Sustainable Land Management	
SLM-1	Targeted Capacity Building
SLM-2	Implementation of Innovative and Indigenous Sustainable Land Management Practices
Integrated Approach to Ecosystem Management	
EM-1	Integrated Approach to Ecosystem Management
Small Grants Programme	
SGP-1	Small Grants Programme

(Source: GEF Business Plan FY04-06, GEF/C.21/9)

VII. The GEF Project Cycle

37. Project proponents seeking GEF support may submit their project idea – typically as a short concept note outlining the rationale and objectives of the initiative – to one or other of the GEF Implementing or Executing Agencies. The GEF Agency will review the idea for conformity with the GEF mandate and its fit within the GEF programming framework as well as its fit with its own areas of comparative advantage. In some cases an Agency may recommend that the proponent seek the support of another GEF Agency. For those that conform, the GEF Agency will work with the proponent to prepare a detailed proposal in a standard format that varies depending on the scale of project conceived, and whether project development funding is required. Standard templates for project proposals are available on the GEF website (www.thegef.org).

38. Once finalized, proposals are submitted by the GEF Agency for review by the GEF Secretariat. Simultaneously, proposals are circulated to the Implementing Agencies, the Scientific and Technical Advisory Panel ("STAP"), the Secretariat of the relevant Convention and, as relevant, to any of the GEF Executing Agencies. Taking into account any comments of these bodies, the GEF Secretariat may require revision of the proposal or will recommend it for approval.

39. Submission of full size projects for approval conforms to a scheduled calendar for compilation of four Work Programmes each year. Two Work Programmes are prepared for review by Council at their meetings held in spring and fall (normally May and November), and two are prepared for review inter-sessionally (normally January and July). A similar calendar applies to the intake to the GEF "pipeline" of new concepts for full size projects, for which normally four intakes are scheduled each year. As a measure to expedite the processing of smaller projects, proposals for medium-sized projects, enabling activities that require no more than $500,000 GEF funding and project development grants, may be submitted at any time. Enabling activities requiring higher levels of funding are processed in the same manner as full size projects.

40. Proposals for full size projects are approved by the GEF Council within the four GEF Work Programmes, prepared and reviewed each year. As another measure to expedite the processing of smaller projects, the Council has delegated authority to the CEO to approve medium-sized projects, expedited enabling activities and PDF-B grants for preparation of full size projects. The CEO also approves concepts for full size projects to the GEF pipeline. Authority has been delegated to the GEF Implementing Agencies to approve smaller preparatory grants (PDF-A) to assist in the

preparation of medium-sized projects or for initial activities needed to prepare full size projects. PDF-A grants sought through the GEF Executing Agencies are approved by the CEO.

41. Once a grant has been approved by the GEF and detailed implementation arrangements have been put in place, the GEF Agency, in accordance with its internal rules and procedures, approves the project for implementation in the form of a legally binding document between itself and the project executing agency. The first tranche of project funds is then transferred and subsequent payments follow the satisfactory preparation and submission to the GEF Agency of progress and financial reports.

1. Full Size Projects

42. To enable the planning of resource allocations across the focal areas and over coming years, all full size projects must, as an initial step, be approved to the GEF pipeline. Application for pipeline entry and approval of a PDF-B grant may be made concurrently. One of the principle outputs of activities carried out with PDF-B funding is the fully elaborated proposal for a full size project. Once a full size project is approved by Council, detailed implementation arrangements are completed during a process of appraisal. A final project document is submitted for endorsement by the CEO (to ensure it conforms with the proposal approved by Council), following which the project is approved officially by the Implementing Agency and the first tranche of funds is transferred to the project executing agency. During implementation, the GEF Agency receives and reviews mandatory progress and financial reports, provides technical and administrative guidance and monitors the progress of the project including preparation of an annual Project Implementation Report. An independent evaluation of the project is carried out at the mid-term and on completion of the project.

2. Medium-Sized Projects

43. Following approval of a medium-sized project by the CEO, implementation arrangements are finalized and the project is approved by the GEF Agency. The GEF Agency provides similar support during implementation to that provided to a full size project and commissions an independent evaluation of the project on completion.

3. Enabling Activities

44. Enabling Activities are initiated through direct request to a GEF Agency from a designated government authority. Global "umbrella" projects have been approved by the GEF Council to fund national enabling activities for the preparation of National Biosafety Frameworks, second national communications to the UNFCCC and third national communications to the CBD. National proposals for these purposes are prepared with support of the GEF Implementing Agency and approved directly by the Implementing Agency who provides support to the national agency throughout project implementation.

4. Small Grant Projects

45. Small Grants projects under the SGP are processed and approved by a national committee and support during implementation is provided by a national office established by UNDP.

VIII. The GEF Project Portfolio Scope and Division of Responsibility among the GEF Agencies

46. Between 1991 and 2004, the GEF provided $5 billion in grants, matched by more than $16 billion in co-financing from other partners, for some 1600 projects (as well as thousands of small grants projects) in developing countries and countries with economies in transition.

47. Of these projects, some 43% are implemented by the World Bank, 39% by UNDP, 11% by UNEP and the remainder through partnership among more than one agency. By focal area, 35% of the resources have been allocated to biodiversity, 35% to climate change, 14% to international waters and the remaining 16% allocated among the other focal areas, including those recently established, and to projects with multiple focal area objectives.

48. The Implementing Agencies and GEF Executing Agencies acting under the policy of expanded opportunities tend to specialize in the type of projects in which they have a comparative advantage. For example, larger investment projects tend to be undertaken by the World Bank and the Regional Development Banks. Projects supported by UNDP are implemented within the context of its country programmes of technical assistance. The UNIDO and FAO support GEF projects related to their expertise in the management of POPs for industrial and agricultural purposes respectively. The International Fund for Agricultural Development ("IFAD") supports projects related to the GEF Operational Programme on sustainable land management. Building on its science base and role in stimulating international cooperation on environmental issues, many UNEP projects focus on the development of tools and methods for environmental management, on environmental

assessment, or promote international cooperation for the management of shared resources.

IX. UNEP as an Implementing Agency of the Global Environment Facility

49. As an Implementing Agency of the Global Environment Facility, UNEP performs three major functions:

    (1) UNEP provides support and the Secretariat to the Scientific and Technical Advisory Panel ("STAP") of the GEF.

    (2) UNEP provides corporate support to the GEF, including contribution to the development of GEF policy and programmes.

    (3) UNEP assists a wide range of project proponents to develop and implement eligible, country driven projects that within the six GEF focal areas, in general, address one or more of the following broad objectives, to:

    • Promote regional and multi-country cooperation to achieve global environmental benefits (management of transboundary ecosystems, transboundary diagnostic analysis and cooperative mechanisms/action);
    • Advance knowledge for environmental decision-making through scientific and technical analysis, including environmental assessments and targeted research;
    • Develop and demonstrate technologies, methodologies and policy tools for improved environmental management;
    • Build capacity to prepare and implement environmental strategies, action plans and reports and environmental management and policy instruments to implement Multilateral Environmental Agreements (MEAs).

50. The areas of focus of UNEP/GEF projects have been defined by the Action Plan on UNEP-GEF Complementarity (UNEP/GC.20/44), adopted by the UNEP Governing Council and the GEF Council in 1999. They relate to UNEP's mandate and areas of comparative advantage and build upon its regular programme of work including environmental assessment, development and implementation of environmental policy and its programmes related to chemicals and energy. The adoption of the Action Plan, together with the establishment, in 1996, of UNEP's GEF Coordination Office (now the UNEP Division of GEF Coordination), have been responsible for the strengthening and growth of the UNEP/GEF work programme of projects in recent years.

51. As of July 2005, UNEP is implementing a GEF work programme financed at US$ 1 billion, including just under US$ 500 million in GEF grant financing. The work programme includes 75 full size projects, 72 medium-sized projects, and 321 enabling activities (including those under a global programme to develop National Biosafety Frameworks in 130 countries) supporting immediate national obligations to the Conventions. Sixty-one projects are under preparation with approved project preparation and development grants. The work programme includes projects in all the GEF Focal Areas and Operational Programmes. 153 countries participate in UNEP/GEF projects, in Africa, Asia, the Pacific, Eastern Europe, Central Asia, Latin America and the Caribbean.

X. The Scientific and Technical Advisory Panel of the GEF

52. The Scientific and Technical Advisory Panel ("STAP") is an advisory body that provides independent strategic scientific advice to the Facility on relevant science and technology issues. UNEP provides STAP's Secretariat and operates as the liaison between the Facility and the STAP.

53. The panel is composed of fifteen internationally recognized experts from both developing and developed countries with expertise relevant to the GEF focal areas. The panel is chaired by a Chairperson, who functions as the spokesperson for the panel and reports to the GEF Council. STAP has a mandate to:

    • Provide objective, strategic scientific and technical advise on GEF policies, operational strategies, and programmes;
    • Conduct selective reviews of projects in certain circumstances and at specific points in the project cycle;
    • Promote targeted research policy and projects and review targeted research projects, and
    • Maintain a roster of experts consisting of internationally recognized specialists in the scientific and technical areas relevant to GEF operations.

54. Meetings of the panel are convened twice a year in spring and fall. Workshops are convened and background reviews commissioned to formulate advise on specific issues. All full size projects are subject to mandatory review by an expert selected from the Roster.

XI. UNEP/GEF Projects

55. The majority of UNEP/GEF projects involve actions in and collaboration with several countries, rather than being limited to a site-specific intervention in a single country. In many cases the rationale for a multi-country approach is to enable regional collaboration for the management of a shared resource. In other cases the rationale is to develop and demonstrate improved management practices under a range of national and ecological conditions, share experiences and promote replication of methodology. UNEP is also implementing several single-country projects in addition to supporting national enabling activities.

56. This section provides some examples of UNEP/GEF projects with specific focus on projects that support the development and implementation of environmental policy and legal frameworks or frameworks of action, and that support implementation of the multilateral environmental agreements for which GEF serves as a financial mechanism.

1. Regional Environmental Frameworks and Programmes of Action

57. Building on UNEP's mandate and experience in promoting international cooperation on global environmental issues and supporting development of environmental legal frameworks, many UNEP/GEF projects seek to develop regional frameworks for cooperation on environmental protection and management.

a) Africa

The Environment Initiative of the New Partnership for Africa's Development

58. Between 2001 and 2003, UNEP supported African countries to prepare an Action Plan for the Environment Initiative of the New Partnership for Africa's Development [NEPAD]. The Action Plan was adopted by the African Union at the second ordinary session of the Assembly of the African Union held in Maputo, Mozambique on 12 July 2003. Delivered through a GEF medium-sized project, an important achievement of this initiative has been to raise the issue of environmental protection to the agenda of the African Heads of State and Government.

59. The Action Plan identifies priority needs for actions on major environmental challenges including climate change, land degradation, and the degradation of the marine environment and freshwater resources, and addresses the links between environment, economic development, health and poverty.

60. In all the thematic areas it addresses, the need for capacity building was identified as crucial for effective implementation of the Action Plan. Accordingly the Action Plan is accompanied by a comprehensive strategy for capacity building, whose objectives the GEF has committed to support. As an initial step, a UNEP/GEF medium-sized project was approved in June 2004 to strengthen the capacity of Africa's Regional Economic Commissions (REC) to implement the NEPAD Environment Initiative and support the preparation of sub-regional environmental action plans.

61. NEPAD Environment Initiative provides a framework for a coherent programming of action aimed at improving environmental management, implementing the global environmental conventions and promoting sustainable development in Africa, including the following UNEP/GEF projects:

   i) Addressing Land-based Activities in the Western Indian Ocean ("WIO-LaB"): A UNEP/GEF project commenced in 2004 to support nine countries in coordinated action to promote environmentally sustainable management and development of the West Indian Ocean region. Addressing land-based activities that harm marine, coastal and inland waters, the project will demonstrate less environmentally damaging development options and strengthen human and institutional capacity to ensure sustainable, less polluting development. The project will strengthen the regional legal basis for preventing land-based sources of pollution by improving policy and legislative mechanisms for effective controls on land-based activities, assisting development of national plans of action and developing a regional protocol.

   ii) Integrated Ecosystem Management ("IEM") of Natural Resources in the Transboundary Areas of Niger Republic and Nigeria: This full size project will commence implementation in 2005 aiming in its first phase to strengthen legal and institutional frameworks for collaboration between the two countries and to carry out pilot demonstrations of integrated ecosystem management. The project will create conditions for sustainable IEM to improve livelihoods in areas covered by the Maiduguri Agreement between Niger and Nigeria. Among other actions, the project will develop an integrated legal and institutional framework for collaboration and coordinated financing from the Niger-Nigeria Joint Commission for Cooperation to community-based organizations and will develop and implement subregional, catchment and community level ecosystem management plans.

iii) Managing Hydrogeological Risk in the Iullemeden Aquifer System: A medium-sized project being implemented in Mali, Niger and Nigeria, is supporting these countries to develop and implement policy to jointly manage the vast transboundary Iullemeden aquifer system currently threatened by reduced recharge, salinization and pollution. The project aims to establish a joint, tri-national, mechanism and cooperative framework to: (a) identify transboundary threats, (b) formulate joint risk mitigation and sharing policy; and (c) implement a joint policy through a legal and institutional cooperative framework.

b) Central Asia

Support to the Implementation of the Central Asia Regional Environment Action Plan

62. A medium-sized project was approved in May 2005 to help remove the main barriers hindering implementation of the Central Asia Regional Environment Action Plan (REAP) and sustainable environmental management at regional level in Central Asia. Among these barriers is lack of a sufficient and adequate regional institutional, political, regulatory and financial mechanism for sustainable environmental management. The project aims to strengthen the political and institutional basis for regional cooperation in sustainable development and land management; strengthen information support to decision-making related to sustainable development and environmental management; engage civil society in strengthening regional cooperation; and catalyze implementation of the REAP.

c) Asia

Reversing Environmental Degradation Trends in the South China Sea and Gulf of Thailand

63. This significant UNEP/GEF project, represents the first attempt to develop regionally coordinated programmes of action for the South China Sea and

Gulf of Thailand designed to reverse environmental degradation particularly in the area of coastal habitat degradation and loss, halt land-based pollution and address the issue of fisheries over-exploitation. The overall goals of the project are: to create an environment at the regional level, in which collaboration and partnership in addressing environmental problems of the South China Sea, between all stakeholders, and at all levels is fostered and encouraged; and to enhance the capacity of the participating governments to integrate environmental considerations into national development planning. Major outcomes will include a Strategic Action Programme, agreed at an intergovernmental level, including a targeted and costed programme of action addressing the priority issues and concerns, and framework for regional cooperation in the management of the environment of the South China Sea. Outcomes will also include national and regional management plans for specific habitats and issues and a regional management plan for maintenance of transboundary fish stocks in the Gulf of Thailand.

d) Latin America

64. UNEP is implementing several projects in Latin America that promote integrated land and water resource management of transboundary river basins. These include the Pantanal and Upper Paraguay River Basin and the Sao Francisco Basin in Brazil, the Bermejo River Basin (Argentina, Bolivia), and the San Juan River Basin (Costa Rica, Nicaragua). Several new projects are under development including international projects for the Amazon Basin and the Plata Basin, described below.

(i) Formulation of a Water Resources Management Framework for the Plata River Basin

65. A major full size project under development in 2005 will strengthen the efforts of the governments of Argentina, Bolivia, Brazil, Paraguay and Uruguay to implement their shared vision for environmentally and socially sustainable economic development of the Plata Basin, specifically in the areas of the protection and integrated management of its water resources and adaptation to climatic change and variability. The project will harmonize and prepare a Programme of Strategic Actions for the sustainable management of the Plata Basin. It will include components to: strengthen institutional arrangements for integrated management of the

Basin; predict the impacts of climatic variability and change on its hydrology; promote a common vision for the Basin and formulate a Basin-level transboundary diagnostic analysis and; elaborate a Framework Strategic Action Programme for the integrated management of the water resources of the Plata Basin.

(ii) Supporting Stakeholder Participation in International Environmental Legal Processes

66. Several UNEP/GEF projects support efforts to strengthen a broad participation of stakeholders, including developing countries, civil society, and indigenous peoples, in international environmental legal processes.

(iii) Fostering Active and Effective Civil Society Participation in Preparations for Implementation of the Stockholm Convention

67. Successful implementation of the Stockholm Convention will require enhanced public awareness about persistent organic pollutants and increased participation, involvement and interest of civil society in the Convention and related activities. UNEP is implementing a medium-sized project that will encourage and enable NGOs in approximately 40 developing countries and countries with economies in transition to engage in activities within their countries that will provide concrete and immediate contributions to national efforts to prepare for implementation of the Stockholm Convention. To support this, eight regional NGOs facilitation hubs are being developed from established NGOs.

(iv) The Global Biodiversity Forum : Multistakeholder Support for the Implementation of the Convention on Biological Diversity ("CBD")

68. An ongoing UNEP/GEF medium-sized project represents the third phase of UNEP/GEF support to the Global Biodiversity Forum ("GBF"). The GBF is a multi-stakeholder forum that, giving particular attention to stakeholders from developing countries, economies in transition and local and indigenous communities, supports implementation of the CBD with specific objectives to:

- Provide an informal mechanism where CBD Parties and major stakeholder groups can explore and strengthen analysis and debate central issues around CBD implementation;
- Expand the CBD constituency to foster broader involvement and commitment of independent, public and business sector

partners in actively supporting and assessing CBD implementation, and;
- Catalyze new cooperative partnerships and initiatives among CBD Parties, among different sectors, and stakeholder groups at global, regional and national levels.

(v) The Indigenous Peoples' Network for Change

69. The Indigenous Peoples' Network for Change project is an initiative of indigenous peoples aimed at advancing the conservation and sustainable use of biodiversity by strengthening the capacity and knowledge of indigenous peoples to participate in processes surrounding the CBD and other relevant international instruments. Submitted in June 2005 for GEF funding, the project will implement an integrated range of activities including capacity building and information sharing at national regional levels, facilitating participation in international processes, and establishing strategic partnerships to strengthen the role of indigenous peoples in conservation and sustainable management of biodiversity.

(vi) Providing Environmental Information for Policy Making

70. Building on UNEP's mandate and experience in environmental assessment, UNEP is implementing several global environmental assessment projects designed to generate or synthesize information on the state of the global environment as a basis for exploring policy options and sound decision making. These include the Global International Waters Assessment ("GIWA") and the Millennium Ecosystem Assessment ("MA").

71. Conducted between June 2001 and March 2005, the Millennium Ecosystem Assessment ("MA") has been designed and implemented to meet the needs of decision makers and the public for scientific information concerning the consequences of ecosystem change for human well-being and options for responding to those changes. The MA has focused on ecosystem services (the benefits people obtain from ecosystems), how changes in ecosystem services have affected human wellbeing, how ecosystem changes may affect people in future decades, and response options that might be adopted at local, national, or global scales to improve ecosystem management and thereby contribute to human well-being and poverty alleviation.

72. The Assessment identifies priorities for action, provides tools for planning and management and

foresight concerning the consequences of decisions affecting ecosystems. It helps identify response options to achieve human development and sustainability goals, and has helped build individual and institutional capacity to undertake integrated ecosystem assessments and to act on their findings. It is anticipated that such integrated assessments will be repeated every five – ten years and that ecosystem assessments will be regularly conducted at national or sub-national scales.

(vii) Building National Capacity to implement Global Environmental Agreements

73. Through 321 national enabling activities, UNEP is supporting 153 countries to meet their direct national obligations to the global environmental Conventions for which GEF serves as a financial mechanism.

a) Biodiversity

74. GEF Biodiversity Enabling Activities assist countries to meet their obligations under the CBD. This includes development of National Biodiversity Strategies and Action Plans ("NBSAP") including the activities necessary to produce quality strategic planning documents (for example, inventories, information gathering, stakeholder consultations and policy, legal and regulatory framework analysis). It includes also participation in a Clearing-House Mechanism ("CHM") for information exchange and support for National Reports to the CBD. Following completion of an initial set of activities, additional funding is available to allow parties to the convention to assess capacity needs for priority areas of biodiversity, undertake CHM activities and prepare their Second National Reports to the CBD. Additional support, for the preparation of Third National Reports, is being made available in 2005. Currently supporting 29 countries with biodiversity enabling activities, UNEP is expected to support up to 50 countries to prepare their third national communications.

b) Biosafety – the Safe Use of Biotechnology

75. UNEP is implementing a global programme of support to build the capacity of eligible countries to implement the Cartagena Protocol on Biosafety, involving support to the development and implementation of National Biosafety Frameworks ("NBF") and participation in the Protocol's Biosafety Clearing House ("BCH").

76. Development of National Biosafety Frameworks: implementation of the Cartagena Protocol requires the establishment of national legal and regulatory structures. A global UNEP-GEF project on Development of national biosafety frameworks is assisting 130 GEF eligible countries that have signed the Protocol to implement it by preparing National Biosafety Frameworks and by promoting regional and sub-regional cooperation through regional and sub-regional workshops.

77. Implementation of National Biosafety Frameworks: UNEP is implementing eight demonstration projects in Bulgaria, Cameroon, China, Cuba, Kenya, Namibia, Poland and Uganda, designed to support these countries to implement their NBF. Based on experience gained through these projects, a number of countries which have finalized their NBF under the global project have now submitted proposals for GEF funding to support implementation of the NBF.

78. Building Capacity for Effective Participation in the Biosafety Clearing House of the Cartagena Protocol: another global project is supporting development of core human resources and establishment of appropriate BCH infrastructure to enable 139 eligible countries to fully participate and benefit from the BCH, as established under article 20 of the Biosafety Protocol. The project facilitates the ability of the eligible countries to access scientific, technical, environmental and legal information on Living Modified Organisms ("LMO"), and thereby assists with implementation of the Protocol in ensuring an adequate level of protection for biodiversity in the field of safe transfer, handling and use of LMOs.

c) Climate Change

79. GEF Climate Change Enabling Activities have been made available to eligible countries to support, initially, the preparation of First National Communications to the UNFCCC. Subsequent to their completion, financing for *interim* measures for capacity building in priority areas is available to support activities between the Initial and the Second Communications. These *interim* activities, including an assessment of national technology needs for implementation of the Convention, are intended to complement activities of the first phase, while at the same time forming a basis for initiation of the Second National Communication. To support preparation of Second National Communications, the GEF Council approved in November 2003, an umbrella project to accommodate support to up to 130 eligible

countries. The programme is jointly administered by the Implementing Agencies, and envisages UNEP supporting an indicative thirty countries. Applications for grants are processed and approved directly by the Implementing Agencies, and UNEP has approved the first of these in 2005.

d) Climate Change National Adaptation Programme of Action

80. The GEF administers a special fund established by the parties to the UNFCCC to support Least Developed Countries ("LDC") prepare National Adaptation Programmes of Action ("NAPA") to address urgent and immediate needs and concerns related to adaptation to the adverse effects of climate change. Since 2002, UNEP has assisted thirteen LDCs prepare NAPA proposals, the first of which was approved early in 2003.

e) Persistent Organic Pollutants

81. Enabling Activities for the Stockholm Convention on Persistent Organic Pollutants (POPs) are intended to create sustainable national capacity to fulfill national obligations for compliance with the Stockholm Convention, particularly the preparation of a National Implementation Plan for POPs. This will enable countries to: (1) prepare the ground for implementation of the Convention; (2) satisfy reporting and other obligations to the Convention and; (3) strengthen national capacity to manage POPs and chemicals generally. UNEP is supporting 54 countries prepare their national implementation plans.

f) National Capacity Needs Self-Assessment for Global Environmental Management

82. Enabling Activities for National Capacity Needs Self-Assessment for Global Environmental Management (NCSA) are intended to identify country level priorities and needs for capacity building to address global environmental issues, in particular biological diversity, climate change and land degradation, and the synergies among them, as well as linkages with wider concerns of environmental management and sustainable development, with the aim of catalyzing domestic and/or externally assisted action to meet those needs in a coordinated and planned manner. UNEP is supporting 35 countries to prepare an NCSA.

XII. Current Developments within the GEF

83. During 2005, donors are negotiating a fourth replenishment of the GEF Trust Fund. A third Overall Performance Study ("OPS-3") of the GEF concluded in June 2005 will inform the replenishment negotiations that are scheduled to conclude in November 2005.

84. Findings and recommendations of OPS-3 are also shaping the development of a programming framework for the fourth phase of the GEF ("GEF-4"), including the identification of strategic objectives for each of the focal areas (Table 3).

85. Emphasis in GEF-4 will be placed on promoting integrated approaches to the management of natural resources, exploiting interlinkages between focal area objectives and synergies among the global environmental conventions to which GEF serves as a financial mechanism. Emphasis will also be placed on strengthening the link between environment and development, through projects that more clearly contribute to sustainable development while at the same time generating global environmental benefits.

86. Since 2003, the GEF Council has been developing a framework for the allocation of resources to countries based on their potential to generate global environmental benefits and their performance. The Resource Allocation Framework will be operational during GEF-4, applied initially to resources in the biodiversity and climate change focal areas.

Neil Pratt, Division Global Environment Facility Coordination, UNEP

Maria Cristina Zucca, Associate Legal Officer, Division of Policy Development and Law, UNEP

Table 3. Proposed Strategic Objectives for the Fourth Phase of the GEF (GEF-4)

Biodiversity
- Catalyzing sustainability of protected area systems at national levels
- Mainstreaming biodiversity conservation within production landscapes and sectors
- Capacity building for the implementation of the Cartagena Protocol on Biosafety
- Generation and dissemination of good practices for emerging issues in biodiversity

Climate Change

Related to operational programme (OP) #5, Energy Efficiency	- Promoting energy-efficient appliances and equipment - Promoting industrial energy efficiency - Promoting building energy efficiency - Promoting re-powering of large power plants (only if replenishment is high)
Related to OP 6, Renewable Energy	- Promoting grid electricity from renewable sources - Promoting renewable energy for rural energy services
Related to OP 7, Reducing long-term Cost of Low GHG-emitting energy technologies	- Supporting deployment of new, low-GHG-emitting energy technologieS
Related to OP 11, Sustainable Transport	- Facilitating sustainable mobility in urban areas

International Waters
- Catalyzing on the ground implementation of management action programmes, regional/national reforms, and stress reduction measures agreed through TDA-SAP or equivalent processes for transboundary water systems.
- Expanding global coverage of foundational capacity building to new transboundary systems with a focus on key programme gaps and integrated, cross focal area approaches as well as undertaking targeted learning with the portfolio.
- Undertaking innovative demonstrations with emphasis on addressing water scarcity/conflicting water uses through IWRM, reducing Persistent Toxic Substances ("PTS") beyond POPs and protecting valuable groundwater supplies, including through public-private partnerships and innovative financing.

POPs
- NIP Programme and dissemination of best practices
- Strengthening capacity for NIP implementation
- Partnering in investments for NIP implementation
- 4 Partnering in demonstration of feasible, innovative technologies & practices for POPs reduction

Ozone
- Addressing HCFCs, residual use of MeBr, and Institutional Strengthening and other non-investment activities

Land Degradation
- Promoting a country partnership framework approach for removing barriers to Sustainable Land Management ("SLM") and foster system-wide change
- Upscale successful SLM practices for the control and prevention of desertification & deforestation through new operations
- Generating & disseminating knowledge addressing current and emerging issues in SLM
- Promote cross focal area synergies and integrated approaches to natural resources management

Resources

GEF Contacts and further Information

UNEP/GEF
Director of the Division of GEF Coordination
United Nations Environment Programme,
P.O. Box 30552, Nairobi 00100, Kenya
Tel: +254-20-624165; Fax: +254-20-624041
www.unep.org/gef
Email : gefinfo@unep.org

Internet Materials

GEF SECRETARIAT available at www.gefweb.org and atwww.gefonline.org

GEF IMPLEMENTING AGENCIES available at www.undp.org/gef, www.unep.org/gef and www.worldbank.org/gef

SCIENTIFIC AND TECHNICAL ADVISORY PANEL OF THE GEF ("STAP") available at http://stapgef.unep.org

TEMPLATES FOR GEF PROJECT PROPOSALS available at
http://thegef.org/Operational_Policies/Eligibility_Criteria/templates.html

UNEP/GEF PROJECTS REFERRED TO IN THIS TEXT:

CHINA SEA AND GULF OF THAILAND available at www.unepscs.org

LAND-BASED ACTIVITIES IN THE WESTERN INDIAN OCEAN available at www.unep.org/GEF/Projects/WIOLAB

THE NAIROBI CONVENTION available at www.unep.org/easternafrica/

UNEP/GEF PROJECT ADDRESSING available at www.unep.org/GEF/Projects/WIOLAB

UNEP/GEF PROJECT DEVELOPMENT OF NATIONAL BIOSAFETY FRAMEWORKS AND OTHER BIOSAFETY PROJECTS available at www.unep.ch/biosafety

UNEP/GEF PROJECT GLOBAL INTERNATIONAL WATERS ASSESSMENT (GIWA) available at www.giwa.net

UNEP/GEF PROJECT MILLENNIUM ECOSYSTEM ASSESSMENT available at www.millenniumassessment.org

UNEP/GEF PROJECT REVERSING ENVIRONMENTAL DEGRADATION TRENDS IN THE SOUTH available at www.unepscs.org

Text Materials

ACTION PLAN FOR THE ENVIRONMENT INITIATIVE OF THE NEW PARTNERSHIP FOR AFRICA'S DEVELOPMENT, (UNEP, 2004).

ACTION PLAN ON UNEP-GEF COMPLEMENTARITY, (UNEP Governing Council Document, UNEP/GC.20/44, UNEP, 1999).

ANNUAL REPORT 2004, (GEF, 2005).

GEF BUSINESS PLAN FY04-06, (GEF Council Document GEF/C.21/9, GEF, 2003).

GEF OPERATIONAL PROGRAMMES, (GEF, 1997, Global Environment Facility, Washington, DC, ppxxx).
INSTRUMENT FOR THE ESTABLISHMENT OF THE RESTRUCTURED GLOBAL ENVIRONMENT FACILITY, (GEF, 1994 and amended and republished, 2004)

OPERATIONAL STRATEGY OF THE GLOBAL ENVIRONMENT FACILITY, (GEF, 1996, Global Environmental Facility, Washington, DC).

UNITED NATIONS CONFERENCE ON ENVIRONMENT & DEVELOPMENT, AGENDA 21. (United Nations, 1992, United Nations, New York).

7. INFORMATION, PUBLIC PARTICIPATION, AND ACCESS TO JUSTICE IN ENVIRONMENTAL MATTERS

I. Introduction

1. Information, public participation, and access to justice in environmental matters are environmental tools set forth in Principle 10 of the 1992 Rio Declaration, ("Principle 10"). More generally, freedom of information, democratic participation in governance, and judicial guarantees are internationally protected human rights contained in constitutions, global and regional treaties. The three legal procedures aim to ensure that every potentially affected person can participate in environmental management at the relevant level. They thus provide transparency in governance and hence serve to strengthen legislation and institutional regimes for environmental management.

2. This chapter examines the scope of "Access to Information," "Public Participation in Decision Making," and "Access to Justice in Environmental Matters" and the understanding of these terms. This chapter will also examine the status of related national legal and institutional regimes and pathways for strengthening them, including, as appropriate, legal and institutional capacities and human resource capabilities. The objectives are to improve the quality of decision-making in environmental matters through increased transparency and to promote the equitable resolution of environmental disputes.

3. Principle 10 of the Rio Declaration refers to the rights of public participation, access to information and access to justice in environmental matters.

**1992 Rio Declaration
(Principle 10)**

"Environmental issues are best handled with participation of all concerned citizens, at the relevant level. At the national level, each individual shall have appropriate access to information concerning the environment that is held by public authorities, including information on hazardous materials and activities in their communities, and the opportunity to participate in decision-making processes. States shall facilitate and encourage public awareness and participation by making information widely available. Effective access to judicial and administrative proceedings, including redress and remedy, shall be provided."

---

4. The term "access to information" in Principle 10 refers to both the availability of information related to the environment (including that on hazardous materials and activities in communities) as well as the mechanisms by which public authorities provide environmental information. Chapter 23 of Agenda 21, on Strengthening the Role of Major Groups, provides that individuals, groups and organizations should have access to information relevant to the environment and development, held by national authorities, including information on products and activities that have or are likely to have a significant impact on the environment, and information on environmental matters.

5. The term "Public Participation" means the availability of opportunities for individuals, groups and organizations to provide input in the making of decisions which have, or are likely to have, an impact on the environment, including in the enactment of laws, the enforcement of national laws, policies, and guidelines, and Environmental Impact Assessment procedures. The Preamble to chapter 23 of Agenda 21 calls public participation "one of the fundamental prerequisites for the achievement of sustainable development." Among human rights instruments, article 25 of the 1966 United Nations International Covenant on Civil and Political Rights enshrines the right to participate "in the conduct of public affairs, directly or through freely chosen representatives" and guarantees related rights, such as freedom of expression in article 19, freedom of assembly in article 21, and freedom of association in article 22.

6. "Access to Justice" refers to effective judicial and administrative remedies and procedures available to a person (natural or legal) who is aggrieved or likely to be aggrieved by environmental harm. The term includes not only the procedural right of appearing before an appropriate body but also the substantive right of redress for harm done. The United Nations Convention on the Law of the Sea specifies the duty of the state parties to ensure that recourse is available for prompt and adequate compensation or other relief in respect of damage caused by pollution of the marine environment by natural or juridical persons under their jurisdiction.

7. In practice, the three elements work together and depend on each other to be effective. Access to environmental information is a prerequisite to public participation in decision-making and to monitoring governmental and private sector activities. It also can assist enterprises in planning for and utilizing the best available techniques and technology. In turn, effective access to justice in environmental matters requires an informed

citizenry that can bring legal actions before informed institutions.

8. The main areas to be examined in determining the effectiveness of access to environmental information, public participation in decision-making and access to justice in environmental matters include:

- The way in which countries handle environmental issues at different levels and the extent to which concerned citizens participate in handling them at the relevant level;
- The extent to which governmental authorities at all levels acquire and hold relevant information concerning the environment and threats to it, including information about private sector activities;
- The extent to which each individual at the national level can have appropriate access to information concerning the environment that is held by public authorities, including information on hazardous materials and activities in his or her community;
- The extent to which the individuals, groups and organizations have opportunity to participate effectively in decision-making processes;
- The efforts made by states to facilitate and encourage public awareness and participation by making information available regarding legislation, regulations, activities, policies and programmes; and
- The extent to which the public in environmental matters is ensured of access to effective judicial and administrative proceedings, including redress and remedy.

9. Principle 10 is not the only instrument that underlines the importance of access to information, public participation in decision-making and access to justice in environmental matters. (See chapter 3, above). Other texts emphasize them as well, including Agenda 21, the United Nations Millennium Development Goals, and the 2002 World Summit on Sustainable Development (WSSD) Plan of Implementation. In addition, the Johannesburg Principles of the Global Judges Symposium 2002 and the decisions of the UNEP Governing Council (especially decisions 20/4, 21/23, 21/24, 22/17), the Programme for the Development and Periodic Review of Environmental Law for the First Decade of the Twenty-First Century ("Montevideo Programme III") and the Malmo Declaration, all express the need to strengthen capacity and related national environmental laws by enhancing the application of Principle 10. Treaties such as the United Nations Framework Convention on Climate Change (article

4.1(i)) and the Convention on Biological Diversity (articles 13, 14, 17), the United Nations Convention to Combat Desertification in Countries experiencing Serious Drought and/or Desertification, particularly in Africa (articles 10, 13, 14, 19, and 25), and the Rotterdam Convention on the Prior Informed Consent Procedure for Certain Hazardous Chemicals and Pesticides in International Trade (article 15) all refer to information, participation and access to justice. A 1998 regional agreement, the (Aarhus) Convention on Access to Information, Public Participation in Decision-Making and Access to Justice in Environmental Matters is entirely devoted to the three procedures. These treaties are discussed in more detail below.

II. International Framework

1. Global Principles

10. In August 2002, members of the Judiciary from around the world agreed on a capacity building programme in environmental law, based in particular on the importance of sensitizing the public and the Judiciary on environmental issues. Building knowledge based on acquisition and dissemination of information, public participation in decision-making and access to justice are key elements of the programme. The Johannesburg Principles on the Role of Law and Sustainable Development which were adopted at the Global Judges Symposium thus included the following statements:

"(...)
We express our conviction that the Judiciary, well informed of the rapidly expanding boundaries of environmental law and aware of its role and responsibilities in promoting the implementation, development and enforcement of laws, regulations and international agreements relating to sustainable development, plays a critical role in the enhancement of the public interest in a healthy and secure environment,

We recognize the importance of ensuring that environmental law and law in the field of sustainable development feature prominently in academic curricula, legal studies and training at all levels, in particular among judges and others engaged in the judicial process,

We express our conviction that the deficiency in the knowledge, relevant skills and information in regard to environmental law is one of the principal causes that contribute to the lack of effective implementation, development and enforcement of environmental law,

We are strongly of the view that there is an urgent need to strengthen the capacity of judges, prosecutors, legislators and all persons who play a critical role at national level in the process of implementation, development and enforcement of environmental law, including multilateral environmental agreements (MEAs), especially through the judicial process,

(...)

For the realisation of these principles we propose that the programme of work should include the following:

(a) The improvement of the capacity of those involved in the process of promoting, implementing, developing and enforcing environmental law, such as judges, prosecutors, legislators and others, to carry out their functions on a well informed basis, equipped with the necessary skills, information and material,

(b) The improvement in the level of public participation in environmental decision-making, access to justice for the settlement of environmental disputes and the defense and enforcement of environmental rights, and public access to relevant information,

(c) The strengthening of sub-regional, regional and global collaboration for the mutual benefit of all peoples of the world and exchange of information among national Judiciaries with a view to benefiting from each other's knowledge, experience and expertise,

(d) The strengthening of environmental law education in schools and universities, including research and analysis as essential to realizing sustainable development,

(e) The achievement of sustained improvement in compliance with and enforcement and development of environmental law,

(f) The strengthening of the capacity of organizations and initiatives, including the media, which seek to enable the public to fully engage on a well-informed basis, in focusing attention on issues relating to environmental protection and sustainable development,

(g) An *Ad Hoc* Committee of Judges consisting of Judges representing geographical regions, legal systems and international courts and tribunals and headed by the Chief Justice of South Africa, should keep under review and publicise the emerging environmental jurisprudence and provide information thereon,

(h) UNEP and its partner agencies, including civil society organizations should provide support to the *Ad Hoc* Committee of Judges in accomplishing its task,

(i) Governments of the developed countries and the donor community, including international financial institutions and foundations, should give priority to financing the implementation

of the above principles and the programme of work,

(j) The Executive Director of UNEP should continue to provide leadership within the framework of the Montevideo Programme III, to the development and implementation of the programme designed to improve the implementation, development and enforcement of environmental law including, within the applicable law of liability and compensation for environmental harm under multilateral environmental agreements and national law, military activities and the environment, and the legal aspects of the nexus between poverty and environmental degradation, ..."

11. UNEP is taking steps in its programme of work to enhance the application of Principle 10 as it implements UNEP GC Decision 22/17, which requested the Executive Director to intensify efforts to provide policy and advisory services in key areas of capacity and institution building, including:

- Access to information regarding legislation, regulations, activities, policies and programmes;
- Public participation in sustainable development policy formulation and implementation, including the promotion of public participation at the local and national levels in policy and programme development and implementation; and
- Cooperation with other organizations, to support efforts by governments who request assistance in the application of Principle 10 at the local and national levels.

The decision also requests the Executive Director to assess the possibility of promoting, at the national and international levels, the application of Principle 10 and to determine, *inter alia*, if there is value in initiating an intergovernmental process for the preparation of global guidelines on the application of Principle 10.

12. The mandate of Principle 10 is not entirely new. The concepts of access to information, public participation in decision-making and access to justice in environmental matters can be found in a large number of international legal instruments adopted before the 1992 Rio Conference, some of them dating back to the 1972 Stockholm Conference on the Human Environment and earlier. The many regional environmental conventions and an even higher number of non-binding instruments are evidence of the existence of the rights contained in Principle 10 prior to 1992, and can be read to demonstrate the development of these concepts over the past

several decades. Relevant examples are given in each of the following parts, which are divided into global conventions, regional conventions, and non-binding international legal instruments.

2. Global Conventions

13. A number of international legal instruments have reflected Principle 10 mandate on access to information, public participation in decision-making and access to justice. In global conventions there is a trend towards including increasingly detailed and explicit provisions. In general, the treaties contain more references to public awareness and access to information than to the other aspects of Principle 10, but public participation in decision-making is also reflected in a large number of instruments and frequently appears with provisions on public awareness and information. Compared to the first two areas, the third element of Principle 10 (i.e., access to judicial and administrative proceedings) is reflected to a lesser extent in environmental treaties but is widespread in human rights instruments. It can be found, basically, in two types of Multilateral Environmental Agreements ("MEAs"): (1) international conventions (or protocols) which set up specific liability regimes for damage resulting from certain environmentally dangerous activities, and (2) conventions which provide for access to justice in a comprehensive manner. The latter type of conventions would include, *inter alia*, obligations to ensure that individuals have the possibility to bring to court violators of environmental laws and regulations.

14. Examples of multilateral environmental instruments containing Principle 10 elements include the 1972 Convention concerning the Protection of the World Cultural and Natural Heritage (article 27), the 1992 United Nations Framework Convention on Climate Change (article 6), the 1994 Convention to Combat Desertification (article 3, 5, and 8), the 1999 Basel Liability and Compensation Protocol (article 8), and the 2001 Stockholm Convention on Persistent Organic Pollutants (article 10). The most elaborate relevant convention, the (Aarhus) Convention on Access to Information, Public Participation in Decision-Making and Access to Justice in Environmental Matters ("1998 Aarhus Convention"), was negotiated under the framework of the United Nations Economic Commission for Europe ("UNECE"), and is the most comprehensive multilateral (regional) environmental agreement in providing concrete obligations and information relating to Principle 10 because it covers all three elements in detail.

15. The first important examples of provisions that illustrate Principle 10 are those contained in the Convention concerning the Protection of the World Cultural and Natural Heritage. This convention, adopted in 1972, recognizes in article 27 the importance of public awareness and information for the protection of the world's cultural and natural heritage as defined in article 1 and 2. It obliges its signatories to "endeavour by all appropriate means, and in particular by educational and information programmes, to strengthen appreciation and respect by their peoples of the cultural and natural heritage" and to "undertake to keep the public broadly informed of the dangers threatening this heritage and of the activities carried on in pursuance of this Convention." The Convention concerning the Protection of the World Cultural and Natural Heritage can thus be seen as an early example of the concern for public awareness later adopted in Principle 10.

16. The 1992 United Nations Framework Convention on Climate Change ("1992 Climate Change Convention") contains provisions on public awareness and information as well as on public participation. It thereby reflects the first and the second elements of Principle 10. Article 6(a) of the 1992 Climate Change Convention addresses the development and implementation of educational and public awareness programmes, and explicitly requires the facilitation of public access to information on climate change and its effects (article 6(a)(i),(ii)). The article refers back to the signatories' main commitments, which also underscore publication of national and regional programmes for climate change mitigation (article 4(b)). Further, the state parties are obliged to promote and facilitate public participation in addressing climate change and its effects and developing adequate responses "in accordance with national laws and regulations, and within their respective capacities." (article 6(a)(iii))

17. The 1992 Convention on Biological Diversity ("1992 Biodiversity Convention") reflects the provisions contained in Principle 10 in both explicit and implicit ways. Environmental information and improving public awareness are reflected in articles 12 and 13. Article 13(a) requires signatories to "promote and encourage understanding of the importance of … the conservation of biological diversity..." As a means to promote public awareness regarding biological diversity, the convention names, in particular, media and educational programmes as well as programmes for scientific research and training (articles 12 and 13(b)). Public participation is implicitly reflected in article 8(j) of the 1992

Biodiversity Convention which aims at stronger involvement of indigenous and local communities as part of its "*in-situ* conservation" objectives. According to this provision, knowledge, innovations and practices of indigenous and local communities relevant for biodiversity conservation is to be preserved, and states shall "promote their wider application with the approval and involvement of the holders of such knowledge, innovations and practices." Article 10(e) adds that cooperation between governmental authorities and its private sector is encouraged with regard to the sustainable use of biological resources. Finally, the 1992 Biodiversity Convention requires "as far as possible and as appropriate," Environmental Impact Assessment ("EIA") procedures to be introduced for proposed projects that are likely to have significant adverse effects on biological diversity (article 14). Such national EIA procedures would reasonably have to involve a certain degree of public participation.

18. The general requirement to involve the public in the process of preparing an EIA can be discerned from several existing legal instruments on EIAs, which demonstrate the participatory character of the EIA procedure. The earliest example is found in the UNEP Goals and Principles of Environmental Impact Assessment of 17 June 1987. According to Principle 17 of the UNEP Goals the public, experts and interested groups should be allowed appropriate opportunity to comment on the EIA. This non-binding principle was later been incorporated into a legally binding Convention of the UNECE Region, the 1991 Convention on Environmental Impact Assessment in a Transboundary Context ("1991 Espoo EIA Convention"), as well in a large number of national laws on EIAs in all regimes.

19. The United Nations Convention to Combat Desertification is probably the most ambitious example of a participatory, or "bottom up," approach. It recognizes the fact that in traditional development planning, programmes have often failed because they were designed with too little reference to the perceptions and capacities of local communities. The 1994 Desertification Convention aims at integrating local communities with their valuable experience and special understanding of their own environment. To this end, article 3(a) of the Convention obliges parties to "ensure that decisions on the design and implementation of programmes to combat desertification...are taken with the participation of populations and local communities..." Action programmes are to originate at the local level and be based on genuine local participation (articles 9 and 10). The participation is to be ensured at all stages, i.e. "...policy, planning, decision-making, implementation and review of the action programmes..." (article 10(2)(f)). (See also articles 6 and 8 of the Regional Implementation Annex for Africa (Annex I)). Affected Parties shall promote awareness and facilitate the participation of local populations, particularly women and youth, with the support of Non-Governmental Organizations ("NGOs") (article 5(d)). Similar provisions of a strong participatory character apply to capacity-building, education and training (article19).

20. The 1997 Kyoto Protocol to the 1992 Climate Change Convention includes a provision on public awareness and access to information relevant to climate change in article 10(e), which requires parties to "promote at the international level ... the development and implementation of education and training programmes, ... and facilitate at the national level public awareness of, and public access to information on, climate change..." This provision is somewhat less comprehensive than the equivalent found in the 1992 Climate Change Convention itself: it is stricter since the obligation in article 10(e) of the 1997 Kyoto Protocol is not limited by a reference to the "respective capacities" of parties.

21. The 1997 Joint Convention on the Safety of Spent Fuel Management and on the Safety of Radioactive Waste Management deals with the siting of proposed facilities in article 6 and 13. The requirements include the obligation of each party to take steps to make relevant safety information available to the public.

22. The objective of the 1998 Rotterdam Convention on the Prior Informed Consent Procedure for Certain Hazardous Chemicals and Pesticides in International Trade ("1998 Rotterdam Convention) is "...to protect human health and the environment from potential harm..." with regard to certain hazardous chemicals and pesticides in international trade (article 1). The prior informed consent procedure, set out in articles 5 through 11 of the 1998 Rotterdam Convention, aims at enhancing transparency, by facilitating information exchange, providing for a national decision-making process on the import and export of the chemicals and pesticides covered by the Convention, and by disseminating these decisions to the parties. The procedural obligations that apply to the parties in relation to each other are complemented by provisions set up to ensure adequate information of the individual importer and of the general public in article 13 through 15, thereby reflecting Principle 10 with regard to access to information.

23. The 1999 Basel Protocol on Liability and Compensation for Damage resulting from Transboundary Movements of Hazardous Wastes and their Disposal ("1999 Liability Protocol") is a good example of the third element of Principle 10, access to justice in environmental matters. "The objective of the Protocol is to provide for a ... regime for liability and ... compensation for damage resulting from the transboundary movement of hazardous wastes..." (article 1). The 1999 Liability Protocol establishes a system of strict liability (article 4) and fault-based liability (article 5) for different categories of damage, as well as proportionate liability in cases of combined cause of damage (article 7). The persons subject to liability according to the 1999 Liability Protocol may be either the exporter or notifier, or the importer, or the disposer of the waste. The important link is article 17, which allows any person who has suffered damage from activities covered by the 1999 Liability Protocol to bring a claim for compensation before the competent national court against those who are liable in accordance with the Protocol. Article 17(2) requires signatories to "...ensure that its courts possess the necessary competence to entertain such claims for compensation". The right of access to justice is further supported by the provisions of mutual recognition and enforcement of judgements contained in article 21 of the 1999 Liability Protocol.

24. Like the 1992 Biodiversity Convention, the Cartagena Protocol on Biosafety to the Convention on Biological Diversity, adopted in 2000, contains several provisions on public awareness and information, though in a more explicit way: parties shall endeavour to ensure access to information on Living Modified Organisms ("LMOs") and are to promote public awareness, education and participation concerning the transfer, handling and use of LMOs (article 23(1)(a),(b)). Parties shall also endeavour to inform their public about the means of public access to the comprehensive information system on Biosafety envisaged by the CBD and set up by the Protocol, namely the Biosafety Clearing-House article 23(3)). The 2000 Cartagena Protocol reflects the element of public participation in article 23(2), which requires that the public shall be consulted in the decision-making process regarding LMOs, and the results of such decision are to be made available to the public.

25. The most recent example of a global environmental convention reflecting Principle 10 is the Stockholm Convention on Persistent Organic Pollutants ("POPs"), ("2001 Stockholm Convention") adopted in 2001. It shows the recent trend of environmental conventions to provide increasing detailed about the state duties concerning information and public participation. The obligation to promote and facilitate the provision to the public "of all available information" concerning POPs in article 10(1)(b) is accompanied by the duty to ensure that the public has access to that information, according to the capabilities of the party. Article 10(1)(d) enshrines public participation with respect to addressing POPs and their effects and the development of "adequate responses," explicitly stating that this also includes "opportunities for providing input at the national level regarding implementation of this Convention." Article 10 of the 2001 Stockholm Convention is also quite elaborate on the issue of public awareness as it mentions the promotion of awareness among policy and decision-makers as well as education and training programmes at the national and international levels including the exchange of education and public awareness materials (article 10(1)(a),(c),(f),(g)). It further states that industry and professional users shall be encouraged to facilitate the provision of relevant information on POPs at the national and international levels, as appropriate (article10 (3)). Different ways of how the information may be provided are illustrated in article 10(4).

26. Conventions of the International Labour Organization ("ILO") provide good examples of the elaboration of Principle 10. Several ILO conventions adopted since 1992 deal with environmental protection and health of workers in the workplace and assign specific rights of information and participation to workers and their representatives. The ILO Convention concerning the Prevention of Major Industrial Accidents of 1993 assigns specific rights to workers and their representatives at "major hazard installations" (article 20) to be consulted "through appropiate cooperative mechanisms in order to ensure a safe system of work..." and the right to be adequately informed of the hazards associated with the workplace and their likely consequences. The ILO Convention concerning Safety and Health in Mines of 1995 contains provisions on rights of workers and their representatives, including the right to access to information on workplace hazards (article 13(1)).

27. The 2001 ILO Convention No. 184 concerning Safety and Health in Agriculture emphasizes consultation and participation throughout. Article 7 requires the national laws and regulations or national authority to ensure that the employer carries out "...appropriate risk assessments in relation to the safety and health of workers and, on

the basis of these results, to adopt preventive and protective measures to ensure that under all conditions of their intended use, all agricultural activities, workplaces, machinery, equipment, chemicals, tools and processes under the control of the employer are safe and comply with prescribed safety and health standards...". In addition, "...adequate and appropriate training and comprehensible instructions on safety and health and any necessary guidance or supervision..." must be provided to workers in "...agriculture, including information on the hazards and risks associated with their work and the action to be taken for their protection, taking into account their level of education and differences in language". In respect to remedies, immediate steps must be taken "...to stop any operation where there is an imminent and serious danger to safety and health and to evacuate workers as appropriate."

28. Article 8 adds that agricultural workers have all the Principle 10 rights, i.e.: "...(a) to be informed and consulted on safety and health matters including risks from new technologies; (b) to participate in the application and review of safety and health measures and, in accordance with national law and practice, to select safety and health representatives and representatives in safety and health committees; and (c) to remove themselves from danger resulting from their work activity when they have reasonable justification to believe there is an imminent and serious risk to their safety and health and so inform their supervisor immediately. They shall not be placed at any disadvantage as a result of these actions...". Finally, "...there shall be prior consultation with the representative organizations of employers and workers concerned" in implementing the Convention.

3. Regional Conventions

29. At the regional level, there are more numerous environmental conventions containing provisions that reflect one or more elements of Principle 10, some of which were adopted before the 1992 Rio Conference. Among the conventions produced by European regional organizations after 1992, the 1993 Convention on Civil Liability for Damage resulting from Activities Dangerous to the Environment ("1993 Lugano Convention") of the Council of Europe, serves as an example of providing for access to justice. Focusing more broadly on access to information, public participation in decision-making and access to judicial and administrative proceedings as its main objectives, the 1998 Aarhus Convention, negotiated under the auspices of the UNECE, is the most comprehensive legally binding instrument elaborating on Principle 10. (See also under

Chapters 1 and 3 above). Other examples in the UNECE region include two Protocols to the 1979 UNECE Convention on Long-Range Transboundary Air Pollution (of 1998 and 1999, respectively), and the 1999 Protocol on Water and Health to the 1992 Convention on the Protection and Use of Transboundary Watercourses and International Lakes.

30. There are also numerous provisions reflecting Principle 10 to be found in environmental conventions in the African region (e.g., in the Lusaka Agreement on Cooperative Enforcement Operations directed at Illegal Trade in Wild Fauna and Flora of 1994, and in the 1995 Agreement on the Conservation of African-Eurasian Migratory Waterbirds). An example of the Near East Region is the 1993 Agreement for the Establishment of the Near East Plant Protection Organization. The 1985 ASEAN Agreement on the Conservation of Nature and Natural Resources of the Asian and Pacific Region is another example of a regional convention that contains the concepts of Principle 10 prior to 1992. In North America, the 1993 North American Agreement on Environmental Cooperation includes all aspects of Principle 10. In the Central American region, the 1992 Convention for the Conservation of the Biodiversity and Protection of Wilderness Areas in Central America, and the 1993 Regional Convention for the Management and Conservation of Natural Forest Ecosystems and the Development of Forest Plantations are identified as treaties containing references to information and public participation. Finally, there are a large number of conventions and protocols on regional seas which demand public awareness and/or public participation, including several instruments prior to 1992.

4. Non-Binding International Legal Instruments

31. A large number of non-binding international legal instruments adopted prior to 1992 already contained the concepts found in Principle 10 inspired, *inter alia*, by human rights instruments and by the 1972 Stockholm Conference on the Human Environment. A rapidly emerging consensus on the three procedural rights led to their incorporation into Principle 10 at the United Nations Conference on Environment and Development in 1992. Most recently, the WSSD Plan of Implementation in its paragraphs 162 through 167 on national laws for sustainable development calls upon governments to promote sustainable development at the national level by, *inter alia*, enacting and enforcing clear and effective laws that support sustainable development. All countries are further called on to strengthen governmental institutions, including by

providing necessary infrastructure and by promoting transparency, accountability and fair administrative and judicial institutions. Paragraph 164 calls upon all countries to "...promote public participation, including through measures that provide access to information regarding legislation, regulations, activities, policies and programmes...".

III. National Implementation

National Actions to Enhance Information, Participation and Access to Justice

32. Public awareness of environmental issues is important if the public is to be involved at every level of environmental management. Principle 10 encourages each country to have informed citizens who can participate in environmental management. The role of the government, the media, schools and other institutions is important in raising awareness on environmental issues if the public is to understand the problems and participate in resolving them at all levels. Public authorities need effective mechanisms for providing environmental information. Where environmental information is lacking, the public is hindered from taking appropriate action to stop environmental degradation. The lack of environmental information also affects public participation in decision-making because the public cannot speak out about environmental degradation and unhealthy conditions in the community if they are not aware of their rights or their situation.

33. State practice shows that a country's constitutional provisions, acts of parliament, and policy documents and guidelines have been used to implement Principle 10. The right to life and/or to a healthy environment provided in national and international law generally extends to procedural rights such as those in Principle 10. In recent years, the right to environment has been recognized in particular to have a procedural aspect, meaning this right includes access to information relating to the immediate environment and/or of projects intended to be undertaken in the area which are likely to adversely affect the environment. These developments have enabled individuals and associations to bring actions on the ground that they have been prevented from getting access to information, or there has been a failure to respond to an information request. The parties can also bring action if they have been prevented from participating in decision-making processes or if they are challenging situations of environmental degradation that have caused them harm.

34. Some countries have adequate laws that provide for the right of the public to access environmental information held by public authorities, but in practice such information may not be easy to retrieve. This problem, caused by lack of capacity to retrieve information as well as inadequate enforcement of the right, causes difficulties in obtaining information on such issues as land ownership, which may be needed for public participation in decision-making or access to justice in environmental matters.

35. The disparity between law and practice and the need to strengthen capacity for retrieving environmental information must be considered when efforts are made to enhance the application of Principle 10. In recent years, UNEP has been reaching out to all the relevant stakeholders including the Judiciary, learning institutions and others in order to expose them to current environmental law and the concept of sustainable development, to strengthen the legal and institutional framework for environmental management.

36. The public can participate in decision-making only if opportunities are made available to the public to participate. The Environmental Impact Assessment ("EIA") procedure mandated by many national laws and policies is a good example of a means to engage the public at the relevant level in decision-making. The EIA process in most countries has a participatory approach that provides opportunities for the public to be involved in decision-making by seeking their input on decisions that are likely to affect their immediate environment. In the process of developing and strengthening environmental laws and policies, the public has also been involved in consensus building stakeholder workshops preceding the enactment of laws or environmental policies, in the process of issuing licences or permits for facilities, and in the enforcement of national laws in courts and the implementation of policies and guidelines.

37. The participation of the public may be either by individual citizens or by the civil society. In particular, Non-Governmental Organizations ("NGOs") are expected to articulate issues and to institute public interest suits if there is a need. There are instances where the law may not restrict public interest litigation, thus allowing it to strengthen environmental legislation, but numerous difficulties may still exist because of the lack of access to information. The public or NGOs may not be adequately involved and informed. The result is an inability to articulate concerns or to act on them. The public or civil society as a whole

thus fails to take action that could change an environmental situation, keeping quiet when they should be pressuring the relevant authorities to act. The Malmo Ministerial Declaration adopted at the First Global Ministerial Environment Forum that was organized by UNEP declared that "The role of civil society...should be strengthened through freedom of access to environmental information to all, broad participation in environmental decision-making, as well as access to justice on environmental issues...".

38. To enhance public participation in decision-making for the purpose of strengthening the legal and institutional framework for environmental management, it is important to advance the capacity of the public to understand environmental issues so that it can participate in an informed manner. The participatory approaches that are used in environmental decision-making to involve major groups, or community-based participation in development activities on such issues as forest, water and land management can be looked into, when seeking to enhance the participation of the public in decision-making. Other relevant issues include the adequacy of laws providing for the involvement of the public in the EIA process as well as the adequacy of existing national legislation for enhancing the application of Principle 10.

39. The WSSD Plan of Implementation identifies actions that can strengthen legislation by the application of Principle 10 in its paragraphs 162 through 167. The Plan of Implementation in its paragraphs 163 and 164 calls on each country to take responsibility for promoting sustainable development and, *inter alia*, "...enacting and enforcing clear and effective laws that support sustainable development. All countries should strengthen governmental institutions, including by providing necessary infrastructure and by promoting transparency, accountability and fair administrative and judicial institutions. All countries should also promote public participation, including through measures that provide access to information regarding legislation, regulations, activities, policies and programmes. They should also foster full public participation in sustainable development, policy formulation and implementation. Women should be able to participate fully and equally in policy formulation and decision-making". This means each country has a responsibility to enhance access to environmental information, public participation in decision-making and access to justice in environmental matters in their country.

40. Obstacles to strengthening the law related to access to justice in environmental matters also may arise. For instance, the public may be capable of articulating environmental issues and may have the required information to file a case in court, but it can still face problems if no effective judicial and administrative remedies and procedures are available. The main issue that hinders access to justice in environmental matters in many countries has been lack of standing for public interest lawsuits when one cannot prove personal interest. However, even in a few countries where public interest suits on the environment are encouraged without proof of personal interest, actual vindication of environmental rights is lacking as many cases brought by the public or NGOs do not succeed. Public interest litigation is frustrated by the cost of litigation, by lack of awareness, and by the substantial difficulties in gathering evidence even where the need to prove personal interest in public interest litigation is not required by courts. Further, in some jurisdictions, advocates taking up public interest litigation are denied the right to sue because significant procedural difficulties stand in the way of the plaintiff's claim even when the law provides for strict liability for violations. Lack of sufficient enforcement of legal remedies is a problem that also frustrates litigation as a preferred option in some countries.

41. Access to justice in environmental matters can be enhanced through legal aid programmes and by building the capacity of the members of the judiciary and prosecutors at all levels to appreciate environmental issues and concerns. The Judiciary and other legal stakeholders creating a greater likelihood that they will be trained in sustainable development and environmental law and should interpret the law and balance the interests in favour of protecting public health and preserving the environment. A citizen who brings suits in court not only is aware of environmental issues around him, but expects to find an informed Judiciary that will consider environmental issues in a knowledgeable manner and provide the appropriate remedy to protect public health and preserve the environment.

42. Mechanisms for avoiding environmental disputes, and judicial, quasi-judicial and administrative mechanisms for avoidance and settlement of environmental disputes, including traditional mechanisms, can also promote access to justice and strengthen the legal and institutional frameworks for sustainable development at the national level. In particular, the human resource capabilities must be strengthened among Government officials to promote and further

develop means through law and practice to increase transparency, strengthen access to information and improve public participation in processes leading to decision-making relating to the environment, and avoid and settle environmental disputes through access to justice.

43. The large number of national and international instruments so far developed provides an opportunity for governments to develop and strengthen national environmental legislation, policy and institutions for the purpose of enhancing the application of Principle 10. Many international legal instruments reflect the different dimensions of Principle 10, including some instruments which incorporate all three elements of the Principle. Access to environmental information includes both ensuring that authorities acquire the relevant information and ensuring the public the right of access to that information. The latter allows for the availability of that information to whoever is interested on any matter concerning the environment, without their having to provide a particular individualized interest. Public participation in decision-making invites the members of the public and other interested parties like non governmental and intergovernmental

organizations to participate in the formulation of the policies and in the execution of those policies. Access to justice requires the provision of legislative safeguards to allow a challenge to any administrative action or decision made regarding the environment.

44. Principle 10 is one of the most widely discussed principles at global, regional and national level, and is to be found throughout the entire Training Manual. Practically every chapter has reference to it as concept, as a tool incorporated in binding and non-binding instruments and their implementation at national level in national legislation, regulations and policies. (See for example chapters 1, 2, 3, 4 and several others). In practice virtually all countries in the different regions embrace the essence and thrust of the principle.

Prof. Dinah L. Shelton, Patricia Roberts Harris Professor of Law, George Washington University Law School

with Sylvia Bankobeza and Barbara Ruis, Legal Officers, Division of Policy Development and Law, UNEP

Resources

Internet Materials

AARHUS CONVENTION INFORMATION available at http://www.unece.org/env/pp/

ENVIRONMENTAL JUSTICE DATABASE available at http://www.msue.msu.edu/msue/imp/modej/masterej.html

THE ENVIRONMENTAL JUSTICE FOUNDATIONS SITE available at http://www.ejfoundation.org/

UNITED NATIONS ENVIRONMENT PROGRAMME: JUDGES PROGRAMME available at
http://www.unep.org/dpdl/Law/Programme_work/Judges_programme/index.asp

UNITED NATIONS ENVIRONMENT PROGRAMME: RESOURCES FOR CIVIL SOCIETY AND NGOs available at
http://www.unep.org/Documents/Default.asp?DocumentID=292

US ENVIRONMENTAL PROTECTION AGENCY, INFORMATION ON ENVIRONMENTAL JUSTICE available at
http://www.epa.gov/compliance/environmentaljustice/

Text Materials

Alexandre Kiss and Dinah Shelton, INTERNATIONAL ENVIRONMENTAL LAW, (3rd edition, Transnational Press, 2004).

Carl Bruch and John Pendergrass, THE ROAD FROM JOHANNESBURG: TYPE II PARTNERSHIPS, INTERNATIONAL LAW AND THE COMMON, (15 Geo. Int'l Envtl. L. Rev. 855, Summer, 2003).

David A. Wirth, PUBLIC PARTICIPATION IN THE INTERNATIONAL PROCESSES: ENVIRONMENTAL CASE STUDIES AT THE NATIONAL AND INTERNATIONAL LEVELS, (7 Colo. J. Int'l Envtl. L. & Pol'y 1, Winter, 1996).

Gary D. Bass and Alair MacLean, ENHANCING THE PUBLIC'S RIGHT-TO-KNOW ABOUT ENVIRONMENTAL ISSUES, (4 Vill. Envtl. L. J. 287, 1993).

Jonas Ebbesson, ACCESS TO JUSTICE IN ENVIRONMENTAL MATTER IN THE EU, (The Hague, Kluwer Law International, 2002).

Katherine M. Harman-Stokes, COMMUNITY RIGHT-TO-KNOW IN THE NEWLY INDEPENDENT STATES OF THE FORMER SOVIET UNION: ENDING THE CULTURE OF SECRECY SURROUNDING THE ENVIRONMENTAL CRISIS, (15 Va. Envtl. L. J 77, Fall 1995).

LeRoy Paddock, ENVIRONMENTAL ACCOUNTABILITY AND PUBLIC INVOLVEMENT, (21 Pace Env. L. Rev. 243, Summer 2004).

Maria Gavouneli, ACCESS TO ENVIRONMENTAL INFORMATION: DELIMITATION OF A RIGHT, (13 Tul. Envtl. L. J. 303, Summer 2000).

Mark A. Drumbl, DOES SHARING KNOW ITS LIMITS? THOUGHTS ON IMPLEMENTING INTERNATIONAL ENVIRONMENTAL AGREEMENTS: A REVIEW OF NATIONAL POLICIES, A COMPARATIVE STUDY OF CAPACITY-BUILDING, (18 Va. Envtl. L. J. 281, 1999).

Neil A.F. Popovic, THE RIGHT TO PARTICIPATE IN DECISIONS THAT AFFECT THE ENVIRONMENT, (10 Pace Envtl. L. Rev. 683, Spring 1993).

Sara Pirk, EXPANDING PUBLIC PARTICIPATION IN ENVIRONMENTAL JUSTICE: METHODS, LEGISLATION LITIGATION AND BEYOND, (17 J. Envtl. L. & Litig. 207, Spring 2002).

Sean T. McAllister, HUMAN RIGHTS AND THE ENVIRONMENT: THE CONVENTION ON ACCESS TO INFORMATION, PUBLIC PARTICIPATION IN DECISION-MAKING, AND ACCESS TO JUSTICE IN ENVIRONMENTAL MATTERS, (1889 Colo. J. Int'l. Envtl. L. Y. B. 187, 1989).

Stephen Stec, THE AARHUS CONVENTION: AN IMPLEMENTATION GUIDE, (New York, United Nations, 2000).

8. TRANSBOUNDARY AIR POLLUTION

I. Introduction

1. "Air pollution" describes the presence of substances that are artificially introduced into the air. Air pollution stems from gases, which in excess are harmful to human health, buildings, ecosystems and the environment in general. This chapter primarily focuses on the problem of long-range transboundary air pollution, mainly in Europe and haze pollution focused on Southeast Asia. The section on national implementation refers to two examples based on Austria and Poland, and one on Indonesia.

II. International Framework

1. Long-Range Transboundary Air Pollution

a) The Problem

2. Sulphur dioxide ("SO_2") and nitrogen oxide ("NO_X") are the primary causes of acid rain. Although some quantities of SO_2 and NO_X are also produced by nature, human activities generate the majority of these gases and the resulting environmental problems. Emissions of SO_2 and NO_X originate from stationary sources, such as coal-fired and oil-fired power stations, and from mobile sources, such as cars and trucks, ships, and aircrafts.

3. Acid rain occurs when SO_2 and NO_X react in the atmosphere with water, oxygen, and other chemicals, forming various acidic compounds. Sunlight increases the rate of most of these reactions. The result is a mild solution of sulphuric acid and nitric acid that is deposited back onto land through wet dispositions like rain, fog or snow, as well as through dry disposition. The atmosphere's acidity is carried by wind, which blows these particles and gases onto buildings, plants and water.

4. Large quantities of acid rain have detrimental consequences for wildlife, forests, soils, freshwater, and buildings. Rain containing SO_2 and NO_X acidifies the soil and water, killing plants and animals. Surface water acidification can lead to a decline in fish population and other aquatic species. Acid rain also harms trees by weakening them through damage to their leaves. A survey of European forests conducted in the mid-1990s revealed that that every fourth tree suffered from abnormal thinning of the crown, which was largely attributed to air pollution. Finally, acid rain can be detrimental to man-made structures, dissolving, for example, certain types of building stone.

b) Smog

5. Smog is a mixture of carbon monoxide, ground level ozone, and particulate matter. Carbon monoxide is a poisonous gas emitted by vehicles and released by forest fires and open burning. Smog is formed from the reaction of sunlight, volatile organic compounds ("VOCs") and NO_X. VOCs come from a variety of sources including industrial operations, vehicles and area sources (e.g., gas station refilling, open burning, paints and solvents in households, incomplete combustion in home heaters, etc.). Smog is a powerful irritant that can cause harm to humans even at levels where it is invisible to the eye. The inhalation of ozone and particulate matter can cause decreased lung capacity, exacerbate cardio-respiratory diseases and worsen asthma. Exposure to smog also decreases the body's defence mechanisms against infections.

6. It is well established that air pollutants such as SO_2 and NO_X, which are often emitted through factory smokestacks, can travel hundreds or even thousands of kilometres. Consequently, the environmental impacts from air pollution may occur in areas far from their sources.

7. Smog has created local, regiona, and international problems since the beginning of the industrial revolution. In the nineteenth century, fumes emitted by a smelter located in Trail, Canada, near the United States border, raised a problem of transboundary air pollution and led to claims of compensation for the harm caused. Some decades later, in 1941, the Trail Smelter Arbitration articulated the "no-harm obligation" for the first time: countries are obligated to avoid causing transboundary air pollution that leads to environmental damage in other nations. The court held that "under the principles of international law…no state has the right to use or permit the use of its territory in such a manner as to cause injury by fumes in or to the territory of another or the properties or persons therein, when the case is of serious consequence and the injury is established by a clear and convincing evidence."

8. International efforts to identify causes and effects of transboundary air pollution were not initiated until

the late 1960s. During the 1970s, research conducted in Europe and North America led to the development of international legislation in this field.

9. While the problem of transboundary air pollution traditionally has been discussed largely in the context of the developed world, it is clear that air pollution is a serious and growing problem around the globe. In many developing countries, emissions are set to rise dramatically in the coming years if the countries follow conventional development paths to industrialization.

c) The Geneva Convention on Long-Range transboundary Air Pollution ("1979 LRTAP")

10. In the 1960s, scientists demonstrated the interrelationship between sulphur emissions in continental Europe and the acidification of Scandinavian lakes, confirming that air pollutants travel several thousands of kilometres and setting the basis of study of long-range transboundary air pollution.

11. In 1972, the United Nations Conference on the Human Environment signalled the start for active international cooperation to combat the problem of air pollution. In November 1979, a ministerial meeting was held in Geneva within the Framework of the United Nations Economic Commission for Europe ("UNECE") on the Protection of the Environment. This meeting resulted in the signature of the Convention on Long-Range Transboundary Air Pollution ("1979 LRTAP") by 34 governments and the European Community. 1979 LRTAP entered into force in 1983 and currently has 49 Parties (as of September 2005), including the United States and Canada.

12. 1979 LRTAP created the framework for controlling and reducing the damage to human health and the environment caused by transboundary air pollution.

d) LRTAP's General Rules

13. 1979 LRTAP defines air pollution as "the introduction by man directly or indirectly of substances or energy into the air, resulting in deleterious effects of such a nature as to endanger human health, harm living resources and ecosystems and material property, and impair or interfere with amenities and other legitimate uses of the environment..."

14. "Long-range transboundary air pollution means air pollution whose physical origin is situated wholly or in part within the area under the national jurisdiction of one State and which has adverse effects in the area under the jurisdiction of another State at such a distance that it is not generally possible to distinguish the contribution of individual emission sources or groups of sources.

15. 1979 LRTAP outlines the general principles of international cooperation for the abatement of air pollution and provides an institutional framework linking science and policy.

16. 1979 LRTAP's overall objective is to protect human health and the environment from air pollution. The Convention seeks to coordinate parties' efforts by means of increased research, monitoring and information exchange on air pollution and its effects and developing emission reduction strategies.

17. 1979 LRTAP sets up a Secretariat and an Executive Body. The Secretariat is provided by UNECE and is based in Geneva. The Executive Body is composed of environmental advisers to UNECE members and meets annually to review the implementation of the Convention and assess the effectiveness of national policies. In doing so, the Executive Body relies on accurate data on SO_2 and NO_X emissions from sources and pollution levels in general communicated by the parties themselves, as required by article 8 of 1979 LRTAP.

18. To provide scientific support to the Convention, the Programme for Monitoring and Evaluation of the Long-Range Transmission of Air Pollutants in Europe ("EMEP") has been established. The Organization for Economic Cooperation and Development ("OECD") initiated EMEP as a special programme in 1977. Since then, EMEP has set up more than ninety monitoring stations in twenty-four countries. EMEP's main functions include the collection of emission data, measurement of air quality, modelling of atmospheric transport and deposition of air pollution, and integrated assessment modelling.

e) Protocols to 1979 LRTAP

19. Within the framework of the 1979 LRTAP eight protocols have been adopted.

20. 1979 LRTAP provides the basis for the development of several protocols addressing transboundary air pollution. The 1985 (Helsinki) Protocol to the 1979 Convention on Long-Range Transboundary Air Pollution on the Reduction of

Sulphur Emissions or their Transboundary Fluxes by at Least 30 per cent ("1985 First Sulphur Protocol") was adopted on 8 July 1985, and entered into force on 2 September 1987. The 1985 First Sulphur Protocol requires its parties to reduce emissions of their transboundary air pollution by 30% by 1993. Europe recorded substantial decreases in sulphur pollution, despite the fact that three important emitters (including the United States, United Kingdom, and Poland) did not initially ratify the Protocol. The then twenty-one parties to the 1985 First Sulphur Protocol reduced the 1980-level sulphur emission by more than 50% from 1987 to 1993. In 1989, the Executive Body began developing a revised protocol incorporating a more sophisticated approach to emission control.

21. The 1994 (Oslo) Protocol to the 1979 Convention on Long-Range Transboundary Air Pollution on Further Reduction of Sulphur Emissions ("1994 Second Sulphur Protocol") was adopted on 14 June 1994 and entered into force on 5 August 1998. The 1994 Second Sulphur Protocol acknowledges the need for precautionary measures to prevent transboundary air pollution from damaging environment and natural resources and is based on the "critical loads" approach. Critical loads are the maximum amount of pollutants that ecosystems can tolerate without being damaged. The Protocol's objective is to reduce sulphur depositions below the level where significant damage is likely to occur. The country-specific loads, which are based on a mapping of actual SO_2 depositions and sources, are specified in Annex I of the Protocol. Each party must meet minimum emission targets within varying time scales. The overall SO_2 emission reduction for all parties is more than 50%.

22. Implementation of the 1994 Second Sulphur Protocol is mainly left to the discretion of the parties but they are required to use the "most effective measures" appropriate to the circumstances of each party. These can include energy efficiency, use of renewable energy such as wind power, reducing the sulphur content of fuel, the application of best available technology and the use of economic instruments such as taxes of tradable permits. Parties are required to report their SO_2 emissions and their implementation measures (article 5).

23. The 1988 Sofia Protocol to the 1979 Convention on Long-Range Transboundary Air Pollution concerning the Control of Emissions of Nitrogen Oxides or their Transboundary Fluxes (the "1988 NO_X Protocol") was adopted on 1 November 1988, and entered into force on 14 February 1991.

The 1988 NO_X Protocol requires its parties to stabilize their NO_X emissions on their transboundary air pollution at 1987-levels by 1994. The 1988 NO_X Protocol covers both major stationary sources such as power plants, and mobile sources such as vehicle emissions.

24. A second step to the 1988 NO_X Protocol requires the application of an effects based and critical loads approach. A new instrument being prepared at present should provide for further reduction of emissions of nitrogen compounds, including ammonia by addressing all significant emission sources.

25. The 1991 (Geneva) Protocol to the 1979 Convention on Long-Range Transboundary Air Pollution concerning the Control of Emissions of Volatile Organic Compounds or their Transboundary Fluxes (the "1991 VOC Protocol") was adopted on 18 November 1991, and entered into force on 29 September 1997. The 1991 VOC Protocol specifies three options for emission reduction targets that have to be chosen upon signature or upon ratification:

(1) 30% reduction in emissions of volatile organic compounds by 1999, using a year between 1984 and 1990 as a basis (this option has been chosen by the majority of countries);

(2) The same reduction as for (1) within a Tropospheric Ozone Management Area ("TOMA") specified in Annex I to the 1991 VOC Protocol and ensuring that by 1999 total national emissions do not exceed 1988 levels. [Annex I specifies TOMAs in Norway; and,

(3) Finally, where emissions in 1988 did not exceed certain specified levels, parties may opt for stabilization at that level of emission by 1999. This option has been chosen by for example Bulgaria, Greece and Hungary.

26. The (Aarhus) Protocol to the 1979 Convention on Long-Range Transboundary Air Pollution on Persistent Organic Pollutants (the "1998 POPs Protocol") was adopted by LTRAP's Executive Body on 24 June 1998, and entered into force on 23 October 2003. The 1998 POPs Protocol focuses on a list of sixteen substances that have been singled out according to agreed risk criteria. The list includes eleven pesticides, two industrial chemicals and three by products/contaminants. The ultimate objective is to eliminate any discharges, emissions and losses of POPs. The 1998 POPs Protocol bans outright the production and use of some products (e.g., aldrin, chlordane, chlordecone, dieldrin, endrin, hexa-bromobiphenyl, mirex and toxaphene). Others are

scheduled for elimination at a later stage (dichlorodiphenyltrichloroethane ("DDT"), heptachlor, hexaclorobenzene ("HCB"), polychlorinated biphenyls ("PCBs")). Finally, the Protocol severely restricts the use of DDT, gamma-hexachlorocyclohexane ("HCH" including lindane) and PCBs. The 1998 POPs Protocol includes provisions for dealing with the wastes of products that will be banned. It also obliges parties to reduce their emissions of dioxins, furans, polycyclic aromatic hydrocarbons ("PAHs"), and HCBs below established base-year levels. Further, the 1998 POPs Protocol contains specific limits for the incineration of municipal, hazardous, and medical waste.

27. The Executive Body adopted the (Aarhus) Protocol to the 1979 Convention on Long-Range Transboundary Air Pollution on Heavy Metals (the "1998 Heavy Metals Protocol") on 24 June 1998 and it entered into force on 29 December 2003. The 1998 Heavy Metals Protocol targets three harmful metals: cadmium, lead and mercury. Parties are required to reduce their emissions for these three metals below established base year levels. The 1998 Heavy Metals Protocol aims to cut emissions from industrial sources (iron and steel industry, non ferrous metal industry), combustion processes (power generation, road transport, and waste incineration. It establishes stringent limit values for emissions from stationary sources and suggests best available techniques for these sources, such as special filters or scrubbers for combustion sources or mercury-free processes. The 1998 Heavy Metals Protocol also requires signatories to phase-out use of leaded petrol. It also introduces measures to lower heavy metal emissions from other products, such as mercury in batteries, and proposes the introduction of management measures for other mercury containing products (e.g., electrical components (thermostats, switches), measuring devices (thermometers, manometers and barometers), fluorescent lamps, dental amalgam, pesticides and paint).

28. The (Gothenburg) Protocol to the 1979 Convention on Long-Range Transboundary Air Pollution to abate Acidification, Eutrophication and Ground-level Ozone (the "1999 Ozone Protocol") was adopted by LTRAP's Executive Body on 30 November 1999 and entered into force on 17 May, 2005. The 1999 Ozone Protocol sets emission ceilings for 2010 in relation to four pollutants: SO_2, NO_X, VOCs, and ammonia. These ceilings were negotiated on the basis of scientific assessments of pollution effects and abatement options. Parties whose emissions have a more severe environmental or health impact and whose emissions are relatively cheap to reduce will have to make the biggest cuts. Once the 1999 Ozone Protocol is fully implemented, Europe's sulphur emissions should be cut by at least 63%, NO_X emissions by 41%, VOC emissions by 40% and ammonia emissions by 17% compared to 1990. The 1999 Ozone Protocol also sets tight limits for specific emission sources (e.g., combustion plant, electricity production, dry cleaning, cars and lorries, etc.) and requires best available techniques to keep emissions at the reduced levels.

29. Scientists estimate that once the 1999 Ozone Protocol is implemented, the area in Europe with excessive levels of acidification will shrink from ninety-three million hectares in 1990 to fifteen million hectares. In addition the area with excessive levels of eutrophication will fall from 165 million hectares in 1990 to 108 million hectares and the number of days with excessive ozone levels will be halved. Consequently, it is estimated that life-years lost as a result of the chronic effects of ozone exposure will be about 2,300,000 lower in 2010 than in 1990, and there will be approximately 47,500 fewer premature deaths resulting from ozone and particulate matter in the air. The exposure of vegetation to excessive ozone levels will be 44% lower than in 1990.

30. Finally, related to the financial aspects of the 1979 LRTAP, the Protocol to the 1979 Convention on Long-Range Transboundary Air Pollution on Long-Term Financing of the Cooperative Programme for Monitoring and Evaluation of the LRTAP in Europe ("EMEP") was adopted on 1984 and entered into force on 28 January, 1988.

31. These protocols demonstrate the aptitude of the treaty system established by the 1979 Geneva Convention to evolve and develop new techniques. The protocols also reflect the permanent negotiations that have become a necessary part of international environmental law.

f) LTRAP Compliance and Supervision

32. 1979 LTRAP and the 1985 First Sulphur Protocol affirm the Executive Body's responsibility to review implementation and require parties to submit reports. However, none of the protocols contain any formal provision for supervision of compliance.

33. Thus, in 1997, the Executive Body established an Implementation Committee for the review of compliance by the parties with their obligations under the protocols to the Convention. The

Implementation Committee has responsibility for reviewing compliance with all of LTRAP's Protocols under a common procedure. It may investigate and report problems of non-compliance. The Executive Body may then decide on non-discriminatory measures to secure compliance. However, its decisions require consensus and thus can be easily blocked.

34. Some countries have criticized 1979 LTRAP for the soft wording of its provisions and the lack of strong institutional framework of its early protocols. Despite this criticism, transboundary air pollution in Europe has fallen substantially, especially in relation to SO_2 pollution. Thus, the overall picture is one of compliance and improvement. The LRTAP regime has not solved the problem of acid rain or transboundary air pollution but it has certainly succeeded in reversing earlier trends.

2. Haze Pollution

a) The Problem

35. Another form of transboundary air pollution is haze, which consists of small particles of dust, smoke, pollen or tiny droplets of water floating in the air. This chapter discusses smoke haze created by forest fires.

36. Southeast Asia is particularly confronted with forest and land fires. The worst fires accompanied by smoke haze broke out in 1997 and 1998, and had severe consequences on human beings and the environment. Smoke haze was spread across national borders and affected especially Brunei, Indonesia, Malaysia and Singapore. Twenty million people were forced to breathe potentially harmful air for extended periods. The haze pollution resulting from these fires imposed enormous economic costs on the region. It has been estimated that the 1997 and 1998 forest fires cost the region approximately $9 billion in lost agricultural products, infrastructure repair, reduced tourism and other economic costs.

37. In addition to regional outfall, forest fires also have consequences for the global environment. The second largest tropical forest in the world is located in Indonesia, which was hit hardest by the 1997 fires. Therefore, the negative effects of haze smoke pose a serious threat to global biodiversity. Furthermore, scientists have warned that the fires' negative impact on global warming may be considerable. Studies suggest that fires in Indonesia could have added as much as one billion tons of carbon dioxide to the atmosphere, equivalent to Western Europe's total CO_2 emissions for a six month period.

38. Several factors seem to interact in causing and exacerbating the effects of forest and land fires. The *El Nino* weather phenomenon interferes with monsoon-rain patterns and thus causes severe droughts, which make land and forests more susceptible to fires. In addition, fires result from farmers' land-clearing activities. The most important factor, however, is man-made logging and deforestation. Logged forests do not retain moisture as well as primary forests, which makes them prone to larger and more extensive fires. Many of Southeast Asia's fires, therefore, are not so much a phenomenon of nature as a consequence of human intervention.

b) Negotiation History

39. Following the 1997 fires, the environment ministers of the Association of Southeast Asian Nations ("ASEAN") intensified their cooperation to prevent and mitigate such devastating forest and land fires for the future. ASEAN is composed of Brunei, Cambodia, Indonesia, Laos, Malaysia, Myanmar, the Philippines, Singapore, Thailand, and Vietnam.

40. The ASEAN governments agreed to a Regional Haze Action Plan ("RHAP") in December 1997. This plan establishes mechanisms to monitor fires and to strengthen regional fire-fighting capabilities, including timely and more accurate weather forecasts, early warning mechanisms and the development of preventive tools, such as monitoring databases and fire danger rating systems. The RHAP also calls for strict enforcement of existing laws, regulation of open fires and training of prosecution and law enforcement officers. A website has been established to more effectively share and manage information relating to early warning and monitoring.

41. At the 2002 World Conference and Exhibition on Land and Forest Fire Hazards held in Kuala Lumpur, the ASEAN ministers signed the ASEAN Agreement on Transboundary Haze Pollution (the "2002 ASEAN Agreement"), an important component of the long-term and broad framework of the RHAP.

42. The 2002 ASEAN Agreement is the first such arrangement in the world. It binds a group of contiguous states to tackle land and forest fires and the resultant transboundary haze pollution and can serve as an example for other regions of the world. Every year around the world, fires destroy approximately 500 million hectares of woodland, open forests, tropical and sub-tropical savannah, as well as 10 to 15 million hectares of boreal and temperate forest and 20 to 40 million hectares of tropical forests.

III. National Implementation

1. EUROPE

a) Austria

43. Austria ratified the 1994 Second Sulphur Protocol in 1998. The 1994 Second Sulphur Protocol requires a licensing procedure for each new or modified installation according to the Industrial Code and the Clean Air Act for Steam Boilers, both of which were introduced in the 1980s. The licensing procedure limits emission values and determines appropriate measurements according to Best Available Technology ("BAT"). For several categories of stationary emission sources, explicit emission limit values and BAT requirements have been set by ordinance. Limit values for the sulphur content of fuels have been adopted. Emission limit values are different depending on the type of fuel and of the thermal input. Almost all of them are more stringent than the values in Annex V of the 1994 Second Sulphur Protocol. As a consequence, Austria's emissions of sulphur dropped by 55% between 1990 and 2000.

44. Austria has not yet implemented market based pollution control mechanisms, such as emissions trading.

45. Measures to increase energy efficiency are included among other energy specific regulations in the 'building code'. For example, there are subsidies for the construction/rehabilitation of residential buildings, the replacement of old heaters and stoves and for energy efficiency measures in the commercial and industrial sector.

46. Austria's energy policy has put special emphasis on the use of renewable energy. For example, the regional energy agency for the federal province of Upper Austria operates energy centres in the Czech Republic and Slovakia and carries out projects together with neighbouring countries. Recent renewable energy initiatives include an annual international symposium (World Sustainable Energy Day) and a competition for best practice projects. Austria also directly supports projects for information transfer, including the hosting of international summer schools on solar energy.

47. Monitoring of ambient air concentrations of sulphur dioxide is performed by about 150 monitoring stations in Austria, out of which three are part of the EMEP network. Research projects are conducted such as the improvement of data on critical loads, deposition of sulphur compounds, dispersion and receptor modelling of air pollutants, and integrated monitoring of air pollution effects on ecosystems.

b) Poland

48. Poland has signed and ratified LTRAP's 1998 Heavy Metals Protocol. The country's National Strategy for the Reduction of Heavy Metal Emission (the "National Heavy Metal Strategy") was elaborated in 1999 and updated in 2002. In addition, Poland's National Environmental Policy for 2003-2006 covers a range of environmental issues, including heavy metal emissions. Poland's National Environmental Policy for 2003-2006 includes wider use of emission standards in the industry, energy and transport sectors and the use of product control measures, introduction of BAT and emission standards for eleven source categories. The country has also developed principles of its energy policy through 2020, that stress the need for reduction of heavy metal emissions through changes in the structure of fuel consumption. This should be achieved by an increase in the use of natural gas, liquid fuels, and renewable sources.

49. Poland's National Heavy Metal Strategy specifically requires:

- Modification of the Polish public system of statistics (emission inventories);
- Detailed prognosis for heavy metal emissions on the national and sectoral level;
- Inventory of major emission sources for the eleven source categories;
- Evaluation of applied technologies and emission control measures;
- Technical and cost-effective analysis of the possibilities of introducing BAT;
- Mandatory and recommended product control measures;
- Analysis of the effectiveness of different economic and market instruments; and
- Preparation of appropriate emission standards for stationary and mobile emission sources.

50. In most of the listed activities initial results have been achieved. Due to industrial restructuring Poland has led to a reduction in the country's heavy metal emissions and in electric energy consumption.

51. The 1998 Heavy Metals Protocol on heavy metals requires parties not to exceed the emission levels of the reference years. In its National Heavy Metal Strategy, Poland chose 1985 as reference year for cadmium and lead and 1988 for mercury. Significantly high emission reduction results have been obtained for lead and cadmium. The lowest

reduction was achieved for mercury. Poland ended the production of leaded petrol in 2002. By 1999, Poland had achieved reduction levels of approximately 57% for cadmium, 63% for lead and 32% for mercury.

52. The use of BAT has become mandatory with the introduction of the new Environmental Protection Law. Source categories considered to be major in Poland are:

- Fuel combustion processes for energy production;
- Iron and steel production (including smelter plants and coke production);
- Non-ferrous metal production (lead, zinc, copper and aluminium);
- Chemical industry (fertilizer production);
- Transport; and
- Waste incineration.

53. So far, in Poland, the main criteria for determining emission ceilings for an individual enterprise has been the air pollution concentration in the vicinity of the emission source. Changes in this approach are being considered. At present, air emission standards are prepared for selected industrial sources (e.g., iron and steel production, foundries, cement production, coke production, cured oil refineries, etc.). According to the updated National Strategy, it is necessary to establish emission limit values for certain source categories and processes such as sinter plants and cement industry. In relation to emission limit values for fuel combustion processes changes are needed in the existing limit values for particulate emission for solid and fuels.

54. Requirements regarding the exchange of technologies and techniques are also included in the new Framework Act on Environmental Protection Law. Introduction of new techniques and technologies are supported by the National Fund for Environmental Protection and Water Management. Transfer of new environmental technologies is also one of the main issues included in multilateral and bilateral cooperation. Poland is preparing to establish a National Centre for BAT.

2. ASIA

Indonesia

55. Since the 2002 ASEAN Agreement was ratified only in 2003, countries have not yet had the opportunity to adopt specific implementing legislation. However, most of the countries, including Indonesia, have some laws in place to combat forest fires and its attendant haze pollution. As of August 2005, seven countries (Brunei, Darussalam, Malaysia, Myanmar, Singapore, Thailand, Vietnam, Lao PDR) have ratified the Agreement.

56. Indonesia is one of the countries hardest hit by forest fires. While it is one of the signatories to the 2002 ASEAN Agreement, it has not yet ratified the agreement. The participation of Indonesia will be crucial to the success of the 2002 ASEAN Agreement and its ratification is expected in the near future. However, Indonesia has policies and legislation in place that directly or indirectly target the problematic of forest fires and haze.

57. Up to 80% of the forest fires that plagued Indonesia in 1997 and 1998 were attributable to agricultural expansion, particularly oil palm plantations. Along with Malaysia, Indonesia accounts for 85% of world palm oil exports. Indonesia adapted its land use policy in order to address the consequences of forest fires. A ministerial decree provides for the criteria for the allocating forestland for oil palm estates and specifies site criteria for new oil palm plantations.

58. Indonesian Government Regulation on Air Pollution Control No. 41/1999 requires the Indonesia Environmental Impact Management Agency ("BAPEDAL") to publish the Air Pollutants Standards Index ("APSI"). This index takes into consideration factors such as the air quality level for human health, animals, plants and buildings. The Minister of Environment is obliged to declare an air pollution emergency situation if the APSI index reaches a certain level (i.e. 300 points).

59. Indonesia has also introduced the 1999 Forestry Law No. 41 ("Forestry Law") in order to address the causes of forest fires and to promote their prevention. Article 49 of the Forestry Law stipulates that the licence holder in the field of forestry and plantation is responsible for the occurrence of the forest fires in his jurisdiction. Article 50 of the Forestry Law states that every person is prohibited from burning the forest unless they hold an authorized licence for special or limited purposes. For example, burning is permitted for forest fire control and combating pest and disease. The Forestry Law also imposes criminal sanctions.

60. Indonesia's Environment Management Act No. 23/1997 provides that a licence for an activity with significant impact on the environment cannot be undertaken unless the proponent can show that EIA has been approved by the responsible agency. The licence must reflect the recommendations and

outcome of the EIA. The licence issuer has the authority to impose administrative sanctions from warning to withdrawal of the licence if the licence holder is found in violation of its obligation.

61. The legal regime also provides for raising public awareness and increased public participation in the prevention, combating and mitigation of forest fires. It further provides for notification of and cooperation with countries that are affected by the consequences of forest fires in Indonesia.

IV. The 2002 ASEAN Agreement

62. The 2002 ASEAN Agreement entered into force in 2003. Its objective is to prevent and monitor transboundary haze pollution as a result of land and forest fires within the context of sustainable development, Principle 2 and 15, the precautionary principle of the Rio Declaration. Parties to the 2002 ASEAN Agreement undertake to manage their natural resources, including forests, in an ecologically sound and sustainable manner and to involve local communities in addressing the issue of transboundary haze pollution.

63. Specifically, the 2002 ASEAN Agreement commits its parties to:

   • Cooperate in developing and implementing measures to prevent, monitor, and mitigate transboundary haze pollution by controlling sources of land and/or forest fires;
   • Establish early warning systems;
   • Exchange information and technology;
   • Provide mutual assistance;
   • Respond promptly to requests for relevant information sought by a state or states that are or may be affected by such transboundary haze pollution when the transboundary haze pollution originates from within their territories; and
   • Take legal and administrative measures to implement their obligations under the 2002 ASEAN Agreement.

64. The parties to the 2002 ASEAN Agreement also facilitate the transit of personnel, equipment, and materials used in fire-fighting and participate in search and rescue operations through their respective territories.

65. The parties have to set up focal points and competent authorities that are entitled to act on behalf of the party in carrying out the administrative measures required by the 2002 ASEAN Agreement. Furthermore, each party is required to install a national monitoring centre, which communicates data about fires, fire prone areas, environmental conditions conductive to fire and data about haze pollution resulting from such fires.

66. The 2002 ASEAN Agreement requires the support of all members before direct action can be taken on a regional threat. This is to ensure that activities avoid violating an individual member country's national sovereignty. Firefighters or other personnel may respond to forest fires in a second country only if requested to do so by the government affected. Responsibility for protecting resources thus remains at a national level.

67. A Conference of the Parties ("COP") and a Secretariat were created under the 2002 ASEAN Agreement. The COP is responsible for reviewing and evaluating the Agreement's implementation and adopts protocols and amendments. The Secretariat arranges the meetings of the bodies established under the Agreement and acts as an interface between these bodies and the member countries. The existing ASEAN Secretariat serves as the Secretariat to the 2002 ASEAN Agreement.

68. The 2002 ASEAN Agreement further establishes the ASEAN Coordinating Centre for Transboundary Haze Pollution Control ("Coordinating Centre"), which facilitates cooperation and coordination to manage land and forest fires, in particular haze pollution arising from such fires. The Coordinating Centre provides assistance upon the request of a signatory nation once it has declared an emergency situation.

69. The ASEAN Transboundary Haze Pollution Control Fund ("Haze Fund") is the 2002 ASEAN Agreement's main financial institution. Contributions to the Haze Fund are voluntary. Pending the establishment of the Coordinating Centre, the 2002 ASEAN Agreement's signatory states have agreed on a set of *interim* arrangements, which rely on existing institutions and resources.

Prof. Alexandre Kiss, Director of Research, Centre for Environmental Law, Robert Schuman University, France

Eva Maria Duer, Associate Legal Expert, Division of Policy Development and Law, UNEP

Resources

Internet Materials

1994 SULFUR PROTOCOL, SUBMISSIONS BY PARTIES available at
http://www.unece.org/env/documents/2002/eb/eb.air.2002.1.q.18-27.pdf

1998 PROTOCOL ON HEAVY METALS, SUBMISSIONS BY PARTIES available at
http://www.unece.org/env/documents/2002/eb/eb.air.2002.1.q.28-36.pdf

ACID RAIN IN EUROPE: BACKGROUND INFORMATION available at http://greennature.com/

ASEAN AGREEMENT ON TRANSBOUNDARY HAZE POLLUTION available at http://www.haze-online.or.id

CONVENTION ON LONG RANGE TRANSBOUNDARY AIR POLLUTION available at http://www.unece.org/env/lrtap/

ENCYCLOPEDIA OF ATMOSPHERIC ENVIRONMENT, ATMOSPHERE, CLIMATE & ENVIRONMENT INFORMATION PROGRAMME - ACID RAIN
available at http://www.doc.mmu.ac.uk/aric/eae/english.html

EUROPEAN STATISTICAL LABORATORY, THE PRESSURE INDICES PROJECT: INTRODUCTION TO THE POLICY FIELDS – AIR POLLUTION
available at http://esl.jrc.it/envind/pf_intro/pf_int01.htm

HAZE ONLINE available at http://www.haze-online.or.id/

SPECIAL REPORT ON FOREST FIRE AND HAZE SITUATION IN INDONESIA AND ACTION TAKEN available at
http://www.aseansec.org/9003.htm

Text Material

TRAIL SMELTER ARBITRATION, (United States v. Canada, 3 R. Int'l Arb. Awards 1911, 1938).

9. OZONE DEPLETION

I. Introduction

1. The Earth's atmosphere is composed of three regions: the troposphere, which extends up to about ten kilometres from the Earth's surface; the stratosphere, which is found between approximately ten and fifty kilometres from the Earth's surface; and the ionosphere, which extends up to 350 kilometres from Earth.

2. Ozone, which has the chemical formula of "O_3," is a molecule composed of oxygen and is found mainly in two regions of the Earth's atmosphere. Most ozone (approximately 90%) is found in the stratosphere. This stratospheric ozone is commonly known as the "ozone layer." The remaining ozone is contained in the troposphere, also known as surface-level ozone.

3. The amount of ozone present in the Earth's atmosphere has critical implications for the environment, human health and national economies. Since not one country can control ozone depletion, it is an important issue in international environmental law.

4. The ozone molecules in the two regions above are chemically identical; however, they have different sources and their effects are very different on humans and other living beings.

5. Surface-level ozone is a result of chemical reactions involving emissions from vehicles, industrial pollution and sunlight. Because ozone reacts strongly with other molecules, high levels of ozone are toxic to living systems. Several studies have documented the harmful effects of ozone on crop cultivation, forest growth and human health. Low-lying ozone is a key component of photochemical smog, a common problem in many cities around the world. Higher amounts of surface level ozone are increasingly being observed in rural areas as well.

6. Stratospheric ozone, in contrast, plays a highly beneficial role. It absorbs most of the sun's biologically damaging ultraviolet radiation and only allows a small amount to reach the Earth's surface. The ozone layer screens out almost all the harmful ultraviolet rays of the sun and thus can be described as our planet's sunscreen.

7. During the 1970s, scientists observed a significant destruction of ozone in the stratosphere. The emergence of evidence peaked in 1985, when a large "ozone hole" was discovered above Antarctica. This has reappeared annually during the springtime, generally growing larger and deeper each year. In 1992, ozone over Antarctica had depleted by 60% from previous observations; and the size of the hole had increased, covering twenty-three million square miles. The overall decline in stratospheric ozone levels was estimated at 3% per decade. By the mid-1990s, ozone depletion extended over latitudes including North America, Europe, Asia, and much of Africa, Australia and South America. Thus, ozone depletion had become an issue of global concern.

8. Scientific evidence has shown that human produced chemicals are responsible for the observed depletions of the ozone layer. These chemicals are used in solvents, foam, aerosol, mobile air conditioning, refrigeration and fire protection and contain various combinations of chemical elements, of which chlorofluorocarbons ("CFCs") are most prominent.

9. CFCs are so stable that only exposure to strong ultraviolet ("UV") radiation breaks them down. When this happens, the CFC molecule releases atomic chlorine. One chlorine atom can destroy over 100,000 ozone molecules, depleting ozone faster than it is naturally created. Chlorine that reaches the stratosphere is also produced by natural occurrences such as volcanic eruptions or large fires, with high concentrations of chlorine fluctuate. It has been shown, however, that natural sources only create approximately 15% of chlorine in the stratosphere and thus have minimal impact on the depletion of the ozone layer.

10. Protecting the ozone layer, the Earth's protective screen against ultraviolet radiation, is essential. Any damage to the ozone layer leads to increased UV radiation reaching the Earth's surface. This can cause a variety of human health problems such as skin cancers, eye cataracts and a reduction in the body's immunity to disease. A 1% decrease in ozone would lead to about a 4% increase of skin cancer and 100,000 to 150,000 additional cases of cataract blindness. Ultraviolet radiation can also affect plant life, damage forests and certain varieties of crops including rice and soya. Ultraviolet radiation can be damaging to microscopic life in the surface oceans (such as plankton, fish larvae, shrimp, crab, and aquatic plants) that form the basis of the world's marine food chain.

11. Several methods have been investigated regarding the replacement of ozone lost in the stratosphere, starting with options such as shipping low-level ozone out of smog burdened cities or producing new ozone and introducing it into the stratosphere. Since ozone reacts strongly with other molecules, however, it is too unstable, expensive and impractical to transport into the stratosphere. Therefore, the only cure to the problem of ozone depletion is to regulate and eliminate the production of CFCs and other ozone-depleting substances.

II. International Framework

1. The 1985 Vienna Convention for the Protection of the Ozone Layer

12. 1975, the World Meteorological Organization ("WMO") conducted the first international assessment of the global ozone situation. The alarming results demonstrated a need for swift response and led to the creation of a Plan of Action on the Ozone Layer, a result of the collaboration between UNEP and WMO. In 1981, UNEP initiated negotiations of a Global Framework Convention for the Protection of the Ozone Layer.

13. Since the impact of ozone depleting substances affects all states, a regime would likely only work if it was global in scope. In order to achieve global adherence to the treaty, the interests of different States had to be reconciled during the negotiation process. Developing countries feared that constraints on producing certain ozone-depleting substances might inhibit their industrial development. Countries with industries heavily relying on ozone-depleting substances, like those of the European Community, were reluctant to accept the high costs associated with measures that regulate production and consumption of these substances. Some states resisted costly measures and controls, arguing that harmful effects had not been proven. However, countries which had already reduced production and consumption of CFCs did not want to see others using them in refrigerators and sprays.

14. The Vienna Convention for the Protection of the Ozone Layer, 1985 ("Vienna Convention") was adopted after consensus was reached on 22 March 1985. The overall objective of the Vienna Convention is to protect human health and the environment against the effects of ozone depletion. As a framework convention, it does not establish any specific controls on ozone depleting substances. Instead, it establishes a general

obligation upon the parties to protect the ozone layer (article 2) and emphasizes the need for international cooperation.

15. The Vienna Convention requires parties to take "appropriate measures" against the adverse effects of human made ozone depletion. These measures include the adoption of legislative and administrative measures, cooperation on research and scientific assessment, information exchange and development and transfer of technology.

16. The Convention provides for the creation of a Conference of the Parties ("COP"), meeting at regular intervals, and a Secretariat. The COP reviews implementation of the Convention and establishes the necessary programmes and policies. It is the body that amends the Convention and adopts new protocols and annexes. The Secretariat organizes and services meetings, prepares and transmits reports on countries and their implementation measures and ensures coordination with other relevant international bodies.

17. The Convention does not impose many concrete obligations nor does it enumerate any substances that these measures might relate to. Rather, it establishes a framework that needs to be filled in through further action. However, it was the first convention to acknowledge the need for preventive action before firm proof of the actual harmfulness of ozone depleting substances was established. Thus, it remains an important indicator of the emergence of the precautionary principle or approach.

2. The 1987 Montreal Protocol on Substances that deplete the Ozone Layer

18. In light of the necessity for more concrete action under the Vienna Convention, countries reconvened in Montreal in 1987 to adopt a protocol regarding the phase out of ozone depleting substances ("Montreal Protocol"). During the negotiations of the Montreal Protocol, three issues were of major importance. First, broad adherence to the Montreal Protocol was essential and there was considerable concern about the financial abilities of developing countries to implement the Montreal Protocol. Second, the Montreal Protocol needed to be drafted in a flexible way in order to timely adjust to new scientific evidence and to the changing needs of its parties. The third issue was to determine an economically feasible and detailed time schedule for the phase out of ozone depleting substances.

19. The Montreal Protocol on Substances that deplete the Ozone Layer is a significant milestone in international environmental law. It establishes firm targets for reducing and eventually eliminating consumption and production of a range of ozone depleting substances. These substances are enumerated in Annexes A-E to the Protocol and are to be phased out within the schedules given in articles 2A-2I. The Montreal Protocol controls both consumption and production of ozone depleting substances in order to protect the interests of producers and importers, who otherwise would have had to sustain high price inflation or overproduction during the phase out period of the targeted gases.

20. The Montreal Protocol includes special provisions for the needs of developing countries. It takes into account that developing countries have hardly contributed to ozone depletion and thus provides for a ten year delay for developing countries in phasing out of production and consumption. This exemption is granted under article 5 of the Protocol, which applies to developing countries and countries whose annual calculated level of consumption of the controlled substances in Annex A is less than 0.3 kilograms per capita on the date of the entry into force of the Montreal Protocol or any time thereafter until 1 January 1999. Furthermore, new financial and technical incentives were adopted to encourage developing countries to switch as quickly as possible to alternative substances and technologies.

21. The Montreal Protocol further attempts to address the problem of trade with countries that are not yet parties to the agreement ("non-parties"). It bans trade in controlled substances with non-parties unless they are found by the Meeting of the Parties ("MOP") to be in compliance with the Protocol's agreements. Furthermore, the parties must discourage the export of CFC production technology. Despite the fact that the Montreal Protocol bans export and import of ozone depleting substances, it remains compatible with the General Agreement on Tariffs and Trade ("GATT"). Article XX (b and g) of GATT allows trade restriction in support of environmental goals and health measures as long as they are not disguised restrictions to trade or applied in a discriminative manner.

22. In the light of new scientific evidence it soon became apparent that the standards adopted in were insufficient to reduce ozone depletion. Therefore, amendments were adopted that incorporated additional substances into the Annexes and provided for a more stringent timetable. At the Second MOP in London in 1990, restrictions on CFCs and halons were made more stringent, and two new substances, tetrachloromethane and 1,1,1,-trichloroethane were included. 179 countries have ratified (as of September 2005) the 1990 London Amendment to the Montreal Protocol.

23. At the Fourth MOP in Copenhagen in 1992, restrictions on CFCs, halons, tetrachloromethane and 1,1,1,-trichloroethane were made considerably more stringent. In addition HCFCs, HBFCs and methyl bromide were included in the list of controlled substances with phase out dates. 168 parties (as of September 2005) have ratified the 1992 Copenhagen Amendment to the Montreal Protocol.

24. In 1997, the parties adopted the Montreal Amendment, deciding to advance the phase out date of methylbromide for the industrial countries from 2010 to 2005. Also, in order to assist the parties in preventing illegal traffic of controlled substances, the parties were now required to establish and implement a system for licensing the import and export of ozone-depleting substances. 135 parties (as of September 2005) have ratified the 1997 Montreal Amendment to the Montreal Protocol.

25. After intensive negotiations at the twelfth meeting of the parties in Beijing in 1999, the parties agreed to include production control of hydrochloroflurocarbons (HCFCs) for industrial as well as developing countries, ("Beijing Amendment"). A new ozone depleting substance, bromochloromethane was added to the Protocol and was to be phased out by 2002. The Beijing Amendment also establishes a ban on trade of imports and exports in HCFCs with countries that have not yet ratified the 1992 Copenhagen Amendment to the 1987 Montreal Protocol. 98 parties (as of September 2005) have ratified the 1999 Beijing Amendment to the Montreal Protocol.

a) Institutions

26. To ensure its effective implementation, several bodies have been established under the 1987 Montreal Protocol. The MOP must keep the Protocol's implementation under continuous review. It is the organ that adopts amendments to the Protocol, makes adjustments in time schedules and additions to or removal from any Annex of substances. The MOP must consider and undertake any additional action that may be required for the achievement of the purposes of this Protocol.

1987 Montreal Protocol's "Phase-Out" Timetable

Substance	Industrial Countries' Reduction (%)	Developing Countries' Reduction (%)
CFCs	100% in 1996	0% in 1999 20% in 2003 50% in 2005 85% in 2007 100% in 2010
Halons	100% in 1994	0% in 2002 50% in 2005 100% in 2010
Carbon tetrachloride	100% in 1996	85% in 2005 100% in 2010
1,1,1,-trichloroethane	100% in 1996	0% in 2003 30% in 2005 70% in 2010 100% in 2015
HBFCs	100% in 1996	100% in 1996
HCFCs	0% in 1996 35% in 2004 65% in 2010 90% in 2015 99,5% in 2010 100% in 2030	0% in 2016 100% in 2040
Methyl bromide	0% in 1995 25% in 1999 50% in 2001 70% in 2003 100% in 2005	0% in 2002 20% in 2005 100% in 2015
Bromochloromethane	100% in 2002	100% in 2002

27. In order to further secure the flexibility of the Protocol in relation to ongoing scientific research decisions, the MOP may make further adjustments in the time schedule or evaluation of ozone-depleting substances. Such decisions should be taken by consensus. However, if after exhaustion of all efforts consensus cannot be reached, a two-thirds majority of the parties can take this decision, which is binding even on those parties that voted against it. To maintain an equitable balance between developed and developing states, these decisions must be supported by separate majorities of both groups. The same rule applies to decisions concerning financial mechanisms.

28. The Vienna Convention and the Montreal Protocol share the same Secretariat, called the Ozone Secretariat, based in Nairobi, Kenya.

b) The Multilateral Fund, its Executive Committee and Secretariat

29. A Multilateral Fund was established by a decision of the Second MOP to the Montreal Protocol in June 1990, and began its operation in 1991. Its aim is to promote technology transfer and technical cooperation. Due to this regime (article 10), developing countries should no longer need to rely on the ten-year delay for the phase out greenhouse gases provided for in article 5 and thus can comply with the Protocol's provisions at an earlier stage. The Multilateral Fund is financed by non-article 5 parties, which are mainly industrialized countries. Thus the Montreal Protocol can be seen as to effectively implement the concept of common but differentiated responsibilities.

30. The Fund is administered by the Executive Committee, which consists of seven parties operating under article 5 and seven parties from developed countries. The Committee develops the plan and budget of the Multilateral Fund and monitors expenditures incurred under the Fund. It must determine criteria and conditions for funding and review the performance reports on the implementation of the Protocol, as far as these are supported by the Fund. The Committee meets at least twice a year in Montreal.

31. The Fund Secretariat was established in 1991 in Montreal and assists the Executive Committee in carrying out its functions. Its activities include the development of the three year plan and budget, the management of the business planning cycle, and monitoring the expenditures and activities of the implementing agencies.

32. Four international agencies have contractual agreements with the Executive Committee to assist article 5 countries by preparing country programmes, feasibility studies and project proposals. They provide technical assistance for project development and implementation and for information dissemination. These agencies are the United Nations Development Programme ("UNDP"), the United Nations Environment Programme ("UNEP"), the United Nations Industrial Development Organization ("UNIDO") and the World Bank. Additionally, several developed countries also provide similar assistance on a bilateral basis.

33. In 2002, approximately 100 governments agreed on a major funding package that will channel hundreds of millions of US dollars to developing countries so they can reduce their reliance on CFCs and other ozone-depleting substances and meet their phase out targets. The table below shows the timetable for article 5 countries in relation to ozone-depleting substances.

c) Non-Compliance Procedure

34. The Montreal Protocol's formal non-compliance procedure was introduced by the Copenhagen Amendment. It attempts to bring non-complying states into compliance by engaging them in a cooperative manner.

35. The formal non-compliance procedure can be invoked by any party to the Protocol, by the Secretariat or by the party itself. The matter is then referred to the Implementation Committee. This

SUBSTANCE	YEAR	CONTROL MEASURE
Annex A, Group I Chlorofluorocarbons (CFCs)		Base Level: Average of 1995 – 1997
	1.1.1999	Freeze both production and consumption levels
	1.1.2005	50% reduction
	1.1.2007	85% reduction
	1.1.2010	100% phase out (with possible essential use exemptions)
Annex A, Group II (Halons)		Base level: Average of 1995-1997
	1.1.2002	Freeze both production and consumption
	1.1.2005	50% reduction
	1.1.2010	100% phase out (with possible essential use exemptions)
Annex B, Group I (Other fully halogenated CFCs)		Base level: Average of 1998-2000
	1.1.2003	20% reduction
	1.1.2007	85% reduction
	1.1.2010	100% phase out (with possible essential use exemptions)
Annex B, Group II (Carbon Tetrachloride)		Base Level: Average of 1998-2000
	1.1.2005	85% reduction
	1.1.2010	100% phase out (with possible essential use exemptions)
Annex B, Group III (Methyl Chloroform)		Base Level: Average of 1998-2000
	1.1.2003	Freeze both production and consumption
	1.1.2005	30% reduction
	1.1.2010	70% reduction
	1.1.2015	100% phase out (with possible essential use exemptions)

SUBSTANCE	YEAR	CONTROL MEASURE
Annex C, Group I Hydrochlorofluorocarbons (HCFCs)		Base Level Consumption: 2015 consumption Base Level Production: average of production and consumption in 2015
	1.1.2016	Freeze both production and consumption
	1.1.2040	100% phase out

Implementation Committee consists of ten parties elected on the basis of equitable geographical representation. The Implementation Committee considers information and observations submitted to it with a view to securing an amicable solution. A report is then submitted to the MOP, which then decides which measures should be taken to bring about full compliance. Such measures can include financial, technical or training assistance. If these measures are insufficient, cautions can be issued. As a last resort, rights and privileges under the Montreal Protocol can be suspended. Developing countries, for instance, could lose their article 5 status if they fail to fulfil their reporting requirements.

36. The MOP also decides on appropriate action in case a developing country informs the Secretariat that it is not able to implement the protocol due to the failure of developed countries to provide financial or technological support. As seen at the description of the Multilateral Fund, financial support provided by developed countries is an essential tool to induce compliance in developing countries and reflects the concept of common but differentiated responsibilities.

37. The international ozone regime has been successful in several ways. The Vienna Convention has currently (September 2005) 190 parties and the Montreal Protocol has 189 parties, including Brazil, China, the European Community, India, Russia and the United States. The amendments to the Protocol, together with the availability of financial means, have helped to ensure very high participation among developed countries. Second, the regime has operated in a dynamic and flexible way. Controls on ozone depleting substances were strengthened in 1990, 1992, 1997 and 1999, and new substances have been added. Third, since the formal non-compliance procedure has been successful, compliance in developed countries has been very high. Most importantly, the flexible compliance mechanism of the Montreal Protocol is often considered to be a role model in environmental agreements.

38. There seems to be an evident need to coordinate the Ozone Regime with the Climate Change Regime, since some of the substitute substances to ozone-depleting gases are classified as greenhouse gases under the 1997 Kyoto Protocol to the United Nations Framework Convention on Climate Change ("UNFCCC"). For more discussion of global climate change issues see chapter 10 herein. It should be noted, however, that the Vienna Convention and the Montreal Protocol have provided one of the most sophisticated and effective models of international environmental regulation. If the Montreal Protocol is fully adhered to, global ozone losses will be eradicated and the Antarctic ozone hole will have recovered by approximately 2045.

III. National Implementation

1. Malaysia

39. To oversee the implementation of its national action plan, the Government of Malaysia created a National Steering Committee for Environment and Development ("NSCED"), which paved the way for Malaysia's ratification in 1989. The NSCED is comprised of a Technical Committee and Industrial Working Groups on solvents, foam, aerosol, mobile air conditioning, refrigeration and fire protection. Other IWGs were established later to keep pace with the Protocol's amendments. In 1996, the Department of the Environment created the Ozone Protection Unit ("OPU") to serve as the focal point and monitor Malaysia's phase-out activities.

40. A key feature of Malaysia's response and implementation strategy is the concept of integrated stakeholder partnership with the industrial sector. Active involvement of Civil Society and Non Governmental Organizations also contributed greatly to the success of implementing the Action Plan. The Department of the Environment has initiated various activities during the phase-out process with IWGs, manufacturers, suppliers and users.

41. Although Malaysia fell under article 5(1) of the Protocol, which extended a grace period of ten years to developing countries to meet international commitments, the government pursued a proactive strategy to reduce and limit the use of the controlled substances ahead of schedule.

42. Based on the work of the Industrial Working Groups, Malaysia submitted its original Country Programme and the Action Plan to phase out ozone depleting substances to the Executive Committee of the Multilateral Fund in December 1991. The plan aimed to progressively reduce the consumption of ozone depleting substances in each sector by 2000 through multiple means. These means included control measures like enforcement of the Customs Duties Order, incentives like exemption of import taxes on ozone depleting substances recycling machines, partnerships for awareness activities, road shows and training, as well as project implementation and monitoring.

43. As a result of its proactive approach and financing through the Multilateral Fund, Malaysia succeeded in phasing out more than 50% of CFCs and halon in its manufacturing sector by 2000. Thus, it met it obligations well in advance of the timetable of the 1987 Montreal Protocol for article 5(1) countries. At the end of 1999, 121 projects and activities for phasing-out CFCs were financed through the Multilateral Fund, totalling US $30.7 million. Malaysia has also ratified the London, Copenhagen, Montreal and Beijing Amendments to the Montreal Protocol.

44. Malaysia's Environmental Quality Order 1993 (i.e., Prohibition on the Use of Chlorofluorocarbons and other cases as Propellants and Blowing Agents) ("Order") prohibits by various dates commencing 1 June, 1994 to 1999, the use of specified ozone depleting substances, in the following processes:

   • As propellant in the manufacture or trade of aerosols, and portable fire extinguishers;
   • As propellant in any manufacturing process, trade or industry of aerosol in certain pharmaceutical products; and
   • As a blowing agent in any manufacturing process (subject to later deadlines applicable to polystyrene foam, thermoformed plastic packaging and molded flexible polyurethane foam).

45. The Order also prohibits, from 1999, the use of combustible petroleum gas or other combustible gas as propellant in any manufacturing process.

46. The administering authority can waive the prohibitions on using controlled substances and combustible petroleum or other combustible gas (as applicable), where satisfied that the use of the relevant substance is essential for human health or safety, and an alternative to the substance is unavailable. The Customs Order 1988 (Prohibition of Imports), amended by the Customs Order 1994 (Amendment No. 4), also prohibits the import of chlorofluorocarbons listed in Annex A to the 1987 Montreal Protocol on Substances that deplete the Ozone Layer, without an import licence.

47. Malaysia has received various awards over the past several years for its exceptionally successful implementation of the 1987 Montreal Protocol's CFC phase-out. The example can be applied to other countries with different levels of development and sociocultural contexts. Malaysia has also shared its experience with other countries, including China, Indonesia, Egypt and Kazakhstan. One of the essential ingredients for success has been Malaysia's commitment to international cooperation and assistance.

2. Canada

48. As one of the early signatories to the 1987 Montreal Protocol, Canada ratified it in June 1988. The country has since made significant progress in reducing the emissions of ozone-depleting substances. Canada implemented the 1987 Montreal Protocol through strong control measures by federal, provincial and territorial governments, changes in technologies and voluntary actions by industry.

49. Canada has adopted regulations to meet its Montreal Protocol commitments. The Ozone-Depleting Substances Regulations (1998) and subsequent amendments are administered under the Canadian Environmental Protection Act (1999). These regulations control the import, manufacture, use, sale and export of ODS. They require gradual reductions of production and import of these substances according to fixed schedule established by the Montreal Protocol.

50. As part of the ongoing process to fulfil its commitments under the Montreal Protocol, Canada has adopted the Strategy to accelerate the Phase-Out of CFC and Halon Uses and to dispose of the Surplus Stocks (Phase-Out Strategy), which was approved in May 2001.

51. There are two separate components of the Phase-Out Strategy. The first is general in nature and provides the "infrastructure" needed to achieve the objectives of the Phase-Out Strategy, which consists of extended producer responsibility programmes, consideration of market force instruments and communication of information to stakeholders. The second component of the Phase-

Out Strategy consists of specific phase-out approaches for individual industry sectors. These phase-out approaches will become regulatory requirements once the federal, provincial and territorial governments adopt regulations to implement the Phase-Out Strategy.

52. A summary of the sector-specific approaches for air conditioning and refrigeration applications is provided in the following table:

Sector	Approach
Mobile Air Conditioning	Prohibit refill with CFCs as soon as possible.
Mobile Refrigeration	Prohibit refill with CFCs effective 2003.
Household Appliances	Enhance implementation of existing recovery programmes. If necessary, add a ban on converting equipment using CFCs.
Commercial Refrigeration and Air Conditioning	Staged CFC refill ban effective by year: equipment < 5 HP: 2004 equipment 5 - 30 HP: 2005 equipment > 30 HP: 2006
Chillers	Limit releases from low pressure purges to less than 0.1 kg/kg air effective 2003. Require conversion or replacement of CFC-containing chillers at next overhaul effective 2005.

53. Canada has developed and implemented a National Action Plan ("NAP") for the Environmental Control of Ozone-Depleting Substances and their Halocarbon Alternatives to ensure that a national framework for the implementation of Canada's ozone layer protection program is realized. The NAP identifies tasks necessary to ensure that consistent, progressive actions take place to control all aspects of pollution prevention and all industry sectors using ozone-depleting substances and their halocarbon alternatives (HFCs and PFCs). The NAP was updated and approved by the Canadian Council of Ministers of the Environment in May 2001 to reflect the status of previous tasks and identify new tasks for the implementation of the Phase-Out Strategy. These new tasks include:

- Encouraging industry to develop Extended Producer Responsibility programmes and participate in their development;
- Developing and implementing control measures needed to support the extended producer responsibility programmes;
- Developing awareness programmes to inform stakeholders of the Phase-Out Strategy;

- Ensuring that control measures developed to implement the Phase-Out Strategy form a clear and comprehensive backdrop among jurisdictions; and,
- Implementing the sector specific control measures and other activities identified in the Phase-Out Strategy.

54. As part of the regulatory development process, amendments (SOR/2002-100) to the Ozone-Depleting Substances Regulations were published by the Minister of Environment in March 2002. These amendments:

- Abolish the current exemption for both human and animal health care products; and
- Establish a phase-out schedule for CFC inhalers.

55. More than 95% of commercial and residential air conditioning units and more than 50% of commercial refrigeration equipment in Canada operate on hydrochlorofluorocarbons ("HCFC") refrigerants (primarily R-22). Many commercial refrigeration units were converted to HCFCs from CFCs. By 1 January 2010, 65% of HCFC refrigerants currently imported into and manufactured in Canada on an annual basis will be eliminated from the supply chain and no HCFC-22 ("R-22") equipment will be manufactured in or imported into Canada. These important environmental steps could create significant service and maintenance issues for the refrigeration and air conditioning industry and their customers. Canada has adopted a phase-out schedule for HCFCs based on the terms of the 1987 Montreal Protocol. (See table on the following page).

Canada's Ozone Compliance Schedule

Date	Activity
Jan. 1, 1996	baseline annual allowable amount of HCFCs based on Montreal Protocol
Jan. 1, 2004	annual allowable amount of HCFCs reduced by 35%
Jan. 1, 2010	annual allowable amount of HCFCs reduced by 65%
Jan. 1, 2010	no new R-22 equipment manufactured or imported
Jan. 1, 2015	annual allowable amount of HCFCs reduced by 90%
Jan. 1, 2020	annual allowable amount of HCFCs reduced by 99.5% except HCFC-123, which can be imported or manufactured until 2030 to service large air conditioning units (chillers) under the remaining 0.5% allowance. No new HCFC equipment to be manufactured or imported.
Jan. 1, 2030	HCFCs no longer permitted to be imported or manufactured

3. South Africa

56. South Africa signed the Montreal Protocol in 1990, the 1990 London Amendment in 1992 and the 1992 Copenhagen Amendment in 2001. To date, South Africa has phased out CFCs, halons, methyl chloroform and carbon tetrachloride, the only developing country in the world that has achieved so much and in line with the phase-out schedule. Although South Africa is classified as a developing country, its consumption of these substances is equal to some of the developed countries. For this reason, South Africa did not hesitate to comply with the requirements of the Montreal Protocol. The following control measures constitute the overall position of South Africa on the Montreal Protocol:

- Working Groups were constituted under a neutral chairmanship to assist the government to implement the Montreal Protocol;
- Regulated ODS's can only be imported or exported after having obtained an import/export permit through the Department of Trade and Industry under their Import and Export Control Act, Act 45 of 1963;
- As a disincentive for the use of regulated ODS's, they could only be imported after an environmental levy of R5, 00 per kg of CFC, was paid;
- Dissemination of information to interested and affected parties is managed and controlled; and
- Contributions to Africa Networking Meetings, as arranged by UNEP, towards improvement and cooperation within the region, were established.

57. South Africa's National Committee on Ozone Layer Protection ("NCOLP") was created to advise the Department of Environmental Affairs and Tourism on matters relating to national responsibilities with respect to ozone layer protection, including monitoring and verification process or issues of implementation and adherence to the Vienna Convention and the 1987 Montreal Protocol and its Amendments, of which South Africa is signatory. Its purpose is also to promote education, training and awareness on ozone layer protection issues.

58. The NCOLP's functions include:

- Making recommendations to the Department on issues related to ozone layer protection and also to express the concerns of key stakeholders;
- Designing and participating in a process leading to the formulation and implementation of a national ozone layer protection strategies;
- Ensuring a structured process of capacity building;
- Assisting with coordination and exchange of information regarding the national activities;
- Assisting with the enhancement of the national awareness of this important environmental issues;
- Addressing the legislation to be in relation to ozone depleting substances; and
- Promoting objectives of NEPAD in relation to the ozone layer protection.

59. The NCOLP consists of many important stakeholder groups, including the national government, business and industry, labour, NGOs, academic institutions, scientists and the South African Weather Services. The group meets four times per year, unless additional meetings are urgently needed.

Prof. Alexandre Kiss, Director of Research, Centre for Environmental Law, Robert Schuman University, France

Eva Maria Duer, Associate Legal Expert, Division of Policy Development and Law, UNEP

Resources

Internet Materials

ENCYCLOPEDIA OF ATMOSPHERIC ENVIRONMENT, OZONE DEPLETION available at
http://www.doc.mmu.ac.uk/aric/eae/english.html

ENVIRONMENT CANADA STRATOSPHERIC OZONE WEB SITE available at http://www.ec.gc.ca/ozone/EN/index.cfm

INTEGRATING ENVIRONMENTAL CONSIDERATIONS INTO ECONOMIC POLICY MAKING PROCESSES ESCAP VIRTUAL CONFERENCE, MALAYSIA IMPLEMENTING MONTREAL PROTOCOL available at
http://www.unescap.org/drpad/vc/conference/ex_my_235_imp.htm

OZONE LAYER PROTECTION IN SOUTH AFRICA available at http://www.environment.gov.za/

OZONE SECRETARIAT available at http://www.unep.org/ozone

THE MONTREAL PROTOCOL ON SUBSTANCES THAT DEPLETE THE OZONE LAYER available at
http://www.unep.org/ozone/montreal.shtml

WHAT CAUSES OZONE DEPLETION? available at http://www.uow.edu.au/arts/sts/sbeder/HoleStory/intro/intro3.html

Text Material

Durwood Zaelke, Donald Kaniaru & Eva Kruzikova, MAKING LAW WORK ENVIRONMENTAL COMPLIANCE AND SUSTAINABLE DEVELOPMENT, (Cameroon May, 2005). In particular Chapter 3 Multilateral Environmental Agreements in action sub 3.2 Case Studies K. Madhava Sarma, Compliance with the Montreal Protocol.

10.   GLOBAL CLIMATE CHANGE

I. Introduction

1.   The Earth's climate is affected by the interaction of radiation from the sun and the Earth's atmosphere. The atmosphere consists of nitrogen and oxygen and a number of natural greenhouse gases (including carbon dioxide, methane, nitrous oxide, ozone gas, and chlorofluorocarbons ("CFCs")). The atmosphere and the surface of the Earth absorb part of the sun's radiation but the remainder is reflected back into space. The greenhouse gases have the important function of trapping this radiation in the lower layers of the Earth's atmosphere. This process is called the "greenhouse effect" without which the Earth would be as cold as the moon. It is now understood that increased concentrations of greenhouse gases in the atmosphere will increase this greenhouse effect and lead to changes in the Earth's climate.

2.   Natural events can also cause changes in the climate. For example, volcanic eruptions or variations in ocean currents can alter the distribution of heat and precipitation. The periodic warming of the central and eastern Pacific Ocean (better known as the *"El Niño"* phenomenon) can affect weather patterns around the world, causing heavy rains in some places and drought in others.

3.   Human activities are now recognized as contributing to climate change. During recent years, scientists have been able to collect evidence of changes in temperature, rainfall and other weather variables. This data suggests that over the twentieth century the average world temperature increased by 0.6° Celsius. The data also demonstrates an increase in the quantity of greenhouse gases in the atmosphere of up to 30%, especially carbon dioxide.

4.   Carbon dioxide ("CO_2") is partly produced as a result of human activities such as burning coal, oil and natural gas ("fossil fuels"), as well as agricultural activities and deforestation. CFCs and methane are also being emitted to the atmosphere as a result of human activities. The increase in the emission of these greenhouse gases can be attributed to the general economic growth which has taken place since the industrial revolution, especially after the 1950s, as well as increased levels of consumption, including the increased demand for electricity and the use of cars.

5.   Oceans and forests can absorb CO_2 and other greenhouse gases, and are therefore referred to as greenhouse gas "sinks." Deforestation, however, releases previously stored greenhouse gases, thus contributing further to the increase of greenhouse gases in the Earth's atmosphere.

6.   Most greenhouse gases remain in the atmosphere for a long period of time. This means that even if emissions from human activities were to stop immediately, the effects of the emissions already accumulated may persist for centuries. Though the temperature increase over the last century has been relatively moderate at around 0.6° Celsius, scientists estimate that the global average surface temperature could rise by between 1.4° to 5.8° Celsius over the next 100 years.

7.   Such a significant increase in the average world temperature will lead to serious impacts on the environment. Climate change experts predict that this global warming will cause increased rainfall in many areas, increased desertification in others, and the loss of ice cover in the polar regions. The average sea level is predicted to rise by up to eighty-eight centimetres by the end of the twenty-first century, posing a serious threat to low lying delta systems and small island states.

8.   Global warming will also have impacts on natural vegetation and fauna. Seasonal patterns will change, leading to longer and hotter summers. Some species will not be able to adapt well to this change of environment and may slowly die out. The most serious consequence is likely to be the impacts on agriculture and thus food safety, especially due to increased water shortages.

9.   While there has been some debate over the degree to which human influenced emissions have contributed to climate change, there is now general consensus that concerted action needs to be taken to minimize and mitigate the problems which global warming is starting to cause.

II. International Framework

1. The Climate Change Convention Regime

10.   International conferences on the phenomenon of global warming were first held in the 1980s. In 1988, the UN General Assembly determined that "climate change is a common concern of mankind" which required urgent action by all states. This initiated political negotiations, which led to the completion of an international convention regime to address the issue.

11. Around the same time, the United Nations Environmental Program ("UNEP") and the World Meteorological Organization ("WMO") established and still cosponsor an independent scientific body called the Intergovernmental Panel on Climate Change ("IPCC"). This body consists of over 2000 scientific and technical experts from around the world who collect scientific information about the causes of climate change, its potential effects and possible ways to mitigate these effects. The IPCC issued its First Assessment Report in 1990, describing the likely threats of climate change, and subsequently produced its Second Assessment Report in 1995, and Third Assessment Report in 2001. The IPCC is currently working on a Fourth Assessment Report, and its findings continue to inform international action to combat climate change. This Report will be completed in 2007.

12. The negotiation process for the climate change regime has proved to be one of the most challenging in the history of Multilateral Environmental Agreements ("MEAs"). Most developing countries have been unwilling to take on onerous commitments, arguing that it was mainly the developed states which had contributed to the increase in global warming as part of their economic development. The tates most threatened by the effects of global warming, such as small island tates, have argued for strong and effective commitments. However, several developed states were concerned about the impact a firm commitment to reducing emissions would have on their economies. Despite these different positions, public concern was strong enough to motivate political leaders towards achieving an international regime to address the problem.

13. By 1992, sufficient scientific and political consensus had been reached to allow 154 states to sign the United Nations Framework Convention on Climate Change ("1992 UNFCCC") ("Convention"). Key to the Convention's completion was the explicit reliance on the concept of 'common but differentiated responsibilities'. This concept allowed commitments to be fixed according to the economic status of each country with the result that, at present, only developed states and countries with economies in transition have a fixed obligation to achieve specified emission reductions. These countries are detailed in Annex I of the 1992 UNFCCC ("Annex I Parties"). In contrast, developing countries can voluntarily take on commitments to limit emissions, but are not required to do so. However, all state parties to the Convention are obliged to develop national programmes in order to generally mitigate the causes and effects of climate change. The key stages in the complex and protracted negotiation process are summarized below:

Key Stages in the Climate Change Convention Regime

1988	UNGA Resolution 43/53 recognizes climate change a "common concern of mankind".
1988	UNEP and WMO establish the Intergovernmental Panel on Climate Change ("IPCC").
1990	The UN launches negotiations on a framework convention on climate change.
1992	The United Nations Framework Convention on Climate Change is adopted in New York and opened for signature at the Earth Summit in Rio de Janeiro, Brazil; the Convention receives 154 signatures and enters into force in 1994.
1995	The first Conference of the Parties ("COP-1") in Berlin, Germany launches a new round of negotiations to strengthen the targets of Annex I Parties ("Berlin Mandate"). IPCC Second Assessment Report concludes that the balance of evidence indicates a discernable human influence on the global climate.
1996	COP-2 in Geneva, Switzerland clarifies the scope of the Berlin Mandate.
1997	COP-3 Kyoto, Japan, adopts the Kyoto Protocol.
1998	COP-4 Buenos Aires, Argentina adopts the 'Buenos Aires Plan of Action' setting out a program of work on the Kyoto Protocol's operational rules and the implementation of the Convention; the deadline for achieving these rules is set for 2000.
2000	COP-6 meets at the Hague but negotiations break down.

2001	January: the IPCC Third Assessment Report is released.

March: US President George W Bush announces that the United States will not become a Party to the Kyoto Protocol.

July: At the resumed session of COP-6 Parties adopt the 'Bonn Agreements,' a political deal on the Kyoto Protocol rules and the implementation of the Convention.

November: COP-7 in Marrakesh, Morocco adopts the 'Marrakesh Accords,' a set of detailed rules for the Kyoto Protocol and the implementation of the Convention.

2002	The World Summit on Sustainable Development ("WSSD") meets in Johannesburg, South Africa, to review progress since the 1992 Earth Summit.

COP-8 in New Delhi, India, seeks to clarify the rules of the regime.

2003	At least 55 states ratify the Kyoto Protocol, but the necessary 55% of total CO_2 emissions is still to be achieved, so that the Protocol is still not in force.

COP-9 in Milan, Italy, continues to consider the rules of the regime.

2004	Russia ratifies the Kyoto Protocol, allowing the Protocol to come into force 16.02.2005.

COP-10 in Buenos Aires, Argentina.

The Convention receives 189 instruments of ratification (August 2005).

2005	Kyoto Protocol enters into force, as of August 2005 there are 155 parties.

COP-11 and COP-1 of the Kyoto Protocol take place in Montreal. A Working Group was established to discuss future commitments for developed countries for the period after 2012.

Abbreviation: COP (Conference of the Parties, the annual meeting of Parties under the Convention).

2. The United Nations Framework Convention on Climate Change ("1992 UNFCCC")

14. The objective of the 1992 UNFCCC is to tackle the negative effects of climate change. The Convention's stated aim is to stabilize greenhouse gas concentration at a level that allows ecosystems to adapt naturally to climate change so that food production is not threatened, while enabling economic development to proceed in a sustainable manner (article 2).

15. In achieving this aim, the parties to the Convention are to be guided by a range of principles that reflect the understanding of global environmental responsibility elaborated in the Rio Declaration on Environment and Development and Agenda 21. These principles include inter-generational equity, the precautionary approach, the right to sustainable development and, as mentioned above, the principle of common but differentiated responsibilities (article 3).

16. The Convention provides that all parties make general commitments regarding:

- The establishment of national inventories of greenhouse gas emissions and sinks;

- The promotion of scientific and technical cooperation;
- The sustainable management of forests, oceans and ecosystems; and
- The integration of climate change considerations in national social, economic and environmental policies (article 4(1)).

17. Certain parties to 1992 UNFCCC, classified as Annex I parties, have taken on additional commitments. Annex I parties include industrialized nations that have committed to return their anthropogenic emissions to 1990 levels by 2000. To this end, the Annex I parties are required to adopt national policies and measures to mitigate the negative effects of climate change by both limiting the emission of greenhouse gases and by protecting greenhouse gas sinks. However, the wording of the 1992 UNFCCC is considered to be rather vague and the extent to which it represents a binding obligation has therefore been questioned (article 4(2)).

18. In meeting these commitments, parties are able to take account of their different starting points, resources, economies and other individual circumstances. Parties may also jointly implement the policies and measures. In order to monitor

progress, the Parties are required to deliver reports covering the ongoing implementation of their policies and measures and their projected emission levels (article 12(1)). In recognition of the fact that these commitments are only the first step in addressing the problem of climate change, the Convention provides for the review of the adequacy of the commitments at an early stage, and then at regular intervals (article 4(2)(d)). This provision led to the further negotiations on setting the specific emission reduction targets found in the 1997 Kyoto Protocol.

19. The Conference of the Parties ("COP") to the Convention serves as the principal supervisory institution for the Convention, and meets regularly to review the adequacy, implementation and effectiveness of the Convention and the Kyoto Protocol. The COP receives advice from the Subsidiary Body for Scientific and Technological Advice ("SBSTA") which reviews and advises on the state of scientific and technical knowledge (article 9), and the Supplementary Body for Implementation ("SBI"), which makes recommendations on policy and implementation issues (article 10). A Secretariat provides organizational support and technical expertise for the COP negotiations, and facilitates the flow of authoritative information on the implementation of the Convention. Now that the Kyoto Protocol has entered into force, the COP may also serve as the formal Meeting of the Parties ("MOP") for the Protocol, referred to as the "COP/MOP". The first meeting of the MOP was held together with COP-11 in November-December 2005.

a) Capacity building and financial mechanism

20. Article 4 of the Convention includes important provisions dealing with capacity building in order to encourage compliance by developing country parties. A range of measures is identified, including the provision of "new and additional" financial resources, the transfer of technology and support for national reporting. Article 4(5) of the Convention states that the developed country parties "shall take all practicable steps to promote, facilitate and finance, as appropriate, the transfer of, or access to, environmentally sound technologies and know-how to other Parties, particularly developing country Parties, to enable them to implement the provisions of the Convention..."

21. The Convention's financial mechanism, provided for in article 11, is designed to be a major source of such funding. Its role is to transfer funds and technology to developing countries on a grant or concessional basis. The mechanism is guided by and accountable to the COP, which decides on policies, programme priorities, and eligibility criteria. The Convention states that the operation of the financial mechanism can be entrusted to one or more international entities with "an equitable and balanced representation of all Parties within a transparent system of governance." The COP has delegated this responsibility to the Global Environment Facility ("GEF") (for more discussion on this see chapter 6), an independent financial institution which provides grants to developing countries for environmental projects.

22. In July 2001, the COP created three new funds to further assist developing countries. A Special Climate Change Fund ("SCCF") and a Least Developed Countries Fund ("LDCF") have been established under the Convention to help developing countries adapt to climate change impacts, obtain clean technologies and limit the growth in their emissions. In addition, an Adaptation Fund was under the 1997 Kyoto Protocol to finance concrete adaptation projects and programmes. The COP would guide this Fund until the 1997 Kyoto Protocol enters into force. The industrialized countries, listed in Annex II of the Protocol, also pledged to make a combined contribution of ¤450 million per year by 2005 through these funds and existing avenues to help developing countries manage their emissions and adapt to climate change.

b) Compliance and Dispute Settlement

23. The Convention establishes three steps to manage compliance: reporting; review; and assessing and responding to non-compliance. This process is overseen by the COP. It also allows for the creation of a multilateral consultative process for the parties to resolve questions of implementation (article 13). The compliance process has been developed under the 1997 Kyoto Protocol, details of which are discussed below.

24. The Convention also contains relatively standard international dispute settlement provisions under article 14, which are similar to those found under the 1985 Vienna Convention/1987 Montreal Protocol. In the case of a dispute between any two or more parties concerning the interpretation or application of the 1992 UNFCCC, the Parties concerned are to seek a settlement of the dispute through negotiation or any other peaceful means of their own choice. Recourse can also be taken in certain circumstances to arbitration or the International Court of Justice.

3. The Kyoto Protocol to the United Nations Framework Convention on Climate Change ("1997 Kyoto Protocol")

a) The Negotiations

25. At the first COP ("COP-1") held in Berlin in 1995, the parties to the 1992 UNFCCC recognized that in light of further scientific evidence (most prominently the Second Assessment Report released by the IPCC), the commitments in the Convention were "not adequate" to achieve its goal. The outcome of this COP provided a strong political mandate ("the Berlin Mandate") for strengthening the commitments in the Convention, which led to the adoption of the text of the first Protocol to the Convention at the third COP ("COP-3") in Kyoto, in December 1997.

26. Although agreement was reached on the specific terms of the Kyoto Protocol to the United Nations Framework Convention on Climate Change ("1997 Kyoto Protocol"), many crucial technical and political issues were left unresolved, including, for example, emissions trading and the use of 'sinks'. Most countries felt they could not ratify the 1997 Kyoto Protocol until these issues were settled. After further negotiations, the Buenos Aires Plan of Action was adopted at COP-4 in 1998. This Plan set out a programme of work on the 1997 Kyoto Protocol operational rules and the implementation of the 1992 UNFCCC, which was scheduled for finalization in 2000.

27. The outstanding issues continued to prove highly controversial, and negotiations eventually broke down at COP-6 in the Hague. In 2001, President Bush officially announced that the United States, the world's largest emitter of CO_2, would not ratify the 1997 Kyoto Protocol on the basis that it would be detrimental to the country's economy and did not include binding emission reductions for developing countries. Despite this, the negotiation process was reassumed and culminated in 2001, with the achievement of political agreement in the Bonn Agreements, which allowed completion of the Marrakesh Accords later that year.

28. The Marrakesh Accords contain extensive and complex provisions to guide the practical implementation of the 1997 Kyoto Protocol. These provisions cover the 'flexible mechanisms', the establishment of a compliance mechanism and the elaboration of rules on permissible land-use, land-use change and forestry ("LULUCF"). The Marrakesh Accords also consolidate matters under the Convention relating to funding arrangements and capacity building for developing countries.

The following description of the main aspects of the 1997 Kyoto Protocol therefore includes reference to the provisions of the Marrakesh Accords where appropriate.

b) Commitments

29. As intended by the Berlin Mandate, the 1997 Kyoto Protocol covers the period beyond the year 2000 and requires stronger commitments from Annex I parties to achieve quantified emission reductions within a specific timeframe. These commitments cover the six greenhouse gases listed in Annex A of the 1997 Kyoto Protocol (carbon dioxide, methane, nitrous oxide, hydrofluorocarbons, perfluorocarbons and sulphur hexafluoride), and each Annex I party's particular 'quantified emission reduction target' is listed in Annex B. These targets are designed to ensure that combined emissions from these 'Annex B parties' are reduced to at least 5% below 1990 levels between 2008 and 2012. However, since emission levels have risen substantially since 1990, this measure is still unlikely to stabilize human induced global warming.

30. In accordance with article 4(2) of the Convention, differentiated targets were set for Annex B parties taking into account their particular circumstances, including for example their ability to access clean technology. The differentiated emission reduction targets were based on 1990 emission levels, and range from an 8% reduction for the EU to a 10% increase for Iceland (called "assigned amounts"). Changes in land use or forest plantations which result in emission reductions can also be used in principle to meet a party's emission reduction target, provided such changes do result in a real reduction (the 'sinks' must become permanent). Emissions of greenhouse gases other than carbon dioxide are converted to carbon dioxide-equivalent emissions by using Global Warming Potential factors published by the IPCC.

31. All Annex B parties are obliged to make demonstrable progress in meeting their emission reduction targets by 2005. However, the 1997 Kyoto Protocol does not actually prescribe how the targets are to be achieved. Instead, a range of indicative measures are proposed, such as:

- Promoting energy efficiency
- Promoting renewable energy
- Phasing out subsidies that contravene the objectives of the Convention
- Protecting and enhancing sinks
- Promoting sustainable forms of agriculture

32. Under Article 4 of the 1997 Kyoto Protocol, two or more Annex B parties can jointly fulfil their commitments by aggregating their emissions. As long as the total amount of emissions is within the total assigned amount limits of those parties as a group, it does not matter that some members have exceeded their individual limits.

c) The Flexible Mechanisms

33. In order to facilitate implementation of the commitments described above, the 1997 Kyoto Protocol provides for the use of an innovative set of tools, called the "flexible mechanisms," designed to help the Annex I parties maximize the cost-efficiency of meeting their emission reduction targets. These flexible mechanisms allow state parties (and authorized private or public sector organizations or businesses) to reduce emissions by undertaking projects in other countries or by trading in emission reduction credits, and then counting these reductions towards their own emission reduction targets. The use of the flexible mechanisms is subject to the condition that the emission reductions achieved are supplemental to national action to reduce emissions. The 1997 Kyoto Protocol establishes three flexible mechanisms: Joint Implementation ("JI"), the Clean Development Mechanism ("CDM") and Emissions Trading ("ET").

34. Joint Implementation, as outlined in article 6, provides that one Annex I party can receive credits for financially supporting (and therefore jointly implementing) appropriate projects to reduce emissions in another Annex I party. Such projects result in the generation of "Emission Reduction Units" ("ERUs"), which can be used by the first Annex I party to meet its own 1997 Kyoto Protocol target. This flexible mechanism is designed to encourage the transfer of technology and to promote energy efficiency or forest conservation schemes. However, the reductions must be 'additional' to any that would have otherwise occurred and must also be supplemental to domestic action.

35. A Supervisory Committee ("SC") will be elected at the first COP/MOP to oversee the operation of JI projects. Projects which started after 1 January 2000 are still eligible as authorized JI projects, though valid ERUs will only be issued for the emission reductions achieved after 1 January 2008.

36. In order to be eligible to take part in a Joint Implementation project, a country must:

- Be an Annex I party and a party to the 1997 Kyoto Protocol;

- Have an assigned amount that has been calculated and recorded;
- Have a national registry in place;
- Have in place a national system for estimating greenhouse gas emissions;
- Have submitted annual greenhouse gas inventory reports; and
- Have submitted necessary supplementary information on its assigned amount.

37. Following decisions taken at COP-7, there will be two kinds of JI projects ("twin track"). Track 1 covers projects where a 'host' party meets all the JI eligibility requirements listed above. In this case, the host country can certify the ERUs itself without recourse to the Supervisory Committee. Track 2 covers projects where a host party only meets the first three JI eligibility requirements. Here the procedures are determined by the SC. The ERUs achieved in any JI project must be independently certified by approved organizations called "Independent Entities."

38. The Clean Development Mechanism is designed to encourage emission-reduction projects that assist in achieving sustainable development in developing countries. Using this mechanism, an Annex I party can invest in appropriate projects in non-Annex I parties, leading to the generation of Certified Emission Reductions ("CERs"). The CDM, established under article 12 of the 1997 Kyoto Protocol, is the only flexible mechanism open to participation by developing States.

39. Under the CDM, Annex I parties receive credit for achieving greenhouse gas emission reductions in non-Annex I countries through financial investment or technology transfer. In order to encourage a 'prompt start' to the CDM, CERs obtained during the period from the year 2000 up to the end of the first commitment period in 2008 can be used in achieving compliance for the first commitment period. An Executive Board ("EB") has been set up to oversee the operation of the CDM.

40. In order to participate in the Clean Development Mechanism, a host country must have ratified the 1997 Kyoto Protocol and set up a designated national authority to oversee the approval of the project. This national authority must decide whether a CDM project activity contributes to sustainable development in the host country, and whether the participants have voluntarily agreed to be involved in the project.

41. For the Certified Emission Reductions to be valid, the project's funding must be in addition to existing

development aid provided by the Annex I party, and the CERs achieved by the CDM project must be in addition to those that would have occurred without the project. For this purpose, project baselines have to be developed, which describe the most likely course of development and the situation that would have prevailed in the absence of the CDM project. A project methodology (including the baseline) must be approved for each project. Alternatively, an existing approved methodology can be adopted. A list of proposed and approved CDM methodologies can be found at the website of the UNFCCC.

42. A template for the CDM Project Design Document ("PDD"), which the project participants must prepare to get CDM project approval, is also available at the UNFCCC website. The first CDM projects are currently in the process of being approved.

43. Once prepared, the PDD must be validated by an independent Designated Operational Entity ("DOE"), which has been accredited by the EB (and which in practice will usually be a financial auditing firm). The PDD must then be sent for registration by the EB, together with confirmation from the host country that the project activity will assist in achieving sustainable development and that the host country voluntarily agrees to participate in the project. The CDM project will then be able to proceed, during which it must be monitored by the project participants, and also independently reviewed from time to time. At the end of the CDM project, a DOE must certify the resultant CERs by subtracting the emissions achieved from the previously approved baseline emissions (subject to taking account of "leakage"). Once the certified CERs are verified, they can be allocated on the basis agreed between the project participants and issued by the registry of the CDM to be offset against a country's emissions reduction target.

44. Article 17 of the 1997 Kyoto Protocol allows Annex B Parties to undertake emissions trading internationally by buying emission reduction credits from another Annex B country in the form of Assigned Amount Units ("AAUs"). Each AAU represents the "right" of that country to emit one ton of CO_2 (or its equivalent in the form of other greenhouse gases). A party that has achieved more emission reductions than it is obliged to achieve under its target under the 1997 Kyoto Protocol can therefore sell the additional credits to a party that might otherwise fail to meet its emissions target. National entities (such as individuals or companies) can also participate in the trading of

emission reduction units if authorized by a state party.

45. In order to be eligible to participate in Emissions Trading, parties have to fulfil the reporting requirements. Each country is obliged to keep a reserve that cannot be traded under article 17 of the Protocol, and should not be allowed to drop beyond 90% of each party's assigned amount. Any such trading must also be supplemental to domestic emission reduction programmes. The option of international emissions trading will be available from 2008, though action has already being taken to set up a trading system in the European Union (see below).

46. A 'sink' stores atmospheric carbon in a carbon 'pool.' Examples of carbon pools are forest biomass, wood products and soils. The inclusion of carbon sinks in the 1997 Kyoto Protocol has been very controversial. Article 3 of the 1997 Kyoto Protocol provides that parties must count both the sequestration (storage) and the emission of greenhouse gases from eligible land use change and forestry activities ("LULUCF"), in measuring performance towards their 1997 Kyoto Protocol targets.

47. Only net changes from human induced activities relating to afforestation, reforestation or deforestation can be legitimately counted. Parties are required to account for the net changes on which they are relying in meeting their commitments, and must include emissions from land use change in the baseline used for calculating their assigned amounts. Some parties have wanted to include additional types of sinks, but it was agreed during negotiations on the 1997 Kyoto Protocol that this would have to be decided at a later stage.

48. Further rules on LULUCF were agreed at COP-7 in Marrakesh, where a new trading unit, a Removal Unit ("RMU"), was created specifically for sink credits. It will be possible to convert RMUs into, for example, Emission Reduction Units ("ERUs"). Nevertheless the serial number of each ERU will include information about the LULUCF activity for which it was issued, and this identification will remain even when the RMU is converted into an ERU. General principles governing the validity of LULUCF activities were also confirmed at COP-7, as follows:

• The assessment of LULUCF activities should be based on 'sound science';
• Consistent methodologies are to be used for estimating and reporting these activities;

- The mere presence of carbon stocks is to be excluded from accounting, as are increased removals due to faster growth caused by increasing concentrations of atmospheric CO_2;
- Any reversals of LULUCF removals are to be accounted for at the appropriate time; and
- LULUCF activities must contribute to biodiversity conservation and the sustainable use of natural resources.

49. The quality of greenhouse gas inventory reporting is the cornerstone of the compliance system. The reporting rules provided under the Convention and the 1997 Kyoto Protocol have therefore been designed to facilitate transparency, comparability, completeness and accuracy of information. Review of reported information is undertaken in two steps. First, there is a technical check conducted by the Secretariat to compile and synthesize the information reported by each Party. The second step involves an in-depth review by Expert Review Teams that have been set up to ensure objectivity and fairness.

50. The 1997 Kyoto Protocol draws on and enhances the approach to compliance adopted under the Convention. Article 18 of the 1997 Kyoto Protocol specifically provides for the negotiation of a detailed non-compliance procedure; and in 1998, a Joint Working Group on compliance was established to formulate a sufficiently robust means of ensuring that the Protocol's emission reduction targets are achieved.

4. Compliance Mechanism – Compliance Committee

51. Compliance was one of the most contentious issues at COP-7 in Marrakesh, but the parties eventually adopted compliance procedures which represent the 'teeth' of the climate change regime. The Marrakesh Accords provide for the creation of a new institution, the Compliance Committee, charged with promoting compliance, providing advise and assistance to the parties, determining cases of non-compliance and applying appropriate "consequences" for non-compliance.

52. The Compliance Committee will have two branches; a 'Facilitative Branch' and a more judicial-like 'Enforcement Branch.' The Facilitative Branch will provide advise and assistance on the implementation of the Kyoto Protocol, giving out 'early-warnings' in cases where a party is in danger of not complying with its emission reduction target. The Facilitative Branch will be able to make recommendations and mobilize financial and technical resources to help the party comply. The Enforcement Branch will determine whether an Annex I party has met its emissions target,

complied with its monitoring and reporting requirements, and met the eligibility tests for participation in the flexible mechanisms.

53. The compliance procedures will be triggered primarily by the results of the review of Parties' annual reports; and a Bureau of the Compliance Committee will be responsible for allocating questions of implementation to the appropriate branch. The Enforcement Branch makes decisions by double majority voting, so that majorities from each bloc of the members of a branch (i.e., both Annex I and non-Annex I parties) must approve it. Public participation in the proceedings will be possible. If a party feels that it has been denied due process during the enforcement proceedings, it can lodge an appeal with the COP/MOP.

54. When a party does not comply with the monitoring and reporting requirements of the 1997 Kyoto Protocol, the Enforcement Branch can require the relevant party to submit an action plan that includes an analysis of the causes of non-compliance, undertake corrective measures to remedy the non-compliance, and set a timetable for the implementation of the action plan. If an Annex I party is not in compliance with the eligibility requirements for the Protocol's flexible mechanism, the Enforcement Branch will be able to order the suspension of the Party's eligibility to participate in the mechanisms until the party has achieved compliance.

55. If an Annex I party fails to meet it emission reduction target, the Enforcement Branch will be able to apply the following consequences:

- For every ton of emissions by which a party exceeds its target, 1.3 tons can be deducted from its emissions allocation (assigned amount) for the subsequent compliance period;
- The party will have to prepare a detailed plan explaining how it will meet its reduced target for the subsequent compliance period; and
- The party will not be able to use international emissions trading to sell any of its emissions allocation until it has demonstrated that it will be able to comply with its current target.

56. It is clear therefore that the compliance regime of the 1997 Kyoto Protocol could be very hard hitting and it has certainly set a new precedent in the level of control that could be applied to States under Multilateral Environmental Agreements ("MEAs").

57. Per article 25 the 1997 Kyoto Protocol would enter into force on the ninetieth day after the date that two conditions are fulfilled:

- Fifty-five countries have ratified the Protocol;
- Sufficient Annex I countries to account for at least fifty-five percent of the total CO_2 emissions from Annex I countries in 1990 have ratified the Protocol.

The ratification of Russian Federation, deposited on 18 November 2004, secured that the Protocol entered into force on 16 February 2005.

III. National Implementation

58. With a detailed international regime almost in place, it is worthwhile considering the manner in which the obligations in the 1992 UNFCCC and the 1997 Kyoto Protocol are being or would be addressed in a national context.

1. Europe

59. As mentioned above, the European Community ("EC") has formed a "bubble" in order to fulfil the respective commitments of its member states, by aggregating their combined emissions as provided for under article 4 of the 1997 Kyoto Protocol. The EC joined the Convention as a party in its own right, and has to report annually on all greenhouse gas emissions within its area of jurisdiction. The EC greenhouse gas inventory includes data for the EC as a whole ("EU15") as well as the individual member states, and has to be submitted annually to the Convention Secretariat. Within the framework of a 'burden sharing agreement' concluded in 1998, the member states have taken on the following individual targets:

Burden-Sharing Targets in the EU

Country	% Targets Below 1990 Levels to be Achieved Between 2008 and 2012
Austria	-13
Belgium	-7.5
Denmark	-21
Finland	0
France	0
Germany	-21
Greece	25
Ireland	13
Italy	-6.5
Luxembourg	-28
Netherlands	-6
Portugal	27
Spain	15
Sweden	4
UK	-12.5

60. In combination, the target for the EU as a whole is to achieve emission reductions of 8% below 1990 levels between 2008 and 2012.

Emission Trading

61. In response to article 17, the Member States adopted the European Union Emissions Trading Scheme Directive ("EU ETS") in July 2003. It is intended that the EU ETS will cover twenty-eight European countries, including the existing fifteen EU Member States, the ten new accession countries as well as Norway, Liechtenstein and Switzerland. It will be the world's first multinational emissions allowance trading scheme for major CO_2 emitters, and may serve as a template for emissions trading schemes covering companies and individuals in other regions.

62. Under the EU ETS each member state will have to impose binding caps on emissions of CO_2 from installations within their jurisdiction involved in:

- Energy activities;
- Production and processing of ferrous metals;
- The mineral industry (e.g., cement, glass or ceramic production); and
- Pulp, paper or board production.

63. Under the Integrated Pollution Prevention and Control ("IPPC") Directive (96/61/EC), each operator of such an installation that carries out activities above the relevant threshold is already required to hold an IPPC permit. The EU ETS Directive will require that each such operator also holds a site-specific and non-transferable GHG Permit. Under this permit, the operator will be obliged to hold emission allowances in its compliance account in the member state's national registry which at least equals the actual GHG emissions emitted by the installations, as reported and verified.

64. Each member state has to develop National Allocation Plans ("NAPs"), which will allocate allowances for each individual installation, thereby setting an emissions cap. The Commission will retain a right of veto over NAPs, restricting individual member states' discretion in setting targets and allocations.

65. The first period of trading will take effect between 2005 and 2007. The second period, operating from 2008 to 2012, coincides with the first commitment period under the 1997 Kyoto Protocol. Further trading periods of five years beyond 2012 are envisaged in the Directive and will be framed according to international agreement on future emissions reductions.

66. Substantial penalties will be imposed in the case of failure to meet an emissions cap. In the first period, this will be ¤40 for each ton of CO_2 by which an installation exceeds its emission cap (rising to ¤100 in the second period). However, the installations concerned will be able to trade EU emission allowances credits in order to achieve compliance. These EU allowances will be a common carbon currency recognized in all member states, which will enable companies to trade them across the whole of the EU. Whether this EU allowance will be considered to be a distinct unit or an Assigned Amount Unit under the 1997 Kyoto Protocol is yet to be seen.

67. Under the Directive, a system of registries has to be established to govern the use of these EU allowances. This will allow the holding and transfer of all EU allowances, as well as Protocol units and units recognized by a member state's domestic trading scheme) to be recorded in each member state in order to achieve a transparent and efficient trading market.

68. As described above, Emission Reduction Units ("ERUs") generated by JI projects, Certified Emission Reductions ("CERs") generated by CDM projects and Removal Units ("RMUs") generated pursuant to LULUCF may be used by Annex I parties to assist in meeting their emission reduction commitments under the Kyoto Protocol. If such units are given recognition within the EU ETS, then the credits generated by JI or CDM projects could also be used by operators (as well as sovereign states) to fulfill their domestic obligations under the EU ETS. The linking of JI and CDM projects to the EU ETS is therefore considered important in creating a global market demand for emission reduction credits, and the EU Commission adopted a proposal for an amendment to the EU ETS to provide for this in July 2003.

69. Upon joining the EU in 2004, the first wave of accession countries are also agreeing to be legally bound by the EU ETS. In addition, Switzerland, Norway and Liechtenstein have expressed their interest in linking their emissions trading schemes to the EU ETS. A clear European price for 'carbon' is expected to emerge as the volume of trade expands. The establishment of an effective emissions trading market under the EU ETS and similar schemes could well be key to successfully achieving the main goal of the Convention, which is to stabilize the impacts of climate change.

2. Japan

70. Having chaired the important COP-3 in Kyoto, Japan ratified the Kyoto Protocol at the beginning of June 2002. Japan is obliged to reduce its overall emissions of greenhouse gases by six percent below 1990 levels in the first commitment period from 2008 to 2012. Since Japan's energy efficiency is already of a high standard, it may not be straightforward for Japan to achieve this goal.

71. Subsequent to COP-3, Japan established its Global Warming Prevention Headquarters where it produced its Guidelines for Measures to prevent Global Warming ("Guidelines") in 1998, which were revised in March 2002. The Guidelines set out the following main principles governing Japan's action on addressing climate change:

- Balance between the environment and the economy: Japan wishes to foster technological innovation and creative initiatives in business circles and to link efforts to prevent global warming to encourage economic revitalization and employment creation;
- Step-by-step approach: Japan has undertaken to assess and review progress on measures it is taking at regular intervals and to implement these measures step by step. The Global Warming Prevention Headquarters intends to carry out a further review of the Guidelines in 2004 and 2007;
- Promotion of combined effort by all sectors of society: Japan recognized that it will not be straightforward for it to achieve its Kyoto Protocol target and it is therefore considered essential that all national stakeholders join forces in their respective roles to achieve this goal. Voluntary business initiatives are considered to be of the highest importance, as well as measures to be taken in the residential, commercial and transportation sectors; and
- Ensuring international cooperation to prevent global warming: Japan is committed to making the utmost effort to establish a common regime in which all countries (including the United States and developing countries) will participate.

72. The measures in the Guidelines cover each type of greenhouse gas (including CO_2 emissions methane, HFCs, PFC and SF6). The following paragraphs provide details of the measures that Japan has implemented in relation to CO_2 emissions.

73. In order to promote reductions in CO_2 emissions, Japan's measures concentrate on energy supply and demand. On the demand side, Japan currently applies measures in the industrial, residential, commercial and transportation sectors. On the supply side, the measures focus on new energy, nuclear power and fuel switching. The new energy

measures include the promotion of photovoltaic power generation and support by way of taxation and financing.

74. Fossil fuels still account for about 83% of the total primary energy supply in Japan. Fuel switching is therefore considered to be an important tool to promote efficient energy supply. For example, the conversion of industrial coal-fired boilers to natural gas, or promoting the conversion of old coal-fired power generation to efficient natural gas combined cycle power generation. New energies are being promoted including solar energy, solar thermal utilization, wind power generation, waste power generation and biomass energy. Legislation concerning the promotion of the use of new energy is planned, as well as the introduction of safety standards for gas pipelines.

75. In relation to sinks, the Guidelines provide for measures covering the development of healthy forests through planting, weeding and thinning, the promotion of the use of wood and wood biomass and the promotion of urban greening.

76. The Steering Committee of the Global Warming Prevention Headquarters have developed guidelines for the approval of projects relating to Joint Implementation in its Decision "Institutional Arrangements in Japan for Utilization of the Kyoto Mechanisms" of July 2002. The Ministry of the Environment Japan also intends to establish a domestic support centre, which will collect and consolidate general and specific information for those who wish to participate in the Flexible Mechanisms of the 1997 Kyoto Protocol. The support centre will collect information about potential host countries including their project needs; legal validity and supporting methodology; and the availability of technology and finance to the project participants.

3. China

77. China's ratification of the 1997 Kyoto Protocol was announced at the 2002 Johannesburg World Summit for Sustainable Development ("WSSD"). Although China has not accepted a mandatory emissions reduction target under the 1997 Kyoto Protocol, Chinese governmental agencies have been working to define and develop programmes to reduce carbon emissions in cooperation with international partners.

78. China's State Development and Planning Commission, Ministry of Science and Technology, State Economic and Trade Commission and Ministry of Foreign Affairs have jointly prepared draft guidelines for setting up a National Clean Development Mechanism Management Office.

The State Council formally issued these guidelines at the end of 2002, and has sought funding from numerous multilateral and international donors for capacity building and technical programmes related to the CDM programme.

79. China intends to have a one-stop CDM project approval process. The four governmental agencies mentioned above will form an inter-ministry CDM Project Review Board, which will be the decision-making body for CDM projects and policy. A CDM Secretariat/Administrative Centre will serve the Board and carry out daily administrative work. The Board will ideally review each proposal within a week to ten days, before forwarding each project to a Minister or Vice Minister for final approval. The senior official approving each project will be responsible for issuing approval letters to project participants.

80. China has had significant interaction with several other countries on CDM-related projects, with Canada being its most active international partner. Canada's International Development Agency ("CIDA") has already applied US $11.5 million to fund six projects related to capacity building and technology transfer, in order to help China kick-start its CDM process. Canada has also made an additional U.S. $3.2 million available for projects in China, to be implemented through the Canada Trust Fund on Climate Change managed by the Asian Development Bank ("ADB"). ADB and CIDA have so far implemented a handful of small-scale renewable energy and energy efficiency projects in Gansu and Guangxi. The Gansu projects focus on small-scale hydroelectric and solar energy facilities, while the Guangxi projects involve energy efficiency, animal waste, biomass and industrial innovation.

Michael Woods LLM, Senior Research Fellow, Centre for Law and Environment, University College of London

Eva Maria Duer, Associate Legal Expert, Division of Policy Development and Law, UNEP

Resources

Internet Materials

CANADA'S NATIONAL CLIMATE CHANGE PROCESS available at http://www.nccp.ca/NCCP/index_e.html
This site contains information about how the Canadian government is responding to climate change. Many of the federal, provincial and territorial governments in Canada have built a National Implementation Strategy on Climate Change, and agreed to the First National Climate Change Business Plan, containing measures to address climate change. The Government also holds National Stakeholders Meetings to discuss issues regarding climate change and get insight from experts.

CLIMATE CHANGE SOLUTIONS available at http://www.climatechangesolutions.com/
Climate Change Solutions is a Canadian website providing information on potential methods for the reduction of greenhouse gases. The site breaks potential solutions down by sector, such as agriculture, electricity and municipalities.

EUROPA: Climate Change available at http://europa.eu.int/comm/environment/climat/home_en.htm
This site contains information about the 1992 UNFCCC, 1997 Kyoto Protocol, the science behind global warming, etc. Most relevant, however, it contains information about the European Climate Change Programme (ECCP). The ECCP provides more specific measures for the EU to take to meet their obligations under the 1997 Kyoto Protocol. A portion of the ECCP, the emissions trading scheme, is outlined in the chapter.

GLOBAL WARMING: EARLY WARNING SIGNS available at http://www.climatehotmap.org/
This website contains an interactive global map tracking the consequences of global warming.

GLOBAL WARMING INTERNATIONAL CENTRE available at http://www.globalwarming.net/
This site is produced by Global Warming International Centre (GWIC). It contains information regarding science and policy and is aimed at both governmental and non-governmental organizations. GWIC also sponsors an annual global warming conference and expo.

INDONESIA: MAJOR STUDIES IN CLIMATE CHANGE available at http://www.ccasia.teri.res.in/country/indo/proj/projects.htm
This site outlines a number of studies in which Indonesia is involved regarding climate change and ways to combat it. It contains information regarding Indonesia's greenhouse gas levels, the impacts of climate change on different ecosystems in the country, and mitigation efforts.

INTERGOVERNMENTAL PANEL ON CLIMATE CHANGE available at http://www.ipcc.ch/
This website contains links to many different types of documents prepared by IPCC. The site contains reports outlining scientific findings, reports prepared for the COPs, speeches and presentations.

NEW ZEALAND CLIMATE CHANGE OFFICE available at http://www.climatechange.govt.nz/
The site contains information about the 1992 UNFCCC and the 1997 Kyoto Protocol, but it also contains extensive information about how the New Zealand government plans to meet its limits set by the Protocol.

PEW CENTRE FOR GLOBAL CLIMATE CHANGE available at http://www.pewclimate.org/
Pew's site contains in depth information regarding the science behind global warming. It also contains policy information, which tends to focus on happenings in the United States. However, the site contains a description of the Kyoto Protocol and the COPs. Finally, the site contains information about the role of private business in combating climate change.

TYNDALL CENTRE FOR CLIMATE CHANGE available at http://www.tyndall.ac.uk/
The Tyndall Centre is a national UK centre promoting a trans-disciplinary approach to evaluating climate change. The Centre brings together scientists, economists, engineers and social scientists in an attempt to develop realistic policies to combat climate change that are individually applicable to varying sectors.

UNITED NATIONS FRAMEWORK CONVENTION ON CLIMATE CHANGE available at http://unfccc.int/
1992 UNFCCC homepage, which contains full text of the Convention and the 1997 Kyoto Protocol, documents from various COPs, current events regarding the Convention, including up-to-date information about Parties.

WORLD METEOROLOGICAL ORGANIZATION (WMO) HOMEPAGE available at http://www.wmo.ch/index-en.html
The WMO homepage contains information about changes in climate and weather patterns. WMO also has programmes contained within it, such as the World Climate Programme. Links to these sites are provided and they contain a wealth of information regarding global weather and climate and evidence of climate change.

WORLD RESOURCES INSTITUTE available at http://climate.wri.org, in particular: Building on the Kyoto Protocol: Options for Protecting the Climate, available at http://climate.wri.org/pubs_pdf.cfm?PubID=3762

11. HAZARDOUS WASTES

I. Introduction

1. This chapter presents an overview of the international instruments and national legislation governing the management of hazardous wastes. It provides guidance on the applicability of the laws to minimize, prevent, remedy or punish actions and consequences involving hazardous and other wastes that can injure the environment and public health. Section II provides an overview of the international law governing hazardous wastes, primarily by examining international, regional and bilateral conventions and other agreements setting out rules and standards for regulation of hazardous and other wastes. Section III provides examples of national implementation through legislation that implement international hazardous waste law at the domestic level.

2. International hazardous waste conventions and other agreements indicate that "wastes" have been understood globally to mean substances or objects that are disposed of, intended to be disposed of, or required to be disposed of under provisions of national law. "Hazardous wastes" are a subset of wastes that include a wide range of wastes capable of causing harm to human health, the environment or both. These include by-products that are explosive, flammable, radioactive, liable to spontaneous combustion, emit flammable gases upon contact with water, poisonous, infectious, corrosive, toxic and those that are capable of yielding another harmful substance after disposal. They also include wastes containing harmful compounds, such as arsenic, cadmium, mercury, lead, acidic solutions, organic phosphorus, halogenated organic solvents and phenols. Such wastes originate from a variety of sources including a wide range of production processes, medical care in hospitals and domestic garbage.

3. The definitions indicate that wastes requiring regulation result from day to day human activities that make societies function. As the world becomes more developed and societies become larger, with affluent consumption patterns, a wide range of industrial, commercial, construction, agricultural, medical and even domestic activities have increased at an unprecedented rate, the inevitable consequence being an accelerated rate of waste generation. For example, reports show that countries of the European Union generate some 1.3 billion tonnes of wastes every year, of which over 36 million tonnes are hazardous wastes. Once

generated, wastes require proper handling and disposal if their adverse impacts on human health and the environment are to be avoided.

4. Concerns have arisen over the amount of wastes generated throughout the world, which has reflected a steady increase in quantity and in improper handling and unsafe disposal. In many countries, large quantities of wastes have been generated that outstrip the countries' capacity to properly dispose of them. For example, the capacities of landfills in many places have been fully utilized and industries and other sectors are in dire need of alternative disposal sites.

5. Following scientific research and studies that revealed and highlighted adverse health and environmental impacts of wastes, concerns about unsafe disposal methods and practices increased. Scientific studies and research have shown that many hazardous substances and their by-products are capable of producing unacceptably high levels of health injury and environmental damage. For example, sulfur can cause chemical burns. And dibromochloropropane, a chemical substance used to control pests, has the propensity to cause toxic effects on the reproductive system, resulting in a reduction in sperm count in men which leads to sterility.

6. Scientific research and studies played a major role in the development of treaties and laws governing hazardous wastes. Although there is no scientific certainty about the hazards of all wastes, studies and research confirmed fears about the dangers of many kinds of wastes by revealing their toxicity, carcinogenicity, mutagenicity, corrosivity and other characteristics harmful to human health and the environment. The revelations, which later provided a basis for international legal actions, led to a tightening of environmental regulations in industrialized countries, beginning in the early 1970s and this, in turn, led to a dramatic rise in the cost of hazardous waste disposal. Inevitably, the situation led to a search for alternative, cheaper ways to dispose of wastes within countries of origin and abroad.

7. In some instances, waste traders resort to unsafe disposal of hazardous and other wastes in unauthorized places within their countries, in coastal areas and in the high seas, causing high levels of water pollution, damage to populations of aquatic organisms and serious health ailments. A search for cheaper ways to dispose of wastes also led to a lucrative but scandalous international commerce in hazardous wastes, basically involving exports of hazardous wastes from

industrialized countries where they could no longer be economically disposed of safely, to developing countries in need of hard currency, but with little knowledge of the hazardous nature of the wastes and no capacity to dispose of them safely. Many of the recipient countries have been in Africa, Eastern Europe and the Caribbean, where hazardous wastes exports have caused severe health and environmental problems to unsuspecting populations, not to mention the accidental spills in the high seas and other environments that have occurred in the course of transit.

8. The situation has been complicated by the practice of manufacturers of concealing information about the nature of wastes generated in their production processes, often in the name of trade and business secrets. Similarly, traders in toxic wastes conceal the nature of wastes they handle, especially waste exports. This makes it even more difficult for recipient countries to take appropriate measures to handle and dispose of the wastes safely.

9. The problems and concerns prompted action within and among countries, which resulted in the development of binding and non-legally binding international agreements setting forth rules, principles and standards for management of hazardous wastes and for the control of transboundary movement of the wastes.

II. International Framework

1. Multilateral Instruments on Hazardous Wastes

a) Basel Convention on the Control of Transboundary Movements of Hazardous Wastes and their Disposal

i. Background and Contents of the Convention

10. The Basel Convention on the Control of Transboundary Movements of Hazardous Wastes and their Disposal ("Basel Convention") is the most important international agreement related to hazardous waste.

11. The origins of the Basel Convention can be traced to the 1972 United Nations Conference on the Human Environment ("1972 Stockholm Conference") which was held to address pollution and other environmental problems which threatened the health and well being of people in many countries and posed risks of damage to ecosystems and species important to life. Prior to

the 1972 Stockholm Conference, a number of international and national scientific organizations had been conducting research which increased understanding of linkages between biological productivity and human welfare, negative impacts of human activities on the environment and, among other things, demonstrated conclusively that worldwide environmental problems could be tackled successfully through international cooperation.

12. Another factor that strengthened calls for the 1972 Stockholm Conference was a number of pollution and other environmental disasters in the 1950s and 1960s. These included the outbreak of Minamata disease, a kind of neurological disorder between 1954 and 1965, among local populations in Minamata, Japan as a result of eating fish contaminated with methyl mercury wastes that had been discharged from a chemical factory into the sea. Another example was to be found at Love Canal, near Niagara Falls in the United States, where homes were built on a former hazardous waste dumpsite containing pesticides and chemicals used in making plastics. Rainwater percolating into the ground resulted in liquid waste that reached many of the homes and contaminated other environments in the area, allegedly causing seizures, learning disabilities and other ailments among residents and killing birds and other organisms in the area.

13. Among the results of the 1972 Stockholm Conference was that government representatives agreed to address a variety of environmental problems, including their undertaking to halt discharges of harmful substances into the environment.

14. In 1981, UNEP identified as one of the subjects of significance to global environmental protection the management and transboundary movement of hazardous wastes. By then, there had been several incidents of improper and illegal dumping of hazardous wastes within countries and at sea, and incidents of exports of hazardous wastes from developed to developing countries where they were inappropriately disposed of, creating adverse environmental problems, were on the increase.

15. UNEP developed the Cairo Guidelines and Principles for the Environmentally Sound Management of Hazardous Wastes ("1987 Cairo Guidelines") addressed to governments with a view to assisting them in the process of developing national policies and measures for environmentally sound management and disposal of hazardous

wastes. When adopting the voluntary 1987 Cairo Guidelines, UNEP's Governing Council requested UNEP to prepare a global legal instrument to control transboundary movement of hazardous wastes and their disposal, because of increasing publicity and awareness of adverse impacts of uncontrolled movement of hazardous wastes, particularly to developing countries. UNEP prepared a draft convention and established a Working Group composed of legal and technical experts to carefully consider and revise the draft, which met five times and subsequently developed a final draft. Then, UNEP convened a meeting of governmental representatives to consider the draft and the proposal for a convention. The Basel Convention was adopted in 1989 and entered into force on 5 May 1992. Currently, it has 166 parties (as of November 2005).

16. The Basel Convention is the first and foremost global environmental agreement that strictly regulates the transboundary movements of hazardous wastes and other wastes. The Convention creates binding obligations for its parties. Article 2 of the Convention defines wastes as "...substances or objects which are disposed of or are intended to be disposed of or are required to be disposed of by the provisions of national law.". Article 1 specifies the scope of the Convention. It regulates hazardous wastes of categories listed in Annex I and III of the Convention, including wastes from particular waste streams such as medical care in hospitals and wastes possessing toxic and other hazardous characteristics as specified in article 1(a). It also regulates wastes that are not covered under article 1(a) but are defined as or considered to be hazardous wastes by the domestic legislation of export, import or transit countries that are parties to the Convention as stated in article1(b). In addition to hazardous wastes, the Convention also regulates "other wastes" of categories listed in Annex II, including wastes collected from households and residues arising from incineration of household wastes, if they are subject to transboundary movement as stipulated in article 1(2).

17. Article 1(3) and (4) of the Basel Convention exempts certain kinds of wastes from its regulatory scope. Article 1(3) states that the Convention does not regulate wastes that, "...as a result of being radioactive, are subject to other international control systems...applying specifically to radioactive materials...". Radioactive wastes are very different in nature and composition and as a result, require very specialized technical and other handling procedures. Therefore, radioactive wastes

are largely regulated by the International Atomic Energy Agency. Further, article 1(4) stipulates that wastes derived from the normal operation of ships whose discharge is already covered by another international instrument are also excluded from the scope of the 1989 Basel Convention.

18. In its Preamble, the Basel Convention recognizes the risk of damage to human health and the environment that is posed by hazardous wastes and other wastes and by the transboundary movement of such wastes. The Preamble expressly states that its purpose is to protect human health and the environment against the adverse effects that may result from the generation and management of hazardous wastes and other wastes. To accomplish its goal, the Convention provides for three key measures with binding obligations on parties, namely:

i. Strict control of transboundary movement of hazardous wastes;

ii. Environmentally sound management of hazardous wastes; and

iii. Enforcement and implementation of the provisions of the convention at international and international levels.

These three measures will be elaborated below.

ii. Strict Control of Transboundary Movement of Hazardous Wastes

19. Transboundary movement of hazardous wastes refers to movement of wastes across international frontiers. Article 4(1)(a) recognizes the right of every party to prohibit the import of hazardous wastes or other wastes for disposal. Therefore, any party can place a ban on the importation of any of the wastes listed in the Annexes to the Basel Convention, or any substances that the party has classified as hazardous waste by national law. A party that has taken such a step is required by articles 4(1)(a) and 13 to inform the Basel Secretariat and other parties of their decision. Once notified of importation prohibitions, parties must prohibit and prevent waste generators and other waste handlers within their countries from exporting wastes to such countries.

20. Moreover, article 4(2)(e) obligates each party to prohibit and prevent movement of wastes to countries, especially developing countries, whether parties to the Basel Convention or not, if it has reason to believe that the wastes will not be

managed and disposed of in an environmentally sound manner in the country of intended destination. In addition, article 4(5) obligates parties not to permit imports of hazardous wastes from countries that are not parties to the Convention or their exports to non-parties, unless bilateral and other agreements allowed by article 11 of the Convention exist between a party and a non-party allowing transboundary movement of hazardous and other wastes between the parties concerned. Where such agreements exist, article 11(2) obligates concerned parties to notify the Basel Secretariat of their existence for purposes of control of any transboundary movement of wastes undertaken. Parties also agreed not to allow wastes exports to Antarctica in article 4(6).

21. Article 4(2)(d) of the Basel Convention obligates parties to take steps to ensure that transboundary movement of hazardous wastes and other wastes is reduced to a minimum. Among other things, this obligates parties to require waste generators in their countries to reduce generation of wastes to a minimum as stipulated by article 4(2)(a). Waste generators can reduce generation of hazardous wastes by, for example, replacing hazardous and non-biodegradable raw materials with less or non-hazardous and biodegradable ones.

22. If movement of wastes is to take place between parties, the Basel Convention obligates parties to ensure that all movements are conducted in accordance with consent and notification requirements and procedures that it establishes. As a first step, article 4(7)(a) requires each party to create a system of national authorization of hazardous waste transporters and other handlers and to prohibit unauthorized persons from engaging in hazardous waste activities. Further, article 4(2)(f) obligates each party to require that information about a proposed transboundary movement of hazardous wastes and other wastes be provided to the governmental authorities in the State of origin, as well as the intended destination countries and countries of transit. To make this possible, article 5 requires each party to designate or establish a competent governmental authority to receive notifications of proposed transboundary movement of wastes and other related information and to respond to it.

23. Parties are also obligated by articles 4(9)(a),(b) and 4(11) to take appropriate measures to ensure that transboundary movements of hazardous wastes are allowed only:

   - If the state of export does not have the technical capacity and/the necessary facilities, capacity or suitable disposal sites to properly dispose of wastes intended for export;
   - The intended destination country has the necessary capacity to dispose of the wastes in an environmentally sound manner; and
   - Any other transboundary waste movement criteria agreed to between the parties concerned (which are not in conflict with the Convention's requirements) and any additional conditions imposed by a party have been met.

24. If the conditions are fulfilled, the proposed destination party, through its competent governmental authority, must be notified in writing of the intended export. Articles 4(1)(c) and 6(1) obligate the exporting party to require the generator or intending exporter to notify the intended destination country and all countries of transit of every intended export of wastes. Under article 6(1), each notification must contain the information specified in Annex V A, including: full name, address and telephone number of the person to be contacted on matters concerning the intended export, reason for the intended export, generator(s) of the waste and site of generation, intended carrier(s) of the waste or their agents, if known, country of export of the waste, name of competent authority, expected countries of transit and their competent authorities, country of waste import and name of its competent authority, projected date(s) of shipment(s), period of time over which waste is to be exported and proposed itinerary, designation and physical description of the waste, information on any special handling requirements including emergency provisions in case of accidents and type of packaging envisaged.

25. Under article 6(3), the exporting parties must not allow the generator or exporter of wastes to commence transboudary movement of wastes until the exporting party receives written confirmation that the notifier has received the written consent from the intended destination state to import and confirmation of the existence of a contract between the exporter and the person or body to dispose of the wastes in the destination party specifying what they propose to do to manage the wastes in question in an environmentally sound manner, including disposal of the waste. In addition, the exporting party must not allow the exporter or generator of wastes to commence shipment until it receives written consent from all destination parties as required by article 6(4).

26. If all required consents are received, the intending exporter is required to comply with labelling, packaging and transportation requirements stipulated by article 4(2)(c),(d) and (7), in

conformity with generally accepted and recognized international rules. With respect to transport, the United Nations Recommendations on the Transport of Dangerous Goods developed by the Committee of Experts on the Transport of Dangerous Goods and other instruments apply. The provisions also require that transboundary movement is to be conducted in an environmentally sound manner to prevent pollution and to minimize adverse consequences to human health and the environment that might result from the movement. In addition, article 4(7)(c) requires that every consignment of wastes intended for transboundary movement be accompanied by a movement document from the point at which the movement commences to the point of disposal.

27. Further, article 6(9) requires that each person who takes charge of the waste consignment in the course of transboundary movement sign the movement document either upon receipt or delivery of the wastes in question. The last person required to sign the movement document is the person who disposes of the wastes in the destination country. The disposer is required to inform the exporter and the competent authority in the exporting state of receipt of wastes and, in due course, of completion of disposal, which must comply with specifications in the notification. If no such information is received by the exporting state, its competent authority is required to notify the importing state.

28. Under article 8, where lawful movements of wastes were commenced but cannot be completed and alternative arrangements cannot be made for the portion of the waste that has already reached the destination country to be disposed of in an environmentally sound manner within a given period of time, the exporting party has a duty to re-import the wastes. In such situations, transit countries have an added obligation not to oppose or hinder re-export.

29. Under article 9, transboundary movements of hazardous and other wastes in certain circumstances constitute criminal violations for illegal traffic in waste. These are transboundary movements of hazardous and other wastes that are not preceded with the required prior notification, without the required consents of the destination or transit countries, with consents obtained from states concerned through falsification, misrepresentation or fraud. Illegal traffic also consists of traffic that does not conform in material ways with the required documents and that results in deliberate dumping of wastes in contravention of the Convention and general principles of international law.

iii. Environmentally Sound Management of Hazardous Wastes

30. In order to protect health and the environment from adverse impacts of wastes, the Basel Convention aims to ensure environmentally sound management of hazardous and other wastes among parties. Article 2 defines environmentally sound management of hazardous and other wastes to mean "...taking all practicable steps to ensure that hazardous wastes and/or other wastes are managed in a manner which will protect human health and the environment against the adverse effects which may result from such wastes". The totality of the Convention's provisions on waste management presents an "integrated life-cycle approach," which involves strong controls from the generation of hazardous wastes to their storage, transport, treatment, reuse, recycling, recovery and final disposal.

31. Article 4(2)(a) requires parties to minimize the generation of hazardous wastes and other wastes within their territories. Waste reduction has two aspects: reduction in the quantity of wastes generated and reduction or elimination of the use of hazardousness substances. For example, article 13(3)(h) obligates parties to share information about any technologies they have adopted and any measures undertaken for the development of technologies for reduction or elimination of production of hazardous wastes. Other hazardous waste reduction technologies that can be adopted in compliance with this provision include cleaner production methods. Waste reduction may also involve educating consumers about the nature of by-products of the products they use, their dangers and safer alternatives.

32. Article 14(1) recognizes the significance of technology transfer, especially to developing countries to enable the minimization of waste generation, and obligates parties to establish regional and sub-regional centres for training and technology transfers regarding the management of wastes and minimization of their generation.

33. Adverse effects on health and the environment can occur as a result of hazardous waste pollution of water and other environments. Therefore, article 4(2)(c) obligates parties to ensure that persons involved in the management of wastes within their countries, such as waste packers, transporters and other handlers, take all necessary steps to prevent waste pollution. This requires, for example, that

proper packaging materials be used to avoid leakage of liquid or other wastes and that wastes be treated before disposal to eliminate their hazardous nature. Article 4(2)(c) further obligates parties to ensure that persons involved in waste management take steps to minimize the consequences of any waste pollution that occurs. For example, one way of reducing the impacts of waste pollution is to develop and implement pollution emergency plans to be followed in the event of pollution incidents.

34. As part of the environmentally sound management of hazardous wastes, parties are further required by article 4(2)(b) to ensure that wastes are disposed of as close to the source as possible, and parties are required to ensure that waste exporters, generators, importers and disposers package, label, transport and handle wastes destined for export in conformity with generally accepted and recognized international rules, standards and practices that can prevent or reduce adverse impacts on health and the environment (article 4(7)(b)).

35. Parties are also required under article 13(3)(d) to gather information and data on effects on human health and the environment of the generation, transportation and disposal of hazardous and other wastes and to share the information with other parties. This may provide valuable basis for national legislation for compliance with the Convention's requirements and any other more stringent measures put in place at the domestic level to protect health and the environment from adverse impacts of wastes.

iv. Enforcement of Provisions for Strict Control of Transboundary Movements and for Environmentally Sound Management of Hazardous Wastes

36. The rules and standards established by the Basel Convention for transboundary movement of wastes are to be enforced at national and international levels. At the national level, article 9(5) obligates each party to introduce appropriate national legislation to prevent and punish illegal traffic in hazardous and other wastes. A party may, for example, create hazardous waste laws expressly prohibiting importation and exportation of hazardous wastes without the prior notifications and consents required by the Convention. A party may also, by law, establish a special police force or customs unit charged with the responsibility of detecting illegal imports and exports of wastes. Further, a party may create laws stipulating fines and/or imprisonment for citizens and others who import hazardous wastes without following the

Convention procedures. Countries can also establish laboratories at their entry points to test the nature of substances exported to their countries to determine whether they are prohibited wastes, in addition to any laws, policies and procedures that may require the return of hazardous wastes to countries of origin in cases where proper procedures have not been followed.

37. Similarly, under article 10(2)(c), parties have an obligation to have effective and efficient methods for environmentally sound management of hazardous wastes as the basis of their national laws, regulations and policies, and the obligation to cooperate in the improvement of existing technologies, and in the development and adoption of new technologies to enable the reduction of waste generation and the management wastes in an environmentally sound manner.

38. If a transboundary movement of hazardous wastes or other wastes occurs in contravention of the Convention's provisions as a result of the conduct of an exporter or generator, article 9(2) requires the exporting state of the wastes in question to ensure that the wastes are taken back by the exporter, or the generator of the wastes, or by the state of export itself. If this is not possible, the state of export has the obligation to ensure that the wastes are otherwise disposed of in accordance with the provisions of the Convention within 30 days of being notified of the illegal traffic. If illegal traffic occurs as a result of the conduct of an importer or disposer, the state of import bears the obligation to ensure that the wastes in question are disposed of in an environmentally sound manner by the importer or disposer. If this is not possible the State of import itself shall, within 30 days of knowing of the illegal traffic, dispose of the wastes in an environmentally sound manner (article 9(3)).

39. In cases where the responsibility for illegal traffic in wastes cannot be assigned to an exporter, generator, importer or disposer, the state of export and the state of import are obligated by article 9(4) to cooperate to ensure that the wastes in question are disposed of in an environmentally sound manner in one of the states concerned, or elsewhere as soon as practicable. Article 12 obligates parties to cooperate with a view to adopting a Protocol setting forth rules and procedures for liability and compensation to apply in cases of damage resulting from transboundary movement and disposal of hazardous wastes. Implementation of this provision is considered in Section vii below under "Developments since the adoption of the Convention".

v. Dispute Settlement Mechanisms

40. In case of any disputes arising as a result of a party's failure to comply with the 1989 Basel Convention, the Convention provides for elaborate dispute resolution mechanisms. Article 20(1) and (2) of the Convention requires parties to resolve disputes through peaceful means. If a party fails to comply with the 1989 Basel Convention and, as a result, a dispute arises between that party and another party concerning the failure to comply, the Convention requires that the parties shall meet and negotiate the matter. If the parties do not agree, the matter shall be resolved through some other peaceful means, such as conciliation. If parties fail to resolve their matters peacefully, they can either refer the dispute to arbitration through the Basel Convention Secretariat, or to the International Court of Justice for resolution.

vi. Institutional Framework for Implementation

41. For its implementation, article 15 and 16 of the Convention establish a Conference of the Parties ("COP") and a Secretariat, and charge them with various responsibilities. Article 15 also allows for the establishment of Subsidiary Bodies to implement its provisions. The COP is the political and decision-making body, which comprises representatives of all the parties to the Convention.

42. Under article 16 of the Convention, a Secretariat was established, responsible for facilitating implementation of the Convention and related agreements by, among other things, coordinating the Convention's system of notification of and consent to transboundary movements of hazardous wastes. The Secretariat monitors transboundary movements of hazardous wastes by receiving information from parties about their exports of hazardous wastes under article 13(3)(b). The Secretariat also works closely with Interpol to prevent illegal transboundary movement of hazardous wastes. The Secretariat is responsible for providing assistance to parties in cases of illegal traffic and for providing information regarding competent persons to consult on technical matters concerning provisions of experts and equipment for rapid assistance to parties in the event of an emergency involving hazardous wastes. The Secretariat is administered by UNEP.

43. In accordance with article 14 of the Convention, the COP has established two types of funds: a general fund, known as a Trust Fund for implementing the Convention's activities generally, and a Technical Cooperation Trust Fund to assist developing countries with the technical aspects of the requirements under the Convention. Technical corporation funds can, for example, be used for technical training of government officials on national regulation of hazardous wastes.

vii. Developments since the Adoption of the Convention

44. During the first decade of the Convention (1989-1999), it was principally devoted to setting up a framework for controlling transboundary movements of hazardous wastes. Among other things, a control system based on prior written notification was put in place in compliance with provisions of articles 4, 5 and 6 of the Convention. The area of focus during the subsequent decade (2000-2010) is the minimization of hazardous waste generation.

45. Recognizing that the long-term solution to the stockpiling of hazardous wastes and the search for across-the-border disposal sites is a reduction in the generation of wastes, the COP in 1999 decided to set out a Strategic Plan and Guidelines for the Convention's activities during the next decade in the "Basel Declaration". Emphasizing minimization of hazardous waste generation, the Plan and strategy for this next decade (2000-2010) include:

- Active promotion and use of cleaner technologies and production methods;
- Creation of awareness to promote the Convention, the aims of the strategy on environmentally sound management of hazardous wastes and other implementation activities; and
- Implementation and promotion of technical capacity-building as well as developing and transferring environmentally sound technologies for management of hazardous wastes, especially for developing countries and countries with economies in transition. For this purpose, regional training centers have been established as discussed in more details below.

46. Building the capacity to manage and dispose of hazardous wastes in an environmentally sound manner is an integral part of implementing the Convention. Through training and technology transfer, parties to the Convention, especially developing countries and countries with economies in transition, can gain knowledge, skills and tools that are necessary to properly manage their hazardous wastes. To this end, the Convention has established an elaborate network of Regional and Sub-regional Centres for Training and Technology Transfer. Activities of the centres are

tailored to meet the needs of the countries in terms of technical and non-technical training.

47. One of the joint obligations created by article 12 of the Basel Convention is for parties to cooperate with a view to adopting a Protocol setting out appropriate rules and procedures for liability and compensation for damages resulting from transboundary movement and disposal of hazardous wastes. Consultations about such a Protocol began in 1993, mainly in response to concerns by developing countries about their lack of funds and technologies for coping with illegal dumping or accidental spills of hazardous wastes. The Basel Protocol on Liability and Compensation for Damage resulting from Transboundary Movements of Hazardous Wastes and their Disposal ("Liability Protocol") was adopted at the fifth COP in 1999. It has not yet entered into force (August 2005).

48. The objective of the Liability Protocol is to provide for a comprehensive regime for liability, as well as adequate and prompt compensation for damage resulting from transboundary movements of hazardous wastes and other wastes, including accidents occurring because of illegal traffic in such wastes. The Protocol establishes rules on liability and compensation for damages caused by accidental spills of hazardous wastes during export, import or during disposal. The Protocol addresses questions as to who is financially responsible in the event of an incident and considers each facet of a transboundary movement of wastes, from the point at which the wastes are loaded on the means of transport to their export, international transit, import and final disposal.

49. Article 15(4) and (5), article 17 and other provisions of the Basel Convention specifically authorize parties to amend the Convention as necessary to assist in fulfilling their responsibilities and to allow effective implementation of its provisions. Pursuant to these provisions, the COP, at its second meeting in 1994, agreed to an immediate ban on the export from the Organization for Economic Cooperation and Development ("OECD") to non-OECD countries of hazardous wastes intended for final disposal. The text of this Amendment to the Basel Convention on the Control of Transboundary Movements of Hazardous Wastes and their Disposal ("1995 Ban Amendment") does not use the distinction OECD/non-OECD countries. Rather, it bans hazardous wastes exports for final disposal and recycling from what are referred to as Annex VII countries (Convention parties that are members of the European Union, OECD, and Liechtenstein) to non-Annex VII countries (all other parties to the Convention). Parties also agreed to ban the export

of wastes intended for recovery and recycling. The Ban Amendment has to be ratified by three-fourths of the parties present at the time of adoption of the Amendment, and has not entered into force yet (August 2005).

b) Marine Environmental Compensation and Liability Agreements and Marine Pollution Prevention Agreements

i. Marine Environmental Compensation and Liability Agreements

50. Besides provisions for liability and compensation in the Convention, the 1972 Convention on the Prevention of Marine Pollution by Dumping of Wastes and other Matter ("1972 London Dumping Convention") and a few other conventions dealing with hazardous wastes, a number of other international agreements set rules specifically dealing with issues of liability and compensation for pollution damage in cases of spills and other discharges in the marine environment, including spills and discharges of hazardous wastes. These include: the International Convention on Civil Liability for Oil Pollution Damage ("Civil Liability Convention"), the International Convention on the Establishment of an International Fund for Compensation for Oil Pollution Damage ("1971 International Fund Convention"), the International Convention on Liability and Compensation for Damage in connection with the Carriage of Hazardous and Noxious Substances by Sea ("Liability and Compensation Convention") and the International Convention on Civil Liability for Bunker Oil Pollution Damage ("Bunker Oil Pollution Convention"). The rules established in these conventions are complementary to those of the Convention with respect to liability and compensation for harm occasioned by hazardous and other wastes. (See also chapters 5 and 13).

51. The Civil Liability Convention was adopted in 1969 to provide for compensation of victims of oil pollution resulting from the escape or discharge of oil from ships and to ensure that ship owners were made liable to pay compensation. It establishes uniform international rules and procedures for determining liability and compensation for damage caused by the escape of discharge of oil from ships. However, the Civil Liability Convention applies only to pollution damage caused in the territorial sea of a party. It also applies to measures taken after the incident to prevent or minimize damage and the liability limits the Convention sets are low. This led to the creation of more agreements to govern liability and compensation for pollution from ships and other sources.

52. The 1971 International Fund Convention entered into force in 1978. The 1971 International Fund Convention establishes an International Oil Pollution Compensation Fund to provide compensation for pollution damage resulting from the escape or discharge of oil from ships. Among other things, the 1971 International Fund Convention outlines the conditions under which the Fund will be used to compensate oil pollution victims, especially where there is inadequate compensation under the Civil Liability Convention. This was followed by the two other liability conventions.

53. The Liability and Compensation Convention, adopted in 1996, has yet to enter into force. The Liability and Compensation Convention will apply to approximately 6000 substances defined by reference to an existing international list of substances, including noxious liquid substances carried in bulk. Article 3 of the Convention stipulates that the Convention shall apply exclusively "(a) to any damage caused in the territory, including the territorial sea of a State Party; (b) to damage by contamination of the environment caused in the exclusive economic zone of a State Party, established in accordance with international law...; (c) to other...damage caused by a substance carried on board a ship...; and (d) to preventive measures..." taken in relation to such damage. It defines damage as including loss of life, personal injury, loss of or damage to property outside a ship, loss or damage by contamination of the environment, the costs of preventive measures, and further loss or damage caused by them. Among other provisions, the Convention introduces strict liability for ship owners, and a system of compulsory insurance to ensure that ship owners meet their liabilities in the event of a pollution incident. The Convention will also introduce a fund financed by cargo interests, to be available in certain circumstances, including where a ship owner is not able to meet liability.

54. The Bunker Oil Pollution Convention, adopted in 2001, has also not yet entered into force. It recognizes the importance of establishing strict liability for all forms of oil pollution, which is linked to an appropriate limitation of the level of liability. The Convention also intends to ensure that adequate, prompt and effective compensation is available to persons who suffer damage caused by oil spills when carried in ships bunkers. Bunker oil is defined by article 1 of the Convention to mean "...any hydrocarbon mineral oil, including lubricating oil, used or intended to be used for the operation or propulsion of the ship, and any residues of such oil". Such residues are wastes and

thus the Convention applies to hazardous and other oil wastes. Among other significant provisions, article 3 of the Convention holds a ship owner, at the time of a pollution incident, to be liable for pollution damage caused by any bunker oil on board or originating from the ship, except under circumstances specified in the provisions, including where the damage results from an act of war, hostilities, civil war, insurrection or a natural phenomenon of an exceptional or inevitable character.

55. It can be concluded that the marine environmental compensation and liability agreements have not yet provided an affective mechanism for liability and compensation for harm resulting from hazardous and other wastes. This makes it necessary that more efforts be made to bring the various schemes provided for into force, and for more efforts to be made to encourage parties to the Basel Convention to ratify its 1999 Liability Protocol.

ii. Marine Pollution Prevention Agreements

56. A number of international agreements for prevention of marine pollution contain provisions for regulation of hazardous and other wastes that are complementary to regulations established in the Basel Convention, which does not specifically regulate ocean dumping. For the marine environment, dumping and discharge of wastes are problems both in the high seas and in coastal areas. Existing agreements setting out rules to address the waste problems, as well as other sources of marine pollution include the International Convention relating to Intervention on the High Seas in Cases of Oil Pollution Casualties, the International Convention for the Prevention of Pollution from Ships, the Convention on the Prevention of Marine Pollution by Dumping of Wastes and other Matter ("London Dumping Convention"), the United Nations Convention on the Law of the Sea ("UNCLOS"), the International Convention on Oil Pollution Preparedness, Response and Cooperation and its 2000 Protocol on Preparedness, Response and Cooperation to Pollution Incidents by Hazardous and Noxious Substances. One of these instruments will be briefly considered below under Section c, namely the London Dumping Convention, to illustrate the applicability of marine pollution prevention agreements to regulate the management of hazardous wastes, especially disposal.

c. Convention for Prevention of Marine Pollution by Dumping of Wastes and other Matter

57. One of the key waste issues that the Basel Convention does not specifically address is dumping in both coastal areas and in the high seas. This is the subject of the Convention for Prevention of Marine Pollution by Dumping of Wastes and other Matter, 1972, which entered into force in August 1975. (See chapters 13 and 17). The London Dumping Convention seeks to prevent marine pollution from waste dumping and from a variety of other sources, including pollution from the air. Regarding hazardous wastes, article 4 of the London Dumping Convention prohibits dumping of such wastes into all marine environments, including the high seas and territorial waters. The London Dumping Convention prohibits all dumping in the marine environment except for the substances listed in an Appendix to the Convention. Hazardous wastes whose dumping in the marine environment is totally prohibited by the London Dumping Convention include wastes containing mercury, organochlorine compounds, plastics, as well as radioactive wastes that are excluded by the Basel Convention.

58. The London Dumping Convention does not create an international enforcement mechanism to ensure that its dumping prohibitions are adhered to. Rather, it obligates parties in articles 4(3) and 7 and other provisions to create national laws, rules and regulations for its implementation. In their national laws, parties are required to prohibit dumping of hazardous wastes in coastal areas and in the high seas and to provide for punishment for infringement of the laws. For example, a party may create national rules prohibiting ships flying its flag from dumping hazardous wastes in the high seas and providing for fines and/or imprisonment in case dumping occurs. In addition, parties are required by article 4(3) to carry out continuous assessments of their coastal waters to determine whether any dumping has taken place and to take remedial measures as appropriate.

59. The London Dumping Convention also sets out binding rules for liability and compensation for damage resulting from dumping of hazardous wastes in the marine environment. In this respect, article 10 of the Convention obligates parties to establish national rules and procedures for assessing liability for damage resulting from dumping of prohibited wastes in the marine environment. National rules may, for example, provide for joint liability in case of discharge of hazardous wastes in the marine environment by more than one production facility.

60. The 1996 Protocol to the London Dumping Convention is intended to replace the Convention though it has yet to enter into force. The Protocol adopts both the precautionary principle and the polluter pays principle. The precautionary principle approach is intended for parties to find solutions for land-based sources of marine pollution and encourages prevention of waste generation.

2. Regional Instruments on Hazardous Wastes

a) Bamako Convention on the Ban of Imports into Africa and the Control of Transboundary Movement and Management of Hazardous Wastes within Africa

61. The Basel Convention gave rise to the development of a number of other conventions on hazardous wastes at the regional level and to the amendment of existing regional conventions on environmental management to specifically include provisions for hazardous wastes. Article 11 of the Basel Convention encourages parties to enter into bilateral, multilateral and regional agreements on hazardous wastes to help achieve the objectives of the Convention. In light of this and other factors, the 1991 Bamako Convention on the Ban of Imports into Africa and the Control of Transboundary Movement and Management of Hazardous Wastes within Africa ("Bamako Convention") was adopted by African states to address certain aspects of hazardous waste problems that the Basel Convention did not cover. The Bamako Convention entered into force in 1998 and its Secretariat is with the African Union.

62. The Bamako Convention regulates substances, especially pesticides, fertilizers and other chemicals that have been banned, cancelled, denied registration by a governmental regulatory action or voluntarily withdrawn in the country of manufacture due to health and environmental reasons. These are considered by the Bamako Convention as hazardous wastes. Efforts to include the specified substances was intended to allow African states to deal with problems of exports of such substances to African countries purportedly for use, when in fact, waste traders and other exporters intend to dispose of them that way. Under article 2, the Bamako Convention also expressly includes radioactive wastes in its definition of hazardous wastes, regardless of whether there exist other international instruments for their control, which means that radioactive wastes are regulated under the Bamako regime.

63. Another significant provision of the Bamako Convention is that it expressly bans the importation of hazardous wastes into African states from non-parties to the Convention. To make this ban effective, articles 4, 6, 8 and 9 of the Convention obliges its parties to take legal, administrative and other measures within their national jurisdictions to prohibit the import of all hazardous wastes into their territories. Any such imports are deemed illegal and the acts involved, criminal. To be able to determine whether illegal exports of wastes into Africa are about to take place and to prevent them, each party is required to set up a "dump watch". Should any such illegal activities take place, the Bamako Convention requires that the illegally imported wastes be exported back to the country of origin and parties have an obligation to inform the Bamako Secretariat and other parties to the Convention of such occurrences.

64. As between parties to the Bamako Convention, article 9 provides that wastes may be moved but only upon receipt from the intended destination country of a written consent, prior to export. Movements of hazardous wastes without such consent amount to illegal traffic. So are movements pursuant to falsified consent, misrepresentation, fraud and those that result it deliberate disposal of wastes in contravention of the Bamako Convention. Under article 8, parties have an added duty to re-import any hazardous wastes exported to another party pursuant to agreements between persons in the countries concerned, if the movement cannot be completed and the portion of hazardous wastes already exported cannot be disposed of in the importing country in an environmentally sound manner.

65. Article 4(3) of the Bamako Convention obliges each party to impose unlimited liability as well as joint and several liability on hazardous waste generators. This means that countries could impose liability for existence of hazardous wastes and for any danger or damage occasioned in the absence of fault or negligence against other parties and non-parties. Under article 12, parties agreed to hold further consultations on matters concerning liability and compensation and to come up with further joint regulations on it. In addition, article 4(3) of the Bamako Convention creates obligations for environmentally sound management of hazardous wastes that are similar to those created under the Basel Convention.

b) Regional Seas Agreements

66. As noted earlier, many international agreements encourage the creation of agreements at regional and sub-regional levels to allow parties to effectively implement rules and regulations created at the international level. For effective management of hazardous wastes in an environmentally sound manner and to ensure strict regulation of transboundary movement of hazardous wastes, article 11 of the Basel Convention authorizes parties to enter into bilateral, multilateral and regional agreements regarding hazardous and other wastes with other parties and non-parties to the Convention. In light of such permissive provisions, regional seas agreements exist in almost every region of the world. (See Chapter 13 for a further discussion on this topic).

67. Although global agreements may apply to every country, and many are useful models for regional instruments, every region has its own environmental problems and its own needs. Therefore, regional agreements are more likely to attract the full interest and commitment of governments in the region. They are tailored to meet some needs in relation to specific environmental problems and issues and provide the legal framework for addressing the issues and problems. Most of the existing regional agreements are similar in structure but different in specifics. Almost every one of them provides for an Action Plan as a mechanism which expresses in clear terms the legal commitment and political will of governments to tackle their common environmental problems and sets forth steps and actions to be taken to address specific environmental problems. Some of the specific differences are included in supplementary protocols to the agreements.

68. With regard to hazardous wastes, the provisions of regional seas agreements complement provisions of the Basel Convention and other global international agreements on hazardous wastes. The following sections provides examples of few of the agreements, pointing out some of the areas in which the agreements can complement international instruments for effective management and control of transboundary movement of hazardous and other wastes.

i. Convention for the Protection and Development of the Marine Environment of the Wider Caribbean Region

69. The Convention for the Protection and Development of the Marine Environment of the Wider Caribbean Region, 1983 ("Cartagena Convention") entered into force in 1986. As of November 2005 it has 21 parties in the region. The regional seas covered by the Cartagena

Convention include the Gulf of Mexico, the Caribbean Sea and adjacent areas of the Atlantic Ocean. For protection of the marine environment of the region, the Convention makes provisions for prevention of pollution from all sources, including pollution by dumping of wastes. Article 6 enjoins parties to take appropriate measures to prevent, reduce and control pollution of the marine environment of the region from dumping of wastes and other matter from ships, aircrafts and other sources. One of the measures introduced in article 12 is the requirement of environmental impact assessment, in relation to pollution prevention. Article 12(1) obligates parties to undertake to develop technical and other guidelines to assist them in the planning of major development projects in a way that prevents or minimizes harmful impacts in the Convention area. In relation to hazardous wastes, this requirement presents a preventive measure before any productive activities that may generate wastes are undertaken. For ongoing projects, article 12(2) obligates parties to conduct assessments of potential impacts of the activities on the marine environment.

70. Further, article 11 complements provisions of the Basel Convention and other conventions on hazardous wastes by providing for measures to deal with pollution emergencies, including emergencies involving hazardous wastes. It obligates parties to cooperate in responding to pollution emergencies in the area, regardless of the cause of such emergencies in order to control, reduce or eliminate pollution, or the threat of it. To be able to respond to pollution emergencies, including those involving hazardous wastes, article 11(1) and (2) further require parties to jointly or individually develop and promote contingency plans for responding to emergencies. They are also obligated to share any information on actual and potential pollution threats with other parties to allow concerted efforts to be taken to prevent, reduce or eliminate impacts.

71. The Cartagena Convention, which preceded the Basel Convention, was not specifically intended to provide for control of pollution by hazardous wastes, but pollution from all sources. The above provisions concerning hazardous wastes were later strengthened by parties by their adoption of a Protocol Concerning Pollution From Land-based Sources and Activities in the Wider Caribbean Region in 1999. Among other things, this Protocol specifically regulates hazardous wastes and lists characteristics that parties should consider in evaluating waste substances for regulation. However, the Protocol has not yet come into force.

ii. Kuwait Region

ii.a. Kuwait Regional Convention for Cooperation on the Protection of the Marine Environment from Pollution

72. The Kuwait region is endowed with valuable natural resources and a great biodiversity of plant and animal species. With all its valuable natural resources, the Kuwait region faces great climatic limitations and major developmental challenges. Its marine waters are shallow and virtually landlocked, experiencing extremes of salinity and temperatures. The rate of evaporation in the region is high, precipitation is poor and freshwater supply is decreasing. Moreover, the risk of oil pollution in the region is one of the highest anywhere, mainly due to the high concentration of offshore installations, tanker terminals, petrochemical industries and the huge volume of oil transported by ships. The offshore installations are located in the inner sea area, a critically balanced ecosystem with higher levels of pollutants, salinity and temperature. The rise in industrialization in the Kuwait region, together with high population growth and rapid urbanization, have resulted in ever-greater impacts from land-based sources of pollution on the region's coastal waters.

73. To meet these challenges, eight governments of the region adopted in 1978 the Kuwait Regional Convention for Cooperation on the Protection of the Marine Environment from Pollution ("Kuwait Convention") and an Action Plan established within the framework of the Convention, making it one of the first regional seas agreements. The Kuwait Convention entered into force in 1979.

74. The Kuwait Convention applies to the Kuwait regional sea as defined in article II but does not apply to internal waters of parties. In the Preamble, parties recognized the growing threat of pollution to marine life, fisheries, human health and recreational uses of beaches, especially pollution through discharge of oil and other harmful substances from human activities on the land and sea. The parties also recognized the need to adopt an integrated development approach to the use of the marine environment and coastal areas so as to allow the achievement of environmental and development goals in a harmonious manner. The Kuwait Convention was to enable parties to carry out land use, industrial and other developmental activities in a way that does not deteriorate the environment. Therefore, one of the key objectives of the Kuwait Convention, as stated in article III, is to prevent, abate and combat pollution of the marine environment in the region.

75. To meet its objectives, the Kuwait Convention does not deal with hazardous wastes specifically but seeks to control pollution of the marine environment from a variety of sources including pollution from ships, by dumping of wastes from ships and aircraft, from land-based sources, and from other human activities. Among other requirements, article XI (a) and (b) desires that each party includes an assessment of potential environmental effects in any planned activity entailing projects within its territory, particularly in the coastal areas and to disseminate information of the assessment of the activities. Article XI requires parties to jointly and/or individually develop guidelines in accordance with sound scientific practice to assist them in planning their development projects in a way that allows them to minimize harmful impacts of projects on the marine environment.

76. The Kuwait Convention also incorporates the Kuwait Regional Action Plan, which mainly covers programme activities relating to oil pollution, industrial wastes, sewage and marine resources. For implementation and coordination of planned activities, article XVI establishes a Regional Organization for the Protection of the Marine Environment ("ROPME") to provide institutional framework for carrying out required measures.

77. In article XXIV, parties agreed to cooperate in the development of procedures for the effective implementation of the Protocol adopted under the Kuwait Convention, including procedures for detection of violations of the Convention, reporting, accumulation of evidence on violation and for monitoring of the environment to detect cases of pollution and for dealing with emergencies. A Marine Emergency Mutual Aid Centre was created in 1982. In the event that a dispute is not settled through peaceful means, the Kuwait Convention provides for settlement of disputes through the Judicial Commission for the Settlement of Disputes, established as an organ within ROPME.

78. Article III(c) of the Kuwait Convention requires parties to establish national laws and standards for implementation of the provisions of the convention and for the effective discharge of the obligations created under it. In article III(e), parties are required to ensure that their pollution prevention measures do not cause transformation of one type of pollution to another which could be more deleterious to the environment.

ii.b. Kuwait Regional Protocol on the Control of Marine Transboundary Movements and Disposal of Hazardous Wastes and other Wastes

79. Pursuant to the Kuwait Convention, parties adopted several protocols, among which the Kuwait Regional Protocol on the Control of Marine Transboundary Movements and Disposal of Hazardous Wastes and other Wastes ("ROPME Protocol") was adopted in 1998. The ROPME Protocol, which entered into force in 2001, was specifically intended to make provisions for the proper management and control of transboundary movement of hazardous and other wastes in the region, which posed dangers to human health and the environment. In the Preamble, the Protocol makes reference to article 11 of the Basel Convention which authorizes parties to enter into bilateral, multilateral and regional agreements.

80. The ROPME Protocol strengthens provisions of articles IV and V of the Kuwait Convention, which provide for control and prevention of the marine environment in the region from pollution from ships and from dumping of wastes and other matter from ships and aircrafts. The substances controlled by the ROPME Protocol include wastes listed in Annex I to the Protocol, which are considered hazardous wastes, and other wastes, as contained in Annex II. It does not apply to a) radioactive wastes under regulation of another instrument; b) wastes from offshore installations that are regulated by the Kuwait Protocol concerning Marine Pollution resulting from Exploration and Exploitation of the Continental Shelf of 1998; c) transboundary movement of wastes overland or airborne; or d) wastes whose movements and disposal do not intrude upon the marine environment in the ROPME area.

81. The ROPME Protocol has various provisions that are similar to those of the Basel Convention. Some provisions provide, for example, for a reduction of the generation of hazardous and other wastes by parties to a minimum (article 9(1)), for prevention of pollution of the marine environment in the area with hazardous and other wastes (article 4(3)), for labelling, packaging and transportation of hazardous wastes in conformity with generally accepted and recognized international standards (article 4(4)), and for all movements of wastes to be accompanied by a movement document as required (article 4(5)).

82. In addition, the ROPME Protocol contains new provisions which complement those of the Basel Convention and other instruments by providing, for

example, that parties shall prohibit all persons under their national jurisdictions from transporting or disposing of hazardous and other wastes unless such persons are authorized or allowed to perform such types of operations. This provision requires that parties put in place a registration system for waste handlers.

83. Further, article 5(1) of the ROPME Protocol prohibits importation of hazardous and other wastes into or through the region for purposes of final disposal. Article 5(2) authorizes parties to import wastes from non-parties into their territories only for purposes of resource recovery, recycling, reclamation, direct re-use or alternative uses. This is allowed only if the state of import has the facilities and technical capacity to manage the wastes in an environmentally sound manner and in compliance with Regional Technical Guidelines developed under the Protocol.

84. Article 8(1) prohibits parties from exporting wastes to other parties unless and until regional technical guidelines for the environmentally sound management of hazardous and other wastes are developed under article 14(c) of the ROPME Protocol. Among other things, the guidelines are to contain a register of disposal facilities within party states that have adequate technical capacities to manage hazardous wastes and other wastes in an environmentally sound manner as required by article 13(5). Thereafter, a notification procedure similar to the one established by the Basel Convention must be followed by parties in the movement of wastes between parties as required by article 8(3)-(8).

85. Article 13 of the Protocol provides that ROPME shall provide institutional framework for the implementation of its provisions. To implement the Protocol, ROPME and its organs are, among other things, required to provide training of national experts, particularly for monitoring and enforcement of the provisions of the Protocol; establish a unified monitoring system for transboundary movement of hazardous and other wastes; and to establish regional reception facilities to receive wastes; and to provide disposal and other services to parties in close cooperation with parties and relevant national and international organizations, such as the Basel Secretariat.

iii. Convention to Ban the Importation into the Forum Island Countries of Hazardous and Radioactive Wastes and to Control the Transboundary Movement and Management of Hazardous Wastes within the South Pacific Region

86. In accordance with article 1, the Convention to Ban the Importation into the Forum Island Countries of Hazardous and Radioactive Wastes and to Control the Transboundary Movement and Management of Hazardous Wastes within the South Pacific Region, 1995 ("Waigani Convention") applies to the South Pacific Region, where many small island states are situated. The vast Exclusive Economic Zones of the South Pacific States are crossed by hazardous and radioactive wastes as vessels move between major producing and consuming countries. Therefore the area is under serious threat of harm to health and the environment from the management and transboundary movement of hazardous wastes. The Waigani Convention came into force in 2001. To date, the Convention has ten parties.

87. The Waigani Convention specifically recognizes the growing threat to human health and the environment posed by the increasing generation of hazardous wastes and their disposal in environmentally unsound manner. Articles 4, 6 and 8 of the Waigani Convention require parties to take appropriate legal, administrative and other measures to ban the importation of radioactive and other wastes from outside the Convention area. Parties are also required to prohibit the dumping of hazardous and radioactive wastes at sea. This could solve problems of illegal dumping at sea as explained in the introductory requirement, but the measure requires very close supervision of waste in each party's jurisdiction.

88. Further, the Waigani Convention makes waste minimization requirements and requires that parties prepare and adopt appropriate arrangements for liability and compensation for hazardous waste damage that are similar to provisions of the Basel Convention. In addition, the Waigani Convention also incorporates important international environmental law principles to guide parties in taking measures to deal with hazardous wastes. For example, article 1 requires parties to apply the precautionary principle in taking measures to deal with hazardous wastes. Parties are obliged to apply the polluter pays principle in taking measures to deal with hazardous wastes (article 12).

3. Bilateral Instruments on Hazardous Wastes

89. In addition to multilateral and regional agreements, there are bilateral agreements setting out rules and regulations for the management and transboundary movement of hazardous wastes. A good example is the 1986 Agreement between the Government of the United States of America and the Government of Canada concerning the Transboundary Movement of Hazardous Wastes ("America/Canada Agreement"). Among other things, the America/Canada Agreement creates an obligation on the two parties to issue prior notification of exports of wastes to the competent authorities of the destination country under article 3. Prior notification of intended transboundary movement of hazardous wastes is an important procedure that has been made a specific requirement in many of the hazardous waste conventions. The rest of the provisions of the Agreement are rather similar to those of the regional and multilateral agreements discussed above. Pursuant to the America/Canada Agreement, 900.000 tonnes of hazardous wastes destined for the nearest recycling, disposal or treatment sites cross the borders of the two countries annually.

4. Non-Legally Binding Instruments on Hazardous Wastes

90. In addition to the legally binding rules and standards established in global, regional and bilateral instruments, there exist a number of hazardous wastes regulations established in non-legally binding agreements. One of the significant instruments in this regard is Agenda 21, agreed to in 1992, at the United Nations Conference on Environment and Development prepared to provide the basic framework and instrumentality for their targets, priorities, goals and responsibility for the protection of various components of the environment.

91. Chapters 20 and 21 of Agenda 21 are devoted exclusively to environmentally sound management and prevention of illegal international traffic in hazardous wastes, including radioactive wastes. The overall objective of governments was to prevent, to the extent possible and to minimize the generation of hazardous wastes, as well as to manage those wastes in such a way as to not cause harm to health and the environment. To meet the objective, countries committed themselves to undertake a number of actions including ratification of the Basel Convention, promoting the minimization of generation of hazardous wastes, establishing domestic standards for hazardous wastes, establishing centres for collection and dissemination of hazardous waste-related information at regional and other levels, and providing financial support for cleaner technology research and development programmes. Among other developments, Agenda 21 has contributed to the wide acceptance and ratification of the Basel Convention, making it a global treaty.

III. National Implementation

92. This section provides two examples of national legislation for implementation of rules, standards and other requirements set out in international conventions and instruments for the management and control of transboundary movement of hazardous wastes, Japan and Kenya. Almost every international instrument on hazardous wastes has provisions requiring legislative implementation at the domestic level by parties and most of the parties have such legislation.

93. For example, article 9(5) of the Basel Convention obligates each party to introduce appropriate national legislation to prevent and punish illegal traffic in hazardous and other wastes. Article 4(4) of the same Convention also obligates parties to take appropriate legal measures to implement and enforce the provisions of the Convention in order to meet set objectives. National legislation may be in the form of laws, rules, regulations, executive orders, decrees and policies for the performance of the requirements set out in the international hazardous waste instruments. What form the national action takes depends on practice and customs of the party concerned.

94. National legislation strengthens compliance with international instruments. Different legislative approaches have been adopted by countries to implement hazardous waste instruments. Some national legislation on hazardous wastes are composed of one framework or primary hazardous waste law, implemented by specific subsidiary regulations, as the Japan example shows. There are also countries with one comprehensive environmental law dealing with a number of environmental subjects and/or components of the environment, within which hazardous wastes are provided for in general provisions. Such laws usually provide for detailed hazardous waste standards and other regulations to be provided for in subsidiary legislation. Kenya provides a good example of this approach. There are also countries that have maintained and improved sectoral or many separate legislation on various sectors -

agriculture, chemicals, water and others, to be administered under separate ministries- health, labour, etcetera and penal laws, within which management and control of transboundary movement of hazardous wastes are provided for.

95. In the various approaches, hazardous waste regulations may be of a command and control type, emphasizing deterrence and punishment. Some of the laws also incorporate the use of economic instruments as incentives or disincentives for environmentally sound management and strict control of transboundary movement of hazardous wastes. It is important to note that in federal governments, one or more of these kinds of laws usually exist at the national as well as state and/or other lower levels. Whichever the approach, a good hazardous waste national legislation should have essential legislative components. These components should include a statement of purpose or objectives, provisions on scope describing who or what the law covers, definitions of terms used, especially unfamiliar terms, an organizational structure, including the means by which the law will be administered, especially bodies or national authorities charged with implementation of the law, powers conferred on the bodies, provisions for building of a knowledge base including collection of information, interpretation and dissemination of information; and a compliance scheme to enforce and promote observance with the legislative provisions and monitor compliance. In order to protect health and the environment from negative impacts, domestic hazardous wastes legislation should be backed by effective enforcement.

1. Japan

96. Japan became a party to the Basel Convention on 17 September 1993. As part of its national implementation efforts, Japan enacted the Law for the Control of Export, Import and other Specified Hazardous Wastes and other Wastes ("Japanese Waste Law"), which took effect in December 1993. The Japanese Waste Law is the main law in Japan on transboundary movement of hazardous wastes. Article 4(5) of the Japanese Waste Law and other provisions provide for the creation of subsidiary regulations for implementation and pursuant to these provisions, two implementing subsidiary legislations, the Enforcement Ordinance of the Law for the Control of Export, Import and other specified Hazardous Wastes and other Wastes, and the Enforcement Regulations of the for the Control of Export, Import and other Specified Hazardous Wastes and other Wastes, have been created. Japan

also has other laws that apply to regulate hazardous wastes, besides the primary law. These include the Waste Disposal and Public Cleansing Law of 1970.

97. Article 1 of the Japanese Waste Law sets out the objectives or purposes of the Law and states that the Law is intended to secure the effective and smooth implementation of the Basel Convention and other international agreements by introducing control measures for the export, import, transportation and disposal of specified hazardous wastes, and thereby, to contribute to the protection of human health and conservation of the living environment.

98. Articles 2, 3 and other provisions of the Japanese Waste Law set out the scope and stipulate that the Law regulates "specified hazardous wastes," importers, exporter, disposers and other waste handlers. Wastes that arise from the normal operation of vessels and radioactive wastes are excluded from the scope of the Japanese Waste Law as stipulated in article 2(1). To clarify the scope of the Law, the definition part in article 2 specifies wastes considered as "specified hazardous wastes" to be regulated by the Law. These include materials listed in Annex I of the Basel Convention, materials to be designated as such by a Japanese Cabinet order (an executive order) and materials designated as such by a joint ordinance of Japanese Ministers of Health and Welfare, and by International Trade and Industry.

99. The Japanese Waste Law's organizational structure includes the Minister of International Trade and Industry and the Director General of the Japanese Environment Agency. They are responsible for issuing all applications for exports of controlled hazardous wastes as provided in article 4(2). The Law requires, in article 4(1) and (2), that any person wishing to export a specified hazardous waste shall obtain prior export permission. One of the matters to be considered by the Director General in processing the application and determining whether to grant an export permit is whether sufficient measures will be taken by the intending exporter to prevent environmental pollution, as stipulated in article 4(3). Article 5(1) requires that where an export permit is issued, the Minister shall also issue an export movement document, whose format is to be defined by the ordinance of the Minister, and include a description of the manner in which transport of wastes is to be executed. Article 6(1) requires all movements of hazardous wastes to be accompanied by the export movement document and to comply with export

movement requirements specified in the export movement document. Imports of regulated wastes are similarly regulated as stipulated in articles 8, 9 and other provisions of the Japanese Waste Law.

100. In accordance with provisions of the Basel Convention, the Japanese Waste Law also strictly regulates disposal of hazardous wastes in articles 12 and 13, provides for re-importation of wastes in certain circumstances in article 14, and provides for penalties for non-compliance. In addition, article 3 provides for building of a knowledge base and requires, among other things, that the Minister and responsible bodies develop and publicize basic issues concerning secure, smooth and effective implementation of the Basel Convention and issues regarding the implementation policies for preventing the damage to human health and/or the living environment which may be posed by the export, import, transportation and disposal of specified hazardous wastes.

2. Kenya

101. In Kenya, it became clear that hazardous wastes form a threat to human health and the environment. For example, by 1989, foreign waste traders had set up an enterprise importing hazardous wastes from industrialized countries for disposal, without having any waste disposal facility in the country. And in 1999, a freighter, Bruma Americana, made several attempts to dock at the port of Mombasa with its load of over 20,000 tonnes of toxic wastes, trying to dispose of it in the country. The vessel was denied entry and it was later discovered that the wastes originated from an industrialized country.

102. To collaborate with other governments in addressing these problems, Kenya became a party to the Basel Convention on 1 June 2000, and therefore had to also take measures to implement the provisions of the Convention. On its part, Kenya enacted the Environmental Management and Co-ordination Act ("EMCA") in 1999, which became operational in January 2000. EMCA provides a comprehensive framework for the management of the environment in Kenya and contains provisions on steps to be taken to implement the government's commitments in international agreements. In particular, Section 124 provides that:

> **1999 Environmental Management and Coordination Act (Section 124)**
>
> "Where Kenya is a party to an international treaty, convention or agreement, whether bilateral or multilateral, concerning the management of the environment, the Authority shall, subject to the direction and control of the council, in consultation with lead agencies: (a) initiate legislative proposals for consideration by the Attorney General, for purposes of giving effect to such treaty convention or agreement in Kenya or for enabling Kenya to perform her obligations or exercise her rights under such treaty, convention or agreement; and (b) identify other appropriate measures necessary for the national implementation of such treaty, convention or agreement... "

103. With regard to the Basel Convention requirements, EMCA contains detailed provisions for regulation of hazardous wastes. Relevant provisions of EMCA include the polluter pays principle and economic incentives for proper management and disposal of hazardous wastes, backed by a number of sanctions.

104. EMCA contains all the essential legislative elements a clear statement of purpose, a comprehensive section which defines terms such as "ecosystem", detailed provisions for regulation of hazardous wastes along the requirements of the 1989 Basel Convention, detailed provisions creating implementing agencies and institutions and creates financial mechanisms for implementation. Among the institutions created to implement the EMCA is the National Environment Management Authority ("NEMA") to exercise general supervision and coordination over all matters relating to the environment and to be the principal instrument of government in the implementation of all policies relating to the environment. Functions of NEMA include the establishment of hazardous wastes and other environmental standards required by EMCA. In carrying out its functions, NEMA is required to collaborate with a number of Lead Agencies, including local authorities and government ministries with functions related to the environment. Section 31 of EMCA also creates a Public Complaints Committee ("PCC") on environmental matters with the responsibility to investigate any allegations or complaints against any person or against NEMA in relation to the condition of the environment in Kenya and to make recommendations for remedial actions to the National Environment Council. In addition, Section 125 of EMCA creates a National Environment Tribunal ("NET") whose functions include hearing appeals on environmental matters.

105. Since the passage of EMCA, Kenya has made appreciable implementation efforts. The government has established NEMA, NET, the PCC and all other bodies created by EMCA and they are in full operation. In collaboration with UNEP, a report on hazardous waste situation in the country has been prepared to help in planning and designing appropriate methods to reduce the generation of hazardous wastes, including the implementation of economic instruments. NEMA is currently developing environmental standards, including standards for hazardous wastes. Further, in compliance with public participation provisions of EMCA, the NEMA, NET and the PCC have been conducting awareness workshops throughout the country to educate the public and government officials on their rights and responsibilities under EMCA and on a variety of environmental law subjects with which the majority of Kenyans are not yet familiar.

106. EMCA applies in addition to sectoral environmental laws in Kenya, such as the Agriculture Act and the Public Health Act. Section 148 of EMCA requires the existing sectoral environmental laws to be modified as necessary in order to give effect to EMCA and that in case of any conflict between the provisions of EMCA and the provisions of the sectoral laws, the provisions of EMCA shall prevail.

Masa Nagai, Senior Legal Officer, Division of Policy Development and Law, UNEP

Dr. Jane Dwasi, UNEP Consultant, University of Nairobi

Barbara Ruis, Legal Officer, Division of Policy Development and Law, UNEP

Resources

Internet Materials

1989 BASEL CONVENTION TEXT available at
http://untreaty.un.org/ENGLISH/bible/englishinternetbible/partI/chapterXXVII/treaty18.asp

ADMIRALITY AND MARITIME LAW GUIDE: INTERNATIONAL CONVENTIONS available at
http://www.admiraltylawguide.com/conven/civilpol1969.html

AUSTRALIAN TREATY SERIES available at http://www.austlii.edu.au/au/other/dfat/treaties/notinforce/2002/25.html

BASEL PROTOCOL ON CIVIL LIABILITY available at http://www.basel.int/meetings/cop/cop5/docs/prot-e.pdf or
http://www.basel.int/pub/protocol.html

CANADIAN/AMERICAN AGREEMENT ON HAZARDOUS WASTE available at
http://stabenow.senate.gov/stoptrash/transboundary.htm

CARTAGENA CONVENTION TEXT available at http://www.cep.unep.org/pubs/legislation/cartxt.html

CHINESE ENVIRONMENTAL PROTECTION LAWS available at http://www.zhb.gov.cn/english/law.php3?offset

CHINESE NATIONAL REPORT ON SUSTAINABLE DEVELOPMENT (1997) available at
http://www.zhb.gov.cn/english/SD/21cn/national_report/nr-c3-s13.htm

DR. ABDUL RAHMAN AL-AWADI, ROPME SEA AREA: MEETING THE CHALLENGE available at
http://www.unep.ch/seas/kapcap.html

ENVIRONMENT CANADA, TRANSBOUNDARY MOVEMENT BRANCH, CANADA-U.S.A. AGREEMENT ON THE TRANSBOUNDARY
MOVEMENT OF HAZARDOUS WASTES available at http://www.ec.gc.ca/tmb/eng/facts/canusa_e.html

GLOBAL MARINE LITTER INFORMATION GATEWAY available at
http://marine-litter.gpa.unep.org/framework/region-13-next.htm

INTERNATIONAL FUND CONVENTION available at
http://www.imo.org/Conventions/mainframe.asp?topic_id=256&doc_id=661 OR http://www.iopcfund.org

JOSEF LEITMAN, INTEGRATING THE ENVIRONMENT IN URBAN DEVELOPMENT: SINGAPORE AS A MODEL OF GOOD PRACTICE
available at http://www.worldbank.org/html/fpd/urban/solid_wm/uwp7.pdf

LONDON CONVENTION available at http://www/londonconvention.org or
http://sedac.ciesin.org/pidb/texts/marine.pollution.dumping.of.wastes.1972.html

REGIONAL AND SUB-REGIONAL CENTRES FOR TRAINING AND TECHNOLOGY TRANSFER regarding the MANAGEMENT OF
HAZARDOUS WASTES and other WASTES and the MINIMIZATION OF THEIR GENERATION available at
http://www.basel.int/pub/regcentrs.html

UNITED NATIONS ENVIRONMENT PROGRAMME, DIVISION OF TECHNOLOGY, INDUSTRY AND ECONOMICS available at
http://www.unepie.org

YEARBOOK OF INTERNATIONAL CO-OPERATION ON ENVIRONMENT AND DEVELOPMENT, TEXT OF WAIGANI CONVENTION available
at http://www.greenyearbook.org/agree/haz-sub/waigani.htm

Text Materials

AMERICAN JOURNAL OF PUBLIC HEALTH, (Vol. 78, at 654-668, 1988).

BULLETIN OF ENVIRONMENTAL CONTAMINATION AND TOXICOLOGY, (Vol. 49, 1992).

BULLETIN OF ENVIRONMENTAL CONTAMINATION AND TOXICOLOGY, (Vol. 53, 1994).

Centers for Investigative Reporting & Bill Moyers, GLOBAL DUMPING GROUND: THE INTERNATIONAL TRADE IN HAZARDOUS WASTES (1990).

EUROPEAN JOURNAL OF PHARMACOLOGY, (Vol. 248, at 166-179, 1993).

Fina P. Kaloianova & Mostafa A. El Batawi, HUMAN TOXICOLOGY OF PESTICIDES, (1991).

INTERNATIONAL DEVELOPMENT RESEARCH & THE UNITED NATIONS ENVIRONMENTAL PROGRAMME, ECOSYSTEM DISRUPTION AND HUMAN HEALTH: SUMMARY REPORT OF A CONSULTATION HOSTED BY IDRC AND UNEP, (March 2002).

Josef Leitmann & World Bank, INTEGRATING THE ENVIRONMENT IN URBAN DEVELOPMENT: SINGAPORE AS A MODEL OF GOOD PRACTICE, (1999).

Jytte Ekdahl, Interpol Secretariat, THE WORK OF INTERPOL IN COMBATING ENVIRONMENTAL CRIME, IN UNITED NATIONS ENVIRONMENT PROGRAMME, ENFORCEMENT AND COMPLIANCE WITH MEAS: THE EXPERIENCES OF CITES, MONTREAL PROTOCOL AND BASEL CONVENTION (1999).

Mark Jaffe, TRACKING THE KHIAN SEA, (Philadelphia Inquirer, July 15, 1988).

Martin W. Holdgate, A REPORT BY THE UNITED NATIONS ENVIRONMENT PROGRAMME, THE WORLD ENVIRONMENT 1972-1982, (Mohammed Kassas & Gilbert F. White Eds., 1982).

PRINCIPLE 6 OF THE DECLARATION OF THE UNITED NATIONS CONFERENCE ON THE HUMAN ENVIRONMENT, UNITED NATIONS, REPORT OF THE UNITED NATIONS CONFERENCE ON THE HUMAN ENVIRONMENT, STOCKHOLM (5-16 JUNE 1972), (U.N. A/CONF.48/14/Rev.1).

RECOMMENDATIONS 4, 5,7, 14 AND 86, UNITED NATIONS, REPORT OF THE UNITED NATIONS CONFERENCE ON THE HUMAN ENVIRONMENT, STOCKHOLM (5-16 JUNE 1972), (U.N. A/CONF.48/14/Rev.1).

SCANDINAVIAN JOURNAL OF WORK AND ENVIRONMENTAL HEALTH, (Vol. 20, at 166-179, 1994).

Stephen O. Anderson & Durwoo Zaelke, INDUSTRY GENIUS: INVENTIONS AND PEOPLE PROTECTING THE CLIMATE AND FRAGILE OZONE LAYER, (2003).

THE UNITED NATIONS CONFERENCE ON ENVIRONMENT AND DEVELOPMENT (UNCED), (Introduction by Stanley P. Johnson), the Earth Summit, International Environmental Law and Policy Series, 1993).

UNITED NATIONS ENVIRONMENT PROGRAMME, ENVIRONMENTAL LAW GUIDELINES AND PRINCIPLES: ENVIRONMENTALLY SOUND MANAGEMENT OF HAZARDOUS WASTES, (June 1987).

UNITED NATIONS ENVIRONMENT PROGRAMME, STATE OF THE ENVIRONMENT AND SPECIAL ASSIGNMENT UNIT, THE STATE OF THE ENVIRONMENT: TEN YEARS AFTER STOCKHOLM, (January 1979).

UNITED NATIONS ENVIRONMENT PROGRAMME, THE STATE OF THE WORLD ENVIRONMENT, (April 1989).

YEARBOOK OF INTERNATIONAL CO-OPERATION ON ENVIRONMENT AND DEVELOPMENT, (2001/2002).

12. CHEMICALS

I. Introduction

1. Chemicals play an important role in daily life and have contributed greatly to human well being. Agricultural chemicals have raised farming yields by killing crop pests and industrial chemicals have made possible an endless array of useful products. Chemical substances are used in virtually every aspect of modern society and are used in many industries, including manufacturing and transportation and service sectors, such as telecommunications, banks, investment firms and coffee houses.

2. However, once released into the natural world, chemicals can persist for years and have long-term health and ecological consequences that were never anticipated or intended. As scientific knowledge and understanding of chemicals have increased, so have concerns about their impacts on human health and the environment. More than 100,000 chemical products, many produced on large scale, have been introduced to commercial markets. Associated risks are often only discovered later, when the damaging effects of certain chemicals have manifested.

3. Chemicals are by no means confined to industrial centres. Due to their sometimes persistent nature, chemicals can be transported in nature thousands of kilometres from where they were used. They move up the food chain and are trapped in fatty tissue of human beings, animals and plants.

4. In 1992, the United Nations Conference on Environment and Development adopted a sustainable development agenda for the 21st century, called Agenda 21. It stated that "Gross chemical contamination, with grave damage to human health, genetic structures and reproductive outcomes, and the environment, has in recent times been continuing within some of the world's most important industrial areas.... The long-range effects of pollution, extending even to the fundamental chemical and physical processes of the Earth's atmosphere and climate, are becoming understood only recently..." (para. 19.2)

5. Today, more chemicals are produced than ever and their production is projected to increase further in the future. (See Table 1). Toxic chemicals are produced worldwide by both developing and developed countries and international trade in chemicals is an important part of today's globalized world.

6. However, the export of chemicals that are subject to strict use controls in the countries of manufacture into countries that have less advanced chemical management schemes has raised grave concerns. These concerns are particularly relevant to developing countries and countries with economies in transition, as they import toxic chemicals often without adequate information on these chemicals and without the infrastructure to manage them in an environmentally sound manner.

II. The International Framework

7. The increase in international trade in chemicals and the realization that their impacts are not

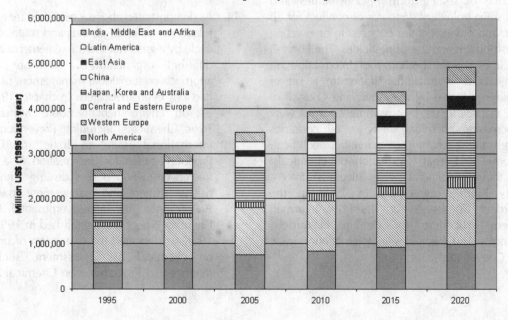

World Chemical Industry Output Projection (OECD)

limited to the country of use but extend regionally, or even globally, stimulated the need for international and multilateral cooperation in their management.

8.   The first legal interventions to manage toxic chemicals took place at the national level and focused on chemicals that were proved dangerous after their production and introduction on the market. These rules usually provided for the reductions of chemical emissions and restrictions on certain forms of their use. They were primarily aimed at the protection of human health, dealing mainly with security at the work place and the safety of consumer goods. In recent years, the focus has shifted from regulation of emissions to a more precautionary approach and from an anthropocentric to a broader environmental approach.

9.   Early international efforts to tackle the environmental and public health problems related to chemicals were generally devoted to improving the availability of information about such substances. In 1976 UNEP established the International Register of Potentially Toxic Chemicals ("IRPTC") to compile and circulate information on chemical hazards.

10. Cooperation between countries was first achieved with voluntary instruments concerning international trade in chemicals. In response to the dramatic growth in chemical production and trade, the United Nations Environment Programme and the Food and Agriculture Organization of the United Nations ("FAO") started developing and promoting voluntary information exchange programmes in the mid-1980s. The International Code of Conduct on the Distribution and Use of Pesticides was adopted in 1985 by FAO, with the objective of setting forth responsibilities and establishing voluntary standards of conduct for all public and private entities engaged in or affecting the distribution and use of pesticides. The London Guidelines for the Exchange of Information on Chemicals in International Trade are a set of guidelines adopted by the Governing Council of UNEP in 1987 for use by governments with a view to increasing chemical safety in all countries through the exchange of scientific, technical, economic and legal information on chemicals. Both these instruments were integrated into a legally binding agreement in 1998 in the Rotterdam Convention on the Prior Informed Consent Procedure for Certain Hazardous Chemicals and Pesticides in International Trade ("PIC Convention").

11. Other legally-binding international instruments were adopted to address specific related issues, such as chemical safety in the workplace, the disposal of hazardous substances and the emission of certain chemicals into the atmosphere. Those instruments are discussed in more detail in other thematic chapters of this Training Manual. The particular instruments that address these specific chemical-related problems are listed below.

12. International agreements relating to safety at work and the prevention of chemical accidents were concluded by the International Labour Organization in 1990 and 1993 respectively in the Convention concerning Safety in the Use of Chemicals at Work and the Convention concerning the Prevention of Major Industrial Accidents. (See chapter 23). The Vienna Convention for the Protection of the Ozone Layer (1985) and its Montreal Protocol (1987) provide control mechanisms for chemicals that deplete the ozone layer. (See chapter 9). The United Nations Framework Convention on Climate Change and its Kyoto Protocol target substances known to cause global warming. (See chapter 10). Some other air pollutants were addressed by the (Geneva) Convention on Long-Range Transboundary Air Pollution and its protocols. (See chapter 8). The 1989 Basel Convention covers those chemical substances defined as "hazardous wastes" under the convention (as discussed in chapter 11).

13. The PIC convention is one of the two global Conventions discussed in this chapter. The other instrument is the Stockholm Convention on Persistent Organic Pollutants ("POPs Convention"), which bans or restricts trade in and use of some of the most dangerous chemical substances known. Two two global conventions are discussed more fully below.

14. As demonstrated above, chemicals are regulated in relation to different aspects and stages of their life cycle by a great number of agreements adopted by different organizations. A more integrated approach on the global management of chemicals had long been advocated. In chapter 19 of Agenda 21, on "Environmentally Sound Management of Toxic Chemicals, including Prevention of Illegal International Traffic in Toxic and Dangerous Products" called for the creation of a forum for intergovernmental bodies dealing with chemical risk assessment and management (para. 19.76). Accordingly, the Intergovernmental Forum on Chemical Safety was established in 1993. Chapter 19 also advocated the expansion of programmes on chemical risk assessment, such as the International Programme on Chemical Safety, run

by UNEP, ILO and the World Health Organization (para. 19.14). Thus, the Inter-Organization Programme on the Sound Management of Chemicals ("IOMC") was established to promote coordination among international organizations involved in implementing chapter 19.

15. Priorities set out in chapter 19 of Agenda 21 are:

   - Expanding and acceleration of international assessment of chemicals risks (programme 19.A);
   - Harmonization of classification and labelling of chemicals (programme 19.B);
   - Information exchange on toxic chemicals and chemical risks (programme 19.C);
   - Establishment of risk reduction programmes (programme 19.D);
   - Strengthening of national capabilities and capacities management of chemicals (programme 19.E); and
   - Prevention of illegal international traffic in toxic and dangerous products (programme 19.F).

16. Since the United Nations Conference on Environment and Development and Agenda 21, dozens of global and regional chemical management agreements and programmes have been initiated, strengthened or completed. In 2002, the World Summit on Sustainable Development agreed to a comprehensive strategic approach for the international management of chemicals. Following this decision, the UNEP Governing Council adopted a plan to develop a Strategic Approach to International Chemicals Management ("SAICM") by 2005. SAICM aims at ensuring that chemicals are used and produced in ways that lead to the minimization of significant adverse effects on human health and the environment. The strategic approach will address a broad array of chemical issues including risk assessment and management, availability and accessibility of information, worker safety, pesticide use and disposal, hazardous wastes, classification and labelling and research and monitoring. It also seeks to enhance the coherency and efficiency among international activities related to chemicals.

1. Rotterdam Convention on the Prior Informed Consent Procedure for Certain Hazardous Chemicals and Pesticides in International Trade

17. Growth of international trade in chemicals during the 1960s and 1970s raised concerns about the potential harmful results of such trade. Developing countries lacking adequate infrastructure to monitor the import and use of toxic chemicals

were seen to be particularly vulnerable. In 1989, FAO's International Code of Conduct and UNEP's London Guidelines (see para. 9 above) were each revised amended to introduce the voluntary Prior Informed Consent ("PIC") procedure. Together, these instruments helped to ensure that governments had the necessary information to assess the risks of hazardous chemicals and to take informed decisions on their future import and management.

18. Concluding that there was a need for mandatory controls, Agenda 21 called for a legally binding instrument on the PIC procedure by the year 2000 (para. 19.38(b)). Negotiations began in March 1996 and were expeditiously completed in only two years. The Rotterdam Convention was adopted on 10 September 1998 and entered into force on 24 February 2004.

19. The Convention creates a legally binding obligation for implementation of the Prior Informed Consent procedure. The procedure is a means for formally obtaining and disseminating the decisions of importing countries as to whether they wish to receive shipments of a certain chemical. It facilitates information exchange about characteristics of chemicals and thereby informs the importing country's national decision-making processes for their importation and use. The Convention does not ban the global trade or use of specific chemicals.

20. The PIC Convention's aim is "...to promote shared responsibility and cooperative efforts among Parties in the international trade of certain hazardous chemicals in order to protect human health and the environment from potential harm and to contribute to their environmentally sound use, by facilitating information exchange about their characteristics, by providing for a national decision-making process on their import and export and by disseminating these decisions to the Parties." (article 1).

21. The scope of the PIC Convention, in terms of the chemicals to be covered, was a difficult issue. A 'chemical' is defined in the Convention as "...a substance whether by itself or in a mixture or preparation and whether manufactured or obtained from nature, but does not include any living organism..." (article 2). The chemicals covered are divided into two categories: industrial chemicals that are banned or severely restricted for health or environmental reasons and severely hazardous pesticide formulations that present problems under conditions of use in developing countries or countries with economies in transition.

22. The Convention covered 41 chemicals including 24 pesticides, 6 severely hazardous pesticide formulation and 11 industrial chemicals (Annex III as amended by the First Meeting of the Conference of the Parties ("COP") by its decision RC 1/3 of 24 September 2004). Many more are expected to be added in the future.

23. Exempt from the PIC Convention are certain groups of chemicals that are regulated under other international regimes. These are narcotic drugs and psychotropic substances, radioactive materials, wastes, chemical weapons, chemicals used as food additives and food. Chemicals in small quantities not likely to affect human health or the environment are also excluded, provided that they are for research and analysis or for personal use.

Major Components of the Rotterdam Convention

a) Institutions

24. The Convention establishes a Conference of the Parties ("COP") to oversee its implementation (article 18). The first Meeting of the COP (COP-1) was held in September 2004.

25. At COP-1, the Chemical Review Committee ("CRC") was formally established to review notifications and nominations from parties and to make recommendations on which nominated chemicals should be included in the PIC procedure (article 18.6). The 31 members of the Committee are appointed by the COP and comprise experts in chemicals management who are appointed on a geographically equitable basis.

26. The COP and its subsidiary bodies are serviced by a Secretariat. Its main functions are to make arrangements for the meetings of the COP and its subsidiary bodies, to facilitate assistance to parties in implementing the Convention, and to ensure the necessary coordination with the secretariats of other relevant international bodies (article 19). It is also the interface between the parties and the Convention's other institutional bodies in the Prior Informed Consent procedure. The Secretariat is located in Geneva, Switzerland and its functions are carried out jointly by the Executive Director of UNEP and the Director-General of FAO.

b) PIC Procedure

27. What is referred to as the PIC procedure can be divided into two phases: (1) the phase of information exchange, and (2) the inclusion of chemicals into Annex III of the Convention and the resulting mandatory procedures governing import decisions, which comprise the core of the PIC procedure.

28. The first requirement of the Convention is that parties establish Designated National Authorities ("DNA") to be the contact points for information exchange and for communication of permissions under the PIC procedure (article 4).

c) Information Exchange

29. The information exchange process is triggered by individual country actions. When a country takes a final regulatory action that bans or severely restricts a chemical within its jurisdiction, it must, through its DNA, inform the Secretariat within 90 days of this action (article 5). The notification must contain information about the action and the chemical itself, as required in Annex I to the Convention. The Secretariat then verifies within six months that the notification contains all necessary information and forwards a summary of this information to all parties. If the notification is incomplete the country is informed about the problem. In addition the Secretariat sends out compilations of the notifications received to the parties every six months as PIC Circulars.

30. As well as notifying the Secretariat about its domestic regulatory action to ban or severely restrict a chemical that it exports, the party has to notify the DNAs in countries intending to import shipments of the chemical (article 12). The required content of this export notification is set out in Annex V of the Convention. Export notification must be provided prior to the first export following adoption of the corresponding final regulatory action and on an annual basis before the first export in each calendar year thereafter. One repeat notification must be sent if the importing country fails to acknowledge receipt of the first notification.

d) Core PIC Procedure

31. At the core of the PIC procedure is the placing of a chemical on the multilateral PIC list in Annex III of the Convention. Parties are then required to provide their 'informed responses' to consent, or not, to import that chemical. Once an informed response has been circulated, export of that chemical can take place only to a country that has explicitly authorized its import.

e) PIC Listing

32. There are two ways to propose the inclusion of a chemical in the PIC list in Annex III: (1) by restriction notification, or (2) by problem pesticide proposal. A party that provides notification of a ban or severe restriction may trigger the PIC listing process, if its notification conforms to Annex I requirements and is supported by another country's notification, as described below (article 5). In addition, a developing country party, or a party with economy in transition, may inform other parties, through the Secretariat, that it is experiencing problems caused by a severely hazardous pesticide formulation under conditions of use in its territory (article 6). The proposal must meet information requirements set out in Annex IV. Part 1. It also should be noted that chemicals previously listed under the UNEP and FAO voluntary codes, prior to the entry into force of the PIC Convention, were considered for listing in Annex III of the Convention independently of the restriction notification or pesticide problem processes (article 8).

33. As soon as the Secretariat has received a problem pesticide proposal or similar regulatory notifications from two countries of two different PIC regions, the core PIC procedure is initiated. At COP-1 the eight PIC regions were identified as: Africa, Asia, Europe, Latin America and the Caribbean, Near East, North America and Southwest Pacific. The Secretariat then forwards the proposal to the Chemical Review Committee ("CRC"). The CRC will then consider (in line with criteria set out in Annex II in case of banned or severely restricted chemicals or Annex IV for severely hazardous pesticide formulations) whether it will recommend to the COP to list the substance in Annex III of the Convention (articles 5.6 and 6.5). The power to list a chemical (article 7) or to remove a chemical from the list (article 9) actually rests with the COP and comes into effect on the date set by the COP (article 22.5).

34. If the CRC intends to recommend the inclusion of a substance, it prepares a draft Decision Guidance Document ("DGD") (article 7). The purpose of a DGD is to help governments to analyze the potential hazards associated with the handling and use of the chemical and to take the decision whether to allow future import of the chemical. Both, the recommendation and the draft DGD are forwarded to the COP. If the COP follows the recommendation and approves the draft DGD the chemical is listed in Annex III and the DGD is forwarded by the Secretariat to the DNA of all parties.

f) Import Decisions

35. The DGD is sent together with an Importing Country Response Form and instructions for completion. Parties are to return their import decisions through this form within 90 days. The Secretariat then summarizes and compiles the responses in the PIC Circular and distributes them to DNAs every six months. The import decision can be a final decision (to consent, to consent subject to specified conditions or not to consent), or an *interim* response (with the statement that a final decision is under consideration), or a request for further information (article 10). If a country fails to provide its import decision, the Secretariat sends a reminder letter and, if necessary, helps the importing country to provide a response within the next 12 months. In the meantime, the *status quo* of trade relations is maintained, which means that export may continue, if the chemical contains a chemical that is registered or has previously been imported and used in the importing country. Without restriction, or explicit consent to the import had been sought and received by the exporter (article 11).

36. Decisions taken by the importing party must be 'trade neutral' to be in line with international trade rules. This means that, if the party decides not to consent to accepting imports of a specific chemical, it must also stop domestic production for domestic use or imports from any non-party.

g) General Obligations

37. Each party is to take measures necessary to establish and strengthen its national infrastructures and institutions for the effective implementation of the Convention (article 15). Implementing measures include legislation and administrative measures and also cover the establishment of national registers and databases compiling safety information for chemicals. They may also entail the encouragement of initiatives by industry to promote chemical safety, such as through voluntary agreements. Countries also are to exchange information generally relevant to the implementation of the Convention (article 14) ensure that importers, relevant authorities and, where possible, users are informed of notifications received (article 11).

h) Technical Assistance

38. The Convention provides for technical assistance to developing countries and countries with economies in transition (article 16). This should facilitate the development of the infrastructure and capacity to manage chemicals in line with the

Convention. The Secretariat is charged with working on a technical assistance strategy to promote implementation of the Convention. For the same purpose, the Secretariat was entrusted by COP-1 with exploring options for a potential financial mechanism.

i) Non-Compliance

39. The COP is charged with the responsibility of developing procedures for dealing with non-compliance (article 17). COP-1 convened an open-ended *ad hoc* working group to conduct deliberations on the issue.

2. Stockholm Convention on Persistent Organic Pollutants

40. A class of chemicals, called persistent organic pollutants ("POPs"), has aroused particular environmental and human health concerns. Most POPs are powerful pesticides. These are chemicals designed to be broadly distributed in the environment, to remain operative over long periods of time and to poison specific aspects of an ecosystem. Other chemicals are produced to serve a range of industrial purposes. Yet others are released as unintended by-products of combustion and industrial processes. While the risk level varies from POP to POP, they share the following four properties:

  - High toxicity;
  - Persistence, lasting for years or even decades before degrading into less dangerous forms;
  - Mobility, as they evaporate and travel long distances through the air and through water; and
  - Higher concentration further up the food chain and accumulation in fatty tissues.

41. POPs are widely distributed throughout the environment. Through global distillation and ocean currents, they travel from temperate and tropical regions (where they are commonly used) to be deposited in the colder regions of the poles. Concentrations there tend to be high because there is less evaporation and transport from colder regions. Thus indigenous peoples in the Arctic have some of the highest recorded levels of POPs even though they have certainly received little benefit from the chemicals' original use.

42. In 1995 UNEP Governing Council initiated an assessment process for a list of 12 POPs. In response, an *ad hoc* Working Group on POPs was convened which developed a work plan for assessing available information on the chemistry,

sources, toxicity, environmental dispersion and socio-economic impacts of these POPs. The Working Group recommended immediate action and an Intergovernmental Negotiating Committee was set up. The Committee drafted the text of the Stockholm Convention, which opened for signature in May 2001 and entered into force on 17 May 2004.

43. The Convention seeks to "...protect human health and the environment from persistent organic pollutants" (article 1). It does so by eliminating the most dangerous POPs, supporting the transition to safer alternatives and by cleaning-up old stockpiles and equipment containing POPs.

44. The Stockholm Convention addresses the challenge posed by POPs by starting with 12 of the worst; also referred to as the dirty dozen. They are divided into three groups:

  (1) Intentionally produced chemicals;
  (2) Unintentionally produced substances (byproducts of chemical processes); and
  (3) Stockpiles.

45. Intentionally produced POPs are listed in Annex A (POPs for elimination) and Annex B (POPs for restriction). Nine of the intentionally produced POPs are pesticides: aldrin, chlordane, DDT (the only chemical in Annex B), dieldrin, endrin, heptachlor, hexachlorobenzene ("HCB") mirex and toxaphene. A family of intentionally produced POPs are industrial chemicals, namely polychlorinated biphenyls ("PCBs"). In addition, the POPs Convention covers two families of unintentionally produced chemical by-products, listed in Annex C of the Convention: polychlorinated dioxins and furans. They are potent cancer-causing chemicals and result from combustion and industrial processes. It should be noted that HCB is also produced as an intermediate industrial chemical and as a unintentional byproduct.

Major Components of the Stockholm Convention

a) Intentionally Produced POPs

46. The Stockholm Convention bans all production and use of the pesticides endrin and toxaphene and requires all parties to stop production of aldrin, dieldrin and heptachlor (artice 3). Those wishing to use remaining supplies of the latter three substances must publicly register for exemptions for narrowly allowed purposes and limited time periods (article 4). The production and use of chlordane, hexachlorobenzene and mirex is

restricted to narrowly prescribed purposes and to countries that have registered for exemption.

47. PCBs are mainly found in electric installation and equipment such as transformers and capacitors. The Stockholm Convention bans the production of PCBs but gives countries until 2025 to phase out the use of in-place equipment containing PCBs (Annex A Part II). However, countries are to exert their best efforts to identify, label and remove PCBs from equipment in use. Recovered PCBs must be treated and eliminated by 2028. Trade in PCB-containing equipment is allowed only for the purpose of environmentally sound waste management. The COP will review the progress on the 2025 and 2028 targets every five years.

48. Production and use of DDT is limited to controlling disease vectors such as malaria mosquitoes in accordance with WHO recommendations and guidelines and only as long as locally safe, effective and affordable alternatives are not available (Annex B, Part II). There are two specific exemptions to allow the use of DDT as an intermediate in the production of the pesticide dicofol. Parties in the DDT register must report on the quantities used, the conditions of use and the relevance to the party's disease management strategy. In addition they have to develop a national action plan to confine use of DDT to disease vector management, explore alternatives to DDT and to strengthen health care. All parties must promote research and development for alternatives to DDT. The COP will review exemptions every three years.

49. Imports and exports of the 10 intentionally produced POPs are restricted and their transport is permitted only for environmentally sound disposal or for specified uses for which the importing country has obtained exemption (article 3(2)).

50. Parties with regulatory and assessment schemes in place for industrial chemicals and pesticides are to regulate new substances with the aim of preventing the production and use of new POPs (article 3(3)). For screening such substances, the criteria set out in Annex D should be applied. These are the criteria used for assessing the potential inclusion of new chemicals to the POPs list (article 8).

b) Unintentionally Produced POPs

51. Governments are further required to take steps to reduce the release of dioxins, furans, hexachlorobenzene and PCBs as by-products of combustion or industrial production, with the view to continue their minimization and eventually, elimination. Within two years after the Convention's entry into force, parties are required to develop National Implementation Plans ("NIPs") to identify, characterize and assess releases of chemicals in Annex C. The NIPs shall include an evaluation of current and projected releases and the efficacy of legislation and policies of management in place. Strategies for reduction of releases, for education and training and a schedule for implementation of the NIP should also be included. Research on alternatives and Best Available Technologies ("BAT") are to be employed. COP-1 established an Expert Group on BAT and Best Environmental Practice to support members in meeting their obligations under the Convention.

c) Stockpiles

52. The Stockholm Convention calls on governments to develop and implement strategies for identifying stockpiles of products and articles containing POPs to ensure that they are managed in an environmentally sound manner (article 6). Wastes containing POPs are to be handled, collected, transported and stored in an environmentally sound manner and in line with international rules. (See Basel Convention, Chapter 11). Their toxic content needs to be destroyed. The Convention does not allow recovery, recycling, reclamation, direct reuse or alternative uses of POPs and prohibits their improper transport across national boundaries. Following a decision by COP-1 the Convention Secretariat is exploring synergies and cooperation options with the Secretariat of the Basel Convention on the Transboundary Movement of Hazardous Wastes and their Disposal.

d) General Obligations

53. Parties must develop a National Implementation Plan (article 7) and designate a National Focal Point (article 9). They are to promote and facilitate a wide range of public information, awareness and education measures (article 10) and are required to encourage and undertake research, development, monitoring and cooperation on all aspects of POPs and their alternatives (article 11). Furthermore, parties have obligations to report on the measures they take to implement the Convention, on the effectiveness of measures taken and on data/estimates for the total quantities of POPs traded and lists of states involved (article 15). COP-1 determined that reports have to be submitted every five years.

e) Institutions

54. The COP reviews and evaluates implementation of the Convention, harmonizes policies and establishes subsidiary bodies as it considers necessary (article 19). Ordinary meetings of the COP are held at regular intervals. The first COP (COP-1) was held in May 2005.

55. The Convention is serviced by a Secretariat located in Geneva, Switzerland. Amongst other tasks it facilitates assistance to parties in implementing the Convention and ensures the necessary coordination with the secretariats of other relevant international bodies, especially the Secretariat of the Basel Convention. It also performs other secretarial functions as specified in the Convention and determined by the COP.

56. The Persistent Organic Pollutant Review Committee ("POPRC") was established by COP-1 (under article 19(6)) to review suggestions for the listing of new POPs that may be submitted by the parties. It comprises 31 members selected on the basis of equitable geographical distribution.

f) Addition of New POPs

57. The POPRC will regularly consider additional candidates for the POPS list. Any government can propose a new listing by providing the required information and stating the reasons for its concern in accordance with Annex D (article 8). The Committee follows a structured evaluation process that incorporates precaution in a number of ways (article 8(7)). It must ensure that all candidate POPs are evaluated using the best available scientific data to determine whether their chemicals properties warrant their inclusion in the treaty. The POPRC moves through several steps of increasing complexity in its assessment of a proposed substance and finishes with an in-depth assessment, in accordance with Annex F, of control options for reducing or eliminating releases of the substance. The Committee then prepares a risk profile for each substance, following the requirements set out in Annex E and makes recommendations to the COP whether to the substance should be listed in the Convention. Then, if the COP agrees, unlike the Rotterdam Convention, inclusion of a new POP requires an amendment of the Stockholm Convention, which each Party needs to ratify.

g) Financial and Technical Assistance

58. Transfer of environmentally sound technologies and technical assistance in line with guidelines and criteria for receiving such assistance are prescribed to facilitate the implementation of the Convention (article 12). Regional and sub-regional centers are being established to closely cooperate with national focal points on technical implementation issues. A financial mechanism is in place, administered by the Global Environment Facility ("GEF") on an *interim* basis (article 14). It provides assistance to developing countries and countries with economies in transition to ensure that incremental costs associated with fulfilling their obligations under the Convention are covered. The financial mechanism particularly supports activities to strengthen capacities to implement, monitor and evaluate the use of DDT and its alternatives.

h) Non-Compliance

59. Pursuant to article 17, an Open-Ended Ad Hoc Working Group was established by COP-1 to consider procedures and institutional mechanisms on compliance. It will draw instruction from compliance mechanisms in other MEAs and on opinions from parties as compiled by the Secretariat.

3. Clustering of Related Agreements

60. Together, the Rotterdam Convention, the Stockholm Convention and the Basel Convention cover all key elements of life cycle management of hazardous chemicals. The concept of clustering them into a more integrated legal programme for chemicals management has merit. The Secretariats of the Rotterdam, Stockholm and Basel Conventions prepared an issues paper in 2001 outlining their current cooperation and the potential for closer cooperation in the future, subject to endorsement by their respective parties. Potential synergies could cover areas such as capacity building, science, technology, legal affairs and institutional matters, monitoring and reporting, and education and awareness raising. In 2002, the UNEP Governing Council endorsed such clustering. Pilot projects are under way to facilitate an integrated life-cycle approach to management of substances covered by the three Conventions.

61. Rotterdam and Stockholm Conventions target strategically important opportunities for chemicals management, namely international trade and persistent pollutants. However, there is much more to the picture. The two conventions form parts of a much larger mosaic of international laws regulating chemical impacts on human health and the environment. They work together with regimes for the management of hazardous wastes, workplace safety, radioactive substances, drugs, foods and other instruments. In particular, it is anticipated that they will work with the Basel Convention on

Hazardous Wastes to provide an integrated management approach to listed chemicals.

62. Rotterdam Convention and Stockholm Convention have much in common. Each adopts a rigorous multilateral approach to identify priority chemicals for international cooperative management. Each recognizes the greater responsibility of developed countries in chemicals management: Rotterdam Convention imposes special responsibilities on manufacturers, mostly located in industrialized countries, to impose controls on exporters; and Stockholm Convention relies on technical and financial assistance to developing countries to implement its obligations. Each Convention is in its early stages of development.

63. The environmentally sound management of chemicals is a global problem that requires international legal cooperation to meet its challenge. The essential legal frameworks have been developed and recently come into force. The next critical steps for convention participants to take are implementation and consolidation.

III. National Implementation

1. The European Union – PIC Procedure

64. The European Union's chemical industry is one of the world's largest. Its products include a wide range of substances that are dangerous to human health and the environment. Some of the chemicals manufactured for export and use in other countries are banned or severely restricted within the European Union ("EU") itself.

65. Regulation (EC) No. 304/2003 of the European Parliament and the Council concerning the export and import of dangerous chemicals implements the Rotterdam Convention. The Regulation has direct application in all EU member states.

66. In addition to dealing with matters relating to the implementation of the Rotterdam Convention, the Regulation seeks to impose the same packaging and labelling requirements for export of all dangerous chemicals as apply to trade within the EU. Thus, the Regulation covers not only chemicals subject to the PIC procedure, but also chemicals that are banned or severely restricted within the EU. In addition, chemicals for export are made subject to EU packaging and labelling requirements.

67. European Union member states are obliged to designate one or more national authorities to carry out the administrative functions under the Regulation and inform the Commission thereof.

The Commission is the common designated authority for the participation of the EU in the Convention, working in close cooperation with the DNAs of the member states. Its functions include the transmission of EU export notifications, submission of PIC notifications, receiving of export notification from third countries, submission of EU import decisions for PIC chemicals and exchange of information with the PIC Secretariat.

68. Under Regulation (EC) No. 304/2003, export notification obligations apply for export to any country, independent of accession to the Rotterdam Convention and irrespective of the intended use of the chemical. There is also a procedure for the import of chemical to the EU from other countries. When the Commission receives an export notification about a chemical from a third country, the marketing or use of which is banned or severely restricted in the country of origin, it registers this in a special database called EDEXIM. In a case where a DNA in a member state receives a notification, it must send it forthwith to the Commission, together with all relevant information.

69. The member states have to designate authorities such as customs offices to control imports and exports of chemicals listed in Annex I of the Regulation. They and the Commission coordinate enforcement activities and member states have to regularly report on such activities. Member states must also ensure correct implementation of the Regulation and have an effective, proportional and dissuasive system of penalties in place.

2. Ghana – PIC and POPs

70. Ghana has warm humid climate most of the year. This creates favorable conditions for a large number of insect-pest species and disease organisms to attack crops, making pest and disease organisms a potential threat to food security in the country. Pests outbreaks are rampant. Hence, a variety of highly toxic pesticides have been resorted to in the past.

71. In contrast to the EU, Ghana is primarily a consumer, rather than a producer, of chemicals in international trade. Until the early 1980s, insecticides, mainly aldrin, dieldrin, DDT and lindane were used to control crop pests. These have now been discontinued, except for lindane, which has been restricted to capsids control in cocoa production.

72. Act 490 of 1994 established an Environment Protection Agency. Its mandate includes the coordination of activities of bodies engaged in

controlling the generation, treatment, storage, transportation and disposal of industrial waste. The Agency is also empowered to issue environmental permits and pollution abatement notices for controlling the volumes, types, constituents and effects of emissions, deposits, waste discharges and of substances that are hazardous or potentially dangerous to the quality of the environment or any segment thereof.

73. Under Section 10 of the Act, a Hazardous Chemicals Committee is established. It is charged, *inter alia*, with monitoring the use of hazardous chemicals by collecting information on importation, exportation, manufacture, distribution, sale, use and disposal of such chemicals.

74. Under Section 28 of the Act, regulations can be adopted on substances that may be released into the environment and on substances that may be hazardous to the environment. Therefore, Act 490 could be interpreted to cover all chemicals in use in Ghana. This fact notwithstanding, there are other laws that are specific to particular chemicals.

75. Concerning pesticides, Act 528, the Pesticides Control and Management Act 1996, as amended in 1997, prescribes measures to minimize the dangers that arise from the misuse of pesticides. It covers all classes of pesticides and provides for registration and additional requirements on labelling. It defines pesticide approval procedures and registration procedures for importers and distributors.

76. The 1997 amendment deals, *inter alia*, with matters relating to certification and approval. It

allows for the issuance of a 3 year temporary importation permit pending full certification. The amendment outlines the procedures and conditions for obtaining approval based on the type of the applicant's activities (importer, formulator/producer, wholesaler/distributor, specialized haulage transporter, public sector operator). Approvals are valid for a year and are renewable.

77. For certification, each applicant must provide the Agency with technical records related to the product (technical characteristics, test findings, dangers to the environment, target crops and parasites, etc.) and pay a fixed fee of US $500 for each application. The certification is issued within 1 to 1.5 years, and is valid for 5 years. The certification is issued for specific formulation of a specific commercial product with specific intended uses. A certification can be extended, but the procedure will need to be repeated.

Eva Maria Duer, Associate Legal Officer, Division of Policy Development and Law, UNEP

Lal Kurukulasuriya, Chief of UNEP's Environmental Law Branch until his retirement in March 2005, currently Director-General of the Centre for Environmental Research Training and Information, Sri Lanka

Gregory Rose, Associate Professor, Faculty of Law, University of Wollongong, Australia

---

Ghana, Pesticides Control and Management Act 1996

1. No person shall import, export, manufacture, distribute, advertise, sell or use any pesticide in Ghana unless the pesticide has been registered by the Environmental Protection Agency in accordance with this Act.
(...)
3. A person seeking to register any pesticide shall submit to the Agency an application for registration which shall be in such form and be accompanied with such fee, information, samples and such other material as the Agency may determine.
(...)
4(2) Pesticides classified under subsection (1) as restricted, suspended or banned shall be subject to the Prior Informed Consent Procedure defined in section 41 of this Act.
(...)
41...."Prior Informed Consent Procedure" means the international operation procedure for exchanging, receiving and handling notification information by the Agency on restricted, suspended and banned pesticides for reasons of health and the environment"

Resources

Internet Materials

EUROPEAN COMMISSION – ENVIRONMENT - CHEMICALS available at
http://europa.eu.int/comm/environment/chemicals/index.htm

GHANA ENVIRONMENTAL PROTECTION AGENCY available at www.epa.gov.gh/

HOMEPAGE OF CREATION OF THE INTERGOVERNMENTAL FORUM ON CHEMICAL SAFETY ("IFCS") available at www.who.int/ifcs/

HOMEPAGE OF THE PIC CONVENTION available at http://www.pic.int

HOMEPAGE OF THE POPs CONVENTION available at http://www.pops.int

INTER-ORGANIZATION PROGRAMME ON THE SOUND MANAGEMENT OF CHEMICALS ("IOMC") available at
http://www.who.int/iomc/

ORGANIZATION FOR ECONOMIC COOPERATION AND DEVELOPMENT available at http://www.oecd.org

UNEP HOMEPAGE ON CHEMICALS available at http://www.chem.unep.ch/

UNEP, REPORT ON THE CONFERENCE OF THE PARTIES OF THE STOCKHOLM CONVENTION ON PERSISTENT ORGANIC POLLUTANTS, (May 2005) availabe at www.pops.int

UNEP, RIDDING THE WORLD OF POPs – A BEGINNER'S GUIDE TO THE STOCKHOLM CONVENTION ON PERSISTENT ORGANIC POLLUTANTS, (April 2005) available at www.pops.int

Text Materials

Jonathan Krueger, INFORMATION IN INTERNATIONAL ENVIRONMENTAL GOVERNANCE: THE PRIOR INFORMED CONSENT PROCEDURE FOR TRADE IN HAZARDOUS CHEMICALS AND PESTICIDES, (Harvard University, September 2000).

UNEP, REPORT ON THE CONFERENCE OF THE PARTIES OF THE ROTTERDAM CONVENTION, (September 2004).

UNEP, THE HAZARDOUS CHEMICALS AND WASTE CONVENTIONS, (September 2003).

13. MARINE POLLUTION

I. Introduction

1. The marine world is both majestic and fragile. Big, beautiful, powerful, life supporting, ancient and mysterious, the world's waters are also delicate and vulnerable. The earth's oceans and seas need protection by and from the planet's dominating species. This chapter presents an overview of international environmental law for protection of the marine environment from pollution.

2. The chapter begins with a description of the environment and of its pollution threats. It proceeds to consider applicable international law, beginning with a brief explanation of the process that built consensus among states to take international legal action. International standards for control of marine pollution are surveyed according to pollution sources. Implementation of international agreements always requires some action at the national level and many agreements require parties to create national laws as a way of implementing the measures required by the agreements. Therefore, this chapter examines some examples of national laws that have been created to implement one or more of the international agreements.

3. The oceans are thought to have been formed as a result of icy comet collisions with the Earth occurring from 4.5 to 3.9 billion years ago, forming steam which gravity condensed and pulled into depressions in the planet's surface. The Earth's major oceanic depressions form the Pacific, Indian, Atlantic, Southern and Arctic Oceans. These oceans are a thin film over the Earth's surface, on average, only a few kilometres deep. Oceans and seas currently cover approximately 71% of the Earth's surface, 360 million square kilometres. This thin layer of oceans forms about 90% of the Earth's biosphere, by volume, and was the original source of life on Earth about four billion years ago. Oceans and seas contain the greatest amount of life by mass.

4. In law, the marine environment is divided into maritime zones. These comprise areas within national jurisdiction, such as the territorial sea, exclusive economic zone and continental shelves, as well as areas beyond national jurisdiction, such as the high seas and deep seabed. The sovereignty of a state extends, beyond its land territory and its internal waters, to a belt of sea adjacent to its coast, described as the territorial sea. This area typically extends 12 nautical miles from the state's coast. The exclusive economic zone is an area beyond and adjacent to the territorial sea, typically extending 200 nautical miles from the state's coast. A continental shelf of a coastal state comprises the submerged prolongation of the land territory of the coastal state - the seabed and subsoil of the submarine areas that extend beyond its territorial sea to the outer edge of the continental margin. A state may be able to assert jurisdiction in some matters to the edge of its continental shelf even if it extends beyond the exclusive economic zone. Areas beyond national jurisdiction must be managed cooperatively. Further, the flows of the ocean's currents run through national jurisdictions but cannot be permanently held or managed there. Accordingly, contaminants cannot be contained within the maritime jurisdiction of one source state. They must also be managed cooperatively.

II. International Framework

1. The Problem

5. Why protect the marine environment from pollution? Seas and oceans perform important ecological functions and provide many benefits to human beings. They are home to numerous animals, plants and other marine organisms that form marine ecosystems and support the livelihoods of hundreds of millions of people. Diverse marine organisms and their genetic resources could hold cures for many of the ailments that we face. Marine fishing is fundamental to the economies of many countries.

6. Fish and many other marine organisms cannot survive in polluted waters that are toxic to them. Marine organisms that are used for food can become contaminated with substances such as mercury, which is harmful to human beings. In addition to chemical substances, items like fishing lines, metal rings, straps, glass and plastics hamper the mobility of marine animals. Once entangled, marine mammals and other organisms have trouble breathing, eating or swimming, all of which can result in their death. Items such as broken glass and chemicals can also harm swimmers and other people using the marine environment.

7. The regulation of marine pollution is usually analyzed according to the identified source producing the marine pollution. The sources and their respective contribution to marine pollution load (by mass) are: land-based (82%), vessel-based (9%), dumping of waste at sea (8%) and off-shore activity (1%).

8. Land-based sources include sewage outfalls, industrial discharges, runoff from urban stormwater and agriculture, river borne and airborne pollution, and litter. Vessel-based sources include operational discharges such as bilge water discharges, but not the operation of a vessel for the purpose of discharging waste, as that is dumping. Pollution from vessels can take the forms of oil, chemicals, lost cargo and equipment, sewage, garbage, fumes and invasive exotic species. Dumping is the deliberate disposal of wastes at sea. Offshore activity generates minor pollution primarily through the use of oily drilling muds and by production blow outs.

Example: Torrey Canyon

On 19 February 1967, the "Torrey Canyon" left Kuwait. She was the first of the big supertankers, carrying a full cargo of 120,000 tons of oil. On 18 March, she struck Pollard's Rock in the Seven Stones reef between the Scilly Isles and Land's End, England. 31 million gallons of oil leaked from the ship and spread between England and France, killing marine life along the Cornish coast of Britain and the Normandy shores of France, blighting the region for many years. The spill left destitute many families and businesses dependent on sea resources for sustenance.

Investigations revealed that the accident resulted from a combination of factors, including:
Poor ship design ,
poor operational scheduling,
incompetence of the crew and
poor navigational procedures.

The ship's operations involved many countries. At the time, the Torrey Canyon was owned by a subsidiary of Union Oil in the United States, registered in Liberia, chartered to BP Shell in the UK, and operated by Italian crew. The vessel left Kuwait for an unknown destination and the slick affected French and English waters. There were no emergency procedures and disaster response strategies stipulated in international law at the time. The situation raised numerous questions, including which state was responsible to check that the vessel was safe.

---

9. The grand scale upon which humans make use of marine resources is placing pressure on various marine ecosystems. In some cases, different uses conflict with and undermine each other. For example, waste disposal has undermined fishing and recreation in some areas. In some cases, over fishing has exhausted marine resources or destabilized part of the marine ecosystem. For example, exotic organisms transported in ship ballast water are invading new ecosystems. As pollution has increased, the assimilative capacity of semi-enclosed seas, in particular, has been nearly exhausted, resulting in negative impacts on related health, and on economic and social activities.

2. The Law of the Sea Process

10. In the mid-twentieth century, international competition over rights to harvest fisheries in outside of territorial waters led to disputes between states. Extraction of hydrocarbons and minerals from the continental shelf and deep sea bed, respectively, also led to disputes among states. Increasing populations and technological advancements created impetus for states to assert claims of national jurisdiction further from the coast, setting them on collision courses. The United Nations took up the issues and, in an effort to find lasting solutions to the problems, tasked its International Law Commission to codify principles customarily applied by states to their uses of the sea. The work of the Commission led to the gradual development of a number of conventions that addressed, *inter alia*, marine pollution issues.

11. The first United Nations Conference on the Law of the Sea, held in 1958, adopted four separate Conventions on laws of the sea. Respectively, they dealt with the high seas, the territorial sea and the contiguous zone, the continental shelf, and fishing and conservation of the living resources of the high seas. A voluntary protocol was also adopted requiring the compulsory settlement of disputes that might arise between parties as a result of interpretation or implementation of the conventions. However, the four Conventions did not address the problem of marine pollution in any detail and were overtaken by subsequent international agreements.

12. A second conference on the Law of the Sea in 1960 was unproductive but a third was a major success in producing agreement. It was convened in 1973 and met twice a year until 10 December 1982, when the omnibus United Nations Convention on the Law of the Sea ("UNCLOS") was adopted. UNCLOS entered into force on 16 November 1994 and has 148 parties (April 2005). In the twelve-year period prior to its entry into force, some of the provisions of UNCLOS had matured into customary international law and became binding on all states.

13. UNCLOS establishes the international legal order of the oceans. The variety of subjects dealt with is covered in a total of 320 articles, divided into seventeen parts, each part dealing with a broad subject concerning the sea. In addition, UNLCOS has nineteen Annexes, each dealing with a specific marine issue. The subject of prevention of marine pollution is covered mainly under part XII of UNCLOS. Some relevant rules are located in other parts, especially part II, concerning the territorial sea, and part XI, concerning the deep sea bed.

3. The Law of the Sea and the Marine Environment

14. Part XII of UNCLOS is a ground-breaking achievement, entirely dedicated to protection of the marine environment. The 45 articles apply to seas and oceans forming the territories of parties, and their exclusive economic zones including the sea bed and to the high seas, ocean floor and ice-covered areas. It is set out in sections that concern general provisions, global and regional cooperation, technical assistance, monitoring and environmental assessment, international rule formation, enforcement, safeguards against inept enforcement, ice-covered areas, responsibility and liability for pollution damage and sovereign immunity.

15. The definition of marine pollution in UNCLOS (article 1(4)) is:

    "...Introduction by man, directly or indirectly, of substances or energy into the marine environment, including estuaries which results or is likely to result in such deleterious effects as harm to living resources and marine life hazard to human health, hindrance to marine activities, including fishing, and other legitimate uses of the sea, impairment of quality for use of sea water and reduction of amenities."

    This definition raises the problem of identifying thresholds for the various threats described in it. Implicit in that problem is identifying what the assimilative capacity of the marine environment is since the scientific understanding of the ocean's assimilative capacity is not well advanced.

16. The key provisions of UNCLOS include:

    • Article 192 which states the obligation to protect and preserve the marine environment;
    • Article 193 which preserves the sovereign rights of states to exploit their own natural resources reflecting the concern of many countries, particularly developing countries, to ensure that they are not obstructed from following the quickest possible path to industrial development;
    • Article 194 which provides that states are to take all measures necessary to prevent, reduce and control pollution of the marine environment using the best practicable means at their disposal and in accordance with their capabilities. The environment protection obligations are heavily qualified by reference to the limits of state capabilities and, later, by reference to their sovereign right to exploit their natural resources. Article 194 also sets out the obligations for states not to cause damage by pollution to other states and their environment or areas beyond those where states exercise sovereign rights, that is, the high seas. Article 194 is based upon obligations in customary international law, as articulated in the Trail Smelter and Corfu Channel cases, and Principle 21 of the Stockholm Declaration; and
    • Article 195 which imposes a duty not to transfer pollution from one type to another, or from one area to another. For example, sewage can be a land-based source when discharged from an ocean outfall, but may be transformed into a dumped source if it is partially treated and the sludge is then dumped at sea by a barge.

17. It has been almost three decades since these general principles were formulated and other, newer principles have since caught the imagination of the international environmental community. In addition to the notion of sustainable development, there are the precautionary principle, integrated ecosystem management, biodiversity conservation, use of best available technologies or environmental practices, and the eclipse of the notion of the right to maximize use of the oceans assimilative capacity. In relation to these newer concepts, UNCLOS is largely silent, but provides a vehicle for separate new legal initiatives. For example, article 194(3)(a) requires the parties to minimise release of toxic substances to reduce the potential of their reaching the marine environment. This provision has relevance to the implementation of the Stockholm Convention on Persistent Organic Pollutants of 2001.

18. Other important aspects of UNCLOS include:

    • Article 198 requiring states to immediately notify others deemed likely to be affected by any form of threatening pollution, whether it emanates from activities or areas under the jurisdiction of the notifying state or not;
    • Article 202 requiring states to cooperate in scientific research and information exchange, and to jointly conduct the research necessary to establish appropriate scientific criteria for the formulation of rules to protect the environment;
    • Article 203 obligating states to provide scientific and technical assistance to developing states to enhance their capacity to protect the marine environment, specifically including the preparation of environmental assessments and assistance in minimizing the effects of major pollution incidents;
    • Article 204 mandating that states keep under particular surveillance the effects of any

activities that they engage in directly or permit in order to determine whether those activities are likely to pollute the marine environment. This is a relatively low threshold for the requirement to identify activities that are to be kept under surveillance;

- Article 205 providing that states must publish reports of the results obtained by their monitoring activities;

- Article 206 requiring states to assess the potential effects of activities which they have reasonable grounds to believe may cause substantial pollution or significant harmful changes to the marine environment and to communicate such reports to the competent international organizations. The latter assessment is also, in effect, an obligation to conduct Environmental Impact Assessments ("EIA");

- Article 213-233 providing for enforcement through investigation of violations, criminal proceedings against offenders, imposition of monetary penalties against offenders and several other sanctions and remedies, as well as limitations on enforcement;

- Article 235 providing that parties shall be responsible and liable for pollution damage under international law should they fail to carry out their duties and responsibilities; and

- Article 237 providing that UNCLOS should be implemented without prejudice to the environmental obligations imposed under other treaties relating to the marine environment.

19. In case any disputes arise as a result of the interpretation or implementation of the provisions of the Convention, they are to be resolved in the manner provided for by the Convention. Parties have an obligation under part XV to settle all their disputes by peaceful means. Part XV sets out a compulsory procedure for binding dispute resolution that is unique among environment protection treaties. First, parties are obliged to conciliate. If conciliation fails, they must resolve the dispute by means of a binding decision handed down by their choice of either the International Tribunal for the Law of the Sea ("ITLOS"), the International Court of Justice ("ICJ") or by an arbitral panel. Either a general panel (Annex VII) or a specialist environmental panel (Annex VIII) can arbitrate the dispute.

20. Chapter XII of UNCLOS sets out a broad framework for comprehensive measures to control marine pollution. Although drafted a quarter century ago and prior to the development of the sustainable development paradigm, its provisions still provide a solid basis for the prescription of standards and for their enforcement regimes. The provisions are supplemented by a range of treaty laws that prescribe standards in much greater detail for more narrowly defined sources of pollution or for particular regions.

4. Land-Based Sources of Marine Pollution

21. The vast majority of marine pollution comes from land-based sources. These include sewage outfalls, industrial discharges, runoff from urban storm water and agriculture, river borne and airborne pollution and litter. Land-based sources of marine pollution can also be transported through the air, such as by vehicle emissions. Enclosed or semi-enclosed seas are especially vulnerable to land-based sources.

22. Recognizing that control of land-based sources of marine pollution was failing, the 1992 United Nations Conference on Environment and Development agreed to advance the subject. Agenda 21 invited the United Nations Environment Programme to convene a meeting on land-based sources as soon as practicable and identified priority actions for control of these sources, including eliminating the discharge of organ halogen compounds that threaten to accumulate to dangerous levels in the marine environment, reducing of discharge of other synthetic organic compounds and promoting controls over anthropogenic inputs of nitrogen and phosphorous, which cause eutrophication. Agenda 21 also recommended updating the 1985 Montreal Guidelines for the Protection of the Marine Environment against Pollution from Land Based Sources, assessing the effectiveness of regional agreements on land-based sources and the formulating of new regional agreements where appropriate, and providing guidance on appropriate technologies and the development of policy guidance for relevant global funding mechanisms.

23. The proposed international conference on land-based sources of marine pollution was held in Washington, DC, in November 1995. It produced a Declaration and an Action Plan, for which UNEP is Secretariat. Financing for some aspects of implementation is available through the International Waters Funds of the Global Environment Facility ("GEF").

24. International management of land-based sources of marine pollution lends itself more to regional approaches than to global ones. As the most intense pollution from land-based sources tends to

be local and its effects magnified in enclosed and semi-enclosed sea areas, and as states located in a common region tend to share a common level of economic development and common environmental conditions, regional arrangements are more apt.

25. The first regional regimes for land-based source of marine pollution were adopted for the Baltic and Northeast Atlantic Seas. These were the 1974 Convention on the Protection of the Marine Environment of the Baltic Sea Area ("Helsinki Convention") and the 1974 Convention for the Prevention of Marine Pollution from Land-Based Sources. In 1992 each was revised and updated. Respectively, they are now the 1992 Convention on the Protection of the Marine Environment of the Baltic Sea Area and the 1992 Convention for the Protection of the Marine Environment of the North-East Atlantic. Regional protocols concerning land-based sources of marine pollution are in place for three regions: Mediterranean Sea ("1980 Athens Protocol"), South-East Pacific ("1983 Quito Protocol"), Arabian Gulf ("1990 Kuwait Protocol") and Protocol concerning Pollution from Land-Based Sources and Activities on 27 October 1999.

26. The regional conventions and protocols each adopt similar definitions of land-based sources of marine pollution and similar regulatory approaches. They cover marine pollution from the coast, watercourses and through the atmosphere. They vary from each other in relation to coverage of offshore installations and waste disposal under the seabed accessed by tunnel or pipeline.

27. The regional conventions also adopt similar approaches to the regulation of land-based sources of marine pollution. Release into the marine environment of "black listed" substances set out in an annex is prohibited. Most of the conventions black list heavy metals such as cadmium and mercury, persistent organic compounds such as organohalogens and organochlorines and radioactive substances. Release into the marine environment of "grey" list substances set out in another annex is typically restricted and subject to authorization by the coastal state. Authorization is conditioned on such factors as the characteristics and composition of the substance, impacts on the receiving environment and the availability of alternatives such as waste production avoidance and alternative disposal methods. Airborne pollution is addressed merely by referring to an obligation to comply with other existing and applicable international standards, of which there are few.

5. Vessel-Based Sources of Marine Pollution

28. Pollution from vessels can take the forms of oil, chemicals, lost cargo and equipment, sewage, garbage, fumes and invasive exotic species. Oil pollution comprises about 71% of vessel-based marine pollution. Discharges may be accidental (9.4%) but are mostly operational, such as through diesel emissions in fumes, or oil residue in bilge and ballast water and hull washings (62%). The total annual oil spillage into the oceans is estimated at one million tonnes dumped in standard operations and 200,000 tonnes spilled in tanker accidents per year. In addition, 250,000 tonnes of oil spill annually results from retirement of oil vessels from transportation activities. Chances of vessel accidents and resultant pollution are increased by inadequate port facilities, poor or improper construction and maintenance of vessels and inadequate capacity of vessel crew to safely operate them.

29. The International Maritime Organization ("IMO") addressed vessel-based marine pollution prior to the negotiation of UNCLOS. As a result, UNCLOS did not elaborate operational controls for vessels, instead referring to standards established by the "competent international organization," in this case the IMO. The IMO was established in 1948, with a mission to promote safer shipping and cleaner seas. It has the responsibility, *inter alia*, to establish rules for prevention of marine pollution from ships.

30. The first of IMO Conventions on marine pollution was the International Convention for the Prevention of Pollution of the Sea by Oil ("OILPOL"), adopted in 1954. It applied to tankers engaged in the transportation of oil. Articles I, II, II, and IV prohibited discharges of oil into the sea except under specified conditions. It prohibited discharge of persistent oil or oily mixtures of greater than 100 parts per million ("ppm") within fifty nautical miles ("nm") of land or within special areas and regulated the rates of discharge (e.g. to a rate of sixty litres/nm to a maximum of 1/15,000 of oil cargo). However, exemptions applied if no oil reception facilities were available in the port of destination and the lack of available reception facilities at oil terminals remains a problem today, especially in developing countries.

31. Requirements introduced in 1969 mandated that new oil cargoes be loaded on top of old ones and that tankers be washed out with high pressure crude oil which is retained rather than sea water that is discharged, resulting in a 30% drop in

discharges. In 1971, separate ballast tanks became mandatory, so that oil cargo tanks did not need to be filled with sea water as ballast. Special areas where no discharges were permitted were declared, including the Great Barrier Reef, the Black Sea, the Baltic Sea and the North Sea.

32. However, OILPOL dealt only with oil, leaving out other contaminants that might be discharged during sea transportation activities. It also left out many issues concerning marine pollution, such as measures to avoid tanker accidents and safety at sea. It did not address matters concerning compensation to those who suffer financially as a result of pollution, proper vessel design and construction and marine rescue systems and crew standards, all of which have a bearing on marine pollution. In light of increased sea transportation activities and steady increases in the sizes of vessels, the threats of pollution loomed prominently. The problem was dramatized by the "Torrey Canyon" disaster, described earlier.

33. The IMO's efforts to develop more comprehensive measures to address marine pollution beyond just oil led to MARPOL, the International Convention for the Prevention of Pollution from Ships. The Convention was adopted in 1973, altered in 1978, and entered into force in 1983 superseding OILPOL. 1973 MARPOL applies to ships flying or entitled to fly the flag of parties and ships operating under the authority of a party but excludes warships, naval auxiliary and/or ships owned or operated by a state and used only on government non-commercial service (article 3). MARPOL has 127 parties.

34. The core of 1973 MARPOL lies in its annexes which deal with all types of pollution by ships (excluding dumping), rather than oil discharges alone. MARPOL's six annexes deal with: (I) pollution by oil, (II) pollution by noxious liquid substances in bulk, (III) pollution by harmful substances carried by in packaged form, (IV) sewage, (V) garbage, and (VI) air pollution. Other than Annexes I and II, Annexes III, IV, V and VI are optional and can be ratified separately from the main body of MARPOL. This results in different parties being signatories to the various Annexes. All the Annexes have entered into force, except Annex VI. Annex I sets out rules for controlling oil pollution, incorporating OILPOL. Annex V prohibits the disposal at sea of certain kinds of garbage, such as rope, plastic and fishing nets, but permits disposal of food and other specified wastes.

35. Key provisions of 1973 MARPOL include:
    • Articles 4, 5 and 6 requiring states to create and

enforce appropriate national laws implementing MARPOL;
    • Article 5 requiring parties to inspect ships flying their flags or operating under their authority to determine their compliance status before issuing them with certificates that authorize operation. Inspection of oil tankers is required before an International Oil Pollution Prevention Certificate is issued and a ship is authorized to operate an oil transporter and, thereafter, at intervals of not more than five years;
    • Article 6 authorizing parties to inspect foreign ships entering their territorial waters to determine whether they have discharged any harmful substances into the territorial waters or elsewhere and, if so, to institute court proceedings;
    • Article 6 authorizing parties to carry out inspection of all ships in their ports to determine whether they have compliance certificates and, if they do not, to deny them sailing rights. Article 7 establishes that inspections are to be conducted in an expeditious manner to avoid undue delay or detention of a ship; and
    • Article 10 requiring disputes concerning the application or interpretation of MARPOL to be resolved through negotiation, and, if parties do not agree, be submitted upon request of any of them to arbitration.

36. Work by the IMO on vessel accidents and emergencies that threaten the marine environment led to the development of the International Convention on Oil Pollution Preparedness, Response and Cooperation ("OPRC") adopted in 1990, which came into force in 1995.

37. The OPRC mandates that parties establish national measures to deal with vessel accidents that threaten to pollute the marine environment that include requirements that:

    • Vessels flying their flags, installations operating in their territorial waters and persons undertaking land-based activities within their jurisdiction that might lead to pollution of the marine environment must prepare plans to deal with oil pollution emergencies (article 3(1)).
    • Vessel operators adopt an oil pollution emergency plan developed by the IMO, known as Shipboard Oil Pollution Emergency Plan and carry it at all times to guide them on what to do in case of emergency.

38. The OPRC also requires parties to establish national systems, including detailed plans, for responding promptly to oil pollution accidents

(article 3(2)) and training and equipping people to combat oil spills and for making oil spill combating equipment available. Parties are also required to establish regulations and procedures for ship operators to report any pollution incidents to coastal authorities and other responsible governmental bodies for action to be taken in accordance with provisions of the Convention (article 4).

39. In addition to pollution emergency control measures at the national level, OPRC require parties to establish systems for cooperation to assist each other in the event of an oil vessel accident or other emergencies threatening to cause marine pollution. Several such systems have been established at sub-regional levels, such as for the Mediterranean Sea.

40. The International Convention on the Control of Harmful Anti-fouling Systems on Ships was adopted in 2001. It is designed to protect the marine environment and human health from the harmful effects of organotin-based anti-fouling systems on ships, such as tributyltin ("TBT"). It has not yet entered into force but prohibits the application of harmful anti-fouling systems on ships from 1 January 2003. By 1 January 2008, all ships will be banned from having such compounds on their hulls or external surfaces or will be required to have a coating that forms a barrier to stop such compounds leaching from the underlying non-compliant anti-fouling systems.

41. The most recent vessel standard developed by the IMO is the International Convention for the Control and Management of Ships Ballast Water and Sediments, adopted on 13 February 2004. Its objective is to minimize and eliminate the international transfer of marine pests and pathogens contained in ships' ballast water and sediments. Vessels must carry a Ballast Water Record Book and a certificate that indicates they are properly equipped. Parties are required to ensure that there are adequate reception facilities in ports where cleaning or repair of ballast tanks occurs so that ballast waster and sediment can be discharged into them.

42. Vessel-based pollution control standards have gradually moved away from discharge limits to design and equipment standards. These are easier to enforce and more effective in preventing pollution. Vessel activities at sea are largely unmonitored and unknowable. Surveillance, boarding, inspections and detentions are resource intensive, cumbersome and expensive. Wise drafting is essential to avoid reliance on

complicated and expensive enforcement actions while still implementing marine environmental standards. A useful technique to promote more cost-effective implementation is to interlink responsibilities and powers for enforcement across an international network of governments. For example, allocating to each flag state, coastal state and port state a share of policing powers and responsibilities can improve policing of vessel-based pollution. Enforcement provisions in UNCLOS seek to achieve this outcome.

43. Under UNCLOS article 217, the role of the flag state in policing vessels remains strong but is not exclusive. Flag states are to adopt laws to effectively enforce international norms and to prohibit vessels which are not in compliance with international norms from sailing. They are also to ensure that their vessels carry the certificates required and issued pursuant to international rules and must immediately investigate violations when requested by other states, regardless of where the violation occurred. Where a vessel is voluntarily in port, the port state may prevent a vessel from sailing where it is in breach of international standards and threatens to cause marine pollution (UNCLOS article 219). The port state is also permitted under article 218 to undertake investigations and institute proceedings related to a polluting discharge by a foreign vessel on the high seas, which violates applicable international rules. Under the Memoranda of Understanding on Port State Control first signed by European States in 1982 and by other regional states in the 1990s, port states agreed to conduct inspections of vessels in port. These undertakings ensure that most vessels are subject to regular examination for compliance with applicable international pollution prevention and safety standards. Non-compliant vessels may be detained until appropriate remedial action has been taken. UNCLOS also authorizes coastal states to physically inspect and to detain vessels within the territorial sea or exclusive economic zone (article 220).

44. International marine pollution liability regimes are agreements that enable persons to receive compensation where an international shipping activity has caused pollution. The fundamental elements are a defined pollution incident which has caused damage to the covered interests of those persons. The ship owner is strictly liable for paying compensation up to a defined limit set out under the liability regime. The compensation is paid through the courts where the injury was suffered.

45. Those liability regimes currently in force are the 1969 International Convention on Civil Liability for Oil Pollution Damage and the 1971 International Oil Pollution Compensation Fund Convention. (See Chapters 5 and 11 of this Training Manual). The latter applies where a ship owner is not financially capable of, providing compensation and provides a limited amount of additional compensation where the pollution damage suffered exceeds the compensation available under the Civil Liability Convention. Article 235 of UNCLOS urges further development of liability regimes.

46. In 1997, the IMO adopted a Convention on civil liability for marine pollution caused by hazardous and noxious substances. However, neither this Convention nor the 2001 Convention on Civil Liability for Marine Pollution caused by Bunker Oils have come in to force.

6. Dumping of Wastes at Sea

47. Dumping is the deliberate disposal of wastes at sea. Typical kinds of dumped wastes include dredged spoils, building construction debris, sewage sludge and municipal garbage. In international law, dumping covers operations by vessels, aircraft or offshore installations for the purpose of waste disposal, including the disposal of the vessels, aircraft or offshore installations themselves. Dumping typically excludes disposal of wastes generated incidentally to the ordinary operations of vessels, aircraft or offshore installations since these activities are primarily covered under regimes specific to these types of operations (UNCLOS article 1(5)).

48. UNCLOS provisions on dumping require that national laws must be no less effective than global rules and standards (article 210.6)). The 1972 Convention on the Prevention of Marine Pollution by Dumping of Wastes and other Matter (known as the "London Convention"), administered through the IMO, establishes the global rules and standards for dumping. For those states not party to the London Convention, UNCLOS has the effect of indirectly bringing the wider community of UNCLOS parties into line with the London Convention.

49. Under UNCLOS, waste dumping is subject to a permit system (article 210(3)) which is to be enforced by coastal states which has veto power over dumping in its territorial sea and exclusive economic zone or onto its continental shelf, flag states and waste loading states (article 216). Therefore, several permits may be needed from the various responsible states. The London Convention provides the details.

50. Article 4 of the London Convention prohibits dumping of hazardous wastes and substances into all marine environments, including high seas and territorial waters. Annex I sets out the "black list" of wastes for which no permits may be granted. The prohibited substances listed in Annex I include organochlorine compounds, mercury and mercury compounds, persistent plastics, high-level radioactive wastes and materials produced for chemical warfare. Article 5 allows the dumping of Annex II substances, for which permits may be issued subject to conditions specified in Annex III. The Annex II "grey list" substances include low concentrations of certain metals and incinerator ash.

51. Article 7 of the London Convention requires parties to enact national laws to provide a basis for their permitting system and to prevent dumping of wastes and other substances into the marine environment in contravention of the Convention. They are authorized to enact more stringent regulations in their national laws and may prohibit dumping of substances that the Convention permits.

52. Parties to the London Convention have adopted a range of important resolutions banning incineration at sea, dumping of low-level radioactive wastes at sea and establishing a process of phasing out dumping of all industrial wastes at sea, among other changes.

53. In 1996 a new Protocol to the London Convention was adopted designed to reduce the practice of waste dumping by introducing waste management and avoidance practices. This Protocol included a new reverse listing that, instead of listing wastes prohibited for dumping, prohibited dumping of all wastes except those specifically listed. The old Annex I "black list" is accordingly replaced by a new Annex 1 "reverse list" of wastes which can be dumped subject to permit. However, the 1996 Protocol has not yet come into force.

54. Regional conventions concerning the dumping of waste have been adopted for the North East Atlantic Ocean (1992) and Baltic Sea (1992), and protocols have been adopted for the Mediterranean (1995), South Pacific (1986), and South East Pacific seas (1989). The North East Atlantic, Baltic and Mediterranean agreements have been revised since 1990 to incorporate the waste management and avoidance approaches of the London Convention's Protocol.

7. Offshore Hydrocarbon and Mineral Recovery

55. UNCLOS article 208(3) expresses a general obligation to prevent marine pollution from offshore activities and to ensure that national measures are no less effective than international measures. In 1979, the IMO adopted a Code for Construction and Equipment of Mobile Offshore Drilling Units. A convention on Civil Liability for Oil Pollution Damage resulting from Oil and Gas Exploration and Exploitation of Seabed Mineral Resources was adopted in 1977 but has not come into force. Regional standards have been adopted in North West Atlantic, where various bilateral agreements have been adopted, especially for dealing with emergencies (e.g., Norway-UK, Canada-Denmark). The various UNEP regional conventions create a general obligation to prevent pollution from offshore activities (e.g., Barcelona Convention article 7) but these are without any detailed content.

56. Currently, deep seabed mining is not a source of marine pollution. Pollution controls concerning activities in the deep seabed area are to be formulated by the International Seabed Authority established in accordance with part XI of the Law of the Sea Convention (UNCLOS article 209). The International Seabed Authority established under the Convention has formulated a Mining Code for deep seabed operations and is developing guidelines for assessment of possible environmental impacts arising from seabed exploration.

8. Regional Seas Agreements

57. UNCLOS requires parties to enter into regional agreements to formulate and establish rules, standards, practices and procedures for the protection of the marine environment, to supplement rules established at the international level (article 197). Framework agreements for protection of the environment have been created in almost every marine region of the world. Ten regional framework agreements have been developed under the UNEP Regional Seas Programme. A legal regime for the North East Atlantic Ocean was developed by regional states prior to the Regional Seas Programme being adopted.

58. The UNEP Regional Seas Programme was initiated in 1974 covering thirteen regions of world's seas involving more than 140 coastal states and territories. They are the Mediterranean Sea, Baltic Sea, Black Sea, Red Sea and Gulf of Aden, West and Central African seas, East African seas, Caribbean region, South Asian seas, East Asian seas, South Pacific, South East Pacific and North West Pacific Oceans. The Regional Seas Programme involves development of an Action Plan for the protection of the marine environment in each region. These facilitate target setting, regional cooperation and capacity building in pollution control. Plans are regularly reviewed and have evolved to address broader sustainable development concerns for coastal zones. (See also under chapter 11, Hazardous Wastes).

59. The eleven regional conventions currently in force are:

- Convention for the Protection of the Marine Environment and the Coastal Region of the Mediterranean ("1976 Barcelona Convention"), adopted on 16 February 1976 and entered into force in 1978;
- Convention on the Protection of the Black Sea against Pollution ("1992 Bucharest Convention") adopted in April 1992 and entered into force in 1994;
- Convention for the Protection and Development of the Marine Environment of the Wider Caribbean Region ("1983 Cartagena Convention") adopted in 1983 and entered into force in 1986;
- Convention on the Protection of the Marine Environment of the Baltic Sea Area ("1974 Helsinki Convention") adopted in 1974 and entered into force in 1980;
- Regional Convention for the Conservation of the Red Sea and Gulf of Aden Environment ("1982 Jeddah Convention") adopted on 14 February 1982 and entered into force on 20 August 1985;
- Kuwait Regional Convention for Cooperation on the Protection of the Marine Environment from Pollution ("1978 Kuwait Convention") adopted in 1978 and entered into force in 1979;
- Convention for the Protection of the Marine Environment and Coastal Area of the South-East Pacific ("1981 Lima Convention") adopted in 1981 and entered into force in 1986;
- Convention for the Protection, Management and Development of the Marine and Coastal Environment of the Eastern African Region ("1985 Nairobi Convention") adopted in 1985 and entered into force in 1986;
- Convention for the Protection of Natural Resources and Environment of the South Pacific Region ("1986 Noumea Convention") adopted in 1986 and entered into force in 1990;
- Convention for the Protection of the Marine Environment of the North-East Atlantic ("1992

OSPAR Convention") adopted on 22 September 1992 and entered into force on 25 March 1998; and,

- Convention for Cooperation in the Protection and Development of the Marine and Coastal Environment of the West and Central African Region ("1981 Abidjan Convention") adopted in 1981 and entered into force in 1984.

60. Legal agreements adopted under the Regional Seas Programme tend to reflect the structure and principles of part XII of the Law of the Sea Convention and provide a framework for more specific standards to be adopted, usually in the form of protocols. The range and kinds of protocols is continually expanding.

a. Convention for the Protection of the Marine Environment and the Coastal Region of the Mediterranean

61. The Mediterranean Region provides the leading model of regional seas agreements, with the oldest and most frequently revised convention, and an extensive range of protocols. The Mediterranean Sea is a virtually closed ocean that is highly vulnerable to pollution. Rapid expansion of large cities around the Mediterranean Sea contributes to the overwhelming pressure on the region's marine, terrestrial and water resources. To address these challenges, states in the region adopted the 1976 Barcelona Convention. So far, the Convention has as 21 country-parties bordering the Mediterranean Sea.

62. The most important features of the 1976 Barcelona Convention include:

- Article 1 which describes the Conventions coverage as the Mediterranean Sea itself and its gulfs and seas but not the internal waters of parties;
- Articles 4 to 8 which declare that the objective of the Convention is to protect the marine environment of the region from pollution from sources including ships, aircrafts, dumping of wastes and from exploitation and exploration of the continental shelf and seabed; and
- Article 8 which requires parties to ensure that activities carried out within their territories do not discharge pollutants into rivers that end up emptying them into the waters in the region. Article 9 which requires parties to cooperate, in the case of an emergency, by taking joint action to mitigate the impacts of pollution from land-based activities or from other sources.

63. As with most of the regional seas conventions, the Barcelona Convention is a framework formed of articles of a general nature which, though adopted of UNCLOS, are consistent with its chapter XII. Protocols and annexes specifying concrete measures must supplement the framework agreement for the Convention to effectively address problems in the region. The Barcelona Convention is complemented by six protocols, more than any other region. These are:

- The Protocol for the Prevention of Pollution by Dumping from Ships and Aircraft was adopted 16 February 1976 and entered into force on 12 February 1978. In 1995, it was amended and renamed Protocol for the Prevention and Elimination of Pollution of the Mediterranean Sea by Dumping from Ships and Aircraft or incineration at Sea. The amendment has not yet come into force.
- The Protocol concerning Cooperation in Combating Pollution of the Mediterranean Sea by Oil and other Harmful Substances in Cases of Emergency was also adopted on 16 February 1976 and entered into force on 12 February 1978. Nearly 30% by volume of all international sea-borne trade originates or is directed to the Mediterranean ports, or passes through the sea, while some 28% of the world's sea-borne oil traffic transits the Mediterranean. To address prevention of pollution from shipping, the Protocol was amended on 25 January 2002, and renamed the Protocol Concerning Cooperation in Preventing Pollution from Ships and in Cases of Emergency, Combating Pollution in the Mediterranean Sea. The amendment has yet to come into force.
- The Protocol for the Protection of the Mediterranean Sea against Pollution from Land-Based Sources was adopted on 17 May 1980 and entered into force on 17 July 1983. Land-based pollution presents 80% of harm done to the Mediterranean Sea. To complement pollution discharge limits operative at the end of the pipe, the Protocol was amended on 7 March 1996. The renamed Protocol for the Protection of the Mediterranean Sea against Pollution from Land-Based Sources and Activities set in place systemic pollution prevention standards that address controls to pollution generating processes. The amendment has not yet come into force.
- The Protocol concerning Mediterranean Specially Protected Areas was adopted on 2 April 1982 and entered into force on 23 March 1986. In June 1995, it was amended and

renamed the Protocol concerning Specially Protected Areas and Biological Diversity in the Mediterranean. The amendment came into force on 12 December 1999.
- The Protocol for the Protection of the Mediterranean Sea against Pollution resulting from Exploration and Exploitation of the Continental Shelf and the Seabed and its Subsoil was adopted on 14 October 1994. It has yet to come into force.
- The Protocol on the Prevention of Pollution of the Mediterranean Sea by Transboundary Movements of Hazardous Wastes and their Disposal was adopted on 1 October 1996. Also this Protocol has not come into force yet.

b. Convention for the Protection and Development of the Marine Environment of the Wider Caribbean Region

64. The Wider Caribbean region, comprising 28 island states and 18 continental countries, is a complex region of natural beauty encompassing both tropical and sub-tropical ecosystems. Ranging from coral reefs to mangrove forests to sea grass beds, each with unique wildlife, it is considered by many scientists to be one of the world's most biodiverse regions. For example, Colombia and Mexico are among the ten richest countries in the world in terms of terrestrial and plant species. Despite wide disparities in the densities of population, levels of economic development and access to resources, all the states in the Caribbean region share similar environmental problems. Nearly 100% of the population of its islands are coastal and the region experiences hurricanes and other devastating climatic and oceanographic conditions. Tourism is a fast-growing industry in many regional states and they are undertaking development activities along the coastline, such as ports and harbours, with negative consequences on their environments.

65. The 1983 Cartagena Convention is of a comprehensive framework type, making requirements on parties, for example, to conduct Environmental Impact Assessments ("EIA") of their planned and on-going projects to determine their potential to cause marine pollution (article 12). Article 15 of the Convention designates UNEP as its Secretariat, responsible for functions including coordination of implementation activities. Disputes arising under the Convention are to be resolved through negotiation and other peaceful means. In the absence of a negotiated resolution, matters are to be referred to arbitration.

66. The 1983 Cartagena Convention has been supplemented by some unique and unusual protocols specifying detailed pollution control measures, namely:

- The Protocol concerning Cooperation in Combating Oil Spills in the Wider Caribbean Region. It requires parties to act individually, as well as to cooperate by providing assistance to each other, to establish and maintain means of responding to oil spill accidents which result in or pose a significant threat of, pollution to the marine and coastal environment.
- The Protocol concerning Specially Protected Areas and Wildlife ("SPAW") was specifically intended to implement article 10 of the Cartagena Convention, which requires the establishment of specially protected areas. Its objective is to protect rare and fragile ecosystems and habitats, including endangered and threatened species.
- The Protocol concerning Pollution from Land-Based Sources and Activities requires parties to take appropriate measures to prevent, control and reduce pollution from transboundary movement of wastes. This Protocol has yet to come into force.

c. Convention for the Protection of the Marine Environment of the North-East Atlantic

67. The 1992 OSPAR Convention was adopted on 22 September 1992 and entered into force on 25 March 1998. It has sixteen parties: Belgium, Denmark, Finland, France, Germany, Iceland, Ireland, Luxembourg, the Netherlands, Norway, Portugal, Spain, Sweden, Switzerland, the United Kingdom, and the European Union. The Convention replaced two earlier conventions: the Convention for the Prevention of Marine Pollution by Dumping From Ships and Aircraft ("Oslo Convention"), which came into force in 1974, and the Convention for the Prevention of Marine Pollution from Land-Based Sources ("Paris Convention"), which came into force in 1978.

68. The objectives of the 1992 OSPAR Convention, as stated in its Preamble, are threefold:

- To safeguard human health from marine pollution in the area;
- To conserve marine ecosystems, particularly by preventing and controlling pollution;
- To restore waters that have been adversely affected by pollution. OSPAR regulations cover all the oil-producing coastal states of Western Europe.

Unlike many of the regional seas agreements, it applies to the internal waters of parties, that is, not only to the territorial sea, high seas, seabeds and subsoil adjacent to parties in the North-East Atlantic and North Sea region.

69. To meet its objectives, article 2(2)(a) of the 1992 OSPAR Convention obligates parties to apply the precautionary principle. This means that parties are to take measures to prevent marine pollution when there is reason to believe that proposed activities in or near the marine environment may create hazards to human health, interfere with legitimate uses of the waters, or harm the living organisms in the waters, even if there is no conclusive evidence that these adverse impacts will definitely occur. Another unique feature of article 2 is that it requires parties to apply the polluter pays principle. Parties are to ensure that the cost of measures taken to prevent, control and reduce pollution as well as the cost of any damage resulting from pollution is borne by the person who pollutes the waters. (See also chapter 3 on Principles and Concepts of this Training Manual).

70. In addition, article 2 of the Convention introduces unusually sophisticated controls on land-based pollution using best available technology standards. Parties are required to ensure that their pollution control programmes make full use of best available techniques and best environmental practices to prevent, reduce and control pollution to the fullest extent.

71. Articles 10, 11 and 12 establish an OSPAR Commission made up of representatives of each party. The Commission has decided to allow Non-Governmental Organizations to participate in the development of its Plan and Programme to facilitate pollution control and other measures. In addition, the Convention provides for the establishment of technical and scientific bodies to implement recommended strategies and to conduct monitoring and assessments.

III. National Implementation

72. International legal obligations are implemented nationally through a range of measures, including legislation, policy and administrative measures. Examples of national legislation drawn from different regions are set out below to illustrate the ways that some countries have implemented the various marine pollution principles and conventions.

1. Romania

73. Romania's Act Number 6 of 1993 authorized the implementation of MARPOL at the national level. Romania's Marine Research Institute, which operates under the Ministry of Waters, Forests and Environment Protection, was designated to act as the focal point for matters concerning the Convention. The Ministry of Water, Forests and Environmental Protection is responsible for enforcement of the law. It drafted a Black Sea Environmental Programme for the Romanian shoreline to facilitate prevention of marine pollution and sustainable development of coastal areas. In addition, Law Number 17 of 1990 governs territorial waters, as required under UNCLOS, and Government Order Number 1907 of 1994 deals with discharge of sewage and wastes at harbour facilities and at sea, and Water Law Number 107 of 1996 deals with accidental oil spills. A National Contingency Plan in case of Marine Pollution by Oil was adopted under that law.

2. South Africa

74. To implement the London Convention, South Africa enacted the "Dumping at Sea Control Act" No. 73 in 1980. In 1985, the Act was amended by the "Prevention and Combating of Pollution of the Sea by Oil Amendment Act" No. 59 of 1985. The amended Act contains detailed provisions prohibiting discharge of oil from ships and other vessels into the sea and imposing penalties for violations and requiring vessel operators and owners to report any accidents leading to oil pollution to the responsible authorities so that appropriate remedial action can be taken. The Act also imposes liability for any damage resulting from oil pollution on the person causing pollution. South Africa has actively participated in the activities of the Scientific Group established by the Convention that are aimed at facilitating technical cooperation and building capacity to combat pollution.

3. Australia

75. Australian marine water quality is administered under complex arrangements that share responsibilities between the national and federated state governments. Under the Offshore Constitutional Settlement, the state governments administer marine waters within 3 nautical miles of the coastline and the national government administers waters from 3 nautical miles to 200

nautical miles of the coastline. The national government requires that activities that might significantly impact on national waters be subject to an environmental impact assessment and approval process, under the Environment Protection and Biodiversity Conservation Act 1999. That legislation goes one step further, to also require long term strategic environmental assessments for cumulative impacts. Within state controlled waters, assessments and approvals for proposed projects that might have significant impacts are required under state legislation.

76. The 1973 MARPOL Convention, however, applies to all Australian waters and is administered by the national government through its Australian Maritime Safety Authority under the Environment Protection (Pollution from Ships) Act 1983 (as amended). The London Convention is also administered by the national government, through its Department of Environment, under the Environment Protection (Sea Dumping) Act 1981 (as amended). Pipelines and other marine structures are also regulated nationally under the Sea Installations Act 1987. In contrast, land-based sources of marine pollution are locally regulated by federated state governments and by municipal governments, which can provide more effective controls over local sources of pollution, albeit there is as yet no national approach to controls.

77. Under the National Oceans Policy 1998, efforts are being made to integrate management of various marine activities in an environmentally sound manner, using large-scale regional marine plans developed through consultation with stakeholders. The national Environment Protection and Biodiversity Conservation Act 1999 applies to marine habitats (as well as terrestrial) and enables the creation of five categories of marine protected areas and provides a range of protections for conservation of threatened or endangered species. Most states have adopted marine park legislation and parks are managed by state authorities in coastal waters, and in those beyond by national authorities. Since 1998, new marine parks are being proclaimed with the objective of creating a National Representative System of Marine Protected Areas for all Australian marine and coastal regions.

Gregory Rose, Associate Professor, Faculty of Law, University of Wollongong, Australia

Dr. Jane Dwasi, UNEP Consultant, University of Nairobi

Barbara Ruis, Legal Officer, Division of Policy Development and Law, UNEP

Resources

Internet Materials

INFORMATION ON REGIONAL SEAS AGREEMENTS available at http://www.unep.org/water/regseas/regseas.htm and at http://www.greenyearbook.org/agree/mar-env/regseas.htm

INFORMATION ON THE BARCELONA CONVENTION available at http://www.greenyearbook.org/agree/mar-env/barcelona.htm

INFORMATION ON THE BUCHAREST CONVENTION available at http://www.greenyearbook.org/agree/mar-env/bucharest.htm

INFORMATION ON THE CARTAGENA CONVENTION available at http://www.greenyearbook.org/agree/mar-env/cartagena.htm

INFORMATION ON THE HELSINKI CONVENTION available at http://www.greenyearbook.org/agree/mar-env/helsinki.htm

INFORMATION ON THE JEDDAH CONVENTION available at http://www.greenyearbook.org/agree/mar-env/jeddah.htm

INFORMATION ON THE KUWAIT CONVENTION available at http://www.greenyearbook.org/agree/mar-env/kuwait.htm

INFORMATION ON THE LAW OF THE SEA CONVENTION available at http://www.un.org/depts/los/index.htm

INFORMATION ON THE LIMA CONVENTION available at http://www.greenyearbook.org/agree/mar-env/lima.htm

INFORMATION ON THE NAIROBI CONVENTION available at http://www.greenyearbook.org/agree/mar-env/nairobi.htm

INFORMATION ON THE NOUMEA CONVENTION available at http://www.greenyearbook.org/agree/mar-env/noumea.htm

INFORMATION ON THE OSPAR CONVENTION available at http://www.greenyearbook.org/agree/mar-env/ospar.htm and at http://www.ospar.org

GENERAL INFORMATION ON MARINE POLLUTION available at http://www.admiraltylawguide.org

REPORTS OF THE UNITED NATIONS SECRETARY-GENERAL ON OCEANS AND LAW OF THE SEA TO THE GENERAL ASSEMBLY available at http://www.un.org/Depts/los/general_assembly/general_assembly_reports.htm

THE INTERNATIONAL MARITIME ORGANIZATION available at http://www.imo.org

THE INTERNATIONAL SEABED AUTHORITY available at http://www.isa.org.jm

THE INTERNATIONAL TRIBUNAL FOR THE LAW OF THE SEA available at http://www.itlos.org

THE LAW OF THE SEA CONVENTION available at http://www.unclos.com

THE LONDON CONVENTION available at http://www.londonconvention.org

Text Materials

Douglas D. Ofiara, Joseph J. Seneca, ECONOMIC LOSSES FROM MARINE POLLUTION: A HANDBOOK FOR ASSESSMENT, (Island Press 2001).

Edgar Gold, LIABILITY AND COMPENSATION FOR SHIP-SOURCE MARINE POLLUTION: THE INTERNATIONAL SYSTEM, (Yearbook of International Co-operation on Environment and Development 31-7, 1999/2000).

ENVIRONMENT CANADA, FEDERAL/PROVINCIAL/TERRITORIAL ADVISORY COMMITTEE ON CANADA'S NATIONAL PROGRAMME OF ACTION FOR THE PROTECTION OF THE MARITIME ENVIRONMENT FROM LAND-BASED ACTIVITIES, IMPLEMENTING CANADA'S NATIONAL PROGRAMME OF ACTION FOR THE PROTECTION OF THE MARINE ENVIRONMENT FROM LAND-BASED ACTIVITIES: NATIONAL REPORT TO THE 2001 INTERGOVERNMENTAL REVIEW MEETING ON IMPLEMENTATION OF THE GLOBAL PROGRAMME OF ACTION, (January 2001).

Michael A. Becker, THE SHIFTING PUBLIC ORDER OF THE OCEANS: FREEDOM OF NAVIGATION AND THE INTERDICTION OF SHIPS AT SEA,. (Harvard International Law Journal, Volume 46, Number 1, Winter 2005).

Nobuyuiki Miyazaki, Zafar Adeel, Kouichi Ohwada, MANKIND AND THE OCEANS, (United Nations University Press 2004).

P.L. Bishop, MARINE POLLUTION AND ITS CONTROL, (McGraw-Hill Book Co. 1983).

Robert Bernard Clark, Chris Frid, Martin Attrell, MARINE POLLUTION, (Fifth Edition, Oxford University Press 2001).

Ronald B. Mitchell, REGIME DESIGN MATTERS: INTENTIONAL OIL POLLUTION AND TREATY COMPLIANCE, (JSTOR 2001).

UNITED NATIONS, THE LAW OF THE SEA BULLETIN.

14. CONSERVATION OF SPECIES AND HABITATS, INCLUDING TRADE IN AND SUSTAINABLE USE OF ENDANGERED SPECIES

I. Introduction

1. This chapter discusses the following instruments:

   - The Convention on the Conservation of Migratory Species of Wild Animals, 1979 ("CMS");
   - The Convention on Wetlands of International Importance especially as Waterfowl Habitat, 1971 ("Ramsar Convention");
   - The Convention on International Trade in Endangered Species of Wild Fauna and Flora, 1973 ("CITES");
   - The Lusaka Agreement on Cooperative Enforcement Operations Directed at Illegal Trade in Wild Fauna and Flora, 1994 ("Lusaka Agreement") and
   - The World Heritage Convention, 1972 ("WHC").

2. Each of these Conventions or Agreements addresses aspects of the conservation of biological diversity and they have many goals in common. Their respective objectives and scope are generally consistent with the text and spirit of the Convention on Biological Diversity ("CBD") (See Chapter 15), which is why these Conventions are often referred to as biodiversity-related Multilateral Environmental Agreements ("MEAs"). However, each MEA has a special mission and a somewhat different concept of conservation. CITES and CMS, for instance, focus on the protection of species while the Ramsar Convention and the WHC focus on sites and, therefore, *in situ* conservation. CITES stresses conservation as a goal similar to the CBD, but focuses on the specific threat of illegal trade and its implications for the conservation of biodiversity. On the other hand, the CBD and the Ramsar Convention focus on sustainable use, taking into account socio-economic concerns such as land use planning and demography. While these conventions, along with the CBD, are the main instruments for achieving biodiversity conservation, there are also regional agreements and treaties that are very important. One such instrument, the Lusaka Agreement is discussed below. Section II underlines the international framework governing the different legal regimes mentioned which have developed over time to regulate the conservation of species and habitats and their relationships, given the different secretariats involved as well as parties.

3. For these agreements to be more effective, it is highly desirable that they be mutually supportive. Thus, coordination between the respective secretariats of the agreements has become very important. The CBD Secretariat, together with the Secretariats of the Ramsar Convention, CITES, CMS and the WHC regularly explore options for a harmonized information management infrastructure for biodiversity related treaties. The Secretariats will continue to cooperate on information management and access, a joint website and a biodiversity-related search engine hosted by the CBD Secretariat. These agreements do not necessarily cover all aspects of biodiversity conservation. For example, the biodiversity of the marine environment is addressed in Chapter 17 below.

4. Section III will briefly examine selected implementing legislation in three countries, namely Uganda on the Ramsar Convention, Singapore on CITES and South Africa on the World Heritage Convention.

II. International Framework

1. The 1979 Convention on the Conservation of Migratory Species of Wild Animals

Introduction

5. Animal migration is a global phenomenon. Migration refers to the periodic movements of animals from one area to another, in a cyclical, generally annual and predictable manner. A wide variety of animals inhabiting the land, sea and air migrate, including antelopes, dolphins, marine turtles, bats and a large number of birds. Many animals migrate due to biological and seasonal requirements, such as the need to find a suitable location for breeding and for raising young and to find favourable areas in which to feed at other times of the year. In extreme cases, animals migrate to locations thousands of kilometres away.

6. Migration allows species to periodically exploit resources in areas that would not be suitable for continuous use. However, animals are biologically dependent on the specific sites they find on their migratory routes and at the end of their journey. As

such, migratory species are particularly vulnerable to a wide range of threats, including habitat shrinkage in breeding areas caused by land and water degradation, residential and industrial expansion, and excessive hunting along migration routes. Because of the wide range of habitats that migrating species require, they tend to be more at risk and in danger than non-migratory species.

7. Migratory species can be considered as representing a common natural heritage. Countries en route thus share a common responsibility to undertake cooperative action for migratory species' conservation throughout their life cycle. The necessity for countries to cooperate in their conservation was recognized in Recommendation 32 of the Action Plan under the 1972 Stockholm United Nations Conference on the Human Environment. This paved the way for the elaboration of the CMS.

Major Components

8. CMS is a global treaty directed at specific listed species. It was adopted in Bonn, in 1979, and entered into force in 1983. 91 countries have ratified the Convention as of July 2005. It recognizes that efficient management of migratory species needs concerted action by all range states and provides a framework within which range states take individual and cooperative action to conserve terrestrial, marine and avian migratory species and their habitats.

9. Article I(1) of the Convention offers key definitions, such as:

- "Endangered" signifies "...that the migratory species is in danger of extinction throughout all or a significant portion of its range."
- "Conservation status" is "...the sum of the influences acting on the migratory species that may affect its long-term distribution and abundance." The conservation status is considered "favourable" when a migratory species is maintaining itself on a long-term basis and its range is neither currently being reduced, nor is likely to be reduced in a long-term basis when there is, and will be in the foreseeable future nor when there is sufficient habitat to maintain the population consistent with wise wildlife management. The conservation status is taken to be "unfavourable" if any of the conditions set out above is not met.
- "Migratory species" is defined as the entire population or any geographically separate part of the population of any species of wild animals ,that habitually and predictably cross one or more national jurisdictional boundaries.

- "Range" means all the areas of land or water that a migratory species inhabits, stays in temporarily, crosses or overlies at any time in its normal migration route.

a. Obligations and Instruments

10. CMS requires countries to adopt strict protection measures for endangered migratory species. Article III indicates that migratory species may be listed in Appendix I of the Convention, "...provided that reliable evidence, including the best scientific evidence available, indicates that the species is endangered...".

11. Countries are encouraged to conclude agreements for the conservation and management of migratory species listed in Appendix II to the CMS. These are species which, under article IV, "...have an unfavourable conservation status and which require international agreements for their conservation and management, as well as those which have a conservation status which would significantly benefit from the international cooperation." Parties also have to undertake joint research and monitoring activities. Species may be listed in both Appendix I and Appendix II.

12. The object of such agreements is to restore or maintain the migratory species concerned to a favourable conservation status or to maintain the species in such a status. The agreements are intended to address all aspects of the conservation and management of the migratory species to achieve restoration or maintenance of the species.

13. The Convention further requires implementation at national and international levels through programmes and direct action, such as research, monitoring and the removal of obstacles that impede the migration of species. Article V refers to the establishment, "if necessary," of appropriate machinery to assist in carrying out the aims of the agreement. This would include the institutional, administrative and legislative mechanisms that serve to achieve the aims of the agreement.

14. Upon becoming a party to the Convention, a party must nominate a focal point and communicate it to the Secretariat of the Convention. The focal point so named would be responsible for communicating all information to the country's institutions. The party must also participate in the Meetings of the Parties ("MOP") or as also called the Conference of the Parties ("COP"). and designate a Scientific Councillor to attend the meetings of the Scientific Council. An annual contribution must be paid to the CMS Trust Fund, which is administered by UNEP.

b. Appendix I Species

15. Appendix I currently lists more than 80 endangered species, including the Siberian crane, the White-tailed eagle and the Dama gazelle. Additional migratory species can be listed on Appendix I if a party considers the species to be endangered and submits a proposal. The statement of reasons for the proposal must include specific information such as biological data, threat data, protection status and needs, range states, comments from range states and references. A migratory species can be removed from Appendix I if reliable evidence indicates that it is no longer endangered and that the species in question is not likely to become endangered again due to its removal from Appendix I.

16. Range states are obliged to prohibit the taking (hunting, fishing, capturing or deliberately killing) of Appendix I species. The states are to conserve and restore important habitats of such species, to counteract factors impeding their migration and are obliged to keep other potentially endangering factors under control. Range states must also report to the COP on measures to implement the Convention's provisions in relation to the species for which they are responsible under Appendices I and II.

c. Appendix II Species and other Species

17. In relation to the species listed at Appendix II, the Convention provides for the development of specific regional agreements. Parties to such a regional agreement need not be parties to the Convention provides for two different kinds of agreements, out of which the more formal agreements are distinguished in the Guide to the CMS (hereinafter, the Guide) as AGREEMENTS, and the less formal ones as Agreements.

18. AGREEMENTS, as provided for in articles IV(3) and V, should deal preferably with more than one species and cover its or their whole range. They should include all necessary instruments to make the AGREEMENT effective and operational. In substance, the AGREEMENTS should coordinate species conservation and management plans, restore and conserve habitats, control factors impeding migration, cooperate in research, monitoring, exchange of information and promote public education.

19. In contrast, Agreements, as defined in article IV (4), provide for the conservation of any population of any species of wild animals that periodically cross jurisdictional boundaries. The geographical coverage does not have to extend to the whole of the migratory range and the species does not have to be listed in any of the Appendices.

20. Less formal legal instruments can also be negotiated under the Convention to achieve similar objectives. A typical example is a Memorandum of Understanding ("MOU") whose aim is to coordinate short-term measures to be taken by the range states at the administrative and scientific level. MOUs allow for the conclusion of legal instruments between Ministries of the range states avoiding lengthy ratification periods. They are aimed at immediate concerted protection measure for seriously endangered species until a more elaborate conservation scheme can be adopted. MOUs may subsequently be converted into more formal Agreements if the members agree, or incorporated as an action plan for conservation.

d. National Implementation

21. The Guide indicates that a new party to the Convention "requires careful examination by the responsible authorities of the respective parties whether their national legislation already includes commitments for the strict protection of endangered migratory species," which are subject to listing under Appendix I, and to which they are a range state, as well as commitments to conservation and restoration of habitat. Any amendments to the Convention's text, or more particularly, the Appendices, may also call for amendment to domestic legislation. The Guide also indicates that beyond domestic legal measures, programmes and direct action are also required.

22. The Convention provides for an institutional structure, consisting of the COP, the Standing Committee, a Scientific Council and a Secretariat. The COP, which is the decision-making organ of the Convention, meets at least once every three years. It monitors the conservation status of migratory species, reviews the progress being made under the agreements and makes recommendations to the parties for improving the conservation status. At the 2002 COP, several species, including the Great White Shark, were added to Appendix I of the Convention. Countries also agreed to adopt bird-friendly techniques when constructing medium-voltage power lines to avoid electrocution of migratory birds.

23. The Standing Committee provides policy and administrative guidance between the regular

meetings of the COP. It consists of one representative from every global region, of the Depositary and of the country that plans to host the next meeting. The Scientific Council gives advice on scientific matters to the institutions of the CMS. The Secretariat provides administrative support under the auspices of UNEP. It develops and promotes Agreements, liaises with governments and organizations and services meetings.

e. Relationship and Cooperation with other Biodiversity related MEAs

24. CMS is the only global convention dealing exclusively with the conservation of migratory species. Even though migratory species in general are included in the Convention on Biological Diversity and migratory fish species are covered by the United Nations Convention on the Law of the Sea ("UNCLOS"), these Conventions do not provide for the special instruments through which conservation work can be done. As seen in other Chapters of this Manual (15 and 17), article 5 of the CBD and articles 65 and 120 of UNCLOS require their parties to implement coordinated international conservation measures for migratory species through existing international legal instruments. In order to promote synergy and avoid possible duplication of work, a Memorandum of Cooperation has been concluded between the Secretariats of the CMS and the CBD.

25. In addition, the CMS Secretariat and the Ramsar Bureau signed a Memorandum of Understanding in February 1997. The Memorandum seeks to ensure cooperation between the two Secretariats in the fields of joint promotion of the two conventions, joint conservation action, data collection, storage and analysis and new agreements on migratory species, including endangered migratory species and species with an unfavourable conservation status. Some concrete results of this relationship have already been observed, particularly with regard to coordinated work between the Ramsar Convention and the CMS's Agreement on the Conservation of African-Eurasian Migratory Waterbirds ("AEWA"). A three-way joint work plan between the Secretariats of the CMS, AEWA and the Ramsar Convention is presently being developed.

f. Agreements concluded under the CMS

i. Agreement on the Conservation of Seals in the Wadden Sea

26. Denmark, Germany and the Netherlands concluded an agreement on the conservation of

Wadden Sea Seals (Phoca vitulina) in October 1990, which entered into force a year later. The agreement was concluded in response to a dramatic decline in the Wadden Sea seal population, as a consequence of the sudden death of thousands of individuals in 1988.

27. This Agreement provides for the development of a conservation and management plan, coordination of research and monitoring, prohibition of taking (with few exceptions), habitat protection, reduction of pollution and public awareness initiatives. The conservation and management plan outlines in simple terms the specific efforts that are needed to implement various aspects of the Agreement, indicates what is presently being done, and outlines specific prescriptions to be undertaken by the parties. Coordination and cooperation between the range states has intensified considerably through the implementation mechanisms of the Agreement. According to the Wadden Sea Secretariat, the seal population has since recovered and has re-established itself at a stable level.

ii. Agreement on the Conservation of Small Cetaceans of the Baltic and North Seas

28. Parties to the 1991 Agreement on the Conservation of Small Cetaceans of the Baltic and North Seas ("ASCOBANS"), which entered into force in 1994, are Belgium, Denmark, Germany, the Netherlands, Poland, Sweden, the United Kingdom, Finland and Lithuania. The ASCOBANS Secretariat is now co-located with the UNEP/CMS Secretariat at the UN premises in Bonn.

29. ASCOBANS encourages cooperation between range states with respect to habitat conservation and management, measures against pollution, surveys, research and public information. An Advisory Committee was established by the first Meeting of the Parties ("MOP"). The Advisory Committee focuses on issues such as by-catch in fishing nets, considered to be one of the greatest threats facing small cetaceans in the Agreement area and the reduction of disturbance to cetaceans by human activities. ASCOBANS has already stimulated a joint research programme to assess the population and distribution of small cetaceans as well as research, monitoring and awareness programmes in individual range states.

iii. Agreement on the Conservation of Populations of European Bats

30. The Agreement on the Conservation of Populations of European Bats ("EUROBATS") was concluded as an AGREEMENT within the meaning of article

IV(3) of the CMS in September 1991 and entered into force on 16 January 1994. EUROBATS presently has more than 25 parties.

31. EUROBATS aims to address threats to 37 bat species in Europe arising from habitat degradation, disturbance of roosting sites and harmful pesticides. Scientific work programmes concentrate on the transboundary programmes for habitat protection and, in particular, for underground and forest habitats of bats. These programmes aim, among other things, to identify sites of European importance and to coordinate data collection throughout the Agreement area as a first step and to develop recommendations for habitat protection and sympathetic forest practices as a follow-up.

iv. Agreement on the Conservation of African-Eurasian Migratory Waterbirds

32. The Agreement on the Conservation of African-Eurasian Waterbird ("AEWA"), the largest agreement developed so far under the CMS, entered into force on 1 November 1999, when 20 contracting parties met in Cape Town, South Africa. The second session of the MOP took place from in 2002, in Bonn. The Agreement covers 235 species of birds that are ecologically dependent on wetlands for at least part of their annual cycle, including many species of pelicans, storks, flamingos, swans, geese, ducks, waders, gulls and terns.

33. Although AEWA only entered into force several years ago, its implementation is well underway. In early 2000, the Global Environment Facility ("GEF") granted US $350,000 for the drafting of a project brief of a full-size African-Eurasian Flyway GEF project. The goal of the project is to develop the transboundary strategic measures necessary to conserve the network of critical wetland areas on which migratory waterbirds depend throughout the Agreement Area. The project will focus on flyway and national protected area planning, capacity-building, demonstration projects, cooperative research and monitoring and communications activities.

v. Agreement on the Conservation of Cetaceans of the Black Sea, Mediterranean Sea and Contiguous Atlantic Area

34. The Agreement on the Conservation of Cetaceans of the Black Sea, Mediterranean Sea and Contiguous Atlantic Area ("ACCOBAMS") entered into force in 2001. The parties had their first meeting in March 2002. The countries that have joined the Agreement so far are Bulgaria, Georgia,

Romania (Black Sea) and Croatia, Malta, Monaco, Morocco, Spain (Mediterranean).

35. ACCOBAMS requires signatories to take coordinated measures to achieve and maintain a favourable conservation status for dolphins, porpoises and whales, and to establish and manage a network of specially protected areas for feeding, breeding and calving "within the framework of appropriate existing instruments." ACCOBAMS calls on its members to implement a comprehensive conservation plan, and to adopt and enforce domestic legislation to prevent the deliberate taking of cetaceans in fisheries by vessels under their flag or within their jurisdiction, and to minimize incidental catches. Governments also undertake to assess and manage human-cetacean interactions, to carry out research and monitoring, to develop information, training and public education programmes, and to put in place emergency response measures. Significantly, membership is also open to non-coastal States of the Agreement area whose vessels are engaged in activities that may affect cetaceans (these are defined as range states for the purposes of ACCOBAMS).

vi. Memorandum of Understanding concerning Conservation Measures for the Siberian Crane

36. The Memorandum of Understanding concerning Conservation Measures for the Siberian Crane ("Siberian Crane MOU") was concluded in 1993 and was the first such instrument to be considered an Agreement under article IV(4) of the Convention. The Siberian Crane MOU now has nine Signatory States: Azerbaijan, China, India, Islamic Republic of Iran, Kazakhstan, Pakistan, Russian Federation, Turkmenistan, Uzbekistan and Mongolia. The remaining Range State (Afghanistan) may become a member in the not too distant future.

37. Originally, the Siberian Crane MOU concentrated on the highly endangered Western and Central Populations of Siberian cranes, which migrate between breeding grounds in Western Siberia and wintering sites in Iran and India. In 1998, however, the scope of the MOU was extended to cover the larger Eastern Population, which winters around Poyang Lake, China, and accounts for over 95% of the species.

vii. Memorandum of Understanding concerning Conservation Measures for the Slender-Billed Curlew

40. The Memorandum of Understanding concerning Conservation Measure for the Slender-Billed Curlew ("Curlew MOU") dates from 1994 and

aims to safeguard the slender-billed curlew, estimated to have declined in number to 200-300 by the time of the MOU's conclusion. The Curlew MOU has 18 range state (Albania, Bulgaria, Croatia, Cyprus, Egypt, Georgia, Hungary, Islamic Republic of Iran, Kazakhstan, Morocco, Oman, Romania, Spain, Ukraine, Uzbekistan, Yemen, Greece and Italy) as well as Bird Life International, the International Council of Hunting and Game Conservation and the UNEP/CMS Secretariat.

viii. Agreement on the Conservation of Albatrosses and Petrels

39. Spain, Australia, New Zealand, Ecuador, Peru, United Kingdom and South Africa have ratified, the Agreement on the Conservation of Albatrosses and Petrels ("Albatrosses Agreement") in force since 2004. It is an AGREEMENT within article IV(3) of the CMS.

40. The purpose of the Albatrosses Agreement is to establish a cooperative and comprehensive framework and process to achieve and maintain a favorable conservation status for albatrosses and petrels. The Agreement aims to stop or reverse population declines by coordinating action to mitigate known threats to albatross and petrel populations. Some of the main threats stem from longline oceanic fishing. The Albatross Agreement calls upon parties to apply the precautionary approach, and in particular, "where there are threats of serious or irreversible adverse impacts or damage, lack of full scientific certainty shall not be used as a reason for postponing measures to enhance the conservation status of albatrosses and petrels."

41. The key potential benefits arising from the development of the Albatrosses Agreement may be summarized as follows:

- Coordinated action to mitigate known threats to albatross and petrel populations;
- Coordination of data collection, analysis and dissemination of information;
- Assessment of the international and regional conservation status of albatrosses and petrels and threats to the species; and
- Communication of the conservation status of albatrosses and petrels to relevant international and regional bodies to promote action.

ix. Memorandum of Understanding on the Conservation and Management of Marine Turtles and their Habitats of the Indian Ocean and South East Asia

42. The Memorandum of Understanding on the Conservation and Management of Marine Turtles ("IOSEA") was finalized in June 2001. The IOSEA entered into force on 1 September 2001. The current fifteen signatory states held their first meeting in Bangkok, in January 2003. The Secretariat is co-located with the UNEP Regional Office for Asia and Pacific, based in Bangkok, and has operated since April 2003. As indicated by the Guide, the IOSEA has a potential membership of at least 40 countries covering the entire Indian Ocean and South East Asia. Threats to marine turtles include the destruction of their habitat, accidental taking through commercial fishing, harvesting of their eggs, eating of their meat and use of their shells by local communities.

43. An associated Conservation and Management Plan was elaborated and adopted prior to the IOSEA. The Plan contains 24 programmes and 105 specific activities, and aims to reverse the decline of marine turtle populations throughout the region. The measures to be taken focus on reducing threats, conserving critical habitat, exchanging scientific data, increasing public awareness and participation, promoting regional cooperation and seeking resources for implementation.

x. Memorandum of Understanding concerning Conservation Measures for Marine Turtles of the Atlantic Coast of Africa

44. The Memorandum of Understanding concerning Conservation Measures for Marine Turtles of the Atlantic Coast of Africa ("Marine Turtle MOU") was concluded in May 1999. Range states gathered again in 2002, to put the finishing touches on a comprehensive Conservation Plan linked to the Marine Turtle MOU. On that occasion, representatives of five countries (Angola, Morocco, Sao Tome and Principe, Senegal and Sierra Leone) added their signatures to those of 12 other signatory states. The Nairobi Declaration, adopted at the conclusion of the conference, sets the stage for further concerted implementation of the Marine Turtle MOU. The Nairobi Declaration draws attention to the problem of marine turtle by-catch in industrial fishing operations and emphasizes the importance of involving resident communities in the development and implementation of conservation activities.

xi. The Memorandum of Understanding on the Conservation and Management of the Middle-European Population of the Great Bustard

45. The Memorandum of Understanding on the Conservation and Management of the Middle-European Population of the Great Bustard ("Bustard MOU") was opened for signature in 2000 and came into effect in June 2001. The Bustard MOU applies to the range states of the Great Bustard, a highly endangered bird in Europe. The MOU calls for cooperation between national authorities for the bird's improved conservation and the strict protection of the species and its habitat through a range of general and specific activities.

xii. Memorandum of Understanding concerning Conservation and Restoration of the Bukhara Deer

46. The Memorandum of Understanding concerning Conservation and Restoration of the Bukhara Deer ("Bukhara Deer MOU") was concluded in 2002, and signed by Kazakhstan, Tajikistan, Turkmenistan and Uzbekistan. The MOU was developed by CMS in collaboration with the Central Asia Programme of the World Wide Fund for Nature ("WWF"). The Bukhara Deer MOU is also signed by cooperating international organizations - WWF, the International Council for Game and Wildlife Conservation and the UNEP/CMS Secretariat, which demonstrates the broad international concern about the loss of Central Asia's biodiversity and its global importance.

47. The Bukhara Deer risks extinction from a number of human threats. Artificial regulation of the water regime, habitat destruction, as well as illegal hunting and poaching are the main reasons for the Bukhara Deer's alarming decline in numbers. The signatories acknowledge their countries' shared responsibility to conserve and restore the Bukhara Deer and the habitats upon which the animals depend. They recognize that they must take concerted, coordinated and immediate action to prevent the disappearance of the remaining populations.

xiii. Memorandum of Understanding and Action Plan concerning Conservation Measures for the Aquatic Warbler

48. The Memorandum of Understanding and Action Plan concerning Conservation Measures for the Aquatic Warbler ("Aquatic Warbler MOU") was adopted by governments and Non-Governmental Organizations in 13 European and African countries in Minsk, in April 2003.

49. The Aquatic Warbler MOU expresses countries' intentions to identify, protect and manage sites where Aquatic Warblers breed (Central Europe and Western Siberia), rest on migration (Western Europe) or spend the winter (Central West Africa). Annexed to the MOU is a detailed Action Plan, which summarizes the distribution, biology and threat status of the Aquatic Warbler, and describes precise actions to be taken by the relevant countries.

2. The 1971 Ramsar Convention on Wetlands of International Importance Especially as Waterfowl Habitat

Introduction

50. Wetlands are among the most complex and productive ecosystems in the world, comparable to rainforests and coral reefs. They can host an immense variety of species of microbes, plants, insects, amphibians, reptiles, birds, fish and mammals. All these species are closely linked to wetlands and to each other, forming a life cycle and a complex set of interactions. If one species disappears, the entire ecological web is endangered, which could lead to the loss of an entire ecosystem over time. For this reason, protecting wetland habitats is essential for maintaining global and national biodiversity.

51. As their name suggests, wetlands are closely linked to the presence of water. Responsible for the balance and purity of the water in lakes and rivers, wetlands also affect the quality of drinking water. They play a role that no other ecosystem can accomplish, since they act like a natural water filtration. Plants, soil and bacteria found in wetlands have a high filtering capacity. When water flows through such areas, plants retain excess nutrients and pollutants, and oxygenate the area.

52. Wetlands also retain excess water. Most of the flooding in urban areas is a result of the disappearance of wetlands in favour of impermeable surfaces such as asphalt roads and tarmacked parking lots. When there is heavy rainfall or snowmelt, large volumes of water rapidly accumulate. Wetlands are like natural sponges—they capture surface runoff water and bring it back to the surface slowly, preventing serious water level control problems. Inversely, during a drought, these water reservoirs are significant sources of water.

53. Wetlands also limit soil erosion. Plants that take root in wetland soils absorb the erosive effects of wind, slow the abrasive current along the shore and mitigate sudden water level variations. They also play an important role in the nutrient recycling processes of elements such as nitrogen and phosphorus. Plants absorb and accumulate these elements in their tissues and in the soil. When the plants die or lose their leaves, the elements are returned to the environment in another form.

54. Wetlands are equally important in maintaining a balanced carbon cycle. Plants, like animals, give off carbon dioxide into the atmosphere through respiration, but also absorb some by photosynthesis in order to transform it into organic matter. Researchers contend that carbon dioxide reserves can offset the negative effects of human-produced greenhouse gases.

55. As wetlands play an essential role in all natural cycles, human disturbances impact natural processes. These impacts are, for example, drinking water deterioration and loss, degradation and disappearance of habitats, animals and plant species, increase in natural disasters and effects on climate change. The Ramsar Convention was the first treaty to recognize that wetlands are among the most productive sources of ecological support on earth. The Convention was concluded in 1971, entered into force in 1975 and has 146 parties as of October 2005. The Convention currently includes 1469 designated sites covering an area of some 126,289,246 hectares.

Major Components

56. Article 1 of Ramsar Convention offers some key definitions of Terms among them the following

    "Wetlands" are defined as "...areas of marsh, fen, peatland or water, whether natural or artificial, permanent or temporary, with water that is static or flowing, fresh, brackish or salt, including areas of marine water the depth of which at low tide does not exceed six meters."

    Another relevant term is wise use, that has been defined as the sustainable utilization of wetlands for the benefit of human kind in a way compatible with the maintenance of the natural properties of the ecosystem.

57. The Convention Manual states that five major wetland types are generally recognized:

    - Marine (coastal wetlands including coastal lagoons, rocky shores and coral reefs),
    - Estuarine (including deltas, tidal marshes and mangrove swamps),
    - Lacustrine (wetlands associated with lakes),
    - Riverine (wetlands along rivers and streams) and
    - Palustrine (meaning "marshy" - marshes, swamps and bogs).

58. The purpose of the 1971 Ramsar Convention is to stop the loss of wetlands and to promote their conservation and wise use as a means to achieving sustainable development. In 1999 and 2002, the mission of the Ramsar Convention was more particularly identified as "the conservation and wise use of all wetlands through local, regional and national actions and international cooperation, as a contribution to achieving sustainable development throughout the world."

a. Obligations

59. Each state party shall designate at least one wetland for inclusion in a List of Wetlands of International Importance ("Ramsar List") and ensure the maintenance of the ecological character of each Ramsar site (article 2(1)). Wetlands should be selected for the List on account of their international biological, ecological, botanical or hydrological significance (article 2(2)). Countries are expected to include in the List as many wetlands as possible. In case of urgent national interests, a state may also delete a wetland from the list or restrict its boundaries. The state then should compensate, however, for the loss by creating additional nature reserves for waterfowl either in the same area or elsewhere. The Convention recognizes human-made wetlands; it now classifies 42 types, in three categories: Marine and Coastal, Inland and Human-made Wetlands.

60. The inclusion of a site on the list does not prejudice the sovereign rights of the territorial state. However, the state must conserve, manage and use wisely the listed wetlands and migratory stocks of waterfowl (article 2(6)).

61. Parties further commit themselves to include wetland conservation within their national land-use planning, with the purpose of promoting the wise use of all wetlands within their territory. Parties are obliged to establish nature reserves, whether they are listed or not, and to endeavor to increase waterfowl populations (article 4). Furthermore, they are obliged to report to the Ramsar Bureau on the status of their listed wetlands (article 3).

62. The Convention also provides for cooperation between state parties. Parties must consult with each other in implementing the Convention,

especially where a wetland extends across the territories of more than one state.

63. Parties are encouraged to establish National Wetland Committees referred to as Ramsar Committees, involving all relevant government institutions at central and state level dealing with water resources, development planning, protected areas, etcetera. NGO participation is also actively encouraged.

b. National Implementation

64. The Convention does not place specific obligations on state parties to enact legislation to protect wetlands. However, the requirement to designate at least one wetland upon signing the Convention, together with the obligation under article 3 to "formulate and implement their planning so as to promote the conservation of wetlands included in the List and as far as possible the wise use of wetlands in their territory" implies a strong need to ensure that a domestic scheme of legislative protection is necessary.

c. Institutions

65. In 1987, an amending protocol established a CoP as a primary Ramsar Convention institution. In its first six meetings, the COP adopted some 120 decisions to give greater precision to the definition of wetlands and to standardize the information form to describe the designated sites.

66. The COP meets every three years and approves resolutions, recommendations and technical guidelines to further the application of the Convention. The Standing Committee includes Regional Representatives of Ramsar geographical regions and meets annually. A Scientific and Technical Review Panel provides guidance on key issues related to the application of the Convention. The Secretariat, called the Ramsar Bureau, shares headquarters with the World Conservation Union/IUCN in Switzerland, and coordinates the day-to-day activities of the Convention. The Ramsar Bureau also administers the annual budget. Each party contributes a percentage related to its contribution of the United Nations budget. The minimum contribution for contracting party is currently US $700 per annum. In addition, many countries and other donors make contributions to special Ramsar Bureau projects.

67. An additional special register, called the Montreux Record, was established to identify Ramsar sites facing problems related to the maintenance of their ecological character. The COP further established a fund in 1990, now known as the Ramsar Small Grants Fund for Wetland Conservation and Wise Use, which provides developing states with financial support for wetlands conservation activities.

d. Relationship and Cooperation with other Biodiversity Related MEAs

68. The Secretariat of the Ramsar Convention has been taking vigorous steps to encourage its administrative authorities and national focal points to build close working relationships with their counterparts of other related conventions at the international level. Such initiatives have proven beneficial for both sides. The Convention works closely with other environmental conventions and institutions. Its Bureau has recently concluded a third Joint Work Plan with the Secretariat of the Convention on Biological Diversity for the period 2002-2006, which was approved by COP-8 in November 2002. This Joint Work Plan provides a blueprint for mutual cooperation between the two Secretariats. The COP of both conventions also promotes increased communication and cooperation between their subsidiary scientific bodies whose members regularly participate in the work and meetings of one another. The Ramsar Bureau also has concluded Memoranda of Cooperation with the Conventions on Desertification and World Heritage, and has signed a Memorandum of Understanding with the CMS Secretariat. The Bureau also works closely with funding institutions such as the World Bank and the Global Environment Facility.

3. The 1973 Convention on International Trade in Endangered Species of Wild Fauna and Flora ("CITES")

Introduction

69. Today, nearly a third of the world's wildlife is in danger of extinction and a major cause, second only to habitat loss, is commercial trade. International trade in endangered species is a highly lucrative business. Improvement in transport facilities has made it possible to ship live animals, plants and their products anywhere in the world. International trade of endangered species involves a wide variety of species, both as live specimens and as products, and concerns millions of animals and plants every year. Trade includes live animals, plants and a vast array of wildlife products derived from them, including food products, exotic leather goods, wooden musical instruments, timber, tourist curios and medicines.

70. In many regions of the world, the level of exploitation of particular animal and plant species is high and the trade in them, together with other factors, such as habitat loss, is resulting in heavy depletion of their populations and even bringing some species close to extinction. A dramatic example is the vicuna, a gazelle-like relative of the camel, which lives in the High Andes. Because of its exceptionally fine and warm wool, which has been in great demand in North America and Europe, nearly half a million were slaughtered after the Second World War before Peru pioneered protection in the 1960 to save the species.

71. Because the trade in wild animals and plants often crosses borders between countries, the effort to regulate such trade requires international cooperation. CITES was conceived in the spirit of such cooperation. The Convention entered in force in 1975. Today, CITES accords varying degrees of protection to more than 30,000 species of animals and plants, whether they are traded as live specimens, fur coats or dried herbs. Not one species protected by CITES has become extinct as a result of trade since the Convention entered into force and 169 parties as of August 2005,with CITES is among the largest conservation agreements in existence.

Major Components

a. Definitions

72. Some definitions from CITES include:

"Species means any species, subspecies, or geographically separate population thereof."

"Specimen means:
(i)   Any animal or plant, whether alive or dead;
(ii)   In the case of an animal: for species included in Appendices I and II, any readily recognizable part or derivative thereof; and for species included in Appendix III, any readily recognizable part or derivative thereof specified in Appendix III in relation to the species; and
(iii) In the case of a plant: for species included in Appendix I, any readily recognizable part or derivative thereof; and for species included in Appendices II and III, any readily recognizable part or derivative thereof specified in Appendices II and III in relation to the species."

"Trade means export, re-export, import and introduction from the sea".

73. The aim of the Convention is to protect endangered species. This is done by banning the trade of endangered species and regulating trade in other commercially exploited species. This should ensure sustainable trade and economic benefits for exporting countries.

b. Obligations and Structure

74. The species covered by the Convention are listed in three Appendices, according to the degree of protection they need:

- Appendix I includes species threatened with extinction. Trade in specimens of these species is permitted only in exceptional circumstances.
- Appendix II includes species not necessarily threatened with extinction, but in which trade must be controlled in order to avoid utilization incompatible with their survival. Article II(2)(b) allows so-called "look-alike" species to be added to Appendix II, even if they are not threatened with extinction, in order to make effective control possible.
- Appendix III contains species that are protected in at least country one that has asked other CITES parties for assistance in controlling the trade.

75. Each party to the Convention must designate a Management Authority and a Scientific Authority. The Management Authority is in charge of administering the licensing system. The Scientific Authority advises the respective party on the effects of trade on the status of the species.

76. A specimen of listed species may be imported into or exported (or re-exported) from a state party only under strict conditions. Appropriate documents must be obtained and presented for clearance at the port of entry or exit.

i. Trade in Appendix I Specimens (article III)

77. In order for trade in Appendix I species to occur, the trade must conform to the provisions of article III. This includes the requirement that an export permit or re-export certificate must be issued by the management authority of the state of export. An export permit may be issued only if the specimen was obtained in a legal way, and if the trade will not be detrimental to the survival of the species and that an import permit has already been issued. If the specimen is a live animal or plant, the specimen must be prepared and shipped so as to minimize any risk of injury, damage to health or cruel treatment. A re-export certificate may be

issued only if the specimen was imported in line with the provisions of the Convention.

78. Further, for such trade to occur, an import permit must be issued by the management authority of the state of import. This may be issued only if a scientific authority of the state of import is satisfied that the purpose of its import is not detrimental to the survival of the species, that the proposed recipient is suitably equipped to house and care for it, and that the management authority of the state of import is satisfied that the specimen will not be used for primarily commercial purposes.

ii. Trade in Appendix II Specimens (article IV)

79. All trade in Appendix II specimens must be in accordance with article. IV. An export permit or re-export certificate needs to be issued by the management authority of the state of export. An export permit may only be issued if the export will not be detrimental to the survival of the species, the specimen was obtained in accordance with the laws of the exporting state for the conservation of flora and fauna. If the specimen in question is a live animal or plant, it must be prepared and shipped in a way that minimizes any risk of injury, damage to health or cruel treatment. A re-export certificate may only be issued if the specimen was imported in accordance with the Convention

80. In the case of specimens introduced from the sea, for species listed in Appendix I or II, a certificate must be issued by the Management Authority of the state into which the specimens are being brought.

iii. Trade in Appendix III Specimens (article V)

81. All trade in Appendix III specimens must be in accordance with article V. In the case of trade from a state that included the species in Appendix III, an export permit can be issued by the management authority under the same conditions as for Appendix species.

82. In the case of export from any other state, the Management Authority of the exporting State must issue a certificate of origin.

83. In the case of re-export, the state of re-export must issue a re-export certificate.

84. The Convention allows or requires parties to make certain exceptions to the general principles described above; however, a permit or certificate will generally still be required. These exceptions are made for specimens in transit or being trans-shipped, for specimens that were acquired before the Convention's provisions applied to them

(known as pre-Convention specimens), for specimens that are personal or household effects, for animals that were bred in captivity and for plants that were bred artificially, for specimens used for scientific research and for animals or plants forming part of a travelling collection or exhibition (such as a circus).

85. Some parties have domestic legislation with trade controls stricter than those required by the Convention. In these cases, compliance with CITES regulations may therefore not be sufficient to ensure that trade is legal.

86. As concerns trade with non-parties, a party may accept documentation equivalent to the permits and certificates described above, in the case that a specimen of a CITES-listed species is transferred between the party and other non-parties. This equivalent documentation however must conform to the requirements of the Convention in a substantial degree (article X).

87. Appendix II specimens do not require an import permit unless this is required under national law.

iv. Compliance and Enforcement

88. Although there is no CITES article specifically dealing with non-compliance, measures to ensure compliance can be drawn from other provisions in the Convention. Measures aim at monitoring and promoting compliance and at identifying cases of non-compliance. To date, CITES has dealt with non-compliance in a consultative and non-judicial manner. However, one suggestion for improving the effectiveness would be the threat, and in cases of persistent non-compliance, the effective suspension of trade.

c. National Implementation

90. While CITES does not specifically require the enactment of legislation, it includes reference at various points to the application of domestic laws of the state of export or import in relation to flora and fauna. Thus, there is a strong expectation that parties will enact legislation which incorporates the obligations taken on when becoming a party to the Convention. Indeed, without appropriate legislation, it would be very difficult for any party to carry out the detailed obligations of appointment of management authorities and scientific committees, listing of species, issue of import and export permits and other onerous requirements of under the Convention.

d. Institutions

90. Every two to three years, the COP meets to review the implementation of the Convention. The COP provides the occasion for the parties to review progress in the conservation of species included in the Appendices, consider proposals to amend the lists of species in Appendices I and II, and to consider discussion documents and reports from the Secretariat, parties, permanent committees and other working groups. The COP may recommend measures to improve the effectiveness of the Convention and make provisions, including the adoption of a budget, necessary to allow the Secretariat to function effectively between the COPs.

91. In order to facilitate the work of the COP and to keep that work in progress between meetings, the COP has established four permanent committees that report to it at each meeting. These are the Standing Committee (which is the senior committee), the Animals Committee, the Plants Committee and the Nomenclature Committee.

92. The Standing Committee provides policy guidance to the Secretariat concerning the implementation of the Convention and oversees the management of the Secretariat's budget. Beyond these key roles, the Standing Committee coordinates and oversees the work of other committees and working groups, carries out tasks assigned to it by the COP and drafts resolutions for consideration by the COP.

93. The Animals and Plants Committees were established to fill gaps in biological and other specialized knowledge regarding species of animals and plants subject to CITES trade controls. Their role is to provide technical support to decision-making about these species. The Nomenclature Committee was established to meet the obvious need to standardize the nomenclature used in the Appendices and in other CITES documents. The Nomenclature Committee recommends standard names for animal or plant species, to the level of subspecies or botanical variety.

e. Relationship and Cooperation with other Biodiversity-Related MEAs

94. The CITES Secretariat makes efforts not only to increase cooperation with other biodiversity-related conventions but also to enhance mutual understanding and cooperation with the Convention's "technical partners." These partners include the UNEP Conservation Monitoring Centre, the World Conservation Union/IUCN and the Wildlife Trade Monitoring Programme of the World Wildlife Fund. CITES aims at increasing coordination in capacity-building, training, awareness raising, fund raising and regionalization.

4. The 1994 Lusaka Agreement on Cooperative Enforcement Operations Directed at Illegal Trade in Wild Fauna and Flora

Introduction

95. In spite of the existence of international instruments such as CITES and the CBD, illegal trade in wild fauna and flora in the African region has continued virtually unabated.

96. Profit margins are high and the risk of being caught is low, giving animal poachers plenty of room to move. Many of the animals being taken from the wild are now worth more dead than alive. The more endangered a species is, the more valuable it is to collectors on the black market. It is estimated that the annual value of illegal international wildlife trade is second in monetary value only to the illegal trade in drugs. International crime syndicates have taken advantage of poor working conditions and limited resources of national law enforcement agencies. These crime syndicates provide monetary incentives, arms and ammunition to poachers.

97. Governments have realized that individual efforts by a government and traditional enforcement methods are no longer capable of providing effective protection to African species from the illegal trade carried out by international organized crime syndicates. The need for closer cooperation among designated national law enforcement agencies to save African wild fauna and flora brought about the adoption of the 1994 Lusaka Agreement on Cooperative Enforcement Operations Directed at Illegal Trade in Wild Fauna and Flora ("Lusaka Agreement"). To date, seven governments are parties to the Lusaka Agreement, which entered into force on 10 December 1996. The parties are Kenya, United Republic of Tanzania, Uganda, Lesotho, Liberia, Congo and Zambia. Other states and invited organizations send observers to the Governing Council meetings.

Major Components

98. Per article 1 key Terms in the Agreement are defined:-

"Agreement area" means the area comprised of the land, marine and coastal areas within the limits of national jurisdiction of the Parties to this Lusaka Agreement and shall include their air space and internal waters.

"Biological diversity" means the variability among living organisms from all sources including, *inter alia*, terrestrial, marine and other aquatic ecosystems and the ecological complexes of which they are part; this includes diversity within species, between species and of ecosystems.

"Illegal trade" means any cross-border transaction, or any action in furtherance thereof, in violation of national laws of a Party to this Agreement for the protection of flora and fauna.

"Specimen" means any animal or plant, alive or dead, as well as any derivative thereof, of any species of wild fauna and flora.

"Wild fauna and flora" means wild species of animals and plants subject to the respective national laws of the Parties governing conservation, protection and trade.

99. The Agreement seeks to reduce and ultimately eliminate illegal trade in wild fauna and flora, and to establish a permanent Task Force for this purpose. It seeks to do so without compromising national sovereignty.

a. Obligations of the Parties

100. Parties are committed to cooperate with one another, and to investigate and prosecute cases of illegal trade. They must provide scientific data and technical assistance to the Task Force, based in Kenya, and also pay their annual assessed contribution to this important institution of the Convention. Parties must return to the country of original export or country of re-export any specimen of wild fauna and flora confiscated in the course of illegal trade. Furthermore, they are obliged to encourage public awareness campaigns.

b. National implementation

101. Under article 4(8), each party is obliged to adopt and enforce such legislative and administrative measures as may be necessary for the purposes of giving effect to the Agreement.

c. Institutions

102. The Task Force is a unique permanent multi-national institution composed of law enforcement officers from each of the parties. It is capable of operating in a transboundary manner against international wildlife smuggling rings. It is composed of field officers, intelligence officers and officers appointed by the Governing Council. These officers are seconded to the Task Force by the parties and will retain their national law enforcement powers in their respective countries. Apart from the annual contribution by the parties, the Task Force receives extra budgetary resources from donor countries such as grants, technical assistance and project funding.

103. The Task Force's functions include the facilitation of activities among the National Bureaus in carrying out investigations of illegal trade and the collection and dissemination of information relating to illegal trade, and the establishment and maintenance of databases. At the request of National Bureaux the Task Force carries out investigations of national laws concerning illegal trade and provides information on the return of confiscated flora and fauna to the country of export or re-export.

104. Each party must designate or establish a National Bureau. The functions of National Bureau are to provide and receive information on illegal trade and to coordinate with the Task Force on investigations thereof. Most governments have designated their national wildlife service authorities for this role.

105. The Governing Council, which is the policy and decision-making body for the Lusaka Agreement, consists of the parties to the Agreement. Each party is represented at ministerial level and with high-ranking officials in the field of wildlife law enforcement.

d. Relationship and Cooperation with other Biodiversity-Related MEAs

106. The Agreement reinforces the work of CITES and the Convention on Biological Diversity. However, unlike CITES, which lists specific species under the Appendices, the Lusaka Agreement is broad in scope, dealing with illegal trade of all species of wild fauna and flora at the regional level. Likewise, the Agreement reinforces the CBD, which aims at, among other things, creating awareness of the need to conserve and sustainably use biological resources before they are further diminished or lost.

5. The 1972 Convention concerning the Protection of the World Cultural and Natural Heritage

Introduction

107. The Great Barrier Reef is the largest coral reef system that has ever existed. The Grand Canyon retraces two billion years of the earth's history. The Galapagos Islands inspired Charles Darwin in his theory of evolution. The Island of Gorée is a reminder of slavery. The Citadel of Haiti is a symbol of liberty, built by slaves who had gained their freedom. These cultural and natural sites are very diverse, yet they have in common the fact that they constitute, together with many others, a common heritage to be treasured as unique testimonies to an enduring past. Their disappearance would be an irreparable loss for humanity.

108. The cultural heritage and the natural heritage represent priceless and irreplaceable possessions, not only of each state, but of humankind as a whole. The loss, through deterioration or disappearance, of any of these prized possessions would constitute an impoverishment of the heritage of all the peoples in the world. Parts of that heritage, because of their exceptional qualities, can be considered to be of "outstanding universal value" and, as such, worthy of special protection against the dangers which increasingly threaten them.

Major Components

109. The Convention Concerning the Protection of the World Cultural and Natural Heritage ("The World Heritage Convention") was adopted by the General Conference of UNESCO in 1972, and has been adhered to by 180 parties (April 2005). The Convention is one of the most complete international instruments that exists in the field of conservation. It is based on the recognition that parts of the cultural and natural heritage of various nations are of outstanding universal significance and need to be preserved as part of the world heritage of humankind as a whole. The Convention also affirms in its preamble that the cultural and natural heritage is increasingly threatened with destruction by changing social and economic conditions. The World Heritage Convention is supplemented by Operational Guidelines drawn up and updated from time to time by its World Heritage Committee.

110. The primary function of the Convention's provisions is to define and conserve the world's heritage, by drawing up a list of sites whose outstanding universal values should be preserved for all humanity and to ensure their protection through a closer cooperation among nations.

111. Article 2 defines 'natural heritage' to include:

- Natural features consisting of physical and biological formations or groups of such formations, which are of outstanding universal value, from the aesthetic or scientific point of view;
- Geological and physiographical formations and precisely delineated areas which constitute the habitat of threatened species of animals and plants of outstanding universal value from the point of view of science or conservation; and
- Natural sites or precisely delineated natural areas of outstanding universal value, from the point of view of science, conservation or natural beauty.

112. Because of the fact that many sites are a combination of natural and cultural sites, as well as "cultural landscapes," it is also important to include here a brief consideration of cultural heritage under the World Heritage Convention. "Cultural heritage" is defined in article 1 as:

- Monuments: architectural works, works of monumental sculpture and painting, elements or structures of an archaeological nature, inscriptions, cave dwellings and combinations of features, which are of outstanding universal value from the point of view of history, art or science;
- Groups of buildings: groups of separate or connected buildings which, because of their architecture, their homogeneity or their place in the landscape, are of outstanding universal value from the point of view of history, art or science;
- Sites: works of man or the combined works of nature and man, and areas including archaeological sites which are of outstanding universal value from the historical, aesthetic, ethnological or anthropological point of view.

113. The international system of protection is ensured on both the national and international level. Cultural and natural property that forms part of the world heritage remains subject to the legislation of the state where it is located. Thus, territorial sovereignty and property rights over elements of the world natural heritage are respected by the World Heritage Convention. However, the country hosting a heritage site has both rights and obligations. Article 4 requires each party to ensure the identification, protection, conservation, presentation and transmission to future generations

of the cultural and natural heritage situated within its territory. Parties periodically have to submit reports to a specially created committee on the measures that they have taken to implement the Convention.

114. At the international level, the entire international community has a duty to cooperate in the protection of the world cultural and natural heritage. This duty includes an obligation not to take any deliberate measures which might damage directly or indirectly the cultural or natural heritage and for other parties to support the requesting state in the identification, protection, conservation and presentation of cultural and natural heritage, recognizing that it constitutes a universal heritage.

a. World Heritage Committee

115. The Intergovernmental Committee for the Protection of the Cultural and Natural Heritage of Outstanding Universal Value, also referred to as the World Heritage Committee, consists of twenty-one members elected by the General Assembly of State parties during the General Conference of UNESCO. Representatives of international intergovernmental and Non-Governmental Organizations ("NGOs") may attend the meetings in an advisory capacity and be invited to participate in particular discussions and problems. The Secretariat of the Committee, which operates as the World Heritage Centre in Paris, is provided by the Director General of UNESCO.

b. World Heritage List

116. A major task of the World Heritage Committee is the establishment, maintenance and publication of the World Heritage List. To be included on the World Heritage List, sites must satisfy the selection criteria. These criteria are explained in the Operational Guidelines. The criteria have been revised regularly by the World Heritage Committee to match the evolution of the World Heritage concept itself. Natural properties should:

- Be outstanding examples representing major stages of the earth's history, including the record of life, significant ongoing geological processes in the development of landforms, or significant geomorphic or physiographic features; or
- Be outstanding examples representing significant ongoing ecological and biological processes in the evolution and development of terrestrial, fresh water, coastal and marine ecosystems and communities of plants and animals; or

- Contain superlative natural phenomena or areas of exceptional natural beauty and aesthetic importance; or
- Contain the most important and significant natural habitats for *in situ* conservation of biological diversity, including those containing threatened species of outstanding universal value from the point of view of science or conservation.

117. The Operational Guidelines state that in principle, a site could be inscribed on the List if it satisfies one of these four criteria and the relevant conditions of integrity. However, it is pointed out that most inscribed sites have met two or more criteria.

118. Sites are listed on the basis of the detailed criteria found in the Guidelines and only with consent of the territorial state. If the listed property is claimed by more than one state, competing rights to the property are not to be prejudiced by inclusion on that list.

119. The World Heritage Committee also has the power to remove properties from the World Heritage List if the property has deteriorated to the extent that it has lost those characteristics which determined its inclusion in the World Heritage List, where the intrinsic qualities of a World Heritage site were already threatened at the time of its nomination by action of man and where the necessary corrective measures as outlined by the state party at the time, have not been taken within the time proposed. The possibility of deletion from the List acts as an incentive on state parties to comply with the Convention's requirements.

c. List of World Heritage in Danger

120. The World Heritage Committee establishes and publishes a List of World Heritage in Danger, which includes property threatened by serious and specific dangers, such as the threat of disappearance caused by accelerated deterioration, large-scale public or private projects, armed conflict, natural calamities, like fires, earthquakes, landslides, etcetera. This List is designed to call the world's attention to natural or human-made conditions that threaten the characteristics for which the site was originally inscribed on the World Heritage List. Endangered sites on this list are entitled to particular attention and emergency action. In urgent cases, such as outbreak of war, the Committee will make the listing itself without having received a formal request. This List currently contains 35 properties.

121. The List of World Heritage in Danger has recently been the subject of discussion between the state parties, with suggestions that properties could only be placed on this List with the consent of the relevant state party. The World Heritage Committee resolved to clarify the situation by indicating in the Operational Guidelines that placing a property on this List is within the discretion of the Committee: the Committee may include a property in the List of World Heritage in Danger when the following requirements are met:

- The property under consideration is on the World Heritage List,
- The property is threatened by serious and specific danger,
- Major operations are necessary for the conservation of the property, and
- Assistance under the WHC has been requested for the property and the Committee is of the view that its assistance in certain cases may most effectively be limited to messages of its concern, including the message sent by inclusion of a site on the List of World Heritage in Danger and that such assistance may be requested by any Committee member or the Secretariat.

d. International Assistance

122. A further major function of the World Heritage Committee is to receive and study requests for international assistance formulated by parties to the World Heritage Convention for conservation presentation or rehabilitation of any part of the world cultural or natural heritage. The Committee decides on action in response to the requests and determines an order of priorities for its operations, taking into account both the intrinsic value of the property, protection and the ability of the state concerned to safeguard such property by its own means. The World Heritage Committee maintains a list of properties for which international assistance has been granted.

e. World Heritage Fund

123. The financial means to carry out assistance is provided through an international trust fund for the Protection of World Cultural and Natural Heritage of Outstanding Universal Value, called the World Heritage Fund. This Fund is used, for example, to finance expert studies to determine and fight the causes of deterioration or to plan conservation measures, to finance training of local specialists in conservation or renovation techniques, to supply equipment for the protection of a natural park or to restore a cultural monument.

124. The World Heritage Fund is replenished from various sources:

- Obligatory contributions from states parties to the World Heritage Convention which are fixed at no more than 1% of their contribution to the budget of UNESCO, and
- Voluntary contributions from states, donations from institutions or private individuals, or earnings from national or international promotional activities.

125. The World Heritage Committee may use the contributions only for defined purposes or accept contributions limited to a particular programme or project, provided no political conditions are attached.

126. A state that seeks international assistance must submit a formal request together with relevant information, supported by experts' reports where possible. This serves to define the operation contemplated, the work necessary, the expected costs, the degree of urgency and the available resources of the state. Assistance can take various forms, including studies, provision of experts and technicians, training of staff, equipment and interest-free loans. However, the contribution by the state being assisted must be substantial.

127. A project or programme for which assistance is granted is defined in an agreement between the World Heritage Committee and the recipient state. This agreement also sets forth the conditions under which the project or programme operates.

f. Advisory Bodies

128. The Convention includes three international organizations which advise the World Heritage Committee in making its decisions: for natural properties, it is IUCN-The World Conservation Union; for cultural properties, it is the International Council on Monuments and Sites; and for advice on restoration and training for cultural properties, it is the International Centre for the Study of the Preservation and Restoration of Cultural Property.

g. Secretariat

129. UNESCO provides the World Heritage Convention's Secretariat. In 1992, UNESCO established the UNESCO World Heritage Centre to carry out this function. The Centre liaises closely with the Advisory Bodies in order to administer the Convention and to advise the World Heritage Committee.

h. National Implementation, Supervision and Compliance

130. Article 29 provides for a measure of international supervision through the establishment of a state reporting system. Each state party submits reports to the General Conference of UNESCO containing information on the legislative and administrative provision that it has adopted and other action that it has taken to apply the World Heritage Convention. These reports are communicated to the World Heritage Committee. Furthermore, the possibility of de-listing from the World Heritage List is an incentive to compliance with the Convention's requirements.

131. While couched in mild language, the Convention contains detailed indications of what state parties should do to implement the Convention's obligations at a national level. Article 5 provides that: "To ensure that effective and active measures are taken for the protection, conservation and presentation of the cultural and natural heritage situated on its territory, each state party to the Convention shall endeavour, in so far as possible, and as appropriate for each country:

(a) to adopt a general policy which aims to give the cultural and natural heritage a function in the life of the community and to integrate the protection of that heritage into comprehensive planning programmes;

(b) to set up within its territories, where such services do not exist, one or more services for the protection, conservation and presentation of the cultural and natural heritage with an appropriate staff and possessing the means to discharge their functions;

(c) to develop scientific and technical studies and research and to work out such operating methods as will make the State capable of counteracting the dangers that threaten its cultural or natural heritage;

(d) to take the appropriate legal, scientific, technical, administrative and financial measures necessary for the identification, protection, conservation, presentation and rehabilitation of this heritage; and

(e) to foster the establishment or development of national or regional centres for training in the protection, conservation and presentation of the cultural and natural heritage and to encourage scientific research in this field."

132. Despite the terms of article 5(d) in relation to taking the appropriate legal, scientific, technical, administrative and financial measures, few state parties have actually adopted specific legislation to implement the obligations of the World Heritage Convention at national level. Most rely on existing legislation policies and administrative mechanisms. The exceptions include South Africa, which is discussed in section III below, and Australia.

i. Relationship and Cooperation with other Biodiversity-Related MEAs

133. A Memorandum of Understanding was signed between the World Heritage Centre and the Ramsar Bureau in 1999. The World Heritage officer in charge and the Ramsar Bureau of natural sites maintain a close working relationship with a view to:

- Promoting nominations of wetlands sites under the two Conventions;
- Reviewing reporting formats and coordinating the reporting about shared sites;
- Contributing to both Conventions' training efforts;
- Coordinating fundraising initiatives concerning shared sites; and
- Encouraging the establishment of joint national committees.

III. National Implementation

134. Examples of implementation of three of the four Conventions and one Agreement in Section II in three countries, namely Uganda, Singapore and South Africa, are given showing some of the varying strategies adopted by states in meeting their obligations under these instruments.These strategies can include incorporation of convention requirements within legislation, as well as through administrative guidelines and policies in line with the practice and procedure of a particular party.

1. Uganda: Implementing the Ramsar Convention

135. Wetland resources in Uganda traditionally have been utilized by the people as a source of materials for construction, crafts, furniture, and as hunting and fishing areas. Traditionally, seasonal wetlands and margins of permanent wetlands have been used for grazing cattle, growing crops and as a source for domestic water. In addition, they are a major habitat for wildlife resources. Despite these values, wetlands have been regarded previously as "wastelands," and many have been reclaimed and degraded.

136. Uganda is a signatory and Contracting Party of the Ramsar Convention on Wetlands of International Importance Especially as Waterfowl Habitat. The

Ramsar Convention entered into force in Uganda in 1988.

137. To carry out its responsibilities with respect to the country's wetlands, the government has outlined broad aims which are also supported by a number of specific goals. Guiding principles will govern the manner in which the National Policy on the Conservation and Management of the Wetland Resources ("National Policy") will be implemented. The National Policy complements the goals and objectives of the National

Environment Action Plan ("NEAP") and sectoral policies such as fisheries, forestry, wildlife, water, land tenure and soils, among others.

138. The Ugandan National Environment Statute (1995), Chapter 153 of the Laws of Uganda, implements the Ramsar Convention by including specific provisions on wetlands:

139. These provisions on wetlands have been implemented through the National Environment (Wetlands, River Banks and Lake Shores

---

Uganda, National Environment Statute (1995), chapter 153

Restrictions on the use of wetlands

37. (1) No person shall-
- (a) reclaim or drain any wetland;
- (b) erect, construct, place, alter, extend, remove or demolish any structure that is fixed in, on, under or over any wetland;
- (c) disturb any wetland by drilling or tunneling in a manner that has or is likely to have an adverse effect on the wetland;
- (d) deposit in, on, or under any wetland any substance in a manner that has or is likely to have an adverse effect on the wetland;
- (e) destroy, damage or disturb any wetland in a manner that has or is likely to have an adverse effect on any plant or animal or its habitat;
- (f) introduce or plant any exotic or introduced plant or animal in a wetland, unless he has written approval from the Authority given in consultation with the lead agency.

(2) The Authority may, in consultation with the lead agency, and upon an application to carry on any activity referred to in subsection (1), make any investigation it considers necessary, including an environmental impact assessment referred to in section 20 to determine the effect of that activity on the wetland and the environment in general.

(3) The Authority shall, in consultation with the lead agency, and by statutory order, specify the traditional uses of wetlands which shall be exempted from the application of subsection (1).

Management of wetlands

38. (1) The Authority shall, in consultation with the lead agency, establish guidelines for the identification and sustainable management of all wetlands in Uganda.

(2) The Authority shall, with the assistance of the Local Environment Committees, District Environment Committees and lead agency, identify wetlands of local, national and international importance as ecosystems and habitats of species of fauna and flora and compile a national register of wetlands.

(3) The Authority may, in consultation with the lead agency and the District Environment Committee declare any wetland to be a protected wetland thereby excluding or limiting human activities in that wetland.

**Uganda, National Environment (Wetlands, River Banks and Lake Shores Management) Regulations in 1999
(No. 3 of 2000)**

4. The objective of this Part of the Regulations is to

- (a) provide for the conservation and wise use of wetlands and their resources in Uganda;
- (b) give effect to clause 2 of article 237 of the Constitution of Uganda;
- (c) ensure water catchment conservation and flood control;
- (d) ensure the sustainable use of wetlands for ecological and touristic purposes for the common good of all citizens;
- (e) ensure that wetlands are protected as habitats for species of fauna and flora;
- (f) provide for the regulated public use and enjoyment of wetlands;
- (g) enhance research and research related activities; and
- (h) minimize and control pollution.

Management) Regulations in 1999 (No. 3 of 2000) ("National Regulations").

140. Part II of the National Regulations provides for the management of wetlands and wetland resources. The objectives of this Part are to provide for the conservation and wise use of wetlands and their resources in Uganda. Regulation 4 provides:

141. A Technical Committee on Biodiversity Conservation, established under Section 11 of the National Legislation, is responsible for advising the Board and the Executive Director on the wise use, management and conservation of wetland resources. Specific functions of the Technical Committee are set out in Regulation 6, whereas functions of District Environment Committees are set out in Regulation 7.

142. The Minister may declare protected wetlands under Regulation 8.

The Minister may, by statutory instrument, and after consultation with the lead agency and with the prior approval from the Policy Committee on the Environment, declare a wetland by stating whether a wetland is fully protected, partially protected or subject to conservation by the local community.

A wetland declared under Sub-Regulation (2)(a) is an area of international and national importance because of its biological diversity, ecological importance, landscape, natural heritage or touristic purposes. The following activities may be permitted: research, tourism and restoration or enhancement of the wetland. Under Sub-Regulation of (2)(c) of the National Regulations, a declared wetland is an area in which a person who has property rights in the land may perform traditional activities, subject to any local environmental restrictions.

143. Other regulations of Part II concern an inventory of wetlands and the use of wetlands and granting of use permits. Part III of these Regulations shall apply to all riverbanks and lake shores in Uganda. Its provisions promote sustainable use and protection of riverbanks, prevent siltation of rivers and lakes and control pollution or degrading activities. An inventory of degraded riverbanks shall be made by local authorities and persons wishing to use river banks shall apply for a permit. Part IV provides for environmental impact assessment and environmental restoration.

2. Singapore: Implementing CITES

144. Singapore ratified CITES in 1986 and has since introduced legislation to control illegal trading of endangered species of animals. The Endangered Species Act ("Import & Export Act") gives effect to CITES by controlling the importation, exportation and introduction from the sea of certain animals

and plants. Section 2 includes definitions of terms within the text. A permit, issued by the Director, Primary Production, is required to import, export or introduce from the sea any species that are listed on the schedule (Section 5). There are penal provisions concerning those who obstruct the execution of this Act or commit an offence under the Act. Under the Import and Export Act, anyone who is convicted of the offence is liable to a maximum fine of not more than US $5,000 or a jail term not exceeding a year or both. Repeat offenders would be fined up to a maximum not exceeding US $10,000 or jailed for not more than a year or both.

145. The Minister may make rules providing for the issue of permits or provisions relating to the purposes of the Import and Export Act. The Act contains a Schedule listing the species that are relevant.

3. South Africa: Implementing the World Heritage Convention

146. In 1997, the Republic of South Africa signed the World Heritage Convention and thus opened the way for recognizing the country's important natural and cultural sites internationally. The World Heritage Committee has since added six South African properties to the World Heritage List. They are: Greater St. Lucia Wetland Park (1999), Robben Island (1999), Fossil Hominid Sites of Sterkfontein, Swartkrans, Kromdraai, and Environs (1999) (known as the Cradle of Humankind), Khahlamba / Drakensberg Park (2000), Mapungubwe Cultural Landscape (2003) and Cape Floral Region Protected Areas (2004).

147. Since ratifying the Convention, South Africa has established an inter-governmental structure, the South African World Heritage Convention Committee, to coordinate the administration and implementation of the Convention. The Committee meets regularly and has compiled a five-year plan for submitting sites to the World Heritage Centre for inscription on the list of World Heritage sites. The national Department of Environmental Affairs and Tourism ("DEAT") is the lead agency for ensuring that the obligations of the Convention are adhered to, and to that end has initiated consultations and the drafting of the South African World Heritage Convention Bill, enacted as the World Heritage Act, No. 49 of 1999. In order to fulfill this role, the DEAT:

- Liaises with UNESCO's World Heritage Centre and the Committee,
- Manages the process of selecting the sites for nomination, and

- Facilitates the process of developing on appropriate legal framework.

148. According to the South African Constitution, as a dualist system, a treaty such as the World Heritage Convention becomes law in South Africa only when it is enacted into national legislation. Specifically incorporating the Convention into South African law ensures that the country can derive maximum benefit from its being a party to the Convention. Thus, the World Heritage Convention was incorporated into South African legislation.

149. The World Heritage Convention Law is designed to create a legal and administrative framework for various cultural and natural sites in South Africa to facilitate the grant of World Heritage Site status by the World Heritage Committee of UNESCO. In the words of the then South African Minister for the Environment, Mr. Valid Moose, in 1999, underscored that the Law sought to create a legal framework that allows the government to:

- Strengthen where appropriate, the powers of bodies currently managing areas to be listed as World Heritage sites;
- Establish, where no such institutions exist, new institutions called Authorities to provide for the cultural and environmental protection, and responsible development of World Heritage Sites;
- Create, where necessary, a Board to oversee the Authority, and an executive staff component responsible for the day-to-day management of the Authority;
- Provide for the preparation of integrated management plans, as required by the World Heritage Convention;
- Provide for proper auditing and financial controls and the preparation of annual reports outlining the activities of each Authority; and
- Ensure that "state of conservation" reports are prepared as required by the World Heritage Convention.

150. This national law therefore ensures that the principles and values of the Convention are given genuine application over South Africa's potential and inscribed World Heritage sites. They also ensures that the national government has the legal means to discharge its responsibilities under the Convention and that these sites are developed in ways that meet the social and development needs of South Africa's citizens. The latter emphasis will bring a South African perspective to the management of country's current and potential sites, and seeks to balance preservation and conservation with job creation and broad economic development.

151. It gives a relevant national authority the powers to liaise extensively with relevant cultural and nature conservation bodies and allows for local and other institutions to act as such Authority. Subject to it being empowered by the Minister, an Authority may facilitate and manage cultural development, nature conservation and related tourism activities at a particular site under its control. Authorities are designed to assist and be assisted by agencies of a province, regional council or local government in the discharge of their duties. At the request of a province, a regional council or a local government, and with the Minister's consent, an Authority may perform functions on contractually agreed terms. The preparation of integrated management plans must be done in a way that ensures consultation with and harmonizes the interests of local, provincial and regional authorities.

152. The national legislation is therefore seen as a seminal example of how development, growth and job creation can be combined with the preservation of cultural heritage and the conservation of biodiversity. The various regulations and institutions allowed for in the legislation are explicitly designed to emphasise sustainable development over constraining forms of protectionism that have sometimes been perceived as being associated with the Convention. This balance between protection and development is particularly important in developing countries such as South Africa.

Prof. Ben Boer, Professor in Environmental Law & Associate Dean International, Faculty of Law, University of Sydney

Eva Maria Duer, Associate Legal Officer, Division of Policy Development and Law, UNEP

RESOURCES

Internet Materials

AGRI-FOOD AND VETERINARY AUTHORITY OF SINGAPORE available at http://www.ava.gov.sg/javascript/main-ie.html

CITES available at http://www.cites.org/

CONVENTION ON MIGRATORY SPECIES available at http://www.wcmc.org.uk/cms/

CRITERIA FOR INCLUSION OF NATURAL PROPERTIES IN THE WORLD HERITAGE LIST available at
http://whc.unesco.org/opgulist.htm#para43

ENDANGERED SPECIES ACT OF SINGAPORE available at http://eelink.net/~asilwildlife/singapore1.pdf

FAOLEX LEGAL DATABASE available at http://faolex.fao.org/faolex/

GUIDE TO THE CONVENTION ON THE CONSERVATION OF MIGRATORY SPECIES OF WILD ANIMALS (JANUARY 2002) available at
http://www.wcmc.org.uk/cms/pdf/CMS_Guide_Jan02_en.pdf

JERRY HARRISON & MARK COLLINS, HARMONIZING THE INFORMATION MANAGEMENT INFRASTRUCTURE FOR BIODIVERSITY RELATED
TREATIES, WORLD CONSERVATION MONITORING CENTRE available at http://www.wcmc.org.uk

KEY DOCUMENTS OF THE RAMSAR CONVENTION available at http://www.ramsar.org/key_guide_nwp_e.htm

LUSAKA AGREEMENT available at www.internationalwildlifelaw.org/lusaka.pdf

NATIONAL POLICY FOR THE CONSERVATION AND MANAGEMENT OF WETLAND RESOURCES, MINISTRY OF NATURAL RESOURCES
(1995) available at http://www.ramsar.org/wurc_policy_uganda.htm

PAUL MAFABI, CASE STUDY 5, NATIONAL WETLANDS PROGRAMME, GOVERNMENT OF UGANDA, REVIEW OF SECTORAL POLICIES
AND LEGISLATION RELATED TO WETLANDS available at http://www.ramsar.org/key_guide_nwp_cs_e.htm

RAMSAR CONVENTION ON WETLANDS available at http://www.ramsar.org/

RAMSAR 'TOOLKIT' FOR THE WISE USE OF WETLAND available at http//www.ramsar.org/wurc_handbook3e_cases.htm

REVIEWING LAWS AND INSTITUTIONS TO PROMOTE THE CONSERVATION AND WISE USE OF WETLANDS, RAMSAR 'TOOLKIT' FOR THE
WISE USE OF WETLANDS available at http//www.ramsar.org/wurc_handbook3e_cases.htm

SOUTH AFRICAN DEPARTMENT OF ENVIRONMENTAL AFFAIRS AND TOURISM available at www.environment.gov.za

THE RAMSAR CONVENTION MANUAL (3RD ED.) (2003) available at http//www.ramsar.og/lib_manual2003.pdf

UGANDA: NATIONAL ENVIRONMENT (WETLANDS, RIVER BANKS AND LAKE SHORES MANAGEMENT) REGULATIONS 1999 (NO. 3 OF
2000) available at http://www.nemaug.org/wetlandsweb.htm

UNESCO WORLD HERITAGE HOMEPAGE available at http://whc.unesco.org/nwhc/pages/home/pages/homepage.htm

WORLD HERITAGE CONVENTION BILL 1999, SOUTH AFRICA available at
http://www.environment.gov.za/PolLeg/Legislation/WrldHerConvAct/WrldHerConvAct.pdf

Text Materials

Alexander Kiss & Dinah Shelton, INTERNATIONAL ENVIRONMENTAL LAW, (2nd ed., Transnational Pubs.).

Durwood Zaelke, Donald Kaniaru & Eva Kruzikova, MAKING LAW WORK, ENVIRONMENTAL COMPLIANCE AND SUSTAINABLE DEVELOPMENT, (Cameroon May, 2005).

GUIDE TO THE CONVENTION ON THE CONSERVATION OF MIGRATORY SPECIES OF WILD ANIMALS, (January 2002).

INTERNATIONAL INSTITUTIONAL ARRANGEMENTS RELATED TO ENVIRONMENT AND SUSTAINABLE DEVELOPMENT, (United Nations General Assembly, 55th session, Report of the Secretary-General, 5 September 2000).

Patricia Birnie & Alan Boyle, INTERNATIONAL LAW AND THE ENVIRONMENT, (2nd ed., Oxford University Press, 2002).

Phillipe Sands, PRINCIPLES OF INTERNATIONAL ENVIRONMENTAL LAW, (2nd ed., Cambridge University Press, 2003).

15. BIOLOGICAL DIVERSITY

I. Introduction

1. All life on earth is part of one great, interdependent system. It interacts with and depends on the non-living components of the planet such as atmosphere, oceans, freshwaters, rocks and soils.

2. Biological diversity is the variety of life in all its forms, levels and combinations. It represents the variability within and among all ecosystems, species and genetic material. Biodiversity is thus an attribute to life, in contrast to "biological resources," which are tangible biotic components of ecosystems. The breadth of the concept reflects the interrelatedness of genes, species and ecosystems. Biodiversity forms the web of life of which human beings are an integral part and upon which they so fully depend.

3. The term biodiversity covers several interrelated aspects. Generally, biodiversity is understood in terms of the wide variety of plants, animals and micro organisms. Biodiversity, however, also includes genetic differences within each species such as, between varieties of plants and breeds of animals. Chromosomes, genes, and DNA, the building blocks of life, determine the uniqueness of each individual and each species. Yet another aspect of biodiversity is the variety of ecosystems such as those that occur in deserts, forests, wetlands, mountains, lakes, rivers, and agricultural landscapes. In each ecosystem, living creatures, including humans, form a community, interacting with one another and with the air, water, and soil around them.

4. Scientists estimate that the number of species, including insects and microorganisms is about 12 million. This diversity of species has emerged through genetic mutation and expansion into new niches over the past 4.5 billion years. Only towards the end of this period did more complex organisms and further significant specification occur. These events are still to be studied but it appears that they have generated the range and dimensions of today's biodiversity. It is thought to be unlikely that further specification will occur, which supports the belief that biodiversity in present times is at its maximum. Therefore, biodiversity must be regarded as a non-renewable resource, whose potential loss would be irreplaceable and could never be reproduced through modern technologies. Biodiversity is therefore valuable not only for the sake of variety itself but also as an output of a four billion years old process of evolution. As a result, biodiversity has fine-tuned resilience to physical conditions and the ability to adapt to changing circumstances. It thus acts as a buffer against future dangers to life supporting ecosystems.

II. International Framework

The Problem

5. The human race had 850 million members when it entered the industrial age sharing the planet with a biodiversity as large as the planet has ever possessed. Today, the world population is nearly eight times as large; and resource consumption and utilisation of biological resources is far greater. Due to human activities, species and ecosystems are more threatened than ever before in recorded history. The losses are taking place in tropical forests, which host 50% to 90% of identified life species, but also in rivers, lakes, deserts and temperate forests, on mountains and islands. (For marine biodiversity, see chapter 17).

6. While the extinction of species and their habitats and the destruction of ecosystems are an ecological tragedy, they also have profound implications for economic and social developments because of the goods and services they provide. Estimates are that at least 40% of the world's economy and 80% of the needs of people in developing countries are derived from biological resources. The loss of the diversity of life diminishes the chances for medical discoveries, economic development and adaptive responses to challenges such as climate change.

7. "Goods and services" provided by ecosystems include:

- Food, fuel and fibre;
- Shelter and building materials;
- Purification of air and water;
- Detoxification and decomposition of wastes;
- Stabilization and moderation of the Earth's climate;
- Moderation of floods, droughts, temperature extremes and the forces of wind;
- Generation and renewal of soil fertility, including nutrient cycling;
- Pollination of plants, including many crops;
- Control of pests and diseases;
- Maintenance of genetic resources as key inputs to crop varieties and livestock breeds, medicines and other products;
- Cultural and aesthetic benefits; and
- Ability to adapt to change.

8. The loss of biodiversity often reduces the productivity of ecosystems, thereby shrinking nature's basket of goods and services. It destabilizes ecosystems, and weakens their ability to deal with natural disasters such as floods, droughts and hurricanes, and with human-caused stresses, such as pollution and climate change. Already, we are spending huge sums in response to flood and storm damage exacerbated by deforestation. Such damage is expected to increase due to global warming.

9. The reduction in biodiversity also hurts in other ways. Cultural identity is deeply rooted in the biological environment. Plants and animals are symbols of the human's world, preserved in flags, sculptures and other images that define humans and human societies. Biodiversity represents a very high economic and social value for local communities and indigenous peoples, who depend on their environment for food, medicines and shelter. Indigenous cultures are often deeply rooted in the belief that the spiritual world resides in nature. This worldview implies a deep respect for the natural world and provides guidance on its use. Thus, degradation of the environment and national biodiversity severely threatens the lifestyles and cultural heritage of indigenous and local communities.

10. Early international treaties addressed specific aspects and components of biodiversity. At the global level, the Convention concerning the Protection of the World Cultural and Natural Heritage, 1972 ("WHC") covers internationally important natural and cultural sites. The specific threat of trade in endangered species is addressed by the 1973 Convention on International Trade in Endangered Species of Wild Fauna and Flora. A specific ecosystem type, namely wetlands, is protected through the 1971 Convention on Wetlands of International Importance Especially as Waterfowl Habitat ("Ramsar Convention"), and a category of species, migratory species, is protected through the 1979 Convention on the Conservation of Migratory Species of Wild Animals . In addition, there are various regional conventions on the conservation of aspects of nature and natural resources such as the 1979 Convention on the Conservation of European Wildlife and Natural Habitats; the 1976 Convention on the Conservation of Nature in the South Pacific; the 1968 African Convention on the Conservation of Nature ,and Natural Resources (since revised in 2003); the 1982 Protocol concerning Mediterranean Specially Protected Areas; the 1985 ASEAN Agreement on the Conservation of Nature and Natural Resources; and the 1986 Convention on the Protection of the Natural Resources and

Environment of the South Pacific. However, in the late 1980s and early 1990s, it became apparent, that all these conventions together could not ensure global conservation of biodiversity. Their sectoral and regional nature resulted in considerable gaps in coverage. A more comprehensive and global approach was deemed necessary to address the continuing loss of biological diversity. These concerns led to the adoption of the Convention on Biological Diversity. This Manual has, in several chapters, discussed different aspects of the above named instruments, for example, chapters 14 and 17.

11. This chapter will first deal with the framework of the Convention on Biological Diversity including access to genetic resources and benefit sharing, and subsequently, discuss the interrelation between the Convention and other relevant international legal regimes, such as the Agreement on Trade Related Aspects of Intellectual Property Rights of the World Trade Organization.

1. The Convention on Biological Diversity

12. The Convention on Biological Diversity ("CBD" or "Convention") was adopted in 1992, and subsequently opened for signature in Rio de Janeiro during the 1992 United Nations Conference on Environment and Development. The adoption of the Convention represented a major breakthrough after lengthy negotiations over more than three years, under the auspices of UNEP whose Governing Council initiated the process in 1989, building upon preparatory work undertaken by IUCN/World Conservation Union.

13. During the negotiations, developing countries envisaged the proposed convention as an opportunity to gain access to technology, financial resources and markets and to promote sustainable economic development. They proposed the establishment of a special system of intellectual property rights, a mechanism for compensating them for access to and the utilization of genetic resources provided by their countries, and mechanisms that would facilitate their access to biotechnology developed through the utilization of these genetic resources. A group of industrial countries was strongly opposed to many of these proposals. They argued that loosening intellectual property rights would threaten and constrain the development of biotechnology and undermine the protection of innovations. The final text of the Convention included many of the proposals made by the developing countries but omitted several substantive proposals on which no agreement could be reached.

14. Issues that could not be agreed upon included the precautionary principle, which is now only referred to in the Preamble, a consolidated intellectual property rights regime, liability and redress for damage to biodiversity and a compilation of global lists of protected areas and species.

15. The Convention is the first international treaty to take a holistic, ecosystem-based approach to the conservation and sustainable use of biological diversity. It is a framework instrument laying down broad goals, key objectives and general principles which are to be operationalized through concrete measures and actions at the national level on the basis of guidance, *inter alia*, provided by the decisions of the Conference of the Parties ("COP") to the Convention. The Preamble sets out the ethical and socio-economic underpinnings of the Convention. These include the intrinsic, ecological and anthropocentric value of biological diversity and its components; the status of biological diversity as a common concern of humankind; the current rate of biodiversity loss due to human activities; and the imperatives of intra- and inter-generational equity.

16. The Convention stipulates in article 1 its three main objectives:

- The conservation of biological diversity;
- The sustainable use of the components of biological diversity; and
- The fair and equitable sharing of the benefits arising out of the utilization of genetic resources, including by appropriate access to genetic resources and by appropriate transfer of relevant technologies, taking into account all rights over those resources and to technologies, and by appropriate funding.

17. The second and third objectives are a clear departure from preceding international biodiversity-related agreements, which were predominantly concerned with conservation. An important aspect of the negotiation of the Convention was the realization that biodiversity rich countries needed to exploit their biological resources for development purposes as well as benefit from the commercial utilization of their genetic resources. Articles 6 to 21 of the Convention set goals, establish general principles, and define measures and mechanisms necessary for the realization of the three objectives.

Major Components

a) General Principles and Concepts

18. The Convention establishes a number of general principles in its preamble and operative provisions. Chapter 3 above discusses some of the general principles outlined below. These principles are calculated to guide and inform action at the national and international levels.

19. Both the preamble and article 3 of the Convention affirm the sovereign right of states over their own biological resources. This provision was a direct reaction to the attempt by developed countries to subsume biodiversity under the common heritage of mankind principle which had been applied to mineral resources in the deep seabed beyond national jurisdiction under the 1982 United Nations Convention on the Law of the Sea ("UNCLOS"). This would have had serious implications regarding the ownership of biological resources within the national jurisdiction of states. However, while affirming national sovereignty over resources, the preamble also underlines the responsibility of states to conserve and sustainably use their biological diversity.

20. Article 3 of the Convention provides that states have the responsibility to ensure that activities within their jurisdiction or control do not cause damage to the environment of other states or of areas beyond the limits of national jurisdiction. The general principle of international law that states are under an obligation to protect, within their own territory, the rights of other states to territorial integrity and inviolability has been progressively extended over the years through state practice and judicial decisions to cover transboundary environmental harm. The general obligation upon states with respect to transboundary environmental harm was reaffirmed in principle 2 of the 1992 Rio Declaration where it is asserted that "States have ... the responsibility to ensure that activities within their jurisdiction or control do not cause damage to the environment of other states or of areas beyond the limits of national jurisdiction." It is this principle that has been restated in article 3 of the Convention. By virtue of this provision, the international responsibility of a state will consequently be engaged in those cases where activities within its jurisdiction or control causes damage to the biological diversity of another state or of areas beyond the limits of national jurisdiction.

21. The preamble affirms that the conservation of biological diversity is a "common concern of humankind." In contrast to the "common heritage of mankind" doctrine, this concept has less implications. States have sovereign rights over their biological resources. However, given the universal value of biological diversity, the global community has certain responsibilities regarding its stewardship.

22. The preamble states that the contracting parties to the Convention are determined to conserve and sustainably use biological diversity for the benefit of present and future generations. The principle of inter-generational equity was first authoritatively articulated in principle 2 of the 1972 Stockholm Declaration and has been reaffirmed in principle 3 of the 1992 Rio Declaration. Equity within and between generations in the use of biological resources is an important underlying postulate of Convention and is implicit in a number of provisions dealing with the rights of local and indigenous communities, access to genetic resources and benefit-sharing, and conservation and sustainable use of biological diversity.

23. There are considerable scientific uncertainties regarding environmental consequences of human production and consumption activities. This uncertainty arises because of gaps in scientific knowledge with respect to the nature and the linkages within the ecosystem and the interplay between ecological factors and socio-economic activities. The precautionary principle articulated in article 15 of the 1992 Rio Declaration demands action in cases of significant risk even where complete scientific evidence regarding probable environmental consequences may be lacking. The preamble to Convention consequently provides that "...where there is a threat of significant reduction or loss of biological diversity, lack of full scientific certainty should not be used as a reason for postponing measures to avoid or minimize such a threat."

b) Measures for Conservation and Sustainable Use

24. In article 6, the Convention provides that parties shall develop national strategies, plans or programmes for the conservation and sustainable use of biological diversity and endeavour to integrate the conservation and sustainable use of biological diversity into relevant sectoral or cross-sectoral plans, programmes and policies. National Biodiversity Strategies and Action Plans ("NBSAPS") have been developed by over 100 countries since the adoption of the Convention and have become the primary tool at the national level

for its implementation. Indeed, a central strategic goal of the Strategic Plan of the Convention adopted by the COP at its sixth meeting is to ensure that NBSAPS and the integration of biodiversity concerns into relevant sectors serve as an effective framework for the implementation of the objectives of Convention.

25. Identification of components of biological diversity and monitoring their conservation status is an important first step in the establishment of measures for conservation and sustainable use. Article 7 of the Convention, therefore, requires parties to identify components of biodiversity important for conservation and sustainable use and to monitor the components so identified, paying particular attention to those requiring urgent conservation measures and those with potential for sustainable use. In addition, parties are required to identify and monitor processes and activities, which may have significant adverse impacts on conservation and sustainable use of biodiversity.

26. Annex I to the Convention contains indicative lists for the identification and monitoring of ecosystems, species, communities and genes and genomes of social, scientific and economic importance.

27. Articles 8 and 9 set out the main conservation commitments under the Convention. Parties are required to meet specific goals relating to *in-situ* and *ex-situ* conservation. "*In-situ* conservation" is defined in article 2 as the conservation of ecosystems and natural habitats and the maintenance and recovery of viable populations of species in their natural surroundings. The *in-situ* conservation commitments outlined in article 8 include, among others, the following:

- The establishment of a system of protected areas;
- The development of guidelines for the selection, establishment and management of protected areas;
- The regulation or management of biological resources important for the conservation of biological diversity within or outside protected areas, with a view to ensuring their conservation and sustainable use;
- The promotion of the protection of ecosystems, natural habitats and the maintenance of viable populations of species in natural surroundings;
- Promotion of environmentally sound and sustainable development in areas adjacent to protected areas with a view to furthering the protection of these areas;
- The rehabilitation and restoration of degraded ecosystems and the recovery of threatened species;

- Management and control of risks associated with living modified organisms resulting from biotechnology;
- Prevention, control and eradication of alien invasive species;
- The respect, preservation and maintenance of traditional biodiversity-related knowledge; and,
- The development of appropriate legislative and regulatory frameworks.

28. *Ex-situ* conservation is defined as the conservation of components of biological diversity outside their natural habitats. Article 9 specifies the main *ex-situ* conservation commitments, including:

- Adoption of measures for *ex-situ* conservation of components of biological diversity, preferably in the country of origin of such components;
- Establishment and maintenance of facilities for *ex-situ* conservation of and research on plants, animals and microorganisms;
- Adoption of measures for the recovery and rehabilitation of threatened species and for their reintroduction into their natural habitats;
- Regulation and management of collection of biological resources from natural habitats for *ex-situ* conservation; and,
- Cooperation in the provision of financial and other support for *ex-situ* conservation.

29. Sustainable use is defined in article 2 of the Convention as "...the use of components of biological diversity in a way and at a rate that does not lead to the long-term decline of biological diversity, thereby maintaining its potential to meet the needs and aspirations of present and future generations." The main sustainable use commitments are outlined in article 10, including:

- Integrating consideration of the conservation and sustainable use of biological resources into national decision-making;
- Adopting measures relating to the use of biological resources to avoid or minimize adverse impacts on biological diversity;
- Protecting and encouraging customary use of biological resources in accordance with traditional cultural practices that are compatible with conservation or sustainable use requirements;
- Supporting local populations in developing and implementing remedial action in degraded areas where biological diversity has been reduced; and
- Encouraging cooperation between governmental authorities and its private sector in developing methods for sustainable use of biological resources.

c) **Access to Genetic Resources and Benefit Sharing**

30. The third objective of the Convention, the fair and equitable sharing of benefits arising from the use of genetic resources, is of particular importance to developing countries. They hold most of the world's biological diversity but feel that, in general, do not obtain a fair share of the benefits derived from the use of their resources for the development of products such a high-yielding crop varieties, pharmaceuticals and cosmetics. Such a system reduces the incentive for the world's biologically richer but economically poorer countries to conserve and sustainably use their resources for the ultimate benefit of mankind.

31. The issue of Access and Benefit-Sharing ("ABS") was one of the central themes during the negotiations of the Convention whose substantive provisions on ABS are contained in article 15 (access to genetic resources); article 16, paragraph 3 (access to and transfer of technology that makes use of genetic resources); and article 19, paragraph 1 (participation on biotechnological research on genetic resources) and paragraph 2 (access to results and benefits from biotechnologies). These provisions address both providers and users of genetic resources and also outline the basic goals and elements of an ABS regime under the Convention.

32. Article 15 of the Convention addresses the terms and conditions for access to genetic resources and benefit sharing. The provisions of the Convention apply only to genetic resources, which are provided by parties that are countries of origin of such resources or by parties that have acquired the genetic resources in accordance with the Convention. In effect, these provisions do not apply to genetic resources acquired prior to the entry into force of the Convention.

33. Article 15 recognizes the sovereign rights of states over their natural resources and provides that the authority to determine access to genetic resources rests with the national governments and is subject to national legislation. It also establishes a number of principles and the conditions governing access to genetic resources and benefit-sharing. These are:

- Parties shall endeavour to create conditions to facilitate access to genetic resources and shall not impose restrictions that run counter to the objectives of the Convention;
- Access, where granted, shall be on mutually agreed terms;
- Access to genetic resources shall be subject to the prior informed consent of the contracting party providing such resources;
- Scientific research on genetic resources

provided by other contracting parties shall be undertaken with the full participation of such parties and, where possible, in the territory of such parties; and

- Parties shall take legislative, administrative or policy measures to ensure the fair and equitable sharing of the results of research and development and the benefits arising from the commercial and other utilization of genetic resources with the contracting party providing such resources; and benefit-sharing shall be on mutually agreed terms.

34. Article 19 of the Convention provides for participation in biotechnological research by countries providing genetic resources and the sharing of benefits arising from the utilization of genetic resources in such research and development. It also contemplates the negotiation of and adoption of a protocol that sets out appropriate procedures, including, in particular, advance informed agreement in the field of safe transfer, handling and use of any Living Modified Organisms ("LMOs") resulting from biotechnology that may have adverse effect on the conservation and sustainable use of biological diversity. The Cartagena Protocol on Biosafety was subsequently adopted in January 2000.

35. Although the Convention entered into force in 1993, it was not until 1999 that work began in earnest to further develop and operationalize its general principles and broad objectives. COP-5 established the "Ad Hoc Open-Ended Working Group on Access and Benefit-Sharing" to develop guidelines and other approaches concerning access to genetic resources and benefit-sharing. The "Bonn Guidelines on Access to Genetic Resources and Fair and Equitable Sharing of the Benefits arising out of their Utilization" ("Bonn Guidelines") were adopted by COP-6 in 2002. The policy choice made by COP-6 to develop international guidelines for ABS was a pragmatic step. Legislative and policy developments in most countries are largely in their embryonic stages. International guidelines would, therefore, greatly assist governments in developing effective national and regional ABS regimes. Also, the political sensitivity of the issue and the lack of political consensus on a number of outstanding items had an influence on any global ambition for the development of a legally binding instrument at that stage. It should be noted, however, that the development of a number of multilateral environmental agreements has been preceded by the adoption of international non-binding regimes.

36. Indeed, COP-7 mandated the Working Group to elaborate and negotiate an international regime on access to genetic resources and benefit-sharing with the aim of adopting an instrument/instruments to effectively implement the provisions in articles 15 and 8(j) of the Convention and its three objectives.

The Bonn Guidelines on Access to Genetic Resources and Fair and Equitable Sharing of the Benefits arising out of their Utilization

37. The 2002 Bonn Guidelines establish detailed procedures to facilitate access to genetic resources and the fair and equitable sharing of benefits on the basis of the 'prior informed consent' of the country providing genetic resources and on 'mutually agreed terms'. The Guidelines provide guidance to parties in the development of benefit sharing regimes and arrangements while promoting capacity building, transfer of technology and the provision of financial resources.

38. Although compliance with the Guidelines is voluntary, they provide the first widely accepted criteria for national licensing of access to genetic resources and the sharing of benefits arising from the utilization of genetic resources. The Guidelines should assist parties, governments and other stakeholders in developing an overall access and benefit-sharing strategy, and in identifying the steps involved in the process of obtaining access to genetic resources and benefit-sharing. More specifically, the Guidelines are meant to assist parties, governments and other stakeholders when establishing legislative, administrative or policy measures on access and benefit-sharing and/or when negotiating contractual arrangements for access and benefit-sharing. The Guidelines are structured as follows:

- Section I on General Provisions covers key features, use of terms, scope, relationship with relevant international regimes and the objectives of the guidelines;
- Section II deals with the role of the national focal point and competent national authority(ies), and responsibilities of parties and stakeholders that are users and providers of genetic resources;
- Section III addresses the participation of stakeholders in the development and implementation of access and benefit-sharing arrangements;
- Section IV covers steps in the process of access and benefit-sharing, including prior informed consent and mutually agreed terms;
- Section V covers other provisions, such as incentives, accountability, monitoring and reporting, verification, dispute settlement and remedies;

- Appendix I contains suggested elements for Material Transfer Agreements; and
- Appendix II provides an illustrative list of monetary and non-monetary benefits.

39. A few issues covered by the Guidelines are still outstanding and may require further clarification. They include the use of terms, the scope of guidelines with respect to products and derivatives and stakeholder involvement.

40. Some of the key features of the Guidelines that will contribute towards the effective implementation by parties, governments and other stakeholders of the relevant provisions of the Convention related to access to genetic resources and benefit-sharing include:

- The definition of the roles and responsibilities of national authorities and of users and providers in the implementation of ABS arrangements: for example, competent national authorities are responsible for granting access in accordance with national legislative, administrative or policy measures and for advising on the requirements for obtaining prior informed consent.
- The participation of stakeholders in the development and implementation of ABS arrangements: the Guidelines recognize that the involvement of relevant stakeholders is essential to ensure the adequate development and implementation of access and benefit-sharing arrangements. However, in view of the diversity of stakeholders and their diverging interests, the nature and level of involvement of different stakeholders remains an issue that will require further clarification and development at the national level.
- The identification of steps in the access and benefit-sharing process: the guidelines re-emphasize the obligation to seek Prior Informed Consent ("PIC") established under article 15 of the Convention. In addition, however, the Guidelines have endeavoured to clarify and define the necessary steps in the ABS process that would facilitate compliance with this basic obligation, and identified the basic principles and elements of PIC, the national entities granting PIC, the procedures for obtaining PIC, and other elements of PIC to be taken into consideration when establishing access and benefit-sharing arrangements.
- The identification of basic requirements for mutually agreed terms: the Guidelines describe the basic requirements and elements of mutually agreed terms and benefit-sharing, to be considered as guiding parameters in

contractual agreements and benefit-sharing arrangements.
- The identification and establishment of measures for the implementation of the Guidelines and ABS arrangements: the Guidelines address the issue of the type of incentives necessary to ensure effective implementation by parties, Governments and other stakeholders. Other issues of particular concern to provider countries with respect to implementation, such as mechanisms to promote the accountability of all stakeholders, national monitoring and reporting of access and benefit-sharing arrangements, means for verification of compliance with the relevant provisions of the Convention, the settlement of disputes and remedies in cases of violation of national measures implementing the relevant provisions of the Convention are also addressed.

d) Access to and Transfer of Technology

41. Access to and transfer of technology is considered in the Convention, as is the case with other post-Rio multilateral environmental agreements, as one of the critical elements for its effective implementation. The Convention expressly recognizes the role that technology transfer and cooperation can play in the realization of its three objectives and is conceived as part of the positive measures to facilitate the effective implementation of the Convention. Issues relating to technology transfer and cooperation are addressed in articles 16, 18 and 19 of the Convention. In addition, issues regarding training and research considered so essential to establishing national capacities to absorb technologies are addressed in article 12 of the Convention.

42. The basic obligation of all parties regarding access to and transfer of technology is set out in article 16(1), which provides that each contracting party "...undertakes...to provide and/or facilitate access for and transfer to other Contracting Parties of technologies that are relevant to the conservation and sustainable use of biological diversity or make use of genetic resources and do not cause significant damage to the environment." The obligation established has a number of important aspects. First, its scope is limited to the categories of technologies specified: that is, technologies relevant to the conservation and sustainable use of biological diversity or that make use of genetic resources. Second, the wording of the paragraph provides flexibility in the manner in which parties can implement it depending on each concrete situation. Parties can "provide and/or facilitate"

access for and transfer of technologies to other parties. This is a necessary and important latitude since for technologies subject to intellectual property rights, parties would have very limited leverage on the private sector to affect transfer. In this regard, therefore, parties can only facilitate transfers through such measures as providing appropriate incentives to the private sector. On the other hand, for technologies in the public domain, a party could directly provide access for and transfer to another party.

43. There are a number of other conditions regarding technology transfer established under article 16. First, under article 16(2), "Access to and transfer of technology...to developing countries shall be provided and/or facilitated under fair and most favourable terms, including on concessional and preferential terms where mutually agreed, and, where necessary, in accordance with the financial mechanism established by Articles 20 and 21..." It would appear that the Convention requires developed country parties to ensure that the terms under which developing country parties' access technologies are fair and most favourable. This would seem to suggest that access to and transfer of technology would be on terms other than those established by the international technology market. How this is to be ensured by parties in cases of proprietary technology, that is, technologies subject to intellectual property rights, is an issue that will need to be further addressed by the COP. However, the paragraph makes an important linkage with the Convention's financial mechanism: it is clear that the resources available through the mechanism could be used to facilitate access to and transfer of proprietary technology to developing countries.

44. Second, in the case of technology subject to patents and other intellectual property rights, access and transfer shall be provided on terms that recognize and are consistent with the adequate and effective protection of intellectual property rights (article 16(2)). In effect, access to and transfer of proprietary technology is made subject to the existence of adequate and effective protection of intellectual property rights. This provision would seem to require that recipient countries have in place adequate and effective domestic intellectual property rights regimes. To what extent strong national intellectual property rights regimes facilitate the transfer of technology is an issue that is currently subject to intense international debate.

45. Third, parties are required to "...take legislative, administrative or policy measures...with the aim that Contracting Parties, in particular those that are

developing countries, which provide genetic resources, are provided access to and transfer of technology which makes use of those resources, on mutually agreed terms, including technology protected by patents and other intellectual property rights, where necessary, through the provisions of Articles 20 and 21 and in accordance with international law (article 16(3))..." The obligation is imposed on user-countries to establish an enabling legal and policy environment for access to and transfer of such technology to countries, which provide genetic resources. This is important to ensure the effective implementation of the third objective of the Convention relating to the fair and equitable sharing of benefits arising from the utilization of genetic resources.

46. Last, parties are required to "...take legislative, administrative or policy measures...with the aim that the private sector facilitates access to, joint development and transfer of technology...for the benefit of both governmental institutions and the private sector of developing countries..." (article 16(4)). The vast amount of global technology is owned by the private sector of developed countries. Developed country parties are therefore required to play a facilitative role through legislative and policy development that would act as an incentive to their private sector actors to provide access to and transfer of technology to developing countries.

47. There are a number of other provisions in the Convention that are relevant to technology transfer. Article 18 on technical and scientific cooperation requires parties to promote international cooperation in the field of conservation and sustainable use of biological diversity and to develop methods of cooperation for the development and use of technologies, including indigenous and traditional technologies and to promote the establishment of joint research programmes and joint ventures for the development of technologies relevant to the objectives of the Convention. Article 19 on biotechnology requires parties to establish "...legislative, administrative or policy measures to provide for the effective participation in biotechnological research activities by the Contracting Parties, especially developing countries, which provide the genetic resources for such research..." and to "...take practicable measures to promote and advance priority access on a fair and equitable basis by Contracting Parties, especially developing countries, to the results and benefits arising from biotechnologies based upon genetic resources provided..."

e) The Role of Indigenous and Local Communities

48. The preamble to the Convention recognizes the close and traditional dependence of many indigenous and local communities embodying traditional lifestyles on biological resources and the need for fair and equitable sharing of benefits arising from the use of traditional biodiversity-related knowledge, innovations and practices. The protection, preservation and maintenance of traditional biodiversity-related knowledge and the sharing of benefits arising from the use of such knowledge is further elaborated upon in article 8(j) of the Convention. It provides that:

> **1992 Convention on Biological Diversity (Article 8(j))**
>
> "Each Contracting party shall:
> (...)
> (j) subject to its legislation, respect, preserve and maintain knowledge, innovations and practices of indigenous and local communities embodying traditional lifestyles relevant for the conservation and sustainable use of biological diversity and promote their wider application with the approval and involvement of the holders of such knowledge, innovation and practices and encourage the equitable sharing of the benefits arising from the utilization of such knowledge, innovations and practices..."

49. In order to address the implementation of this article, COP-4 established the Ad Hoc Open-Ended Inter-session Working Group ("Working Group") on article 8(j) and related provisions of the Convention. The mandate of the Working Group is to provide the COP with advice on the application and development of legal and other appropriate forms of protection of traditional biodiversity-related knowledge, innovations and practices. A programme of work on article 8(j) and related provisions of the Convention was subsequently adopted by COP-5. The programme of work comprises several elements: participatory mechanisms; status and trends in the protection of traditional biodiversity-related knowledge, innovations and practices; traditional cultural practices for conservation and sustainable use; equitable sharing of benefits; exchange and dissemination of information; monitoring; and legal issues. For each element a range of tasks and activities to be undertaken by parties, the Secretariat and the Working Group are identified. Among the tasks the Working Group is currently addressing are guidelines for the conduct of cultural, environmental and social impact assessments regarding proposed developments on sacred sites and on lands or waters occupied or used by indigenous and local communities;

development of *sui generis* systems for the protection of traditional knowledge, innovations and practices; and the development of mechanisms to ensure full and effective participation of indigenous and local communities in decision-making and implementation.

50. The COP has taken a number of decisions in this regard. COP-6 adopted the recommendations of the Working Group on cultural, environmental and social impact assessments regarding projects likely to impact on sacred sites, lands and waters of indigenous and local communities. The COP has further taken decisions on the participation of indigenous and local communities in the operations of the Convention. These include encouraging parties to include representatives of indigenous and local communities in their delegations to meetings organized under the Convention. In order to ensure compliance with the Prior Informed Consent procedure of indigenous and local communities and to guarantee benefit-sharing, the COP has urged parties and governments to encourage the disclosure of the origin of traditional knowledge, innovations and practices in applications for intellectual property rights, where the subject matter of the application concerns or makes use of such knowledge in its development.

51. The seventh meeting of the Conference of the Parties, held in Kuala Lumpur, Malaysia, in February 2004, adopted a series of decisions pertaining to the programme of work on article 8(j) and related provisions, on the respect, preservation and maintenance of knowledge, innovation and practices of indigenous and local communities. One of the main achievements of COP-7 was the adoption (decision VII/16 F) of the Akwé Kon Voluntary Guidelines for the Conduct of Cultural, Environmental and Social Impact Assessment regarding Developments Proposed to take place on, or which are likely to Impact on, Sacred Sites and on Lands and Waters Traditionally Occupied or Used by Indigenous and Local Communities. The Guidelines, which were named with a Mohawk term meaning "everything in creation", provide a collaborative framework ensuring the full involvement of indigenous and local communities in the assessment of cultural, environmental and social impact of proposed developments on sacred sites and on lands and waters they have traditionally occupied. Moreover, guidance is provided on how to take into account traditional knowledge, innovations and practices as part of the impact-assessment processes and promote the use of appropriate technologies. The Guidelines suggest a ten-step process for impact assessment of proposed development.

52. Article 10(c) further requires states to "protect and encourage customary use of biological resources in accordance with traditional cultural practices that are compatible with conservation or sustainable use requirements."

f) International Cooperation and the Financial Mechanism

53. Given the wide-ranging nature of the Convention, there are a number of provisions, which seek to deal with implementation through international cooperation. As such, provisions are made for international cooperation in the field of research and training, particularly taking note of the needs of developing countries; and public education and awareness raising (articles 12(a) and 13(b)). Furthermore, articles 17 and 18 deal with information exchange relevant to conservation and sustainable use of biodiversity and improved international technical and scientific cooperation.

54. Article 18(3) provides for the establishment of a Clearing-House Mechanism ("CHM") to facilitate technical and scientific cooperation. The second meeting of the COP decided that the CHM should start with a pilot phase. A fully operational CHM has since been established and operates as a tool for information exchange and technical and scientific cooperation.

55. Expertise in managing information and technology varies enormously from country to country. The CHM should ensure that all governments have access to the information and technologies they need for their work on biodiversity. The mission of the Clearing House is to:

- Promote and facilitate technical and scientific cooperation, within and between countries;
- Develop a global mechanism for exchanging and integrating information on biodiversity; and,
- Develop the necessary human and technological network.

56. The clearing-house is coordinated by the Executive Secretary of the Secretariat of the Convention and overseen and guided by an Informal Advisory Committee ("IAC") set up by the parties to the Convention. The committee works in a transparent and cooperative manner to promote awareness of the multiple needs and concerns facing various communities, countries and regions.

57. In addition, a network of national focal points for the mechanism has been established to address matters relating to technical and scientific cooperation. The parties have recently emphasized the need to strengthen the role of these focal points. Building a network of Non-Governmental Organizations ("NGOs") and other institutions working on biodiversity could contribute to this goal. Establishing national, regional, sub-regional and thematic clearing-house focal points for specific topics could also help.

58. For the first time in a global conservation agreement, a legal relationship is created between the conservation and sustainable use obligations of developing countries and the financial obligations of developed countries. Developed country parties are required to provide new and additional financial resources to enable developing country parties to meet the full incremental costs to them of implementing their obligations under the Convention (article 20). Such financial resources are to be provided largely but not exclusively through a financial mechanism established under article 21 of the Convention. Developed country parties may also provide resources through bilateral and other multilateral channels.

59. The relationship between developing country implementing obligations and developed country financial and technology transfer obligations is underlined by article 20(4) which states that "the extent to which developing country Parties will effectively implement their commitments under this Convention will depend on the effective implementation by developed country Parties of their commitments under this Convention related to financial resources and transfer of technology and will take fully into account the fact that economic and social development and eradication of poverty are the first and overriding priorities of developing country parties. The funding is to enable developing countries to cover the incremental costs associated with measures to implement the Convention's obligations. Such costs have to be agreed upon between the developing country concerned and the financial mechanism established under article 21. The COP has designated the Global Environment Facility ("GEF") as the *interim* financial mechanism for the Convention. (For a discussion on GEF see Chapter 6). The financial mechanism operates under the authority and guidance of and is accountable to the COP. The COP determines the policy, strategy, programme priorities and criteria relating to access to and utilization of financial resources under the mechanism. It provides regular guidance to the financial mechanism on these matters. In this regard, financial resources and the financial

mechanism are standing items on the agenda of the COP. For the above purposes, a Memorandum of Understanding was concluded between the CBD Secretariat and the GEF Council in 1996.

g) Institutional Arrangements

60. In order to facilitate the implementation of the objectives of the Convention, several bodies have been established under it.

61. The Conference of the Parties is the decision making body of the Convention. It is in charge of policy development, provides guidance to parties on the implementation of the Convention and reviews its implementation (article 23).

62. The Subsidiary Body on Scientific, Technical and Technological Advice ("SBSTTA") has been established to provide scientific and technical advice to the COP. It is mandated to: provide scientific and technical assessments of the status of biological diversity, prepare scientific and technical assessment of the effects of types of measures taken in accordance with the Convention, identify appropriate technologies and know-how relating to the conservation and sustainable use of biological diversity, provide advice on scientific programmes and international cooperation in research and development related to conservation and sustainable use of biological diversity, and respond to scientific, technical and technological questions that may be raised by the COP and its subsidiary bodies (article 25).

63. A Secretariat provides administrative support to the Convention. Its functions include servicing meetings organized under the Convention, reporting to the COP on the execution of its functions; coordination with other relevant international bodies, and any other functions assigned to it by any protocol or by the COP. (article 24) At its first meeting, the COP designated the United Nations Environment Programme ("UNEP") to carry out the functions of the Secretariat of the Convention. The Secretariat of the Convention is hosted by the Government of Canada in Montreal.

h) Compliance, Liability and Dispute Settlement

64. To monitor compliance with Convention obligations, article 26 requires parties to submit to the COP, on a regular basis, national reports on measures taken to implement the provisions of the Convention and their effectiveness in meeting its objectives. The COP provides guidance regarding reporting intervals and the nature, structure and content of the reports. The Convention does not have a non-compliance procedure. It is, however, possible for the COP to assess the extent of compliance by parties on the basis of the national reports.

65. Article 27 lays down the procedure relating to settlement of disputes concerning the interpretation or application of the Convention. Parties are urged to seek a solution to such disputes through negotiation or mediation by a third party. For a dispute not resolved through negotiation or mediation, parties can either resort to arbitration as provided for in part I of Annex II to the Convention or submit the dispute to the International Court of Justice ("ICJ"). In this latter regard, parties are required at the time of ratification or accession to indicate either arbitration or the ICJ as a compulsory means of dispute settlement.

66. The question of liability and redress for damage to biological diversity was one of the critical issues before the negotiators of the Convention. There was, however, no consensus during the negotiations on the nature of a liability and redress regime under the Convention. Decision on this issue was therefore postponed to a later date. Article 14(2) of the Convention consequently provides that the COP "...shall examine, on the basis of studies to be carried out, the issue of liability and redress, including restoration and compensation, for damage to biological diversity, except where such liability is a purely internal matter." A number of studies have been undertaken so far under the authority of the COP and a legal and technical expert group is envisaged to further explore this issue.

i) Relationship with other International Agreements

67. As regards the legal relationship with other international agreements, article 22 of the Convention provides that the Convention "...shall not affect the rights and obligations of any Contracting Party deriving from any existing international agreement, except where the exercise of those rights and obligations would cause a serious damage or threat to biological diversity. In addition, parties are required to "...implement this Convention with respect to the marine environment consistently with the rights and obligations of States under the law of the sea."

68. In relation to access to genetic resources and benefit-sharing, the provisions of the Convention interrelate with the FAO International Treaty on Plant Genetic Resources for Food and Agriculture. As stated in its preamble, the International Treaty has been negotiated in harmony with the Convention. Article 19 of the International Treaty

requires its Governing Body to establish and maintain cooperation with the COP to the CBD; to take note of relevant decisions of the COP; and to inform the COP of matters regarding the implementation of the Treaty.

69. The provisions of the CBD on technology transfer and benefit sharing touch on issues relating to Intellectual Property Rights ("IPR"), and therefore create important inter-linkages with the World Trade Organization's Agreement on Trade-Related Aspects of Intellectual Property Rights ("TRIPs Agreement") and the international agreements administered by the World Intellectual Property Organization ("WIPO"). Indeed, article 16(3) of the Convention expressly recognizes that patents and other intellectual property rights may have an influence on its implementation and calls on parties to cooperate in order to ensure that such rights are supportive of and do not run counter to the objectives of the Convention. The COP has invited the WTO to explore the interrelationship between the Convention and the TRIPs Agreement.

70. The Conference of the Parties to the Convention has, since its fourth meeting, regularly reaffirmed the importance of cooperation and the need to design and implement mutually supportive activities with other conventions, international organizations and initiatives.

2. Intellectual Property Rights and Biological Diversity

71. The reason why industries make investments in research and development is the expectation of a technological advantage in relation to other market competitors and, as a result thereof, higher profits. Intellectual Property Rights provide protection for the results of investment in the development of new technology, thus giving incentives and means to finance research and development activities. IPR are thus a means of promoting and rewarding innovation. However, balancing private and public interests in protecting innovation is the essence of Intellectual Property legislation.

72. Intellectual property legislation recognizes two main categories of protection: "copyright" as rights over the creations of people's minds and expressions of their thoughts and industrial property, like trademarks and geographical indications. Intellectual property can be divided into the protection of distinctive signs like trademarks and geographical indications and the protection of technology and inventions through patents, industrial designs and trade secrets.

73. The importance of biomaterials for industrial purposes is rapidly expanding. Pharmaceutical, biotechnological and agricultural industries undertake expensive research and development efforts to create technologies that allow the effective utilization of natural species' genes and to market the improved products that result. They will thus make intensive use of any IPR regime in force to recover their investments. Many companies have been granted patents on domestically bred plants in developing countries and often also on indigenous knowledge about their use. IPRs are being claimed on plant species long used by Africans, pain killers used by Chinese, Andean crop species, and traditional rice varieties nurtured by Indian farmers.

74. Applying IPRs to plant genetic material can result in constraining farmers in their use of seeds since patented seed varieties cannot be grown for future use as seed by a person not holding patent rights. Thus, farmers face the threat of becoming dependent on commercial supplies for vital inputs such as seeds. Over longer periods this might reduce breeding alternatives for local and indigenous farmers and communities. This could eventually lead to higher genetic uniformity in crops or other commercialized plant species, which would become increasingly vulnerable to pests and diseases. Strong IPRs systems thus can promote genetic erosion, which entail serious implications for the genetic pool.

75. Under their domestic legislation industrial breeders can get the commercial gains of exploited Plant Genetic Resources without necessarily sharing them with the indigenous communities of the countries from which the genetic material originates. However, the sharing of their traditional knowledge and resources with the rest of the world should go hand in hand with the sharing of the relevant benefits derived from their utilization. This should include the rights to control access to their knowledge, its recognition and protection.

76. According to IP law, innovative knowledge must comply with different requirements to enable legal protection. Innovation thus becomes a "formal" procedure, acknowledged merely if it complies with given legal parameters and requirements. This "formal innovation" is appropriate for modern market societies.

77. Indigenous and local communities and local farmers have long had a significant interdependence with the lands and environments within which they live. A wide array of plant species was bred over generations to resist specific pests or simply to enhance the harvest. Healing

properties of many plants have been discovered and developed over years to cure community-specific diseases. Any improvement in knowledge or biodiversity has regularly been sought on behalf of the community, which is why indigenous and local communities and local farmers never deemed protection of their knowledge necessary. This kind of innovation, not recognized within legal structures, is known as "informal innovation."

78. The concepts addressing "formal innovation" are mainly based on the idea that innovation is the product of individuals. This concept is not applicable to indigenous knowledge where contributions are often made by entire communities and therefore cannot be attributed to distinct groups or individuals. The recognition of their rights needs the creation of special or *sui generis* regimes. A further concern is that acquiring and defending IPR protection within the currently established regimes requires access to information, good legal advice and financial resources. These resources are often beyond the capabilities of indigenous and local communities.

79. Recognizing only the known and established IPR also bears the risk that indigenous communities will be forced to buy the products of these companies at high prices. Likewise, farmers might have to pay royalties for using products which they had originally developed, improved, used and protected themselves for centuries. Cultural and intellectual contribution of traditional knowledge to industrial inventions risks being erased and lost forever, with unpredictable consequences for global biodiversity, food security and the environment in general.

80. Under these circumstances, the global community has recognized the need for protection of traditional knowledge, innovations and practices through the establishment of *sui generis* systems, for instance, in the form of Farmer's Rights.

81. Several attempts have been made within the framework of other international agreements and negotiations to introduce a system providing for the protection of farmers' and indigenous communities' rights. The Convention on Biological Diversity recognizes the importance of the respect for preservation, maintenance and recognition of traditional knowledge, innovations and practices and the role of indigenous and local communities and farmers in the conservation and sustainable use of biological diversity. Furthermore, it recognizes the importance of benefit-sharing with indigenous and local communities in recognition of their role in the conservation and sustainable use of biological diversity.

82. Within the conventional IPR systems, the option of the use of "geographical indications" as a potential mechanism for the recognition and protection of "informal innovation" has been raised. Indigenous products derived from long established traditional methods are frequently attributed names of the region where they have been developed or of the communities that have habitually used them. The main advantage of geographical indications as a means of protection for informal innovation is the "relative impersonality" of the right (i.e., the protected subject matter is related to the product itself (its attribute or definition) and is therefore not dependent on a specific right holder). However, since only certain products rely on customarily used indications, especially new products will fail to comply with the demands of IP law for accrediting protection.

83. The Uruguay Round of trade negotiations (from 1986 to 1994) brought intellectual property rights (copyrights, trademarks, patents, etcetera) into the GATT/WTO framework through the Agreement on Trade-Related Aspects of Intellectual Property Rights. The scope of protection of IPRs has varied widely between countries. The growth in international trade, including trade in products subject to intellectual property rights, inevitably led to increasing pressure for the harmonization and strengthening of IPR systems, especially from developed countries with strong high-technology sectors. The TRIPS Agreement is an attempt to narrow the differences in protection between countries and bring such rights under common international rules.

84. The TRIPS Agreement deals with, *inter alia,* (a) the applicability of the basic principles of GATT 1994 (e.g., "most-favoured nation" treatment and national treatment) and of relevant international intellectual property agreements or conventions; (b) the provision of adequate standards and principles concerning the availability, scope and use of trade-related IPRs; (c) the provision of effective and appropriate means for the enforcement of trade-related IPRs; and (d) the provision of effective and expeditious procedures for the multilateral prevention and settlement of disputes between governments.

85. The linkage between the TRIPS Agreement and the international biodiversity regime is mainly at four distinct levels: the protection of the knowledge, innovations and practices of local and indigenous communities; the sharing of the benefits arising from the utilization of genetic resources; the patentability of the forms; and the transfer of technologies.

86. The first issue concerns the capacity of existing IPR regimes to protect traditional biodiversity-related knowledge. Article 8(j) of the Convention requires parties to "...respect, preserve and maintain knowledge, innovations and practices of indigenous and local communities embodying traditional lifestyles relevant for the conservation and sustainable use of biological diversity..." and to "...encourage the equitable sharing of the benefits arising from the utilization of such knowledge, innovations and practices." The TRIPS framework is predicated on the protection of formal and private knowledge in sharp contrast to the "informal, collective and intergenerational" nature of traditional knowledge. In this regard, therefore, there is a direct conflict between the objectives of the Convention and the TRIPS regime. Consequently, proposals have been made to develop alternative *sui generis* IPR systems to protect traditional biodiversity-related knowledge.

87. Second, article 27(1) of the TRIPS Agreement defines the formal legal requirements regarding patentable subject matter and provides that patents shall be available for inventions that are "...new, involve an inventive step and are capable of industrial application..." Indigenous and local communities cannot therefore secure patent protection for their knowledge of the natural attributes of biological resources since such knowledge does not constitute an invention in terms of the TRIPS Agreement. Yet, in many cases such knowledge has constituted an important input to biotechnological innovation by modern industry. In effect, the existing IPR regime is likely to encourage the unauthorized appropriation of traditional biodiversity-related knowledge without concomitant benefit-sharing with the holders of such knowledge. It has been suggested that IPR systems should require, for example, the disclosure of the origin of traditional knowledge where this has constituted an input to a biotechnological invention in order to protect traditional knowledge and promote benefit-sharing. In this respect, COP-6 in its Decision VI/24IICdii invited parties and governments to encourage the disclosure of the origin of relevant traditional knowledge, innovations and practices in applications for intellectual property rights where the subject matter of the application concerns or makes use of such knowledge in its development.

88. The TRIPS regime is primarily concerned with ensuring adequate protection and enforcement of IPRs. Issues of equity are not a central consideration. The Convention, however, requires that the benefits arising from the utilization of genetic resources and related traditional knowledge be shared in a fair and equitable manner with the contracting party providing such resources and the holders of traditional biodiversity-related knowledge. In many instances, the results of research and development ("R&D") in developed countries based on genetic resources and traditional biodiversity-related knowledge from developing countries have been protected through the patent system without any benefits accruing to the countries of origin of such resources or the holders of relevant traditional knowledge. Indeed, the existing IPR systems do not require the disclosure of either the country of origin of genetic resources or of the relevant traditional knowledge used in R&D. In this instance also, the COP has, in its Decision VI/24C, invited parties and governments to encourage the disclosure of the country of origin of genetic resources in patent applications. Such disclosure would promote the tracking of compliance with prior informed consent and mutually agreed terms on which access to genetic resources was granted and contribute to sharing of benefits arising from the utilisation of genetic resources.

89. Article 27(3)(b) of the TRIPS Agreement provides that members may exclude from patentability "plants and animals other than micro-organisms, and essentially biological processes for the production of plants or animals other than non-biological and microbiological processes. However, Members shall provide for the protection of plant varieties either by patents or by an effective *sui generis* system or by a combination thereof..." The provision is largely permissive since it leaves the discretion to members to decide whether to grant patents for plants, animals or essentially biological processes. In any case, the provision provided for the review of the sub-paragraph four years after the entry into force of the WTO Agreement. The process of review is already underway within the TRIPS Council. The fear is that such a review might result in a mandatory requirement for the protection of plants, animals, biological processes and plant varieties through patents.

90. The inclusion of biological material in the TRIPS Agreement, either through patent protection or through other forms of IPR protection raises fundamental issues for the Convention. First, there is the ethical question: is it morally defensible to patent life forms, such as animal and plant species. There has been significant public opposition to genetic engineering on moral grounds in a number of European countries. Second, there is the issue of the privatization of biological resources, that is, the grant of monopoly rights over biological resources.

This could not only create restrictions on continued access to genetic resources, in particular by indigenous and local communities and farmers who are dependent on biological resources for sustenance (economic, social and spiritual), but also lead to a rapid depletion of biological resources. Such privatization may, therefore, not be consistent with the overall objectives of the Convention.

91. Article 7 of the TRIPS Agreement emphasizes, as one of its primary objectives that "The protection and enforcement of intellectual property rights should contribute to the promotion of technological innovation and to the transfer and dissemination of technology, to the mutual benefit of producers and users of technological knowledge..." In this respect, there is significant coincidence with the provisions of the Convention whose article 16 requires parties to provide and/or facilitate the transfer of technology to other parties. Further, that access to and transfer of technology to developing countries shall be "...under fair and most favourable terms, including on concessional and preferential terms where mutually agreed..." and that "...such access and transfer shall be provided on terms which recognize and are consistent with the adequate and effective protection of intellectual property rights..." The provision further underlines that the parties recognize that patents and other IPRs may have an influence on the implementation of the Convention and calls for international cooperation to ensure that IPRs are supportive and do not run counter to the objectives of the Convention. In addition, article 19(2) requires each contracting party "...to promote and advance priority access on a fair and equitable basis by Contracting Parties, especially developing countries, to the results and benefits from biotechnologies based upon genetic resources provided by those Contracting Parties..."

92. It has been argued that IPR systems encourage technology transfer, particularly in those sectors where research and developments costs are high, by reassuring owners of proprietary technology that their rights will be protected. Potential suppliers of technologies are more willing to transfer technology voluntarily if the recipient country has an effective IPR regime in place. On the other hand, it is asserted that the protection of plant varieties through Plant Breeders Rights ("PBRs") and utility patents make elite plant varieties too expensive for indigenous and local communities and farmers in developing countries. In addition, such protection may discourage researchers from exchanging genetic material freely.

3. International Convention for the Protection of New Varieties of Plants

93. The International Union for the Protection of New Varieties of Plants ("UPOV Convention"), is an intergovernmental organization established in 1961 to coordinate the implementation, at the international level, of the Plant Breeder's Rights established by the Convention for the Protection of New Varieties of Plants. The Convention, adopted in Paris in 1961, entered into force in 1968, and was revised in 1972, 1978 and 1991. Currently fifty-eight states (May 2005) are parties to the Convention.

94. The 1961 UPOV Convention, as amended, is aimed at ensuring that member states acknowledge the accomplishments of new plant variety breeders and make available to them exclusive rights of exploitation if their varieties are distinct, homogeneous and stable. It provides a *sui generis* form of intellectual property protection specifically adapted for the process of plant breeding and is calculated to encourage breeders to develop new varieties of plants.

95. From 1961 to 1991, the UPOV Convention provided for a Breeder's Exemption and, at least implicitly, a Farmer's Privilege, where both principles provide flexibility within the IP protection.

96. According to the Breeder's Exemption, authorization by the breeder is not required either for the utilization of the variety as an initial source of variation for the purpose of creating new varieties or for the subsequent exploitation of such new varieties. Under the 1991 Convention, however, the only compulsory exceptions to the exclusive right of the breeder left are: (i) acts done privately and for non-commercial purposes; (ii) acts done for experimental purposes; and (iii) acts done for the purpose of breeding and exploiting other varieties, provided they are not essentially derived. The Breeder's Exemption is thus not applicable to essentially derived varieties, which are varieties predominantly derived from another (initial) variety retaining the expression of the essential characteristics from the genotypes or combination of genotypes of the initial variety.

97. According to the Farmer's Privilege, farmers are allowed to use their own harvested material of the protected varieties for subsequent sowing on their own farms. As implicitly recognized under the 1978 Act a broad interpretation of the "privilege" was allowed. The 1991 Act, however, has

narrowed it down by explicitly including it in its text. According to 1991 Act, the Farmer's Privilege is no longer the general rule but an optional exception, which leaves it up to national governments to decide whether to permit farmers to use the seed of a protected variety. This would be allowed for propagation purposes on their own holdings, within reasonable limits and subject to the safeguarding of the legitimate interest of the breeder (article 15.2).

98. While under the 1978 Act the breeder was entitled to protection whatever the origin of the initial variation from which his variety is derived, thus including the mere discovery of a new plant variety, this is not sufficient under the 1991 Act. The breeder must have developed his variety in order to be entitled to the protection. Unlike the previous Acts, the 1991 Act provides parties with the possibility of simultaneous protection for the same plant variety by more than one type of intellectual property rights (i.e., they can choose both Plant Breeder's Rights and patents).

99. The 1978 Act limits the scope of protection to reproductive or vegetative propagating material of the variety not including harvested products, while the 1991 Act extends it to the commercial use of all material of the variety. Thus, the Breeder's Rights extend to varieties that are not clearly distinguishable from the protected variety; varieties whose production requires the repeated use of the protected variety, and varieties that are essentially derived from the protected variety.

100. The 1978 Act requires the authorization of the breeder for the repeated use of the plant variety only in cases of commercial production. Authorization from the breeder is extended under the 1991 Act to propagating material, harvested material and products made thereof provided a number of conditions are met.

101. The 1978 Act requires member states to protect a minimum of five genera upon becoming a party and to protect genera or species on a progressive basis thereafter, leading to a minimum of twenty-four genera, while again, the 1991 Act requires existing member states to protect all plant genera within a given period of time.

102. According to the 1978 Act, states have to grant Plant Breeder's Rights protection for a minimum period of 18 years for vines, forest trees, fruit trees and ornamental trees, and fifteen years in the case of all other species, while in the 1991 Act it has been extended to 25 and 20 years, respectively.

a) Agenda 21

103. Chapter 14 of Agenda 21 deals with the plant genetic resources of the world within the context of long-term food security, sustainable agriculture and rural development. Chapter 15 addresses the conservation of biological diversity; and Chapter 16 addresses the environmentally sound management of biotechnology. Throughout these chapters, Agenda 21 recognizes the importance of indigenous and local communities, their knowledge and culture, and the potential contribution to the protection of biodiversity.

b) FAO Global System for the Conservation and Sustainable Use of Plant Genetic Resources

104. In 1983, the FAO established the Commission on Plant Genetic Resources (now the Commission on Plant Genetic Resources for Food and Agriculture ("CGRFA")) as a permanent intergovernmental forum to deal with questions concerning plant genetic resources. It also adopted as a formal framework the International Undertaking on Plant Genetic Resources ("IUPGR"). The Commission has since coordinated, overseen and monitored the development of the FAO Global System for the Conservation and Sustainable Use of Plant Genetic Resources for Food and Agriculture and its mandate has been broadened to cover all components of biodiversity of relevance for food and agriculture in 1995. A total of 167 countries and the European Community now are members of the CGRFA (as of January 2006).

105. The objectives of the Global System are to ensure the safe conservation and to promote the availability and sustainable utilization of plant genetic resources for present and future generations by providing a flexible framework for sharing the benefits and burdens. It covers both the conservation (ex situ and in situ, including on-farm) and utilization of plant genetic resources for food and agriculture.

106. The IUPGR was the first comprehensive international agreement governing the conservation and sustainable utilization of agricultural biodiversity. Its objective was to ensure that plant generic resources of economic and social interest will be explored, preserved, evaluated and made available for plant breeding and scientific purposes.

107. Agenda 21 called for the strengthening of the FAO Global System for the Conservation and Sustainable Use of Plant Genetic Resources, and its

adjustment in line with the outcome of negotiations on the CBD.

108. In accordance with the outcome of the negotiations of the UNCED as well as for the realization of Farmers' Rights, the FAO Conference adopted a resolution in 1993 on the "Revision of the International Undertaking on Plant Genetic Resources", which requested the Director-General to provide a forum for negotiations among Governments for (i) the adaptation of the IUPGR, in harmony with the CBD; (ii) consideration of the issue of access on mutually agreed terms to plant genetic resources, including *ex situ* collections not addressed by the Convention; and (iii) the issue of the realization of Farmers' Rights. In this Resolution the Conference urged that the process be carried out through the Commission on Plant Genetic Resources (now "CGRFA"), with the help of its Working Group, in close collaboration with the Governing Body of the Convention. Throughout the negotiation process, the COP adopted decisions underlining the need for ensuring harmony with the Convention.

109. This issue of Farmers' Rights resulted from debates in FAO concerning the asymmetric treatment given to donors of germplasm and donors of technology. The FAO Conference acknowledged in various resolutions "the enormous contribution that farmers of all regions have made to the conservation and development of plant genetic resources, which constitute the basis of plant production throughout the world, and which form the basis for the concept of Farmers' Rights" and defined Farmer's Rights as "rights arising from the past, present and future contribution of farmers in conserving, improving and making available plant genetic resources, particularly those in the centres of origin/diversity."

110. The objective of the development of the concept of Farmers' Rights was to ensure that farmers, farming communities and their countries, receive a just share of the benefits derived from plant genetic resources (which they have developed, maintained and made available) and thereby provide incentives and means for the conservation and further development of these plant genetic resources by farmers, and through cooperation between farmers, breeders and the national and international research services.

111. In order to implement Farmers' Rights, some developing countries are considering the inclusion of a national mechanism as part of the development of a national *sui generis* system of protection of new plant varieties under the TRIPS Agreement. Given the global nature of the values

of germplasm that farmers provide, the implementation of Farmers' Rights needs some form of international action in order to compensate farmers at the global level.

112. The International Treaty on Plant Genetic Resources for Food and Agriculture ("2001 ITPGR") was adopted in November 2001, after seven years of international negotiations for the revision of the 1983 International Undertaking on Plant Genetic Resources.

113. The objective of the 2001 ITPGR is the conservation and sustainable use of plant genetic resources for food and agriculture and the fair and equitable sharing of the benefits arising out of their use, in harmony with the Convention on Biological Diversity for sustainable agriculture and food security. This objective is to be attained by closely linking the International Treaty to the FAO and to the Convention (article 1).

114. The scope of the 2001 ITPGR embraces all plant genetic resources for food and agriculture. The Treaty is at the crossroads between agriculture, trade and the environment, and constitutes a multilateral tool to promote cooperation and synergy in these sectors.

115. The 2001 ITPGR establishes a multilateral system of access and benefit-sharing for plant genetic resources, related knowledge and technologies, for an agreed list of crops, established on the basis of interdependence and food security. It also provides for benefit sharing through information exchange, technology transfer, capacity building, and the mandatory sharing of the monetary and other benefits of commercialization of products incorporating material accessed through the Multilateral System. It also includes a Funding Strategy according to which parties to the International Treaty will take measures, within the governing bodies of relevant international organizations, to ensure the allocation of agreed and predictable resources. Monetary benefits paid on commercialization are part of this funding strategy.

116. The Multilateral System applies to a list of sixty-four plant genera, which include thirty-five crops and twenty-nine forages. The conditions for access and benefit sharing will be set out in a standard Material Transfer Agreement ("MTA"), to be established by the Governing Body, at is first meeting, after entry into force.

117. Access will be provided for utilization and conservation in research, breeding and training for food and agriculture, and subject to property rights

and access laws. A key point is payment of an equitable share of the monetary benefits from the commercialization of a product that uses plant genetic resources from the Multilateral System. This is projected to be voluntary when the product is available without restriction for further research and breeding and mandatory when it is not.

118. The 2001 ITPGR, in article 9, underlines that "...Contracting Parties recognize the enormous contribution that local and indigenous communities and farmers of all regions of the world, particularly those in the centres of origin and crop diversity, have made and will continue to make for the conservation and development of plant genetic resources which constitute the basis of food and agriculture production throughout the world." The International Treaty recognizes Farmers' Rights as being complementary to Plant Breeders' Rights. However, the contracting Parties agree that the realisation of these rights rests with national governments. Therefore, in accordance with their needs and priorities each contracting party should take measures to protect and promote Farmer's Rights through:

• The protection of traditional knowledge relevant to plant genetic resources for food and agriculture;
• The right to equitably participate in sharing benefits arising from the utilization of plant genetic resources for food and agriculture; and,
• The right to participate in national decision-making related to the conservation and sustainable use of plant genetic resources for food and agriculture.

119. Aiming at guaranteeing food security, 2001 ITPGR benefits all humankind. The immediate benefits, however, for plant breeders (particularly for small-scale breeders in developing countries), are that the Treaty ensures access to the plant genetic resources they need, and prevents their monopolization, in particular, by large players. For the private sector, it sets out a clear and predictable framework for access to plant genetic resources, which will promote investment in agricultural research. The Treaty provides the agriculture sector in general with a new forum, in which to address the special needs and problems of agriculture and from which to negotiate with the trade and environment forums. 2001 ITPGR entered into force on 29 June 2004 and has currently 83 parties (as of January 2006).

120. As the specialized United Nations agency responsible for the promotion of IP worldwide, the World Intellectual Property Organization ("WIPO")

administers some twenty-three treaties in the field of intellectual property. These treaties define the internationally agreed basic standards of intellectual property protection and establish a global protection system which ensures that one international registration or filing system will have effect in any of the relevant signatory states. The treaties dealing with standards cover, *inter alia*, patents, copyrights, trademarks and industrial designs and include the Paris Convention for the Protection of Industrial Property (1883), the Berne Convention for the Protection of Literary and Artistic Works (1886), the Patent Law Treaty (2000) (entered into force on 28 April 2005), the Trademark Law (1994) and the WIPO Copyright Law Treaty (2002). The objective of the global protection system treaties is to simplify and reduce the cost of making individual applications or filings in all the countries in which protection for a given intellectual property right is sought. The treaties in this category include the Patent Cooperation Treaty (1970), which implements the concept of a single international patent application which has legal effect in the countries, which are bound, by the treaty.

121. WIPO has only more recently considered specific IP issues related to traditional knowledge and genetic resources. In particular, WIPO undertook fact-finding missions to consult with a wide range of stakeholders such as indigenous and local communities, Non-Governmental Organizations, governmental representatives, academics, researchers and private sector representatives to determine the IP needs and expectations of holders of traditional knowledge.

122. In October 2000, the WIPO General Assembly agreed to establish the Intergovernmental Committee on Intellectual Property and Genetic Resources, Traditional Knowledge and Folklore ("IGC"), a unique intergovernmental body for debate and dialogue concerning the interplay between intellectual property, traditional knowledge, genetic resources and folklore.

123. The IGC's work programme considers issues such as the role of IP systems in relation to traditional knowledge and how to preserve, protect and equitably make use of traditional knowledge. The IGC has also worked on both the defensive and the positive protection of traditional knowledge. The defensive protection of traditional knowledge consists of measures that ensure that other parties do not obtain IP rights over pre-existing traditional knowledge. The positive protection consists of the use of existing legal mechanisms to protect and promote traditional knowledge. In some countries,

legislation has been developed specifically to address the positive protection of traditional knowledge.

124. The work of the IGC has concentrated on examining the relationship between IP and genetic resources in the areas of contractual agreements for access to genetic resources; legislative, administrative and policy measures to regulate access to genetic resources; and the protection of biotechnological inventions. The IGC has furthermore conducted an on-going technical analysis of the use of existing intellectual property and *sui generis* approaches for the legal protection of traditional cultural expressions.

125. As part of the work of the IGC, WIPO is currently in the process of compiling an on-line, searchable database of biodiversity-related Access and Benefit-Sharing Agreements, with a particular emphasis on the intellectual property aspects of such agreements. Other databases and inventories currently being developed by WIPO include Traditional Knowledge Databases and Prior Art; Non-Exhaustive Inventory of Traditional Knowledge-Related Databases; and Non-Exhaustive Inventory of Traditional Knowledge-Related Periodicals.

126. The Conference of the Parties to the Convention on Biological Diversity has, over the years, recognised the important role WIPO may play in the implementation of the provisions of the Convention concerning the protection of traditional knowledge and access to genetic resources and benefit-sharing and has underlined the need for closer cooperation and mutual supportiveness. At its fifth meeting, the COP in decision V/26 requested WIPO, in its work on intellectual property issues, to take due account of the relevant provisions of the Convention, including the impact of IPRs on the conservation and sustainable use of biological diversity, and in particular the value of the knowledge, innovations and practices of indigenous and local communities. In the same decision, it invited WIPO to analyze issues of IPRs as they relate to access to genetic resources, including disclosure of country of origin of genetic resources in patent applications. At its sixth meeting, the COP in decision VI/24 C invited WIPO to prepare a technical study on disclosure issues regarding country of origin of genetic resources, sources of traditional knowledge and prior informed consent where genetic resources and/or traditional knowledge have been utilised in the development of claimed inventions.

III. National Implementation

1. Costa Rica

127. This Central American state covers just 0.04% of the world's total land area, yet is believed to harbour some half a million species, or about 4% to 5% of the estimated terrestrial biodiversity on this planet. To conserve its rich biological heritage, Costa Rica has placed roughly 25% of its land base under some form of protection.

128. The Costa Rican Biodiversity Law ("Costa Rica Law") (1998) is a framework law on sustainable development and biodiversity. It clearly establishes the Mutually Agreed Terms ("MAT") and Prior Informed Consent ("PIC") Principles. Its objectives include:

- The integration of conservation and sustainable use of the biodiversity elements into the development of socio-cultural, economic and environmental policies;
- The promotion of the active participation of all social sectors in the conservation and ecologically sustainable use of biodiversity, in order to attain economic, social and cultural sustainability; and
- The regulation of access to genetic resources and thus to make it possible an equitable sharing of the social, environmental and economic benefits derived from the utilisation of such genetic resources, with special attention to the local communities and indigenous peoples.

129. The Costa Rica Law defines "access to biochemical and genetic elements" as activity to obtain samples of wild or domesticated biodiversity, in *ex situ* or *in situ* conditions as well as the procurement of the associated knowledge. The ultimate goal of access should be basic research, bio-prospecting or economic utilization.

130. Any research programme or bio-prospecting activity to be carried out in the national territory, involving biodiversity genetic or biochemical material requires an access "permit". Certain criteria are established to promote enforcement of the law. Among these criteria the preventive criterion, the precautionary criterion or *in dubio pro natura*, and the environmental public interest criterion.

131. A National Commission for the Management of Biodiversity was established, whose role it is to propose policies concerning access to biodiversity

and genetic and biochemical elements, both *in situ* and *ex situ*. It also performs the role of a compulsory consultation body in processes related to "intellectual rights" claims. The provisions approved by the Commission on this issue constitute the general regulations of access to genetic and biochemical elements as well as for the protection of biodiversity "intellectual rights". In order to obtain an access permit it is necessary to show:

- The prior informed consent of the representatives of the place where access will materialize;
- The ratification of such PIC by the Technical Office of the Commission;
- The terms under which technology transfer and equitable sharing of benefits will take place; and
- The type of protection required by the representatives of the place where access will materialize; and the definition of the way in which such activities will contribute to the conservation of species and ecosystems.

132. The Costa Rica Law also includes a right to cultural objection, according to which the local and indigenous communities are enabled to oppose to access to "their" resources and the associated knowledge on the basis of cultural, spiritual, social, economic or other reasons.

133. The Commission also runs a Technical Office, which issues the access permits. It should organize and keep updated a registry of access rights to genetic and biochemical elements. This Office is also in charge of collecting a deposit from interested countries for the National System of Conservation Areas. Access permits should clearly state:

- The certificate of origin, the possibility or prohibition to extract or export samples or, where applicable, the duplication and deposit of such samples; the periodical reports;
- The necessary monitoring and control;
- The ownership and publicity of results; and
- Any other condition that according to the applicable scientific and technical rules is necessary in the view of the Technical Office of the Commission.

134. The Costa Rican Wildlife Conservation Law ("Wildlife Law") (1992) applies to genetic resources of wild flora and fauna. Although it does not extend to domesticated or cultivated species, the Wildlife Law still applies to wild fauna and flora that are located *ex-situ*. Since they remain state owned or national patrimony, access to them requires authorization from the state. Genetic resources can be removed from Costa Rican national parks only with prior authorization.

135. The activities regulated by the Wildlife Law are related to the ultimate purposes or objectives of physical access to genetic resources. Article 50 of the Wildlife Law makes a distinction between commercial and non-commercial activities. It sets out different requirements for each. This legal instrument for access applies to nationals and non-nationals. However, nationals may be entitled to special treatment: for example, being subject to lower licensing fees or access for longer periods be authorized for nationals than to non-nationals.

136. In order to ensure that prior informed consent requirements fulfilled export controls are used by Costa Rica under the Wildlife Law. The 1992 Wildlife Law requires written permission to export wildlife from the Wildlife Office of the Ministry of Natural Resources, Energy and Mines.

2. India

137. India's Biological Diversity Act ("Diversity Act") (2002) is designed to turn the spirit of the Convention of Biological Diversity into a national instrument with three objectives:

- Conservation of biodiversity;
- Sustainable use of biological resources; and
- Equitable sharing of benefits arising from such use.

138. To this end, the Diversity Act:

- Prohibits transfer of Indian genetic material outside the country, without specific approval of the Indian Government;
- Stipulates that anyone wanting to take a patent or other Intellectual Property Right ("IPR") over such material, or over related knowledge, must seek permission in advance;
- Provides for the levying of appropriate fees and royalties on such transfers and IPRs;
- Provides for the development of appropriate legislation or administrative steps, including registration, to protect indigenous and community knowledge;
- Empowers governments to declare Biodiversity Heritage Sites, as areas for special measures for conservation and sustainable use of biological resources;
- Stipulates that risks associated with biotechnology (including the use of genetically modified organisms), will be regulated or controlled through appropriate means; and
- Provides for the designation of repositories of biological resources, at national and other levels.

139. The Diversity Act proposes to set up bodies at three levels (national, state and local), to carry out the above functions. Importantly, the Diversity Act

provides citizens with the power to approach courts if they detect violations. The Diversity Act presents a bold step by a national government to take the issues of biodiversity conservation and sustainable use seriously in addressing the thorny issues involved:

India, Biological Diversity Act (Article 8(j))

"3(1) ...No person... (...non-citizen, non-resident or non registered or foreign owned corporation...) shall, without previous approval of the National Biodiversity Authority, obtain any biological resource occurring in India or knowledge associated thereto for research or for commercial utilization or for bio-survey and bio-utilization.

4. No person shall, without the previous approval of the National Biodiversity Authority, transfer the results of any research relating to any biological resources occurring or obtained from, India for monetary consideration or otherwise to any person who is not a citizen of India or citizen of India or a body corporate or organization which is not registered or incorporated in India or which has any non-Indian participation in its share capital or management.

6. (1) No person shall apply for any intellectual property right, by whatever name called in or outside India for any invention based on any research or information on a biological resource obtained from India without obtaining the previous approval of the National Biodiversity Authority before making such application...

7. No person, who is a citizen of India or a body corporate, association or organization which is registered in India shall obtain any biological resource for commercial utilization, or bio-survey and bio-utilization except after giving prior intimation to the state Biodiversity Board concerned:

Provided that the provisions of this section shall not apply to the local people and communities of the area, including growers and cultivators of biodiversity, and vaids and hakims, who have been practicing indigenous medicine."

---

140. In certain aspects, the Diversity Act goes further than the CBD. For instance benefit sharing is envisaged not only for indigenous communities for all communities as well as in relation to classical knowledge as contained in the Ayurvedic texts. Furthermore, the Act does not only cover genetic resources of which India is the country of origin but also such resources of which neighbouring countries are hosts.

141. The Biological Diversity Act also responds to the age of biotechnology and information technology. In order to implement the provisions of this Act, a biodiversity information system of unparalleled size and complexity needs to be set up. This Biodiversity Information System will have to compile information on a variety of issues, namely:

- Status of the country's ecological habitats, and the natural as well as anthropogenic processes impacting the habitats;
- Current status of populations of a whole range of biodiversity elements, focusing on the more notable useful and harmful species and varieties, and the impact of natural processes, as well as human harvests, culturing, control and other practices;
- Regimes of legal as well as customary property rights, access rights, and conservation practices as they affect biodiversity;
- Harvest, transport, trade and markets in biodiversity;
- Processing of biodiversity resources to generate value added products;
- Demand for and consumption of biodiversity resources and their products;
- Existing technologies and new innovations pertinent to biodiversity, both at grass-roots, and in the more sophisticated industrial sector; and
- Intellectual property rights, customary as well as through the legal regime, over biodiversity resources.

142. Such a Biodiversity Information System will have to feed into development planning at all levels, from Panchayats, through districts, states and the country as a whole. It will have to help promote sustainable use and economic activities such as local level value addition, as well as serve more sophisticated biotechnology based enterprises. It should help direct proper flows of benefits of commercial uses of biodiversity to holders of traditional knowledge, as well as to grass-roots innovators.

143. It will also be relevant to actualizing the provisions pertaining to farmers' rights in the Protection of Plant Varieties and Farmers' Rights Act of 2001. While organizing information pertaining to plant varieties intellectual property rights concerns have to be kept in mind and guard the interests of all segments of the population, of the tribe and, of the dispensers of herbal medicines, as well as modern enterprises such as pharmaceutical industry.

3. China

144. Unlike Costa Rica and India, China does not have a specific law on biodiversity. National implementation of the Convention on Biological Diversity in China is carried out through different laws and by a broad variety of means and in different sectors of national governance.

145. China has formulated a series of laws, regulations, plans and programmes for the conservation and sustainable use of biological diversity. The Constitution of China regulates that the state shall ensure the reasonable utilization of natural resources and protect the rare and valuable fauna and flora. Laws and regulations concerned with conservation of biological diversity include for example the Law on Environmental Protection, the Law on Forest, the Law on Water, the Law on Marine Environmental Protection, the Law on Grasslands, the Law on Fishery, the Law on Protection of Wild Animals, the Regulation on Nature Reserves and the Regulation on Protection of Wild Plants.

146. Under the support of UNDP/GEF, China compiled its China Biodiversity Conservation Action Plan in 1994, in which the priority of ecosystems for biodiversity conservation and the priority of species under protection are determined. The Chinese government also compiled and promulgated China's Agenda 21 – White Paper on China's Population, Environment and Development in the 21st Century. Chapter 15, "Conservation of Biodiversity," of the White Book defines the policies, targets, priority areas and projects for biodiversity conservation.

147. China set up its Compendium of Development Plan for Nature Reserves in China (1996-2010), specifying the targets and specific programmes for nature reserves planning nationwide. Furthermore, China has formulated Biodiversity Conservation Action Plan for all different kinds of sectors, like forestry, agriculture, marine environment, national wetlands and for *ex situ* Protection of the Giant Panda.

148. In November 2000, the State Council issued the Compendium of National Ecological Environment Conservation. The basic principles of the Compendium are:

- To protect ecosystems, to construct ecosystems, and to attach equal importance to pollution prevention and to ecological conservation;
- To conduct integrated planning, comprehensive decision-making and reasonable development;
- All development activities of natural resources should take the carrying capacity of natural ecosystems into consideration;
- It is not allowed to sacrifice ecological environment for short-term and regional economic benefits; and

- To follow the principle that those conducting the development should be responsible for the conservation, and those making the damages should be responsible for the restoration, those utilising the resources should pay, so as to protect ecological environment according to laws.

149. China has made significant achievements with *in situ* conservation. Nationwide, *in situ* conservation networks have been preliminarily set up. By the end of 2000, there were 1,227 nature reserves, with a total area of approximately 98 million hectares, accounting for nearly 10% of the state territory.

150. Since 1979, China has carried out environmental impact assessment. The industrial construction projects, infra-structure construction projects, regional programming projects and the agriculture, forest, water resources, marine engineering projects should conduct environmental impact assessment.

151. The development of wild animal breeding and wild plant cultivation is an important way to conserve and reasonably utilize biological resources. The permit system has standardized the breeding and cultivation of wild animals and plants, which has provided large amount of fur and pharmaceutical products for markets, reduced the demand for wildlife and promoted the sustainable utilization of these resources.

152. In order to protect spawning fish and baiting fingerling, no-fishing zones and seasons have been designated; and the fishery permit system has been carried out. Great efforts have been devoted to artificial breeding and natural breeding while protecting fishery resources.

153. In order to restore and re-establish damaged and degraded ecosystems, the Chinese government have taken significant measures to implement the projects for conservation of natural forests. Since the implementation of pilot project of natural forest conservation in 1998, approximately 51 million hectares of forests have been protected while nearly 6,000 million hectares of forest vegetation has been restored.

154. The development of new tourism zones and the construction of new tourism sites and tourism reception facilities in the tourism zones should follow environmental impact assessment. In order to support the international ecotourism year, China has conducted various kinds of education activities.

155. Policies and regulation in China respect the rights of minorities and local communities and respect the traditional lifestyle of the local communities that is beneficial to the conservation and sustainable use of biological diversity. They promote the sum-up, inheriting and developing of the traditional knowledge, which has been actively conducted with the assistance of relevant international organizations.

156. Also, with the assistance of international organizations, some nature reserves undertook management with the participation of local communities which are encouraged in the management of the nature reserves. China's Agenda 21 clearly emphasizes the significance of conserving traditional knowledge and encourages the participation of minority nationalities, women, and communities in biodiversity conservation.

157. In April 1997, China issued the Regulation of the Protection of New Varieties of Plants, to conduct protection of new plant varieties by regulation. Based on the regulation, the Implementation Measures of the Regulation of the Protection of New Varieties of Plants (agriculture and forestry parts) and the protected inventory of new agriculture and forestry plant varieties were issued. Since 1996, China has organized the implementation of seed engineering. In order to promote the awareness of the importance of protecting new plant varieties across the country and the enforcement and administration in line with laws, training courses have been conducted. China has also set up the information exchange network of germplasm resources with convenient information inquiry through Internet for overseas users. In the last years China has provided over 8000 copies of various crop germplasm resources for the countries in the world and the international agriculture research institutions, so that the germplasm resources of China could be utilized in the world and thus make contributions to world food safety.

158. China has implemented the protection of biotechnological intellectual property rights since mid-1980s. The Patent Law, enacted on 1 April 1985, protects the invention of biotechnology, including the invention of the production methods of animal and plant varieties and medicines. The Patent Law, amended on 1 January 1993, lists most of the products and materials modified by biotechnology into protection. However, the fourth provision of article 25 of the law stipulates that animal and plant varieties shall not be granted with patents.

159. In connection with the preparation for entry into relevant international treaties and the WTO, China issued the Regulation of New Plant Variety Protection on 30 April 1997. Up to now, eighteen species and genera in the first batch were protected, such as rice, corn, Chinese cabbage, potato, chrysanthemum, dianthus, Calamus, purple flower lucerne, grassland early grain, Chinese white poplar, paulownia, China fir, magnolia, peony, plum, rose and camellia.

Dan Ogolla, Programme Officer, Legal Affairs, Secretariat of the Convention on Biological Diversity

Eva Maria Duer, Associate Legal Officer, Division of Policy Development and Law, UNEP

Rossana Silva Repetto, Legal Officer, Regional Office for Latin America and the Caribbean, UNEP

Resources

Internet Materials

BIOLOGICAL DIVERSITY IN FOOD AND AGRICULTURE available at http://www.fao.org/biodiversity/genres_en.asp

CONVENTION ON BIOLOGICAL DIVERSITY available at www.biodiv.org

INTERNATIONAL UNION FOR THE PROTECTION OF NEW VARIETIES OF PLANTS available at http://www.upov.int/index.html

THE CONVENTION ON BIOLOGICAL DIVERSITY IN CHINA available at http://www.biodiv.org/world/map.asp?ctr=cn

THE CONVENTION ON BIOLOGICAL DIVERSITY IN COSTA RICA available at http://www.biodiv.org/world/map.asp?ctr=cr

THE CONVENTION ON BIOLOGICAL DIVERSITY IN INDIA available at http://www.biodiv.org/world/map.asp?ctr=in

WORLD TRADE ORGANIZATION, TRIPS AGREEMENT, ARTICLE 27.3B (TRADITIONAL KNOWLEDGE AND BIODIVERSITY) available at http://www.wto.org/english/tratop_e/trips_e/art27_3b_e.htm

WORLD INTELLECTUAL PROPERTY ORGANIZATION available at http://www.wipo.int

Text Materials

Brian Groombridge (Ed.), GLOBAL BIODIVERSITY: STATUS OF THE EARTH'S LIVING RESOURCES: A REPORT (First ed, Chapman & Hall, 1992).

Christoph Bail, Robert Falkner & Helen Marquard (Eds.), THE CARTAGENA PROTOCOL ON BIOSAFETY: RECONCILING TRADE IN BIOTECHNOLOGY WITH ENVIRONMENT.

Jack R. Kloppenburg Jr. & Daniel L. Kleinman, *Seeds of Controversy: National Property versus Common Heritage,* in SEEDS AND SOVEREIGNTY: THE USE AND CONTROL OF PLANT GENETIC RESOURCES, (1988).

Michael Bowman & Catherine Redgwell (Eds.), INTERNATIONAL LAW AND THE CONSERVATION OF BIOLOGICAL DIVERSITY, (Kluwer Law International, 1996).

16. BIOSAFETY

I. Introduction

1. Biotechnology which is the use of biological processes to develop products, has a long history and refers to a range of techniques, including selective breeding, cross-fertilization and fermentation. Generally, biotechnology has brought about many economic and human health benefits. For example, the selection and breeding of grains has produced better quality and higher yielding varieties and has expanded the use of diverse crop species well beyond their centres of origin.

2. Over the past four decades, science has evolved rapidly beyond conventional methods of biotechnology. Scientific research into the genetic properties of living organisms has revealed how several biological functions are determined through information encoded in the organisms' genes. Science has made it possible to isolate a gene and transfer genetic code, Deoxyribonucleic Acid ("DNA"), between organisms. Thus, techniques in modern biotechnology now include genetic engineering.

3. Animals, plants, and micro organisms, in which one or more foreign genes are introduced, are called "transgenic organisms". These Genetically Modified Organisms ("GMOs") [in some instances, reference is made to Living Modified Organisms ("LMOs") have combinations of genes or genetic materials that have been altered in a way that does not occur naturally through mating or recombination.

4. GMOs have potential benefits. Modern biotechnology, makes it possible to mass produce therapeutically useful compounds, vaccines, new drugs, diagnostic aids, novel or improved industrial enzymes, and crops with improved agronomic or consumer benefits. Genetic manipulation can improve the quality and quantity of agricultural production and allows the development of plants and animals that are disease- and pest-resistant. Agricultural output better sustains climatic hazards and incorporates additional vitamins and nutrients that can enhance their consumers' health. The environment also benefits from farmers' reduced dependence on fertilizers and herbicides, which, in turn, reduces pollution and allows farmers to reinvest their savings on increasing production. This leads to increased food security for the world's increasing population. Finally, efficiencies made possible by GMOs could reduce the area of land dedicated to agriculture, leaving more habitats and ecosystems undisturbed and preserving biodiversity.

5. GMOs, however, also pose serious risks. Genetic engineering raises issues of misuse, new health risks and the unintended creation of organisms or genetic traits that may irreversibly affect the world's complex ecological cycle. GMOs may also threaten human health by giving rise to new food allergies and unintended immune response to existing antibiotics and medicines.

6. With regard to the environment, use of GMOs raises concerns about the possible transfer of modified genes to naturally occurring plant and animal species. The effects of such transfers are unknown and uncontrollable. Of particular concern is the effect GMOs could have on genetic diversity in plants and animals. Large-scale farming is another potential problem resulting from society's dependence on GMOs. Mass production of identical plants and animals can lead to a loss of indigenous species. Further, as agricultural output is homogenized, it becomes more susceptible to disease and pests. This increased vulnerability could rapidly outweigh the benefits of increased food security.

7. The production of "super crops" in higher-technology countries could have deleterious effect on the agricultural markets in countries relying on more traditionally cultivated food. Small scale farmers could be disadvantaged as modified varieties displace traditional crops.

8. Large seed companies that develop transgenic crop varieties have a strong interest in preventing farmers from harvesting seed for use in the next planting season. In fact, some companies are actively considering the development of GMO technology that would genetically "switch-off" the ability of a plant to re-germinate. Supporters of Genetic Use Restriction Technology ("GURT") view this as a way of preventing growers from pirating the GMO technology, while avoiding the risk of unintended gene flow and potential contamination. Detractors of GURT, however, view it as an unnecessary and potentially exploitative business scheme aimed at forcing farmers to buy a new supply of seeds each year, an expense that many farmers, and particularly the small scale farmers, in the developing world cannot bear. Thus, the GURT issue pits farmers' traditional rights and methods against corporations' new technologies and intellectual property rights.

II. International Framework

The Development of an International Framework on Biosafety

9.   Biosafety has been a matter of concern in the international community since the first GMO field trials took place in the 1980s. The use and release of GMOs into the environment, particularly transgenic plants, has provoked debate around the world.

10. The Organization for Economic Development and Cooperation ("OECD"). In 1986, published a book on Recombinant DNA Safety Considerations ("Blue Book"), which provided guidelines on scientific principles that could be applied in the assessment and management of risks associated with the development and use of GMOs. In the wake of the Blue Book, an increasing number of social groups and governments began to express their views in favour of adopting binding regulations to ensure biosafety.

11. In 1990, the European Council undertook a major step in ensuring biosafety by adopting the first international instruments regulating biotechnology. The Council issued Directive 90/219, on the contained use of genetically modified micro organisms, and Directive 90/220, on the deliberate release into the environment of GMOs ("1990 Directives"). Both of these Directives were issued to underscore the European Council's dual goals of protecting the environment from the potential threats of GMOs, while ensuring the furtherance of biotechnology. Later, Directive 90/220 was repealed and replaced by Directive 2001/18/EC.

12. The United Nations first addressed biosafety in 1991, when the United Nations Industrial Development Organization issued the "Voluntary Code of Conduct for the Release of Organisms into the Environment" ("UNIDO Code"). The UNIDO Code was developed in conjunction with the United Nations Environment Programme ("UNEP"), the World Health Organization and the United Nations Food and Agriculture Organization. The purpose of the UNIDO Code is to provide a framework for member countries in establishing an international network committed to biosafety and facilitating information exchange on the topic.

13. At the United Nations Conference on Environment and Development in Rio de Janeiro. In 1992, United Nations member countries emphasized the importance of international cooperation on biosafety, Chapter 16 of Agenda 21 specifically stresses the need to ensure safety in the development, application, exchange, and transfer of biotechnology while, at the same time, recognizing the potential of GMOs to contribute to sustainable development.

14. The issue of safety in biotechnology found also its way into the 1992 Convention on Biological Diversity ("CBD"). The Convention is, in fact, the first international legal instrument after the EC directives to provide for rules on biotechnology as regards its safe handling. The Convention also deals with the question of access to benefits arising from biotechnology. Specifically its articles 16 and 19 stipulate the importance of biotechnology in achieving the objectives of the Convention and highlight how the results and benefits of biotechnology should be distributed. Article 19 requires parties to consider the need for a protocol on biosafety. It also requires each contracting party to provide information on the potential adverse impact of living modified organisms that cross borders and on any available safety requirements.

15. In May 1992, in Resolution 2 of the Nairobi Final Act in which the Convention was approved, UNEP was invited to prioritize issues arising from the Convention, including Article 19. As a result, UNEP established a small group of experts to consider the need for and modalities of a protocol on biosafety. The experts were generally of the view that international cooperation in the fields of biotechnology and biosafety would be best served by adopting a legally binding instrument.

16. Upon entering into force in December 1993, the question of biosafety was included in the agenda of the first meeting of the Conference of the Parties to the Convention ("COP") of 1994. The first meeting of the COP established an open-ended ad hoc group of experts, nominated by governments, to meet period prior to its second meeting to consider the need for and modalities of a protocol as envisaged under paragraph 3 of article 19 of the Convention. This particular paragraph of the Convention marked both a conclusion and a beginning of international negotiations on biosafety. It reflected the final compromise that the Convention negotiators managed to make then, and provided the basis for the commencement of fresh negotiations by calling upon parties to the Convention to:

     "consider the need for and modalities of a protocol setting out appropriate procedures, including, in particular, advanced informed agreement, in the field of the safe transfer, handling and use of any living modified organism resulting from biotechnology that may have adverse effect on the conservation and sustainable use of biological diversity."

17. The second meeting of the COP was held in 1995, and in Decision II/5 the parties established an open-ended ad hoc working group ("BSWG") with the task of negotiating a biosafety protocol.

18. The BSWG began negotiations in July 1996 and the final text of the biosafety protocol, the Cartagena Protocol on Biosafety to the Convention on Biological Diversity, was adopted on 29 January 2000 ("Protocol" or "Biosafety Protocol"). The Protocol entered into force on 11 September 2003, having been ratified or acceded to by fifty parties to the Biodiversity Convention. It has currently (October 2005) 127 Parties. The first meeting of the Parties to the Protocol took place in February 2004 in Kuala Lumpur, and the second one in May-June 2005 in Montreal, Canada.

The Cartagena Protocol on Biosafety

1. General

19. The Biosafety Protocol consists of forty articles and three annexes. The Preamble explains the genesis of the agreement and sets forth its status and relationship with existing trade agreements. The first six articles outline the Protocol's objective, general provisions, terms and scope; the last six articles stipulate standard final clauses, such as signatories and entry into force. The intervening articles outline specific requirements of the Protocol, including the procedure for advance informed agreement, the procedure for introducing LMOs into the food supply; risk assessment, risk management, documentation, information sharing and the creation of the Biosafety Clearing-House, ("BCH") characterization and treatment of confidential information, capacity-building, liability and redress, and compliance.

20. The objective of the Protocol is to contribute to ensuring an adequate level of safety in the transfer, handling, and use of LMOs. Generally, the Protocol applies to all LMOs, but excludes from the agreement certain transgenics or uses of transgenics, including LMOs used in pharmaceuticals for humans and addressed in other international agreements or by other international organizations.

21. The Protocol focuses on the obligation that requires exporters of LMOs that are intended for direct release into the environment to seek prior agreement from authorities of importing countries, unless the latter agree otherwise. Importing countries, in turn, are required to subject these LMOs to risk assessment before they make decisions regarding the approval or prohibition of imports.

22. The Protocol is only one part of a broader international regime on biosafety. There are a number of other international agreements and arrangements that address various aspects of biosafety. For example, the International Plant Protection Convention addresses plant pest risks and invasive species issues associated with LMOs. The activities of the Codex Alimentarius Commission include the development of standards and guidelines for genetically modified foods, including the labelling of foods derived from LMOs. The World Organization for Animal Health develops standards aimed at preventing the introduction of infectious agents and diseases through international trade in animals; it also sets standards for vaccines, including those that are genetically engineered.

2. Some of the Specific Requirements of the Cartagena Protocol on Biosafety

23. The very adoption of the Biosafety Protocol underscores the precautionary principle that runs throughout the agreement. In regulating the international movement of LMOs, the Protocol seeks to prevent or mitigate risk by requiring that exporters obtain the importing country's prior agreement before the transgenics are introduced into the importer's environment.

a) Advance Informed Agreement Procedure

24. Central to the Protocol is the Advance Informed Agreement ("AIA") procedure that is defined in articles 7, 8, 9, 10 and 12. While article 7 of the Protocol defines the scope of the AIA procedure, the actual procedural rules are described in articles 8 to 10 and 12 of the Protocol. According to these rules, the party of export or the exporter is obliged to notify in writing and to provide minimum information to the party of import, prior to the first shipment of any given type of LMO intended for introduction into the environment of the party of import. The party of import then has 90 days to acknowledge receipt of the notification. The party of import also has to inform the notifier, whether it intends to proceed with the Protocol's decision procedure, or according to its domestic regulatory framework.

25. The decision procedure works as follows: a risk assessment must be carried out for decisions made on the import of LMOs. The exporter has to carry out the risk assessment or bear its cost if the party of import so requires. Within 90 days of notification, the party of import must inform the notifier that either it will have to wait for written consent, or that it may proceed with the import without written consent. If the requirement is to wait for written consent, the party of import has 270 days from the date of receipt of notification to communicate, in writing, its decision. The decision could be either to:
   - Approve the import and add conditions as appropriate, including conditions for future imports of the same LMO;
   - Prohibit the import;
   - Request additional information; or
   - Extend the deadline for response by a defined period.

26. A party of import may, in light of new scientific information, review and change a decision at any time and also a party of export or a notifier (exporter) may request the party of import to review its decisions. The purpose of this procedure is to ensure that importing countries have the opportunity to assess risks associated with the LMO before agreeing to its import.

27. The importing country may also take into account socio-economic considerations as specified by the Protocol, when making its decision to import. Several developing countries consider this possibility to include socio-economic risks into decision taking process as important. They believe that the introduction of a certain LMO might result in considerable risks for local farmers, and national economies, which are based to a large extent on agriculture and biodiversity. The reference to socio-economic considerations also allows for the recognition of the value of biodiversity to indigenous and local communities and thus resonates with the strong link between biodiversity conservation and the recognition and protection of traditional knowledge, innovations and practices as provided for under article 8(j) of the Convention.

28. The Protocol's AIA procedure does not apply to:
   - Pharmaceuticals for humans that are addressed by other relevant international agreements or organizations;
   - LMOs in transit to a third party;
   - LMOs destined for contained use (in a laboratory or other containment facilities only);
   - LMOs intended for direct use as food, feed or for processing (LMO-FFP);
   - LMOs that have been declared safe by a meeting of the parties to the Protocol.

b) LMOs intended for Direct Use as Food, Feed or for Processing

29. LMOs intended for direct use as food, feed or for processing ("LMOs-FFP") represent a large category of agricultural commodities. They are not subject to the AIA procedure but are covered by a separate, less restrictive procedure outlined in article 11 of the Protocol.

30. A party making a decision approving an LMO that may be subject to transboundary movement for direct use as food or feed, or for processing, for a domestic use, including releasing it into the market, must inform others through the Biosafety Clearing-House, within 15 days of its decision. Other

Comparative Summary of the AIA and Article 11 procedures

Features	The AIA procedure	Article 11 Procedure
LMOs covered	Those destined for intentional introduction into the environment	Those intended for direct use as food, feed, or for processing
Trigger	Notification	Information
Actors	• Party of export • Exporter • Party of import	• A party making decision to release (for domestic use, including placing on the market) • A potential party of import
Obligations **1. Provision of information;** **2. Observing time limits;** **3. Ensuring consistency**	• Annex I • Acknowledge receipt of notification (90 days). Communicate decision (270 days) • Consistent with the Protocol	• Annex II • No general requirement exists • Developing countries and countries with economies in transition (270 days) • Consistent with the objective of the Protocol • Any party can request for it • No detailed guidance exists • Does not imply consent or refusal

Additional information	The party of import can request for it	Any party can request for it
Types/content of decision	• Approving without conditions; • Approving with conditions; • Requesting for additional information; • Extending the time for decision taking by a defined period of time.	No detailed guidance exists
Consequence of silence	Does not imply consent	Does not imply consent or refusal
Basis for decision	• Domestic regulatory framework; • The Protocol procedure (article 10); • Risk assessment (article 15, Annex III); • Precautionary approach, • Socio-economic considerations	•Domestic regulatory framework; • Risk assessment (Annex III)-where there is no domestic regulatory framework • Precautionary approach; • Socio-economic considerations.
Review of decision	It is possible to review a decision	There is no explicit provision in this regard. But it should be possible
Simplified procedure	It may be applicable where there are adequate measures for safety in place	The procedure itself is meant to be simplified
Mode of transaction	Direct between the actors (bilateral)	Through the Biosafety Clearing-House (multilateral)

parties, which may be importing the LMO, could take their own decisions regarding whether and how to import such LMO. Decisions by parties of import could be taken under their domestic regulatory framework that is consistent with the objective of the Protocol. A developing country party or a party with an economy in transition may, in the absence of a domestic regulatory framework, declare through the Biosafety Clearing-House that its decisions on the first import of LMOs-FFP will be taken in accordance with risk assessment as set out in the Protocol. In case of insufficient relevant scientific information and knowledge, the party of import may use precaution in making its decision on the import of LMOs-FFP.

c) Risk Assessment and Risk Management

32. Prohibiting or restricting the import of LMOs is a trade measure. In order for a trade measure taken with a view to help protect human, animal or plant life within the importing country to be WTO compatible, it should conform to the 1995 WTO Agreement on the Application of Sanitary and Phytosanitary Measures ("SPS Agreement"). Any such measure, in order to be in conformity with the SPS Agreement, should adopt an internationally sanctioned standard or should be based on risk assessment. The first clause in the decision procedure of the Protocol regarding whether to import LMOs for introduction into the environment establishes that such decisions shall be taken in accordance with risk assessment, which seems to be in accord with the SPS Agreement. The Protocol describes how risk assessment should be carried out and further provides for its parameters.

33. Parties to the Biosafety Protocol are required to establish and maintain appropriate risk management mechanisms, measures and strategies taking into account article 8(g) of the Biodiversity

Convention. They need to take measures to prevent unintentional transboundary movements of LMOs. Risk management measures should be based on risk assessment and imposed to the extent necessary to prevent adverse effects of LMOs on biological diversity and human health. In 2005, parties adopted the "Terms of Reference for the Ad Hoc Technical Expert Group on Risk Assessment."

d) Information Sharing

34. The Protocol relies heavily on the sharing of appropriate and timely information for its effective operation and implementation. In order to facilitate the exchange of information, the Protocol has established a BCH as part of the clearing-house mechanism of Convention. The BCH is a system of information sharing and a tool for implementation. Each Party is required to make available to the BCH information specified in several provisions of the Protocol. For instance, each party has to make available to the BCH:

(a) Any existing laws, regulations and guidelines for implementation of the Protocol, as well as information required for the advance informed agreement procedure under the Protocol;

(b) Any bilateral, regional and multilateral agreements and arrangements;

(c) Summaries of risk assessments or environmental reviews of LMOs, including relevant information regarding processed products of LMO origin;

(d) Final decisions regarding the importation or release of LMOs;

(e) Reports submitted by it pursuant to the Protocol, including those on the implementation of the Advance Informed Agreement procedure.

At the second MOP, the Multi-Year Programmme of Work for the Operation of the Biosafety Clearing-House was adopted.

e) Unintentional Transboundary Movement of LMOs (article 17)

35. When a party knows of the occurrence of an unintentional transboundary movement of LMOs that is likely to have significant adverse effects on biodiversity and human health, it must notify affected or potentially affected states, the BCH and relevant international organizations and give information on the unintentional release. Parties must start immediate consultation with the affected or potentially affected states to enable them to determine response and emergency measures.

f) Identification of LMOs

36. The Biosafety Protocol provides for safe handling, transport, packaging and identification of LMOs. Each party is required, among other things, to take measures to identify LMOs as "LMOs" in documentation accompanying transboundary shipments. The specific documentation requirements are defined in the Protocol in accordance with the intended use of the LMO. In this regard, it is important to note that there are some existing documentation requirements under other regimes that are relevant to some types of LMOs. For example, the United Nations Model Regulations on the Transport of Dangerous Goods specify documentation requirements for certain categories of genetically modified micro-organisms. Depending on the existence of need and appropriate modalities, there is also a possibility of developing standards for identification, handling, packaging and transport practices involving LMOs, under the Protocol in the future, by the CoP serving as the meeting of the parties to the Protocol.

g) Confidential Information (article 21)

37. Each party is required to protect confidential information received under the Protocol and identified as such by the notifier. Each party has to put in place procedures to protect and treat such information in no less favourable manner than it treats confidential information in connection with domestically produced living modified organism. The party of import shall not use confidential information for commercial purposes without the written consent of the notifier. The Protocol does not allow the notifier to identify or withhold, as confidential, any information relating to: (a) the name and address of the notifier; (b) general description of the living modified organism; (c) summary of risk assessment; and (d) methods and plans for emergency response.

h) Capacity Building (article 22)

38. Capacity building is one of the subjects addressed by the Protocol. The preamble recognizes the fact that many countries, particularly developing countries have limited capabilities to cope with the nature and scale of known and potential risks associated with LMOs. In that regard, the Protocol requires the parties to promote international cooperation to help developing countries and countries with economies in transition to strengthen human resources and institutional structure in biosafety. Parties are encouraged to assist with scientific and technical training and to promote the transfer of technology, know-how and financial resources. Parties are also expected to promote private sector involvement in capacity building. The second MOP in 2005 adopted the "Terms of Reference for the Comprehensive Review and Possible Revision of the Action Plan for Building Capacities for the Effective Implementation of the Protocol".

i) Public Awareness and Participation (article 23)

39. The Protocol requires and encourages parties to inform and involve their public in matters relating to living modified organisms. More specifically, parties are required to promote and facilitate public awareness, education and participation, including access to information concerning the safe transfer, handling and use of LMOs. The public has to be consulted in the decision-making process and the results of such decisions should be made available in accordance with domestic legislation and with a respect to confidential information as provided for in the Protocol. The Protocol further requires parties to promote and facilitate public access to information on LMOs that may be imported, as well as access to the Biosafety Clearing-House.

j) Compliance Procedures and Mechanisms (article 34)

40. The Biosafety Protocol anticipates the adoption of procedures and institutional mechanisms to promote compliance and to deal with cases of non-compliance by the Conference of the Parties serving as the meeting of the Parties to the Protocol. The procedures are already determined to be cooperative ones (as opposed to confrontational) that shall include provisions to offer advice or assistance for those parties that may be faced with difficulties to comply with the obligations of the Protocol. The compliance procedures are required to be separate from, and without prejudice to, the dispute-settlement procedures and mechanisms established by the Convention. These procedures

have been adopted by the first meeting of the parties to the Protocol. A Compliance Committee has also been established by a decision of the same meeting to implement or oversee the procedures. The second meeting adopted the "Rules of Procedure for the Meetings of the Compliance Committee under the Cartagena Protocol on Biosafety."

k) Liability and Redress (article 27)

41. The Biosafety Protocol commits the first meeting of the parties to put in place a process to elaborate rules and procedures on liability and redress for damage resulting from the transboundary movements of LMOs. It sets a desirable period of four years for completion of this task. The provision reflects the compromise that was possible at the end of the negotiations of the Protocol between the opposing views of some who sought to have detailed rules of liability and redress in the Protocol on the one hand, and those who wanted to see no provision at all concerning liability and redress, on the other. The parties to the Protocol agreed, at their first meeting, on the nature and timetable of the process envisaged in the Protocol. An open-ended ad-hoc working group of legal and technical experts is established to carry out the process in accordance with its terms of reference provided in Decision BS-I/8.

l) Transboundary Movement of LMOs with Non-Parties

42. The Protocol addresses the obligations of the parties in relation to transboundary movements of LMOs to and from non-parties to the Protocol. Movements between parties and non-Parties must be carried out in a manner that is consistent with the objective of the Protocol. Parties are required to encourage non-parties to adhere to the Protocol and to give relevant information to the BCH.

m) Administration of the Biosafety Protocol

43. The governing body of the Protocol is the COP to the Convention serving as the meeting of the parties to the Protocol ("COP-MOP"). Its main function is to review the status of implementation of the Protocol and to make decisions necessary to promote its effective operation. Only parties can take decisions under the Protocol. Parties to the Conventions that are not parties to the Protocol may only participate as observers in the proceedings of meetings of the COP-MOP. The COP-MOP may decide to use any subsidiary body established by or under the Convention, or establish its own subsidiary bodies as deemed

necessary for facilitating the implementation of the Protocol. The Secretariat of the Convention serves also as the Secretariat to the Protocol.

44. At the national level, each party needs to designate a national focal point to be responsible for exchange with the Secretariat. The functions will include, for example, receiving notifications of meetings relating to the Protocol from the Secretariat and invitations to submit views on matters under discussion. Each party also has to designate at least one competent national authority to perform the administrative functions as required by the Protocol. It shall be authorized to act on the Party's behalf with respect to those functions, which may be dependent on the type of LMO(s), for which the authority is responsible. A party may decide to combine the functions of both focal point and competent national authority in one institution. A list of focal points and competent national authorities is maintained by the Secretariat and is available in the BCH.

3. Relationship of the Cartagena Protocol on Biosafety with other Agreements

45. The relationship between environmental treaties, which prohibit trade in certain goods or allow parties to ban certain goods on environmental grounds, on the one hand, and the trade regime, which seeks to restrict non-tariff barriers to trade, on the other, is increasingly becoming important. The World Trade Organization agreements such as the General Agreement on Tariffs and Trade ("GATT"), Agreement on the Application of Sanitary and Phytosanitary Measures ("SPS") and the Agreement on Technical Barriers to Trade ("TBT"), contain provisions relevant to the Cartagena Protocol. The final text of the Protocol has not settled, in a definitive way, the question of how it relates to the WTO and other international agreements. However, in its preamble, the Protocol states that parties:
   - Recognize that trade and environment agreements should be mutually supportive;
   - Emphasize that the Protocol is not interpreted as implying a change in the rights and obligations under any existing agreements and
   - Understand that the above recital is not intended to subordinate the Protocol to other international agreements.

46. Conflict may well arise over how parties implement the provisions of the Protocol. For instance, WTO rules impose strict limitations on the use of precautionary trade measures. However, a party to the Protocol might decide, based on a small amount of scientific evidence, to ban imports

of, say genetically modified tomatoes, arguing that it is allowed to do so under paragraph 8 of article 11. In the first place this raises a question of jurisdiction. It may lead to the question of where such disputes should be dealt with or adjudicated. The WTO's Committee on Trade and Environment has expressed its preference for disputes arising from a Multilateral Environmental Agreement ("MEA"), to be handled within the proper framework of the latter. However, if the claimant in the example above asserts that the basis of the dispute is not a violation of the rules of the Protocol but that of WTO, then it is likely that the dispute might be handled under the WTO Dispute Settlement Procedure.

47. The last paragraph of the Protocol, which states that the Protocol is not intended to be subordinate to other international agreements, is very important. This language appears to be relatively strong as compared to a similar one used in another MEA adopted prior to the Protocol. Thus, in case a dispute over the implementation of the Protocol is brought to the WTO, it would be very difficult for the dispute panel to ignore the Protocol's wording even if the same preamble simultaneously states that the Protocol will not be interpreted as changing the rights and obligations of a party under any existing agreements. In any event, like any other agreement, reasonable interpretation of the Protocol depends on the understanding of its context, which includes the text, the preamble and its annexes.

III. National Implementation

48. As a party to the Protocol, a country is expected to put in place domestic implementing legislation that will allow it to adhere to the terms of the international agreement. This section presents the programmes of Indonesia, Australia, and Cuba, as examples of national biosafety frameworks. See under chapter 2 above as well of which this part is a reinforcement.

49. The number of countries that have ratified or acceded to the Protocol is growing. Each country joining the Protocol, as a party, is required to take necessary legal and administrative measures to implement its obligations under the Protocol. As implied in the previous section, the design and implementation of biosafety frameworks at national level should take into account not only the Protocol, but also a range of issues and concerns addressed by other regimes that have relevance to biosafety.

Some Examples of National Experiences in the Development and Implementation of Biosafety Frameworks

1. Indonesia

50. As one of the centres of mega biodiversity, Indonesia seeks to utilize its immense biological resources in a sustainable manner as well as to develop biotechnology. Indonesia has placed a high priority on the development of biotechnology since 1985 in order to address the need for sufficient food production in a more sustainable and performing agricultural system. It ratified the Cartagena Protocol in December 2004.

51. Indonesia established a national committee for biotechnology in 1993 at the State Ministry for Science and Technology. The purpose of the committee is to formulate policies and programmes relating to biotechnology which are overseen through a system of four national centres for excellence in agriculture and industrial and medical biotechnology. As a result of this initiative, Indonesia now has plant transformation programmes carried out at public and private research institutes, a public university, and an industrial laboratory.

52. Indonesia's biotechnology efforts are focused on a long-term strategy that involves drug discovery, genomics, conservation of germ plasma, genetic improvement of agricultural output, and marine and environmental biotechnology.

53. In 1993 the State Ministry on Research and Technology released guidelines for genetic engineering research, which control research of GMOs/LMOs. The guidelines include specific provisions that cover plants, cattle, fish and microbes.

54. Further it adopted biosafety regulations in 1997, through the Decree for Genetically Engineered Agricultural Biotechnology Products (the "Biosafety Decree"). The Biosafety Decree established Indonesia's Biosafety Commission, which advises the government on the safe release of GMOs/LMOs. The Biosafety Decree also created an expert technical team to assist the Biosafety Commission in the evaluation and implementation of procedures around the release of GMOs/LMOs.

55. Based on the early experience of the Biosafety Commission, the Ministries of Agriculture, Estate Crop and Forestry, Food, and Health issued, in

1999, a joint agreement expanding the scope of the Biosafety Decree to food safety. In that year, Indonesia also adopted specific food safety laws and regulations, including mandatory labelling of genetically engineered food.

2. Australia

56. The centerpiece of Australia's national biosafety framework is the Gene Technology Act of 2000 ("Gene Act"), which came into force on 21 June 2001. The Gene Act introduced a new regulatory system for GMOs in Australia, which replaced the country's previously voluntary system. The purpose of the Gene Act is "[to protect the health and safety of people, and to protect the environment, by identifying risks posed by or as a result of gene technology, and by managing those risks" through the regulation of GMO transactions.

57. The Gene Act encompasses all GMO activities undertaken in Australia, from contained research to intentional release into the environment. The regulatory system uses a science-based approach to risk assessment and management, while allowing for the consideration of socio-economic and ethical issues. It has to be noted that Australia has not signed or ratified the Cartagena Protocol.

58. Key functions of the Gene Act include:

- Prohibition of GMO-related activities unless they are undertaken in accordance with the legislation (e.g., the intentional release of a GMO into the environment requires a permit);
- Establishment of a process for assessing the risks to human health and the environment posed by GMOs;
- Provision for extensive public participation in any programme related to GMOs;
- Establishment of the Gene Technology Regulator (the "Gene Regulator") to administer the Gene Act;
- Establishment of a scientific advisory committee, an ethics committee and a community consultative committee to advise the Gene Regulator;
- Provisions for monitoring and enforcement of the Gene Act; and
- Creation of the Record of GMO and Genetically Modified Product Dealings, a centralized, publicly available database of all approved GMOs and genetically modified products ("Gene Database").

59. Through the Gene Act, the Gene Regulator assesses GMO applications and issues licences for the intentional release of transgenics into the environment. If the Gene Regulator believes that such release may pose a significant biosafety risk, he must invite public comment through the publication of a notice in the Commonwealth Gazette, relevant newspapers and on the website of the Office of the Gene Regulator. The Gene Regulator must then prepare a draft risk assessment and management plan, taking into account any public comment received, as well as any input from the Gene Technology Technical Advisory Committee, the Federal Environment Minister, relevant local councils, and state and territory governments. Once developed, the risk assessment and management plan is again submitted for public comment and, following the appropriate period, the Gene Regulator may approve the application and issue a licence. The public must again be notified of the Gene Regulator's final decision.

60. The Gene Act provides the Gene Regulator with extensive inspection, monitoring, and investigative authority over approved GMO licencees. The Gene Regulator conducts inspections of at least 20% of all field trial sites annually to ensure that transgenic crop field trials are being conducted in accordance with conditions contained in the underlying licence. Monitoring activities confirm the exact location of the approved field trial and the condition of any buffer zones used to isolate the GMO crop. The Gene Regulator also monitors past field trial sites to ensure that the GMO field trial crop has been eradicated.

3. Cuba

61. Cuba initiated its national biosafety framework in 1984 and, in 1996, formalized its regulations through Ministerial Resolution 67/96, which established the National Biosafety Centre ("CNSB") under the Ministry of Science, Technology and the Environment ("CITMA"). It ratified the Cartagena Protocol in September 2002.

62. Under Resolution 67/96, CNSB's purpose is to organize, direct, implement, supervise, and control the "national biosafety system," including Cuba's participation in relevant international biosafety agreements. In its regulatory capacity, CNSB develops the legal instruments and technical standards necessary for the implementation and strengthening of biosafety measures in Cuba.

63. CNSB has developed Cuba's national biosafety strategy, which is focused on the following goals:

- Establishment of procedures for the assessment and issuance of authorizations for activities involving a high biological risk;

- Preparation of a national inventory of facilities and areas where releases of GMOs/LMOs into the environment occur, including a specification of the biological agents handled at such facilities;
- Conduct of on-site inspections;
- Development and implementation of capacity-building programmes through the conduct of educational courses, development of skills and other measures, including the organization of national biosafety workshops;
- Establishment of technical committees on GMO/LMO food products, as well as the adoption of biosafety standards;
- Development of contingency plans and emergency procedures; and
- Compliance with the biosafety-related commitments in relevant international instruments to which Cuba is a party.

64. Cuba adopted the Decree-Law No. 190 ("Law 190") in 1999, as the legal basis for its national biosafety framework. The objective of Law 190 is to establish the general principles regulating the use, research, testing, production, importation, and exportation of biological agents and GMO/LMO products and organisms. Law 190 also establishes the regulatory regime that guarantees Cuba's compliance with international biosafety commitments and sets forth measures for the prevention of accidents and environmental protection.

65. In addition to Law 190, Cuba's national biosafety framework is comprised of a number of other legislative instruments. Resolution No. 42/99 classifies biological agents and toxins that affect human and animal health according to their risk profile. Resolution No. 8/2000 outlines the general biosafety regulations for facilities that handle transgenics and GMO/LMO products. Finally, Resolution No. 76/2000 regulates procedures for the granting of biosafety permits and licences.

66. Working with CNSB, CITMA designs, implements, and controls national biosafety policies. The relevant agencies of Cuba's Central State Administration are required to work with CITMA to regulate GMOs/LMOs. These groups are also responsible for providing public outreach and the appropriate implementation of relevant policies.

67. Law 190 charges CITMA with oversight responsibilities for all aspects of GMOs/LMOs. In general, all entities dealing with GMOs/LMOs and genetically modified products are subject to inspection and regulation by CITMA. CITMA's oversight authority is further defined in Resolution No. 8/2000.

Worku Damena Yifru, Legal Officer, Biosafety Programme, Secretariat of the Convention on Biological Diversity

Eva Maria Duer, Associate Legal Officer, Division of Policy Development and Law, UNEP

Resources

Internet Materials

AUSTRALIAN GOVERNMENT DEPARTMENT OF HEALTH AND AGEING, OFFICE OF THE GENE TECHNOLOGY REGULATOR, GENE TECHNOLOGY ACT 2000 available at http://www.health.gov.au/ogtr/index.htm and http://www.austlii.edu.au/au/legis/cth/consol_act/gta2000162/

BIOSAFETY CAPACITY BUILDING INITATIVE, IUCN REGIONAL BIODIVERSITY PROGRAMME, ASIA available at http://www.rbp-iucn.lk/biosafety/CouStatus_Indonesia.htm

COMMONWEALTH OF AUSTRALIA CONSOLIDATED ACTS available at www.austlii.edu.au/au/legis/cth/consol_act

http://www.biodiversityasia.org/

http://www.codexalimentarius.net/web/index_en.jsp

THE CARTAGENA PROTOCOL available at http://www.biodiv.org/biosafety/default.aspx

THE CENTER FOR INTERNATIONAL DEVELOPMENT AT HARVARD UNIVERSITY, GLOBAL TRADE NEGOTIATIONS HOME PAGE, BIOTECHNOLOGY PAPERS available at http://www.cid.harvard.edu/cidtrade/issues/biotechnologypaper.html

THE WORLD CONSERVATION UNION available at www.iucn.org

Text Materials

Alexandre Kiss, Dinah Shelton, INTERNATIONAL ENVIRONMENTAL LAW, (2nd Edition, Transnational Publishers).

Cosbey, Burgiel, THE CARTAGENA PROTOCOL ON BIOSAFETY - AN ANALYSIS OF RESULTS, (IISD Briefing Note)

Louise O. Fresco, GENETICALLY MODIFIED ORGANISMS IN FOOD AND AGRICULTURE: WHERE ARE WE? WHERE ARE WE GOING?

Patricia Birnie, Alan Boyle, INTERNATIONAL LAW AND THE ENVIRONMENT, (2nd Edition, Oxford University Press).

Phillip Sands, PRINCIPLES OF INTERNATIONAL LAW, (Volume 1: Frameworks, Standards and Implementation, Manchester University Press, Manchester, 1995).

17. PROTECTING AND PRESERVING MARINE BIODIVERSITY, INCLUDING THROUGH SUSTAINABLE FISHERIES

I. Introduction

1. The broad subject of biological diversity, or biodiversity, is examined primarily in chapter 15 of this Training Manual. This chapter provides an overview of the international legal framework for the protection and preservation of marine biodiversity, including through sustainable fisheries. The focus is exclusively on biodiversity in the marine environment, on marine biodiversity. Usage of the term (marine) biodiversity follows the definition laid down in article 2 of the Convention on Biological Diversity ("CBD"). Accordingly, biodiversity does not just include diversity at the species-level, such as marine plants, mammals, fishes and other living organisms, but also diversity of the ecosystems of which these species are part and genetic diversity within species. Concrete components of biodiversity are habitats, ecosystems, communities of species and genetic material. The term "marine environment" herein is used in a broad sense, and encompasses seas and oceans and its marine life, including gulfs and coastal areas, but not inland waters. The chapter has a special focus on marine capture fisheries (excluding therefore aquaculture) and the way in which these fisheries are managed in order to protect and preserve marine biodiversity.

2. The chapter first discusses the current threats to marine biodiversity posed by certain human activities. As the 2004 Kuala Lumpur Ministerial Declaration, made within the framework of the 1992 CBD, notes: "biological diversity is being lost at an unprecedented rate as a result of human activities." This certainly also applies to marine biodiversity.

3. Law, both international and national, is an indispensable tool for regulating human activities with the object of preventing or minimizing threats to marine biodiversity. Section II below examines the current international legal regime for the protection and preservation of marine biodiversity, with a special focus on marine capture fisheries. The international regime consists of legally binding and non-legally binding instruments, adopted at the global level or at the regional or sub-regional level. While the primary objective of many of these instruments may not always be the protection and preservation of marine biodiversity, they do contribute to that objective. The discussion concentrates on the main global and (sub-)regional instruments even though relevant instruments adopted at the bilateral level and those within the European Union are certainly no less relevant.

4. Ensuring that international instruments, whether legally binding or not, are effective, usually requires implementation at the national level and most often by means of legislation. Section III of this chapter, entitled National Implementation, therefore provides examples of the way in which states have implemented relevant international instruments through national legislation. These examples are also helpful for demonstrating how national legislation is applied to address marine biodiversity problems.

5. Our seas and oceans cover about 70% of the earth's surface and play important functions in maintaining and sustaining the earth's ecological balances. The seas and oceans produce a third of the oxygen that we breathe, offer a valuable source of protein and moderates global climatic change. Marine and coastal areas are home to a wide variety of ecosystems, for example, coral reefs found in both tropical and temperate areas, sea-grass beds and mangrove forests. Most of these ecosystems support a diverse spectrum of marine life, ranging from top predators such as marine mammals to organisms such as algae, which are at the bottom of the food web. Maintaining the abundance within and the biodiversity of these ecosystems is crucial for fisheries worldwide, including aquaculture. For many people throughout the world, the marine environment is not only a vital source of protein, but the activities which it sustains, such as fisheries, transport and tourism, also provides them with an income.

6. The need for the protection and preservation of marine biodiversity is especially necessary for organisms and habitats that are highly endemic, meaning they are found in very few places in the world. For example, the Indian Ocean is known to have 482 different species of coral, 27% of which live only at one location. Another example is the Baltic Sea, which is the largest body of brackish water in the world and contains many unique habitats that support rare marine organisms. Seamounts on the deep sea-bed are known for their endemism as well.

7. It is not just living marine resources that are beneficial to humans. The exploitation of non-living marine resources such as oil, gas, sand, gravel, and diamonds and other precious minerals provides states with substantial revenues. The benefits of the marine environment are also not limited to tangible resources. Other uses include the laying of submarine telecommunication cables and pipelines, maritime transport, tourism and various types of building activities. These latter building activities do not necessarily have to be related to resource exploitation, for example by oil rigs, but could also take the form of land reclamation, artificial islands or installations for producing energy from the water, currents or winds. Another use of the marine environment is marine scientific research, which has provided actual and potential benefits to all states on issues such as weather forecasting, the study of effects of ocean currents, and natural forces at work on the ocean floor. Marine bio-prospecting is a newly emerging use, which is aimed at identifying applications or uses of marine living organisms, parts thereof or their genetic material. While some regard it as marine scientific research, others prefer to treat it as a resource activity.

8. Many human activities that take place on land eventually also have an impact on the marine environment. Industrial activity and modern agricultural practices produce many pollutants that are either discharged directly into the marine environment or end up in the marine environment through the atmosphere or through rivers. Examples of pollutants are agricultural chemicals, heavy metals and nuclear waste. Once in the marine environment, these pollutants can cause ailments and death of living organisms, destroy marine habitats and otherwise have adverse effects on the functioning of marine ecosystems. If affected organisms in one way or another are consumed by humans, serious human health concerns can also arise.

9. Increasing global human population in recent decades and demographic trends of increasing population densities in coastal areas pose further problems to the marine environment. An estimated 67% of the current global population lives on the coast, or within 60 kilometres of the coast, and that percentage is still increasing. Many of the cities that currently experience the highest population growth, such as São Paulo, Shanghai, Hong Kong, Manila and Djakarta, are on or near the coast. These burgeoning populations do not only increase pressure on the utilization of resources in coastal areas but are also a continuously growing strain on the marine environment due to increased human activity both at sea and on land. The impact of untreated human waste alone is already a serious concern.

10. All of these uses, whether related to resources or not and whether they take place on land or at sea, have an impact on the marine environment and possibly on biodiversity. The expansion in types of uses of the marine environment as well as their intensity has not always been accompanied with adequate regulation at the national, regional or global levels. Also, if such regulation was in fact in place, compliance has often been inadequate to prevent serious adverse consequences for marine biodiversity. The most serious threats to marine biodiversity are degradation and loss of habitats, overexploitation and indiscriminate fishing practices, marine pollution, invasive alien species and climate change. The following paragraphs discuss marine biodiversity threats in relation to deforestation and mining, tourism, fishing and invasive alien species.

11. Deforestation and mining, even if occurring many hundreds of kilometres inland, often lead to widespread erosion and thereby large increases in sediment load in coastal areas. This has smothered coral reefs and other coastal habitats in Indonesia, Malaysia, the Philippines, Sri Lanka and in many other places in the world. Conversely, the construction of dams for hydro-electricity generation or for irrigation purposes has led to dramatic reductions in sediment loads, but with equally severe consequences for coastal ecosystems. The Nile Delta is reported to be sinking at an alarming rate due to a combination of lack of sediment input, enhanced erosion and severe reduction in nutrient load. Such problems have led to the collapse of fisheries in many places, including in the eastern Mediterranean region.

12. As a considerable segment of tourism occurs in coastal areas, it poses a sizeable threat to marine biodiversity. Such tourism can be land-based or vessel-based. Land-based tourism in coastal areas commonly requires permanent infrastructure, such as hotels and marinas. The establishment of this infrastructure has often led to the destruction of critical coastal habitats such as mangrove forests, wetlands, estuaries and coral reefs. Infrastructure development is often undertaken without proper evaluation of the functions and benefits of these habitats to local or regional ecosystem processes. Once constructed, the use of this infrastructure may also affect marine biodiversity, for example through the discharge of sewage, and tourism activities carried out in the marine environment, such as boating, recreational fishing, diving,

snorkelling and marine wildlife viewing. Coral reefs also suffer from extraction of coral for jewellery or souvenirs. This practice has resulted in the extinction of red and black corals in the Mediterranean and in the tropics. In Sri Lanka, reef cover is declining at an annual rate of 10% due to indiscriminate extraction methods. Vessel-based tourism, or cruise tourism, has grown considerably in recent decades. The environmental concerns of the increasing use of ever bigger vessels are largely similar to those of merchant ships. Once cruise vessels call in port, however, the environmental impact differs fundamentally. While supplying cruise vessels with large amounts of food, fresh water and fuel, collecting and processing huge quantities of various types of garbage and receiving many short-time visitors provides ports with financial benefits, these activities also lead to environmental and biodiversity concerns.

13. The essence of many of the problems currently faced by marine capture fisheries is caused by the fundamental characteristics of marine fish, namely that they are a common property and renewable natural resource that moves around freely. Failure to regulate will therefore inevitably lead to over-exploitation and economic inefficiency and ultimately to conflict at the national and/or the international level. As many fish stocks are not confined to single regulatory areas and cannot therefore be regulated by one single authority, it is often essential that fisheries management authorities cooperate in order to align their regulatory efforts. Non-alignment will eventually lead to declining catches in transboundary stocks on both sides of a maritime boundary. As the successful regulation of marine fisheries often depends on cooperation at the international level, the sovereign equality of states under international law is often perceived as a stumbling block. As no state, in principle, can be forced to do something against its will, international regulation may often be at the level of the 'lowest common denominator' and experience 'free rider' problems. This does not mean, as is by now widely recognized, that unilateral coastal State authority is a sufficient guarantee for sustainable fisheries.

14. According to figures released by the United Nations Food and Agriculture Organization in 2002, about 50% of the world's fish stocks are fully exploited and about 30% are over-exploited or depleted. However, those dramatic figures may be misleading due to massive over-reporting by China and El Niño fluctuations in the Peruvian anchoveta fishery. Consequently, the true situation is probably one of steadily declining global catches since the late 1980s. A well-known but sad case is that of the Northwest Atlantic cod stocks that collapsed in the early 1990s, and have not recovered since. Collapses of populations and extinction of species will often bring about changes in ecosystems. A very famous example is the North Eastern Pacific sea otter, which was hunted down to near extinction at the end of the 19th century. As sea otters prey on urchins, and urchins feed on kelp, this resulted in a loss of many kelp beds that are crucial habitats for fish and invertebrates. Intensive fishing activity can also lead to changes in the composition of fish stocks and loss of genetic diversity.

15. Fishing can also cause the local or regional extinction of species. For example, incidental and accidental catches of the pre-historic Coelacanth off the coast of the Comoros have finally brought the species on the brink of extinction. A form of fishing that is currently highly criticized for its threat to biodiversity is deep-sea fishing, in particular those fisheries that use techniques like bottom-trawling or that target seamounts. Some extremely destructive fishing practices, such as those involving the use of explosives or poison, such as cyanide, are sometimes still used by fishermen in developing states. While this satisfies short-term nutrition or financial needs, such desperate behaviour kills many non-target species, destroys entire habitats and has severe mid-term and long-term nutrition and financial implications. Generally, by-catch of commercial uninteresting species, which is commonly discarded, is acknowledged to be a huge problem. Media attention to this problem is nevertheless frequently limited to by-catch of high profile species, such as marine mammals, birds and sea turtles.

16. The intentional or accidental introduction of aquatic organisms into the marine environment is certainly not a new phenomenon, but has received continuously increasing attention in recent years. Intentional introduction of alien or new species usually occurs for perceived benefits, for example resource exploitation, but often overlooks the risks associated with limited scientific knowledge about the impacts of introduction. There are various so-called pathways of accidental introduction. One of these is by means of large merchant vessels up-taking and discharging water used for ballast tanks, which mainly serve to ensure a vessel's stability once it has offloaded its cargo. Due to the global nature of merchant shipping, the biodiversity threats and consequences of accidental introduction of alien species through ballast water are experienced throughout the globe. For

example, the introduction of the North American comb jelly by ballast water into the Black and Azov Seas has contributed significantly to the collapse of fisheries, with massive economic and social impacts. The Caspian Sea is presently facing the same threat.

II. International Framework

1. Global Legally Binding Instruments

a) United Nations Convention on the Law of the Sea

17. The rapid pace of technological development following, and in part triggered by, the Second World War, effectively disclosed the ocean's huge reserves of non-renewable resources, dramatically increased fishing effort, and led to a quickly expanding number of large vessels and volumes of hazardous cargo that traversed the oceans. This coincided with a growing global demand for resources, a widening awareness of environmental degradation, and a fundamental change in the nature and composition of the international community as a consequence of the process of decolonization and the Cold War.

18. Under these circumstances, the then existing international law of the sea was regarded as inadequate. This was partly because it was unable to deal with some of the new issues and uses of the oceans that had emerged but also because it no longer reflected the needs and interests of the predominant part of the international community. This created considerable friction, which sometimes led to heated skirmishes (e.g., the 'cod wars' between Iceland and the United Kingdom between 1958 and 1976). The need for a legal order for the oceans that would be both general (relating to all ocean space) and comprehensive (for covering all uses and resources) was eventually widely recognized. After a lengthy process of negotiation, this need resulted in the adoption of the United Nations Convention on the Law of the Sea ("UNCLOS") on 10 December 1982. UNCLOS entered into force on 16 November 1994. (See also generally chapter 13 above).

19. The overarching objective of UNCLOS is to establish a universally accepted, just and equitable legal order - or 'Constitution' - for the oceans that lessens the risk of international conflict and enhances stability and peace in the international community. The fact that UNCLOS had, in September 2005, attracted 149 parties suggests that this objective has been achieved. However, UNCLOS is in many ways a framework convention that relies on implementation at the global and

regional levels through various international organizations. In the sphere of vessel-source pollution, for example, this implementation mandate was entrusted to the International Maritime Organization ("IMO") while fisheries were foreseen to be managed at the regional level through Regional Fisheries Management Organizations ("RFMOs"). Moreover, in view of the constantly changing needs and interests of the international community, UNCLOS would need to be amended or complemented by new international instruments. While some of these instruments adopted since 1982 are closely connected with the UNCLOS, for others this is less so.

20. UNCLOS is a massive treaty. It consists of 320 articles in 17 separate parts and has 9 Annexes. As a 'Constitution for the Oceans,' the Convention deals with a much broader range of issues than those related to marine biodiversity and sustainable fisheries, but those are not discussed in this chapter. The parts in UNCLOS have either a zonal scope or a thematic scope. The zonal scope is used for part II 'Territorial Sea and Contiguous Zone,' part III 'Straits used for International Navigation,' part IV 'Archipelagic States,' part V 'Exclusive Economic Zone,' part VI 'Continental Shelf,' part VII 'High Seas,' and part XI 'The Area.' Of the remaining thematic parts, part XII 'Protection and Preservation of the Marine Environment' is particularly important for this chapter and is also covered in chapter 13.

21. International law recognizes that the "territory" of a state consists of the following components: the land (including islands and rocks), internal waters, territorial sea, archipelagic waters, and the subsoil below and the airspace above these. A state enjoys sovereignty within its territory but beyond that a state can only have less than sovereignty, for example sovereign rights, jurisdiction, rights or freedoms. States can establish a territorial sea with a maximum breadth of 12 nautical miles (1 nautical mile = 1,852 kilometres) measured from the baselines along the coast, as provided in article 2. Archipelagic waters are the waters enclosed by drawing lines around groups of islands according to specific conditions as provided in article 47. A coastal state's sovereignty within its territorial sea and archipelagic waters entitles it to all the living and non-living resources therein. It also gives the coastal state practically unlimited jurisdiction to prescribe and enforce its own laws and regulations with respect to all activities occurring therein, including those by foreign ships and aircrafts. The main exception to that jurisdiction is the right of innocent passage for ships of all states under article 17.

22. Coastal states are also entitled to an Exclusive Economic Zone ("EEZ") with a maximum width of 200 nautical miles, measured from the baselines. In their EEZs, coastal states have sovereign rights for the purpose of exploring, exploiting, conserving and managing the living and non-living natural resources, and for other economic activities (articles 55-57). These resources include those in the water column, such as fish, and on or under the sea bed, for example abalone, oil and gas. In their EEZs coastal states also have jurisdiction for the protection and preservation of the marine environment but this can only be exercised by taking account of the freedoms of other states in the EEZ, for instance navigation, over flight, and the laying of sub-marine cables and pipelines.

23. In certain circumstances, coastal states have a continental shelf that extends beyond the EEZ, sometimes even beyond 350 nautical miles measured from the baselines (article 76). Over its continental shelf, a coastal state has sovereign rights for the purpose of exploring it and exploiting its natural resources, including relevant jurisdiction. These natural resources consist of the non-living resources of the sea-bed and subsoil together with sedentary species, such as clams and abalone, as provided in article 77.

24. Those parts of the sea that are not internal waters, territorial sea, archipelagic waters or EEZ, are high seas. All states enjoy the freedoms of the high seas mentioned in paragraph 22 of this chapter in addition to the freedoms of scientific research, construction of artificial islands and fishing, except for sedentary species on a coastal state's juridical (legal) continental shelf as provided by articles 76 and 77. The 'Area' is the sea-bed and ocean floor beyond the coastal states' legal continental shelves. The non-living mineral resources in the area are part of the common heritage of mankind and subject to an internationalized management regime as provided by articles 1(1)(1), 133 and 136.

25. UNCLOS does not only grant rights but also imposes obligations. Whenever the Convention acknowledges or grants a right to states, whether in their capacity as flag state (the state where a ship is registered) or as a coastal state, it is commonly followed by an obligation for other states to respect these rights. In addition, UNCLOS imposes obligations on states acting in their different capacities that are owed to the international community. The most important of these are obligations on the conservation and utilization of marine living resources, and on the protection and preservation of the marine environment.

26. The obligations on the conservation and utilization of marine living resources are included in part V on the EEZ and Section 2 of part VII on the high seas, but (rather strangely) not in relation to sedentary species (article 68). Articles 61 and 62 contain obligations on conservation and utilization that apply to any category of species that occurs within a coastal State's EEZ. Article 61 requires a coastal state to establish a Total Allowable Catch ("TAC") to ensure that the harvesting of living resources within the state's EEZ is aimed at producing the Maximum Sustainable Yield ("MSY") and does not lead to over-exploitation. Serious over-exploitation often leads to the collapse of stocks and thereby affects the mid- and long-term interests of present and future generations. These obligations also require the coastal state to gather a wide range of relevant data to ensure that the TAC is based on the best scientific evidence available. A TAC can take many forms, for instance a maximum amount of fish that can be caught, a maximum number of licensed ships or a fixed fishing season. In the context of this chapter, it is important to note that article 61 does not just deal with targeted fish. The TAC should take account of the interdependence of stocks. Therefore, the conservation measures of the coastal state are also required to take into consideration the effects of fisheries on associated species (by-catch) and dependent species (predator-prey relationships), as well as environmental factors. However, these obligations still fall short of a firm obligation to engage in the recently emerging holistic notion of ecosystem-based fisheries management.

27. Article 62 contains a type of obligation that is very different from that in article 61. Article 62 requires the coastal state to promote the objective of optimum utilization of the living resources in its EEZ. In case the coastal state has insufficient capacity to harvest the entire TAC, it must give other states access to the surplus of the TAC. The coastal state is normally given compensation, monetary or otherwise, for allowing other states to harvest the surplus. In addition, under article 62(4), a coastal state's sovereign rights in its EEZ allow the coastal state to require foreign ships that harvest the surplus in its EEZ to comply with a wide range of laws and regulations. The objective of optimum utilization was inserted with concerns of global food security in mind. However, there are currently very few stocks that are under-utilized. Article 62 recognizes that the objective of optimum utilization is "without prejudice to" article 61, meaning that the objective must give way to the obligation to conserve and avoid over-exploitation.

28. Maritime boundaries only exist on maps. They do not impede the movement of marine species and they are also not drawn or negotiated with the range of distribution of marine species in mind. The need for states to cooperate in order to align their management of marine living resources with other states is therefore evident. Articles 63-67 lay down regimes for international cooperation for various different categories of species whose ranges of distribution are not confined to a single coastal state's EEZ. These categories are: shared stocks within the EEZs of two or more coastal states under article 63(1), straddling stocks between EEZs and the high seas under article 63(2), the highly migratory species listed in Annex I to the UNCLOS that are presumed to occur both in the EEZ and the high seas, for instance tuna species under article 64, marine mammals under article 65, anadromous species, such as salmon, which spawn in rivers but spend most of their life in the marine environment under article 66, and catadromous species, such as certain eel species, which spawn in the ocean but spend most of their life in rivers under article 67. Whereas the regimes for anadromous and catadromous species reserve harvesting for coastal states in their maritime zones and prohibit flag states to harvest these species on the high seas, the other regimes do not give preference to one or the other. They essentially require the states involved to cooperate either directly or through appropriate international organizations. Regional Fisheries Management Organizations are currently the most widely used vehicles for cooperative international management.

29. Articles 116-120 in Section 2 of part VII on the high seas contain the regime for the conservation and management of the living resources of the high seas. Article 116 recognizes the freedom of fishing on the high seas but makes this right explicitly subject to the obligation to respect the rights, duties and interests of coastal states under articles 63(2) and 64-67, the obligation to avoid over-exploitation and cooperation with other high seas fishing states. This regime therefore also applies to stocks whose range of distribution is confined to the high seas (discrete high seas stocks). Article 119 repeats many of the obligations that are also laid down in article 61 on the EEZ. For instance, those on the objective of MSY, science-based management and taking account of the effects on associated and dependent species and environmental factors.

30. The obligations in UNCLOS on the protection and preservation of the marine environment are largely laid down in part XII. It commences with article 192, which lays down a, by now, universally accepted legal norm: "states have an obligation to protect and preserve the marine environment." This is immediately followed by the overarching objective of sustainable development, which requires a balancing of economic, social and environmental considerations for present and future generations. It reads: "states have the sovereign right to exploit their natural resources pursuant to their environmental policies and in accordance with their duty to protect and preserve the marine environment." Part XII does not define 'their natural resources.' To determine what these are and which states have sovereign rights or freedoms over them, it is necessary to go back to the zonal parts of UNCLOS.

31. Part XII deals with 'pollution of the marine environment'. This term is defined in article 1(1)(4). Pollution as an activity is obviously very different from fishing. The object of fishing or hunting for marine mammals is expressly aimed at removing species from the natural environment. If unregulated, this intentional activity will therefore pose a risk to marine biodiversity. In addition, fishing activities may have side-effects that are not expressly intended, for instance by-catch of commercially uninteresting species that are discarded, or bottom trawling that has negative effects on the ecosystem. The actual object of pollution, on the other hand, is to get rid of substances or energy but not to cause environmental damage or pose a threat to marine biodiversity, even though it may have that effect.

32. Chapter 13 above discusses how UNCLOS deals with pollution of the marine environment. While UNCLOS does not embrace the notion or objective of marine biodiversity, or even define 'marine environment,' the definition of 'pollution of the marine environment' encompasses "harm to living resources and marine life." Whereas measures to prevent, reduce or control pollution of the marine environment are undeniably also beneficial to the protection and preservation of marine biodiversity, they are not often specifically designed for that purpose. Rather, these measures are intended to protect and preserve the marine environment in general.

33. Two provisions in part XII are exceptions to this general rule. First, article 194(5) requires all states, when they take measures to prevent, reduce or control pollution of the marine environment, to "include those (measures) necessary to protect and preserve rare or fragile ecosystems as well as the habitat of depleted, threatened or endangered species and other forms of marine life." Measures

would be required in relation to any source of pollution, for example pollution by ships through dumping and operational discharges, from land (through rivers) or from the exploitation of the non-living resources on the sea-bed. Second, article 196(1) requires states to "take all measures necessary to prevent, reduce and control pollution of the marine environment resulting from … the intentional or accidental introduction of species, alien or new, to a particular part of the marine environment, which may cause significant and harmful changes thereto." It seems that the words "resulting from" are intended to qualify the introduction of new or alien species as 'pollution of the marine environment' or at least that it be treated as such. Regardless of the correctness of this interpretation, article 196(1) clearly imposes an obligation on states to prevent, reduce and control significant and harmful changes to the marine environment caused by the introduction of new or alien species. It is noteworthy that the IMO 2004 Ballast Water Convention, discussed below in paragraphs 49-50 of this chapter, does not refer to pollution.

b) Fish Stocks Agreement and other Developments

34. Even though UNCLOS was intended to be a Constitution for the Oceans, this did not mean that it was cast in stone. It was understood that the needs and interests of the international community would be constantly changing and that UNCLOS had to be adjusted accordingly. One such adjustment already took place before UNCLOS entered into force in 1994. The adjustment concerned the regime for the exploitation of the deep sea-bed in the area in part XI of UNCLOS. An important group of developed states that were expected to actually engage in such exploitation, including the United States, was dissatisfied with the regime. As these dissatisfied states were therefore unlikely to become parties to UNCLOS and would thereby effectively block universal acceptance and effectiveness, an Implementation Agreement was adopted in 1994 that met their concerns. This Agreement allowed for the current near-universal participation in UNCLOS.

35. In the early 1990s, the international community agreed that something needed to be done concerning international cooperation in the conservation and management of straddling fish stocks and highly migratory fish stocks. This eventually led to the adoption of the United Nations Agreement for the Implementation of the Provisions of the United Nations Convention on the Law of the Sea of 10 December 1982 relating to the Conservation and Management of Straddling

Fish Stocks and Highly Migratory Fish Stocks ("1995 Fish Stocks Agreement") in New York, on 4 August 1995. The 1995 Fish Stocks Agreement entered into force on 11 December 2001, and has currently 56 parties (as of September 2005). The 1995 Fish Stocks Agreement only deals with straddling and highly migratory fish stocks, and therefore not with the other categories of species in articles 63(1) and 65-68 and discrete high seas species. However, some of the provisions and concepts in the 1995 Fish Stocks Agreement would be very useful for the international management and conservation of some of these categories of species as well. Some of these provisions could even be argued as already being part of customary international law.

36. The 1995 Fish Stocks Agreement does not fundamentally change the balance of rights of UNCLOS between coastal states and states that fish on the high seas. As the full title of the Agreement reveals, it implements certain provisions of UNCLOS. While building on the balance of rights of UNCLOS, it makes the obligations of states broader, stronger and more detailed. In addition, part VIII of the 1995 Fish Stocks Agreement contains a robust dispute settlement procedure which is largely linked to the similarly robust procedure of UNCLOS.

37. The widening of the obligations is, among other things, evident in the obligation to apply the precautionary approach and to protect marine biodiversity under articles 5(c) and 5(g) of the Agreement. The precautionary approach is described in article 6, noting that "The absence of adequate scientific information shall not be used as a reason for postponing or failing to take conservation and management measures." The remainder of the provision, as well as Annex II, give states very detailed guidance on how the precautionary approach needs to be implemented. The 1995 Fish Stocks Agreement places marine capture fisheries in a much wider context in comparison with UNCLOS. In addition to the need to take account of associated and dependent species, paragraphs (d), (e) and (f) of article 5 require states to take account of a wide range of ecosystem considerations, for instance assessing the impacts of non-fisheries activities on target stocks, minimizing pollution, waste, discards, catch by lost or abandoned gear and catch of non-target species. Together, the provisions require states to pursue a much more holistic approach to fisheries management. This is undoubtedly a significant advance of international law, even though the real litmus test remains, as always, implementation at the national and regional level.

38. The strengthening of obligations is, among other things, reflected in the concept of compatibility. Accordingly, article 7 stipulates that the conservation and management measures that the coastal state applies in its EEZ with respect to straddling and highly migratory fish stocks should be compatible with the conservation and management measures applied by states fishing on the high seas for those stocks. Moreover, article 8 firmly recognizes the role of the Regional Fisheries Management Organizations ("RFMOs") as international vehicles for fisheries governance. Only states that are members of RFMOs or that cooperate with them "shall have access to the fishery resources" (paragraph (4)). While this is a treaty provision that applies in principle only between states that are parties to the 1995 Fish Stocks Agreement, many RFMOs already take measures against non-cooperating states.

39. Article 312 of UNCLOS contains a procedure for the amendment of the Convention that can be used after it has been in force for ten years. As the article 312 procedure has become available in 2004, the international community is currently looking at issues that would be suitable for such a procedure. It should be observed, however, that the two implementation agreements of 1994 and 1995 show that there are alternatives to this procedure. Regarding marine biodiversity, there were already some calls to negotiate a more comprehensive regime to ensure high seas biodiversity or a more specific regime for high seas fishing or deep-sea fishing, as well as a specific instrument on biodiversity and genetic resources of the deep sea-bed.

c) Convention on Biological Diversity

40. The Convention on Biological Diversity ("CBD") was negotiated under the auspices of UNEP, adopted in 1992 and entered into force on 29 December 1993. It has 188 parties (as of November 2005), therefore, its application is even more universal than UNCLOS. CBD is one of the outcomes of the United Nations Conference on Environment and Development, held in Rio de Janeiro in 1992, and establishes a global legally binding framework for the conservation of biodiversity, the sustainable use of its components and the fair and equitable sharing of the benefits arising out of the utilization of genetic resources. Since the Convention on Biological Diversity is examined in Chapter 15 above, this chapter's discussion focuses on the applicability of CBD to marine biodiversity, as well as relevant implementation efforts by its governing body, the Conference of Parties ("COP") and its Subsidiary Body on Scientific, Technical and Technological Advice ("SBSTTA").

41. The applicability of CBD to marine biodiversity is primarily determined by articles 4 and 22. Article 22 on 'Relationship with other International Conventions' stipulates in paragraph (1) that the Convention shall not affect rights and obligations under other existing international agreements except where their exercise "would cause a serious damage or threat to biological diversity." Paragraph (2) determines that parties to the CBD "shall implement this Convention with respect to the marine environment consistently with the rights and obligations of States under the law of the sea." Whereas paragraph (1) could be regarded as establishing the supremacy of biodiversity obligations, paragraph (2) ensures that this supremacy does not affect the balance between rights and obligations (or jurisdictional balance) within the law of the sea, most importantly UNCLOS. It does not say that the rights and obligations under the law of the sea are not constrained by the supremacy of biodiversity obligations; which they are! But the threshold of "serious damage or threat" ensures that this supremacy is not automatic. The manner in which they are constrained is indicated by article 4 on 'Jurisdictional Scope'. This provision effectively distinguishes between 'areas within the limits of national jurisdiction' and beyond.

42. Beyond the limits of national jurisdiction, *inter alia*, the high seas and the area, only the CBD provisions on processes and activities carried out under the jurisdiction or control of states are applicable. Fishing on the high seas is an obvious example of such an activity. Flag states that become parties to the CBD thereby accept certain obligations in relation to fishing by their nationals, both natural and juridical, and vessels on the high seas. The limitation mentioned at the outset is a significant one as the CBD's obligations on processes and activities contained in articles 3, 5, 7(c) and 8(l) are not very specific. Article 3 obliges states "to ensure that activities within their jurisdiction or control do not cause damage to the environment of other States or of areas beyond the limits of national jurisdiction." The wording of this obligation is similar to that in article 194(2) of the UNCLOS Convention. However, the biodiversity-focus of the CBD means that the term "environment" has a broader meaning here in comparison with the UNCLOS Convention. The obligation has therefore broadened as well. Article 7(c) of the CBD requires states to "identify processes and categories of activities which have or are likely to have significant adverse impacts on the conservation and sustainable use of biological diversity, and monitor their effects through sampling and other techniques." Article 8(l) requires states to regulate or manage processes and activities where a significant adverse effect on biological diversity has

been determined pursuant to article 7. These three provisions are complemented by article 5, which obliges states to cooperate "in respect of areas beyond national jurisdiction and on other matters of mutual interest, for the conservation and sustainable use of biological diversity."

43. In areas within the limits of national jurisdiction, which, *inter alia*, include the EEZ and the legal continental shelf, the provisions of the CBD are fully applicable. That is, they apply to components of biodiversity (for example a particular species or habitat) as well as to processes and activities carried out under the jurisdiction or control of states. With regard to processes and activities, the obligations identified in paragraph 42 of this chapter are applicable. Regarding components of biodiversity, the provisions of the CBD apply in principle in a similar way to the marine environment as to the terrestrial environment. The discussion in chapter 15 above would therefore be just as relevant to the maritime zones of coastal states. States are required, for example, by article 6 to "develop national strategies, plans or programmes for the conservation and sustainable use of biological diversity" and to integrate these, as far as possible and as appropriate, into relevant sectoral or cross-sectoral plans, programmes and policies. Moreover, article 7 lays down identification and monitoring obligations, and article 8 obligations on 'in-situ conservation,' for example, through the establishment of a network of protected areas where measures apply to conserve one or more components of biodiversity, or by preventing the introduction of, controlling or eradicating alien species which threaten ecosystems, habitats or species.

44. As a framework convention, the CBD needed further implementation efforts to tailor it to concrete issues and to set priorities. For this purpose, the COP has so far developed seven Thematic Programmes and fourteen Cross-Cutting Issues, which are integrated into the Thematic Programmes. The Thematic Programme on the Conservation and Sustainable Use of Marine and Coastal Biological Diversity (Jakarta Mandate) was adopted by Decision II/10 at COP-2 (1995). The programme of work for the Jakarta Mandate was first adopted at COP-4 (1998) but has been elaborated at later COPs, most recently at COP-7 (2004). The programme of work aims at assisting the implementation of the Jakarta Mandate at the national, regional and global levels. It identifies key operational objectives, priority activities and time-schedules within each of the five programme elements: (1) integrated marine and coastal area management, (2) marine and coastal living resources, (3) marine and coastal protected areas,

(4) mariculture, and (5) alien species and genotypes. A specific work plan on coral bleaching has been integrated into programme element (2). At this time, the Jakarta Mandate does not seriously address the shortcoming identified above, namely the non-applicability of the CBD to components of biodiversity beyond the limits of national jurisdiction. However, the Decision VII/5 'Marine and Coastal Biodiversity, adopted at COP-7 (2004), could be seen as a modest first step to address this in relation to the conservation and sustainable use of deep sea-bed genetic resources.

45. The cross-cutting issues that seem especially relevant to the Jakarta Mandate are the Ecosystem Approach, Protected Areas and Alien Species. Important COP decisions on these Cross-Cutting Issues include: Decision V/6 of COP-5 (2000) 'Ecosystem Approach', which contains a description (instead of a definition), offers operational guidance and recommends the application of 12 principles of the ecosystem approach; a Decision VII/11 on 'Ecosystem Approach' adopted at COP-7, whose Annex contains a refinement and elaboration of the ecosystem approach and annotations to the 12 ecosystem principles; the Decision VII/5 on 'Marine and Coastal Biodiversity' adopted at COP-7 (2004) which gives higher priority to marine protected areas, both within and beyond areas of national jurisdiction; the Decision VII/28 on 'Protected Areas (articles 8(A) to (E))' adopted at COP-7, whose Annex lays down a Programme of Work on Protected Areas; and Decision VI/23 of COP-6 (2002) 'Alien Species that threaten Ecosystems, Habitats or Species,' whose Annex contains 'Guiding Principles for the Prevention, Introduction and Mitigation of Impacts of Alien Species that threaten Ecosystems, Habitats or Species.'

46. The further implementation of the CBD at the national, regional and global levels goals is also addressed in Decision VI/26, by which COP-6 adopted the Strategic Plan for the Convention on Biological Diversity ("Strategic Plan"). The Strategic Plan's mission is "to achieve by 2010 a significant reduction of the current rate of biodiversity loss at the global, regional and national level as a contribution to poverty alleviation and to the benefit of all life on earth." It also identifies various strategic goals and objectives. In relation to subgoals 1.1-1.3 on international cooperation, mention should also be made of the Decision on 'Cooperation with other Conventions and International Organizations and Initiatives,' adopted at COP-7. The general issue of cooperation between the CBD and other international organizations is discussed in Chapter

15 of this Manual. In the context of marine biodiversity, the CBD cooperates with global organizations like the FAO and with regional organizations such as the OSPAR Commission (see below) and other regional seas agreements, as well as with RFMOs.

d) Global Conventions on Marine Pollution

47. Chapter 13 on marine pollution discusses a number of global conventions aimed at the prevention, reduction and control of marine pollution. As noted in paragraph 32 above, however, these conventions are not specifically aimed at the protection and preservation of marine biodiversity, even though their effective implementation may lead to significant benefits in that regard. There are nevertheless some exceptions to this general rule. For instance, MARPOL 73/78 uses a system of special areas in which more stringent discharge and emission standards for polluting substances apply. The designation of such special areas and the more stringent standards could be justified on account of the need to protect marine biodiversity.

48. Also, a coastal state or a group of coastal states that have identified an area within their EEZ where marine biodiversity is threatened by international merchant shipping could ask the International Maritime Organization ("IMO") to designate this area as a Particularly Sensitive Sea Area ("PSSA") and have one or more associated protective measures applied therein. Appropriate protective measures could, for instance, be the designation of areas to be avoided or precautionary areas. As there is no exhaustive list of these measures, states could propose innovatory measures as well. Most of these measures would also be available without PSSA identification but not without IMO approval. In recent years, the IMO bodies with competence to approve such protective measures have appeared to be both pragmatic and broad-minded. This is reflected in the adoption of a ship reporting system aimed at avoiding ship strikes of the North Atlantic right whale off the Atlantic coast of the United States and the 'no-anchoring area' to protect coral reefs in the Flower Garden Banks Marine Sanctuary in the United States EEZ in the Gulf of Mexico. Neither of these measures was linked to a PSSA.

49. In February 2004 the International Convention for the Control and Management of Ships' Ballast Water and Sediments ("2004 Ballast Water Convention") was adopted within the IMO. The Convention is made up of 22 articles and a single

Annex consisting of Regulations and two Appendices. Pursuant to its core obligation in article 2(1), states are obliged to give full and complete effect to all provisions in order to prevent, minimize and ultimately eliminate the transfer of harmful aquatic organisms and pathogens through the control and management of ships' ballast water and sediments. Article 1(8) defines 'harmful aquatic organisms and pathogens' as "aquatic organisms and pathogens which, if introduced into the sea including estuaries, or into fresh water courses, may create hazards to the environment, human health, property or resources, impair biological diversity or interfere with other legitimate uses of such areas". This explicit reference to "biological diversity" is probably the first of its kind in an IMO convention. As was already noted in paragraph 33 above, the 2004 Ballast Water Convention does not address impacts of ballast water in terms of pollution. This is also why it was regarded as inappropriate to lay down its substance in an Annex to MARPOL 73/78. Treatment in this subsection on 'Global Conventions on Marine Pollution' is therefore not strictly correct.

50. The 2004 Ballast Water Convention, which has not entered into force yet, establishes a minimum level of regulation for certain types of ships that carry ballast water. Among other things, ships are to have on board and implement a Ballast Water Management Plan, to carry a Ballast Water Record Book and to meet ballast water management requirements. The latter necessitates existing ships to meet ballast water exchange standards and new ships to meet performance standards or alternatives that offer equal levels of protection. Vessels using the ballast water exchange method should not discharge ballast water within 200 nautical miles from the nearest land or in waters with depths lower than 200 meters and must meet an efficiency of at least 95% volumetric exchange (Regulations B-4 and D-1). Interestingly, article 2(3) and Section C of the Annex allow states individually or in concert to regulate more stringently above this minimum level. The extent to which this Convention contributes to global uniformity in the regulation of international merchant shipping therefore remains to be seen. This concern is especially pertinent as IMO conventions take a long time to enter into force, and this convention is not expected to be any different. The residual regulatory competence of states pursuant to article 2(3) and Section C not only acknowledges existing mandatory and voluntary regulation but also that further regulation does not have to await entry into force of the Convention.

e) International Convention for the Regulation of Whaling

51. The International Convention for the Regulation of Whaling ("1946 ICRW") is presently the only instrument at the global level that deals specifically with both the conservation and utilization of marine living resources. The Preamble to the 1946 ICRW identifies this dual purpose as "to provide for the proper conservation of whale stocks and thus make possible the orderly development of the whaling industry." The ICRW was adopted on 2 December 1946 and came into force on 10 December 1948. The negotiation of the ICRW built on the 1937 International Agreement for the Regulation of Whaling and its 1938 and 1945 Protocols. At the time of writing, there were 51 states parties to the 1946 ICRW. The Schedule attached to the 1946 ICRW and which is an integral part of it contains the agreed definitions and technical conservation and management measures.

52. Marine mammals can be grouped together in three orders: the Cetacea (whales, dolphins and porpoises), the Sirenia (dugongs, manatees and seacows) and the Carnivoria (sea otters and polar bears and the species belonging to the Pinnipedia (seals, sea lions and walruses)). As most commentators regard the species coverage of the ICRW as being limited to baleen whales and large toothed whales (paragraph I of the Schedule), smaller types of whales, such as dolphins and porpoises and species from the other orders of marine mammals are excluded. Many of these species nevertheless fall within the coverage of the Convention on the Conservation of Migratory Species of Wild Animals ("CMS"). The CMS is largely a framework instrument which relies for its implementation on the creation of regulatory instruments at the regional level. In contrast with the ICRW's dual objectives of conservation and utilization, these regional instruments have so far been primarily or exclusively concerned with conservation. Chapter 14 above deals in detail with the CMS and the regional instruments that have been adopted under it.

53. 1946 ICRW predates UNCLOS by several decades. It is therefore no surprise that the coverage of the ICRW is not influenced by the division of the oceans in the maritime zones and the rights of coastal states and flag states therein as recognized by UNCLOS. 1946 ICRW "applies to factory ships, land stations and whale catchers under the jurisdiction of the Contracting Governments and to all waters in which whaling is prosecuted by such factory ships, land stations and whale catchers" as provided by article I(2). However, it should be realized that the ICRW does not affect the sovereign rights of coastal states over marine mammals in their EEZs under article 65 of UNCLOS. This means that whether or not a coastal state is a party to 1946 ICRW, it has a right under article 65 to regulate the exploitation of marine mammals more strictly than the ICRW. If, for instance, 1946 ICRW would in the future allow commercial whaling in the Indian Ocean, a coastal state like India could nevertheless prohibit all whaling within its EEZ. The reverse is not possible. That is, a party to the ICRW cannot authorize whaling in its own EEZ by invoking article 65 of UNCLOS if it is also legally bound to a ban on whaling under 1946 ICRW.

54. 1946 ICRW establishes the International Whaling Commission ("IWC") as its regulatory body. The main duty of the IWC is to review and revise as necessary the measures laid down in the Schedule that governs the conduct of whaling throughout the world. These measures, among other things, provide for the complete protection of certain species; designate specified areas as whale sanctuaries (for example, the Indian Ocean Sanctuary established in 1979 and the Southern Ocean Sanctuary established in 1994); set limits on the numbers and size of whales which may be taken; prescribe open and closed seasons and areas for whaling; and prohibit the capture of suckling calves and female whales accompanied by calves (see article V(1)). Parties to 1946 ICRW are required by article IX(1) to take appropriate measures to ensure the application of the provisions of this Convention and the punishment of infractions of its provisions in operations carried out by persons or by vessels under its jurisdiction. This will require states to enact the necessary national legislation.

55. As the IWC has become a highly politicized body where decisions are often not just based on science but also on political and cultural grounds, it is useful to look at the ICRW's decision-making procedures. Each contracting party to 1946 ICRW has one member in the IWC and one vote, as provided under article III(1). The IWC meets once a year in one of its member states to amend the Schedule. The core-decisions under article V(1) must be taken by a three-fourths majority; other decisions are taken by a simple majority, as required under article III(2). There is also an 'opting-out' procedure under article V(3), which enables parties to avoid becoming legally bound to amendments that were adopted with the necessary majority. This procedure currently allows, for instance, Norway to be legally engaged in

commercial whaling despite the general moratorium on commercial whaling that is in force. The IWC is assisted by a Scientific Committee, which assesses the status of the world's whale stocks and offers the IWC advice on the need for regulation. However, the IWC is not bound by that advice.

56. In the last decade, the Scientific Committee has also recognized the need for scientific research on the effects of environmental change on whales. The need to place the management and conservation of whales in a broader ecosystem context has, among other things, led to several workshops (including one on the interactions between whales and fish stocks), research programmes, and closer cooperation with the Secretariat of the CMS and the Commission for the Conservation of Antarctic Marine Living Resources ("CCAMLR"). At its 55th Annual Meeting in 2003, the IWC adopted the Berlin Initiative on Strengthening the Conservation Agenda of the International Whaling Commission, which established a permanent Conservation Committee. The efforts of this Committee may strengthen the conservation agenda of the IWC and place whaling in a broader ecosystem context. In 2001, the IWC recognized the importance of habitat protection and integrated coastal zone management for whales and urged states to take appropriate action within and under relevant international conventions.

57. Marine mammals have relatively low levels of reproduction and this especially holds true for large whales. Intensive hunting therefore brings a high risk of over-exploitation, the collapse of stocks and even extinction. By the late 1970s, there was a well-founded concern that centuries of whaling had brought most of the large whale species to the brink of extinction. In 1982, the IWC eventually agreed to a pause in commercial whaling on all whale stocks from the 1985/86 season onwards. This moratorium on commercial whaling has been in effect ever since. In the meantime, the IWC has developed a Revised Management Procedure ("RMP") which seeks to ensure that once the moratorium is lifted, sufficient account is taken of the high risks to over-exploitation and thereby loss to marine biodiversity. The moratorium will not be lifted until the completion of the Revised Management Scheme ("RMS"), which complements the RMP on matters of supervision, control and data-gathering to ensure that catch limits are not exceeded. Currently, the RMS appears to be nearing completion.

58. Today, whaling still continues despite the moratorium on commercial whaling. Some whaling is allowed for the purpose of aboriginal subsistence whaling, for example, in Greenland, the Russian Federation, St. Vincent and the Grenadines and the United States. Moreover, Norway continues commercial whaling on the northeast Atlantic minke whale stock after Norway opted-out of the moratorium; and both Iceland and Japan are engaged in scientific whaling pursuant to article VIII of 1946 ICRW. These three states are continuously criticized for their whaling activities. Finally, small numbers of large whales are occasionally taken by nationals of states that are not parties to 1946 ICRW.

59. It is difficult to predict what will happen with the IWC in the future, even in the near future. It is hard to deny that some stocks of some of the large whale species would allow limited commercial whaling. Some argue, however, that even if this were true, shortcomings in monitoring and control would inevitably lead to excess catches of authorized stocks and illegal catches of stocks for which the moratorium would still apply. The polarization of the IWC in a pro-whaling and an anti-whaling camp is, however, more than anything caused by cultural and political factors. Some members of the IWC have openly stated that they will never agree on a resumption of commercial whaling under any circumstances. At the closure of the 55th Annual IWC Meeting in 2003, a group of 17 members, including Iceland, Japan and Norway, issued a statement in which they concluded that the establishment of the Conservation Committee and the failure to adopt the RMS have "provoked an increased interest in examination of alternatives that would provide for the sustainable use of abundant whale resources." But as the IWC's collapse has been predicted so often in the past already, only time will tell. The key to a healthy IWC lies in the diligence by which the participating states respect each other's views and legitimate rights and interests in light of the overarching need for conservation of whale species.

60. One global instrument that should not be left unmentioned here is the Convention on International Trade in Endangered Species of Wild Fauna and Flora ("CITES"). Trade regulation by CITES can complement the efforts in the protection and preservation of marine biodiversity of the IWC and RFMOs. Chapter 14 above deals in detail with CITES while specific aspects, such as trade, are alluded to in other chapters and in particular chapter 24 on Trade and Environment.

2. Regional Legally Binding Instruments

a) Regional Fisheries Management Organizations

61. As most fish stocks are not confined to the maritime zones of a single coastal state, management and conservation needs to take place at the bilateral, regional or sub-regional level. The framework character of the UNCLOS and the Fish Stocks Agreement envisages this as well. Article 8 of the Fish Stocks Agreement clearly confirmed the international community's preference for RFMOs as the appropriate international vehicles for fisheries governance. There are currently more than 30 international fisheries bodies. However, not all of these have a management mandate that allows them to determine a TAC or allocate the TAC between the participating states. The fisheries bodies established under article VI(1) and (2) of the Constitution of the United Nations Food and Agriculture Organization have, for instance, merely an advisory role. Other bodies only have a scientific advisory role, such as the International Council for the Exploration of the Sea ("ICES"). Table 1 lists some of the main RFMOs.

a general observation, however, many RFMOs take account of associated and dependent species as required by the UNCLOS Convention but only CCAMLR and the IBSFC take a more holistic, ecosystem-oriented approach.

i. International Convention for the Conservation of Atlantic Tunas

63. The International Convention for the Conservation of Atlantic Tunas ("1966 ICCAT") was adopted on 14 May 1966, and entered into force on 21 March 1969. The 1992 Protocol with the new calculation scheme for annual financial contributions had not yet entered into force at the time of writing. There were 40 contracting parties to 1966 ICCAT at the time of writing. In addition, the special status known as 'Cooperating Party, Entity or Fishing Entity' was created, which was enjoyed by Chinese Taipei (Taiwan) at the time of writing.

64. The objective of 1966 ICCAT, as stated in the Preamble, is to maintain the populations of tunas and tuna-like fishes caught in the Convention Area at levels which will permit the maximum sustainable catch, or yield for food and other

---

Table 1: Some Regional Fisheries Management Organizations

- Commission for the Conservation of Antarctic Marine Living Resources ("CCAMLR")
- Commission for the Conservation of Southern Bluefin Tuna ("CCSBT")
- General Fisheries Commission for the Mediterranean ("GFCM")
- Inter-American Tropical Tuna Commission ("IATTC")
- International Baltic Sea Fishery Commission ("IBSFC ")
- International Commission for the Conservation of Atlantic Tunas ("ICCAT")
- Indian Ocean Tuna Commission ("IOTC")
- International Pacific Halibut Commission ("IPHC")
- Northwest Atlantic Fisheries Organization ("NAFO")
- North Atlantic Salmon Conservation Organization ("NASCO")
- North-East Atlantic Fisheries Commission ("NEAFC")
- North Pacific Anadromous Fish Commission ("NPAFC")
- Pacific Salmon Commission ("PSC")
- South East Atlantic Fisheries Organization ("SEAFO")*
- Western and Central Pacific Fisheries Commission ("WCPFC")*

Constitutive instrument in force but Commission not yet fully operational

---

62. While all the RFMOs that are listed in Table 1 have management powers, there are numerous important differences between them. These differences relate to, among other things, their geographical scope of operation, the type or categories of species for which they have competence and their management and conservation mandates. To illustrate some of these differences, two of these RFMOs will be discussed in more detail. These are ICCAT and CCAMLR. As

purposes. The Preamble and article IV of 1966 ICCAT stipulate that the species covered by the Convention are the tuna and tuna-like species and such other species of fish exploited in tuna fishing in the Convention area that are not under the auspices of any other international organization. About 30 species are of direct concern, including yellowfin, skipjack, bigeye, albacore and bluefin tuna. The Convention applies to "all waters of the Atlantic Ocean, including the adjacent Seas" (such as the Mediterranean Sea and the Caribbean Sea). There is no precise definition in terms of longitude and latitude.

65. 1966 ICCAT establishes as its main regulatory body the International Commission for the Conservation of Atlantic Tunas ("Tunas Commission"). While the Tunas Commission takes decisions by a simple majority, as provided by article III(3), there is also an opting-out procedure under article VIII(3). The Tunas Commission works through a variety of Committees, Subcommittees, Working Groups and Panels, which deal with a wide range of issues, such as stock assessment, compliance and allocation.

66. The recommendations adopted by the Commission include TACs, minimum size limits and vessel effort limitations. The Tunas Commission has also introduced statistical documentation programmes for swordfish, and bigeye and bluefin tuna. These programmes require contracting parties to ensure that imports of these species are accompanied by validated statistical documents. The Tunas Commission occasionally also imposes import prohibitions on consignments from non-complying states. The research mandate of the Tunas Commission encompasses the oceanography of the environment in which the target species live and the effects of natural and human factors upon their abundance, as provided by article IV(1). While the Tunas Commission compiled data on by-catch, principally for certain species of sharks, there has been little progress towards ecosystem-oriented management. However, two Resolutions adopted by the Tunas Commission in 2003 may change this. Resolution 03-10, 'On the Shark Fishery,' is aimed at supporting the implementation of FAO's 1999 International Plan of Action for the Conservation and Management of Sharks and requests data on directed shark fishing carried out in the 1966 ICCAT Convention area. Resolution 03-11, 'On Sea Turtles,' calls for data collection on interactions between sea turtles in the Tunas Commission fisheries and on impacts on sea turtles in the 1966 ICCAT Convention area, and supports FAO's efforts towards a more holistic approach on the management and conservation of sea turtles.

ii. Convention on the Conservation of Antarctic Marine Living Resources

67. The Convention on the Conservation of Antarctic Marine Living Resources ("1980 CAMLR") was adopted on 20 May 1980, and entered into force on 7 April 1982. At the time of writing, there were 32 parties to the CAMLR Convention, 24 of which were Members of the convention's regulatory body, the Commission for the Conservation of Antarctic Marine Living Resources ("CCAMLR").

68. The objective of 1980 CAMLR the "conservation of Antarctic marine living resources," while "the term 'conservation' includes rational use," as provided by article II. Paragraph (3) of article II lists the three principles of conservation that are to be observed for harvesting and other activities in the CAMLR Convention Area. Even though these principles are not named, it is generally accepted that they embrace ecosystem-based (fisheries) management and a precautionary approach avant la lettre. This addresses the concerns that led to the negotiation of the convention, namely that large-scale krill harvesting would threaten the Antarctic marine ecosystem as a whole. In view of the relatively low biodiversity and the few trophic levels in the Southern Ocean, an ecosystem approach was a logical choice and - it was probably expected - also a relatively feasible one. After more than 20 years after 1980 CAMLR entered into force, it appears that this expectation was optimistic. Today, CCAMLR is nevertheless widely credited for its efforts in ecosystem-based fisheries management and is regarded as the leading RFMO in this respect. Among CCAMLR's successes in this context are its measures to minimize by-catch of birds, in particular albatrosses and petrels, in long-line fishing and CCAMLR's Ecosystem Monitoring Program ("CEMP").

69. 1980 CAMLR applies to Antarctic marine living resources, which are defined in article I as "the populations of fin fish, molluscs, crustaceans and all other species of living organisms, including birds, found south of the Antarctic Convergence." Article IV recognizes the primacy of the International Convention for the Regulation of Whaling and the Convention on the Conservation of Antarctic Seals in relation to whaling and sealing. The main fisheries that took place at the time of writing targeted Patagonian and Antarctic toothfish, krill and mackerel icefish. While the estimates of the total annual removals of toothfish in recent years indicate a serious risk of over-exploitation of some or all stocks, the annual catches of krill have remained well below the annual TAC. This is not to say that technological innovations and changing market forces may not bring an end to the under-utilization of the krill resources in the future.

70. Under article I, the geographical scope of 1980 CAMLR includes large areas north of the Antarctic Treaty Area (south of 60° South latitude) and is based on an approximation of the Antarctic Convergence, which separates the warmer northern waters from the cooler southern waters. The CAMLR Convention Area is therefore regarded as one of the few RFMOs whose regulatory area largely overlaps with that of a Large Marine Ecosystem ("LME"), with all the consequential

advantages that should offer for ecosystem-based management. In reality, however, several species managed by CCAMLR also occur outside the Convention Area. The actual and alleged occurrence of Patagonian toothfish outside the Convention Area has in recent years caused serious difficulties in combating illegal, unreported and unregulated fishing for this species.

71. CCAMLR is charged with giving effect to the Convention's objective and principles of conservation. The various ways by which it can fulfill its mandate are listed in paragraph (1) of article IX. These include facilitating research, compiling data, adopting and reviewing conservation measures. The non-exhaustive list of types of Conservation Measures in paragraph (2) of article IX include the designation of TACs, protected species and open and closed seasons for harvesting.

72. CCAMLR takes decisions by consensus on matters of substance while on other matters decisions are taken by a simple majority of the Members present and voting as required by article XII(1) and (2). To accommodate members that do not want to oppose consensus, but nevertheless want to avoid becoming legally bound by Conservation Measures, article IX(6)(c) and (d) of 1980 CAMLR contains an opting-out procedure. Instead of blocking consensus, members often prefer to voice their informal objections and concerns in Commission Reports. Consensus decision-making is a characteristic of the Antarctic Treaty System ("ATS"), of which CCAMLR is part. While the advantages and disadvantages of this method of decision-making are well known, the prospects for majority decision-making in the ATS are especially bleak in view of the sensitive Antarctic sovereignty issue. A state that becomes party to 1980 CAMLR or even a Member of CCAMLR, but not party to the Antarctic Treaty, should realize that CCAMLR is more than 'just' another RFMO. This is evident in article IV of 1980 CAMLR, which makes the agreement to disagree as laid down in article IV of the Antarctic Treaty applicable to states that are parties to 1980 CAMLR, and reiterates its substance.

73. The Commission is assisted by a Scientific Committee, whose recommendations and advice must be taken fully into account as provided by article IX(4). This leaves the Commission a margin of discretion that is quite common in RFMOs. Since 1980 CAMLR came into force, the Commission has established two permanent subcommittees: the Standing Committee on Administration and Finance ("SCAF") and the Standing Committee on Implementation and Compliance ("SCIC"). The Secretariat of 1980 CAMLR is based in Hobart, Australia, which is also the venue for all the annual meetings of the Commission and the Scientific Committee. The challenges for CCAMLR in the future are likely to be related on the one side to its ambitious commitment to ecosystem-based fisheries management and on the other side to dealing with illegal, unreported and unregulated fishing, which at the time of writing was carried out by ships flying the flag of both parties and non-parties to 1980 CAMLR.

b) Regional Seas Agreements

74. Regional seas agreements have been extensively examined in Chapter 13 above with respect to their provisions on the protection and preservation of the marine environment from pollution. However, some of these agreements also have provisions that relate more specifically to the protection and preservation of marine biodiversity. Two of these are discussed below for illustrative purposes.

i. Convention for the Protection and Development of the Marine Environment of the Wider Caribbean Region (Cartagena Convention)

75. The Convention for the Protection and Development of the Marine Environment of the Wider Caribbean Region ("Cartagena Convention") has been discussed in detail in Chapter 13. It establishes a broadly oriented framework for cooperation on the protection and development of the marine environment of the Wider Caribbean Region. The Preamble to the Cartagena Convention identifies "the protection of the ecosystems of the marine environment of the wider Caribbean region" as one of its principal objectives and recognizes the need to strive for sustainable development. In furtherance of these objectives, article 10 requires parties to "individually or jointly, take all appropriate measures to protect and preserve rare or fragile ecosystems, as well as the habitat of depleted, threatened or endangered species, in the Convention area." This wording is clearly inspired by article 194(5) of UNCLOS. Article 10 of the Cartagena Convention complements these provisions by stating, "To this end, the Contracting Parties shall endeavour to establish protected areas." However, the activities that would need to be regulated in these protected areas are not indicated. Although the primary focus of the Cartagena Convention is pollution, nothing in the Convention prevents the parties from imposing restrictions on harvesting of marine living resources in these protected areas.

76. Evidence of a focus that is broader than pollution is the Protocol concerning Specially Protected Areas and Wildlife in the Wider Caribbean Region ("SPAW Protocol"). The SPAW Protocol was adopted on 18 January 1990, and entered into force on 18 June 2000. While article 3(1) of the SPAW Protocol essentially repeats the obligation articulated under article 10 of the Cartagena Convention, article 5(2) contains a long list of activities that should, where appropriate, be regulated. This list includes vessel-source pollution, dumping, navigation, fishing, introducing non-indigenous species, tourism, and "any other measure aimed at conserving, protecting or restoring natural processes, ecosystems or populations for which the protected areas were established."

ii. OSPAR Convention

77. The Convention for the Protection of the Marine Environment of the North-East Atlantic ("1992 OSPAR Convention") was adopted on 22 September 1992, and entered into force on 25 March 1998. The 1992 OSPAR Convention consists of a Preamble and Articles, five Annexes and three Appendices. Annexes I-III deal with pollution from various sources, Annex IV deals with the assessment of the quality of the marine environment and, most relevant for our purpose, Annex V concerns 'the protection and conservation of the ecosystems and biological diversity of the maritime area,' while Appendix 3 contains 'criteria for identifying human activities for the purpose of Annex V.' Annex V and Appendix 3 were adopted in 1998, and entered into force on 30 August 2000. At the time of writing, the 16 contracting parties to the Convention were Belgium, Denmark, the EU, Germany, Finland, France, Iceland, Ireland, Luxembourg, the Netherlands, Norway, Portugal, Spain, Sweden, Switzerland and the United Kingdom. Of these, Belgium, France, and Portugal were not yet parties to Annex V and Appendix 3.

78. Geographically, the 1992 OSPAR Convention applies to the 'Maritime area', which is defined in article 1(a) as the marine waters (including internal waters) of the North-East Atlantic, excluding the Baltic Sea and the Belts and the Mediterranean Sea and its dependent seas. Article 2(1)(a) contains the core obligation, which is for contracting parties "to prevent and eliminate pollution and ... to protect the maritime area against the adverse effects of human activities so as to safeguard human health and to conserve marine ecosystems and, when practicable, restore marine areas which have been adversely affected." The OSPAR Commission is established to facilitate and supervise the implementation of this objective. As article 4 of Annex V recognizes, the competence of the Commission does not extend to vessel-source pollution and fisheries, for which primacy lies with the IMO, the EU, ICCAT, the North Atlantic Salmon Conservation Organization ("NASCO") and the North-East Atlantic Fisheries Commission ("NEAFC"). Where the Commission has, for instance, through Quality Status Reports ("QSRs") drawn up pursuant to Annex IV, identified threats posed by these activities to marine ecosystems and marine biodiversity, it can do little else than bring these threats to the attention of these organizations. The 2000 QSR lists fisheries among the human activities with the most adverse impacts on the marine environment.

79. Annex V builds on the general obligation in article 2(a) of the 1992 OSPAR Convention "...to protect and conserve the ecosystems and the biological diversity in the maritime area..." It also serves to implement the 1992 Convention on Biological Diversity and its Jakarta Mandate at the regional level. Contracting parties are required, *inter alia*, to take the necessary measures in this regard to restore adversely affected marine areas and cooperate in adopting programmes and measures for the control of the human activities identified by the application of the criteria in Appendix 3. The OSPAR Commission is, among other things, charged with drawing up such programmes and measures, to gather relevant data on the impacts of human activities on ecosystems and biodiversity and to aim for an integrated ecosystem approach. OSPAR's Biological Diversity and Ecosystems Strategy, which was updated in 2003, provides the Commission further guidance on these tasks and sets priorities. Presently, these tasks are mainly carried out by the Biodiversity Committee ("BDC"). The main priorities include assessing which species and habitats need protection, assessing which human activities are likely to have an actual or potential adverse effect on these species and habitats or on ecological processes, and developing Ecological Quality Objectives, for which the North Sea has been selected as a pilot project. These will eventually have to culminate in programmes and measures designed to regulate human activities and restore areas.

80. Progress under Annex V so far includes the Texel-Faial criteria for the selection of threatened and declining species and habitats; the OSPAR List of Threatened and Declining Species and Habitats; the OSPAR Guidelines for the Identification and Selection of Marine Protected Areas in the OSPAR Maritime Area; the OSPAR Guidelines for the

Management of Marine Protected Areas in the OSPAR Maritime Area; and OSPAR Recommendation 2003/3 on a Network of Marine Protected Areas. The development of the latter network is carried out in cooperation with the Helsinki Commission (established under the Convention on the Protection of the Marine Environment of the Baltic Sea Area).

3. Global Non-Legally Binding Instruments

a) Rio Declaration and Agenda 21

81. The Rio Declaration and Agenda 21 are two non-legally binding instruments adopted by the international community at the 1992 UNCED. UNCED was another incremental step in the evolution of international environmental law. While the Rio Declaration contains general principles and objectives, Agenda 21, the Action Plan for the 21st Century, contains detailed guidance on their practical implementation. See also chapters 3 and 7 above.

82. Although general support existed as to the need to balance social, economic and environmental factors within the overarching objective of sustainable development, the interests of developed and developing states in the 1992 Rio Declaration differed significantly. While developed states lobbied strongly for the incorporation of Principles 10, 15 and 16 on public participation, precaution, and the polluter-pays principle, developing states insisted on Principles 3, 5, and 7, which emphasised the right of development, poverty alleviation and 'common but differentiated responsibilities'.

83. Agenda 21 is a massive document consisting of forty chapters. For our purposes, Chapter 15 on 'Conservation of Biological Diversity' and chapter 17 on 'Protection of the oceans, all kinds of seas, including enclosed and semi-enclosed seas, and coastal areas and the protection, rational use and development of their living resources' are especially relevant. Each Chapter usually consists of several programme areas, which are in turn broken down into a basis for action, objectives, activities, and/or means of implementation. Activities include management-related recommendations, data and information requirements, and requirements for international and regional coordination and cooperation. Means of implementation include financial and cost evaluations, scientific and technological means, human resource development and capacity building.

84. One of the main elements of Chapter 15 is its support for the Convention on Biological Diversity, which was adopted during UNCED. The states also committed themselves to its early entry into force. Paragraph 1 of chapter 17 refers to UNCLOS, thereby respecting its jurisdictional framework. Also noteworthy are paragraph 17.30(vi) which calls on the development of rules on ballast water exchange, paragraphs 17.50 and 17.80 which call for the conference which eventually culminated in the Fish Stocks Agreement; paragraph 17.54 on destructive fishing practices; and paragraph 17.75 which, inter alia, emphasises the need to preserve rare or fragile ecosystems.

b) FAO Code of Conduct for Responsible Fisheries

85. The Code of Conduct for Responsible Fisheries ("1995 FAO Code of Conduct") was adopted at the Twenty-eight Session of the FAO Conference on 31 October 1995. The drafting of the Code occurred parallel to the negotiations of the Fish Stocks Agreement and the 1993 FAO Agreement to promote Compliance with International Conservation and Management Measures by Fishing Vessels on the High Seas ("1993 FAO Compliance Agreement"). Care was taken to ensure that these three instruments would not contradict each other. In fact, the 1993 FAO Compliance Agreement forms an integral part of the Code of Conduct. Even though there are non-contradictory overlaps, the three instruments largely complement each other. The principal purpose of the FAO Code of Conduct is to offer practical guidance to states and all those involved in fisheries. The Code of Conduct is therefore essentially a 'Responsible Fisheries. How to do it?'

86. The scope of the FAO Code of Conduct is much broader than the Fish Stocks Agreement or the Compliance Agreement. First, it is not just limited to marine capture fisheries, but extends to all fisheries, including inland (freshwater) fishing and aquaculture. Consequently, unlike the Fish Stocks Agreement, its application is not limited to the EEZ and the high seas, but also extends to internal waters, territorial seas and archipelagic waters. Second, the guidance offered is not limited to aspects of conservation and management but also covers fisheries development, marketing, trade, energy use, food hygiene and quality, a safe working environment, marine pollution and integrated coastal zone management. Third, the FAO Code of Conduct is not just directed to states but also specifically at persons, financial institutions and vessel-owners and charterers.

87. As the Introduction to the Code already emphasizes, due respect for the ecosystem and biodiversity is fundamental to responsible fishing. Specific references to biodiversity occur in articles 6.6, 7.2.2(d), 8.4.8 and 12.10. But indirect acknowledgment of the importance of biodiversity is present throughout the code, for example in articles 2(i), 6.2, 6.5, 6.6, 7.2.2(g), 7.2.3, 7.5.2, by way of taking account of associated and dependent species and ecosystems and, of course, by way of striving for sustainable and responsible fishing.

88. Apart from implementation efforts by all those directly involved, including states, the implementation of the FAO Code of Conduct is also fostered by three other main processes. First, FAO's Committee on Fisheries ("COFI") monitors the implementation and application of the Code. Second, article 2(d) of the Code of Conduct envisages the development of international agreements in furtherance of the Code's objectives. So far, this has led to four non-legally binding International Plans of Action ("IPOAs"): the 1999 IPOA for Reducing Incidental Catch of Seabirds in Longline Fisheries, the 1999 IPOA on the Management of Fishing Capacity, the 1999 IPOA on the Management and Conservation of Sharks, and the 2001 IPOA to Prevent, Deter and Eliminate, Illegal, Unreported and Unregulated Fishing. Third, the FAO Fisheries Department has developed various technical guidelines in support of the implementation of the Code of Conduct, among them we can find, 'Fisheries Management'. The Ecosystem Approach to Fisheries,' was finalized in 2003.

c) Johannesburg Plan of Implementation

89. The 2002 World Summit on Sustainable Development was held in Johannesburg, South Africa, to assess the progress made in implementing Agenda 21 and to expedite the realization of the remaining goals. It culminated in two instruments: the Johannesburg Declaration on Sustainable Development ("Declaration") and the Johannesburg Plan of Implementation of the World Summit on Sustainable Development ("JPOI").

90. While the Declaration refers to the protection and management of the natural resource base for economic and social development as one of the overarching objectives, and to the protection of biodiversity as a basic requirement for humans, these issues appear to have less priority than for instance poverty eradication. The first substantive Chapter (II) of the JPOI is in fact devoted to the latter issue. Unlike Agenda 21, the JPOI does not have a separate chapter on oceans and seas. Issues

of marine biodiversity and sustainable fisheries are integrated into chapter IV 'Protecting and Managing the Natural Resource Base of Economic and Social Development,' in particular in paragraphs 29-34 and 42. These paragraphs advocate sustainable fisheries, integrated coastal and ocean management, the maintenance of the productivity and biodiversity of important and vulnerable marine and coastal areas as well as more specific actions, including adherence to international instruments and the establishment of marine protected areas. Target dates of 2010 and 2012 are set for the application of the ecosystems approach, a significant reduction in the current rate of loss of biological diversity and the establishment of representative networks of marine protected areas.

III. National Implementation

91. As stated in paragraph 4 above, international agreements usually require implementation at the national level to give effect to their provisions. This is commonly done by means of national legislation and some international agreements in fact specifically stipulate this. Therefore, this section presents three examples of national legislation, two implementing UNCLOS, and one the Convention on Biological Diversity, all related to the protection and preservation of marine biodiversity, including through sustainable fisheries.

a) China: Implementation of UNCLOS

92. China ratified UNCLOS on 7 June 1996, and thereby committed itself to act in accordance with the Convention and implement it by means of national legislation where required. In part, this has been achieved by China's Exclusive Economic Zone and Continental Shelf Act ("EEZ Act"), which was adopted on 26 June 1998 and came into force on the same day. By means of articles 2 and 3 of the Act, China establishes an EEZ and claims therein sovereign rights related to natural resources and other economic uses and jurisdiction for various purposes in accordance with articles 56 and 57 of the UNCLOS. Article 4 of the EEZ Act confirms China's sovereign rights and jurisdiction over its continental shelf. Articles 6 and 10-12 of the Act, the last three of which are reproduced below, claim rights that are relevant to the protection and preservation of marine biodiversity. Article 15 of the EEZ Act provides a basis for the Chinese Government to enact relevant regulations.

93. The State Oceanic Administration of China is one of the bodies entrusted with implementation of the EEZ Act. In collaboration with other governmental

---

**The People's Republic of China:
Law on the Exclusive Economic Zone and the Continental Shelf**

Article 10: "The competent authorities of the People's Republic of China shall have the right to take the necessary measures to prevent, reduce and control pollution of the marine environment and to protect and preserve the marine environment of the exclusive economic zone and the continental shelf."

Article 11: "Any State, provided that it observes international law and the laws and regulations of the People's Republic of China, shall enjoy in the exclusive economic zone and the continental shelf of the People's Republic of China freedom of navigation and overflight and of laying submarine cables and pipelines, and shall enjoy other legal and practical marine benefits associated with these freedoms. The laying of the submarine cables and pipelines must be authorized by the competent authorities of the People's Republic of China."

Article 12: "The People's Republic of China may, in the exercise of its sovereign rights to explore, exploit, conserve and manage the living resources of the exclusive economic zone, take such measures, including boarding, inspection, arrest, detention and judicial proceedings, as may be necessary to ensure compliance with its laws and regulations. ..."

---

bodies, the Administration has taken a number of measures to implement the Act. For example, to guard against adverse consequences to the marine ecosystem that might result from the exploration of mineral resources of the deep-sea bed, China has, through the Administration, been closely collaborating with the International Seabed Authority established by UNCLOS.

b) Belize: Implementation of UNCLOS

94. Belize ratified UNCLOS on 13 August 1983, and became a party upon the Convention's entry into force on 16 November 1994. To be able to implement the conservation requirements of UNCLOS, Belize undertook major amendments to its Coastal Zone Management Act ("Coastal Zone Act"), Chapter 329. The amendments took effect on 31 December 2002. One of the Coastal Zone Act's key provisions is Section 1, which creates a body known as the Coastal Zone Management Authority, which is charged with the responsibility of taking specific steps and actions to implement the Act.

95. The Authority has the statutory mandate to assist in the development and implementation of programmes and projects that translate policies of the government related to conservation of the marine environment into activities that contribute to sustainable development of coastal resources. The Coastal Zone Act also requires the Authority to assist in the development and execution of programmes and projects that foster and encourage regional and international collaboration in the use of marine resources. In addition, the Authority is required to undertake research and monitoring activities in Belize's coastal areas to determine activities that may have adverse impacts on the marine environment. It also requires the Authority to promote public awareness of the unique nature of Belize's coastal zone and the need for effective and sustainable conservation and management of its resources.

96. The Coastal Zone Act also establishes an Advisory Council, which works with the Authority and is in charge of the country's fisheries. It also establishes

---

Belize: Coastal Zone Management Act (Chapter 329)

"The objects of the Institute are: (a) to stimulate and advance the conduct of marine scientific research in Belize; (b) to promote the utilization and conservation of the marine resources for the economic and social benefit of Belize, and to enhance the national capabilities of Belize in the conduct of marine scientific research; (c) to promote a public understanding of the appreciation for all aspects of the marine and related environment..." (Section 9).

"The functions of the Institute are: (a) to conduct research and development on the marine environment of Belize, the Caribbean and adjacent regions; (b) to collaborate in the maintenance of a centralized accessible centre for information and research related to the coastal zone; ... (d) to study the multiple uses of the sea and coastal zones, their resources and potential use in Belize, the Caribbean and adjacent regions, and to evaluate and promote such studies with a view to minimizing possible conflicts which may result from such uses; ...(j) to assist the Authority in the development of technical guidelines for the sustainable use of coastal resources;...(l) to provide advice, as required, on development activities within the coastal zone;..." (Section 10 (a) -(l)).

---

a Coastal Zone Management Institute ("Management Institute"), and charges it with the responsibility of managing the country's coastal areas, promoting utilization and conservation of marine resources and conducting marine scientific research.

97. Through collaboration, the Coastal Zone Management Authority, the Management Institute and other institutions have provided technical guidance to the Fisheries Department of Belize on matters related to conservation and sustainable fisheries. They have also assisted the Fisheries Department in developing a project for the construction and deployment of safe fish aggregating devices that will allow for the exploitation of commercially important fish species in the maritime zones of Belize, and in the high seas without threatening to deplete the resources.

98. The Ecosystems Management Unit of the Fisheries Department has been conducting monitoring activities for lobsters and other commercially important species to detect any reductions in their populations for necessary restorative measures. It has also implemented programmes for on-site protection of species of fish, for protection of the marine ecosystems and for enforcement of fisheries regulations to promote sustainable fisheries. A heightening of enforcement activities has led to a 50% increase in patrols compared to 1999-2000; resulted in more arrests and prosecutions; had a significant impact on illegal fishing activities; led to sixty-seven convictions in the year 2001; resulted in a total of US $120,720 in fines, resulted in the confiscation of US $137,020 worth of fishing equipment and curbed non-compliance with

fisheries regulations. Areas where enforcement activities have been regular include Bacalar Chico Marine Reserve, Hol Chan Marine Reserve, Glovers Reef Marine Reserve and Sapodilla Cayes Marine Reserve.

c) Australia: Implementation of the Convention on Biological Diversity

99. Australia ratified the CBD on 18 June 1993, and became a party upon the CBD's entry into force on 29 December 1993. In order to implement the CBD, the federal government ("Commonwealth") of Australia passed the Environment Protection and Biodiversity Conservation Act ("EPBC Act"), Number 91 of 1999, which entered into force on 16 July 2000. The EPBC Act, which has been amended several times since its adoption, is a massive piece of legislation comprising 528 Sections. The EPBC Act establishes a national framework for environment protection through a focus on protecting matters of national environmental significance and on the conservation of Australia's biodiversity, including marine biodiversity. Among other things, the EPBC Act requires the preparation of lists of endangered, threatened and critically endangered species of animals, plants and other organisms so that appropriate action can be taken to conserve, preserve and restore their populations. Particular attention is given to the tool of the establishment of protected areas. In addition, the EPBC Act creates specific offenses in relation to the export or import of endangered and threatened species.

100. Chapter 5, part 12 of the EPBC Act establishes a system for identifying and monitoring biodiversity

---

Australia: Environment Protection and Biodiversity Conservation Act, Number 91 of 1999

Section 171: "(1) The Minister may, on behalf of the Commonwealth, co-operate with, and give financial or other assistance to, any person for the purpose of identifying and monitoring components of biodiversity. ...the co-operation and assistance may include co-operation and assistance in relation to all or any of the following: (a) identifying and monitoring components of biodiversity that are important for its conservation and ecologically sustainable use."

Section 171(3): "In this Act: *components of biodiversity* includes species, habitats, ecological communities, genes, ecosystems and ecological processes."

Section 178(1): "The Minister must, by instrument published in the *Gazette*, establish a list of threatened species divided into the following categories: (a) extinct; (b) extinct in the wild; (c) critically endangered; (d) endangered; (e) vulnerable; (f) conservation dependent."

Section 196: "(1) A person is guilty of an offence if: (a) the person takes an action; and (b) the action results in the death or injury of a member of a native species or a member of an ecological community; and (c) the member is a member of a listed threatened species (except a conservation dependent species) or of a listed threatened ecological community; and (d) the member is in or on a Commonwealth area.... (3) The offence is punishable on conviction by imprisonment for not more than 2 years or a fine not exceeding 1,000 penalty units, or both."

to allow necessary actions to be taken for conservation and preservation. Part 12 requires approval of activities involving the marine environment through a permitting system, which allows conditions to be placed on the permits to prevent human activities from causing harm to marine organisms and their environment.

101. The administration of the EPBC Act and the Environment Protection and Biodiversity Conservation Regulations of 2000 (as amended) is one of the key functions of the Commonwealth's Department of Heritage. The Approvals and Wildlife Division is the body responsible for the implementation of the Act of 1999. The Division consists of three Branches: the Environment Assessment and Approvals Branch, the Policy and Compliance Branch and the Wildlife Branch. These bodies have undertaken a number of activities aimed at implementing the EPBC Act. For example, action plans have been developed to guide the government in undertaking conservation measures that the EPBC Act stipulates. The plans include strategies to be undertaken by scientists to review the conservation status of different categories of Australia's marine organisms, identify any threats to their conservation and recommend appropriate response actions. Such plans assist not only governmental bodies, but also non-governmental organizations to set priorities for conservation of threatened species.

102. In addition, the EPBC Act recognizes a Biodiversity Day, which is celebrated in Australia in September of each year. There is also a National Threatened Species Day every year. On these days, the government makes specific efforts to create awareness of the need and obligation to protect and conserve biodiversity in Australia. On such days, the Commonwealth Government involves Australians in practical measures to conserve their unique and valuable species by holding workshops and conferences, planting trees, and conducting school projects on biological diversity, among other conservation activities.

Dr. Erik Jaap Molenaar, Senior Research Associate, Netherlands Institute for the Law of the Sea ("NILOS")

Dr. Jane Dwasi, UNEP Consultant, University of Nairobi

Resources

Internet Resources

A.G. OUDE ELFERINK, THE IMPACT OF ARTICLE 7(2) OF THE FISH STOCKS AGREEMENT ON THE FORMULATION OF CONSERVATION & MANAGEMENT MEASURES FOR STRADDLING & HIGHLY MIGRATORY FISH STOCKS, FAO LEGAL PAPERS ONLINE #4 (AUGUST 1999) available at http://www.fao.org/Legal/pub-e.HTM

COMMISSION FOR THE CONSERVATION OF ANTARCTIC MARINE LIVING RESOURCES ("CCAMLR") available at http://www.ccamlr.org

CONVENTION ON BIOLOGICAL DIVERSITY ("CBD") available at http://www.biodiv.org

CONVENTION ON MIGRATORY SPECIES ("CMS") available at http://www.wcmc.org.uk/cms

ECOSYSTEM-BASED MANAGEMENT OF FISHERIES. OPPORTUNITIES AND CHALLENGES FOR COORDINATION BETWEEN MARINE REGIONAL FISHERY BODIES AND REGIONAL SEAS CONVENTIONS, (FAO DOC. RFB/II/2001/7) available at www.fao.org/documents

FISHERIES DEPARTMENT OF THE UNITED NATIONS FOOD AND AGRICULTURE ORGANIZATION ("FAO") available at http://www.fao.org/fi

HIGH NORTH ALLIANCE available at http://www.highnorth.no

INTERNATIONAL COMMISSION FOR THE CONSERVATION OF ATLANTIC TUNAS ("ICCAT") available at http://www.iccat.es

INTERNATIONAL MARITIME ORGANIZATION ("IMO") available at http://www.imo.org

INTERNATIONAL WHALING COMMISSION ("IWC") available at www.iwcoffice.org

OSPAR COMMISSION available at http://www.ospar.org

UNEP, HANDBOOK OF THE CONVENTION ON BIOLOGICAL DIVERSITY (2ND ED., 2003) available at www.biodiv.org

UNITED NATIONS DIVISION FOR OCEAN AFFAIRS AND THE LAW OF THE SEA ("DOALOS") available at http://www.un.org/Depts/los

UNITED NATIONS ENVIRONMENT PROGRAMME ("UNEP") available at http://www.unep.org

UNITED NATIONS ENVIRONMENT PROGRAMME, CARIBBEAN REGIONAL CO-ORDINATING UNIT, CARIBBEAN ENVIRONMENT PROGRAMME available at http://www.cep.unep.org

Text Resources

Alan Boyle, INTERNATIONAL & COMPARATIVE LAW QUARTERLY, (Volume 54, Part 3, July 2005 - Further Development of the Law of the Sea Convention: Mechanisms for Change).

E.J. Molenaar, ECOSYSTEM-BASED FISHERIES MANAGEMENT, COMMERCIAL FISHERIES, MARINE MAMMALS AND THE 2001 REYKJAVIK DECLARATION IN THE CONTEXT OF INTERNATIONAL LAW, (17 INTL.L J. of Marine & Coastal L., 2002, pp. 561-595).

E.J. Molenaar, THE CONCEPT OF "REAL INTEREST" AND OTHER ASPECTS OF CO-OPERATION THROUGH REGIONAL FISHERIES MANAGEMENT MECHANISMS, (15 INTL. J. of Marine & Coastal L., 2000, pp. 475-531).

F. Orrego Vicuña, THE CHANGING INTERNATIONAL LAW OF HIGH SEAS FISHERIES, (Cambridge University Press, 1999).

J.A. de Yturriaga, THE INTERNATIONAL REGIME OF FISHERIES FROM UNCLOS 1982 TO THE PRESENTIAL SEA, (Martinus Nijhoff Publishers, 1997).

R.R. Churchill & A.V. Lowe, THE LAW OF THE SEA, (Manchester University Press, 1999).

S.J. Bache, MARINE WILDLIFE BYCATCH MITIGATION. GLOBAL TRENDS, INTERNATIONAL ACTION AND THE CHALLENGES FOR AUSTRALIA, (Ocean Publications, Centre for Maritime Policy, University of Wollongong, 2003).

W.C.G. Burns & A. Gillespie (Eds.), THE FUTURE OF CETACEANS IN A CHANGING WORLD, (Transnational Publishers, 2003).

W. Edeson, D. Freestone & E. Gudmundsdottir (Eds.), LEGISLATION FOR SUSTAINABLE FISHERIES. A GUIDE TO IMPLEMENTING THE 1993 FAO COMPLIANCE AGREEMENT AND 1995 UNITED NATIONS FISH STOCKS AGREEMENT, (the World Bank, 2001).

18. FRESHWATER RESOURCES

I. Introduction

1. Water is essential to human and other forms of life. Therefore, attention should be paid not only to regulating the exploitation of water and diminishing or halting pollution of single water bodies, but also protecting and preserving the entire ecosystems of which water resources constitutes integral part. For example, deforestation in a watershed can affect its streams, which in turn can affect fish and other aquatic life and lead to flooding. The cascade of social and economic consequences that can flow from the loss of healthy ecosystems demonstrates that freshwater ecosystems should not be seen as something separate from human society and well being. They are, in fact, an integral part of a country's economy and should be both protected and enhanced accordingly.

2. This chapter focuses on the protection, conservation and management of freshwater resources, both at the international and national level. Freshwater resources have been the object of regulation long before the emergence of environmental protection and sustainable development concerns. International rules and principles, as well as national regimes, have been developed to regulate their navigational and other uses. These regimes, perhaps with the exception of sanitation standards, mostly treated water as an economic resource, and dealt largely with the quantitative aspect of water resources.

3. The emergence of environmental protection obligations and of the principle of sustainable development, as well as the increased awareness that water resources have to be managed in a holistic approach, have highlighted the need to integrate existing water regulation regimes with rules and principles concerning the environmental aspects of freshwater resources, and to regulate the quantitative and qualitative aspects in an integrated manner. Therefore, in order to reflect the evolution of the law in this area and the interlinkages between the regulation of the use of water and the protection and conservation of water resources and their ecosystems, this Chapter will also address the issue of water allocation rights, falling under what is traditionally referred to as water law.

1. The Hydrological Cycle

4. Most freshwater on Earth is in constant motion in the hydrologic cycle. (See table, above). This expression refers to the process whereby water evaporates into the atmosphere and returns to Earth's surface through condensation and precipitation. Evaporation may occur from any wet surface. Most water evaporates from the oceans, since they cover about 70% of the planet, but also from other bodies of water, such as lakes, reservoirs and rivers, as well as from moist soil and other surfaces. Considerable amounts of water vapour enter the atmosphere through transpiration and evaporation from vegetation in a process referred to as evapotranspiration. Thus crops, trees and other vegetation act as virtual "pumps," transferring water from the ground into the atmosphere. Therefore, large-scale elimination of vegetation can affect local and regional climate patterns.

5. When water returns to land through precipitation, it may either remain on the surface, as standing water or as runoff, or soak into the ground through infiltration. Runoff flows into streams, lakes and other forms of surface water, generally finding its way into the ocean. Water entering the ground through infiltration may be held in the soil, to eventually return to the surface through capillary action and evaporate, or may percolate downward to become groundwater. The area on the land surface where infiltration occurs is called the recharge area. This may lie a considerable distance from the place where groundwater is withdrawn or emerges naturally, for example, by flowing into a river, or emanating from the ground in the form of a spring. The underground geologic structures containing water are often referred to as aquifers. These porous, permeable water-bearing formations are composed of such material as sand, gravel or limestone. The water contained in these aquifers is called groundwater. The upper surface of groundwater is the water table. Water moves not only from Earth's surface to the atmosphere and back again, but also from the surface into the ground and back again to the surface. For example, considerable water seeps from streams through their beds into the ground, changing from surface water to groundwater. This groundwater may later rejoin the stream, emerge as a spring or flow underground into a lake or the ocean. However, there are certain aquifers containing what is sometimes called confined groundwater, or fossil water, that do not interact with surface water or other aquifers, but these are highly exceptional.

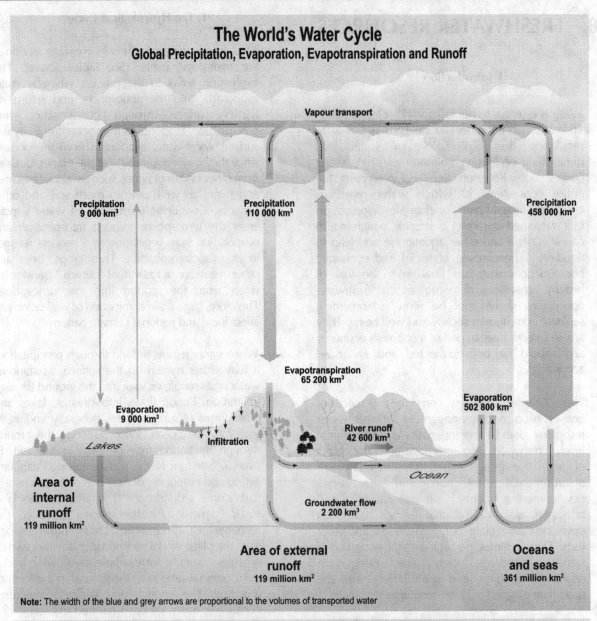

The World's Water Cycle
Global Precipitation, Evaporation, Evapotranspiration and Runoff

Vapour transport

Precipitation
9 000 km³

Precipitation
110 000 km³

Precipitation
458 000 km³

Evapotranspiration
65 200 km³

Evaporation
502 800 km³

Evaporation
9 000 km³

River runoff
42 600 km³

Lakes

Ocean

Infiltration

Area of
internal
runoff
119 million km²

Groundwater flow
2 200 km³

Area of external
runoff
119 million km²

Oceans
and seas
361 million km²

Note: The width of the blue and grey arrows are proportional to the volumes of transported water

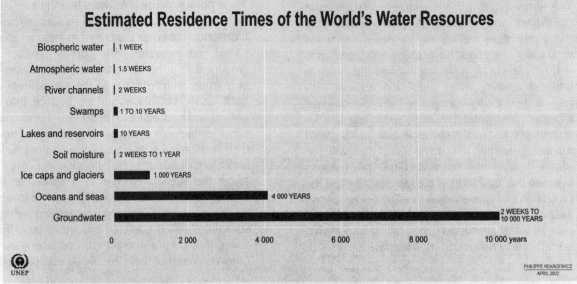

Estimated Residence Times of the World's Water Resources

Biospheric water	1 WEEK
Atmospheric water	1.5 WEEKS
River channels	2 WEEKS
Swamps	1 TO 10 YEARS
Lakes and reservoirs	10 YEARS
Soil moisture	2 WEEKS TO 1 YEAR
Ice caps and glaciers	1 000 YEARS
Oceans and seas	4 000 YEARS
Groundwater	2 WEEKS TO 10 000 YEARS

0   2 000   4 000   6 000   8 000   10 000 years

UNEP

PHILIPPE REKACEWICZ
APRIL 2002

Source: Igor A. Shiklomanov, State Hydrological Institute (SHI, St. Petersburg) and United Nations Educational, Scientific and Cultural Organisation (UNESCO, Paris), 1999;
Max Planck, Institute for Meteorology, Hamburg, 1994; Freeze, Allen, John, Cherry, *Groundwater*, Prentice-Hall: Engle wood Cliffs NJ, 1979.

6. It is estimated that over three-quarters of all freshwater on Earth is frozen in polar ice-caps and glaciers and is inaccessible as a practical matter. Approximately 97% of the remaining water consists of groundwater, while surface water accounts for a surprisingly small percentage of the total of freshwater on earth. Therefore, a high percentage (about one-third) of the global population depends upon groundwater, much of which is drawn from shallow aquifers, which are more subject to pollution than deep aquifers.

2. Water Scarcity

7. Although water has been the same for billions of years, as it neither grows nor diminishes over time, concerns about its scarcity derive largely from intensified human demand for a finite supply and deterioration of its quality caused by human activities. Intensified human demand largely due to rapid population growth. If about one-third of the global population lives today in countries under moderate-to-high water stress, studies have estimated that by the 2015, nearly half the world's population will live in countries lacking sufficient water.

8. Water quality is an important consideration for its intended use. Therefore, water quality and quantity are interrelated: water resources may be plentiful but unsuitable for human use because of contamination. This problem is becoming more serious, particularly in urban areas where the need to provide adequate and safe supplies of water and dispose of the increasingly large quantities of wastewater in a safe and environmentally sound way is becoming an increasingly pressing concern.

9. An additional factor that may have profound effects on water supplies is global climate change, whose consequences, as estimated by the Intergovernmental Panel on Climate Change ("IPCC") created by the WMO and UNEP to assess scientific, technical and socio-economic information relevant for the understanding of climate change, its potential impacts and options for adaptation and mitigation) include not only higher temperatures but also rising sea levels, altered precipitation patterns, and an increase in extreme climatic events and storm surges, among other effects. All of these factors will impact on the availability and quality of freshwater resources and be exacerbated by human demand for freshwater.

10. The world's water is unevenly distributed. Some geographic regions have more water than they can possibly use while others do not have enough. Governments have sometimes responded to this phenomenon by transferring water from places where it is abundant to those where it is scarce. While water transfers may address needs of the present and short-term future, they may also have unforeseen and harmful longer-term effects on ecosystems and even human populations.

3. Water Pollution

11. Principal sources of freshwater pollution include untreated sewage, agricultural run-off and discharge of chemical substances. These affect all forms of freshwater and marine water in coastal areas, degrade associated ecosystems and threaten the health and livelihoods of people dependent upon them.

12. The lack of adequate sanitation is the primary cause of water contamination and water-related diseases, such as cholera, dengue fever, diarrhoea and typhoid fever. Some 2.3 billion people are afflicted with these diseases each year. Children are particularly vulnerable since their immune systems are not fully developed. The poor are the most likely to have inadequate sanitation facilities and to suffer consequent adverse effects on their health and environment.

13. Substances deposited on land surfaces (for example, fertilizers, pesticides and other chemicals used in agriculture), may filter into groundwater, which could be affected by other sources of pollution affecting streams that eventually replenish the aquifer. Once contaminated, groundwater is very difficult to purify unless it is extracted and treated which process would be experience as well.

14. The quality of groundwater in coastal areas may also be affected by over-pumping, or mining. Mining of groundwater occurs when withdrawals exceed the average rate of replenishment. Because coastal aquifers are often geologically connected with the adjacent ocean, these withdrawals can cause sea water to be drawn into the aquifers, increasing the salinity of the freshwater and making it unfit for many uses.

4. Water Uses

15. Humans use freshwater in a wide variety of ways. Nevertheless, it is possible to identify several broad categories of uses for convenience: domestic uses; industrial uses; agricultural uses; recreational uses; navigational uses; waste-disposal uses; and in-stream uses (such as fishing, conservation of fish and other aquatic life, recreation, safeguarding aesthetic values and preservation of aquatic ecosystems). These categories may be further

subdivided. For example, domestic uses include the use of water for drinking, washing, food preparation, sanitation and subsistence farming, among other uses.

16. It is important to bear in mind the potential for different uses of water to come into conflict with each other. Thus, for example, the use of water for drinking would conflict with any other use, for instance waste-disposal use - that made the water unfit for drinking.

17. Conflicts between uses of land and water must also be confronted. For example, deforestation can increase runoff, causing erosion of soil which can lead to increased turbidity of streams and sedimentation of their beds; sedimentation can, in turn, cause flooding and decrease infiltration of water from streams into aquifers. Agriculture may result in the direct or indirect discharge of pollutants into water sources and affect the extent to which those sources are available for other uses. More broadly the interest of the international community in environmentally sound management of water resources is to provide a framework of peaceful cooperation and avoidance of conflicts that could jeopardize peace and security among countries sharing the resource. Conflict resolution mechanisms are at all times at the core of underlying cooperation.

18. The relationship between fresh, coastal and marine water resources must also be borne in mind. Nearly one-third of the world's population lives in coastal zones. Since most watercourse systems eventually reach the sea, coastal residents bear the effects of freshwater management practices in the relevant basins. Thus, freshwater systems, wetlands, and coastal and marine waters should be managed holistically.

19. Estuaries, partly enclosed aquatic zones where seawater mixes with freshwater from rivers, deserve special protection, as they provide sanctuaries, breeding and feeding grounds for many important species and serve as nurseries for half of the living organisms in the world's oceans. Also marshes and wetlands serve critical ecological functions, by regulating water regimes, and by providing habitats for flora and fauna as well as important water purification services. They are often relied upon by local populations for food and even shelter.

II. The International Framework

1. Major Developments in the Field of Cooperation on Freshwater

20. The issues of water availability, use, management, and conservation, with all their implications, are at the centre of concern at national and international levels. In the past decade, water has been at the center of international conferences and initiatives as well as the object of international cooperation, including through the development of legally-binding agreements.

21. The International Conference on Water and the Environment, a meeting of water specialists held in Dublin in 1992, adopted the Dublin Statement on Water and Sustainable Development and a set of four Guiding Principles. The first of these principles reads: "Fresh water is a finite and vulnerable resource, essential to sustain life, development and the environment." The other principles concern the need for a participatory approach to water development and management, the central role of women in the provision, management and safeguarding of water, and the need to recognize water as an economic good.

22. At the United Nations Conference on Environment and Development, held in Rio de Janeiro in 1992, Governments adopted a detailed plan of action, Agenda 21, whose chapter 18 outlines the action needed at the national level to safeguard freshwater resources. Agenda 21 adopts the concept of integrated water resource management, based on the idea that water is "...an integral part of the ecosystem, a natural resource and a social and economic good..." and that "Freshwater is a unitary resource" and the "complex interconnectedness of freshwater systems demands that freshwater management be holistic (taking a catchment management approach) and based on a balanced consideration of the needs of people and the environment." It also contains useful recommendations on activities and means of implementation with regard to the impacts of climate change on water resources.

23. At the Millennium Summit, held in 2000, the General Assembly adopted the Millennium Declaration (UNGA Resolution 55/2 of 8 September 2000), by which states resolved to reduce by half the proportion of people without sustainable access to safe drinking water by 2015. World leaders also agreed to adopt in all

environmental actions a new ethic of conservation and stewardship and, as a first step, to "stop the unsustainable exploitation of water resources by developing water management strategies at the regional, national and local levels, which promote both equitable access and adequate supplies. (See Paragraph 23 of the Millennium Declaration). These commitments have been translated into the Millennium Development Goal 7: Ensure environmental sustainability.

24. Water was at the centre of several international conferences, such as the Bonn International Conference on Freshwater (December 2001) and the Second (March 2000) and Third (March 2003) World Water Forums.

25. Furthermore, one of the major priority areas at the World Summit on Sustainable Development ("WSSD", Johannesburg 2002) was water. In the Johannesburg Plan of Implementation states not only reaffirmed the Millennium Development Goal mentioned above, but additionally committed to halving the proportion of people without access to basic sanitation services within the same period. They also called for the development of integrated water resources management and water efficiency plans by 2005. The United Nations Commission on Sustainable Development decided at its eleventh session (April 2003) to monitor progress and promote the further implementation of the water agenda in the first cycle of its new multi-year programme of work.

26. At the eighth special session of the Governing Council / Global Ministerial Environment Forum of the United Nations Environment Programme held in Jeju, Republic of Korea in March 2004, Ministers and other heads of delegations engaged in a dialogue on the priority environmental dimensions of the water related themes and associated targets stemming from the Millennium Declaration and the World Summit on Sustainable Development, and in particular on integrated water resource management, water and sanitation and water, health and poverty. The summary of the discussions held is known as the Jeju initiative.

2. Freshwater Regulation at the International Level

27. Water is one of the most widely shared resources of the planet. Rivers often constitute the border between states or flow across different countries and lakes often lie on the territory of different states. Therefore water can be a factor for competition as well as a reason of cooperation among states. Disputes for the control of water resources have a

long history. Also major water development projects (e.g. the construction of a dam) have caused violence and civil strife.

28. But shared waters can also be a source of cooperation: throughout history, states have manifested their interest in cooperating for the management of water resources and have recognized the need to establish rules and principles for a peaceful cooperation.

29. The body of rules and principles that have been developed to respond to similar situations is impressive, due to the extensive state practice in this field, both in terms of agreements and other forms of rules of conduct. Historically, rules and principles of international law relating to international watercourses first developed in the field of navigation. One of the first European agreements relating to shared water resources, the Final Act of the Congress of Vienna (1815), stipulated that there was to be freedom of navigation on all navigable rivers. However, other uses of shared water resources, such as irrigation, the generation of hydroelectricity and waste disposal, have become increasingly important. The practice of states sharing freshwater resources has led to the development of general rules and principles concerning the non-navigational uses of international watercourses. This body of law finds its most recent and authoritative expression in the 1997 United Nations Convention on the Law of the Non-Navigational Uses of International Watercourses ("International Watercourses Convention").

30. The International Watercourses Convention is based on preparatory work done by the United Nations International Law Commission ("ILC"), whose objective is the progressive development of international law and its codification. The ILC's work on international watercourses was based on a wide variety of sources, including treaties and other forms of state practice, and the work of international organizations. One of these organizations, the International Law Association ("ILA"), adopted an unofficial but influential draft in 1966 entitled the Helsinki Rules on the Uses of the Waters of International Rivers, which helped to clarify the law in the field.

31. While the International Watercourses Convention is not yet in force, a number of the rules it contains reflect customary international law, which is binding on all states. Of these rules, the three most fundamental include:
   • Obligation to utilize an international watercourse in an equitable and reasonable manner;

- Duty to prevent significant harm to other riparian states; and
- Obligation to provide prior notification of planned measures that might affect other states sharing a watercourse.

32. The fundamental nature of the principle of equitable utilization was underscored by the International Court of Justice ("ICJ") in its 1997 judgment in the Gabcikovo-Nagymaros Case. In that decision, the ICJ referred to what it called a state's "basic right to an equitable and reasonable sharing of the resources of an international watercourse".

33. Two other obligations, which have begun to receive attention only relatively recently, may be added to the three just mentioned:
- The emerging substantive obligation to protect international watercourses and their ecosystems against degradation; and
- The procedural duty of riparian states to cooperate with each other in their relations concerning shared freshwater resources, a duty that encompasses a variety of forms of cooperation ranging from sharing of data and information to cooperation in the joint management of shared water resources.

34. Considering the authoritative character of the International Watercourses Convention as a codification of basic principles of international watercourse law, states sharing freshwater resources have referred it as a source of standards governing their relations and as a model for ad hoc agreements regulating specific water bodies. In view of the Convention's influence and because it conveniently summarizes the generally applicable principles, the following section examines the content of this instrument in more detail.

a) The 1997 United Nations Convention on the Law of the Non-Navigational Uses of International Watercourses

35. The Convention on the Law of the Non-Navigational Uses of International Watercourses ("International Watercourses Convention") originated from the work of the International Law Commission, mandated by the General Assembly in 1970 to "take up the study of the law of international watercourses with a view to its progressive development and codification." The ILC adopted a complete set of draft articles in 1994, which was submitted to a Working Group for its finalization in the form of a multilateral agreement. As a result of this process, the International Watercourses Convention was adopted by the General Assembly on 21 May 1997, as an annex to

Resolution 51/229. The Convention is not yet in force; it will enter into force when it has been ratified by thirty-five states (article 36). As of November 2005, sixteen states have signed and fourteen are parties to the Convention.

36. The International Watercourses Convention defines the term "watercourse" (article 2) as "a system of surface waters and ground waters constituting by virtue of their physical relationship a unitary whole and normally flowing into a common terminus" and an "international watercourse" as a watercourse "parts of which are situated in different States." This definition takes into consideration the reality of the hydrological cycle and suggests the need for states to take into account the physical unity of interconnected surface water and groundwater when managing shared freshwater resources. However it does not apply, strictly speaking, to groundwater that is not connected in some way with surface water, so-called "confined" groundwater. Nevertheless, the ILC annexed a Resolution on Confined Transboundary Groundwater to the set of draft articles it adopted in 1994, recommending that states be "guided by the principles contained in the draft articles" in regulating confined transboundary groundwater. Subsequently the ILC took up the study of the law applicable and to confined transboundary groundwater. Its work is ongoing at the time of this writing.

37. Part II of the International Watercourses Convention contains a number of general principles. The first of these principles is the principle of equitable utilization and participation (article 5), which provides:

Convention on the Law of the Non-Navigational Uses of International Watercourses (Article 5)

"1. Watercourse States shall in their respective territories utilize an international watercourse in an equitable and reasonable manner. In particular, an international watercourse shall be used and developed by watercourse States with a view to attaining optimal and sustainable utilization thereof and benefits therefrom, taking into account the interests of the watercourse States concerned, consistent with adequate protection of the watercourse.

2. Watercourse States shall participate in the use, development and protection of an international watercourse in an equitable and reasonable manner. Such participation includes both the right to utilize the watercourse and the duty to cooperate in the protection and development thereof, as provided in the present Convention."

38. The principle of equitable utilization, as set forth above, is chiefly concerned with apportionment, or allocation, of water between states sharing an international watercourse. It therefore relates primarily to water use, and thus to water quantity, rather than to water quality. However, as is clear from that text that equitable utilization incorporates the concepts of sustainable use and adequate protection of the watercourse. The ensuing paragraph expresses the duty of states to participate equitably in the use, development and protection of an international watercourse.

39. The International Watercourses Convention sets forth (article 6) a non-exhaustive list of factors to be taken into account by a state to ensure that its utilization of an international watercourse is equitable and reasonable. These factors include:

- Geographic, hydrographic, hydrological, climatic, ecological and other factors of a natural character;
- Social and economic needs of the watercourse states concerned;
- Population dependent on the watercourse in each watercourse state;
- Effects of the use or uses of the watercourses in one watercourse state on other watercourse states;
- Existing and potential uses of the watercourse;
- Conservation, protection, development and economy of use of the water resources of the watercourse and the costs of measures taken to that effect; and
- Availability of alternatives, of comparable value, to a particular planned or existing use.

The weight to be given to each factor "is to be determined by its importance in comparison with that of other relevant factors". In determining what is a reasonable and equitable use "all relevant factors are to be considered together and a conclusion reached on the basis of the whole."

40. Another fundamental principle governing states' conduct in relation to international watercourses is the obligation not to cause significant harm, set forth in article 7 of the Convention. According to paragraph 1 of that provision, states sharing a watercourse must "in utilizing an international watercourse in their territories, take all appropriate measures to prevent the causing of significant harm to other watercourse States." Paragraph 2 provides that

---

Convention on the Law of the Non-Navigational Uses of International Watercourses
Article 7(2)

"Where significant harm nevertheless is caused to another watercourse State, the States whose use causes such harm shall, in the absence of agreement to such use, take all appropriate measures…to eliminate or mitigate such harm and, where appropriate, to discuss the question of compensation."

---

41. As mentioned above, the cornerstone of relations between states sharing water resources is cooperation with regard to specific watercourses. This is captured in article 8, according to which states sharing a watercourse must "cooperate on the basis of sovereign equality, territorial integrity, mutual benefit and good faith in order to attain optimal utilization and adequate protection of an international watercourse", and "may consider the establishment of joint mechanisms or commissions...to facilitate cooperation on relevant measures and procedures in the light of experience gained through cooperation in existing joint mechanisms and commissions in various regions."

42. Another form of cooperation is provided for in article 9, according to which states sharing a watercourse should regularly "exchange readily available data and information on the condition of the watercourse" and related forecasts, in particular those relating to the hydrological, meteorological, hydrogeological and ecological nature of the watercourse, including its water quality. If the required information is not readily available, the requested state should "employ its best efforts to comply with the request," although it may condition compliance upon payment of the reasonable costs of collecting and processing the data or information.

43. The conventions established (article 10) that none of the different categories of uses of the watercourses (e.g., navigation, irrigation, hydroelectric power production, industrial uses and so on) has priority over other kinds of uses in the absence of an agreement or custom to the contrary and it provides that, whenever different uses of an international watercourse conflict with each other, such conflict "shall be resolved with reference to [the principles of equitable and reasonable utilization and participation and obligation not to cause significant harm], with special regard being given to the requirements of vital human needs." According to a "statement of understanding" adopted by the states that negotiated the UN Convention, " in determining

'vital human needs,' special attention is to be paid to providing sufficient water to sustain human life, including both drinking water and water required for production of food in order to prevent starvation."

44. According to the International Watercourses Convention, a riparian state must provide timely notification to other watercourse States of planned measures which may have a significant adverse effect upon them. These measures may include, for instance, new irrigation schemes, dams, plants discharging their waste into the stream, etc. to the other riparian states. This will allow the other riparian states to synchronize their existing uses with the new use or to determine whether the new use will cause them harm or will be inequitable. In the latter case, the states concerned will have an opportunity to reach an appropriate resolution before the plans are implemented and it becomes more difficult to do so. Articles 11-19 of the Convention establish detailed notification procedures for such cases.

45. The International Watercourses Convention contains a general obligation and several specific ones relating to the protection and preservation of international watercourses. The general obligation, set forth in article 20, provides as follows: "Watercourse States shall, individually and, where appropriate, jointly, protect and preserve the ecosystems of international watercourses".

46. The specific obligations related to pollution, alien species, and the marine environment include that States must "prevent, reduce and control the pollution of an international watercourse that may cause significant harm to other watercourse States or to their environment, including harm to human health or safety, to the use of the waters for any beneficial purpose or to the living resources of the watercourse..." (article 21). This may be seen as a specific application of the general obligation to prevent harm reflected in article 7. Furthermore, states are to "take all measures necessary to prevent the introduction of species, alien or new, into international watercourses" (article 22) and to take all measures with respect to an international watercourse that are necessary to protect and preserve the marine environment, including estuaries..." (article 23).

47. The International Watercourses Convention also contains provisions on the prevention and mitigation of harmful conditions and emergency situations (articles 27 and 28 respectively), dealing with the prevention of such harmful conditions as floods, ice hazards, water-borne diseases, erosion, salt-water intrusion, drought and desertification, and with emergency situations that may be brought on by such phenomena as floods, landslides and industrial accidents.

3. Freshwater Regulation at the Regional and Subregional Levels

a) The 1992 UNECE Convention on the Protection and Use of Transboundary Watercourses and International Lakes

48. The rules governing shared watercourses have also been established in regional contexts, and have resulted in several conventions, protocols and agreements, which represent the reference point for states which share watercourses and intend to cooperate in their conservation, management and use.

49. An important example of regulation of transboundary water resources at the regional level is the 1992 Convention on the Protection and Use of Transboundary Watercourses and International Lakes ("Helsinki Convention"), which was concluded under the auspices of the Economic Commission of Europe ("UNECE") at Helsinki. The Convention entered into force on 6 October 1996, with 26 signatories and 35 parties as of November 2005.

50. The Helsinki Convention deals with the prevention, control and reduction of transboundary impacts relating to international watercourses and lakes, with a strong emphasis on pollution prevention. It establishes a framework for cooperation between the member countries of the UNECE on the prevention and control of pollution of specific transboundary watercourses by ensuring rational use of water resources with a view to sustainable development. Transboundary waters are defined as any surface or ground waters that mark, cross or are located on the boundaries between two or more states.

51. Under the Convention, the Parties shall take all appropriate measures:
   • To prevent, control and reduce pollution of waters causing or likely to cause transboundary impact;
   • To ensure that transboundary waters are used with the aim of ecologically sound and rational water management, conservation of water resources and environmental protection;
   • To ensure that transboundary waters are used in a reasonable and equitable way, taking into particular account their transboundary character, in the case of activities which cause or are likely to cause transboundary impact;
   • To ensure conservation and, where necessary, restoration of ecosystems.

52. Actions designed to deal with water pollution must address pollution at source, and measures adopted on this basis must not result directly or indirectly in a transfer of pollution to other parts of the environment.

53. The Helsinki Convention establishes that parties must be guided, in their actions, by the following fundamental principles:

   • The precautionary principle, according to which action to avoid the release of hazardous substances must not be postponed, despite the lack of a proven causal link between the substances and the transboundary impact;

   • The "polluter pays" principle, according to which the costs of pollution prevention, control and reduction measures must be borne by the polluter; and

   • Water resources must be managed so that the needs of the present generation are met without compromising the ability of future generations to meet their own needs.

54. The Convention also establishes obligations in the field of monitoring, research and development, consultations, warning and alarm systems, mutual assistance, institutional arrangements, and the exchange and protection of information, as well as public access to information.

55. Two Protocols were adopted under the Helsinki Convention: the Protocol on Water and Health and the Protocol on Civil Liability and Compensation for Damage caused by the Transboundary Effects of Industrial Accidents on Transboundary Waters. The main aim of the Protocol on Water and Health, adopted in London on 17 June 1999, is to protect human health and well being by better water management, including the protection of water ecosystems, and by preventing, controlling and reducing water-related diseases. It is the first international agreement of its kind adopted specifically to attain an adequate supply of safe drinking water and adequate sanitation for everyone and effectively protect water used as a source of drinking water. To meet these goals, the parties are required to establish national and local targets for the quality of drinking water and the quality of discharges, as well as for the performance of water supply and wastewater treatment. They are also required to reduce outbreaks and the incidence of water-related diseases.

56. The Protocol on Civil Liability and Compensation for Damage caused by the Transboundary Effects of Industrial Accidents on Transboundary Waters was adopted and signed by 22 countries in Kiev, Ukraine, on 21 May 2003, under both the Helsinki Convention and the ECE Convention on the Transboundary Effects of Industrial Accidents. The Protocol is open for ratification by parties to one or both Conventions, but any other Member state of the United Nations may accede to the Protocol upon approval by the Meeting of the Parties. The Protocol on Civil Liability will enter into force once 16 states have ratified it.

57. The Protocol on Civil Liability allows individuals affected by the transboundary impact of industrial accidents on international watercourses to bring a legal claim for adequate and prompt compensation. Companies can be held liable for accidents at industrial installations as well as during transport via pipelines. The liability covered by the Protocol includes physical damage, damage to property, loss of income, the cost of reinstatement and response measures. The Protocol contains provisions ensuring non-discriminatory treatment of pollution victims, by ensuring that victims of the transboundary effects cannot be treated less favourably than victims from the country where the accident has occurred.

b) Protocol on Shared Watercourse Systems in the Southern African Development Community

58. The Southern African Development Community ("SADC") is a regional economic community that has the goal of promoting the integration of the regional economy and poverty alleviation, food security and industrial development. It was established in 1992 and comprises fourteen countries: Angola, Botswana, the Democratic Republic of Congo, Lesotho, Malawi, Mauritius, Mozambique, Namibia, Seychelles, South Africa, Swaziland, Tanzania, Zambia and Zimbabwe. It is based on a treaty that is supplemented by sectoral protocols.

59. The first SADC Protocol on Shared Water Course Systems ("SADC Protocol"), developed with the assistance of UNEP, was signed in 1995, and ratified in September 1998. Following adoption of the United Nations Convention on the Law of the Non-Navigational Uses of International Watercourses in 1997, a revised Protocol was developed, in line with the provisions of the UN Convention. The Revised Protocol was signed on 7 August 2000, and entered into force on 22 September 2003. At the time of writing, the following countries had ratified the Protocol: Botswana, Lesotho, Mauritius, Mozambique, Namibia, South Africa, Swaziland, Malawi and Tanzania.

60. Overall objective of the Revised Protocol is:

> **Protocol on Shared Watercourses Systems in the Southern African Development Community (Article 2)**
>
> "[…] to foster closer cooperation for judicious, sustainable and co-ordinated management, protection and utilisation of shared watercourses and advance the SADC agenda of regional integration and poverty alleviation."

61. In order to achieve this objective the Protocol seeks to:
    • promote and facilitate the establishment of shared watercourse agreements and Shared Watercourse Institutions for the management of shared watercourses;
    • advance the sustainable, equitable and reasonable utilisation of the shared watercourses;
    • promote a co-ordinated and integrated environmentally sound development and management of shared watercourses;
    • promote the harmonisation and monitoring of legislation and policies for planning, development, conservation, protection of shared watercourses, and allocation of the resources thereof; and
    • promote research and technology development, information exchange, capacity building, and the application of appropriate technologies in shared watercourses management.

62. The Protocol introduces the principle of "unity and coherence of each shared watercourse" which implies the need to harmonize uses of the water in the interests of sustainability and regional integration. It requires member states to undertake to respect and apply the existing rules of general or customary international law relating to the utilization and management of the resources of shared watercourse systems and, in particular, to respect and abide by the principles of community interests in the equitable utilization of those systems and related resources."

63. The Protocol also requires member states to establish appropriate institutions necessary for the effective implementation of the provisions of the protocol, which include, among others, River Basin Commissions between Basin States and River Authorities or Boards in respect of each drainage basin, with the following objects:
    • Develop a monitoring policy for shared watercourse systems;
    • Promote the equitable utilization of shared watercourse systems;

    • Formulate strategies for the development of shared water course systems; and,
    • Monitor the execution of integrated water resource development plans in shared watercourse systems.

c) Agreements concerning Specific Watercourses

64. The international regimes described previously in this Chapter establish general rules to be followed by states sharing freshwater resources. States will therefore normally be guided by those rules in the management of such shared resources, and on their basis they will develop mechanisms for cooperation, often in the form of legally binding agreements regulating the specific water bodies, containing the rights and duties of the respective states and relevant institutional arrangements.

65. Riparian states are becoming increasingly aware of the need to cooperate with other riparian states for the management of shared water resources at the basin level, based on the recognition that the hydrological linkage between land, freshwater river basins and coastal waters does not allow for the management of these resources in isolation. From this perspective, for certain water systems not only states whose territory directly adjoins the water body but also all those whose water resources contribute to or are affected by such a water body should be involved in any cooperative arrangement, whether legally binding or not.

66. In the case of the Nile basin, for instance, ten countries (Kenya, Tanzania, Uganda, Sudan, Egypt, Burundi, Rwanda, Ethiopia and the Democratic Republic of Congo) are involved in the Nile Basin Initiative, which was established in 1998 as a dialogue to create a regional partnership to facilitate the common pursuit of sustainable development and management of Nile waters and in the context of which a number of significant steps have been taken towards closer and more stable cooperation.

67. Based on the recognition of this widespread form of cooperation and considering the high number of basin organisations existing in the world, an International Network of Basin Organizations was established in 1996, with the following objectives:
    • Establishing a network of organizations interested in global river basin management, and facilitate exchanges of experiences and expertise among them;
    • Promoting the principles and means of sound water management in sustainable development cooperation programmes;

- Facilitating the implementation of tools for institutional and financial management, for programming and for the organization of data banks;
- Promoting information and training programmes for the different actors involved in water management including local elected officials, users' representatives and the executives and staff of member organizations;
- Encouraging education of the population, the young in particular; and
- Evaluating ongoing actions and disseminate their results.

68. Although there exist many examples of basin-wide cooperation, of the more than 260 international water basins existing today, more than 150 still lack any type of cooperative management framework. Furthermore, the majority of those basins enjoying some form of cooperation do not have comprehensive agreements including all the riparian states in the basin. And among the existing agreements, the majority lack the tools necessary to promote long-term holistic basin-wide resource management. Therefore, much work still needs to be done before adequate legal regimes are developed throughout the world.

69. Although the general rules on cooperation and management of shared water resources are provided in the International Watercourses Convention as well as, when applicable, in relevant regional and subregional instruments, each river basin has its own characteristics, and it is therefore difficult to provide a brief overview of the existing agreements regulating specific watercourses. Anyone interested in a specific arrangement has to check that instrument directly.

III. National Implementation

70. Not all river basins are international, and not all aspects of international river basins are regulated at the international level. Indeed, nearly every state in the world has set in place a legal regime regulating the use of water resources in their territory. Many existing legislations have not been updated to take into consideration environmental protection and sustainable development considerations that have been integrated in national policies and legislation relatively recently where water policies have been developed followed by new consolidating Water Acts and regulations. Hence, many countries are undertaking a process of integration of such considerations in their respective water laws, or developing additional legislations dealing with the environmental aspects of water management. Many countries are also working to ensure that the institutions responsible for water management and the environment collaborate so as to ensure that environmental considerations are taken into account when decisions are made that concerns the use and management of national waters. Rather than reviewing specific recent Acts (such as Kenya, 2002), major trends and lessons learnt are outlined below. Diversity in conditions and circumstances in different regions and countries necessitate such treatment, thus leaving it to an interested party to critically examine the situation in their own country and other countries they may be interested in.

1. Major Trends in National Legislation

71. Governments have taken several different approaches to the protection and conservation of freshwater resources. The two most prominent approaches are water quality standards and effluent limitations. The first approach prescribes a specific quality standard for a particular watercourse, effectively proscribing pollution that would cause water quality to fall below that standard. The second approach sets the quantity of pollutants that may be legally discharged from a specific source. While the two approaches are fundamentally different, they may be combined, as some states have done. Thus, it is possible, for example, to rely principally upon effluent limitations but to calibrate them according to what is needed to meet overall water quality standards.

72. While law, policy and the literature concerning the protection of freshwater have traditionally focused on the control of pollution of water in rivers, lakes or aquifers, many experts have become convinced that it is essential to include the entire freshwater ecosystem in protection and preservation programmes. Various uses of land may affect water quality. The United Nations General Assembly has recognized the urgency of developing and implementing water resource protection approaches based on the principle of integrated watershed management, that recognize the interrelationship between water and land and provide for the preservation of aquatic ecosystems. Similarly, Agenda 21 identifies the maintenance of the integrity of aquatic ecosystems, and their protection from degradation on a drainage basin basis, as the primary objective of freshwater management. In summary, the protection of freshwater from pollution and the preservation of aquatic ecosystems are not ends in themselves. They are not objectives appropriate only for rich countries. They can actually sustain and increase the quantity of water available for a variety of uses, from domestic to agricultural and industrial. Safeguarding water supplies is a key objective of water resources management in today's world.

73. There are several important trends and issues in national water policies and legislation. The most obvious and significant trend is the incorporation of sustainable development into legislation concerning freshwater resources. Sustainable development may appear explicitly in relevant statutes or may be incorporated implicitly through an emphasis on the need to strike a proper balance between economic development and environmental protection. Other aspects of sustainable development, including a participatory approach to water management, transparency in public decision-making, and the need to ensure that minorities, women and children are not subject to discrimination, also feature in this trend.

74. An increasingly important aspect of the trend toward incorporation of sustainable development into national water legislation is the conservation of freshwater resources. The rapidly declining supply of freshwater on a per capita basis, coupled with increasing pollution and other forms of degradation, as well as the impact of global climate change, are leading governments to emphasize the need to conserve precious water resources and protect them against contamination.

75. Another important trend is integrated water resources management. Countries are increasingly deciding to manage basins holistically. This entails conducting an inventory of available water resources and of the ecosystems within which they are situated and the uses that are made of the watercourses and the surrounding land. Surface and groundwater are then used and managed conjunctively and water systems themselves are managed as an integral part of their drainage basins rather than as a separate resource. This avoids problems and inefficiencies created by separate and often conflicting regulatory regimes for different uses of water, and for uses of land and water.

76. A crucial aspect of environmental protection and natural resource management is impact assessment. The notion of Environmental Impact Assessment is widely recognized as an indispensable element of legislation in these fields at regional and national levels. See chapters 3 and 21 herein. This is an important part of the preventive approach to environmental protection. Impact assessments are often broadened to consider effects other than those on the environment, per se, such as those on groups that may be affected by the planned project or activity. The World Commission on Dams final report advocates for a new decision-making framework based on a rights and risks approach.

77. Finally, many governments are moving in the direction of various forms of water pricing and privatization of water service, seeking for greater efficiency and as a mechanism for generating the financing needed to solve public health problems caused by inadequate water supply and sanitation systems.

2. Lessons Learned

78. A wealth of lessons has been learned over the past several decades concerning the management of freshwater resources and legislative approaches to regulating the management, use and protection of this vital resource. Some of these lessons derive from past experience, which has revealed the kinds of approaches that work well and those that have not performed up to expectations. Other lessons are based upon a better understanding of both the functioning of natural systems, of which water forms a critical part, and of how these systems serve to support human life and contribute to economic development. These latter lessons are thus based not so much on experience with actual water legislation, as on knowledge that did not exist when a number of water laws were drafted.

79. Manage freshwater for sustainable development: The World Commission on Environment and Development has defined sustainable development as "development that meets the needs of the present without compromising the ability of future generations to meet their own needs." Sustainable development includes not only equity between generations (inter-generational equity) but also equity among members of Earth's, and individual countries,' present populations (intra-generational equity). More generally, sustainable development entails taking care in managing freshwater resources to ensure that efforts to raise living standards do not compromise the sustainability of those resources and associated ecosystems over time. Economic development that degrades the resource base on which it directly or indirectly depends will be short-term development only. Degradation of freshwater will threaten the livelihoods of many, if not all, and especially the poor.

80. Manage freshwater in a holistic manner: an ecosystem approach. In the words of Agenda 21, "Freshwater is a unitary resource. Long-term development of global freshwater requires holistic management of resources and a recognition of the interconnectedness of the elements related to freshwater and freshwater quality." Management of water resources is holistic when it is done on a catchment or drainage basin basis. This includes

both land and water resources, since land use can have significant impacts on freshwater and related ecosystems. A holistic approach also implies that water resources management will be integrated. Integrated Water Resources Management takes into account not only the ecosystem of which water forms an integral part but also the many different human activities, both existing and proposed, that use and affect freshwater resources. It also has a technical component (i.e., the optimal operation of a watershed or a region's entire system of water diversion, storage, conveyance, treatment and discharge works). Holistic water management is a cornerstone of sustainable development because without it, gaps, overlaps and conflicts among different sectoral management and regulatory efforts are bound to occur, impairing their effectiveness. A holistic approach also means that the different aspects of water management (i.e., its qualitative and quantitative aspects) should be managed and regulated in an integrated and consistent manner because they are strictly interdependent. This approach, also known as the ecosystem approach, is gaining consensus at the international level and is increasingly followed in many national contexts.

81. Ideally, treat all matters concerning freshwater in a single, integrated water law. The lessons that have already been discussed have shown that sustainable development and holistic water management require an integrated approach to the stewardship of freshwater resources. Following such an approach in a coherent manner may be difficult if the relevant laws are contained in scattered statutes. Therefore, as far as practicable, all aspects of water use and protection should be dealt with in a single piece of legislation. There is a tendency in some recently enacted water legislation to follow this approach. The greater the integration of law, the greater the facilitation of holistic management, since all aspects of water regulation may be harmonized in one document. It also helps the drafter to avoid gaps, overlaps, inconsistencies and conflicts in the statutory scheme.

82. Several countries have gone beyond the integration of water resources statutes into a single law by enacting laws that address the sustainable development of multiple resources (e.g., water resources, forestry resources, land use, biological

communities), in a single law. The same benefits that come from integration of all the laws governing a particular resource into a single law may be multiplied by the integration of all the laws governing multiple natural resources into a single law.

83. Conserve water through rational urban development policies: There are well-known examples of large population centres that are located in arid areas, far from sources of freshwater. These cities have, typically, experienced fast growth and inadequate local water supplies, and have therefore been forced to transport water over long distances. This usually results in losses of water through evaporation and seepage, and often works to the serious detriment of ecosystems and even populations at the water's source. While there are well-recognized limits on the authority of governments to control where people live, this sort of situation should be anticipated and avoided wherever possible.

84. Build in ways to collaborate with stakeholders: A participatory approach to freshwater resources management should be ensured, one that includes all stakeholders in relevant decision-making processes that provides opportunities for meaningful collaboration between water planners and managers, and interested public and private sector stakeholders. By harnessing the interest, the knowledge, the financial and staff resources, and the political support of stakeholders, water planning and management authorities can leverage their own limited ministerial resources. Among other benefits, such an approach allows those with knowledge of specific local needs and conditions to inform planning and management processes, helping to forestall potential future difficulties. This approach also fosters a sense of legitimacy of those processes and hence of ownership of the results they produce. Ultimately, it can help ensure a more robust solution to planning and management challenges in a given area.

85. Inclusion of environmental impact assessment in project approval processes: Many countries today have legislation requiring the assessment of environmental and other impacts of proposed projects. Impact assessment is an integral part of the preventive approach to environmental protection and thus, sustainable development.

86. <u>Groundwater and surface water should not be treated separately:</u> While there are differences between surface and groundwater that make some provisions applicable only to one water body and not the other, water codes should treat surface and groundwater as parts of a unified planning and permit system. This is especially important for aquifers that are hydrologically connected with a surface watercourse. In such circumstances, groundwater extraction and surface water diversion can have mutually reinforcing effects.

Stephen C. McCaffrey, Distinguished Professor and Scholar, University of the Pacific, McGeorge School of Law

Maria Cristina Zucca, Associate Legal Officer, UNEP

Resources

<u>Internet Materials</u>

FAO Land and Water Development Division, Water Resources, Development and Management Services available at http://www.fao.org/landandwater/aglw/index.stm

International Network of Basin Organizations available at www.riob.org

International Year of Freshwater 2003 available at www.wateryear2003.org/en/

Nile Basin Initiative available at www.nilebasin.org

Patricia Wouters, The Legal Response to International Water Scarcity and Water Conflicts: the United Nations Watercourses Convention and Beyond available at www.thewaterpage.com

The International Law Commission ("ILC") available at http://www.un.org/law/ilc/

The United Nations Treaty Database available at http://untreaty.un.org/

The Water Page website available at www.thewaterpage.org

The World Bank, Water Resources Management available at http://lnweb18.worldbank.org/ESSD/ardext.nsf/18ByDocName/WaterResourcesManagement

United Nations Development Programme, UNDP and Water available at http://www.undp.org/water/

United Nations Economic Commission for Europe, Activities on Water available at http://www.unece.org/env/water/

United Nations Educational Scientific and Cultural Organization, the Water Portal available at http://www.unesco.org/water/

United Nations Environment Programme, Activities in Freshwater available at http://www.unep.org/themes/freshwater/

United Nations Environment Programme, Environmental Law Programme available at www.unep.org/dpdl/law

World Health Organization, Water homepage available at http://www.who.int/health_topics/water/en/

Text Materials

Alexander Kiss, Dinah Shelton, INTERNATIONAL ENVIRONMENTAL LAW, (third edition, Transnational Publishers Inc., 2004).

Attila Tanzi, THE UNITED NATIONS CONVENTION ON THE LAW OF INTERNATIONAL WATERCOURSES: A FRAMEWORK FOR SHARING, (Kluwer Law International, 2001).

ATLAS OF INTERNATIONAL FRESHWATER AGREEMENTS, (UNEP, 2002).

Augusto Dante Caponera, THE LAW OF INTERNATIONAL WATER RESOURCES: SOME GENERAL CONVENTIONS, DECLARATIONS AND RESOLUTIONS ADOPTED BY GOVERNMENTS, INTERNATIONAL LEGAL INSTITUTIONS, AND INTERNATIONAL ORGANIZATIONS, ON THE MANAGEMENT OF INTERNATIONAL WATER RESOURCES, (Food and Agriculture Organization of the United Nations, 1980).

Bryan Randolph & Ruth Suseela Meinzen-Dick, NEGOTIATING WATER RIGHTS, (ITDG Pub., 2000).

Edward H.P. Brans, THE SCARCITY OF WATER: EMERGING LEGAL AND POLICY RESPONSES, (Kluwer Law International, 1997).

Gerhard Loibl, AGREEMENTS FOR MANAGEMENT OF SHARED GROUNDWATER RESOURCES, IN GROUNDWATER LAW AND ADMINISTRATION FOR SUSTAINABLE DEVELOPMENT, (edited by Sergio Marchiso, Fatma Bassiouni and Maria Cristina Zucca).

GLOBAL ENVIRONMENTAL OUTLOOK 3, (UNEP, 2002).

GUIDEBOOK FOR POLICY AND LEGISLATIVE DEVELOPMENT ON CONSERVATION AND SUSTAINABLE USE OF FRESHWATER RESOURCES, (UNEP, 2005).

Giuseppe Cataldi, LEGAL ASPECTS OF GROUNDWATER: SOURCES AND EVOLUTION OF INTERNATIONAL LAW, IN GROUNDWATER LAW AND ADMINISTRATION FOR SUSTAINABLE DEVELOPMENT, (edited by Sergio Marchiso, Fatma Bassiouni and Maria Cristina Zucca).

International Bureau of the Permanent Court of Arbitration, RESOLUTION OF INTERNATIONAL WATER DISPUTES, (Aspen, 2003).

Patricia Birnie and Alan Boyle, INTERNATIONAL LAW AND THE ENVIRONMENT, (second edition).

Patricia Wouters, INTERNATIONAL WATER LAW: SELECTED WRITINGS OF PROFESSOR CHARLES B. BOURNE, (Kluwer Law International, 1997).

Stephen C. McCaffrey, THE LAW OF INTERNATIONAL WATERCOURSES – NON NAVIGATIONAL USES – (Oxford, 2001).

THE RELATIONSHIP BETWEEN THE 1992 UN/ECE CONVENTION ON THE PROTECTION AND USE OF TRANSBOUNDARY WATERCOURSES AND INTERNATIONAL LAKES AND THE 1997 UN CONVENTION ON THE LAW OF THE NON-NAVIGATIONAL USES ON INTERNATIONAL WATERCOURSES - REPORT OF THE UN/ECE TASK FORCE ON LEGAL AND ADMINISTRATIVE ASPECTS, prepared by Attila Tanzi.

VITAL WATER GRAPHICS – AN OVERVIEW OF THE WORLD'S FRESH AND MARINE WATERS, (UNEP).

UNEP ENVIRONMENTAL LAW TRAINING MANUAL, (UNEP, 1997).

19. DESERTIFICATION

I. Introduction

1. In all countries of the world, land is a critical resource and the basis for survival. Its degradation, therefore, threatens not only economic but also the physical well-being. Soils in drylands are particularly vulnerable to degradation because they are deficient in moisture, humus and nutrients. New soils in these habitats are formed over long periods of time, from a few thousand to millions of years. A single centimetre of soil may take from twenty to a thousand years to form. Yet, this centimetre can be, and is often destroyed or lost within seconds when the land is mistreated through chemical pollution, over-irrigation, or eroded by water or wind.

2. This chapter discusses desertification, a negative transformation that results primarily from man's over-dependence, overuse and/or mismanagement of inherently fragile lands, especially dry lands. Land degradation, which result from the poor land use practices is of global occurrence, leaves no continent unaffected. UNEP has estimated that globally, about fifty-one million square kilometres is threatened by desertification, which supports one fifth of the world population. There are over 110 countries, including more than 80 developing countries affected by desertification. In Africa alone, some 36 countries are seriously affected by desertification. Globally, there are over 250 million people who are directly affected by desertification.

3. This chapter reviews and discusses the problem of desertification: what it is, its causes, manifestations, effects and scope. It proceeds to provide an overview of international law that has been developed to address desertification and the attendant ecological and socio-economic problems, primarily by examining the scope of the 1994 United Nations Convention to Combat Desertification in Countries experiencing Serious Drought and/or Desertification, particularly in Africa ("Convention") and the applicability of non-legally binding instruments for prevention and control. In establishing rules and regulations to address a particular environmental problem, international instruments, including the Convention, require parties to enact and implement laws at national level and examples of national laws to implement the Convention.

II. International Context

1. The Problem

4. Desertification is defined as the reduction or loss of biological or economic productivity of land resulting from land use or from processes such as water or wind erosion. The United Nations General Assembly coined the term desertification when it decided to convene a conference on the subject in the wake of several years of harsh drought and famine in Africa, particularly in the Sahel region. Desertification does not refer to the expansion of existing deserts. The Convention defines desertification as, "land degradation in arid, semi-arid and dry sub-humid areas resulting from various factors, including climatic variations and human activities." The Convention is also concerned with dryland areas, which are susceptible to desertification.

5. Dryland areas are conventionally defined in terms of water stress so that the *ratio* of mean annual precipitation ("P") to the mean annual potential evapotranspiration (PET) is less than 1.0. The P/PET for arid, semi-arid and dry sub-humid drylands falls within the range of 0.05 to 0.65. (See also article 1(g) of the Convention). The hyperarid regions (true deserts) where P/PET is less than 0.05, as well as areas that lie within humid ecosystems with P/PET of more than 0.65, are excluded from the Convention areas of concern although they may also be affected by land degradation.

6. The arid, semi-arid and dry sub-humid areas cover 6,150 million hectares, or about 47% of total land area in the world. Drylands are ecologically fragile areas; they are characterized by low rainfall that is also seasonal, high rates of evapotranspiration that exceed the rate of precipitation, highly variable rainfall and high potential for water logging and salinization, especially of irrigated lands.

7. Drylands are particularly vulnerable to desertification because they recover slowly from disturbance. With a limited supply of water, new soils form very slowly; salts once accumulated tend to remain where they are; and soils that are dry, poorly held together, and sparsely covered by vegetation are susceptible to erosion. Infrequent rains are particularly erosive, especially where vegetation cover is sparse. Despite the harsh environmental conditions prevailing in the drylands, they still provide much of the world's grain and livestock and constitute critical habitats that support much of the game animals including large mammals and migratory birds.

2. Causes and Consequences

8. Desertification is the result of complex interaction between physical, chemical, biological, socio-economic and political factors of local, national and global nature. The main causes of desertification include: deforestation, clearance of marginal lands for cultivation, poor management of arable land including over use of fertilizers and pesticides, poor irrigation practices, uncontrolled dumping of wastes, deposition of pollutants from the air, encroachment of desert sands onto croplands and poor land-use planning. Such human activities degrade soil fertility and other useful components, loosen soil structure and reduce vegetation cover, thereby exposing land to erosion by rain and wind. Landslides also occur easily.

9. Similarly, maintaining large numbers of livestock leads to overgrazing and to soil compaction due to constant trampling of the ground by animals. The impact loosens the soil structure, affects the health of plant communities, and exposes soil to erosion by wind and water. These ultimately render the land useless.

10. Climate change could also affect agriculture by causing long-term changes in agro-ecosystems through increased frequency and severity of extreme weather events, such as heat waves, droughts, flooding and cyclones, all of which could exacerbate soil erosion and affect patterns of plant diseases and pest infestation.

11. Another factor is chemical degradation of soils, which causes loss of nutrients and/or loss of organic matter, salinization, pollution and acidification. The physical processes involved include compaction, sealing and crusting, waterlogging, and subsidence of organic soils. The other agents of soil degradation include rising sea-level due to either subsidence or climate warming, flooding of valleys for hydroelectric purposes, tourism development of long beaches and in the mountains, and expansion of urban and industrial areas.

12. In addition, international trade patterns can lead to short-term exploitation of land resources for export purposes, leaving negligible profit at the community level for land rehabilitation. Similarly, the development of an economy based on cash crops results in the distortion of local markets and promotes overexploitation of land.

3. Scope and Magnitude of the Problem

13. The three examples (Chile, China and Africa) below demonstrate that the processes of land degradation leading to the loss or reduction of fertility and productivity of land are not limited to one country or continent. They have continued, and continue to take place, in varying degrees, all over the world, making desertification a global problem in terms of occurrence. Besides occurrence, the problem of desertification is global in many other respects. For example, there are close linkages between desertification and poverty, which has implications for global humanitarian assistance.

14. In Africa, an estimated 500 million hectares of land have been affected by soil degradation since 1950, including 65% of the regions agricultural land. In Latin America, land degradation affects 300 million hectares of land as a result of soil erosion, loss of nutrients, deforestation, overgrazing and poor management of agricultural land. In Europe, approximately 12% of the land (115 million hectares) is affected by water erosion. In North America, about ninety-five million hectares are affected by land degradation mainly due to erosion. In Asia, out of a total land area of 4.3 billion hectares, the region contains some 1.7 billion hectares of drylands.

15. Desertification problems raise a number of environmental issues requiring effective laws at the international and national levels to provide basis for joint and individual actions to address them. These issues include:

- Recognizing that some lands are ecologically fragile and require proper management to avoid turning them into deserts;
- Controlling of human activities on ecologically fragile lands to prevent desertification;
- Creating regulatory control of deforestation and soil erosion, among others, to reduce and prevent land degradation;
- Controlling population growth to prevent and reduce negative population impacts on fragile lands;
- Rehabilitating desertified lands and lands experiencing impacts of drought that might eventually lead to desertification;
- Acting to address socio-economic impacts of desertification and drought in affected areas;
- Integrating the development of lands in environmentally sensitive areas to sustainable development of the areas; and
- Encouraging of diversification of cropping

systems as well as the adoption of appropriate agricultural technologies, among others, to halt and reverse land degradation.

III. National/Regional Examples

1. Chile

16. Part of Chile, which lies between the Pacific Ocean to the West, Argentina to the South and Atacama desert to the North, is arid. It receives rainfall for short periods in the winter and experiences long dry periods of eight to nine months. Its topography consists of many rugged ranges. These features make the land fragile. As a result of mining activities in the region, large areas were cleared and agricultural activities and livestock raising were intensified by the local people, especially in the short wet periods to meet demands of the increasing populations, without proper soil management measures.

17. Over time, human activities led to massive loss of vegetation cover and organic matter and exposed the light-textured soils to the heat of the sun during the dry season and to the direct action of heavy rains in the short wet seasons. Heavy soil erosion set in throughout the entire area, especially where there were human settlements, resulting in the decimation of vegetation. In addition, heavy losses of top soil occurred. These changes led to reduction in productivity of the land and to reduced human development activities, making the area to be declared by the Chilean government, "a zone of extreme poverty". Because subsistence and development activities could no longer take place on the land, there has been continuous emigration of people from the area, a phenomenon that has created a distortion in the population distribution by age and sex, with accompanying effects on family structures.

2. China

18. Much of the land in China to the north of the country where the Gurbantunggut, Taklimakan, Komdag, Badin Jaran and other deserts in the country are found is dry. Most of the lands receive less than 200 millimetres of annual rainfall with evaporation reaching as high as 4,000 millimetres. Prior to 1956, the country had gone through a century of political turmoil, during which desertification advanced unhindered across the northern dry lands as wind-driven sand dunes swept across the northern part of the country, covering agricultural lands on the river banks and causing people to retreat southwards.

19. The impacts of the shifting dunes were exacerbated by intensive deforestation and plundering of agricultural and other activities of the colonizing powers that occupied China at the time. These activities removed vegetation cover, caused heavy soil erosion and exposed more lands to moving sand dunes, thus, rendering more land unproductive. Upon regaining its status the Chinese government took several measures to combat the process of desertification with appreciable success.

3. Africa

20. In the areas south of the Sahara desert covering Burkina Faso, Mali, Niger, Chad, Gambia and other countries, rainfall is very scanty, evapotranspiration far exceeds precipitation during most months of the year and only one rain-fed crop can be grown in a normal year without irrigation. The climate is generally harsh- a short rainy season, often characterized by violent and unpredictable showers followed by a long dry season. Therefore, the area is ecologically fragile.

21. For many years, people living in these areas practiced shifting cultivation- cutting down trees, slashing and burning portions of land for cultivation for a certain length of time and then abandoning them to regenerate while they moved to newer areas. The increasing population led to the extension of agricultural lands closer to the desert margins without allowing enough time for vegetation regeneration. Areas along rivers in the area were also intensively and extensively irrigated without proper checks on water logging and salinization. Over time, these activities exposed much of the soil to the sun, heat, heavy rains and soil erosion during the wet seasons, and to sweeping desert sand dunes during the long dry periods.

22. As more land became useless and productivity reduced, famine and poverty set in and many migrated from their homelands to urban centres. The situation worsened due to the long periods of drought between 1968 and 1973, and between 1982 and 1985, which led to the drying up of major rivers in the area. The entire belt was turned into a desert adjoining the Sahara desert, which resulted in loss of livestock due to lost pastures, severe famine, deaths to many people in the countries, massive migration, and the desperate need for food aid for millions of people in these areas. According the Report of the United Nations Conference on Desertification (Nairobi, 1977), between 100,000-250,000 people died and 3.5 million heads of cattle perished as a result of the

Sudano-Sahelian drought of 1968-1973. No disaster of a similar magnitude had occurred elsewhere in the world.

IV. The International Legal Regime

23. As a result of the problems explained above, especially the situation in Africa, the international community took steps to develop legally and non-legally binding instruments establishing rules and regulations that provide the basis for action to combat desertification and mitigate the impacts of drought. There are a number of conventions dealing with matters related to land degradation, desertification and/or drought, such as the United Nations Framework Convention on Climate Change, which is discussed in more detail in Chapter 10 above. However, the only binding international agreement focusing specifically on the problem of desertification, land degradation and drought is the United Nations Convention to combat Desertification in Countries experiencing Serious Drought and/or Desertification, particularly in Africa, adopted in Paris, France, on 17 June 1994, and entered into force on 26 December 1996. It consists of a preamble, six parts and five Regional Implementation Annexes for Africa, Asia, Latin America and the Caribbean, Northern Mediterranean and Central and Eastern Europe respectively. It has currently (as of November 2005) 191 parties, making it a global treaty.

24. The objective of the Convention, provided in article 2, is "to combat desertification and mitigate the effects of drought in countries experiencing serious drought and/or desertification, particularly in Africa, through effective action at all levels, supported by international cooperation and partnership arrangements..." The article further calls on all parties to take appropriate measures to prevent and mitigate the problems in those areas that are considered to be environmentally sensitive and prone to drought and desertification and to restore areas that have, or are experiencing negative impacts that might eventually lead to desertification. Parties are also required to address underlying causes of desertification, such as high rates of population growth and lack of necessary information on the part of local communities. In addition, parties are required to address the social and economic effects of desertification, such as famine and poverty. The Convention requires that all steps and actions be integrated as part of sustainable development of affected areas.

25. The Convention creates three types of obligations on parties to be fulfilled as they are guided by the established principles (1) general and specific

obligations of all parties, (2) obligations of affected parties, and (3) obligations of developed countries that are parties to the Convention.

26. Article 4(1) and (2) requires that any plans and other strategies to address the problems shall be coherent, integrated, long-term and coordinated. Strategies to address the causes as well as the socio-economic aspects of drought and desertification would, for example, include soil erosion control measures, famine relief programmes, and poverty eradication measures. Parties are also obliged to give priority to affected African countries, without neglecting affected parties in other developing regions.

27. Further, article 4(2)(d)-(f) obligates parties to promote cooperation amongst them at all levels: national, sub-regional, regional and international. Cooperation allows them to create appropriate institutional mechanisms and to use existing bilateral and multilateral financial mechanisms and arrangements to facilitate their efforts to protect and conserve the environment in ways that can prevent or minimize desertification and drought. This would require, for example, that countries establish joint funds to finance programmes and projects undertaken to combat desertification.

28. By the time the Convention entered into force, some countries had already taken some measures to combat desertification and the effects of drought. For example, African States had already established the Cairo Programme of Action during their Ministerial Conference on Environment in 1985, through which pilot projects were being undertaken in some countries with support of the Club du Sahel, UNSO, CILSS and other partners. In recognition of this fact, article 4(1) of the Convention places an obligation on all parties to make use of such existing and future arrangements of a similar nature between two or more countries to jointly or individually carry out agreed plans, actions and strategies for combating desertification and the effects of drought, including rehabilitation of degraded lands.

29. In article 8, the Convention recognizes that other international agreements with similar objective exist. Such other agreements have objectives that relate to the integrated development of land, control of soil erosion, deforestation, reclamation of degraded land and prevention of degradation of biological productivity of land. They include the Convention on Biological Diversity and the United Nations Framework Convention on Climate Change. Article 8(1) of the Desertification Convention therefore directs that where parties have made commitments to conduct activities

under such other international agreements, the activities shall be coordinated with those under the Convention in order to derive maximum benefits and to avoid duplication of effort.

30. There can be little doubt that implementation of the various agreed measures would be costly. In recognition of this fact, parties agreed that, depending on their capability, they would make financial resources available for establishment of training centres; and for scientific research and other actions that the convention requires. However, because of the limited financial resources of developing countries, especially those in Africa, developed countries that are parties to the Desertification Convention have an obligation under articles 20 and 21 to financially support their developing counterparts. The Convention further requires developed country parties to mobilize funds from the Global Environment Facility ("GEF"), and from other sources, and to channel the resources to developing country parties in order to meet this requirement. For example, the government of Canada may individually provide funds and technological assistance to the government of Burkina Faso to develop appropriate soil erosion control techniques. The government of Canada may also, jointly with the government of the Netherlands, provide similar support. Developed country parties can also collaborate with the Conference of the Parties ("COP") under the Convention to create other financial mechanisms and sources for funds from multilateral financial institutions such as the World Bank and the International Monetary Fund. To allow parties to work with institutions created by the Convention to implement its provisions, each party is required to appoint a representative to serve as the focal point to liaise with the Convention Secretariat and the COP.

31. The Convention's obligations for preventing and/or minimizing the effects of desertification and drought make it necessary for parties to have ample accurate and relevant information on various matters. Availability of accurate and sufficient information and its proper utilization requires research on various aspects of the desertification problem and adoption of appropriate technologies. Capacity to gather information, conduct research and adopt appropriate technologies varies greatly between developed countries, developing countries, and least developed countries. Therefore, articles 17(1) and 18 require parties, according to their respective capabilities, to promote technical and scientific cooperation in the fields of combating desertification and mitigating the effects of drought through appropriate national and sub-regional institutions.

32. In addition to obligations of all parties, article 5(c) requires parties affected by desertification and drought to take steps and actions within their countries to address the problems of desertification and drought and their underlying causes, including ecological and socio-economic factors. For example, to minimize the intensive cultivation of marginal lands that leads to soil erosion and desertification, parties are responsible for taking measures to reduce the rate of population growth. Further, article 5(a) and (b) obligates them to give priority to addressing the problems. This means, for example, that in government budgets, combating desertification and drought should be given funding priority.

33. Articles 9 and 10 of the Convention introduces obligations with respect to National Action Programmes ("NAPs"), which are key instruments for implementing the Convention. Affected countries are required to develop NAPs that will combat the problem of desertification in their particular country. The NAPs should suit each country's domestic circumstances. The information to be contained in the NAPs is stipulated in article 10 and includes: factors identified by each party as contributing to desertification and drought; measures necessary to combat them; specification of roles to be played by governments, local communities and other users of natural resources in combating desertification and drought; resources available to combat desertification and drought and necessary resources that are still lacking. The programme areas for combating desertification and drought that may be included in NAPs are stipulated in article 10(2), (3) and (4) and include: improvement and/or establishment of the early warning systems and food security; development of sustainable irrigation programmes; establishment of institutional and legal frameworks; promotion of capacity-building, promotion of environmental education; and strengthening capabilities for assessment and observation of hydrological and meteorological services. Once NAPs are developed, article 9(1) requires parties to make them public and implement programmes stipulated in them.

34. To harmonize, complement and increase the efficiency of NAPs, affected countries that are parties to the Convention are also required under article 11 to jointly prepare and implement sub-regional and regional action programmes ("SRAPs" and "RAPs"). In formulating the SRAPs and RAPs, parties are called upon to ensure that the programmes are trans-boundary in nature, and that they do not duplicate efforts of national programmes but rather complement them and increase their efficiency. The five regional

implementation Annexes to the Convention contain specific guidelines on the content, steps and actions that need to be taken depending on the particular circumstances of each region.

35. Under article 17 and 18, the Convention requires parties to collect and analyze relevant information and data through studies and research for practical application. Parties are also required to facilitate and strengthen a global network of institutions for collecting, analyizing and exchanging information; to link national, sub-regional and regional data and information collection centres to the global institutions; and to promote and support research activities on relevant areas depending on their capacities. In addition, developed countries that are parties to there to are required to develop and transfer relevant technologies, information, know-how and best practices on desertification prevention and control to developing parties as necessary.

36. Article 19 obligates parties to build the capacity of national institutions, especially of developing countries, as well as the capacity of intergovernmental organizations through training, financial support, establishment of extension services and by disseminating information on environmentally sound methods that can facilitate measures to combat desertification and mitigate the effects of drought.

37. To provide the basis and legitimacy for necessary steps and actions, articles 5(e), 10(4) and 16(g) require parties to strengthen and enforce existing national laws on subjects related to prevention and control of desertification and drought, and to create and enforce relevant laws where laws are lacking. Relevant laws may be created, for example, in the form of acts of parliament, local authority regulations and executive orders and decrees providing for programmes and actions for combating desertification and the effects of drought.

38. Further, parties are required by articles 5(d) and 10(e)-(f), among other provisions, to fully involve local citizens, NGOs and Community-Based Organizations ("CBOs") in formulating the plan of action for combating desertification and mitigating the effects of drought. The NGOs and the CBOs have major roles to play in participatory processes, particularly in the organization of local communities for effective participation in combating desertification. The Convention, therefore, advocates a bottom-up approach and stresses the crucial roles of NGOs and CBOs in its implementation.

39. To allow effective implementation of agreed steps, actions and programmes, the Convention establishes a number of key institutions, including a Conference of the Parties, to be the political decision-making body. This supreme body comprises of representatives of all parties to the Convention. Under articles 22, 30 and 31, the COP is the organ responsible for reviewing reports submitted by parties detailing how they are carrying out their commitments as well as facilitating the exchange of information and other matters mandated by the Convention.

1. Committee on Science and Technology

40. The steps, actions and programmes that are mandated by the Convention require substantial scientific and technological studies, research and information, as well as development, adoption and transfer of appropriate technologies to developing countries. To these ends, a Committee on Science and Technology ("CST") was established under article 24 as a subsidiary body to the COP. The Committee is composed of governmental representatives who have expertise and competence in fields relevant to desertification and drought and is the key organ with respect to these matters.

41. In accordance with articles 18 and 19 of the Convention, functions of the CST include giving advice and providing the COP with information on scientific research, and on specific issues concerning the state of the art in technology that is relevant to combating desertification and mitigating the effects of drought.

42. The COP may also appoint ad hoc panels to provide, through the CST, relevant information, data and advice on specific issues. The CST also provides advice to the COP on the structure, membership and maintenance of the roster of independent experts as well as suggesting possible research priorities for particular regions and sub-regions.

43. The other functions of CST relate to data and information collection, analysis and exchange, as well as evaluating the application of science and technology to research projects aimed at the implementation of the Convention. Some of the key issues that the CST has been concerned with in the context of its implementation of the Convention include establishment and testing of benchmarks and indicators, integration of traditional knowledge and technologies with modern science, and establishment of the Early Warning Systems for drought and crop forecasting through remote

sensing, atmospheric weather monitoring and water conservation monitoring, among others.

2. Resolution of Disputes

44. Disputes are likely to arise on matters concerning the interpretation or applicability of a global convention such as the Desertification Convention. Issues concerning technology transfer, funding and many others that the Convention authorizes are likely to generate disputes and claims among parties that would require resolution. As a first step, article 28(1) of the Convention requires that a party that has a dispute or claim against another party must inform that other party that there exists a dispute between them. Subsequently, the Convention provides that disputes are to be settled in one of three ways.

45. First and foremost, disputes are to be settled through negotiation, or other peaceful means of choice to the parties involved. If one or more parties to a dispute do not wish to resolve their claims or disputes through negotiation, they are mandated to pursue other peaceful means, such as conciliation.

46. Second, under article 28(2)(a), disputes can be settled through arbitration. This provision is applicable to a party that is a government, or a regional economic integration organization, such as the European Community, if, at the time of becoming a party to the Convention, or at any other time thereafter, it declares in writing and submits the written declaration to the Convention Secretariat, stating that it recognizes arbitration as a compulsory means of resolving disputes in relation to any party that also accepts arbitration.

47. Third, disputes may be resolved by the International Court of Justice ("ICJ") upon submission to it by the disputing parties. This option is open to state parties if they have submitted written declarations to the Secretariat, stating that dispute settlement between the state issuing a declaration and any other state that also accepts compulsory resolution by the Court shall be submitted to the Court.

48. If parties fail to resolve disputes between themselves within a period of twelve months of the notification of one party by another that a dispute exists between them, the Convention mandates that the dispute shall be resolved through conciliation at the request of any of the parties involved. This provision applies to governments, as well as regional economic integration organizations that are parties. Disputes shall also be referred to conciliation at the request of a party, if parties to the dispute are governments and one or more of them have not, by declaration, accepted resolution by arbitration or by submission to the ICJ.

3. Developments since Adoption

49. Since the Convetion was adopted and entered into force, a number of activities have been undertaken by parties and by the Convention's organs to implement its provisions. For example, many countries have developed, implemented and submitted reports on their NAPs to the Convention Secretariat, in addition to creating and strengthening a variety of domestic laws to implement the Convention. As of May 2005, more than 75 NAPs had been prepared. In Africa, all the sub-regions have developed the SRAPs in the context of UNCCD implementation.

50. In addition, some (sub-)regions have prepared resource mobilization strategies to support the implementation of SRAPs. Among other activities, the fourth COP adopted Annex V, the Regional Implementation Annex for Central and Eastern Europe, which became the latest addition to the text of the Convention. The Annex provides guidance to parties in the regions on the development of NAPs and on other matters concerning implementation of the Convention.

51. A total of seven sessions of the COP have been held since the adoption of the Convention: in Rome (1997), Dakar (1998), Recife (1999), Bonn (2000), Geneva (2001), Havana (2003), and Nairobi (2005). With effect from 2001, COP sessions were to be held on a biannual basis, interchanging with sessions of the Committee for the Review of the Implementation of the Convention.

52. Other notable developments of the Convention since its adoption include:

- The establishment of the Committee for the Review of the Implementation of the Convention ("CRIC");
- COP-6 accepted the GEF as the financial mechanism of the Convention and in 2005 a MOU between the GEF and the Convention was concluded as enhanced collaboration; and
- Convening the first meeting of the Group of Experts in Hamburg, Germany, in November 2002.
- In 2005, the establishment of Ad Hoc Working Group to improve the procedures for communication and information, as well as reporting.

V. National Implementation

53. The Desertification Convention creates obligations on parties to take legal and regulatory measures to accomplish its objectives, namely the prevention and/or reduction of land degradation, the rehabilitation of degraded land, the reclamation of desertified land and the mitigation of the effects of drought. Parties are required to take legal and regulatory measures to meet these ends as part of sustainable development of ecologically sensitive habitats, namely arid, semi-arid and dry sub-humid areas. In this respect, the Convention particularly obligates parties to:

- Strengthen relevant existing legislation, to establish long-term policies and action programmes, to provide an enabling environment to combat desertification and mitigate the effects of drought under article 5(e);
- Create laws, where appropriate, to establish and facilitate long-term policies and actions to combat desertification and mitigate the effects of drought under article 5(e);
- Create legal and institutional frameworks to facilitate the implementation of National Action Programmes for combating desertification and the effects of drought under article 10(4);
- Develop national legislation on the basis of which information may be exchanged on local traditional knowledge on combating desertification and mitigating the effects of drought under article 16(g);
- Promote, finance, transfer, acquire, adapt and develop environmentally sound and economically viable technologies that are relevant for combating desertification and mitigating the effects of drought through appropriate legislation under article 18(1);
- Create legal frameworks to build the capacity of people, educate them and raise their awareness on measures to combat desertification and mitigate the effects of drought as required by article 19(1)(j); and
- Incorporate into the National Action Programmes, institutional, legal and regulatory frameworks that would, among other things, ensure proper natural resource management and provide security of land tenure for local people under article 8(3)(c) (iii) of the Regional Implementation Annex for Africa.

54. Legislation on steps, actions and activities to achieve the obligations of the Convention may, for example, contain provisions for soil erosion control and prohibition of deforestation. Three examples (China, Malawi and Cameroon) demonstrate

various legal measures that have been taken to implement the Convention and how legal measures can be used to address desertification, drought and related problems. The examples also highlight essential components of implementing national legislation, including purposes or objectives of the legislation, definitions, especially of unfamiliar words used, provisions for key measures stipulated in the Convention, provisions for implementing bodies and organs, and financial and enforcement mechanisms.

1. China

55. China has been seriously impacted by desertification. An estimated 27% of the country's land mass is desertified with an average of 2,460 square kilometres of land being lost to deserts each year. Nearly 400 million people live in these areas, and the economic loss to China has been estimated at around US $6.5 billion per year. China signed the Convention on 14 October 1996, and ratified it on 18 February 1997, becoming the sixty-fourth party thereto.

56. In its implementation of the Convention's provisions on creating and strengthening appropriate legislation on desertification and drought, China passed a Law of the People's Republic of China on Desert Prevention and Transformation ("Desert Prevention Law") in August 2001, which took effect on 1 January 2002.

57. In addition to providing the guiding principles, it requires a number of specific prevention and control measures, including support by the state of scientific research and technological development on desert prevention and transformation as stipulated in article 7.

58. Further, article 33 provides for the application of economic instruments such as fund subsidies, financial discounts and tax exemptions to encourage people to take measures to prevent desertification and transform desertified and degraded lands. Article 38 and other provisions of the Desert Prevention Law also provide for penalties for activities that lead to desertification and those that tend to defeat land restoration measures.

59. Articles 4, 5 and other provisions of the Desert Prevention Law provide for its implementation and enforcement by a number of Chinese institutions and organs, including the State Council with overall leadership, local governments at county and other levels and the administrative departments in charge of forestry, agriculture, irrigation works, land, environment protection, and

meteorology. Among other sources, funds for implementation of desertification control and prevention measures in affected areas are to be derived from financial budgets and allocations for the areas as stipulated in article 32.

60. Sample provisions of China's national legislation dealing with desertification are as follows:

China, Desert Prevention Laws articles 1-3

1. This Law was formulated in order to prevent land desertification, to transform desertified land, to protect the safety of environment and to promote the sustainable development of economy and society.

2. Desertified land referred to in this Law means the land that has already been desertified and the land that is obviously going to be desertified. The specific scope shall be clarified by the planning on national desert prevention and transformation approved by the State Council.

3. Desert prevention and transformation shall follow the following principles: (1) planning desert prevention and transformation uniformly, adjusting it according to the circumstances, carrying it out step by step, and insisting on the combination of regional and key prevention and transformation.

---

61. Pursuant to the provisions of China's law on desertification, China, in October 2002, forged a very important partnership with the Council of the GEF in which the Council endorsed in Beijing a "Country Programming Framework" ("CPF") covering a ten-year period beginning in 2003. The Framework between the GEF and China will support a sequenced set of priority activities that strengthen the enabling environment and build institutional capacity for integrated approaches to combat land degradation, desertification and to mitigate the effects of drought.

62. The programme adopts an integrated ecosystem management model for widespread replication. The total estimated cost of the CPF over a ten-year period is US $1.5 billion. The Chinese Government will contribute US $700 million and mobilise an additional US $615 million from other donors to finance baseline activities. Work on the project commenced in 2003.

2. Malawi

63. Malawi occupies the southern part of the East African Rift Valley. Malawi has an area of approximately 119,140 square kilometres, 20% of which is covered by water. Its topography and climatic conditions are greatly varied. Out of a total population of over 9,838,486, 29% of Malawi's citizens live in dry lands, mainly in the Rift Valley floor districts. Despite disappointing results, the majority of its population has over the years cultivated maize. Wood fuel constitutes 90% of their domestic energy source, especially in the dry lands. This means that the rate of degradation of vegetation and subsequently soils has been very high. These factors describe Malawi's susceptibility to desertification and drought-related problems that have been discussed in this chapter.

64. In order to facilitate its efforts to combat desertification, Malawi became a party to the Desertification Convention in June 1996, and has since taken a number of legislative and other implementing measures. In this respect, a National Environmental Management Act was enacted in 1996, to provide a comprehensive framework for the management of its environment and natural resources. In addition, the Forestry Act of Malawi enacted in 1997, and took effect the same year as part of the country's implementation of the Convention. The preamble to the Forestry Act specifically states that the purpose of the Act is, among other things, to provide for the protection and rehabilitation of environmentally fragile areas.

65. Malawi's Forestry Act, Sections 4, 5, 15 and 16, establishes a number of offices, institutions and mechanisms for implementation of its provisions. These include the office of the Director of Forestry charged with the responsibility of planning for the activities intended to meet to set objectives, and a Forestry Management Board. Section 55 of the Forestry Act establishes a Forest Development and Management Fund as a financial mechanism to support the various implementation and enforcement activities provided for.

66. Sample provisions of the Forestry Act of Malawi are as follows:

Preamble: "An Act to provide for...protection and rehabilitation of environmentally fragile areas..."

Purposes of the Act (section 3): "(a) to identify and manage areas of permanent forest as protection or production forest in order to maintain environmental stability; to prevent resource degradation and to increase social and economic benefits; (b) to augment, protect and manage trees and forest on customary land in order to meet basic fuelwood and forest produce needs of local communities and for the conservation of soil and water; (c) to promote community involvement in conservation of trees and forests in forest reserves and protected forest areas in accordance with the provisions of this Act; (d) to empower village natural resource management committees to source financial and technical assistance from the private sector, Non-Governmental Organizations and other organisations; (f) to promote optimal land use practices through agroforestry in smallholder farming systems; (g) to upgrade the capacity of forestry institutions in the implementation of their resource management responsibilities and in development of human resources in forestry; (i)to protect fragile areas such as hill tops, river banks, water catchment and to conserve and enhance biodiversity; and (l) to promote bilateral, regional and international cooperation in forest augmentation and conservation."

3. Cameroon

67. Cameroon is one of the Central African countries that has been adversely impacted by the effects of desertification and drought. Cameroon signed the Desertification Convention on 14 October 1996, and ratified it on 29 May 1997. The approach adopted by Cameroon in meeting its obligations under the Convention and other international environmental agreements is slightly different from that of China and Malawi.

68. In 1996, the government of Cameroon established a framework environmental law, Law Number 96/12 of August 1996 Relating to Environmental Management ("Environmental Management Law"), which lays down the general legal framework for environmental management in the country and sets out basic provisions for protection of various components of the environment, such as the atmosphere, coast and marine waters, soils and sub-soils and management of wastes. The provisions are to be supplemented by detailed regulations on the various components of the environment in the form of enabling decrees.

69. Section IV of the Environmental Management Law deals with protection of soils and the sub-soil and resources therein against any form of degradation. Within the Law's provisions for protection of soil,

there are included specific requirements for protection and fight against desertification. The relevant provision, Section 36 (2) states that, "An enabling decree of this law, prepared in collaboration with the Administrative units concerned, shall lay down: the specific conditions for the protection and fight against desertification, erosion, loss of arable land and pollution of the soil and its resources by chemicals, pesticides and fertilizers."

70. Further, Section 38 subjects agricultural, industrial, urban and other activities that are likely to degrade the soil to an authorization system which shall prohibit any activities likely to lead to soil degradation. Where activities are authorized but result in soil degradation, the Environmental Management Law also provides for rehabilitation at the cost of permit holders responsible for the damage in Section 37(2).

71. In addition, Section 9 of the Environmental Management Law contains detailed provisions for guiding environmental law principles, including the precautionary principle and the principle of public participation, which entitles every citizen of Cameroon to information on activities that can damage the environment. The Law also provides for a number of environmental protection measures, including environmental impact assessment. Part VI deals with issues of liability and sanctions for non-compliance with statutory provisions.

72. Section 10(2) and other provisions of the Environmental Management Law provide for the institutional framework for its implementation and enforcement by an Inter-Ministerial Committee on the Environment, a National Consultative Committee on the Environment and Sustainable Development, decentralized territorial authorities and administrative units, as well as grassroots communities and environmental associations whose functions are to be detailed by an enabling decree of the Law. Section 11 establishes a National Environmental and Sustainable Development Fund as a financial mechanism for implementation and enforcement of the Law.

Prof. Simeon Kedogo Imbamba, Environmental Consultant, Nairobi

Dr. Jane Dwasi, UNEP Consultant, University of Nairobi

Resources

Internet Resources

CANADA COMBATS DESERTIFICATION available at http://www.acdi-cida.gc.ca/desertification-e.htm

COMBATING DESERTIFICATION IN NAMIBIA available at http://www.namibia-desertification.org/

ENVIRONMENTAL PROTECTION LAWS IN CHINA available at http://www.zhb.gov.cn/english/law.php3?offset

FOOD AND AGRICULTURE ORGANIZATION OF THE UNITED NATIONS available at http://www.fao.org/desertification/default.asp?lang=en

ISRAEL MINISTRY OF FOREIGN AFFAIRS, COMBATING DESERTIFICATION AND DESERT REHABILITATION available at http://www.israel-mfa.gov.il/mfa/go.asp?MFAH024v0

LAW OF THE PEOPLE'S REPUBLIC OF CHINA ON DESERTIFICATION AND TRANSFORMATION, ENVIRONMENTAL PROTECTION LAWS OF CHINA available at http://www.zhb.gov.cn/english/law.php3?offset

MARY TIFFEN & MICHAEL MORTIMER, DRYLANDS RESEARCH, "DESERTIFICATION"- INTERNATIONAL CONVENTIONS AND PRIVATE SOLUTIONS IN SUB-SAHARAN AFRICA IN SUSTAINABLE DEVELOPMENT: PROMOTING PROGRESS OR PERPETUATING POVERTY?, (PROFILE BOOKS, 2002) available at http://www.sdnetwork.net/pdfs/tiffen_mortimer_chapter14.pdf

MEDITERRANEAN DESERTIFICATION AND LAND USE available at http://www.medalus.demon.co.uk/

NATURAL RESOURCE ASPECTS OF SUSTAINABLE DEVELOPMENT IN MALAWI available at http://www.un.org/esa/agenda21/natlinfo/countr/malawi/natur.htm

THE FIRST NATIONAL MALAWI REPORT ON THE PREPARATION AND IMPLEMENTATION OF THE UNITED NATIONS CONVENTION TO COMBAT DESERTIFICATION PROGRAMME available at http://www.unccd.int/cop/reports/africa/national/1999/malawi-eng.pdf

UNITED NATIONS CONVENTION TO COMBAT DESERTIFICATION available at http://www.unccd.int/main.php

UNITED NATIONS DEVELOPMENT PROGRAMME DRYLANDS DEVELOPMENT CENTRE available at http://www.undp.org/drylands/

USGS DESERTIFICATION PAGE available at http://pubs.usgs.gov/gip/deserts/desertification/

Text Materials

C.J. Barrow, LAND DEGRADATION, (Cambridge University Press, 1991).

DEPARTMENT OF DESERT RESEARCH, LANZHOU INSTITUTE OF GLACIOLOGY, CRYOPEDOLOGY AND DESERT RESEARCH, THE TRANSFORMATION OF DESERTS IN CHINA: A SUMMARY VIEW OF THE PEOPLE'S EXPERIENCE IN CONTROLLING SAND IN UNITED NATIONS ENVIRONMENT PROGRAMME, (UNEP Reports and Proceedings Series 3, Combating Desertification in China, James C. Walls, Ed., 1982).

DOWN TO EARTH: A SIMPLIFIED GUIDE TO THE CONVENTION TO COMBAT DESERTIFICATION, WHY IT IS NECESSARY AND WHAT IS IMPORTANT AND DIFFERENT ABOUT IT, (Centre for Our Common Future in Collaboration with INCD, 1995).

Elisabeth Corell, THE NEGOTIABLE DESERT: EXPERT KNOWLEDGE IN THE NEGOTIATIONS OF THE CONVENTION TO COMBAT DESERTIFICATION, (1999).

M. P. Petrov, DESERTS OF THE WORLD, (Translated from Russian by IPST Staff, 1976).

MANAGING FRAGILE ECOSYSTEMS: COMBATING DESERTIFICATION AND DROUGHT, THE EARTH SUMMIT: THE UNITED NATIONS

Conference on Environment and Development ("UNCED"), Stanley P. Johnson & Gunther Handl (Eds.) (1993).

Mostafa Kamal Tolba, Desertification in African Land Use Policy, (October 1998).

Mostafa K. Tolba, Saving our Planet, (Chapman & Hall, 1992).

Pagiola Stephen, The World Bank, the Global Environmental Benefits of Land Degradation Control on Agricultural Land, (1999).

Perez F. Trejo, European Commission EPOCH Programme, Environment and Quality of Life: Desertification and Land Degradation in the Mediterranean, (October 1992).

Protecting the Environment from Land Degradation: UNEP's Action in the Framework of Global Environment Facility, (1998).

The Forestry Act of Malawi, UNEP/UNDP Joint Project on Environmental Law and Instructions in Africa: Compendium of Environmental Laws of African Countries, Sectoral Environmental Laws and Regulations, (Volume VI) (1998).

UNESCO/UNEP/UNDP, J.A.Mabbutt & C. Floret, (Eds.), Case Studies on Desertification 52, (1980).

United Nations Environment Programme (Stiles, Daniel, Ed.), Social Aspects of Sustainable Dryland Management, (John Wiley & Sons, 1995).

United Nations Environment Programme, Success Stories in the Struggle against Desertification: a Holistic and Integrated Approach to Environmental Conservation and Sustainable Livelihoods, (December 2002).

United Nations Environment Programme, United Nations Convention to combat Desertification in those Countries experiencing Serious Drought and/or Desertification, particularly in Africa (1995).

20. MOUNTAIN, FOREST, AND POLAR ECOSYSTEMS

I. Introduction

1. Ecosystems require preservation and protection from human interference that might harm and adversely affect their vital functions. This chapter focuses on three examples that illustrate the unique demands that ecosystems place on efforts at protection and preservation: mountain ecosystems, forest ecosystems and polar region ecosystems. Each of these types of ecosystems is comprehensively examined in a self-contained part, virtually as a sub-chapter. Each type of ecosystem displays significant differences in the composition of the communities that comprise them, the differences in the vital functions they perform, and the importance of these functions to nature and to human beings. In each case, many or even all of the plant or animal species or organisms are unique to the relevant environment. These differences notwithstanding, all these ecosystems have in common the geographic and climatic features that support communities of plants, animals, and other mutually dependent organisms. They all perform certain vital functions that are dependent upon the community remaining largely intact.

2. A growing understanding of the unique features and protective demands of ecosystems has prompted the making of ecosystem-oriented laws at international and national levels. Notably, ecological systems, processes, and regions often do not overlap with political boundaries and protective efforts have the potential to clash with individual states' concerns regarding sovereignty over their territories or natural resources. In response to these challenges, certain international environmental law principles and concepts, including the concept of sustainable development and the precautionary principle, have developed. Many of the principles and concepts applicable to the protection and management of ecosystems are discussed in detail in chapter 3 of this Manual.

3. Alongside the development of international environmental law principles and concepts, various treaty-based legal regimes for the protection of ecosystems have emerged. While some treaty regimes incorporating ecosystem-oriented management principles and concepts

have a broad approach to environmental issues concerning, for example, protection of the marine environment and biodiversity protection, only a small number of regimes actually aim to govern entire ecosystems. The scope of the existing legal regimes depends partly on the urgency of the ecological concerns at hand, the perceived importance of the threatened ecosystem and the extent to which ecosystem protection and management implicate state sovereignty.

II. Mountain Ecosystems

1. Ecosystem Characteristics and Vulnerabilities

4. Webster's New Collegiate Dictionary describes a mountain as a landmass that projects conspicuously above its surroundings and is higher than a hill. Mountains are found on every continent and cover 26% of the Earth's surface. Because of their physical and ecological characteristics, mountains perform crucial ecological functions and provide many benefits to humans. For example, many mountains originate from volcanic activities, which, during formation, lead to an outpouring of lava on the outer surface of the mountains. Over time, the lava and rock particles develop into rich volcanic soils that support the growth of many plants and trees that develop into forests that are home to diverse species of animals, plants and other organisms.

5. Mountains have also become the water towers of humanity. Because air ascends mountains, cools, condenses and falls as rain, mountain areas usually receive more rainfall than low-lying areas. This is one of the reasons many rivers, including trans-boundary ones, originate from mountains and mountain ranges. Many of these rivers play important roles in supporting regional economies. For example, the Indus River, which originates from the Himalayan Mountains, supports rice irrigation for more than 130 million people in Pakistan alone and flows through India and Bangladesh, supporting the world's largest irrigation network. In Central America, the entire economic development of the Atacama Desert area depends on small streams that originate from the Andes Mountains. In Europe, the Alps supply water to major European rivers including the Rhine, Rhone, Danube and the Po. In Eastern Africa, the Mara River, which is the only permanent water source in Northern Tanzania and supports millions of diverse species of wildlife in the Serengeti, originates from the Rift Valley mountain ranges in Kenya. All the major rivers in the world,

from the Rio Grande to the Nile, have their headwaters in mountains. As a consequence, more than half of the world's population rely on mountain water to grow food, produce electricity, sustain industries and, most importantly, to drink.

6. In addition, because of their topography and aesthetic beauty, mountains are increasingly popular destinations for tourism, the world's biggest industry. In the Alps, there has been a steadily growing two-season tourism since the 1950s. Mountains can also be reservoirs of a number of precious minerals. In the United States' Rocky Mountains, for example, there are substantial traces of silver, cadmium, zinc, and other minerals that are in high demand. Mountains are also home to much of the world's population, especially in mountainous countries such as Kyrgyzstan, Kazakhstan, Tajikistan, and the Carpathian region of Europe, which contains more than sixteen million people.

7. The pressures on mountain ecosystems are manifold. They are very fragile because of their steep slopes, high altitude and other attributes. In many regions, human activities are threatening to destroy them and to seriously undermine their ability to perform ecological functions and provide benefits to humans.

8. Human factors such as population pressure, combined with natural hazards such as climate change, have pushed poor agricultural practices ever higher up the mountains, especially in countries that are largely mountainous. In many regions, many health problems in mountain wildlife and in people living downstream have resulted. Mountain forests have been cut down and the areas cultivated, prompting cycles of deforestation, soil erosion, downstream flooding, water flow changes and pollution of rivers with agricultural chemicals. Availability of minerals on some mountains has also led to heavy mining activities, resulting in the pollution of the headwaters of many rivers, including those that flow through more than one national boundary. The resulting negative impacts on ecosystems have created disputes between countries where mining activities take place and downstream countries that experience adverse consequences. In addition, mountains have been made toxic waste dumping grounds in many places. For example, dangerous nuclear wastes have been dumped high up in the mountains of Kyrgyzstan. The wastes threaten to spill into rivers that flow into the fertile valleys below, much of which are in neighbouring Uzbekistan and are home to almost 20% of Central Asia's entire population.

9. Tourism is another human activity that is threatening to destroy mountain ecosystems. Even mountains in remote corners of the world are becoming popular destinations for tourists, with many negative results. Often, large mountain forests are cleared to create room for mountain hotels and other tourist resorts. Not only does this affect biological diversity, but also, once built, waste discharges emanate from the hotels to the sources of many rivers that originate from the mountains. In addition, tourist activities on mountains and glaciers have weakened the stability of the mountain ecosystems, resulting in avalanches, snow slides, landslides and ice slides.

10. Wars and civil strife in mountainous regions have also had severe consequences on wildlife and human populations living there. The United Nations Food and Agriculture Organization reports that many of the world's wars are being fought in mountainous regions. Recent examples include Afghanistan, Kurdistan and Kashmir, to name but a few from a long list. In these wars, explosives destroy mountain landscapes and vegetation that have been habitats for many unique species of wildlife, including endangered species.

2. International Environmental Regime relating to Mountain Ecosystems

a) Convention on the Protection of the Alps

11. The Alps are the most significant mountain areas in Western Europe, running at heights between 2,000 and 3,000 metres high and stretching across the borders of a number of countries including Switzerland, France, Germany, Italy, Austria, Liechtenstein and Slovenia. The Convention on the Protection of the Alps ("1991 Alpine Convention") makes the Alps the world's first mountain region to be legally protected at the international level.

12. The Alpine Convention was adopted on 7 November 1991, by Austria, France, Germany, Italy, Liechtenstein, Switzerland, Slovenia and the European Economic Community. The Alpine Convention came into force on 6 March 1995. As of November 2005, it has nine parties, including all of the initial signatories, plus Slovenia and Monaco.

13. The parties agreed to establish a comprehensive policy for the protection and sustainable development of the Alps in their entirety. The range of issues addressed by the 1991 Alpine Convention include: protection of the region's landscape and its diverse species of animals, plants and other

organisms, regulation of agriculture in the mountain region, mountain tourism, proper land use planning for the mountain areas, prevention of pollution of the mountain ecosystems and avoidance of competition over use of the mountains along national lines.

14. The 1991 Alpine Convention is a framework agreement, which sets out the basic principles and procedures according to which the regime is to be fleshed out, and establishes the institutions through which the parties are to cooperate. Specific obligations are contained in nine issue-specific protocols that have been adopted since 1994, to complement the 1991 Alpine Convention.

15. The 1991 Alpine Convention's substantive provisions set out a general obligation to pursue a comprehensive policy for the protection and preservation of the Alps. To this end, the parties agree in article 2(1) to apply the principle of prevention, the "polluter pays" principle and the principle of cooperation at national and international levels, after carefully considering the interests of all the Alpine states, regions and the European Community. For example, parties should take measures to ensure that manufacturing facilities and other entities that cause pollution of the Alpine environment take responsibility for cleanup and for any pollution damage.

16. Additionally, article 2(2) requires parties to take appropriate measures in eleven areas of concern that reflect an ecosystem-oriented approach: population and culture, planning for sustainable development of the region, prevention of air pollution impacting the region, soil conservation, management of Alpine water resources, conservation of nature and the countryside, regulation of farming in the mountain areas, preservation of mountain forests, regulation of tourism and recreation, control of transport through the region, consideration of energy-related matters, and waste management. For example, with respect to conservation of nature, article 2(2)(f) of the 1991 Alpine Convention obliges parties to take appropriate measures to protect, conserve, and, where necessary, rehabilitate the natural environment and the countryside. The goal is to allow ecosystems to function, to preserve animal and plants species and their habitats, to maintain nature's capacity for regeneration and sustained productivity and to preserve the variety, uniqueness and beauty of nature and the countryside on a permanent basis.

17. Also, under articles 3 and 4, the 1991 Alpine Convention requires parties to cooperate in carrying out research activities, scientific assessments, and the exchange of legal and technical information that would enable them to meet their obligations.

18. At an institutional level, the 1991 Alpine Convention creates the Alpine Conference, which meets once every two years. This plenary body is made up of representatives of the parties. It serves as a forum for the discussion of the common concerns of and cooperation between the parties. It is also responsible for examining the implementation of the convention and for making decisions regarding further development of the Alpine Convention. The regular work of the Alpine Convention is carried out by the Standing Committee, assisted by "Groups of Experts", as provided for in articles 5 through 8.

19. As already noted, the 1991 Alpine Convention requires parties to take appropriate measures to address a variety of concerns. However, the Convention does not contain detailed obligations in this respect. The necessary detail for the implementation of the 1991 Alpine Convention was to be achieved through the adoption of individual sub-agreements, or "protocols," as provided under article 2(3). Between 1994 and 2000, parties adopted nine protocols on mountain agriculture, nature protection and landscape conservation, land use planning and sustainable development, mountain forests, tourism, soil conservation, energy, transport, and dispute settlement. The Protocol on Land Use Planning and Sustainable Development, for example, requires parties to develop and implement regional plans for sustainable development. In the context of regional economic development, such plans are to be aimed at, among other things, conservation and management of important environmental and cultural areas, and reducing the risk of natural calamities. By December 2002, all of the nine protocols had come into force and parties are in the process of developing three more.

b) Framework Convention on the Protection and Sustainable Development of the Carpathians

20. The Carpathian Mountains are a range of mountains straddling the Czech Republic, Hungary, Moldavia, Poland, Romania, Slovakia and Ukraine. The Framework Convention on the Protection and Sustainable Development of the Carpathians ("2003 Carpathian Convention") was adopted on 22 May 2003. It entered into force on 4 January 2006.

21. In its Preamble, the 2003 Carpathian Convention expressly recognizes the Alpine Convention as its model. Its primary objective is the protection and sustainable development of the Carpathian Mountains region with a view to improving the quality of life of the people living there, to strengthening local economies of the region and its communities, and to conserving the natural resources thereon and the cultural values of the mountain people.

22. To meet these objectives, the 2003 Carpathian Convention sets out a number of guiding principles in article 2, including the precaution and prevention principles, the polluter pays principle, the principle of public participation and stakeholder involvement, transboundary cooperation, ecosystem approach, programatic approach and integrated planning and management of the land and water resources. The 2003 Carpathian Convention obliges parties to apply these principles in taking steps, actions, and measures on a number of matters specified in articles 4 through 13. These include conservation and sustainable use of biological and landscape diversity, landscape planning, sustainable water resource development, integrated rive basin development, and sustainable agriculture, forestry, tourism, transport, infrastructure, industry and energy. For example, on industry and energy, parties are required by article 10 "...to promote cleaner production technologies, in order to adequately prevent, respond to and remedy industrial accidents and their consequences, as well as to preserve human health and mountain ecosystems".

23. For its implementation, article 14 of the 2003 Carpathian Convention establishes a Conference of the Parties to be responsible for a number of matters, including amendments to the 2003 Carpathian Convention and adoption of protocols thereto. In articles 15 and 16, the Convention also establishes a Secretariat to be responsible for compilation and submission of reports to parties and other matters, and subsidiary bodies to provide technical assistance. Parties shall settle disputes arising from the interpretation or implementation of the Carpathian Convention by negotiation and by other means that are in accordance with international law as provided by article 20.

c) Non-Legally Binding Instruments

24. Agenda 21 is one of the instruments that, although non-legally binding, has produced practical results with respect to protection of mountain ecosystems. It sets a plan of action and measures that representatives of 180 governments agreed to take on various areas of environmental conservation. With respect to protection of mountain ecosystems, its Chapter 13 is the most relevant.

25. In Chapter 13 of Agenda 21, UNCED recognised that the world's mountains have significant natural resources, provide essential ecological goods and services to humans, and therefore, should be preserved, restored and sustainably managed. Fresh mountain water conservation, conservation of biological diversity in mountain areas, conservation of mountain forests, and prevention of negative impacts of climate change on mountains and sustainable tourism are some of the mountain issues that were identified as requiring conservation actions. The representatives of governments agreed to raise awareness of mountain people on these issues and to support their efforts to prevent, reduce and reverse the trend of degradation of mountain ecosystems. They also agreed to provide mountain people with alternative livelihoods to avoid over-exploitation of mountain resources and to undertake other programmes to address mountain issues.

26. On the basis of Agenda 21, a number of actions have been taken, including creation of agreements that specifically address mountain ecosystem issues in specific regions. For example, parties to the Framework Convention on the Protection and Sustainable Development of the Carpathians expressly stated in the Preamble to the Convention that they recognized the importance of and were acting pursuant to mountain issues highlighted in Chapter 13 of Agenda 21.

27. Agenda 21 has also stirred a number of non-governmental organization initiatives for protection, preservation and sustainable development of mountain areas, including:

- Charter for the Protection of the Pyrenees of 1995, whose objective, inter alia, is to preserve the mountain range's ecological values;
- African Mountains and Highlands Declaration of 1997, which highlights major problems affecting Africa's mountain ecosystems and provides policy recommendations to address them;
- Kathmandu Declaration of 1997, which calls for, inter alia, effective protection of the mountain environment and respect for the culture and dignity of mountain peoples; and
- Draft World Charter of June 2000, which sets out conditions that are crucial to meeting the needs of mountain populations while preserving their environment.

28. There are also many examples of non-legally binding instruments that were developed through governmental fora pursuant to Chapter 13 of Agenda 21, with much input by Non-Governmental Organizations. These include the Cusco Declaration on Sustainable Development of Mountain Ecosystems, which was drawn up by representatives of eighteen countries from various continents gathered in Cusco, Peru, in 2001. In their deliberations, parties identified sustainable mountain development as one of the mountain issues requiring careful consideration, and recognized that social and economic measures are necessary in addressing the issues.

29. Since the adoption of the Alpine Convention in 1991 and the inclusion of Chapter 13 on mountain ecosystems in Agenda 21, binding and non-binding instruments focusing on the protection and sustainable development of mountain areas have proliferated. This trend is indicative of a growing recognition that the delicate balance between ecological and developmental needs requires comprehensive, ecosystem-wide approaches. Although ratification and implementation remain works in progress, the Alpine Convention is the most advanced legal regime for mountain protection so far. It is a landmark agreement and provides a solid basis for transboundary collaboration. Recent developments regarding other mountain areas suggest that this framework convention may be a suitable model for the gradual evolution of legal regimes, and for the tailoring of regimes to the specific concerns of a particular mountain region. Work is underway to develop comparable agreements for the Altai Mountain range involving Kazakhstan, Mongolia, and Russia, and the Caucasus Mountain range involving Armenia, Azerbaijan, Georgia and Russia.

3. National and Local Initiatives relating to Mountain Ecosystems

30. Legislative protection of mountain ecosystems is an area that is still developing and only a few countries have passed laws, rules, standards and policies that specifically deal with mountain issues. While relevant legislation exists in various countries, this section of this chapter is limited to laws related to the Alpine Convention in order to illustrate how that particular agreement is being implemented.

31. Although France, Italy, Austria and other parties to the 1991 Alpine Convention have laws or policies that address issues related to mountain ecosystems,

Switzerland is particularly illustrative, since most of its territory is mountains. For Switzerland, national implementation of the 1991 Alpine Convention and the protocols did not require any additional legislative measures because it already had in existence a number of laws at different levels of government addressing mountain agriculture, social and sustainable development of mountain areas, mountain tourism, infrastructure and other issues covered by the 1991 Alpine Convention. When Switzerland became a party to the 1991 Alpine Convention, it gave its commitment to improve its existing mountain legislation where necessary. Switzerland does not have a single, unitary piece of legislation that covers its mountain ecosystems. Instead, it has a number of laws covering various issues concerning protection and sustainable development of mountain areas, which tend to link the protection of mountain ecosystems with the right of the people to adequate economic development. Some of these laws include:

- *The Federal Law on Assistance regarding Investments in Mountain Areas.* This is the main sectoral legislation, also called Swiss Mountain Law of 1974. It was revised substantially in 1998, to provide for some of the measures required by the Alpine Convention, especially pollution control, protection of the mountain landscape and sustainable development of the mountain areas. On the sustainable development aspect of the law, for example, article 1 provides for incentives for the development of mountains. Among other things, the law provides for subsidies from the government for development projects in the mountain communities to facilitate environmental protection, including establishment of refuse disposal facilities. The law also provides subsidies to support trades that would provide alternative livelihoods to the people and prevent over-utilization of the fragile mountain lands.
- *The Federal Mountain Region Housing Improvement Act 844 of 1970.* This law contains a number of provisions that relate to mountain protection. For example, article 4 requires any work undertaken for home improvement in mountain regions to be done in accordance with the requirements of physical planning, protection of nature and landscape, and environmental conservation. The provisions strengthen the purpose of the infrastructure loans under the Swiss Mountain Law to promote the sustainable development of mountain regions.

- *The Federal Agriculture Act and the 1998 Ordinance on Direct Payment to Agriculture.* In furtherance of the Alpine Protocol on Mountain Farming, these laws contain provisions for financial aid to mountain communities for sustainable promotion of agriculture in the mountain areas.

32. The various Swiss mountain laws are implemented by bodies responsible for enforcing and applying the various laws, such as the Swiss Agency for the Environment, Forests and Landscape. As a federal state, Switzerland's responsibility for natural resource management and protection of the environment is shared between different levels of government: the Confederation, the cantons and, to a small extent, municipal authorities.

III. Forest Ecosystems

1. Ecosystem Characteristics and Vulnerabilities

33. Forest ecosystems perform important ecological and economic functions. Internationally, there are several different definitions of a forest. Some definitions depend on the actual vegetation on the ground. For example, the European Union has defined forestland as having at least 20% canopy closure and a minimum area of 0.5 hectares. For Mediterranean regions, the 10% canopy cover is the adopted definition. Similarly, the United Nations Food and Agriculture Organization, which undertakes considerable work on forest protection, defines forests as land with 10% tree cover. Other definitions depend on legal designation of areas as forests, or legal classification of land use as forest, agricultural or urban.

34. Regardless of the definition, it is important to bear in mind that forests are more than simply "areas with trees." Trees are but one component of a forest ecosystem, which comprises various species of plants, animals, mammals, and other organisms that interact amongst themselves and with their physical environment.

35. Forests perform vital ecological services and provide ecological goods that provide many benefits to humans. Scientific research and direct observation in many areas of the world show that forests make water available because undisturbed forests tend to maintain high rates of infiltration that ensure ground water recharge. Therefore, removal of forests, especially in tropical areas, results in a reduction of dry season flows of rivers, notably those originating in forest catchment areas. Scientific studies and research also show that in certain circumstances, for example where forests

cover extensive areas, like in the Amazon basin, forest increase precipitation and their removal may result in less rainfall. Removing forests also degrades water quality because forest vegetation can no longer reduce and eliminate water-borne pollutants that would be carried in surface run off, or immobilize or transform pollutants through chemical and biological processes.

36. Forests also prevent soil erosion, especially on steep slopes. This function is particularly important because many forests are found in mountainous areas that receive heavy rainfall that could easily cause soil erosion if not protected by vegetation. If the presence of forest vegetation helps prevent erosion, it follows that removal of forests promotes erosion, with attendant high run off, downstream sedimentation and siltation, degradation of water quality, and increased flooding, especially of low-lying areas.

37. The World Commission on Forests and Sustainable Development has articulated the importance of forest ecosystems as follows:

> The whole forest issue is about people, sometimes illustrated in a direct and brutal way. When some 10,000 people drowned in mud and water in Central America in November 1998 the blame was on Hurricane "Mitch," the worst of its kind in a long time. This was only half of the truth about the tragic event. The other half is about land mismanagement in the region. Big cash crop farms, often multinational, have gradually taken over the fertile plains and driven poor families to cultivate and collect firewood from marginal lands and forested mountain hillsides. As expected, these lands have become eroded, causing unprotected soil to wash away by forceful rains, forming mudslides which killed everything in their path.

38. Moreover, forests help to maintain climatic balances, and to avert or slow climate change by storing carbon in their living matter and soils and by absorbing atmospheric carbon dioxide. Conversely, forests are a source of destructive greenhouse gases when burned and destroyed. Burning and destruction of forests lead to emission of carbon and carbon dioxide into the atmosphere where the gases contribute significantly to global warming by trapping heat from incoming solar energy in the atmosphere. The relationship between forest cover and climate change is one of the global dimensions of forest ecosystem protection.

39. In addition, forests are home to millions of indigenous people in many countries in the world and are habitat to numerous diverse species of animals, plants and other organisms. Forests contain at least two thirds of the Earth's terrestrial species and 70% of the world's plant and animal species. The biotic diversity of forests serves as a foundation for selection and breeding of plants and animals. The genetic bank is also drawn upon to strengthen the yield and resistance of food crops and for materials of medicinal and industrial value. Forest dwellers are dependent on forests for their economic, social, cultural and spiritual well-being.

40. These vital functions of forests and the delicate ecological balance that forests maintain are being greatly upset and undermined by a variety of human activities. Increasing human populations have resulted in accelerated deforestation in many countries as forest lands are cultivated or cleared to grow food crops or raise cattle, or cut simply for fuel. For example, an estimated two billion people in developing countries still rely on wood as their source of fuel. The quest for development has also resulted in massive logging for timber for domestic consumption and export and turning forest lands into cash crop farms. There is also the problem of illegal logging in national and other publicly owned forests, which not only destroys forest ecosystems, but also distorts timber markets, acts as a disincentive to sustainable forest management, and robs forest owners and governments of massive revenues due to them from forestry activities.

41. Lack of, or negative, governmental forestry policies have had a share in the reduction of forest cover. In many countries, regular and uncontrolled forest clearing are authorized by governmental authorities, usually without any consideration of adverse impacts or consultation with affected communities.

42. Ironically, although it is usually assumed that the greatest value can be extracted from a forest by maximizing timber and pulp products or by converting it to agriculture, the ecological functions of forests that are generally regarded as free or simply not noticed are highly valuable. For example, when alternative management strategies for the mangrove forests of Bintui Bay in Indonesia were compared, taking into account the value of fish, locally used products, and erosion control, it was found that it would be most profitable to keep the forests to yield US $4800 per hectare, instead of cutting them down for timber, which would only yield US $3600 dollars per hectare.

2. International Environmental Regime relating to Forest Ecosystems

43. To date, there is no comprehensive legally binding international agreement dealing specifically with forests and the environmental, social, and economic aspects of the management and preservation of forest ecosystems.

44. Some critics of an all-encompassing forest convention approach point to the great diversity of the world's forests and the challenge of arriving at an agreement that would be a meaningful contribution to global forest protection.

45. However, the fragmented nature of forest-related provisions under existing international agreements is one of the key reasons proponents of a legally binding forest agreement argue for a comprehensive, ecosystem-oriented approach to the protection and sustainable development of forests.

a) The Ramsar Convention on Wetlands of International Importance, especially as Waterfowls Habitat

46. The Ramsar Convention on Wetlands of International Importance especially as Waterfowl Habitat ("1971 Ramsar Convention") was adopted on 2 February 1971, and entered into force on 21 December 1975. As of November 2005, the 1971 Ramsar Convention has 147 parties.

47. The 1971 Ramsar Convention applies to forest ecosystems to the extent that they fall within the Convention's definition of "wetland" under article 1. Article 2 of the Convention requires each party to designate suitable wetlands within its territory for inclusion in a "List of Wetlands of International Importance" which is maintained by a bureau established under article 8 of the Convention. Selection of wetlands of international importance is based on set criteria including their international significance in terms of ecology, botany, zoology, limnology or hydrology. For example, Brazil, which became a party to the Ramsar Convention on 24 September 1993, has included Varzea Forest in the Mamiraua area as a wetland of international importance under article 2 of the Convention.

48. Once designated as wetlands of international importance, forests are to be conserved in the manner stipulated by articles 3, 4, 5 and other provisions of the 1971 Ramsar Convention. Among other conservation actions, article 4 obligates parties to establish designated forests as nature reserves to be protected and preserved.

b) The Convention concerning the Protection of the World Cultural and Natural Heritage

49. The Convention concerning the Protection of the World Cultural and Natural Heritage ("1972 World Heritage Convention") was adopted in November 1972, entered into force on 17 December 1975, and has 180 parties as of November 2005).

50. The 1972 World Heritage Convention requires parties to protect natural and cultural heritage of "outstanding universal value." Under articles 1 and 2, natural and cultural heritage include natural sites and areas which are of outstanding universal value from the point of view of science, conservation and natural beauty, regardless of whether such areas have been delineated by a party as forest reserves, nature reserves, or some other conservation area. Article 3 requires each party to delineate such areas within their territories as "World Heritage Sites" to be included in a "World Heritage List". To date, the World Heritage List includes 812 properties, of which forty-eight are tropical forests covering more that 32.3 million hectares. Once an area is designated as a World Heritage Site, article 4 of the 1972 World Heritage Convention requires each party to protect, conserve, and transmit the forests to future generations. To meet these requirements, article 5(d), *inter alia*, of the agreement requires parties to take appropriate legal, scientific, technical, administrative, and financial measures.

c) The Convention on International Trade in Endangered Species of Wild Flora and Fauna

51. The Convention on International Trade in Endangered Species of Wild Flora and Fauna ("1973 CITES") was adopted in 1973, and protects a number of timber species and plants through regulation. 1973 CITES is discussed in more detail in Chapter 14 of this Manual.

d) The Rio Conference Instruments

52. At the 1992 Rio Conference, forest issues moved closer to the centre of international attention. Each of the three conventions discussed at Rio addresses important aspects of global forest conservation: (i) the 1992 United Nations Framework Convention on Climate Change and its Kyoto Protocol (the latter one adopted in 1997), (ii) the 1992 Convention on Biological Diversity, and (iii) the 1994 United Nations Convention to combat Desertification in Countries experiencing Serious Drought and/or Desertification, particularly in Africa, whose issues were raised in Rio but was

concluded after the Rio Conference. These Conventions are addressed more fully in chapters 10, 15, and 19. The Forest Principles are covered in section f) below.

53. The first multi-party convention is the United Nations Framework Convention on Climate Change ("UNFCCC"), which entered into force in March 1994, and its Kyoto Protocol, which entered into force on 16 February 2005 and has as of November 2005, 189 parties. An overarching objective of UNFCCC is the reduction of greenhouse gas concentrations in the atmosphere. Within a specified time frame, the levels of greenhouse gases will be reduced so they do not dangerously interfere with the international climate system, while enabling economic development of nations to proceed in a sustainable manner.

54. To the extent that forests constitute sinks for greenhouse gas emission, their preservation and enhancement is touched upon by the global climate change regime in UNFCCC. Article 4.1(d) calls upon parties to promote sustainable management and cooperate in the conservation and enhancement of greenhouse gas sinks and reservoirs, including forests. This focus on forests as carbon sinks and reservoirs, as opposed to ecosystems, is pursued in the 1997 Kyoto Protocol to UNFCCC. The 1997 Kyoto Protocol sets out binding targets for reducing emission of greenhouse gases and a range of methods for meeting these targets. One of these methods, provided for by article 2.1(a) (ii) is the protection and conservation of forests. This option is further outlined in article 3 of the 1997 Kyoto Protocol, which enshrines parties' emission reduction and limitation commitments. Article 3.3 highlights that parties performances will be measured against the net changes in greenhouse gas emissions, be they from actual changes in emissions or changes in absorption by "carbon sinks" resulting, *inter alia*, from afforestation, reforestation or deforestation. Under the 1997 Kyoto Protocol, measures such as afforestation and reforestation, which increase living plant matter that absorb carbon dioxide and other green house gases, can be used by developed countries to offset their green house gas emissions. On the other hand, changes in land use activities such as deforestation that deplete carbon sinks will be subtracted from the amount of permitted emissions. However, methodologies for achieving and measuring changes in a country's carbon sinks continue to be a sensitive topic.

55. In contrast to UNFCCC, the second multi-party convention, the Convention on Biological

Diversity focuses on a significant aspect of ecosystem protection: the conservation of biological diversity. The Biodiversity Convention has three goals: (i) conservation of biological diversity, (ii) sustainable use of components of biological diversity, and (iii) the fair and equitable sharing of benefits arising from the use of genetic resources. For example, article 8 of the Biodiversity Convention requires parties to take appropriate measures for *in situ* conservation of biological diversity, which applies to natural settings of forest ecosystems. Since its adoption, the scope of the Biodiversity Convention has expanded to specifically include forest ecosystems.

56. In 1995, the COP to the Biodiversity Convention adopted a statement in which they stressed that forests have a crucial role to play in maintaining global biological diversity. This led to the development of a work programme for forest biological diversity in 1996, which focuses on the development of technologies and research necessary for the conservation and sustainable use of all types of forests. Further, in 1998, the COP decided to consider forest protection and conservation as one of the priority themes for its future activities. It established a technical expert group on forest biological diversity with mandate to review available information on status, trends, and threats to forest biological diversity and to suggest action to address them. The group has the potential to become an important forum for developing more specific forest conservation and protection rules under the Biodiversity Convention.

57. In addition, a Subsidiary Body on Scientific, Technical, and Technological Advice supports the work of the COP to the Biodiversity Convention. This panel works on a variety of issues concerning conservation of biological diversity, including impacts of forest fires on forests and harvesting of non-timber forest resources. The Global Environment Facility also strengthens measures taken under the Biodiversity Convention by providing funding for the agreement's forest biological diversity conservation projects. In 2002, the COP adopted Decision VI/22 that set out a programme of work for forest biological diversity.

58. The third convention adopted in the aftermath of Rio, the United Nations Convention to combat Desertification in those Countries experiencing Serious Drought and/or Desertification, particularly in Africa ("Desertification Convention"), also addresses forest issues. In pursuit of its objectives to combat desertification, to mitigate effects of drought, and to contribute to sustainable

development, the regime must consider deforestation, as it is one of the significant factors contributing to desertification. Specifically, article 10 of the Desertification Convention requires parties to prepare and implement national action programmes identifying factors contributing to desertification and indicating practical measures that they intend to take to combat desertification and mitigate the effects of drought. Many of the national action programmes that have been prepared and adopted include measures to prevent and mitigate the effects of deforestation.

e) The International Tropical Timber Agreement

59. The International Tropical Timber Agreement ("1994 ITTA") was originally adopted in 1983, renegotiated in 1994 and entered into force on January 1, 1997. As of November 2005, it has 60 parties, including countries that produce and those that consume timber.

60. In the International Timber Agreement, parties recognize the need for effective conservation and development of tropical timber forests with a view to ensuring their optimum utilization while maintaining the ecological balance of the regions concerned and of the biosphere. 1994 ITTA provides an effective framework, which enables:

- Cooperation and consultation between tropical timber producing and consuming members with regard to all relevant aspects of the tropical timber economy;
- Promotion of research and development with a view to improving forest management and wood utilization; and
- Encouragement of members to support and develop industrial tropical timber reforestation and forest management activities.

61. To meet those objectives, articles 1 and 3 of 1994 ITTA establish an International Timber Organization to adopt necessary rules and regulations, to utilize the services and expertise of existing intergovernmental, governmental, or non-governmental organizations, and to exercise such powers and perform such functions as necessary. The ITTA is currently being renegotiated.

62. Since its creation, the International Timber Organization has developed sustainable forest management indicators for parties to the Agreement, served as a forum for consultation on tropical forest matters; undertaken a number of forest conservation activities, and assisted members

to meet their year-2000 objective. The objective was that, by 2000, all tropical timber products traded internationally by member states would originate from sustainably managed forests.

f) The Rio Forest Principles

63. Because forest issues proved to be so sensitive that negotiations at the Rio Conference fell short of a legally-binding instrument on forests, negotiators instead reached consensus on a number of forest issues that they committed themselves to address and on actions that they would take to conserve and sustainably manage forests. These were set out as the Non-Legally Binding Authoritative Statement of Principles for a Global Consensus on the Management, Conservation and Sustainable Development of all types of Forests ("1992 Rio Forest Principles"). The 1992 Rio Forest Principles reflect the negotiators' efforts to balance a wide range of competing concerns. Much of the balancing fell within the broad theme of "environment development" tensions, along with the accommodation of the needs and aspirations of forest-dwelling populations.

64. The 1992 Rio Forest Principles affirmed states' sovereignty to exploit their own natural resources pursuant to their own environmental policies. The principles also capture states' responsibilities to ensure that activities within their jurisdiction or control do not cause damage to the environment of other states or areas beyond their national jurisdictions. With respect to forests, this means, for example, that governments must ensure that deforestation does not cause erosion or flooding in other states. However, as environmental concerns regarding the decline of forest ecosystems often are cumulative or global in nature, it will tend to be difficult to attribute adverse effects to individual states. For that reason, the 1992 Rio Forest Principles place certain, limited constraints on parties' forest management and exploitation activities.

65. Further, the 1992 Rio Forest Principles call upon states to sustainably manage their forests, forest resources and forest lands to meet the needs of people that are directly dependent on timber and non-timber products, as well as forest ecosystem needs. Governments committed to provide citizens with accurate and reliable information about forests and forest ecosystems and to promote participation by local communities, non-governmental organizations, forest dwellers, industries, and other interested persons in decision-making on matters concerning forests and on efforts to conserve, preserve and sustainably

manage forests. For example, before governments make decisions to construct roads and dams through forests or to convert forest lands to farmlands and settlement areas, they shall hold public hearings and dialogue with and collect views from all interested parties. In addition, states committed to take specific steps and actions to maintain the ecological balances of forests. Among other actions, they agreed to undertake afforestation and reforestation and create national regimes to ensure sustainable management, development and conservation of forests.

66. Chapter 11 of Agenda 21 flanks the Rio Forest Principles by providing a comprehensive action plan for regional and global efforts to find a sustainable balance between the ecological and economic functions of forests. The Commission on Sustainable Development ("CSD") was established to facilitate the implementation of these commitments made at the Rio Conference. The CSD then established the Open-Ended Ad Hoc Intergovernmental Panel on Forests ("IPF"), which is comprised of CSD member-government representatives.

67. In June 1997, the IPF submitted its final report to the CSD, which adopted it, and forwarded a set of recommendations to the UN General Assembly Special Session ("UNGASS" or "Rio Plus Five"). The UNGASS decided to continue the intergovernmental policy dialogue on forest issues through the establishment of an ad hoc open-ended Intergovernmental Forum on Forests ("IFF"), which operates under the aegis of the CSD. In 2000, the IFF was replaced by the United Nations Forum on Forests ("UNFF"), whose work programme encompasses a broad range of issues relating to sustainable development and conservation of forests, including ongoing exploration of suitable international arrangements and mechanisms. Thus, though the question of a legally binding forest agreement remains alive, it has not come any closer to a resolution. In the five sessions the UNFF has held (most recently June 2005), it was not possible for states to achieve agreement if negotiations on a legally-binding instrument on forests should start.

68. Leaving aside the issue of a legally binding forest agreement, it is important to note that the Rio Conference did serve to catalyze international, regional, and national action for sustainable management of forests and set the stage for continued work on appropriate solutions to threats to forests. It at once led to a global acceptance of the pivotal role that sustainable management of forests plays and underscored that the concept of

sustainable development of forests lacked clear definition. As a result, a number of international processes and other actions have been initiated in which countries and other interested parties have defined criteria and corresponding indicators to evaluate, monitor, and certify the sustainability of forest management activities. Of these international processes, the Montreal Process and the Pan-European Process on Protection of Forests provide good examples.

69. In September 1993, the Conference on Security and Cooperation in Europe sponsored an international seminar in Montreal on sustainable development of forests ("Montreal Process"). During the Montreal Process, the attending governments, including Australia, Canada, Chile, Japan and Mexico, developed seven international criteria and indicators for the sustainable management of forests. These criteria are essential components of the conservation and sustainable management of forests in temperate regions and include, *inter alia,* conservation of biological diversity, maintenance of forest contribution to the global carbon cycle, and maintenance of the health of forest ecosystems, and vitality and maintenance of productive capacity of forest ecosystems.

70. The Montreal Process requires that any party's management of its forest resources must include efforts to conserve the biological diversity of the forest ecosystem. The Montreal Process established a list of sixty-seven "indicators," including the extent to which a party's national legal framework supports the conservation and sustainable management of forests. Public participation in policy- and decision-making is an important "indicator."

71. In 1995, the Montreal Process was followed the Santiago Declaration, a statement of political commitment to sustainable forestry. Through the Santiago Declaration, parties agreed to be guided by internationally developed criteria and indicators in their national efforts to sustainably manage forests. Since endorsing the Santiago Declaration, countries participating in the Montreal Process have taken steps to apply the agreed criteria and indicators. A Working Group was created to clarify any issues that might arise in the process of implementation and to facilitate national efforts. One of the group's activities is to undertake an initial survey to determine availability of data for indicators in each country and the capacity of countries to report on indicators. Interim survey results suggest that most countries have data for and can report on 50% or more of the sixty-seven indicators of the Montreal Process.

72. The Montreal Process also developed a set of Pan-European Criteria and Indicators for Sustainable Forest Management ("Pan-European Process"), which is a European policy framework for sustainable forestry for use at the national level. The Pan-European Process has significantly enhanced European countries' management of their forests. The Pan European Process consists of six criteria, twenty-seven quantitative indicators, and 101 descriptive indicators. Components of the criteria requiring care include general conditions of forest biodiversity, rare and vulnerable ecosystems, and threatened forest species. For example, Criterion 4 requires the maintenance, conservation, and appropriate enhancement of biological diversity in forest ecosystems. The Pan-European Process also allows for forest certification, through which on-the-ground forestry operations by governments and other forest owners can be assessed against the predetermined set of standards.

73. These examples of non-legally binding instruments on sustainable forestry demonstrate that there is a growing international web of activities on forest conservation and management. These are to be welcomed as they help build consensus on how to address the international aspects of forest issues. These instruments represent efforts to slow deforestation, to provide for sustainable forest management, to preserve remaining forests, to increase forest cover, to specify tenure and land use rights and liabilities, and to allow active involvement of people at local and national levels in decision-making processes. However, they also illustrate the need for some oversight, to avoid overlapping and/or contradictory initiatives.

3. National Initiatives relating to Forest Ecosystems

74. This discussion highlights efforts by the United States and Japan to implement international regimes because, given the non-binding nature an international forest instrument to date, it is hard to track domestic "implementing" efforts.

a) United States

75. The United States has endorsed Agenda 21 and, in doing so, committed itself also to implementing the 1992 Rio Forest Principles. The United States was expected to create, maintain and enforce national laws that captured principles of sustainable forestry, including laws that:

- Incorporate principles and methods for ensuring sustainable forestry management;
- Enhance protection and sustainable

management of all forests;

- Combat deforestation;
- Provide citizens with accurate and reliable information about forests and forest ecosystems; and,
- Promote participation of all stakeholders in sustainable forest management.

76. The United States had implemented forestry laws long before it committed itself to the 1992 Rio Forest Principles. Despite its early legislative initiatives, the United States has long-struggled with balancing competing concerns between the economic exploitation of its forest resources and the environmental conservation of their ecosystems. In 1905, for example, the U.S. Forest Service was created to manage 156 designated forests. The wide discretionary powers granted to the U.S. Forest Service and ambiguity in the statutory provisions created conflicts between increased timber production to meet increasing housing demands and conservationists' desire to protect forest resources. This prompted the enactment of the Multiple-Use Sustainable Yield Act of 1960 ("Multiple-Use Act"), which called upon the U.S. Forest Service to apply a multiple-use approach to the management of forests. This multiple-use approach was defined as utilization in the combination that will best meet the needs of the American people.

77. Despite positive efforts taken under the Multiple-Use Act, the U.S. Forest Service did not de-emphasize the importance of timber production. This created further conflicts over unsustainable timber practices within the United States' national forests. As a result, the U.S. Congress created additional forestry laws, including the Forest and Rangeland Renewable Resources Planning Act of 1974 and the National Forest Management Act of 1994.

78. Although these laws contained substantive and procedural provisions that covered a range of forestry issues, the United States' forest management activities focused more on harvesting forest products than on programmes sustaining healthy forest ecosystems. Therefore, by the time the Earth Summit was held at Rio, the United States had yet to fully incorporate an ecosystem approach to the management of its forests.

79. Subsequently, the U.S. Forest Service participated in a conference attended by ecologists, foresters, economists, and sociologists in its effort to develop the idea of an ecosystem approach to forest management. The U.S. Forest Service and other

participants documented their commitments in "Defining Sustainable Forestry." In the document, the U.S. Forest Service announced that the principles adopted at the conference, including the commitment to environmentally-sensitive production of wood and other natural resources, were consistent in spirit with the principles from the United Nations Conference on Environment and Development. This is an acknowledgement by the U.S. Forest Service of its partial fulfillment of the commitments the United States made on forests at Rio.

80. To further the ecosystem management approach to forestry, the U.S. Forest Service published proposed rules to amend its forest planning regulations in April 1995. The proposed rules streamlined the forest planning system and revised certain sections to incorporate principles of ecosystem management. Such principles include the significance of landscapes and the preservation of biological diversity to recover and conserve endangered and threatened species. The rules were adopted by the U.S. Congress on 1 November 2000.

b) Japan

81. As part of its implementation of the Rio Forest Principles and other forest initiatives, Japan formulated the Basic Plan for Administration and Management of National Forests in 1998 ("Basic Plan"). Among other things, the Basic Plan is intended to ensure that the public benefits from forests and introduces three new types of classification for national forests, based on the purpose of their management: (i) Forests for Water and Land Conservation, (ii) Forests for Humans and Nature, and (iii) Forests for Recycling Use of Resources. The first two categories of forests are for public benefit. The last category is for ecological purposes, including functions as wildlife habitat. Japan's forestry management efforts have resulted in the expansion of its Forests for Water and Land Conservation and Forests for Humans and Nature to include 80% of the country's national forests under its protection. Such an approach satisfies the Rio Forest Principles, as well as the requirements of the Biodiversity Convention. Japan's improved management system for forests has also substantially expanded the acreage of land under forest cover in the country.

82. As part of its Basic Plan, Japan conducted a comprehensive review of its forest and forestry policy, which resulted in a revision of its Forestry Basic Law in 2001. The revision resulted in the

enactment of the Basic Law on Forest and Forestry in June 2001, which incorporates the Rio Forest Principles and principles of sustainable forestry management as emphasised in Agenda 21.

83. The Basic Plan complements other Japanese legislation that provide for forest pest control and other various forestry issues, including the Forest Pests and Disease Control, Law No. 53 of 1950, the Law concerning Management of National Forest, No. 246 of 1951, the Forest Consolidation Law No. 84 of 1954, and the Emergency Measures Law for Soil and Water Conservation Law No. 21 of 1960.

84. Article 2 of the Basic Plan recognizes the multifunctional roles of forests, including conservation of water resources and prevention of global warming. Article 3(1) and (2) provides for encouragement of a better public understanding of forests and forestry and for public involvement in forest management decisions and expands the roles of municipalities. Article 11 provides for the government's responsibility to establish and implement a Basic Plan for forest management. It stipulates that targets for the fulfillment of multifunctional roles of forests and for the supply and use of forest products shall be established. These targets will guide forest management and conservation, the operation of forestry and wood industries, and forest products consumption. The Basic Plan shall also identify issues that forest owners and other relevant parties should address.

85. For implementation, Articles 28 and 29 of the Basic Plan establish a Forestry Policy Council within the Ministry of Agriculture, Forestry and Fisheries to undertake the various measures relating to forests and forestry. Further, pursuant to article 18, Japan has undertaken a number of international initiatives for sustainable forestry management through official development assistance to developing countries to combat deforestation and forest degradation, promote sustainable forest management in beneficiary countries, prevent forest fires, and promote social forestry, among other things. As of April 2002, the government of Japan was implementing twenty-two such activities.

IV. Polar Ecosystems

1. Ecosystem Characteristics and Vulnerabilities

86. The Arctic and Antarctic are collectively referred to as the world's Polar Regions. The Arctic encompasses a total area of approximately 14,056 million square kilometres and is located between the North Pole and latitude 60 degrees north. It includes the Arctic Ocean, northern Alaska, Greenland, the Barents Sea, the Beaufort Sea, Hudson Bay and the tributaries of some rivers and water bodies originating in adjacent areas. Portions of the region fall within the territorial jurisdictions of eight countries: Canada, Norway, Sweden, Finland, Denmark, Russia, Iceland and the United States.

87. The Antarctic is located around the globe's South Pole, south of latitude 60 degrees south. It comprises an ice-covered land mass surrounded by a body of water known as the Southern Ocean. It is the world's fifth largest continent and covers an area of roughly fourteen million square kilometres. The body of water surrounding Antarctica forms a natural boundary between the region and the rest of the world.

88. The Arctic and Antarctic share climatic and ecological characteristics that are peculiar to the Polar Regions. The most distinctive features of the Polar Regions are extremely low temperatures averaging minus-30 degrees Celsius in the winter in the Arctic, and even colder in Antarctica. Large portions of both Polar Regions are also covered with permanent, thick ice and snow, even in the summer. In Antarctica, vast permanent ice cover averages 200 metres thick; unlike the Arctic, snow and ice have continued to accumulate in the Antarctic over the years, making it stand at a high elevation. In the Arctic, only about 10% of the Arctic Ocean is ice-free, even in the summer months. The Polar Regions also experience large seasonal variation in the amount of sunlight and solar radiation that they receive. In the long winter, they receive very little sunlight and are mostly dark, but in the summer, they receive twenty-four hours of continuous sunlight. The climatic conditions in the Polar Regions are compounded by winds that can blow at up to 100 kilometres per hour.

89. The Regions' extreme climatic conditions perform important ecological functions. For example, the extensive ice and snow cover of the oceans and land in the Polar Regions helps cool the Earth by reflecting energy from the sun back into space. Also, the cold, dense, salt water that is created as ice forms tends to sink to lower reaches of the ocean; thereby helping to drive ocean currents, which distribute heat around the Earth, and regulates the exchange of heat, moisture, and salinity in the oceans. Thus the Polar Regions help to maintain the weather systems and climate all over the world.

90. The Polar Regions also comprise a variety of unique landscapes of great aesthetic beauty, making them important tourist destinations that deserve to be preserved. For example, the Arctic boasts of "cordillera", areas that feature some of the world's most spectacular glaciers, boreal forests, meadows, ice shattered rugged mountains. The Arctic is also replete with "tundra," low-lying, treeless plains that are covered with ice and snow all winter, with a permanently frozen sub-soil known as "permafrost". Likewise, Antarctica's spectacular scenery consists of huge ice cliffs and dramatic mountain ranges, cut by immense glaciers that spill out into a coastal maze of islands, inlets, and waterways, and icebergs of all shapes and sizes, some as big as islands, others exquisitely sculpted.

91. The Regions' extensive ice and snow cover also provides important wildlife habitat that have adapted to living in the cold conditions. The Arctic is home to several species of bears, including the rare Kodiak, the world's second largest bear; seals, including endangered fur seals, whales, including the endangered Beluga Whale and the bow-head whale, the Laysan Albatross, which is the largest flying bird in the world, and many other kinds of birds, and large herds of caribou. The Antarctic is also rich in fauna, including penguins, fur seals, petrels, albatrosses, various types of fish, and other marine mammals. The Polar Regions are also important wildlife breeding grounds, especially in the summer. In addition, certain marine areas, especially in the Arctic, remain ice-free year round or for much of the year, and are richly-endowed with cod, salmon, trout, and several other types of fish.

92. There are also precious minerals in the Polar Regions. In the Arctic, oil has been found in the Barents Sea and there are other minerals in the continental shelves and other areas, making mining an important economic activity in the region. For many years, the Antarctic has also been seen as a possible treasure trove of mineral wealth because of its geological ties to the vast mineral resources of South Africa and the rich oil fields of Australia's southern coast.

93. Because of the relatively pristine conditions of the Arctic, the wilderness status of Antarctica, inaccessibility, and other characteristics, the Polar Regions are also important places to conduct scientific research and experiments. This research can provide benefits on a range of important issues, such as the understanding of weather patterns, possible impacts of global climate change, continental drift, and biological adaptability. The best known example is research on impacts of manufactured compounds, especially chrorofluorocarbons, on the ozone concentrations in the Earth's atmosphere. Research conducted in Antarctica has revealed that these substances, which were first thought to be safe and were commonly used in spray cans and air conditioners, lead to loss of ozone gas, which protects living things from damage by high levels of ultraviolet radiation from the sun. Research has shown that loss of atmospheric ozone over Antarctica has allowed more ultraviolet radiation to reach the Earth's surface in increasingly large areas in the Southern hemisphere. These findings were crucial in promoting international agreement on the phase-out of ozone depleting substances that has been discussed in more detail in Chapter 11 of this Manual. There are currently eighteen countries operating research stations in Antarctica, making the preservation of Antarctica for scientific research one of the issues to be addressed by law.

94. Both Polar Regions' ecosystems are fragile and have been faced with a number of environmental threats originating mainly from outside the regions. One of the problems is that of climate change. It results from the release of carbon dioxide, methane, and other green house gases into the atmosphere from deforestation, industrial, agricultural, and other economic activities taking place in Europe and other parts of the world. There is ample scientific data showing that as a result of accelerated rates of warming in Polar Regions due to increased release of harmful substances in the atmosphere, the regions have warmed alarmingly in a short period of time in recent years. As the Polar Regions warm, they can drive and amplify global temperatures, causing areas of the world that are currently cold to be warm. Warming has also caused a dramatic reduction in thickness of the ice sheets as they melt increasingly, threatening to destroy coastlines surrounding the Arctic and accelerating rates of erosion, flooding, and damage to buildings and infrastructure. It is also likely to adversely affect polar bears and other species adapted to living in polar conditions.

95. In addition to the dangerous hole in the ozone layer over Antarctica, the Arctic has, since the 1950s, experienced an air pollution phenomenon known as arctic haze. This is a reddish-brown haze composed of very small particles containing a wide variety of man-made and natural compounds including sulphate compounds, persistent organic pollutants, heavy metals, soot, and hydrocarbons. Winter winds carry the deadly contaminants from the industrialized regions of Europe, Asia, and America to the Arctic. Here, the haze reduces visibility in the winter, and, coupled with increased blackness of snow on the ground, threatens to

change incoming and out-going radiation levels and to modify the climate in the region and surrounding countries.

96. Petroleum and chemical shipments from one country or continent to another through the waters in the Polar Regions add to the risks of pollution damage from spills and leakage. Reports indicate that between 1971 and 1997, there were 2,742 accidental spills of petroleum products in the region. The disastrous shipwreck of the Argentinean vessel Bahia Paraiso in Antarctic waters in January 1989 illustrates the seriousness of the threats posed by sea transportation of hazardous substances. The accident was, unfortunately, followed by the even graver Exxon Valdez oil spill in Alaska, which dramatized concerns about hazardous industrial and transport activities in Polar Regions. The susceptibility of Polar Regions to contamination by oil and other hazardous substances is exacerbated by the fact that, at present, technology for cleaning up spilled petroleum is not adequate to remove oil from ice-covered waters.

97. In addition to the Regions' shared characteristics, they have distinct characteristics that create distinct challenges. For instance, while the Arctic straddles the territories of several countries, Antarctica is isolated, and both the continent and the surrounding high seas are not subject to the territorial jurisdiction of any state that might exercise national protection over its ecosystem. As a result, uncontrolled extraction of its fish, seals, whales, and other resources has led to over-exploitation of resources over which no individual state can lay claim. As early as 1892, ships from Norway and other countries were already heavily extracting whales in Antarctica. By 1934, large Japanese whaling ships and ships from other countries had also become a more or less permanent feature in the region. These were joined by whaling and sealing ships from the United States of America in 1948, and extraction of living resources continued in the region unabated, threatening to deplete the resources.

98. Since no single state could exert control over the use of Antarctica, its environment was also subjected to military activities by a number of countries that conducted not only military training, but also made it a site for testing nuclear and other weapons and for uncontrolled dumping of all kinds of wastes, threatening to destroy its ecosystems. Whereas Antarctica is non-militarized, the activities of submarines, notably during the Cold War, made the Arctic a highly strategic region. Military forces of Russia, and other countries that operated nuclear sub-marines bases, left behind, dumped, or sank radioactive nuclear waste materials in their bases in the Arctic. Radioactive materials have also been generated by fallout from weapons testing that took place, especially between 1945 and 1980, and from nuclear accidents, such as the 1986 Chernobyl accident. In addition, there have been discharges of nuclear wastes from nuclear storage facilities and nuclear power plants in Siberia, and from other parts of the region that have polluted the Barents Sea and other environments in the region.

99. A further significant difference between the two poles rests in the fact that Antarctica has no permanent population except for research scientists whose number average 200 per year, and summer tourists. By contrast, portions of the Arctic are inhabited by indigenous populations, including the Eskimo of Alaska and the Saami of northern Scandinavia, with a total population of approximately 3.8 million. The indigenous people undertake various economic activities including agriculture, fisheries, mining, and manufacturing. They have also opened up the region to accelerated rates of oil and gas exploration and exploitation in the Barents Sea and other areas, and to accelerated rates of mining of zinc, cadmium, and other minerals. These activities have contributed to the discharge of harmful substances such as wastes, polychlorinated biphenyls and mercury into the Arctic environment. Recent surveys indicate that more than two million litres of waste oil and fuel, and approximately 260 tonnes of other hazardous wastes, are produced annually by some communities and that their poor disposal threatens to damage the ecosystems of the region. Therefore, the presence of these populations raises the need in the Arctic, unlike in the Antarctica, to balance the economic needs of the population, including mineral exploitation, with ecological needs. More generally, the presence of indigenous populations also raises issues related to indigenous rights, rather than simply state rights.

100. Because of the global nature of the problems originating from outside the Polar Regions, the environmental issues they raise are likely best addressed by global agreements that focus on the root causes of the problems. The relevant regimes, including the Vienna Convention for the Protection of the Ozone Layer and Protocol, the United Nations Convention on Climate Change and its Kyoto Protocol, the Stockholm Convention on Persistent Organic Pollutants, and the Basel Convention on Hazardous Wastes are covered in chapters 11, 12, and 13 of this Manual.

2. International Environmental Regime relating to Antarctica

a) The Antarctic Treaty

101. The availability of free-for-all minerals, fish, and other resources in Antarctica and the potential to use the region for all kinds of purposes free of charge also led to a scramble by many nations to own portions of it. By the end of the second World War, there were conflicting claims of territorial sovereignty over portions of Antarctica by a number of these states, including Argentina, Australia, Chile, France, New Zealand, Norway, the United Kingdom, the Soviet Union, and potentially, the United States.

102. In order to resolve disputes arising out of the various claims, to protect the various interests, and to prevent war between the wrangling nations, the United States spearheaded consultative efforts to eliminate territorial dispute over Antarctica and to preserve pending claims, non-military status of the region, and scientific research opportunities. Collaborative efforts between the states, with input from world scientists, culminated in the adopting in1959 of the Antarctic Treaty in Washington by the twelve states that had been actively undertaking research activities in Antarctica, including Argentina, Australia, Belgium, Chile, France, Japan, New Zealand, Norway, South Africa, United Kingdom, United States, and the former Soviet Union.

103. Since adoption, it has 28 consultative parties and 17 acceding states, making a total of 45, as of November 2005. The 1959 Antarctic Treaty applies to the area south of latitude 60 degrees south, including ice shelves. In the Preamble, the parties recognize that "it is in the interest of all mankind that Antarctica shall continue forever to be used exclusively for peaceful purposes and shall not become the scene or object of international discord." The Antarctic Treaty thus created new ground by aiming to cooperatively govern the status and conservation of an entire continent. Some commentators would suggest that the treaty laid the foundation for the status of Antarctica as "common heritage of humankind," an international environmental law concept discussed in more detail in Chapter 3 of this Manual.

104. The main thrusts of the treaty as provided in articles I, II, and IV are to ensure that Antarctica is used for peaceful purposes only; to ensure the freedom of scientific investigation and international cooperation in scientific research on the continent; and to freeze any claims of territorial sovereignty over Antarctica. To meet these key objectives, parties agreed in article I to prohibit military activities, such as the establishment of military bases or weapons testing in Antarctica. Article III (1) looks to promote international scientific cooperation, including the exchange of research plans and personnel, and requires that results of research be made freely available. In article IV (1) and (2), the 1959 Antarctic Treaty provides that no activities will enhance or diminish previously asserted rights or claims to territorial sovereignty in Antarctica, and that no new or enlarged claims can be made.

105. The only express reference to environmental protection in the 1959 Antarctic Treaty itself is article IX(1)(f), which provides that parties may make recommendations on measures regarding "preservation and conservation of living resources in Antarctica." However, other parts of the treaty are also relevant to environmental protection. Aside from the above mentioned preservation of Antarctica for the purposes of research, the most relevant provisions are those prohibiting nuclear explosions and the disposal of radioactive waste in Antarctica under article V. These provisions made Antarctica the first nuclear weapons-free zone in the world. Although nuclear power was not prohibited, detonation of nuclear bombs, testing of nuclear weapons and storage of wastes from nuclear facilities in Antarctica were banned entirely. On the whole, the provisions aim to promote the idea of peaceful use of Antarctica and to reduce the danger of contamination of the Antarctic environment.

106. Article VII provides for the inspection, at any time and without prior notice, of other parties' ships, stations, installations, and equipment in Antarctica to ensure the observance of, and compliance with, the 1959 Antarctic Treaty. In article VIII (1), the Antarctic Treaty clarifies that, irrespective of the parties' positions regarding jurisdiction over all other persons in Antarctica, observers and scientific personnel are subject to the jurisdiction of the party to which they are nationals in respect of all acts or omissions occurring while they are in Antarctica. Under article X, parties undertake to exert appropriate efforts to the end that no one engages in any activity in Antarctica that is contrary to the Antarctic Treaty's principles and purposes.

107. Articles VIII (2) and XI, in turn, provide for the settlement of disputes. They require that all disputes and claims arising between parties concerning use or rights and claims over Antarctica and any other disputes arising as a result of interpretation or implementation of the agreement

be resolved through peaceful means. If parties fail to reach agreement through peaceful means, they are free to refer matters to the International Court of Justice.

108. Article IX provides for the parties to meet periodically to discuss recommended measures to further the objectives of the Treaty. The parties can also consider further arrangements on specific issues and adopt necessary amendments to the treaty, which under article XII, enter into force for each party as it ratifies or accedes to it. Only consultative parties can participate in the meetings that adopt recommendations or amendments. This group of parties comprises the original twelve signatories to the treaty, and fifteen additional parties that have acquired this status by joining the treaty and conducting scientific research in Antarctica as provided under article IX(2). The remaining seventeen parties merely have observer status at the meetings of the consultative parties.

109. Since the 1959 Antarctic Treaty entered into force on 23 June 1961, parties have held regular consultative meetings. In addition to helping reduce the tensions surrounding territorial claims and strategic interests in Antarctica, these consultations have resulted in the gradual development of what has become known as the Antarctic treaty system. It comprises the original treaty, two treaties on the conservation of Antarctic Seals and Antarctic Marine Living Resources, respectively, and a ground-breaking protocol on environmental protection.

b) Convention for the Conservation of Antarctic Seals

110. The first additional agreement to be adopted was the Convention for the Conservation of Antarctic Seals ("1972 Seals Convention"). The Seals Convention was adopted on 1 June 1972, and entered into force on 11 March 1978. As of November 2005, the Seals Convention has 16 parties.

111. The Seals Convention is concerned with various species of seals in the marine environment of Antarctica, specifically in the Southern Ocean. Antarctic seals are vulnerable to over-exploitation for commercial purposes, especially because Antarctica is not subject to the jurisdiction of any government that could exercise control over harvesting of marine living resources. Parties were concerned that due to over-exploitation, the population of Antarctic seals was threatened with depletion.

112. To address this concern, the 1972 Seals Convention establishes a number of rules regarding harvesting and implementation of various species of seals that apply to nationals of parties and to vessels flying the flags of parties. Article1 includes a prohibition on the killing or capture of various species of seals, including southern fur seals, unless the killing or capture is done in accordance with the requirements stipulated by the convention. Articles 2(2) and 4 require each party to create laws establishing a permitting system for their nationals and vessels flying their flags that are engaged in seal harvesting in Antarctica. In the permits, parties would, for example, set catch limits and /or open and closed seasons or areas to ensure that harvesting of the various species of seals does not cause their populations to fall below sustainable levels. In setting any limits, parties are required by article 3(2) of the 1972 Seals Convention to base decisions on the best scientific and technical evidence available. Article 5 requires them to share information on any such measures with other parties through the Scientific Committee on Antarctic Research, an independent body that helps to address various environmental issues on Antarctica.

113. An Annex to the 1972 Seals Convention contains specific rules on catch limits, places total bans on the catch of four species of seals, establishes open and closed seasons for harvesting other species seals, and outlines other rules that parties have established. These rules are to be observed by parties in creating and implementing measures that the Seals Convention requires to assure sustainable harvesting of seals and to prevent depletion of their species. However, since there has been no commercial sealing in the Antarctic area covered by the treaty since 1964, activity under the Seals Convention has been limited to collecting information on annual kills or captures for scientific purposes.

c) Convention on the Conservation of Antarctic Marine Living Resources

114. The Convention on the Conservation of Antarctic Marine Living Resources ("1980 CCAMLR") was the second agreement negotiated to complement the Antarctic Treaty. Notwithstanding the diversity of species of living plants, mammals, fish, and other organisms in Antarctica, there initially was no agreement among Antarctic Treaty parties specifically dealing with all living resources. Recognizing the gap, after consultation and negotiation, parties adopted the CCAMLR on 20 May 1980, and the agreement entered into force on 7 April 1982. In contrast to the 1972 Seals

Convention, article IV of 1980 CCAMLR provides that the agreement is open also to non-parties to the Antarctic Treaty. As of November 2005, it has 30 parties.

115. 1980 CCAMLR has been heralded as one of the first global conventions to reflect both the ecosystem and precautionary approaches to environmental protection. It was intended to create a framework for cooperation among parties to balance conservation and rational use of Antarctic marine living resources. The preamble squarely places the protection of marine living resources in the context of the protection of the integrity of the Antarctic marine ecosystem. According to article I(2), the term "Antarctic marine living resources" includes populations of fin fish, molluscs, crustaceans, birds, and other living organisms found South of the Antarctic Convergence. Article I(3), in turn, defines the Antarctic marine ecosystem as "the complex of relationships of Antarctic marine living resources with each other and with their physical environment." In keeping with this ecosystem approach, article I(1) extends the scope of the CCAMLR's application to include Antarctic marine living resources in an area that is larger than that covered by the 1959 Antarctic Treaty.

116. Article II of 1980 CCAMLR sets a number of ecosystem-oriented principles to guide parties in undertaking steps to conserve resources and to govern harvesting of the resources. The first principle in article II (3)(a) is sustainable utilization of the resources, which requires, among other things, that parties take steps to prevent decrease in the size of any harvested population to levels below that which ensures its stable increment. Parties may, for example, establish catch limits and open and closed harvesting seasons to maintain populations of commercial and other species and to prevent over harvesting. Under article II (3)(b), parties must also work to maintain the ecological relationships between harvested and dependent and related populations of Antarctic marine living resources. Reflecting a precautionary approach, article II(3)(c) further highlights the need for "prevention of changes or minimization of the risk of changes in the marine ecosystem which are not potentially reversible over two or three decades, taking into account the state of available knowledge of the direct and indirect impact of harvesting..." and related activities.

117. In article V, the 1980 CCAMLR parties that are not parties to the Antarctic Treaty agreed to abide by measures for conservation of living resources in Antarctica that have been agreed to under the Antarctic Treaty. Among other things, the measures under article XXIV and other provisions of 1980 CCAMLR include monitoring by parties of fish catches, fishing vessels, and use of appropriate fishing gear to ensure that fish stocks are not depleted; designation of closed and open fishing seasons; and use of scientific survey techniques to study the behaviour, breeding patterns, and other characteristics of marine living resources so as to preserve their populations.

118. Article VII creates the Commission for the Conservation of Antarctic Marine Living Resources ("Commission") to facilitate cooperative conservation efforts and to perform various conservation-related functions. According to articles IX and X, these functions include facilitating research into and comprehensive studies of Antarctic marine living resources and of the Antarctic marine ecosystem, compiling data on the status of and changes in population of Antarctic marine living resources and on factors affecting the distribution, abundance and productivity of harvested species and dependent species, and setting catch limits that are applicable to all parties. Managed fisheries exist, *inter alia*, for finfish, krill and squid. In keeping with CCAMLR's ecosystem-oriented conservation approach, the Commission is also to seek cooperation with respect to the conservation of associated species that straddle the Convention area and adjacent areas as provided by article XI. The Commission is supported by a permanent secretariat based in Hobart, Tasmania, Australia.

119. In addition to the Commission, articles XIV and XV establish a Scientific Committee for the Conservation of Antarctic Marine Living Resources ("Scientific Committee"). The Scientific Committee is a consultative body whose responsibilities include the collection, study, and exchange of information with respect to the marine living resources in the area to which the Convention applies. It also assists the Commission by gathering and assessing information, establishing criteria and methods pertaining to conservation measures and harvesting limits, and by making other recommendations that the Commission may adopt.

120. Article XXI requires all parties to take appropriate measures to ensure compliance with 1980 CCAMLR. The Convention reinforces its approach to compliance by providing, in article XXIV for a system of observation and inspection designed both to promote the Convention's objectives and to ensure observance of its provisions. CCAMLR's focus on compliance notwithstanding, its efforts at

effective ecosystem protection are being undermined by illegal, unreported, and unregulated fishing in the convention area. In response to the challenge, a variety of steps have been taken within the framework of CCAMLR regime to address the problem of illegal fishing. In 1999, parties adopted a Catch Documentation Scheme for toothfish. The Scheme helps to monitor international trade, identify the origins of imports, and assists in determining if imports from the Convention Area are consistent with the CCMALR's conservation measures. It also provides catch data for assessing fish stocks.

d) Protocol on Environmental Protection to the Antarctic Treaty

121. The Protocol on Environmental Protection to the Antarctic Treaty ("1991 Madrid Protocol") is intended to fill the remaining gaps in the Antarctic Treaty System, and to complement the 1959 Antarctic Treaty with respect to environmental protection as provided in the Preamble and article 4 thereof. Like the 1980 CCAMLR, the Madrid Protocol adopts an ecosystem-oriented approach. The Madrid Protocol was adopted on 4 October 1991, and entered into force on 14 January 1998.

122. Under articles 21 and 22 of the Protocol, the 1991 Madrid Protocol is open to all parties to the Antarctic Treaty. To date, the Protocol has twenty-nine parties, including the twenty-seven consultative parties. Five Annexes to the 1991 Madrid Protocol, which detail specific environmental protection measures and requirements, are also in force: on environmental impact assessment (Annex I), on the conservation of Antarctic flora and fauna (Annex II), on waste disposal and management (Annex III), on prevention of marine pollution (Annex IV), and on area protection and management (Annex V).

123. In addition to concerns over a growing tourist industry and pollution emanating from research facilities, the impetus for the 1991 Madrid Protocol was provided by the contentious issue of mineral resource mining in Antarctica. Attempts to resolve conflicting state interests in mining and exploration of the Antarctic mineral resources had led to the negotiation of a Convention on the Regulation of Antarctic Mineral Resource Activities in 1988. This agreement would have permitted mining in Antarctica. However, due to many parties' strong resistance to any mineral exploitation in Antarctica, the Convention never came into force. Instead, article 7 of the Madrid Protocol bans mining and other mineral resource activities in Antarctica. Article 25(2) allows for the possibility of review of

the situation only after fifty years of its entry into force.

124. In the 1991 Madrid Protocol, Antarctica is designated as a nature reserve, and in article 2, "devoted to peace and science." Article 3 sets out environmental principles that provide rules to govern all human activities in the Antarctic treaty area. It requires that in the planning and implementation of all activities, fundamental consideration be given to the intrinsic value of the Antarctic environment, including its wilderness and aesthetic values and its value as an area for the conduct of scientific research. Parties are also required to conduct activities in a way that avoids adverse effects on the Antarctic climate, weather patterns, or air and water quality; and to avoid significant changes in the atmospheric, terrestrial, aquatic, glacial, or marine environments. They are also required to avoid causing detrimental changes in the distribution, abundance or productivity of species or populations of species of fauna and flora including endangered or threatened species or populations of such species. Article 3 also requires that all activities be planned and conducted so as to give priority to scientific research and to preserve the value of Antarctica as a site for research, notably research related to the global environment. Under article 6, parties must cooperate in the planning and conduct of activities in the treaty area.

125. Article 8 brings a precautionary approach to the Madrid Protocol. It identifies, according to significance of potential impact, the activities that are subject to prior environmental impact assessment pursuant to Annex I. This article obligates parties to ensure application of the assessment processes set out in the Annex to all new or significantly changed activities. These anticipatory requirements are backed up by articles 13, 14, 15 and 16, which require parties to ensure compliance with the 1991 Madrid Protocol through appropriate regulatory and enforcement measures at the domestic level, to arrange inspections of activities and equipment in Antarctica, to provide for prompt and effective response action to environmental emergencies in the treaty area, and to create an Annex on rules and procedures relating to liability for environmental damage in the treaty area. Parties are in the process of negotiating this Annex.

126. Article 11 establishes a Committee for Environmental Protection composed of party representatives, and their experts and advisers. In 1988, it met for the first time during the Twenty-Second Antarctic Treaty Consultative Meeting and

serves as the advisory body for the implementation and observance of the Madrid Protocol and its Annexes as provided under article 12.

3. International Environmental Regime relating to the Arctic

127. Unlike the Antarctic, for which a comprehensive treaty regime developed over a number of decades, the Arctic is not governed by a binding legal regime. The region has no history of comprehensive multilateral cooperation, perhaps due to the strategic and antagonistic efforts that prevailed throughout the Cold War. Besides a number of bilateral agreements between individual Arctic states on individual issues such as fisheries, wildlife, and protection from pollution, the Arctic legal regime consists primarily comprised of non-legally binding declarations, plans of action, strategies for environmental protection and similar arrangements between states in the region.

a) Declaration on the Protection of the Arctic Environment

128. The Declaration on the Protection of the Arctic Environment ("Arctic Declaration") was the first step in developing a pan-Arctic approach to environmental protection. It was adopted in 1991, at a Ministerial Conference held in Finland by the eight countries with portions of their territories lying in the Arctic: Canada, Denmark, Finland, Iceland, Norway, Russia, Sweden and the United States. The Arctic Declaration established the Arctic Environmental Protection Strategy ("AEPS"), joint action plan that outlined cooperative steps and actions to protect and preserve the Arctic environment. In its objectives, the AEPS reflected the need to balance protection of Arctic ecosystems and sustainable use of natural resources by local populations.

129. In the AEPS, the Arctic countries undertook to cooperate in conducting scientific research to identify sources, pathways, sinks and effects of pollution, and to share available data. Priority was given to identification of the various aspects of pollution by persistent organic pollutants, oil, heavy metals and radioactive materials for possible action to reduce their adverse impacts on the environment. The countries also agreed to conduct assessments of potential environmental impacts of development activities on the Arctic environment and to give due regard to traditional and cultural needs, values, and practices of Arctic indigenous peoples in their cooperative efforts.

130. The AEPS was criticized for its piecemeal approach to environmental concerns and the absence of concrete commitments and timelines. Nonetheless, the AEPS has been important in focusing attention on the need for a coordinated approach to the protection of the Arctic environment, and in laying the foundations for subsequent cooperative efforts. The AEPS also launched a series of cooperative programmes that continue to operate, including:

- Arctic Monitoring and Assessment Programme, which was intended to assess the levels and impacts of key Arctic pollutants;
- Emergency Preparedness, Prevention, and Response Programme, which was to provide a framework to address the threat of environmental emergencies;
- Conservation of Arctic Flora and Fauna, which was to facilitate the exchange of information and coordination of research into species and habitats; and
- Protection of the Arctic Marine Environment, which was to take measures to prevent marine pollution.

b) The Arctic Council

131. In 1996, in the Ottawa Declaration, the Arctic countries established an Arctic Council to be in charge of promoting and coordinating actions and steps for environmental protection. The Arctic Council grew out of the cooperative context of the AEPS and maintains the four AEPS programmes that were outlined above, but also places environmental protection in a much wider context, notably the need for sustainable development in the region. Most of its sessions and activities are open to participation by and input from local populations, with a particular role being accorded to indigenous peoples in the Arctic and their representative groups. Military matters are explicitly excluded from its purview.

c) The Barrow Declaration

132. In 1988, the Arctic Council adopted the Barrow Declaration in 1998, in which the eight Arctic states adopted an Arctic Council Action Plan to eliminate Pollution of the Arctic ("ACAP"). The ACAP set forth a number of activities specifically intended to deal with pollution of the Arctic environment with hazardous substances. It recommended and endorsed specific measures including biodiversity protection in the region, calling upon UNEP to initiate a global assessment of mercury that could form the basis for appropriate international action in which the Arctic states

would participate actively. It also encouraged Arctic states to ratify the convention on persistent organic pollutants, established a committee to evaluate and synthesize knowledge on climate change and increased ultraviolet radiation, and supported the work of the intergovernmental panel on climate change.

d) Regional Programme of Action for the Protection of the Arctic Marine Environment from Land-Based Activities

133. On 18 September 1998, the Arctic Council adopted the Regional Programme of Action for the Protection of the Arctic Marine Environment from Land-Based Activities ("RPA"), a non-legally binding environmental instrument. Key considerations in the RAP include recognition that 80% of marine pollution is land-based and that certain Arctic populations of plants and animals are amongst the most exposed populations in the world to certain environmental contaminants. In the RPA, the Arctic Council recognized that, notwithstanding existing efforts at national and international levels, it would not be possible to eliminate pollutants in the eight countries all at once. Therefore, the Arctic Council chose to gradually phase-out pollutants from the Arctic, beginning with persistent organic pollutants and heavy metals. The Arctic Council seeks funding from donors to carry out their proposed activities.

e) Sub-Regional Regimes

134. Non-legally binding agreements on the environment in the Arctic also exist at sub-regional level. Cooperation at the sub-regional level in the Arctic began in the 1990s, building on and reinforcing earlier bilateral contacts. The Barents Euro-Arctic Region was established under the 1993 Kirkenes Declaration and operates at two levels - between the governments of Finland, Norway, Russia and Sweden, and between the eight northernmost counties and/or provinces in these countries. The Barents Regional Council created under the 1993 Kirkenes Declaration is comprised of representatives from local governments and representatives of the Saami, an indigenous group of people in the region seeking to make joint efforts in addressing environmental issues in the region.

f) Legally Binding Instruments

135. There exists a body of legally binding agreements, which, although not focused on the Arctic ecosystem as such, applies to aspects of Arctic environmental protection, including the following:

- 1973 Agreement on Conservation of Polar Bears between Canada, Denmark, Norway, the former Soviet Union, and the United States to protect polar bears and the flora and fauna of the Arctic;
- Convention on Conservation of North Pacific Seals adopted by Canada, Japan, the former Soviet Union and the United States on 9 February 1957; and
- Agreement on the Conservation of African-Eurasian Migratory Waterbirds ("AEWA"), which was negotiated within the framework of the Convention on the Conservation of Migratory Species of Wild Animals and entered into force on 1 November 1999.

136. The existence of many non-legally binding agreements seeking to address environmental issues in the Arctic shows that concerned parties have the will to take steps and actions to prevent harm. However, a comprehensive legally binding instrument that would integrate sustainable development and environmental protection as a key policy requirement is necessary. The various topics covered in the non-legally binding declarations, plans of actions, and strategies, as well as other strategies by Arctic communities should now be incorporated into a binding agreement to promote sustainable development of the region. In this regard, the Antarctic Treaty system that is well developed should provide examples to the Arctic Council on steps forward. For the Antarctic, the disarmament of nations, the maintenance of peace over Antarctica, and its preservation for peaceful purposes only, are remarkable achievements of the Antarctic Treaty system, which shows the significant role international law can play in addressing environmental problems. All parties to the agreements under the Antarctic Treaty system should be encouraged to make efforts to implement them at national levels to continue to preserve the uniqueness of the Polar Region and its ecological significance.

4. National and Local Initiatives relating to the Polar Regions' Ecosystems

137. At the moment, all is not well with mountain, forest, and polar regions ecosystems, even in some of the countries where implementing legislation exists. A lot more effort should be made at national levels to protect, conserve, and sustainably manage ecosystems. This chapter demonstrates that there is political will to implement international instruments at national levels and this can serve as a useful enforcement mechanism. Examples of national legislations provided show that different

approaches have been taken by nations in their implementation of international instruments. While some countries have created new implementing laws, others have strengthened existing laws to provide for actions and measures agreed at the international level. While some countries' implementing laws have comprehensive provisions providing for ecosystem conservation, protection, and sustainable development, others have framework implementing laws making general provisions and allowing for creation of implementing regulations at national and lower levels. Effective domestic enforcement of the laws can make all of the different approaches work to ensure sufficient protection, conservation and sustainable management of ecosystems. Efforts should also be made to encourage parties that do not yet have domestic implementing legislation to take measures to put it in place. The sample legislation examined in this chapter provides useful models for implementation.

138. Although a number of countries have taken legislative actions for the protection and conservation of Polar Regions' ecosystems, not all these laws indicate clearly whether or not they were intended to implement the international instruments at domestic levels. In addition, given the non-legally binding nature of most international arrangements regarding the Arctic, "implementing legislation" in the strict sense of the term is difficult to identify. Therefore, the following discussion focuses on examples of United States and Australian legislation that explicitly pertains to the implementation of the Convention on the Conservation of Antarctic Marine Living Resources ("Antarctic Marine Resource Convention").

a) United States

139. The United States became a party to 1980 CCAMLR on 7 April 1982. In November 1984, it passed the Antarctic Marine Living Resources Convention Act, 16 U.S.C. Sections 2431-2444, to provide the legislative authority to implement the CCAMLR ("Marine Resources Act").

140. Sections 2433, 2436 and 2441 of the Marine Resources Act require the Director of the United States National Science Foundation and the Secretary of Commerce to conduct and support basic research of the Antarctic marine ecosystem for purposes of implementing appropriate conservation measures for the Antarctic living resources and in doing so, to consult with other agencies and the Marine Mammal Commission as appropriate. Under Section 2434 of the Marine Resources Act, the United States Secretary of State

is responsible for establishing a system of observation and inspection pursuant to Art. XXIV of the Convention, receiving communications from the Commission, and to taking appropriate conservation action on them.

141. Under Section 2436, the Secretary of Commerce, in consultation with the Secretary of State and other United States agencies, has the authority to promulgate necessary and appropriate regulations for implementation of the Marine Resources Act. In exercise of this authority, the Secretary has promulgated federal regulations creating a permitting system for all United States nationals, vessels, and others operating under United States jurisdiction for harvesting of marine living resources in the Antarctic, for importation of such resources into the United States, and for their re-exportation from the United States to other countries. Specifically, the Codes of Federal Regulations appearing at Title 50, Part 300, Section 300 prohibit importation into the U.S of any marine living resources without an import and harvesting permit. Further, the regulations implement a Catch Documentation Scheme for Patagonian toothfish, adopted by the Antarctic Marine Resource Convention to control its illegal harvest. Anyone who wishes to import or harvest the fish must possess a harvest or dealer permit. Section 300.103(3) of the regulations require that conditions be placed on the permits limiting the amount of catch and/or requiring compliance with specified conservation measures.

142. Section 2435 creates a number of offenses in relation to marine living resources of Antarctica, including: engaging in harvesting or other associated activities in violation of the Antarctic Marine Resource Convention or a conservation measure in force in the United States pursuant to article IX of the Convention, which requires parties to undertake various conservation measures, including designation of protected marine species and a quantity of species which may be harvested from the Convention area; violating a regulation promulgated under the Marine Resources Act; transporting, offering for sale, selling, purchasing, importing, exporting, or possessing Antarctic marine living resources (or part or product thereof) which the person knows or reasonably should have known were harvested in violation of a conservation measure in force in the United States pursuant to article IX of the Antarctic Marine Resource Convention or in violation the Marine Resources Act's regulations; and refusing to permit an authorized officer of the United States to board a United States vessel or a vessel subject to United States jurisdiction to conduct a search or inspection

to enforce the Convention, the Act, or regulations made there under Sections 2437 to 2439 of the Act provide for civil and criminal penalties for its violation, as well as seizure and forfeiture of Antarctic marine living resources, vessels, and equipment. The responsibility for enforcing the Act lies with the United States Secretary of Commerce and the U.S. Coast Guard.

143. Since 1988, all United States importers of Patagonian toothfish and all other Antarctic marine living resources harvested in the area to which the CCAMLR applies have been required to hold an Antarctic import permit. In addition, the United States has been continuously monitoring and controlling the harvesting and associated activities of its nationals and vessels flying its flag in the Convention area to ensure compliance with the regulations.

b) Australia

144. As a party to the Antarctic Marine Resource Convention, Australia enacted the Antarctic Marine Living Resources Act, Number 30 of 1981 ("Australian Marine Resources Act") to give effect to the Convention on Conservation of Antarctic Living Resources and to the conservation measures that Australia accepted in accordance with article IX of the Convention. It applies to Australian nationals, including businesses registered in Australia that are engaged in harvesting of living resources in Antarctica.

145. One of the means by which the Australian Marine Resources Act regulates harvesting of living resources to assure their conservation and preservation is by establishing a permitting system for harvesting for all purposes. Activities for which permits are required under the Act include: harvesting living marine organisms of a specified kind or kinds, carrying out research with respect to living marine organisms of a specified kind or kinds, and fishing for recreational purposes. Section 9(3) of the Act requires that in considering the granting of a permit, due regard must be given to the conservation of Antarctic marine living resources. Conservation includes rational use of the resources to maintain population size and ecological balance, avoiding significant impacts on the marine ecosystem, and environmental impact assessment for certain activities, including research activities near shores as stipulated under article II of CCAMLR.

146. Carrying out any of the listed activities without a valid permit is a punishable offence under the Australian Marine Resources Act. The Antarctic Treaty and Government Section of the Australian Antarctic Division is the Australian governmental body responsible for administering the permitting system. Once a permit is granted, Sections 9(1)-(7) and 10 of the Act require any restrictions on harvesting and any conditions placed on the permit to control harvesting.

Prof. Jutta Brunnee, Professor of Law and Metcalf Chair of Environmental Law, Faculty of Law, University of Toronto

Dr. Jane Dwasi, UNEP Consultant, University of Nairobi

Resources

Internet Materials

ALPMEDIA INFORMATION SERVICE available at http://www.alpmedia.net/index1.html

ALPINE CONVENTION available at http://www.convenzionedellealpi.org/page1_en.htm

ANTARCTIC MARINE LIVING RESOURCES CONVENTION ACT OF 1984 available at http://ipl.unm.edu/cwl/fedbook/amlrca.html

ANTARCTIC WEB DIRECTORY available at http://dir.ansme.com/regional/831095.html

ARCTIC ALIVE WEBSITE available at http://www.arcus.org

ARCTIC COUNCIL available at http://www.arctic-council.org/

ARCTIC MONITORING AND ASSESSMENT PROGRAMME available at http://www.amap.no

AUSTRALIA ANTARCTIC MARINE LIVING RESOURCES ACT NO. 30 OF 1981, SECTIONS 9 & 10 available at http://www.antdiv.gov.au/MediaLibrary/asset/MediaItems/ml_375314273263889_AntMarineLRC81.pdf

BICKSHEK GLOBAL SUMMIT 2002 available at http://www.mtnforum.org/resources/library/faoun02ea.htm

CADMIUM TOXICITY THREATENING WILDLIFE IN ROCKY MOUNTAINS, OSU NEWS (DECEMBER 2000) available at http://oregonstate.edu/dept/ncs/newsarch/2000/Jul00/cadmium.htm

CODE OF FEDERAL REGULATIONS TITLE 36, CHAPTER 2, FOREST SERVICE available at http://www.access.gpo.gov/nara/cfr/waisidx_00/36cfrv2_00.html

CONVENTION ON THE PROTECTION OF THE ALPS available at www.mtnforum.org/resources/library/eurco91a.htm

COUNTRY REPORTS ON FORESTS UNDER AGENDA 21 available at http://www.un.org/esa/agenda21/natlinfo/agenda21/issue/natur.htm#forest

FOREST WEB PORTAL OF THE CONVENTION ON BIOLOGICAL DIVERSITY available at https://www.biodiv.org/programmes/areas/forest/portal/home.shtml

FRAMEWORK CONVENTION ON THE PROTECTION AND SUSTAINABLE DEVELOPMENT OF THE CARPATHIANS available at www.mtnforum.org/resources/library/cpsdc03a.htm

HISTORY AND OBJECTS OF FOREST RESERVES available at www.lib.duke.edu/forest/usfscoll/publications/1905_Use_Book/007-011.htm

INTERNATIONAL COOPERATION OF JAPAN TO PROMOTE SUSTAINABLE FOREST MANAGEMENT IN DEVELOPING COUNTRIES BY MEANS OF ODA available at http://www.mofa.go.jp/policy/environment/forest/coop0211.html

INTERNATIONAL TROPICAL TIMBER ORGANIZATION available at http://www.forestry.sarawak.gov.my/forweb/sfm/fres/ip/itto/mission.htm and http://www.itto.or.jp

MOUNTAIN FORUM ON-LINE LIBRARY AND REFERENCE DATABASE available at http://www.mtnforum.org/resources/library/liblevels/lib315a.htm#law

MOUNTAIN PARTNERSHIP available at www.mountains2002.org/files/pdf/faolawstudy.pdf

NATIONAL (DOMESTIC) LAWS AND POLICIES available at http://www.mtnforum.org/resources/library/mlp_03.htm#National Laws

NATIONAL SCIENCE FOUNDATION available at http://www.nsf.gov/od/opp/antarct/anttrty.htm

OPENING REMARKS BY MR. MUTSUYOSHI NISHIMURA, AMBASSADOR FOR GLOBAL ENVIRONMENT, MINISTRY OF FOREIGN AFFAIRS AT THE FIRST MEETING FOR THE PROMOTION OF ASIA FOREST PARTNERSHIP, TOKYO, JAPAN (11 NOVEMBER 2002) available at http://www.mofa.go.jp/policy/economy/fishery/afp/remark0211-2.html

PRESSURES ON THE ARCTIC ECOSYSTEM FROM HUMAN ACTIVITIES available at http://www.gov.nt.ca/RWED/library/eps/envscn.pdf

RICHARD TARASOFSKY, ED., ASSESSING THE INTERNATIONAL FOREST REGIME, IUCN ENVIRONMENTAL LAW AND POLICY PAPER NO. 37 (1999) available at http://www.iucn.org/themes/law/info04.html

SWISS AGENCY FOR THE ENVIRONMENT, FORESTS AND LANDSCAPE available at www.buwal.ch/inter/e/ea_alpen.htm#Scheiz

TITLE 50-WILDLIFE AND FISHERIES, CHAPTER III- INTERNATIONAL FISHING AND RELATED ACTIVITIES, PART 300-INTERNATIONAL FISHERIES REGULATIONS, SUBPART G--ANTARCTIC MARINE LIVING RESOURCES available at http://frwebgate5.access.gpo.gov/cgi-bin/waisgate.cgi?WAISdocID=11491446112=1=0=0& WAISaction=retrieve

UNEP, GEO-3 GLOBAL ENVIRONMENT OUTLOOK 2002-2003, CH. 2, SECTION ON FORESTS available at http://www.unep.org/GEO/geo3/english/177.htm

UNEP GLOBAL ENVIRONMENT OUTLOOK: THE ANTARCTIC available at http://www.unep.org/geo2000/english/0126.htm

UNITED NATIONS FOOD AND AGRICULTURE ORGANIZATION, FORESTRY DEPARTMENT available at http://www.fao.org/forestry/fo/country/nav_world.jsp?lang_id=1

UNITED STATES CODE, TITLE 16: CONSERVATION available at http://caselaw.lp.findlaw.com/casecode/uscodes/16/chapters/44a/toc.html

UNITED STATES CODE, TITLE 50, CHAPTER III: INTERNATIONAL FISHING AND RELATED ACTIVITIES available at http://www.access.gpo.gov/nara/cfr/waisidx_00/50cfr300_00.html

UNITED STATES CODE, TITLE 50: WILDLIFE AND FISHERIES available at http://www.access.gpo.gov/cgi-bin/cfrassemble.cgi?title=200050

WORLD COMMISSION ON FORESTS AND SUSTAINABLE, DEVELOPMENT, OUR FORESTS, OUR FUTURE, CODE OF FEDERAL REGULATIONS, TITLE 36, VOL. 2, PART 200 (UNITED STATES GOVERNMENT PRINTING OFFICE, 1999) available at http://frwebgate.access.gpo.gov/cgi-bin/multidb.cgi

WORLD HERITAGE CENTER available at http://whc.unesco.org/nwhc/pages/doc/mainfsearch.htm

Text Materials

Arni Finnson, CONTROVERSIAL DECISION ON MINING LAKE MYVATN, (WWF Arctic Bulletin, Vol. 4).

"ARCTIC ECOZONES" IN THE STATE OF CANADA'S ENVIRONMENT, ENVIRONMENT CANADA: OTTAWA, (1996).

ARCTIC POLLUTION ISSUES: A STATE OF THE ARCTIC ENVIRONMENT REPORT, (AMAP: Norway, 1997).

Ayesha Ercelawn, END OF THE ROAD – THE ADVERSE ECOLOGICAL IMPACTS OF ROADS AND LOGGING: A COMPILATION OF INDEPENDENTLY REVIEWED RESEARCH, (NRDC: New York, 1999).

Barbara M.G.S. Ruis, NO FOREST CONVENTION BUT TEN TREE TREATIES, UNASYLVA NO. 206 ON GLOBAL CONVENTIONS RELATED TO FORESTS, (2001).

Canadian Council of International Law, ed., GLOBAL FORESTS AND INTERNATIONAL ENVIRONMENTAL LAW, (Kluwer, 1996).

Christopher C. Joyner, GOVERNING THE FROZEN COMMONS: THE ANTARCTIC REGIME AND ENVIRONMENTAL PROTECTION, (1998).

Donald Rothwell, The Polar Regions and the Development of International Law, (1996).

Giles Whittell, Russia to Accept Nuclear Waste for $30 Billion, Vancouver Sun, (December 22, 2000).

Hal Salwasser et al., An Ecosystem Perspective on Sustainable Forestry and New Directions for the United States National Forest System, in Defining Sustainable Forestry, (Gregory H. Aplet et al., eds., 1993).

IUCN Draft Framework Strategy and Action Plan for IUCN Work in the Circumpolar Arctic, (September 2000).

Janet N. Abramovitz, Taking a Stand: Cultivating a New Relationship with the World's Forests, Worldwatch Paper, (April 1998).

Jutta Brunnée & André Nollkaemper, Between the Forests and the Trees - an Emerging International Forest Law, (23 Envtl. Conservation 307, 1997).

Jutta Brunnée & Stephen J. Toope, Environmental Security and Freshwater Resources: a Case for International Ecosystem Law, (5 Yearbook of Intnl. Envtl. L. 41, 1994).

Linda D. Kozaryn, United States, Russia, Norway Sign Arctic Environmental Pact, American Forces Press Service, (October, 1996).

Mark Floyd, Cadmium Toxicity threatening Wildlife in Rocky Mountains, (News Communication Servs., July 12, 2000).

Mia Soderland & Alan Pottinger, eds., Rio+8: Policy, Practice and Progress towards Sustainable Management, (2001).

Preamble to the Antarctic Treaty, reproduced in Lakshman D. Guruswamy, Sir Geoffrey W.R. Palmer, Burns H. Weston & Jonathan C. Carlton, International Environmental Law and World Order: a Problem-Oriented Course Book, (2d Ed.) (1999).

Report of the World Commission on Forests and Sustainable Development, our Forests, our Future, (1999).

SOAER, AMAP Report on Issues of Concern: Updated Information on Human Health, Persistent Organic Pollutants, Radioactivity, and Mercury in the Arctic, (September 2000).

State of the Arctic Environment Report (SOAER), (1997).

The Montreal Process, Progress on Implementation of the Montreal Process on Criteria and Indicators for the Conservation and Sustainable Management of Temperate and Boreal Forests, (February, 1997).

Thomas Nilsen, Floating Nuclear Plants in the Siberian Arctic? (WWF Arctic Bulletin, 2000).

UNEP, GEO-2000, Global Environment Outlook, Chapter 2, The Polar Regions, (2000).

21. ENVIRONMENTAL IMPACT ASSESSMENT

I. Introduction

1. Development can have, and has had over the years, major impacts on the environment, by degrading soils and waterways, altering landscapes and threatening biodiversity. In addition to harming our surroundings, these impacts can and do have significant economic costs and negatively affect human health. Environmental Impact Assessments ("EIA") provides a tool that would assist in the anticipation and minimization of development's negative effects. Undertaken in the early stages of project planning and design, EIA could help shape development in a manner that best suits the local environment and is most responsive to human needs.

2. EIA arose out of the pollution and unnecessary degradation of natural resources caused by rapid population growth, industrialization, agricultural development, and technological progress. EIA recognizes that natural resources are finite and incapable of absorbing the unchecked demands of modern society.

3. EIA assesses the impacts of a proposed project before work on the project begins. In some circumstances, where the impact of policies, plans and programmes is under consideration, EIA is carried out as a Strategic Environmental Assessment ("SEA") and provides decision makers with information about the consequences of the development programmes under consideration. In addition to helping formulating proper development policy, EIA also provides for public involvement in the decision making process. Thus, EIA serves three main functions:

   • Integration of environmental issues into planning and decision-making;
   • Anticipation and minimization of environmental damage; and
   • Public participation in decision-making and environmental conservation.

4. The conservation ideas that gave rise to EIA are central to international environmental law. In the wake of public outcry about environmental degradation from development, the United States passed the first EIA-related legislation in 1969. Since then, more than 100 countries have adopted some form of EIA legislation and policy.

5. EIA concepts are also supported at the international level. In 1987, the United Nations issued the Goals and Principles of Environmental Impact Assessment. Similarly, in 1989, the World Bank issued its Environmental Assessment Directive and has routinely screened funded projects for their potential domestic, transboundary and global environmental impacts. In 1991, the United Nations Economic Commision for Europe, further developing the EIA Guidelines adopted by UNEP, adopted the Convention on Environmental Impact Assessment in a Transboundary Context, the most comprehensive international agreement on EIA.

6. EIA's focus on environmental conservation and sustainable development echoes general principles and concepts of customary law. The focus is embodied in many Multilateral Environmental Agreements, including the Convention on Biological Diversity and the United Nations Convention on the Law of the Sea. Environmental Principle 17 of the UNCED Rio Declaration states that "Environmental impact assessment, as a national instrument, shall be undertaken for proposed activities that are likely to have a significant adverse impact on the environment and are subject to a decision of a competent national authority." Thus, EIA reflects the "no-harm" obligation of customary law in the transboundary context.

7. One of EIA's strengths is its ability to be tailored to meet specific needs of any development situation. Nevertheless, the steps included in EIA are similar across many applications and include:

   • Screening to determine whether a certain project should be subject to EIA;
   • Scoping to decide which impacts should be taken into account by EIA;
   • Impact analysis to evaluate the type of likely environmental impacts;
   • Mitigation and impact management to develop measures to avoid, reduce or compensate for negative environmental effects;
   • Reporting to catalogue and track the results of EIA for decision makers and other interested parties, including the public;
   • Review of EIA quality to examine whether the EIA report includes all of the information required by decision makers and the public;
   • Decision making to approve or reject project proposals and, if needed, to set the terms and conditions under which a certain project can proceed; and
   • Implementation and follow-up to ascertain whether the project is proceeding as planned,

monitor the effects of the project, and take actions to mitigate problems that arise during the course of the project.

In many cases the steps as above are embodied in national legislation, regulations and policies. National legislation might be specific on EIA, or an integral part of environmental management and coordination additionally buttressed by EIA regulation. Numerous framework laws of developing countries do take such an approach as examples from Uganda, Kenya, Tanzania, Guyana demonstrate. Three examples are given in section III below

8. Development projects may not only have environmental impacts but may also have social, cultural and economic effects, which can be analyzed through a Social Impact Analysis ("SIA"). Decision makers often undertake EIA and SIA at the same time, defining the "environment" and "environmental impacts" broadly to include social and cultural aspects of development. For example, the construction of a hotel complex will not only have environmental impacts depending on the site selection but will also have social and economic impacts through the creation of jobs or the displacement of traditional commerce. SIAs generally include the analysis of impacts on local lifestyle, culture, community dynamics, and human health.

9. Finally, both social and environmental issues can be addressed in SIA, which assesses the impacts of a proposed policy, plan or programme, and their alternatives. Recent developments in international environmental law seek to promote the adoption of SIA as a planning tool during the initial stages of decision-making.

II. International Framework

1. Convention on Environmental Impact Assessment in a Transboundary Context

10. Initiated through a seminar on EIA held in Warsaw, the Convention on Environmental Impact Assessment in a Transboundary Context ("Espoo Convention") is the most comprehensive international agreement on EIA. It entered into force in 1997 and has currently (as of November 2005) 41 parties. Although the Espoo Convention is a regional agreement of the United Nations Economic Commission for Europe, it is open for signature to all members of the United Nations.

11. The main objective of the Espoo Convention is the creation of EIA-based mechanisms to effectively monitor and control trans-boundary pollution. Article 2(1) of the Convention provides that "The Parties shall, either individually or jointly, take all appropriate and effective measures to prevent, reduce and control significant adverse transboundary environmental impact from proposed activities."

12. The Espoo Convention is overseen by the Meeting of the Parties ("MOP"), which convened in 1998, 2001 and 2004. The MOP's Bureau and the Convention Secretariat support the MOP.

13. The Espoo Convention stipulates the obligations of its parties to assess the environmental impact of certain development activities early in the decision making process. Each party must establish an EIA procedure for the development projects listed in Annex I of the convention (e.g., waste processing plants, infrastructure construction, deforestation, etcetera).

14. The scope of the Espoo Convention is generally limited to projects listed in its Annex I. However, when an unlisted project may cause a significant transboundary environmental impact, the affected signatories are entitled to request an EIA. Should the parties disagree about the likelihood or severity of a transboundary environmental impact, the affected party can call for the establishment of an Inquiry Commission to advise the affected parties. The parties initiating the disputed project is not obligated to follow the advice of the Inquiry Commission.

15. The Espoo Convention also obligates its parties to notify and consult with each other on all major projects under consideration that are likely to have a significant transboundary environmental impact. The procedure must allow for public participation and preparation of an EIA. The affected party and its citizens have the right to participate in the preparation of the proposed project's EIA.

16. Public participation in the development of an EIA figures heavily in the Espoo Convention. In accordance with Rio Principle 10, the Espoo Convention foresees that public participation in the development of transboundary EIA will:

- Improve relations between peoples and countries and prevent transboundary environmental conflicts;
- Develop civil society and democracy;
- Promote the timely disclosure of relevant information to participants in the

environmental decision-making process;

- Help people understand, respect, and accept final decisions on projects; and

- Provide insight into environmental protection and the mitigation of long-term environmental problems that result from development decisions.

17. Article 4 of the Espoo Convention requires the EIA to contain certain information, including (Appendix II):

- Description of the proposed activity and its purpose;

- Description of reasonable alternatives, where appropriate, including a "no-action" alternative;

- Description of the likely environmental impacts resulting from the proposed activity and its alternatives;

- Description of available mitigation measures;

- Explicit indication of predictive methods and underlying assumptions, as well as relevant environmental data relied upon for development of the EIA;

- Identification of gaps in knowledge encountered in developing the EIA;

- Outline for monitoring and management programmes and plans for post-project assessment; and

- Non-technical summary, including presentation of visual aides.

18. The Espoo Convention does not contain a compliance mechanism. As such, while a party initiating a project is required to undertake an EIA, it is not held to the outcome of the analysis.

2. Protocol on Strategic Environmental Assessment

19. Strategic Environmental Assessment ("SEA") has been described to be "The formalised, systematic and comprehensive process of evaluating the environmental impacts of a policy, plan or programme and its alternatives, including the preparation of a written report on the findings of that evaluation, and using the findings in publicly accountable decision-making" (Thievel).

20. The Protocol on Strategic Environmental Assessment to the Convention on Environmental Impact Assessment in a Transboundary Context ("2003 SEA Protocol") is an initiative of the second MOP of the Espoo Convention that met in February 2001. The SEA Protocol was adopted in 2003, and is open for adoption by all members of the United Nations. It has not yet entered into force. The first meeting of the signatories took place in June 2004.

Pending the Protocol's entry into force, activities under the 2003 SEA Protocol are decided upon by the Meeting of Signatories.

21. The 2003 SEA Protocol requires its signatories to evaluate the environmental consequences of their official draft development plans and programmes, but not policies. The SEA Protocol provides for extensive public participation in governmental decision making in areas such as land use, transportation, agriculture, and industrial activities. Again, in accordance with Rio Principle 10, public participation includes public comment and accountability of the final decision-makers.

22. The SEA Protocol not only covers typical environmental effects of plans and programmes, but also places a special emphasis on human health effects. This is the result of the participation of the World Health Organiszation ("WHO") during the agreement's negotiations, as well as the commitments made at the 1999 London Ministerial Conference on Environment and Health.

23. The SEA Protocol's objective is to utilize Strategic Environmental Assessment-concepts to fully integrate environmental objectives into development plans and programmes in a manner that will support sustainable development and further environmental conservation. The 2003 SEA Protocol defines an SEA to be "The evaluation of the likely environmental, including health, effects, which comprises the determination of the scope of an environmental report and its preparation, the carrying-out of public participation and consultations, and the taking into account of the environmental report and the results of the public participation and consultations in a plan or programme".

24. Article 4 of the SEA Protocol outlines those instances in which an SEA must be undertaken. Articles 8, 9 and 10 of the SEA Protocol deal with public participation in the SEA process, which must be provided "early" in the project assessment and in a manner that is "timely and effective." Public health officials and environmental authorities are similarly entitled to "early, timely and effective" submission of their opinions on the effects of a proposed project.

25. The 2003 SEA Protocol requires decisions on plans and programmes take due account of the conclusions of any EIA, as well as comments of the public, health and environmental officials and the affected parties. A final project decision must disclose how environmental considerations were

taken into account and the *rationale* for the adoption of the plan or programme in light of the SEA.

26. Like the Espoo Convention, the 2003 SEA Protocol seeks to mitigate the effects of transboundary pollution, but focuses more on a parties domestic plans and programmes in the context of Strategic Environmental Assessment.

III. National Implementation

27. In general, countries that have adopted EIA legislation and regulations provide for a multi-step process that encourages public participation prior to any final decision. Countries with EIA legislation differ in delineating which party is responsible for the preparation of the EIA. Some countries, like Kiribati and Uganda, allow to the developer of the proposed project to conduct the EIA. Brazil, on the other hand, requires that the statutory EIA is prepared by an independent third-party that does not have a stake in the proposed development project.

1. Brazil

28. Brazil has two main pieces of legislation concerning with EIA, including the Order Conama No. 1 Concerning Environmental Impact Assessments of 1986 ("Brazil EIA Order") and the Resolution SMA-42 establishing the Procedures for the Analysis of Environmental Impact Studies of 1996 ("Brazil EIA Resolution").

29. The Brazil EIA Order contains the statutory definitions relating to "environmental impacts" resulting from development, as well as the licensing requirements of the regulated activities. The Brazil EIA Order is administered by the SEENV, the federal government's licensing agency and contains the scope of SEENV's authority under the act.

30. The Brazil EIA Order also provides that a statutory environmental impact study is to be executed by a qualified multidisciplinary team that is independent from the project's developer. Nevertheless, the developer must cover the costs of both the initial study and the final preparation of the Report on Environmental Impact Assessment ("REIA"). The Brazil EIA Order specifies the type of information that must be included in the REIA.

31. The Brazil EIA Order vests SEENV with authority to approve the REIA after a public notice and comment period.

32. The Brazil EIA Resolution outlines the procedure for determining when a proposed development project requires an EIS and SEENV licence. A developer of a proposed project must first submit a preliminary environmental report and a licence request. These materials are then published and open to public comment. SEENV then either requires or waives the submission of an EIS. If SEENV requires an EIS, the developer of the proposed project prepares and submits a work plan for the EIS and undertakes a REIA. Upon approval of the plan by SEENV, and after public notice and comment, SEENV either grants or denies the requested development licence.

2. Uganda

33. Uganda's basic EIA requirements are set forth in the National Environment Statute of 1995 ("National Environmental Statute," Chapter 153 of the Laws of Uganda) and are further elaborated upon in the Environmental Impact Assessment Regulations of 1998 ("Uganda EIA Regulations"). In 1999, Uganda also issued the Environmental Impact Assessment Public Hearing Guidelines ("Public Participation Guidelines") that detail the public notice and comment process in relation to EIA.

34. The Uganda EIA Regulations provide the statutory definitions of "environmental impact assessment," "environmental impact statement" and "environmental impact study." The Uganda EIA Regulations also outline the tasks of Uganda's Technical Committee on Environmental Impact Assessment and list the development activities to which the regulations apply.

35. As provided by the Uganda EIA Regulations, the developer seeking regulatory approval must first provide a description of the proposed project to the Lead Agency. Upon review of the project brief, the Lead Agency then files comments on the brief with the Executive Director, who has authority to approve those projects that will not significantly negatively affect the environment. If the proposed project is expected to harm the environment, the Executive Director will require the developer, in consultation with the Lead Agency, to develop an Environmental Impact Study ("EIS").

36. The Uganda EIA Regulations require that the developer, in addition to undertaking the EIS with the Lead Agency, identify entities that will be involved in any mitigation measures. The developer is also required to initiate and manage the public comment process.

37. Once the developer completes the process around the EIS, the Executive Director may issue an EIS as prescribed by the Uganda EIA Regulations. The Lead Agency, general public, and other interested parties then have standing to provide comments on the EIS. After appropriate consideration of any comments, the Executive Director can either approve or reject the project, or require the developer to redesign the project or to provide further information on its expected environmental impact.

3. Kiribati

38. Kiribati's Environment Act of 1999 ("Kiribati Environment Act") sets forth the country's national EIA procedure. The Environment Act provides statutory definitions of "environmental impact assessment" and "Environmental Impact Statement" ("EIS"). The Kiribati Environment Act also requires the relevant governmental minister consider the environmental impacts arising from any development decision. For example, before any development project is undertaken, the law requires the responsible minister to consult with all relevant parties to the decision.

39. Governmental ministers are also required to determine whether an Initial Environmental Evaluation Report ("IER") or EIS is needed based on the likely impact of the subject development project on the environment. The Kiribati Environment Act outlines the information that should comprise an IER or EIS.

40. The Kiribati Environment Act provides for public participation both during and after the development of an IER or EIS. While the final decision to proceed with a development project is that of the relevant minister, the Environment Act does provide for some degree of governmental accountability.

41. The entity responsible for the development project is also responsible for the costs and preparation of an IER or EIS.

42. The Kiribati Environment Act contains some monitoring and information gathering provisions, which are enforceable both during and after project development. The Act also contains sanctions for developers acting in contravention of the Act.

Charles E. Di Leva, Chief Counsel, ESSD and International Law, The World Bank Legal Department

Eva Maria Duer, Associate Legal Officer, Division of Policy Development and Law,

Resources

Text Materials

Alan Gilpin, ENVIRONMENTAL IMPACT ASSESSMENT: CUTTING EDGE FOR THE TWENTY-FIRST CENTURY, (Cambridge University Press, 1995).

Christopher Wood, ENVIRONMENTAL IMPACT ASSESSMENT: A COMPARATIVE VIEW, HARLOW, ESSEX, ENGLAND: LONGMAN SICENTIFIC AND TECHNICAL, (Wiley, 1995).

David B. Smith & Mieke van der Wansem (Eds.), STRENGHTENING EIA CAPACITY IN ASIA: ENVIRONMENTAL IMPACT ASSESSMENT IN THE PHILIPPINES, INDONESIA AND SRI LANKA, (World Resources Institute, 1995).

Environmental Law Network International (Ed.), INTERNATIONAL ENVIRONMENTAL IMPACT ASSESSMENT: EUROPEAN AND COMPARATIVE LAW AND PRACTICAL EXPERIENCE: CONTRIBUTIONS OF THE INTERNATIONAL CONFERENCE HELD IN MILAN IN OCTOBER 1996, S.1.: CAMEROON, (May 1997).

Hubert Heinelt, et al. (Eds.), EUROPEAN UNION ENVIRONMENT POLICY AND NEW FORMS OF GOVERNANCE: A STUDY OF THE IMPLEMENTATION OF THE ENVIRONMENTAL IMPACT ASSESSMENT DIRECTIVE AND THE ECO-MANAGEMENT AND AUDIT SCHEME REGULATION IN THREE MEMBER STATES, (Ashgate, 2001).

Ian Thomas, ENVIRONMENTAL IMPACT ASSESSMENT IN AUSTRALIA: THEORY AND PRACTICE, (3d Ed., Federation Press, 2001).

Ray Clark & Larry Canter (Eds.), ENVIRONMENTAL POLICY AND NEPA: PAST, PRESENT AND FUTURE, (St. Lucie Press, 1997).

SLOVENIA, EUROPEAN BANK FOR RECONSTRUCTION AND DEVELOPMENT, ENVIRONMENTAL IMPACT ASSESSMENT LEGISLATION; CZECH REPUBLIC, ESTONIA, HUNGARY, LATVIA, LITHUANIA, POLAND, SLOVAK REPUBLIC, LONDON, GRAHAM & TROTMAN/M. NIJHOFF FOR THE EUROPEAN BANK FOR RECONSTRUCTION AND DEVELOPMENT (Eds.), (1994).

Prasad Modak & Asit K. Biswas (Eds.), CONDUCTING ENVIRONMENTAL IMPACT ASSESSMENT IN DEVELOPING COUNTRIES, TOKYO, (United Nations University Press, 1999).

Timo Koivurova, ENVIRONMENTAL IMPACT ASSESSMENT IN THE ARCTIC: A STUDY OF INTERNATIONAL LEGAL NORMS, (Ashgate, 2002).

22. HUMAN RIGHTS AND THE ENVIRONMENT

I. Introduction

1. General

1. More than two million annual deaths and billions of cases of disease are attributed to pollution. Nearly half a billion of people, mainly women and children in poor rural areas, live in severely polluted environments. Annually, 500 million premature deaths can be attributed to the high levels of pollution in cities. It is estimated that the deterioration of the ozone layer will lead to more than 300,000 additional cases of skin cancer in the world and 1.7 million cases of cataracts.

2. All over the world, people are experiencing the effects of ecosystem decline, from water shortages and fish kills to landslides on deforested slopes. Environmental degradation has adverse impact on the quality of human life, and more specifically on the full enjoyment of human rights. The victims of environmental degradation typically belong to more vulnerable sectors of society. Children, racial and ethnic minorities and the poor regularly carry a disproportionate burden of such abuse.

3. Indigenous peoples are particularly vulnerable to environmental threats, as they are often completely dependent on their immediate environment for survival. Indigenous cultures are often deeply rooted in the belief that the spiritual world resides in nature. This worldview implies a deep respect for the natural world and provides guidance on its use. Thus, degradation of environment and national biodiversity severely threatens the lifestyle of indigenous peoples. Indigenous peoples not only depend on their environment for food and shelter, but erosion of biodiversity goes hand in hand with vanishing of cultural diversity, such as the disappearance of languages. More than half of the 6,000 languages currently spoken are unlikely to survive this century. Thus, indigenous peoples have a special need for protection when violation of their human rights results from irreparable harm to their environment and special consideration will be given to their cause in this chapter.

4. Despite the interrelationship and the interaction between environmental issues and human rights, most organizations and governments have treated, until recently, human rights violations and environmental degradation as unrelated issues. Just as human rights advocates have emphasized civil and political rights, environmentalists have tended to focus primarily on natural resource preservation without addressing human impacts of environmental abuse. In recent years, however, the right to a healthy environment has been increasingly acknowledged and the use of human rights to further environmental objectives has become widespread.

2. The Relationship between Human Rights and Environmental Law

5. Taking into account the strong factual relationship between environmental degradation and impairment of human rights, it is important to consider how these two fields interrelate within the law. Is there a human right to a clean environment or are environment and human rights best protected through different legal regimes?

6. Approaching environmental problems from a human rights point of view can have several advantages. In contrast to most areas of international environmental law, the human rights system already provides for various courts, commissions and other bodies, where individuals can raise human rights and associated environmental issues. Second, unlike environmental considerations, human rights are less likely to be subordinated in bureaucratic decision-making when they are compared to other considerations such as development or full employment. Third, human rights can provide access to justice in a way that other regulations or tort law simply cannot. Also, concerned citizens and Non-Governmental Organizations ("NGOs") are more likely to support general statements of rights than a highly technical regulation expressed in complex legislation.

7. Many environmentalists argue for the recognition of a specific environmental right based on the fundamental human needs for clean air and water, a stable climate system and, more generally, an environment conducive to human life and health. The right to a healthy environment does exist, in fact, in the African and Inter-American human rights systems, as will be discussed later in this chapter.

8. There are three main positions on the interrelationship between human rights and environmental protection. The first position views environmental protection as a pre-requisite to the enjoyment of existing human rights and thus sees human rights obligations of states as including the duty to ensure the level of environmental

313

protection necessary to allow full exercise of protected rights. The second position sees certain human rights, especially rights of information, participation in governance, and the right to a remedy, as essential to good environmental decision-making. Thus, these human rights must be implemented in order to ensure environmental protection. The third position, now reflected in nearly half the constitutions of the world and two regional human rights instruments, sees the right to a safe, healthy and ecologically-balanced environment as an independent human right. However, this last approach is not accepted by all countries and is not included in any global human rights instrument at present.

9. Regardless of whether one favours a rights-based approach to environmental protection or not, the field of human rights will remain vital for environmental protection and achieving sustainable development.

3. Human Rights Relevant to the Environment

10. There are several different ways to categorize human rights. One common method of listing rights is according to subject matter: civil, political, economic, social or cultural rights. Civil and political rights include the right to life, the right to privacy and home life, and the right to equality and non-discrimination, all of which may be impacted by environmental conditions. Economic, social and cultural rights lay down a minimum standard for human living and well-being. Implementation of these rights above the level of basic needs characteristically depends on the level of economic development each country has reached. The right to health, the right to food and water, and the right to an adequate standard of living have served as vehicles to further environmental protection when the fulfillment of the rights is hampered by environmental degradation.

11. Human rights can further be divided into substantive and procedural rights. From a human rights perspective, the following substantive rights can be affected by environmental degradation:

- The Right to Life is the most important and fundamental human right. In its broadened scope it entails the right to health and well being.
- The Right to Respect for Private and Family Life and Home has been successfully invoked against severe pollution within the European Human Rights System.
- The Right to Use and Enjoy Property.

- The Right to a Decent Environment is expressly recognized by two regional human rights treaties, namely the African (Banjul) Charter on Human and Peoples' Rights and the San Salvador Protocol to the American Convention on Human Rights.
- The Right to Self-Determination.
- The Right to Cultural Expression and Right to Religion.

The last two rights are particularly important to indigenous peoples.

12. Procedural rights are a critical complement to substantive rights. Procedural rights are enabling rights in that they make it possible for people to contribute actively to the protection of their environment. Procedural rights that further the environmental cause include:

- The Right to Information,
- The Right to Participation,
- The Right to Equal Protection and to be Free from Discrimination, and
- The Right to Judicial Remedy.

13. Human rights may also be categorized according to the scope of the protection afforded. Some rights are deemed so fundamental that they may never be suspended whatever the national emergency. The "non-derogable" rights common to all human rights instruments are the right to life, the right to be free from torture, the right of non-discrimination and freedom from slavery. Other rights are drafted in precise terms without qualification or limitation, but they may be suspended when strictly required by the exigencies of a national emergency threatening the life of the nation. A third category of rights is normally defined and its scope set forth, but it is accompanied by a "limitations" clause setting forth the permissible grounds for the State to qualify the right or balance it against other public interests, including public order, health, safety, morality, or in some cases economic well-being.

II. International Framework

1. Human Rights Instruments

14. On 10 December 1948, the General Assembly of the United Nations adopted and proclaimed the Universal Declaration of Human Rights ("1948 Universal Declaration"). The 30 articles of the 1948 Universal Declaration proclaim in clear and simple terms the fundamental rights which equally apply to all human beings. Through its adoption, individuals became subjects of international law in their own right.

15. Within the United Nations, human rights activities are pursued by bodies under the authority of the UN Charter or established by human rights treaties. In addition, several specialized agencies of the UN have important human rights functions, such as the International Labour Organization ("ILO") and the UN High Commissioner for Refugees ("UNHCR"). The principal Charter-based bodies with a human rights role are the Security Council, the General Assembly, the Economic and Social Council ("ECOSOC") and the Commission on Human Rights ("CHR").

16. The Commission on Human Rights is a "functional commission" of ECOSOC. The CHR has become responsible for monitoring existing international standards, recommending new international human rights standards, investigating violations, submitting proposals for new programmes and policies related to human rights, providing advisory and technical services to countries needing assistance in protecting human rights and pursuing other related objectives.

17. The 1948 Universal Declaration was followed in 1966 by the adoption of two human rights covenants. The first is the International Covenant on Civil and Political Rights ("1966 ICCPR"), which details the basic civil and political rights of individuals and groups. Eighteen independent experts on the UN Human Rights Committee supervise state implementation of and compliance with the 1966 ICCPR, primarily through a system of state reporting. The Committee may make comments and recommendations to the state individually or issue General Comments to all state parties. In this context, the Committee has indicated that state obligations to protect the right to life can require positive measures designed to reduce infant mortality and protect against malnutrition and epidemics, which clearly implicate environmental protection. If the state has also accepted the first Optional Protocol to the 1966 ICCPR, the Human Rights Committee may hear individual complaints against this state party. In such a case, the Committee found that allegations of Canadian citizens that the storage of radioactive waste near their homes threatened the right to life of present and future generations raised "serious issues with regard to the obligation of states parties to protect human life" even though the case was declared inadmissible for formal reasons.

18. The second covenant is the International Covenant on Economic, Social and Cultural Rights, which describes the basic economic, social, and cultural rights of individuals and groups. The Committee on Economic, Social and Cultural Rights supervises implementation of this Covenant. In this context, Ukraine reported in 1995, on the environmental situation consequent to the explosion at the Chernobyl nuclear reactor, with regard to the right to life. Committee members may also request specific information about environmental harm that threatens human rights. Poland, for example, was asked to provide information in 1989 about measures to combat pollution, especially in Upper Silesia. The Committee may pose questions and make recommendations in response to the state report. In 2000, the Committee issued General Comment No. 14 on "Substantive Issues arising in the Implementation of the International Covenant on Economic, Social and Cultural Rights" (article 12) Paragraph 4 states that "the right to health embraces a wide range of socio-economic factors that promote conditions in which people can lead a healthy life, and extends to the underlying determinates of health, such as...a healthy environment." It added that "any person or group victim of a violation of the right to health should have access to effective judicial or other appropriate remedies at both national and international levels and should be entitled to adequate reparation."

19. Other important United Nations agreements on human rights are the UN Convention against Genocide (1948), the Convention against Torture (1975) and the Convention on Elimination of all Forms of Discrimination against Women (1979). The latter stipulates that state parties shall ensure women the right to "enjoy adequate living conditions, particularly in relation to … water supply..." The UN Convention on the Rights of the Child, adopted on 20 November 1989, is the most widely ratified human rights treaty with 192 parties (as of November 2005). It addresses the need for clean drinking water and the dangers and risks of pollution, and requires parties to combat disease and malnutrition.

United Nations Convention on the Rights of the Child (Article 24)

1. States Parties recognize the right of the child to the enjoyment of the highest attainable standard of health and to facilities for the treatment of illness and rehabilitation of health. States Parties shall strive to ensure that no child is deprived of his or her right of access to such health care services.
(…)
c) To combat disease and malnutrition, including within the framework of primary health care, through, inter alia, the application of readily available technology and through the provision of adequate nutritious foods and clean drinking-water, taking into consideration the dangers and risks of environmental pollution;
(...)

20. In 1994, an international group of experts on human rights and environmental protection convened at the United Nations in Geneva, and drafted the first declaration of principles on human rights and the environment. This Draft Declaration of Principles on Human Rights and the Environment ("1994 Draft Declaration") was included in the Final Report on Human Rights and the Environment to the Sub-Commission on Prevention of Discrimination and Protection of Minorities, which was issued by Special Rapporteur Madam Ksentini in the same year.

21. The 1994 Draft Declaration is the first international instrument that comprehensively addresses the linkage between human rights and the environment. The Draft Declaration demonstrates that accepted environmental and human rights principles embody the right of everyone to a secure, healthy and ecologically sound environment.

22. On the question of whether a specific environmental right exists, the Report on Human Rights and the Environment further supports the intermediary position described above. The Report concludes that environmental rights are contained in and can be derived from existing human rights instruments of both a substantive and procedural nature.

2. Environmental Law Instruments

23. Environmental law instruments that link the environment and human rights began to appear as early as 1972, in the Stockholm Declaration on Human Environment, which states that "Man has the fundamental right to freedom, equality and adequate conditions of life, in an environment of quality that permits a life of dignity and well being..."

24. In comparison, Principle 1 of the 1992 Rio Declaration on Environment and Development provides that "Human beings are at the centre of concerns for sustainable development. They are entitled to a healthy and productive life in harmony with nature."

25. An important consensus reached at the Rio Summit in 1992 was that sustainable development and environmental protection cannot be achieved independently from human development.

26. With regards to procedural rights, the 1982 World Charter for Nature was one of the first declarations that recognized the right of individuals to participate in decision making and to have access

to means of redress when their environment had suffered damage or degradation. Ten years later, Principle 10 of the 1992 Rio Declaration on Environment and Development stated the need for these participatory rights:

> **Rio Declaration on Environment and Development (Principle 10)**
>
> "Environmental issues are best handled with the participation of all concerned citizens, at the relevant level. At the national level, each individual shall have appropriate access to information concerning the environment that is held by public authorities, including information on hazardous materials and activities in their communities, and the opportunity to participate in decision-making processes. States shall facilitate and encourage public awareness and participation by making information widely available. Effective access to judicial and administrative proceedings, including redress and remedy, shall be provided."

27. The Convention on Access to Information, Public Participation in Decision-Making and Access to Justice in Environmental Matters ("1998 Aarhus Convention") was adopted under the auspices of the United Nation Economic Commission for Europe ("UNECE") in 1998. The Aarhus Convention entered into force in 2001, and the first MOP took place in 2002.

28. The Aarhus Convention builds on above cited Principle 10 of the Rio Declaration and on Principle 1 of the Stockholm Declaration. The Preamble states that every person has the right to live in an environment adequate to his or her health and well-being, and the duty, both individually and in association with others, to protect and improve the environment for the benefit of present and future generations.

29. The Aarhus Convention provides for a comprehensive right to public participation in environmental decision-making and a right of access to environmental information. This right includes a right to request and obtain information and an obligation upon states to collect and disseminate information. The Aarhus Convention also provides for a right of access to the courts in environmental matters, ensuring that decisions relating to participation and access to information may be challenged. Another very important feature is the explicit assertion of the interests of Non-Governmental Organizations ("NGOs"). In most cases, NGOs are entitled to participation in decisions making, to require disclosure of information and to litigate.

30. The WHO-UNECE Protocol on Water and Health to the 1992 Convention on the Protection and Use of Transboundary Watercourses and International Lake touches upon the right to a healthy environment. The Protocol is the first major international legal approach for the prevention, control and reduction of water-related diseases in Europe. Cleaner water and better sanitation could prevent over 30 million cases of water related diseases in Europe alone.

3. The International Framework from an Indigenous Peoples' Perspective

31. The survival of indigenous peoples depends upon the integrity of their environment. One way in which environmental degradation violates indigenous rights is through direct and indirect harm to the people and the resources that sustain them. Yet destruction of the environment not only affects indigenous peoples in their right to life, health and well being but also in their right to self-determination and right to cultural expression and right to religion.

32. Article 27 of the 1948 Universal Declaration and other instruments, such as article 13 of the American Declaration of the Rights and Duties of Man, contain articulations of the Right to Culture. In addition, article 27 of the 1966 International Covenant on Civil and Political Rights states:

1966 International Covenant on Civil and Political Rights
(Article 27)

"In those States in which ethnic, religious or linguistic minorities exist, persons belonging to such minorities shall not be denied the right, in community with the other members of their group, to enjoy their own culture, to profess and practise their own religion, or to use their own language."

---

33. The ILO Convention concerning Indigenous and Tribal Peoples in Independent Countries ("1989 Tribal Peoples Convention") calls for adoption of special measures to protect and to preserve the environment of indigenous and tribal peoples. It entered into force in 1991, and has been ratified by 17 states (as of November 2005), mainly from Latin America. The 1989 Tribal Peoples Convention contains numerous references to the lands, resources, and environment of indigenous peoples.

34. Article 2 of the 1989 Tribal People's Convention provides that actions respecting indigenous peoples shall be developed with the participation of the peoples concerned. In accordance with articles 6 and 7, parties must consult indigenous peoples and provide for their participation in formulating national and regional development plans that may affect them. Environmental impact assessment must be done of planned development activities with the cooperation of the peoples concerned, and "Governments shall take measures, in cooperation with the peoples concerned, to protect and preserve the environment of the territories they inhabit." Rights to remedies are provided in article 12. Part II of the 1989 Tribal Peoples Convention addresses land issues, including the rights of the peoples concerned to the natural resources pertaining to their lands. According to article 15, land rights include "the right of these peoples to participate in the use, management and conservation of these resources." Article 30 requires the governments to make known to the peoples concerned their rights and duties.

35. The United Nations Sub-Commission on Prevention of Discrimination and Protection of Minorities adopted a Draft Declaration of the Rights of the World's Indigenous Peoples in 1994 ("1994 Draft Declaration"), which it submitted to the Commission on Human Rights for further action. In 1995, the Commission decided to establish an intergovernmental Working Group to review the draft. The Working Group has become an important center of indigenous rights activities in the United Nations.

36. According to article 12 of the 1994 Draft Declaration:

1994 Draft Declaration of the Rights of the World's Indigenous Peoples
(Article 12)

"Indigenous peoples have the right to practise and revitalize their cultural traditions and customs. This includes the right to maintain, protect and develop the past, present and future manifestations of their cultures, such as archaeological and historical sites, artifacts, designs, ceremonies, technologies and visual and performing arts and literature, as well as the right to restitution of cultural, intellectual, religious and spiritual property taken without their free and informed consent or in violation of their laws, traditions and customs."

---

37. Part VI of the 1994 Draft Declaration includes the right of indigenous peoples "to maintain and strengthen their distinctive spiritual and material relationship with the lands, territories, waters and coastal seas and other resources which they have traditionally owned or otherwise occupied or used, and to uphold their responsibilities to future

generations in this regard" (article 25). Specific protection is also afforded to medicinal plants, animals and minerals. Indigenous peoples have the right to special measures to control, develop and protect their genetic resources, including seeds, medicines, and knowledge of the properties of fauna and flora. Indigenous peoples are given the right to own, develop, control and use the total environment of the lands, air, waters, coastal seas, sea-ice, flora and fauna and other resources, which they have traditionally owned or otherwise occupied or used. The 1994 Draft Declaration also requires restitution of or compensation for lands taken without free and informed consent. Article 28 provides that "Indigenous peoples have the right to the conservation, restoration and protection of the total environment and the production capacity of their lands, territories and resources...." Part V of the 1994 Draft Declaration contains procedural rights, including the right of indigenous peoples to fully participate at all levels of decision-making in matters which may affect them.

38. The UN General Assembly, in the context of the International Decade of the World's Indigenous Peoples (1994-2004), noted that the goal of this Decade is to strengthen international cooperation for the solution of problems faced by indigenous peoples in various areas, including the environment. The General Assembly has called for increased participation of indigenous peoples in activities for the decade. In 2001, the UN Human Rights Commission appointed a special rapporteur on the situation of human rights and fundamental freedoms of indigenous peoples. The rapporteur's mandate includes receiving communications on violations of human rights.

39. The chapter of Agenda 21 on indigenous populations mentions existing treaties and the draft universal declaration on indigenous rights. It provides that indigenous people and their communities "...may require, in accordance with national legislation, greater control over their lands, self-management of their resources, participation in development decisions affecting them, including, where appropriate, participation in the establishment or management of protected areas..." It makes no reference to the fact that the 1989 Tribal Peoples Convention contains environmental rights for the indigenous peoples, requiring states parties to take special measures to safeguard the environment of indigenous peoples (article 4).

40. As demonstrated below, the case law of the Inter-American human rights system has contributed considerably to recognizing the rights of indigenous peoples in respect to their environmental and natural resources.

III. Regional Human Rights Systems

1. The European Convention on Human Rights

41. The Council of Europe, a regional intergovernmental organization, adopted the European Convention on the Protection of Human Rights and Fundamental Freedoms ("1950 ECHR") in 1950, which entered into force in 1953, to give effect to some of the civil and political rights contained in the 1948 Universal Declaration of Human Rights. In 1961, the Council adopted a companion treaty for economic and social rights, the European Social Charter. Both treaties have been revised numerous times. The 1950 ECHR established a European Commission on Human Rights, which ceased to exist with the procedural reforms of 1998, and the European Court of Human Rights. Individuals and groups who claim to be victims of violations of rights in the 1950 ECHR can file cases at the European Court after exhausting all domestic remedies. Inter-State cases can also be filed. The European Social Charter has its own supervisory institutions, which in limited circumstances may hear complaints from certain groups. It does not have an individual complaint mechanism.

42. The 1950 ECHR does not contain any specific rights to a clean environment. Likewise, the European Social Charter does not contain any right to environmental quality and the former European Commission on Human Rights held that such a right cannot be directly inferred from the 1950 ECHR.

43. A similar approach to the environment was taken by the European Union at its Nice Summit. The Charter of Fundamental Rights of the European Union, adopted during the Summit on 7 December 2000, omits environmental protection from its listed rights of persons and duties of member states. The Charter simply provides in article 37 that "A high level of environmental protection and the improvement of the quality of the environment must be integrated into the policies of the Union and ensured in accordance with the principle of sustainable development."

44. However, the European Court of Human Rights has considered environmental issues in relation to other provisions of the 1950 ECHR, including:

- Article 2 (right to life);
- Article 3 (prohibition of torture and degrading treatment);
- Article 5 (right to liberty and security as a person);

- Article 6 (right of tribunal);
- Article 8 (right to privacy);
- Article 11 (right to freedom and peaceful assembly); and
- Article 1 of the First Protocol (peaceful enjoyment of possessions).

45. One of the most important cases under the 1950 ECHR was Lopez-Ostra vs. Spain (1994).

46. Ms. Ostra's flat in Lorca, Spain was situated within 12 meters of a waste disposal plant. She alleged that the plant emitted fumes, noise and smell that made her family's living conditions intolerable and caused her and her family serious health problems. Expert evidence stated that hydrogen sulfide emissions from the plant exceeded the permitted limit and could endanger the health of those living nearby. This supported the contention that there could be a causal link between these emissions and the applicant's daughter's illness.

47. The Court applied a test based on article 8 of the ECHR, the right to privacy, which attempts to balance competing interests of individuals against those of the community as a whole. The Court further stated that severe environmental pollution, even without causing serious damage to health, could affect the well being of individuals and impede their enjoyment of their homes in such a manner as to have an adverse effect on their private and family life.

48. The Court found that Spain has not fulfilled its duty to take reasonable and appropriate measures to secure the applicant's rights. This notion is most valuable since it poses an obligation on the state to not only refrain from interfering but to actively protect human rights. The Court concluded that the state did not strike a proper balance as between the individual and public interests, in other words between private well being and general economic concerns and that Spain had violated article 8 of the ECHR.

49. The Court stated that the state had a positive duty to take reasonable and appropriate measures to secure the applicants' rights under article 8 and to strike a fair balance between the competing interests of the individual and of the community as a whole. In the particularly sensitive field of environmental protection, mere reference to the economic well being of the country was not sufficient to outweigh the rights of others.

50. In a subsequent case, Maria Guerra v. Italy (1998), the Court reaffirmed that article 8 can impose positive obligations on states to ensure respect for private or family life. Citing the Lopez Ostra case, the Court reiterated that "severe environmental pollution may affect individuals' well-being and prevent them from enjoying their homes in such a way as to affect their private and family life."

51. Other important ECHR cases are Arrondelle v. United Kingdom, Powell & Raynor v. United Kingdom, Hatton and Others v. United Kingdom, Chapman v. United Kingdom.

2. The Inter-American Human Rights System

52. The Inter-American System of Human Rights consists of general and specialized human rights instruments. The basic texts are:

- The Charter of the Organization of American States ("OAS"),
- The American Declaration of the Rights and Duties of Man (1948), and
- The American Convention on Human Rights (1969) with its two Protocols.

53. The American Convention on Human Rights ("1969 American Convention") has been ratified by 25 countries, predominantly in Latin America. For states that are not party to the Convention, the rights in the American Declaration of the Right and Duties of Man ("1948 American Declaration") provide the basic standards they are expected to uphold. The Inter-American Human Rights System uses a Commission and a Court (for states that are party to the Convention and accept its jurisdiction) to protect and promote human rights. The Commission can hear individual petitions and conduct country studies to investigate widespread human rights abuses. The Commission also can refer cases to the Court.

54. The 1948 American Declaration, as the principal normative instrument of the system, and the 1969 American Convention, provide a series of individual rights particularly relevant to environmental issues. The Preamble of the 1948 American Declaration states:

1948 American Declaration of the Right and Duties of Man

"All men are born free and equal, in dignity and in rights, and, being endowed by nature with reason and conscience, they should conduct themselves as brothers one to another.

(...)

Since culture is the highest social and historical expression of ...spiritual development, it is the duty of man to preserve, practice and foster culture by every means within his power.

(...)"

---

55. The Commission and the Court may also apply special international instruments as complementary provisions, as for instance the 1969 Tribal Peoples Convention.

56. The principal organ of the system is the Inter-American Commission on Human Rights, which plays a unique role in assisting the member states in their efforts to respect and ensure the rights of the individuals subject to their jurisdiction. Among its many functions, the Commission promotes awareness of human rights, provides member states with advisory services in this field and monitors the situation of human rights in each member states carrying out on-site observations. The Commission acts in individual petitions alleging human rights violations, prepares studies and reports and makes recommendations to OAS member states for the adoption of progressive measures promoting human rights.

57. Any person or group can file a petition alleging the violation of the 1969 American Convention by a state party or the 1948 American Declaration by an OAS member state. The identity of the petitioner may be kept in confidence. The alleged victims must have exhausted all available domestic remedies, the petition has to be submitted in a timely manner and should not represent a complaint that essentially duplicates a petition pending or previously settled.

58. The Inter-American Human Rights Court has jurisdiction to hear contentious cases submitted by the Commission or States accepting its jurisdiction. The Court also can render advisory opinions. Beyond submitting to the General Assembly of the OAS a report specifying which states have not complied with its judgments, the Court has no enforcement mechanisms.

59. With respect to the cause of indigenous peoples, the 1969 American Convention protects minorities and prohibits discrimination against them. Article 24 requires all persons to be regarded as equal before the law and be accorded equal protection of the law. This is reinforced by the obligation (in article 1.1) to respect and ensure guarantees "without any discrimination for reasons of race, color, sex, language, religions, political or other opinion, national or social origin, economic status, birth or any other social condition."

60. When indigenous representatives complained that processes against indigenous defendants were conducted in Spanish and that translation was not provided for those who understood only their native language, the Inter-American Commission expressed its expectation that the recognition of indigenous languages in their areas of use will ensure translation in every case required. This should come through amendments to the Constitution.

61. The case law of the Inter-American human rights system has contributed considerably to recognizing the rights of indigenous peoples in respect to their environmental and natural resources. The case of Awas Tingni Mayagna (Sumo) Indigenous Community v. Nicaragua involved the protection of Nicaraguan forests in lands traditionally owned by the Awas Tingni. The case originated as an action against government-sponsored logging of timber on native lands by Sol del Caribe, S.A. (SOLCARSA), a subsidiary of the Korean company Kumkyung Co. Ltd.. The government granted SOLCARSA a logging concession without consulting the Awas Tingni community, although the government had agreed to consult them after to granting an earlier concession. The Awas Tingi filed a case at the Inter-American Commission, alleging that the government violated their rights to cultural integrity, religion, equal protection and participation in government.

62. The Commission found in 1998 that the government had violated the human rights of the Awas Tingni and brought the case before the Court. On 31 August 2001, the Court issued its judgment on the merits and reparations, deciding by seven votes to one that the state violated the 1969 American Convention's right to judicial protection (article 25) and the right to property (article 21). The Court unanimously declared that the state must adopt domestic laws, administrative regulations and other necessary means to create effective surveying, demarcating and title mechanisms for the properties of the indigenous communities, in accordance with customary law and indigenous values, uses and customs. Pending the demarcation of the indigenous lands, the state must abstain from realizing acts or allowing the realization of acts by its agents or third parties that could affect the existence, value, use or enjoyment of those properties located in the Awas Tingni lands. The Court also declared that the state must invest U.S. $50,000 in public works and services of collective benefit to the Awas Tingni as a form of reparations for non-material injury and U.S. $30,000 for legal fees and expenses.

63. The Additional Protocol to the American Convention in the area of Economic Social and Cultural Rights ("Additional Protocol") was signed in San Salvador in 1988, and entered into force 10 years later. The Additional Protocol's article 11 is

highly relevant to the environment, and states that "1. Everyone shall have the right to live in a healthy environment and to have access to basic public services. 2. The State Parties shall promote the protection, preservation, and improvement of the environment."

64. The Additional Protocol sets out a series of useful and enforceable obligations, but it does not allow individual petitions to be filed concerning article 11. Thus, the main function of the Commission regarding this right will be to review the state reports that are filed concerning implementation and compliance.

3. The African Human Rights System

65. Africa has the youngest of the regional Human Rights systems. The African (Banjul) Charter of Human and Peoples' Rights ("1981 African Charter") was adopted by the Organization of African Unity ("OAU") and entered into force in 1986. The 1981 African Charter enumerates the traditional list of civil and political rights, but also includes economic, social and cultural rights and was the first to include a right to environment.

66. Article 24 of the 1981 African Charter states that "All peoples shall have the right to a general satisfactory environment favorable to their development."

67. The current system consists of a Commission alone, whose role is to promote and monitor human rights in member states by researching specific situations, organizing seminars, giving recommendations to states, laying out human rights principles and cooperating with other international organizations. The Commission also hears individual complaints.

68. The African Commission on Human and Peoples' Rights was the first international human rights body to decide a contentious case involving violation of the right to a general satisfactory environment on 27 May 2002. The case is a landmark not only in this respect, but also in the Commission's articulation of the duties of governments in Africa to monitor and control the activities of multinational corporations. Acting on a petition filed by two Non-Governmental Organizations on behalf of the people of Ogoniland, Nigeria, the African Commission found that Nigeria had breached its obligations to respect, protect, promote, and fulfill rights guaranteed by the 1981 African Charter.

69. The Communication alleged that the military government of Nigeria was involved in oil production through NNPC in consortium with SPDC, and that the operations produced contamination causing environmental degradation and health problems. The Communication also alleged that the consortium disposed of toxic wastes in violation of applicable international environmental standards and caused numerous avoidable spills near villages, consequently poisoning much of the region's soil and water, and that the government aided these violations by placing the state's legal and military powers at the disposal of the oil companies.

70. After finding the petition admissible, the Commission acknowledged four separate but overlapping duties with respect to guaranteed rights: to respect, protect, promote, and fulfill them. These obligations universally apply to all rights and entail a combination of negative and positive duties. Assessing the claimed violations of the rights to health under article 16 and to a general satisfactory environment under article 24, the Commission found that the right to a general satisfactory environment imposes clear obligations upon a government, requiring the state to take reasonable and other measures to prevent pollution and ecological degradation, to promote conservation, and to secure an ecologically sustainable development and use of natural resources. Applying these obligations to the facts of the case, the Commission concluded that although Nigeria had the right to produce oil, the state had not protected the articles 16 and 24 rights of those in the Ogoni region.

71. The suggestion of a broadly justiciable right to environment is reinforced by the Commission's final comment that all rights in the 1981 African Charter may be applied and enforced. The Commission gives the right to environment meaningful content by requiring states to adopt various techniques of environmental protection, such as environmental impact assessment, public information and participation, access to justice for environmental harm, and monitoring of potentially harmful activities. The result offers a blueprint for merging environmental protection, economic development and guarantees of human rights.

IV. National Implementation:
National Legislation/Judicial Decisions

72. The Supreme Court of the Philippines has produced a ruling of utmost importance on human rights that furthered environmental objectives. Therefore the section on application of human rights in the Philippines will mainly focus on this ruling. The discussions of the employment of

human rights in the sections on India and South Africa will then focus on how specific human rights relevant to environment have been implemented in the national legal systems and interpreted by the national courts.

1. Philippines

73. The Minors Oposa v. Secretary of the Department of Environment and Natural Resoures (1993) case is based upon a substantive procedural right to a clean environment contained in article II, Section 16, or the Philippine Constitution, which states that "The State shall protect and advance the right of the people to a balanced and healthful ecology in accord with the rhythm and harmony of nature."

74. The plaintiffs were a number of minors together with the Philippine Ecological Network, a non-profit organization. After their claim was dismissed at the first instance, the plaintiffs petitioned the Supreme Court to reverse that ruling. The Supreme Court reversed the ruling and the case returned to the lower court.

75. On the question of standing, the Supreme Court points out that the fact that some of the plaintiffs are minors adds a novel element. The minors represent their generation as well as generations yet unborn and can file a class suit. The Supreme Court stated:

> "Their personality to sue on behalf of the succeeding generation can only be based on the concept of intergenerational responsibility insofar as the right to a balanced and healthful ecology is concerned. (…) Needless to say, every generation has a responsibility to the next to preserve that rhythm and harmony for the full enjoyment of a balanced and healthful ecology."

76. The Supreme Court based its judgment on two pillars, the human right to a clean environment as enshrined in the Constitution and the concept of intergenerational equity. The case contains fundamental statements on the issue of intergenerational equity and responsibility. The Court stated:

> "While the right to a balanced and healthful ecology is to be found under the Declaration of Principles and State Policies and not under Bill of Rights, it does not follow that it is less important than any of the civil and political rights enumerated in the latter. Such a right belongs to a different category of rights altogether for it concerns nothing less the self-preservation and self-perpetuation aptly and fittingly stressed by the petitioners, the advancement of which may even be said to predate all governments and constitutions.

> As a matter of fact, these basic rights need not even be written in the Constitution for they are assumed to exist from the inception of humankind."

77. It is most significant that the Supreme Court states that the right to a sound environment is a self-executing constitutional policy. By itself, independent of specific statutory right, this right is actionable against the Secretary of the Department of Environment and Natural Resources.

2. India

a) The Right to Life

78. The right to life has been employed in a diversified manner in India. It includes, among other things, the right to survive as a species, quality of life, the right to live with dignity and the right to livelihood. Article 21 of the Indian Constitution states: "No person shall be deprived of his life or personal liberty except according to procedure established by law".

79. In its jurisprudence, the Supreme Court interpreted the right to life guaranteed by article 21 of the Constitution to include the right to á wholesome environment. In Subash Kumar (1991), the Court observed that the "right to life guaranteed by Article 21 includes the right of enjoyment of pollution-free water and air for full enjoyment of life". This was reaffirmed in M.C. Mehta v. Union of India (1998). The case concerned the deterioration of the world environment and the duty of the State government, under article 21, to ensure a better quality of environment. The Supreme Court ordered the Central Government to show the steps they have taken to achieve this goal through national policy and to restore the quality of environment.

b) Equality before the Law

80. The Constitution of India provides that all are equal before the law and shall be accorded equal protection of the law. Article 14 states that "The State shall not deny to any person equality before the law or the equal protection of the laws within the territory of India."

81. Urban environmental groups frequently resort to article 14 to quash 'arbitrary' municipal permissions for construction that are contrary to development regulations. Article 14 can be used to challenge government sanctions for mining and other activities with high human rights and environmental impact, where the permissions are arbitrarily granted without adequate consideration of environmental impacts.

c) The Right to Property

82. In India, the right to property was formally removed from the fundamental rights in 1979. This right is now protected by article 300A of the Indian Constitution and does not have the same procedural advantages as other fundamental rights. This amendment was created in response to multiple lawsuits brought against different government agencies by indigenous peoples who were being evicted from their property as their lands were being used for other development projects.

d) Environmental Laws and Policies

83. Indian national legislation is sectoral; therefore, human rights and the environment are dealt with by separate legislation. However, framework environmental legislation in recent years took account of human health and safety aspect and sustainable development. The general environmental framework laws tend to be enabling in nature, and mainly charge a competent national authority to provide more specific guidelines and regulations in future.

84. The Constitution Act of 1976 (Forty Second Amendment) explicitly incorporated environmental protection and improvement as a part of state policy. Article 48A provides that "[t]he state shall endeavor to protect and improve the environment and safeguard the forests and wildlife of the country." Article 51A(g) imposes a similar responsibility on every citizen "to protect and improve the natural environment including forests, lakes, rivers and wildlife, and to have compassion for living creatures...." Thus, protection of natural environment and compassion for living creatures were made the positive fundamental duty of every citizen.

e) Procedural Rights

85. There are several regulations guiding the procedures of environmental impact assessment. Some provisions in the framework legislation deal with access to environmental information. Provisions for complaints from "any person" under environment legislation and Asian Development Bank-Funded Projects show increased public participation in decision-making. However, there is no general duty on the state to collect environmental information. With regard to access to justice and standing in Court, the Indian High Courts moved from the "aggrieved person" test to the "sufficient interest" test in the early 1970's.

f) Right to Remedy

86. The Indian courts have made several directions on payment of compensation for damage and payment of costs required for the remedial measures. The courts ordered the relevant Ministry to adopt necessary measures in order to broadcast information relating to environment in the media. The courts also drew the Government's attention to areas where legislation was necessary and established a committee to monitor the directions of the court.

3. South Africa

87. The Constitution of the Republic of South Africa was approved by the Constitutional Assembly on May 1996, and took effect on 4 February 1997. South Africa's Constitution is one of the most progressive in the world, and enjoys high international acclaim. The Preamble of the Constitution states that the aims of the Constitution are to:

- Heal the divisions of the past and establish a society based on democratic values, social justice and fundamental human rights;
- Improve the quality of life of all citizens and free the potential of each person;
- Lay the foundations for a democratic and open society in which government is based on the will of the people and every citizen is equally protected by law; and
- Build a united and democratic South Africa able to take its rightful place as a sovereign State in the family of nations.

88. Fundamental rights are contained in Chapter Two of the South African Constitution and seek to protect the rights and freedoms of individuals. The Constitutional Court guards these rights and determines whether or not actions by the state are in accordance with constitutional provisions.

a) Right to Life

89. Section 11 of Chapter 2 of the South African Constitution deals with the right to life, a nonderogable right. Under Section 24 of Chapter 2 of the South African Constitution, everyone has the "right to an environment that is not harmful to health or well-being...". Section 24 adds that the government must act reasonably to protect the environment by preventing pollution and ecological degradation, promoting conservation, and securing ecologically sustainable development, while building the economy and society.

90. Under the South African Constitution, the state has a duty to protect, promote, respect and fulfill socio-economic rights. Section 24 demonstrates that the right to a healthy environment is part of the socio-economic right of South Africa. This right is often applied by the courts to give a meaningful interpretation to the right to life. Section 27(1)(b) of Chapter 2 of the Constitution guarantees the right of everyone to have access to sufficient food and water. Section 28(1)(c) of the Constitution also gives children the right to basic nutrition. The environmental rights protected under the South African Constitution are closely related to the right of access to sufficient water and place duties on the state to prevent pollution and ensure conservation of water resources. One of the central goals of the Government's water policy is to ensure equitable access by all South African's to the nation's water resources and to end discrimination in access to water on the basis of race, class or gender.

b) Equality before the Law

91. Section 9(2) of Chapter 2 of the South African Constitution deals with right to equality. The Constitution defines equality to include the "full and equal enjoyment of rights and freedoms". The state may take steps to protect or advance individuals or groups that have been disadvantaged by unfair discrimination with the aim of promoting the achievement of equality.

c) Right to Property

92. Section 25 of Chapter 2 of the South African Constitution, which deals with the right to property, including land rights, aims to protect an individual's property rights and to promote land reform. This right is still a hotly debated issue due to the property imbalances in South Africa after the apartheid. Under Section 25(1), the property rights may not be interfered with unless it is done under a "law of general application." Therefore, it protects the property rights of named or easily identifiable individuals or groups. Section 25(1) also prohibits the arbitrary deprivation of property. The Interim Protection of Informal Land Rights Act (1996) allows for the protection of certain rights to and interests in land, where they are not properly protected by law. Informal rights to land mean the use, occupation or access to land following the practice of a tribe or indigenous law. No person or community may be deprived of this land right without consent. Appropriate compensation must be paid if the person or community is deprived of land.

93. With regard to access to justice and standing in Court, Section 38 of Chapter 2 of the Constitution provides that persons who may approach a court can be:

- Anyone acting in their own interest;
- Anyone acting on behalf of another person who cannot act in their own name;
- Anyone acting as a member of, or in the interest of, a group or a class of persons;
- Anyone acting in the public interest; or
- An association acting in the interest of its members.

94. Section 32 deals with right of access to information and Section 33 deals with right to a just administrative action. Section 32 can be used by community groups to find out more about harmful industrial development, which will have a detrimental effect on their life and well-being. These rights are not absolute and may be limited if the limitation is reasonable and justifiable in a democratic society based upon human dignity, equality and freedom (Section 36 of the South African Constitution).

95. The National Environment Management Act 1998 ("NEMA"), amongst other things, requires that the public must be actively involved when decisions are made that affect the environment. NEMA also obliges the government to examine all environmental impacts before going ahead with any development.

96. The Promotion of Access to Information Act (2000) further outlines which information would be available and how to submit information requests from the government and from private individuals. There are also regulations under the Environmental Conservation Act (1989) providing for impact assessments for certain activities. Moreover, women and other vulnerable and disadvantaged groups must be encouraged to get involved in decisions about their environment.

97. In its jurisprudence, the Supreme Court promotes the notion of public participation. In "The Director, Mineral Development Gauteng Region and Sasol Mining (pty) Ltd v. Save the Vaal Environment and Others (1994)", the Supreme Court of Appeal held that before a permit is given for mining, the government must be prepared to listen to the views of people concerned with potential environmental impacts. The types of environmental concerns that can be raised include destruction of plants and animals, pollution, loss of jobs and small businesses and property values.

Prof. Dinah L. Shelton, Patricia Roberts Harris Professor of Law, George Washington University Law School

Eva Maria Duer, Associate Legal Officer, Division of Policy Development and Law, UNEP

Resources

Internet Materials

EUROPEAN COURT OF HUMAN RIGHTS available at http://www.echr.coe.int/Eng/General.htm

INTER-AMERICAN COMMISSION ON HUMAN RIGHTS available at http://www.cidh.oas.org

Text Materials

Antonio G.M. La Vina, THE RIGHT TO A SOUND ENVIRONMENT IN THE PHILIPPINES: THE SIGNIFICANCE OF THE MINORS OPOSA CASE, (RECIEL Vol. 3 No. 4, 1994).

BACKGROUND PAPERS 1-6 TO THE JOINT UNEP-OHCHR EXPERT SEMINAR ON HUMAN RIGHTS AND THE ENVIRONMENT, (14-16 January 2002, Geneva).

CASE OF HATTON AND OTHERS V. THE UNITED KINGDOM, (decided 2 October 2001).

David Hunter, INTERNATIONAL ENVIRONMENTAL LAW AND POLICY, CHAPTER 16, (Foundation Press, 2002).

Guenter, Handl, Eide, Krause & Rosas (Eds.), HUMAN RIGHTS AND PROTECTION OF THE ENVIRONMENT, ECONOMIC, SOCIAL AND CULTURAL RIGHTS, (2001).

Kate Cook, ENVIRONMENTAL RIGHTS AS HUMAN RIGHTS, (EHRLR Issue 3, Sweet & Maxwell Ltd., 2002).

Kiss & Shelton, INTERNATIONAL ENVIRONMENTAL LAW, (3rd ed. Transnational Press, 2004).
Malgosia Fitzmaurice, THE RIGHT OF THE CHILD TO A CLEAN ENVIRONMENT, (So. Ill. Univ. L. J., Vol. 23 No. 3, Spring 1999).

Margaret de Merieux, DERIVING ENVIRONMENTAL RIGHTS FORM THE EUROPEAN CONVENTION FOR THE PROTECTION OF HUMAN RIGHTS AND FUNDAMENTAL FREEDOMS, (Oxford J. of Legal Studies, Vol. 21 No. 3, 2001).

Philippe Sands, HUMAN RIGHTS, ENVIRONMENT AND THE LOPEZ-OSTRA CASE: CONTEXT AND CONSEQUENCES, (EHRLR Issue 6, Sweet & Maxwell Ltd., 1996).

23. INTERNATIONAL LABOUR, HEALTH AND THE ENVIRONMENT

I. Introduction

1. According to the International Labour Organization ("ILO"), approximately 1.2 million people die each year as a result of occupational accidents and work-related diseases. The ILO estimates that workers suffer from 250 million occupational accidents and from 160 million occupational diseases each year. Deaths and injuries take a particularly heavy toll in developing countries, where large numbers of workers are concentrated in some of the world's most hazardous industries.

2. This social and economic burden is not evenly distributed among countries. For example, fatality rates in some European countries are twice as high as in some others, and in parts of the Middle East and Asia fatality rates soar to four times greater than those in the industrialized countries. Certain hazardous jobs can increase the risk of workplace accidents or death by 10 to 100 times. Similarly, insurance coverage for occupational safety and health varies widely in different parts of the world: workers in Nordic countries enjoy nearly universal coverage while only 10% or less of the workforce in many developing countries is likely to enjoy any sort of coverage.

3. Clearly, workplace health is a global concern. Accordingly, in addition to international agreements setting forth rules and regulations that apply specifically to environmental issues, international conventions have also established standards and procedures to safeguard human health within the workplace environment. In addition to UNEP, the primary international bodies active in this area are the ILO and the World Health Organization ("WHO"). Although the conventions, recommendations and strategies of the ILO and the WHO cover a variety of labour-related topics, many of them are specifically intended to safeguard workplace health and safety and are applicable in the absence of specific environmental instruments. The primary objectives of the ILO and the WHO in this area are to create global awareness of the dimensions and consequences of work-related accidents, injuries and diseases, to promote the goal of basic protection for all workers in conformity with international labour standards, and to enhance the capacity of their member states to design and to implement effective preventive and protective policies and programme.

4. The world's workplaces contain hazards to the health and safety of employees and the environment. Consequently many countries are addressing these hazards with the assistance of the ILO and the WHO, whose conventions and recommendations provide a basis for legislative action at the national level. Further, the establishment of collaborative programmes with the ILO and the WHO provides countries with access to technical and scientific expertise that allows them to better provide for worker health and safety. Overall, the ILO and the WHO can help improve occupational health, safety and the environments of their member states.

5. This chapter discusses hazards in the workplace and introduces the initiatives that the ILO and the WHO have undertaken to address those problems. This chapter also presents examples of national legislation developed and adopted by China, South Africa and Kenya to provide for healthy workplace environments.

II. International Framework

1. The Problem

6. About 45% of the world's total population and 58% of the population over ten years of age belong to the global workforce whose efforts sustain the economic basis of society. However, the workplace is a hazardous environment. Health hazards, accidents, disease, and unsafe working conditions put workers at risk. The health and the well-being of working people are fundamental prerequisites for productivity and are crucial for overall socioeconomic and sustainable development.

7. Workplace health and safety hazards are common in many economic sectors and affect large numbers of workers. According to the WHO, approximately 30% to 50% of workers report hazardous physical, chemical or biological exposures, or overload of unreasonably heavy physical work or ergonomic factors. An equal number of working people report psychological overload at work resulting in stress. Many individuals spend one-third of their adult life in such hazardous work environments. About 120 million workplace accidents resulting in some 200,000 fatalities are estimated to occur annually

and up to 157 million new cases of occupational disease may be caused by various exposures at work.

8. The United Nations estimates that only 5% to 10% of workers in developing countries have access to workplace health services. With approximately 80 % of the world's workers residing in these countries, the need for a focus on occupational health is acute. According to the principles of the UN, the WHO and the ILO, every citizen has a right to healthy and safe work and to a work environment that enables him or her to live a productive life.

9. There are several benefits to creating healthy work environments. Proper attention to workplace health and safety results in more productive workers who can raise healthy families and work their way out of poverty. Safe workplaces contribute to sustainable development by controlling pollution and reducing hazards from industrial processes.

10. Workplace health and safety can also contribute to improving the employability of workers, through worker training, assessment of work demands, medical diagnosis, health screening and assessment of functional capacities. Finally, workplace health is fundamental to public health, for it is increasingly clear that major diseases, such as HIV/AIDS, heart disease and others, require workplace programmes as part of a country's overall disease control strategy.

2. International Regulatory Bodies

11. The ILO and the WHO have established rules, regulations, standards and procedures to safeguard human health within the workplace environment. Both the ILO and the WHO promulgate standards that act as global models for workplace rights and responsibilities. As such, it is the obligation of member states to realize those standards as far as possible and the missions of the ILO and the WHO are to promote their realization. Once adopted, international labour standards are intended to be implemented and conventions ratified by the member states. The ILO and the WHO intend that international labour standards be systematically used as a guide in the design and implementation of labour and social policy at the national level.

12. The ILO was created in 1919, primarily for the purpose of adopting international standards to cope with the problem of labour conditions involving "injustice, hardship and privation". With the incorporation of the Declaration of Philadelphia into its Constitution in 1944, the Organisation's standard setting mandate was broadened to include more general, but related, social policy, human and civil rights matters. International labour standards are essentially expressions of international tripartite agreement on these matters. The ILO has 178 member countries (as of November 2005), and has adopted more than 180 Conventions and 185 Recommendations covering a broad range of workplace-related topics.

13. The WHO was established in 1948, as the UN's specialized agency for health. The WHO's objective is the "attainment by all peoples of the highest possible level of health". Health is defined in the WHO's Constitution as a "state of complete physical, mental and social well-being and not merely the absence of disease or infirmity". WHO is governed by 192 member states through the World Health Assembly. The Health Assembly is composed of representatives from the WHO's member states.

14. The main tasks of the World Health Assembly are to approve the WHO programme and the budget for the following biennium and to decide major policy questions. The WHO is more directly health-related than the ILO but does undertake initiatives to improve environmental health. Among other things, the WHO's activities in this area focus on protection of the human environment, provision of clean water and sanitation. With regard to the workplace environment, the WHO seeks to assist its member states achieving a sustainable basis for health, ensuring an environment that promotes health and making individuals and organizations aware of their responsibility for health and its environmental basis.

3. Selected ILO Conventions relating to the Workplace Environment

15. The standards of the ILO take the form of international labour conventions, recommendations, codes of practice and resolutions. The ILO's conventions are international treaties, subject to ratification by ILO member states. Its recommendations are non-binding instruments, typically dealing with the same subjects as conventions, which set out guidelines that can orient national policy and action. The ILO's recommendations outline general or technical guidelines to be applied in implementing the conventions. The codes of practice relate to various types of dangerous workplace equipment or agents, such as the Code

of Safety in the Use of Chemicals at Work. Finally, the ILO's resolutions are less formal agreements between the organization and committees of experts, special conferences and other bodies covering topics that are both general in nature and more technical. All of the ILO's instruments are intended to have a measurable impact on working conditions and practices in every country of the world.

16. ILO's Occupational Safety and Health Convention No. 155 ("ILO Convention No. 155") (1981), and its accompanying Recommendation No. 164, set forth the standards prescribing the application of comprehensive workplace safety measures and a country's adoption of a coherent national policy on occupational health and safety. ILO Convention No. 155 also provides a framework for establishing the responsibility of employers for providing a safe workplace and the duties and rights of workers.

17. Specifically, ILO Convention No. 155 requires ratifying states to formulate, implement and periodically review a coherent national policy on occupational safety, occupational health and the working environment. Among other things, the ratifying state's policy should take into account the arrangement of elements of the work environment, relations between elements of the work environment, training, communication and cooperation, protection of workers and their representatives from disciplinary measures as a result of actions properly taken by them in conformity with the policy.

18. In 2002, the ILO supplemented its Convention No. 155 by adopting a Protocol that requires member states to adopted certain procedures, means and methods regarding the recording and reporting of workplace accidents and diseases.

19. In additional to workplace safety measures, the ILO also addresses occupational health. Occupational health is the promotion and maintenance of the highest degree of physical, mental and social well-being of workers in all occupations by preventing departures from health, controlling risks and the adaptation of work to people, and people to their jobs. In 1985, the ILO issued the Occupational Health Services Convention No. 161 and its accompanying Recommendation No. 171. The ILO Convention No. 171 sets forth standards stressing the preventative nature of occupational health services, including a regulatory body's responsibility for advising employers, employees and their representatives on the maintenance of a safe and healthy working environment, as well as the adaptation of an employee's tasks to his specific

capabilities. It also stresses the relative roles of employers and employees, the best use of resources and cooperation between the two groups to provide for occupational health.

20. Specific areas covered by ILO Convention No. 171 include:

- Identification and assessment of the risks arising from health hazards in the workplace. This involves surveillance of the factors in the workplace and work practices that may affect the health of employees. It also requires a systematic approach to the analysis of occupational accidents and diseases;
- Advice on the planning and organization of work and working practices, including workplace design and on the evaluation, choice and maintenance of equipment and on substances used at work;
- Advice, information, training and education, on occupational health, safety and hygiene and on ergonomics and protective equipment;
- Surveillance of workplace employees' health; and
- Organization of first aid and emergency treatment.

21. An example of an ILO standard that is more directly related to a worker's physical environment is the ILO Convention No. 170 concerning Safety in the Use of Chemicals at Work (1990) ("ILO Convention No. 170"). The purpose of this Convention is to protect the health of workers, the general public and the environment from the potentially harmful effects that could result from the use of chemicals in the workplace. Through this Convention, member states are required to formulate and implement national policies and laws regulating the safe handling of chemicals at work, classifying the degree of risk posed by chemicals used in the workplace and adopting emergency plans in to address accidents involving chemicals. This Convention is important not only to countries with a significant manufacturing sector but also to those that depend primarily on agriculture. Overall, the Convention calls for the creation of laws prohibiting or restricting the use of DDT, polychlorinated biphenyl, mercury, cyanide and other chemicals that have been found to endanger workers' health and safety, and to contaminate the environment.

4. The WHO and "Environmental Health"

22. According to the WHO, environmental health "comprises those aspects of human health,

including quality of life, that are determined by physical, chemical, biological, social, and psychosocial factors in the environment." Environmental health also refers to the theory and practice of "assessing, correcting, controlling, and preventing those factors in the environment that can potentially affect adversely the health of present and future generations".

23. The WHO has proposed the Global Strategy on Occupational Health for All ("1994 Global Strategy"), which is based on available occupational health indicators and identifies the most evident needs for the development of occupational health and safety. The 1994 Global Strategy outlines priority areas at both national and international levels and proposes the priority actions for the WHO's Workers' Health Programme. The priority objectives proposed by the 1994 Global Strategy include:

- Strengthening international and national policies for health at work;
- Developing healthy work environments;
- Developing healthy work practices and promoting of health at work;
- Providing increased occupational health services;
- Establishing support services for occupational health;
- Developing occupational health standards based on scientific risk assessment;
- Developing human resources for occupational health;
- Establishing registration and data systems, including information services for experts and effective means of transmission of data and information; and
- Developing collaboration between international bodies and non-governmental organizations around issues relating to occupational health.

24. A specific example of a WHO convention that is health-related, but has ramifications for the creation of healthy workplaces is the Framework Convention on Tobacco Control ("2003 Tobacco Convention"). Arising out of the recognized need to regulate the adverse health effects of tobacco, the 2003 Tobacco Convention requires WHO member states to take specific measures to limit smoking in the workplace. The WHO intends that measures taken at the national level will save workers' lives and prevent diseases that result from tobacco use.

III. National Implementation

25. Member states must enact legislation or adopt national measures in order to implement the conventions and recommendations of the ILO and the WHO. China, South Africa and Kenya are all member states of the ILO and the WHO, and have implemented a number of laws regulating workplace hazards. As such, these three countries are demonstrating their commitment to create healthy workplace environments.

1. China

26. Spurred in part by a rash of accidents and explosions in the country's coal mining industry, China's State Administration of Work Safety ("Administration of Work Safety") has taken a variety of measures to implement labour laws and regulations that protect the health of workers and the environment. On 12 December 2001, China's State Economic and Trade Commission adopted the country's first "Guidelines on Occupational Safety and Health Management Systems" ("2001 Guidelines") as the basis of its Work Safety Law that took effect in November 2002.

27. Referencing the "ILO Guidelines on Occupational Safety and Health Management Systems," the Guidelines encouraged employers to adopt principles of occupational health and safety ("OHS") to reduce workplace hazards and improve worker safety. The 2001 Guidelines also required the Administration of Work Safety to develop, implement and regularly evaluate employers' OHS programmes. Enterprises involved in exceptionally dangerous work, as well as companies that had a history of serious accidents, were charged with special responsibilities to establish and maintain OHS management systems.

28. The Work Safety Law of 2002 ("Work Safety Law") codifies China's OHS guidance. The law requires that employers whose operations include the handing of dangerous substances and materials or dangerous conditions must hire full-time OHS personnel to administer safe practices at work. The law also stipulates that employees have the right to be made fully aware of all hazards present in their workplace, as well as the associated preventative and emergency measures. Employees also have the right to refuse orders that violate OHS rules and to take action against employers who violate the rules. The Work Safety Law also obligates employees to avail themselves of education and training in matters pertaining to OHS and take steps to render themselves fully aware of the appropriate

and necessary OHS knowledge. Workers must also improve their skills and capabilities in safe working practices, as well as accident prevention and emergency procedures.

2. South Africa

29. In 1996, South Africa passed the Mine Health and Safety Act ("1996 Mine Act") in response to a number of health and environmental problems that were caused by the country's mining activities. At the time the law was passed, South Africa's mining industry employed over 500,000 people, exposing them to harmful effects of coal mine dusts and dangerous mining operations. One of the 1996 Mine Act's objectives was to give effect to the public international law obligations of the Republic of South Africa with regard to mining health and safety, including the country's obligations as a member state of the ILO.

30. The 1996 Mine Act delegates responsibility for creating a healthier and safer mining industry between the government, employers and employees. Specifically, the law requires employers to provide and maintain a safe workplace, to identify and assess workplace hazards to which non-employees may be exposed, and to ensure non-employees are not exposed to health or safety hazards. An employer's mining operations are to be periodically inspected to assurance compliance with the law. Violation of the law by anyone who, by a negligent act or omission, endangers the health or safety of or causes serious injury to anyone at a mine is punishable by imposition of a fine or imprisonment.

31. Since the Mine Health and Safety Act was passed, employee representatives have met with South Africa's Minister of Minerals and Energy to discuss methodologies for the implementation of the Act. As a result of the law, representatives of employers and employees are now involved in the regulation of mineworkers' health and safety and provide education and training to new mine workers.

3. Kenya

32. Kenya has been expanding its commitment to the creation of healthier work environments by revising existing legislation and collaborating with the ILO. Until 1990, the country's main labour-related legislation was contained in chapter 514 of the Factories Act of 1951. As initially enacted, chapter 514 was applicable only to manufacturing

facilities and few provisions that addressed the issue of workplace health and safety. In order to improve the health and safety of its workforce, however, Kenya began collaborating with the ILO, which provided the country with technical, financial and advisory assistance on measures that Kenya could take to adopt more meaningful occupational health and safety measures consistent with its economic, social and industrial development aspirations.

33. Kenya's work with the ILO led to major amendments to chapter 514, which included comprehensive provisions for worker health and safety. Now entitled the Factories and other Places of Work Act, the law specifically recognizes, for example, the dangers posed by chemicals in the workplace and requires employers to undertake management and treatment programmes to mitigate potential harm to employees and the environment. The law specifically requires employers to label chemicals correctly to ensure their safe handling by workers, to provide workers with adequate protective clothing, and to record and report cases of chemical-related workplace accident and illnesses.

34. The Directorate of Occupational Health and Safety Services ("DOHSS") is one of the regulatory bodies created to implement the Act. Representatives of the DOHSS periodically inspect Kenya's factories and other places of work to ensure that workplaces are in compliance with the requirements of the statute. The representatives carry out medical examinations of employees and site inspections to ensure compliance with safety regulations. Many of the objectives and activities of the DOHSS are the result of Kenya's collaboration with the ILO.

Prof. Malgosia Fitzmaurice, Professor of Public International Law, Queen Mary University of London

Dr. Jane Dwasi, UNEP Consultant, University of Nairobi

Resources

Internet Materials

CHINA'S WORK SAFETY LAW available at http://www.zhb.gov.cn/english/law.php3?offset

PROJECT UNDER GROUND, DRILLBITS & TAILINGS: OCTOBER 22, 1996: PAGE SIX available at
http://www.moles.org/ProjectUnderground/drillbits/1015/96101506.html

SOUTH AFRICA'S MINE HEALTH AND SAFETY ACT available at http://natlex.ilo.org/txt/E96ZAF01.htm

THE INTERNATIONAL LABOUR ORGANIZATION WEBSITE available at http://www.ilo.org

WORLD HEALTH ORGANISATION FRAMEWORK CONVENTION ON TOBACCO CONTROL (2003) available at
http://www.who.int/tobacco/en

WORLD HEALTH ORGANIZATION GLOBAL STRATEGY ON OCCUPATIONAL HEALTH FOR ALL available at
http://www.who.int/oeh/OCHweb/OCHweb/OSHpages/OSHDocuments/GlobalStrategy/GlobalStrategy.pdf

Text Materials

Building Safety in Asia: Sitting in a TinderBox, available in LEXIS, News Library, CURNEWS File (September 1993).

David Weir, THE BHOPAL SYNDROME: PESTICIDE MANUFACTURING AND THE THIRD WORLD, (1986).

Deadly Blaze Leads to Safety Checks, available in LEXIS, News Library, CURNEWS File, at page 17 (March 1993).

Herbert Nigg, et al, Bulletin of Environmental Contamination and Toxicology (Springer-Verlag ed., Vol. 53)(1994).

James H. Colopy, Poisoning the Developing World: The Exportation of Unregistered and Severely Restricted
Pesticides from the United States, IN UCLA JOURNAL OF ENVIRONMNTAL LAW & POLICY, (1994/1995).

Maarit Raution, Dr. Sakari would like to establish a Center for Studies in Occupational Medicine in Kenya, IN
AFRICAN NEWSLETTER ON OCCUPATIONAL HEALTH & SAFETY, VOL. 8, NO. 2, (September, 1998).

Mitchel Zukof, The Trade Human Rights Clashes over GATT, IN BOSTON GLOBE, (October 30, 1994 at 77).

N.M. Kiama, Occupational Health Services in Kenya, IN AFRICAN NEWSLETTER ON OCCUPATIONAL HEALTH & SAFETY,
VOL. 8, NO. 2, (September, 1998).

The Directorate of Occupational Health and Safety Services ("DOHSS"), Ministry of Labour, IN A TRAINING MANUAL
ON HAZARDOUS CHILD LABOUR IN KENYA (with Support from ILO-IPEC Programme on the Elimination of Child Labour)
(1991).

United Nations Industrial Development Organization, FORMULATION OF PESTICIDES IN DEVELOPING COUNTRIES (U.N.
sales No. E.83.II.B.3) (1993).

World Bank, POLICY RESEARCH AND EXTERNAL AFFAIRS & INDUSTRY DEVELOPMENT DIVISION, Export Processing Zones
(1992).

24. TRADE AND ENVIRONMENT

I. Introduction

1. In 1999, when the World Trade Organization ("WTO") held its Third Ministerial Meeting in Seattle, many civil society organizations held widely publicized demonstrations via which they attempted to pressure the global trading system to take into account other issues as well, such as labour rights, health, environmental issues and the widening gap between rich and poor people. Since then, globalization, which may be described as a process of increasing political and economical integration among states, has been a phenomenon which has continued to receive growing attention globally.

2. At the very core of the globalization trend lies economic integration through trade, investment and capital flows. An enormous flow of capital, goods and services crosses the border of each country daily. The WTO advocates the continuous elimination of trade barriers in order to achieve free trade. The WTO, therefore, is seen as one of the embodiments of globalization, besides other organizations such as the Bretton Woods institutions (i.e. World Bank Group and International Monetary Fund).

3. Advocates of free trade argue that trade liberalization promotes sustainable development. Various arguments are employed to support this claim. One argument proposes that, through liberalizing trade, the efficient use of the world's scarce resources would be stimulated. This theory, known as 'comparative advantage,' reasons that each country will specialize in goods and services, which it produces more efficiently than other countries. Furthermore, it is argued that free trade will generate economic growth and wealth. More wealth and an increase in income will, in turn, provide the necessary means for increased environmental protection. Moreover, through generating wealth and increased incomes, international trade would have the potential to reduce or alleviate poverty.

4. Until 1994, when new arrangements were agreed, the liberalization of trade was the objective of the General Agreement on Tariffs and Trade ("GATT"), which was adopted in 1947, after the Second World War with the aim to establish a new international trading system. It was the intention to create another institution, besides the Bretton Woods institutions, to handle international economic cooperation. However, the attempt to create an International Trade Organization failed, and as a result, the GATT remained as the only multilateral instrument governing international trade. The GATT's objective was to liberalize trade and to have goods move as freely as possible by lowering and/or eliminating trade barriers.

5. Trade barriers can appear as tariffs that countries impose on goods when these are imported, or as non-tariff barriers, such as quotas and bans, which are quantitative restrictions.

6. From 1947 to 1994, the elimination of trade barriers has taken place in eight rounds of trade negotiations under auspices of the GATT. These rounds were often rather lengthy; for example, the Uruguay Round consisted of ten intergovernmental meetings spread out over almost eight years (1986-1994) to review and discuss all the trade issues under the GATT.

7. The Uruguay Round led to the establishment of the WTO in 1995, which replaced the GATT as the international organization overseeing the multilateral trading system. The Agreement from 1947 was revised, which led to a new agreement, the GATT 1994. It should be noted that the WTO did not replace the GATT as an agreement. The GATT 1994 was integrated within the WTO. The main functions of the WTO are administering WTO trade agreements, serving as a forum for trade negotiations, handling trade disputes, monitoring national trade policies, cooperating with other international organizations and assisting developing countries in trade policies issues. Its main objective is similar to that of the GATT, namely to ensure that trade moves freely and predictably.

8. The relationship between international trade and the environment is rather complex. Some claim that international trade is responsible for environmental degradation, since it causes increased global economic activity, which accelerates environmental degradation. Illegal trade in wildlife, unsustainable harvesting of tropical forests, non-sustainable exploitation of fisheries, increased transboundary movement of hazardous wastes, and acceleration of climate change processes through emission of greenhouse gases are seen as results of free trade.

9. The linkages among environmental protection and conservation, broader sustainable development issues and trade topics gained increased attention

in particular since the 1992 Rio Earth Summit, during which governments emphasized the importance for trade and environmental policies to be mutually supportive in order to encourage sustainable development. Agenda 21, adopted in Rio, states in chapter 39.3(d): "...States recognize that environmental policies should deal with the root causes of environmental degradation, thus preventing environmental measures from resulting in unnecessary restrictions to trade...". Further, the Rio Declaration on Environment and Development includes Principle 12, which provides that

---

**Rio Declaration
Principle 12**

"[S]tates should cooperate to promote a supportive and open international economic system that would lead to economic growth and sustainable development in all countries, to better address the problems of environmental degradation. Trade policy measures for environmental purposes should not constitute a means of arbitrary or unjustifiable discrimination or a disguised restriction on international trade. Unilateral actions to deal with environmental challenges outside the jurisdiction of the importing country should be avoided..."

---

10. The link between environment and trade is also addressed in many Multilateral Environmental Agreements ("MEAs"), such as article II of the 1973 Convention on International Trade in Endangered Species of Wild Fauna and Flora ("CITES"), which lists under its Fundamental Principles: "Appendix I shall include all species threatened with extinction which are or may be affected by trade. Trade in specimens of these species must be subject to particularly strict regulation in order not to endanger further their survival and must only be authorized in exceptional circumstances."

11. More recently, the 2000 Cartagena Protocol on Biosafety includes among its preambular paragraphs: "Recognizing that trade and environment agreements should be mutually supportive with a view to achieving sustainable development".

12. The 1998 Convention on the Prior Informed Consent Procedure for Certain Hazardous Chemicals and Pesticides in International Trade ("PIC Convention") is immersed with the relationship between trade and environment. Its first preambular paragraph reads, "[a]ware of the harmful impact on human health and the environment from certain hazardous chemicals and pesticides in international trade;" and it also contains "[R]ecognizing that trade and

environmental policies should be mutually supportive with a view to achieving sustainable development". Article 1 states the objective of the PIC Convention:

**PIC Convention
Article 1**

"The objective of this Convention is to promote shared responsibility and cooperative efforts among Parties in the international trade of certain hazardous chemicals in order to protect human health and the environment from potential harm and to contribute to their environmentally sound use, by facilitating information exchange about their characteristics, by providing for a national decision-making process on their import and export and by disseminating these decisions to Parties."

---

13. The 2001 Convention on Persistent Organic Pollutants ("POPs") includes in its Preamble, "[R]ecognizing that this Convention and other international agreements in the field of trade and the environment are mutually supportive." The same idea is also included in a variety of regional agreements.

14. The 1995 Agreement establishing the WTO includes the following guidance in the first paragraph of the Preamble:

"Recognizing that their relations in the field of trade and economic endeavour should be conducted with a view to raising standards of living, ensuring full employment and a large and steadily growing volume of real income and effective demand, and expanding the production of and trade in goods and services, while allowing for the optimal use of the world's resources in accordance with the objective of sustainable development, seeking both to protect and preserve the environment and to enhance the means for doing so in a manner consistent with their respective needs and concerns at different levels of economic development."

---

15. There is uncertainty about the implications when a state is a party to a MEA but not a member of the WTO, and viceversa. The use of trade sanctions to implement international environmental obligations raises possible conflicts between obligations under MEAs and obligations under the WTO. Such conflicts would be subject to the general rules of international law, as reflected in the 1969 Vienna Convention on the Law of Treaties (as discussed in chapter 1 of this Manual).

16. Applying these rules, it would follow that the trade restrictions established under post-1994 agreements, such as the 2000 Biosafety Protocol and the 2001 POPs Convention, would prevail

over inconsistent obligations established under the 1994 GATT (to the extent that they are inconsistent) when the states involved are parties to both the MEA as well as the GATT. In the case when a state is not a party to the relevant MEA, the obligations of the GATT might prevail, to the extent that the GATT obligations are inconsistent. The situation is slightly more complex in the case of pre-1994 MEAs, such as the 1987 Montreal Protocol and the 1989 Basel Convention. With the GATT 1947 being re-adopted as the GATT 1994 at the Uruguay Round of trade negotiations, the trade agreement is, at least technically, *the lex posterior*. However, the ruling of the WTO Appellate Body in the Shrimp/Turtle dispute suggests that trade restrictions in most MEAs, like the 1987 Montreal Protocol or the 1989 Basel Convention, are unlikely to fall afoul of the GATT 1994 requirements. Moreover, some MEAs may also be seen as *lex specialis* rules (i.e., more specific rules) than those embodied in the GATT.

17. Trade and environment are intertwined with one another. Indeed, trade rules can have a degrading impact on the environment, and environmental measures can interfere with free trade, by prohibiting trade in certain products or impose trade barriers in their aim to protect the environment. But besides this more negative and more visible correlation, the two regimes also have the possibility to coexist and to reinforce one another. The multi-faceted interrelation between the multilateral trading system and environmental regimes will be the focus of this chapter.

II. International Framework:
the Pillars of the World Trade Organization System - the Agreements and the Dispute Settlement Understanding

1. The Agreements of the World Trade Organization

18. As mentioned above, the WTO was established by the 1994 Marrakesh Agreement, which entered into force on 1 January 1995, and superseded the GATT as the international institution to regulate international trade. At its heart are the WTO Agreements, negotiated and ratified by the bulk of the world's trading nations. These documents form the legal basis for international commerce. Parties have to keep their trade policies within agreed limits. Although negotiated and signed by governments, the goal of the WTO Agreements is to help producers of goods and services, exporters, and importers to conduct their business, while attempting to allow governments to meet social and environmental objectives.

19. The WTO Agreements cover goods, services and intellectual property. The Agreements are structured in such a way that all members have to accept the whole 'package' which consists, in general, of: (a) the 1994 GATT, which comprises of the 1947 GATT as well as subsequent decisions on the application of its provisions, and which is augmented by twelve multilateral agreements such as the Agreement on Technical Barriers to Trade and the Agreement on Sanitary and Phytosanitary Measures, (b) the General Agreement on Trade in Services;,(c) the Agreement on Trade-Related Aspects of Intellectual Property Rights, and (d) the Understanding on Rules and Procedures governing the Settlement of Disputes. Some of the provisions of these agreements may have an impact on environmental issues and will be discussed in this chapter.

2. 1994 General Agreement on Tariffs and Trade

20. The 1994 General Agreement on Tariffs and Trade ("1994 General Agreement"), formally adopted at the 1994 Marrakesh Conference establishing the WTO, covers international trade in goods. The 1947 General Agreement is based on the 1947 GATT, and the developments and decisions adopted since that time. Promotion and liberalization of free trade has been the purpose of GATT since its inception. At the core of GATT are three principles:

i) The most-favoured-nation clause,
ii) The national treatment obligation, and
iii) Non-tariff barriers, quantitative restrictions and licenses.

21. The most-favoured-nation clause, found in article 1 of the 1994 General Agreement, ensures equality of treatment, and prohibits discrimination between the products of different importing states. A specific privilege or treatment given to products from one country is subsequently also granted to similar products from all WTO members. This rule tries to avoid different tariffs for different countries. For example, Country A favours the import of a certain product from Country B, by providing it cheaper custom charges and duties. At the same time, Country A imposes higher custom charges and duties on similar (the GATT language is 'like') imported products from other countries. The GATT does not allow this and the most-favoured-nation principle has to be applied to the like products of the other countries. The consequence for Country A is that it has to impose the same favoured custom charges and duties that Country B enjoys on the imported similar products of other countries.

22. The second key principle is included in article III of the 1994 General Agreement, the principle of national treatment. The essence of this principle is to prevent discrimination between imported and domestically produced goods. It requires importing countries to treat imported products the same as domestically 'like products.' Country X produces a product, but also imports 'like products' from Country Z. However, at the same time, Country X is posing an excessively high tax on the imported like products and a lower tax on their home-produced product. In such a case, the GATT's national treatment principle says that Country X has to apply the same taxes or regulations on imported like products from Country Z as they do on their own national products. No domestic laws should be applied to imported products to protect domestic producers.

23. The issue of 'like products' has given rise to long and intensive discussions. In each specific case, the term 'like product' has to be determined by taking into account a number of factors (e.g., the product's end use in a given market or the properties of the product). Moreover, discussions arose on another factor that has to be taken into account, namely the way products are produced or harvested, the so-called 'process and production methods' ("PPMs"). An example where the issue of PPMs became relevant was the catching of tuna in nets that killed dolphins as well. When the USA banned import of tuna from Mexico, which was caught with nets that also killed dolphins, the Dispute Settlement Panel ruled in 1991, that this action discriminated against 'like products'. In other words, an importing country cannot impose a ban on the like products of an exporting country member with a similar product, but which is produced or harvested in a different way. It is claimed that this encourages countries to maintain lower production standards concerning environmental conditions and animal, human or plant life, or health and safety. Environmentalists regarded this ruling as a setback for protecting the environment.

24. The third and final key principle is article XI, which aims to encounter non-tariff barriers. It prohibits quantitative restrictions to trade such as bans and quotas on imported and exported goods. This means that a country cannot enforce a regulation that imposes a quota on goods – for instance, to import not more than 5,000 pieces of a specific product - from another country to protect their own domestic 'like products'. Such a non-tariff barrier is considered to be an obstruction to international trade.

25. Moreover, members are obliged to transparency pursuant to article X (i.e., they have to publish all trade and trade-related measures to ensure certainty, predictability and accountability of governmental measures).

26. The international trading system (including its basic principles) is subject to a number of exceptions. Article XX of the 1994 GATT, entitled 'general exceptions', exempts from the obligations of the General Agreement measures that are necessary for achieving certain public objectives such as protection of public morals and protection of human, animal or plant life, health, national treasures, or exhaustible natural resources. Quantitative restrictions can be used to achieve these objectives, subject to the requirement that such measures are not applied in a manner that would constitute a means of arbitrary or unjustifiable discrimination between countries or as a disguised restriction on international trade.

27. For example, two exceptions to the most favoured-nation clause apply. The first exception applies to regional trade agreements. A large number of WTO members are party to one or more regional trade agreements; and preferential tariffs may be established between the parties of those agreements. Another exception applies to the least-developed countries. The WTO allows members to apply favoured tariff rates, or zero tariff rates, to products coming from these countries while applying higher rates for similar products from other countries. The objective of this exception is to promote economic development where it is most needed (article XVIII).

28. The possibility for a security exception also exists under article XXI, which allows a general deviation from the WTO obligations in cases where the security interests of a country are concerned. A member is allowed to take any action that it considers necessary for the protection of its essential security interests, and members are not required to furnish any information the disclosure of which would be contrary to their essential security interests. For example, quantitative restrictions are permissible in respect of trade in products which impinge on a country's security interests (e.g. arms and ammunition).

29. Environmental exceptions are also allowed. Article XI, which prohibits non-tariff barriers, may lead to conflicts with the provisions included in some MEAs. For example, the 1989 Basel Convention on the Control of Transboudary Movements of Hazardous Wastes and their Disposal ("Basel

Convention") and the 1973 Convention on International Trade in Endangered Species of Wild Fauna and Flora ("CITES") both contain regulations that impose license or permit requirements for trade in the materials that they control. For example, CITES has three appendices that limit the trade of endangered species listed in those appendices. Countries, however, are allowed to trade in these species on the condition that they have an export permit and, in the case of Appendix I, also an import permit. The use of permits to regulate trade is obviously a limitation to international trade, but it protects the environment. This measure falls within the scope of exemptions found in article XX of the GATT.

30. The two paragraphs of article XX that are relevant for environment-related measures are:

> "Subject to the requirement that such measures are not applied in a manner which would constitute a means of arbitrary or unjustifiable discrimination between countries where the same conditions prevail, or a disguised restriction on international trade, nothing in this Agreement shall be construed to prevent the adoption or enforcement by any contracting party of measures:
> ...(b) necessary to protect human, animal or plant life or health; and
> ...(g) relating to the conservation of exhaustible natural resources if such measures are made effective in conjunction with restrictions on domestic production or consumption"
> [...]

31. Before a country can apply these exceptions it must establish a provisional justification and a final justification. Paragraph (b) requires the party to prove that the rule is 'necessary' to protect the environment. The word 'necessary' requires that: (i) the state must prove the necessity of protecting its environment, (ii) in order to protect the environment, a rule that affects the free trade is needed, and (iii) the state must demonstrate that the used measure is the least trade-restrictive option.

32. Paragraph (g) allows countries to take action to conserve exhaustible natural resources. A state claiming an exception under this paragraph must first prove that the measure relates to the conservation of the exhaustible natural resource. Furthermore, the state must demonstrate that the measure is in conjunction with national restrictions on the exhaustible natural resource and is aimed primarily at the objective of conservation. When a measure passes this provisional justification, it must comply with the opening paragraph (the 'chapeau') of article XX, which addresses how the measure is applied. This is called the final justification.

33. The exceptions in article XX (b) and (g) of the GATT are being mirrored in the Agreement on Technical Barriers to Trade ("TBT") and the Agreement on the Application of Sanitary and Phytosanitary Measures ("SPS"). As discussed previously, the exceptions of article XX are a reason to apply a technical barrier, or a sanitary or phytosanitary measure. Such measures are only applicable if the exception threatens human, animal or plant life, or health. For instance, when a country uses growth hormones to raise chickens resulting in meat containing hormone residue that can be harmful for human health, a country could opt to prevent imports by citing the exception possibility. Another example, relating to the TBT Agreement, is where a country allows only CFC-free refrigerators to be imported. This is a technical barrier to international trade, to protect human, animal and plant life by decreasing the amount of CFC-gasses that deplete the ozone layer.

3. General Agreement on Trade in Services

34. The General Agreement on Trade in Service ("GATS") is the first agreement to set multilateral rules and commitments that direct government measures regarding trade in services. The GATS covers all services such as water, health, energy, tourism and education. Ranging from architecture to telecommunications and air transport, services are often the largest and most dynamic component of many developed and developing country economies. Important in their own right, these services also serve as crucial inputs into the production of most goods.

35. Part II of the GATS sets out "general obligations and disciplines", which are basic rules that apply to all members and, for the most part, to all services. The GATS article II, on most-favoured-nation treatment, directly parallels the centrally important article I of the GATT. The first paragraph states that "With respect to any measure covered by this Agreement, each member shall accord immediately and unconditionally to services and service suppliers of any other member treatment no less favourable that it accords to like services and service suppliers of any other country". This classical statement of the most-favoured-nation principle is, however, qualified. A member is permitted to maintain a measure inconsistent with the general most-favoured-nation requirement if it has established an exception for this inconsistency.

36. A second basic principle carried over from the GATT is transparency. Traders will be disadvantaged in doing business in a foreign country unless they know what laws and regulations they face. The GATS requires each member to publish promptly "all relevant measures of general application," that is, measures other than those which involve only individual service suppliers that affect operation of the Agreement.

37. The GATS provisions on general and security exceptions are similar to their GATT equivalents. This similarity reflects the fact that the overriding considerations which are recognized as allowing a country to ignore specific international obligations will apply as strongly to one aspect of its trade as to another. The general exceptions (article XIV) are, as in the GATT, preceded by the chapeau that makes the right of a member to adopt or enforce measures for the purposes listed subject to the condition that they are not applied as "a means of arbitrary or unjustifiable discrimination between countries where like conditions prevail, or a disguised restriction on trade in services...".

38. One general obligation of the GATS that has no GATT counterpart is article IX, which pioneers in a multilateral trade agreement in recognizing that "certain business practices" of service suppliers may restrain competition and thereby restrict trade in services. Members agree to consult on such practices, when so requested by another member, and to exchange information with a view to eliminating them.

39. Governments can make their own schedule of commitments related to services and determine the level of obligations they will require of foreign suppliers. This flexibility is in favour of developing countries, as they are expected to liberalize fewer service sectors in line with their development situation. The obligation schedules of developing countries are, in general, less extensive than those of developed countries.

40. There are four levels of flexibility within the GATS. First, governments decide in which sectors they will make commitments guaranteeing the foreign supplier to provide the service. Second, governments can set limitations on the services that are committed and can define the level of market access and degree of national treatment that they are prepared to give. Third, governments can renegotiate or even withdraw commitments. Finally, governments are allowed to provide more favourable treatment to some trading partners. In this regard, the governments can make exemptions from the most-favoured nation principle, which is otherwise applicable to all services. Since 2000, a new round of negotiations is underway "with a view to achieving a progressively higher level of liberalization" of trade in services.

4. Agreement on Trade-Related Investment Measures ("TRIMs")

41. Between 1990 and 2000, a significant rise in the mobility of capital has occurred. There was, notably, an increase of international investment in general, and of Foreign Direct Investment ("FDI") in particular. An example of FDI is an investment of a company based in Country A, which contributes to the equity of a company in Country B. Other types of investment are currency speculations and international portfolio investment, which is investment in stocks and shares. Increased capital flows and FDI may have an impact on the environment. Liberalizing investment measures may lead to the creation of 'pollution havens,' meaning that companies invest in another country to take advantage of less stringent environment measures or non-enforced environmental standards in that country.

42. TRIMs applies only to investment measures that affect trade in goods. Acknowledging that investment measures can have trade-restrictive effects, this Agreement prohibits a WTO member from applying a measure that is prohibited by the provisions of GATT article III (national treatment obligation) or XI (quantitative restrictions). In 1996, a Working Group was established to examine the relationship between trade and investment.

43. Many developing countries have made it clear that they consider that the Working Group had not completed however, analysis and study of the subject. They argue that the existing bilateral investment treaties (UNCTAD estimates that over 2,100 bilateral treaties are in operation) already provide adequate legal protection to investors, and question whether a WTO agreement would indeed increase investment flows. They have expressed concern that a multilateral agreement would add obligations to developing countries while limiting their ability to align investment inflows with national development objectives.

44. In the mid 1990s, efforts were made, under the auspices of the Organization on Economic Cooperation and Development ("OECD"), to establish a Multilateral Agreement on Investment ("MAI") which would allow for the free movement of capital across international borders by imposing

a new set of rules restricting countries from using legislation, policies and programmes as obstructions to the free flow of capital. In October 1998, the negotiations on MAI failed for a number of reasons, such as social and environmental concerns. The draft MAI was criticized by environmentalists for not providing adequate safeguards for the environment.

45. At the 2001 WTO Doha Ministerial Conference, the ministers recognized that "the case for a multilateral framework to secure transparent, stable and predictable conditions for long-term cross-border investment, particularly foreign direct investment". The ministers gave the Working Group a new and more ambitious mandate on this subject, and agreed that negotiations on an investment agreement would take place after the next ministerial conference in Cancun "on the basis of a decision to be taken, by explicit consensus at that Session on the modalities of negotiations (i.e., how the negotiations are to be conducted)".

46. However, in Cancun, no consensus was reached, in particular because of the major controversies surrounding the so-called 'Singapore issues.' Because the mandate came from the 1996 Singapore Ministerial Conference, trade and investment is sometimes described as one of four 'Singapore issues'. The other 'Singapore issues' are trade and competition policy, transparency in government procurement, and trade facilitation.

5. Agreement on Technical Barriers to Trade

47. The Agreement on Technical Barriers to Trade ("TBT Agreement") covers technical regulations and standards. Its objective is to ensure that WTO Members do not use technical regulations or standards in such a way that international trade is obstructed. The TBT Agreement tries to ensure that regulations, standards, testing and certification procedures do not create unnecessary obstacles. Technical regulations and product standards may vary from country to country. Having many different regulations and standards poses difficulties for producers and exporters. If regulations are set arbitrarily, they could be used as an excuse for protectionism. The TBT Agreement defines a technical regulation as a document that lays down the characteristics of the product or their related process and production measures. The TBT Agreement also deals with labelling and/or packaging as these methods apply to the production or process methods.

48. Article 2.2 of the TBT Agreement also includes environmental-related possibilities for exception:

> "Members shall ensure that technical regulations are not prepared, adopted or applied with a view to or with the effect of creating unnecessary obstacles to international trade. For this purpose, technical regulations shall not be more trade-restrictive than necessary to fulfil a legitimate objective.... Such legitimate objectives are, *inter alia*: national security requirements; the prevention of deceptive practices; protection of human health or safety, animal or plant life or health, or the environment..."

49. An example of a TBT measure is the use of hazardous or toxic materials in the packaging of products. If an exporting country uses toxic or hazardous materials, it may be subjected to a ban on its products by countries that ban products containing or being processed using toxic or hazardous wastes. Before a TBT measure can be applied, certain conditions have to be fulfilled. Technical regulations should not be more trade restrictive than necessary to fulfill their legitimate objective of article 2.

50. The TBT Agreement seeks harmonization of technical regulations and standards. The imposed regulations and standards should be based on available and relevant standards from an international body. The Agreement also requires that, when the objective that gave rise for the application of the regulation or standard no longer exists, then the regulation or standard has to be removed. The same applies when there is a less trade restrictive regulation available.

6. Agreement on the Application of Sanitary and Phytosanitary Measures

51. The Sanitary and Phytosanitary Agreement ("SPS Agreement") governs regulations aimed at protecting human, animal and plant health. Almost all states have regulations to ensure that food is safe for consumers, and to prevent the spread of pests or diseases among animals and plants. These sanitary (human and animal health) and phytosanitary (plant health) measures can take many forms, such as requiring products to come from a disease-free area, inspection of products, specific treatment or processing of products, setting of allowable maximum levels of pesticide residues or permitted use of only certain additives in food. The measures usually apply to domestically produced food or local animal and plant diseases, as well as to products coming from other countries.

52. Sanitary and phytosanitary measures may result in restrictions on trade. All governments accept the fact that some trade restrictions may be necessary to ensure food safety and animal and plant health protection. However, sometimes governments go beyond what is needed for health protection and use sanitary and phytosanitary restrictions to shield domestic producers from economic competition. The basic aim of the SPS Agreement is to maintain the sovereign right of any government to provide the level of health protection it deems appropriate, but to ensure that these sovereign rights are not misused for protectionist purposes and do not result in unnecessary barriers to international trade.

53. The SPS Agreement still allows countries to set their own standards, but it also states that regulations must be based on science. They should be applied only to the extent necessary to protect human, animal or plant life or health (article 2.(2)). Further, regulations should not arbitrarily or unjustifiably discriminate between countries where identical or similar conditions prevail.

54. The SPS Agreement includes provisions on control, inspection and approval procedures. Governments must provide advance notice of new or changed sanitary and phytosanitary regulations, and establish a national enquiry point to provide information.

55. Due to differences in climate, existing pests or diseases, or food safety conditions, it is not always appropriate to impose the same sanitary and phytosanitary requirements on food, animal or plant products coming from different countries. Therefore, the SPS Agreement recognizes that sanitary and phytosanitary measures sometimes vary, depending on the country of origin of the food, animal or plant product concerned.

7. Agreement on Trade-Related Aspects of Intellectual Property Rights

56. For a discussion of the Agreement on Trade-Related Aspects of Intellectual Property Rights ("TRIPS"), reference is made to chapter 15 of this Training Manual on Biological Diversity.

8. Dispute Settlement Understanding ("DSU")

57. Besides the WTO Agreements, an important pillar of the World Trade System is WTO's Dispute Settlement Understanding, which can be seen as the central element of the WTO to provide security and predictability to the international trading system. The DSU was agreed upon during the Uruguay Round, and is in many ways more evolved than it was under the trading system before 1994. The DSU sets out the various stages in the settlement procedure and the timetable to be followed in resolving disputes. However, the time limits are not rigid. For example, when a case is considered urgent, if it involves perishable goods, then the case should be decided upon in less time. Furthermore, the DSU makes it impossible for the country that looses the case to block the adoption of the ruling. The ruling, in the initial as well as in the appeal stage, is automatically adopted unless there is consensus on rejecting the ruling. This is a big step forward from the 1947 GATT, where consensus was needed to adopt the ruling, so it could be blocked by a single objection.

58. The body that deals with the settlement of disputes is the Dispute Settlement Body ("DSB"), which is actually the General Council meeting as the Dispute Settlement Body, made up of all member governments. The Dispute Settlement Body is solely authorized to establish the 'Panels' that will consider the case, and to accept or reject the Panels' findings or the results of an appeal. The Dispute Settlement Body also monitors the implementation of the rulings and the recommendations; and it also has the power to authorize sanctions if the country that lost the case does not comply with the ruling.

59. Before it is decided to establish a Panel to contemplate the case, the countries in the dispute at hand have to enter into negotiations to see if they can settle their differences by themselves. They can request the WTO Director-General to mediate or try to help in any other way. If this stage (up to 60 days) of consultation fails, the complaining country can request the DSB to appoint a Panel. Within 45 days, the Panel is to be established and the panellists are to be appointed. The final report of the Panel has to present to the parties within six months, and three weeks later it has to be circulated to all WTO members. Panels, which mostly consist of three experts, examine the evidence and decide on the case. The Panel's report, which contains the rulings or recommendations, is submitted to the DSB. Despite the 'assisting role' of the Panels, their conclusions are difficult to overturn, as this can only be done by consensus within the DSB.

60. If the ruling does not satisfy a party to the dispute, it may appeal against the ruling. The appeal has to be based on points of law such as raising questions about the legal interpretation of the provisions in question. It may not request the re-examination of evidence or provide new evidence. The appeal procedure is handled by the Appellate Body,

consisting of seven permanent members, of which three members will hear the appeal. The Appellate Body can uphold, reverse or modify the Panel's ruling. It should take the Appellate Body between 60 and 90 days to come up with an appeals report. The appeals report will be accepted unconditionally by the DSB after 30 days from the issuance to the members. The report can only be rejected through the DSB by consensus.

61. If the report, the 'Panel's report' if there is no appeal and the 'Appeals report' if there is an appeal, is accepted, the affected party has to bring its law and/or policy in 'prompt' compliance with the recommendations or rulings. The country must state its willingness to do so at a DSB meeting to be held within 30 days after the report's adoption. If it is impossible to comply promptly, the country will be given a 'reasonable period of time' to do so. When the country fails to comply with the recommendations and rulings within the reasonable time period, it has to negotiate with the complainant to determine mutually acceptable compensation, such as, for example, elimination or

reduction of quotas or licenses. If there is then no agreement within 20 days then the complaining country can ask for limited trade sanctions.

62. Despite the numerous suggestions for improvements or clarifications, underlying these proposals is the shared conviction amongst all members that overall the DSU has served them well since it started operating. This is illustrated by the fact that more than 300 cases have been brought to the DSB since 1995, compared with the final total of 300 cases filed during the entire 47 years of the former GATT. At the Doha Ministerial Conference, member states agreed to negotiate to improve and clarify the DSU. Originally, it was agreed to conclude these negotiations before May 2003. On 24 May 2003, acknowledging the fact that the DSB special session needed more time to conclude its work, the General Council agreed to extend teh special sessions timeframe by one year to May 2004. A futher extension was agreed by the General Council on 1 August 2004 current setting a new deadline. However, no consensus has been reached yet.

Table 1: Dispute Settlement Understanding Stages

These approximate periods for each stage of a dispute settlement procedure are target figures - the agreement is flexible. In addition, the countries can settle their dispute themselves at any stage. Totals are also approximate. (source: www.wto.org)

60 days	Consultations, mediation, etc
45 days	Panel set up and panellists appointed
6 months	Final panel report to parties
3 weeks	Final panel report to WTO members
60 days	Dispute Settlement Body adopts report (if no appeal)
Total = 1 year	(without appeal)
60-90 days	Appeals report
30 days	Dispute Settlement Body adopts appeals report
Total = 1 year 3 months	(with appeal)

9. Institutional Structure of the World Trade Organization

63. As of December 2005, the WTO has 149 members, which all have one vote in the system. Decisions in the WTO are normally taken by consensus. A majority vote is also possible, but this option is hardly ever used.

64. The highest authority in the WTO belongs to the Ministerial Conference ("MC"). This body meets at least once every two years and is composed of the relevant ministers of the WTO countries, such as ministers for economic affairs, foreign affairs, industry, etcetera. Since the establishment of the WTO in 1994, they have met five times. The first MC was held in 1996, in Singapore, and the most recent MC was held in Cancun, in September 2003. The MC can take decisions on all issues dealt with under the multilateral trade agreements.

65. The next level is the General Council. This body meets several times a year at WTO's Geneva Headquarters and consists of government representatives (usually ambassadors or equivalent) of all members. The Council acts on behalf of the MC in all WTO affairs, it is handling the day-to-day work in between Ministerial Conferences. The Council also meets as the Trade Policy Review Body, to review members' policies, and as the Dispute Settlement Body, to settle disputes between WTO members. The Council reports to the MC.

66. The next level is composed by Councils: the Goods Council, the Service Council and the Intellectual Property ("TRIPS") Council. They all report to the General Council, and are responsible for the functioning and implementation of the agreement related to their area of expertise. The Councils have committees who keep them informed about developments in issues relating to trade, services or intellectual property.

67. Six other committees and working groups are also reporting to the General Council. The WTO members are all represented in these committees. The committees deal with issues such as development, environment, regional trade agreements, investment, competition policy and government procurement.

68. The Committee on Trade and Environment ("CTE") has been established during the Uruguay Round in 1994. The objective of the CTE is to study the relationship between trade and environment and to make recommendations on the need for rules to enhance the positive interaction between trade and environment measures for the promotion of sustainable development.

69. The CTE's work is focused on two principles. First, the WTO Members do not want the WTO to intervene in the setting of national and international environmental standards, as it is not an environmental agency. This should be left to the competent organs of MEAs, such as the Conference of the Parties ("COP"). The WTO is solely competent to deal with international trade and in the area of environment, and its main task is to raise questions when environmental measures have significant impact on trade and viceversa. The second important principle where the CTE is based upon is to uphold the WTO rules in case a conflict arises between environmental regulations and multilateral trade agreements.

70. At the Fourth Ministerial Conference in Doha in 2001, Ministers instructed the CTE to focus particularly on three issues: the effects of environmental measures on market access, the relevant provisions of the TRIPS Agreement, and labelling requirements for environmental purposes. It was also agreed that the CTE should deal with (i) the relationship between existing WTO rules and specific trade obligations set out in Multilateral Environmental Agreements ("MEAs"), (ii) procedures for regular information exchange between MEA Secretariats and the relevant WTO committees, and the criteria for the granting of observer status, and (iii) the reduction or, as appropriate, elimination of tariff and non-tariff barriers to environmental goods and services.

71. The CTE has not come up with effective solutions for the interlinked issues of trade and environment, but merely discussed and analyzed the problems. While its mandate was broad, its powers were less so. It is institutionally separated from the WTO Committees that have direct responsibility for the ongoing development of the specific agreements most relevant to environmental issues, such as the Committees on Technical Barriers to Trade, and on Sanitary and Phytosanitary Measures, and the Councils for TRIPS and Services. The CTE has not been able to move many of the trade and environment issues within its mandate very far forward. However, the lack of significant progress in the CTE did not always lead to stagnation in the broader debate. For example, some topics of the CTE agenda have been addressed with success outside the WTO. It may be possible for the CTE to become more powerful through the mandate to conduct the trade and environment-related negotiations in special negotiations sessions. Also, the ongoing meetings of the CTE with several MEA Secretariats focusing on exchange of information, technical assistance and capacity building could provide a further basis to enhance the mutual supportiveness between the multilateral trading system and international environmental law.

72. The broad agenda launched at the fourth WTO Ministerial Conference in Doha in 2001 was expected to conclude and provide results by 1 January 2005, but the pace of negotiations is rather slow and did not meet this deadline. A Sixth Ministerial Conference was held in Hong Kong, China from 13 - 18 December 2005, and the aim is to complete the Doha Round in 2006. One of the issues that is scheduled to have been agreed upon is the definition of the concept of an "environmental good", and to identify environmental goods that are in the export interest of developing-country members, whilst bearing in mind the potential for these negotiations to deliver "environmental" as well as "trade" gains.

10. Examples of cases dealt with by the Dispute Settlement System of the GATT/WTO concerning Environmental Issues

73. The GATT and the other additional agreements do not provide a straightforward framework for if a conflict occurs between free trade and environmental protection. The application of article XX to trade-restrictive rules in multilateral environmental agreements and national legislation has been proven difficult. This problem of settling competing social and economic values is being addressed by the Committee on Trade and Environment, as mentioned above. Further, the GATT/WTO introduced an extensive system, the Dispute Settlement Understanding, to deal with trade-related disputes. A dispute may arise when one country adopts a trade policy measure or takes some action that one or more fellow-WTO members considers to be breaking the WTO agreements, or to be a failure to live up to obligations.

74. Only a small number of cases brought to the dispute settlement system of GATT/WTO raised questions on environmental measures or human health. Although the number of cases before the WTO Dispute Settlement Body has increased significantly in comparison to the GATT, environmental issues have only been raised in a very limited number of cases. Among the landmark cases on the relationship between trade and environment (since 1948) are the Thai cigarettes case, the Asbestos case, the Reformulated gasoline case, the Beef hormones case, the Tuna-Dolphin cases and the Shrimp-Turtle case, of which the latter two will be discussed into more detail below. They dealt with a variety of environmentally-related issues such as health, the interpretation of 'like products,' PPM-based measures, etc.

75. Tuna-Dolphin cases (1991, 1993). Since, on the high seas, some specific species of Tuna swim in the proximity of dolphins, fishermen caught dolphins when catching tuna. Unless special protective measures are used, dolphins die in the process and since they have no commercial value, they are just discarded as bycatch. The GATT Dispute Settlement Panel ruled that a United States unilaterally imposed import embargo of 'tuna not caught in a dolphin-friendly manner' was in contradiction with the GATT rules (article XI). Article XX of the GATT, which provides exceptions for measures that are 'necessary' to protect human and animal life and health (XX(b)) and that are 'in relation to' the 'conservation of exhaustible natural resources' (XX(g)), could not be used as a justification. The Tuna/Dolphin Panel held that these exceptions applied to measures which were the least trade restrictive. The Panel found that other less-trade restrictive measures, such as negotiation of an international agreement, might have been undertaken in place of the unilateral measure. Widely criticized, the Tuna/Dolphin rulings were never adopted by the competent the GATT organ.

76. In the Shrimp/Turtle case (1998), the Appellate Body ("AB") took a different approach than the Panel in the Tuna/Dolphin cases to unilaterally imposed trade measures with the aim to protect the global environment. The US banned import of shrimps from some south-east Asian countries, major shrimp exporters, in accordance with US legislation, which prohibited the import of shrimps caught without the use of a so-called 'Turtle Excluding Device'. This Device is a specific net that prevent the incidental catch and killing of turtles, because many sea turtles are killed in nets that shrimp trawlers use to catch shrimp.

77. The US listed all sea turtles as endangered or threatened under the Endangered Species Act, and prohibited the taking of all endangered turtles not only within the US and its territorial sea, but also on the high seas. Further, a US law instructed the US Secretary of State to initiate negotiations dealing with international agreements for the protection and conservation of sea turtles and prohibited the import of shrimps harvested with wrong technology. Four states –India, Pakistan, Malaysia and Thailand– brought a complaint under the DSU arguing that the US measure violated Article XI.

78. The AB held that the import ban was not consistent with article XI. With regard to article XX, the AB ruled that this provision imposes two requirements on trade measures that condition market access on other countries' policies. First, such measures must fit within one of article XX's specific exceptions. Second, such measures must be applied in a manner consistent with article XX's chapeau. That is, their application must neither give rise to unjustified or arbitrary discrimination between countries where the same conditions prevail, nor create a disguised restriction on international trade.

79. In the Shrimp/Turtle case, the AB held that the US measure, which prohibited imports of shrimp from any country that did not have a turtle-conservation programme comparable to that of the US, fits within the article XX(g) exception for conservation of exhaustible natural resources, and so decided that sea turtles are an exhaustible natural resource:

"132. We turn next to the issue of whether the living natural resources sought to be conserved by the measure are "exhaustible" under Article XX(g). That this element is present in respect of the five species of sea turtles here involved appears to be conceded by all the participants and third participants in this case. The exhaustibility of sea turtles would in fact have been very difficult to controvert since all of the seven recognized species of sea turtles are today listed in Appendix 1 of the Convention on International Trade in Endangered Species of Wild Fauna and Flora ("CITES"). The list in Appendix 1 includes "all species threatened with extinction which are or may be affected by trade"."

80. However, the AB also found that the US measures had been applied in a way that violated the Chapeau of article XX, which requires that an applied measure should not constitute 'arbitrary or unjustifiable discrimination between countries where the same conditions prevail' or a 'disguised restriction on international trade'.

81. The AB ruled that the US measure was not falling within the scope of the Chapeau. The trade ban by the US forced other countries to comply with US legislation, through implementing the same policy, in order to qualify for export to the US, and did not take into consideration the different conditions that may occur in the territories of other members. Furthermore, the US had not undertaken the same efforts to reach an international agreement with the southeast Asian states as it has done with American and Caribbean states. The AB therefore found that the US measures did not fall within the Chapeau and qualified the ban as 'unjustifiable discrimination,' even more so while there were other appropriate measures available with a similar impact.

82. In 2001, three years after its Shrimp/Turtle ruling, the AB clarified and elaborated on its original holding. One of the 1998 Shrimp/Turtle complainants, Malaysia, challenged the measures the US had taken in response to the AB decision. This 2001 AB ruling was in favour of the US and held that the measures taken by the US in implementing the earlier ruling (e.g., in entering a Memorandum of Understanding with southeast Asian states, had brought its turtle-friendly trade measures in conformity with article XX).

Table 2: MEAs and their impact on trade

Environmental agreement	Trade measures
Ozone Layer	
Vienna Convention for the Protection of the Ozone Layer (1985)	No explicit trade provisions. However, the obligation to take appropriate measures against the further depletion of the ozone layer can have implications for international trade
Montreal Protocol on Substances that deplete the Ozone Layer (1987)	Import and export restrictions of certain substances to and from non-parties and export restrictions to non-parties of technology that produce ozone-depleting substances
Climate Change	
United Nations Framework Convention on Climate Change (UNFCCC) (1992)	No direct trade restrictions, but actions of countries implementing the UNFCCC could have significant trade implications
Kyoto Protocol (Protocol to UNFCCC) (1997)	Implementing policies with the objective of reducing greenhouse-gas emissions will have an impact on international trade
Biological Diversity	
Convention on International Trade in Endangered Species of Wild Fauna and Flora (CITES) (1973)	Regulation of trade in certain species through permits and quotas
Convention on Biological Diversity (1992)	No explicit reference to any trade measures, but several articles create obligations that may result in such measures
Cartagena Protocol on Biosafety (Protocol to the Convention on Biological Diversity) (2000)	Importing countries need to give consent for the introduction of living modified organisms
International Tropical Timber Agreement (1994)	There are no trade-measures in the ITTA itself. However, ITO's mandate, promoting trade in tropical timber from sustainable managed sources, could have an impact on trade
Transboundary Movement of Hazardous Wastes	
Basel Convention on the Control of Transboundary Movements of Hazardous Wastes and their Disposal (1989)	Import and export restrictions on hazardous wastes to and from both parties and non-parties
Rotterdam Convention on the Prior Informed Consent Procedure for Certain Hazardous Chemicals and Pesticides in International Trade (PIC) (1998)	Information requirements and need to obtain consent from the importing party for certain the import of certain chemicals
Stockholm Convention on Persistent Organic Pollutants (POPs)(2001)	Import and export restrictions for certain persistent organic pollutants

11. Trade and Multilateral Environmental Agreements

83. As the amount of Multilateral Environmental Agreements ("MEAs") continues to grow, the number of such agreements that have an impact on free trade continue to rise as well. At the moment, the WTO distinguishes almost forty multilateral environmental agreements that include trade measures, the most important of which can be found in Table 2.

12. Trade-Restrictive Measures in Multilateral Environmental Agreements

84. A wide variety of reasons for why trade measures are included in Multilateral Environmental Agreements ("MEAs") can be given. One of these is that MEAs may simply want to control trade, because free trade provides incentives that threaten the environment or encourage unsustainable exploitation of natural resources. For example, there might be a high demand for a bird that is an endangered species. Allowing free trade would scatter these birds all over the world and destroy any reproducing population that still exists. Not tolerating the trade in this species may then be necessary to ensure its survival.

85. Another reason can be that the MEA aims to discourage environmentally harmful production processes and the migration of industries to countries with lower environmental standards. For example, environment polluting production processes may be cheaper than environmentally friendly ones. To prevent environmental damage, a MEA may be agreed upon that contains measures which stimulate the use of the environmentally friendlier processes. Subsequently, trade measures are needed to prevent industries from moving to another country that is not a party to the MEA, producing there with environmentally damaging processes, which could be followed by exporting the product to countries that are party to the MEA.

86. Additional objectives are to create market opportunities and incentives to use or dispose of a good in an environmentally sound manner, and to induce producers to internalize the costs to the environment caused by their products or production processes. Finally, the MEA may want to limit the entry of a harmful substance into a country.

87. Very detailed classifications of different kinds of trade measures in MEAs do not exist. However, the distinction between party and non-party measures is frequently made, as well as the difference between specific and non-specific trade measures.

Party measures are measures that only apply to parties to the agreement, whereas non-party measures apply to countries that are no party to it. The terms 'specific trade measures' and 'non-specific trade measures' specify the difference between measures that can literally be read in the MEA (specific trade measures), and measures that are not laid down in the MEA itself, but are introduced by parties to fulfil the obligations of the agreement (non-specific trade measures).

13. Reconciling Trade-Restrictive Provisions with GATT 1994

88. Although no conflict between MEAs and the GATT/WTO has arisen so far in practice, the 1987 Montreal Protocol, with its objective of phasing out chlorofluorcarbons ("CFCs"), may be used to illustrate how trade provisions in a MEA might, in the future, conflict with the GATT/WTO, in particular with articles I, III and XI of the 1994 GATT. The examples given below are hypothetical and should be regarded as describing areas of potential future conflict.

89. The Montreal Protocol allows its parties to trade with other parties as well as non-parties, but with the latter group only if certain conditions are met. The Montreal Protocol imposes restrictions on parties to trade with non-parties with products that contain CFCs. These trade provisions can conflict with articles I and III of the 1994 GATT if the non-party is a WTO member. For instance, Country A - party to the Montreal Protocol and a WTO member - trades with Country B, also a party to the Protocol and a WTO-member, in a CFC-free product. However, Country C, a non-party to the Montreal Protocol but a WTO member, has 'like products' but these are produced by using CFCs. Therefore Country A bans the trade with Country C, because the products were produced using CFCs, and it will only trade with Country B, whose products are CFC-free.

90. As mentioned before, the GATT Dispute Panels ruled that 'like products' using different manufacturing methods do not affect the characteristics of the product. Hence the above-mentioned products are the same, even if the country uses a production method that involves CFCs. Therefore, Country C can bring a claim of discrimination (article I of the GATT). The same applies regarding article III of the GATT. However, the difference is that the imported product should be treated the same as the domestic product. An example is when Country A imposes an environmental tax on the products of Country C,

because they are produced using CFCs, and not on their own CFC-free product. Country C can then file a claim of discrimination. Both products are 'like products' and therefore the product of Country C should be treated equally as Country A's domestic product, if there would be no environmental exception in the GATT.

91. The trade rule can also be in conflict with article XI of the GATT, because the imposed trade ban by Country A on the products of Country C forms a quantitative restriction according to article XI.

92. As noted, article XX(b) of the GATT provides an exception that can permit the trade measure. The measure, however, must be necessary to protect human, animal and plant life or health and it has to be the least trade restrictive measure available. To qualify for this exception there must be no alternative available that is less inconsistent with the GATT Agreement. If the trade provisions in the Montreal Protocol can qualify for the necessity test and there are no less trade restrictive measures available, then the trade provision can be approved under the WTO.

14. Regional Trade Agreements and the Environment

93. The WTO provides a global framework for international trade. Alongside the WTO, there is an increasing number of regional and bilateral trade agreements. Various reasons have been given for this trend, one of them being that it appears increasingly difficult to come to trade agreements on the global level. Thus, a number of states revert to bilateral agreements regulating certain trade aspects between them.

94. Further, regional free trade zones have been or are being established. In this Section, four regional trade agreements will be discussed, especially regarding their provisions dealing with environmental concerns. Regional trade agreements have been concluded also in other regions of the world. Examples are the Association of Southeast Asian Nations ("ASEAN"), the Economic Community of West African States ("ECOWAS"), the Common Market for Eastern and Southern Africa ("COMESA"). The agreements aim, in general, at a closer economic cooperation between their member states. Until now, they have not yet discussed the relationship between trade and environment in detail (e.g., as has been done in the North American Free Trade Agreement or the European Union), but it is supposed that similar questions will arise in the future.

a) North American Free Trade Agreement

95. The North American Free Trade Agreement ("NAFTA") is a free trade agreement between Canada, Mexico and the USA. It was adopted in 1992 and entered into force on 1 January 1994. It was one of the first regional trade agreements that took environmental concerns elaborately into account.

96. NAFTA allows environmental measures that influence trade on two different grounds. The first ground includes standard-related measures as well as sanitary and phytosanitary measures. The starting point for these measures is that each of the three countries is allowed to set its own levels of protection. If a party believes that a certain product is too dangerous it can even ban it, without breaking any NAFTA rules. Of course, this party will have to ensure that the ban is imposed on all 'like products' and not only on, for example, imported ones.

97. The second category of measures is those taken to implement some listed international environmental agreements. Unfortunately, this list of international environmental agreements contains only a few of the international environmental agreements that influence free trade.

98. Apart from these provisions, NAFTA contains some general provisions on the environment, like the ones in the Preamble and article 1114(2) in which parties recognize that "it is inappropriate to encourage investment by relaxing... environmental measures." However, no enforcement measures apply to this Article.

99. NAFTA also contains much-commented provisions that were made to protect investors' interests, but have been used to attack environmental legislation. Article 1110, for example, provides protection against uncompensated expropriation of investments. This has led, among others, to the case of S.D. Myers vs Canada, in which Myers, a company specialized in treating toxic waste, was awarded damages for not being allowed to export toxic waste out of Canada. The Tribunal held that the Canadian law banning the export of PCBs was not for a legitimate environmental purpose, but for protection of Canadian enterprises from US competition. Canada breached its NAFTA obligations and was liable to pay compensation. In January 2004, the Federal Court of Canada rejected a Canadian request to set aside the NAFTA arbitration decision.

100. One of the side agreements to NAFTA, the North American Agreement on Environmental Cooperation ("NAAEC") focuses on environmental effects of trade. However, negotiations about this side agreement only started after those on NAFTA had been finished. It was then agreed that no changes to NAFTA would be made anymore. This made it difficult to actually address trade-related issues in NAAEC.

101. In general, NAAEC can be divided into two parts. The first part establishes a framework for environmental cooperation between the three participating governments by, for example, establishing a North American Commission on Environmental Cooperation ("NACEC"). This part also lays down the broad environmental agenda for the NAFTA countries and enumerates the ecological challenges they face. The second part contains a dispute settlement procedure. This dispute settlement procedure is to be used when anyone claims that a party is not effectively enforcing its environmental laws.

102. The NAAEC's main objectives are the promotion of sustainable development, the encouragement of policies preventing pollution, and improving the compliance of environmental laws and policies. Furthermore, the NAAEC also promotes public participation and transparency in the development and enhancement of environmental laws and policies. An important provision of the NAAEC is that parties are obligated to maintain high environmental laws and are not allowed to lower their environmental standards to attract investment. In addition, each party agreed to enforce its environmental laws and as support for that they can establish a monitoring system.

b) Free Trade Agreement of the Americas

103. At the 1994 First Summit of the Americas held in Miami, the 34 states of the region started to negotiate the Free Trade Area of the Americas ("FTAA"), in which barriers to trade and investment will be progressively eliminated. The states also agreed to finalize these negotiations before 2005. They adopted the Miami Summit's Declaration of Principles and Plan of Action. Since then, eight FTAA Trade Ministerial meetings have taken place, as well as three other Summits of the Americas, most recently in January 2004.

104. A Trade Negotiations Committee has been established and the various drafts of the FTAA have been elaborately discussed. There is currently a third draft, dated November 2001. The FTAA can co-exist with bilateral and sub-regional agreements, to the extent that the rights and obligations under these agreements are not covered by or go beyond the rights and obligations of the FTAA, and that the FTAA will be consistent with the rules and disciplines of the World Trade Organization ("WTO").

105. The FTAA draft, as it stands now, contains almost the same investment provisions as NAFTA. As mentioned previously, this gives corporations the option to hold the government liable for any damages occurred through the implementation of legislation. Another important area that the FTAA is focusing on is that of liberalization of services, such as education, environmental services, health and energy.

106. The original 1994 mandate for the FTAA contained a promise to promote economic integration of the hemisphere in such a way as "to guarantee sustainable development while protecting the environment". A major Summit on Sustainable Development was held in Bolivia, in 1996, to ensure that the principles of the 1992 Rio Earth Summit would be integral to the FTAA process. Out of that meeting, at which civil society groups and environmentalists were notably absent, came 65 initiatives know as the 'Santa Cruz Action Plan,' and a new body, the OAS Inter-American Committee on Sustainable Development. However, no clear mandate for action evolved from this process and as result it was dropped from the FTAA's new mandate at the Santiago Summit in 1998.

107. The Draft FTAA includes chapter VI, entitled 'Environment Provisions,' but there are also states who do not wish to see the inclusion of such a chapter at all. These states argue that environmental issues are outside the FTAA negotiation mandate. Also taking into account that the Declaration of Nuevo León which was adopted in January 2004, at the Special Summit of the Americas, which hardly includes any references to environment, it remains a highly contentious issue. What the final contents of the FTAA will be is still very much open to debate, as is its date of adoption.

c) Mercado Común del Sur

108. The MERCOSUR, or *Mercado Común del Sur* (Southern Common Market), was created by Brazil, Uruguay, Paraguay and Argentina in March 1991, by the Treaty of Asunción. The MERCOSUR originally was set up with the ambitious goal of

creating a common market/customs union between the participating countries on the basis of various forms of economic cooperation that had been taking place between Argentina and Brazil since 1986. It is now a customs union, meaning that all members have the same tariffs to the outside world and is committed eventually to becoming a full common market. In this sense the MERCOSUR aspires to regional integration like the EU, rather than a free trade area like NAFTA.

109. The Protocol of Ouro Preto of 1994 added much to the institutional structure of MERCOSUR. A transition phase was set to begin in 1995, and to last until 2006, with a view to constituting the common market. In 1996, association agreements were signed with Chile and Bolivia establishing free trade areas with these countries. Furthermore, a dispute settlement system has been established with a view to strengthen MERCOSUR's institutionalization.

110. Regarding the environment, MERCOSUR only contained a general goal that the environment was to be preserved. The MERCOSUR structure, though still evolving, provides several environment-related innovations. Mechanisms for public participation were provided in the original Protocol of Ouro Preto, through a Social and Economic Advisory Council, which exists as part of the MERCOSUR institutional structure. This Council receives information from labour, business and consumer representatives.

111. More explicit environment and trade linkages are made through various legal mechanisms that combine as elements of a developing regime. Several resolutions of the *Grupo Mercado Común* (Common Market Group) and decisions of the *Consejo de Mercado Común* (Common Market Council) have touched upon issues such as pesticides, energy policies and transport of hazardous products.

112. In 1992, the informal *Reunión Especializada de Medio Ambiente* ("REMA") (Special year Meeting of the Environment), was established to analyze and, if possible, harmonize, the environmental laws of the parties. Later, REMA was elevated to an official subgroup of the Common Market Working Group, called 'the Environment'. The objective of this subgroup is to propose ways to protect the environment while avoiding violation of the concept of free trade and similar conditions of competitiveness apply in all member countries. This group has discussed issues such as environment and competitiveness, non-tariff barriers to trade, and common systems of environmental information.

113. Because of the work of this Working Group, the parties accepted a Framework Agreement on the Environment in 2001. The objective of the Framework Agreement is 'sustainable development and environmental protection through the development of economic, social and environmental dimensions, contributing to a better quality of environment and life for the people'.

114. The Framework Agreement focuses on increased cooperation on shared ecosystems and upward harmonisation of environmental management systems, among others, through cooperation on the development of instruments for environmental management. Besides, the Agreement contains provisions for dispute settlement and for the future development of protocols in three areas: quality of life and environmental management, sustainable management of natural resources and environmental policy.

115. In 2003, several events contributed to the further strengthening of MERCOSUR. The newly elected presidents of Argentina and Brazil put MERCOSUR at the top of their political agenda. Among the initiatives is the appointment of the ex-president of Argentina as the President of the newly established Committee of Permanent Representatives of MERCOSUR.

d) European Union

116. In 1957, six European countries adopted the Treaty of Rome establishing the European Economic Community, with the objective to establish an economic union between its member states. Since then, a number of major treaty revisions have taken place, such as the Single European Act (1986), the Treaty on European Union (Maastricht 1992), and the Amsterdam Treaty (1997).

117. These revision created a legal system between the member states which goes far beyond those established between sovereign states until now. The European Union ("EU") is itself generating legislation which directly applies to European citizens and confers specific rights on which they can rely. The strengthening of the political ties, besides the economics, has become a significant policy of the EU as well.

118. The boost given to community integration had the effect of prompting a vast enlargement process to include countries of central and eastern Europe. As of 1 May 2004, the EU has been enlarged to 25 members, and more accessions are expected in 2007.

119. At the heart of the EU lies a single market with common external tariffs. This makes the EU, in the first place, a regional trade agreement. An extensive harmonization process of health, safety and environmental standards has been taking place, mainly in an 'upwards' direction, that is, most standards were put at a rather high level. States that want to join the EU have to adapt their standards to the EU standards.

120. The EU allows its member states to ban imports from other member states that do not comply with standards for health, safety and environmental protection. Most important EU trade and environment cases before the European Court of Justice have addressed the conflict between the treaty articles ensuring the free movement of goods and services and exceptions for environmental protection.

121. EU member states are allowed to impose higher standards that restrict trade, but this restriction has to be proportional to the threat that is posed to health, safety or environment. Nevertheless, as in NAFTA, (disproportional) trade restrictions imposed to protect the environment have led to court rulings against certain environmental legislation of EU member states.

122. The 1997 Amsterdam Treaty included the principle of sustainable development as one of the European Community's aims and makes a high degree of environmental protection one of its absolute priorities. To promote global sustainability, the EU endeavours to integrate environmental concerns in its external relations and trade policies. They attempt to focus on developing stronger global cooperation on environmental issues and on bettering the balance between liberalized trade rules and multilateral environmental agreements. The 2002 sixth action programme for the environment sets out the priorities for the European Community up to 2010. Four areas are highlighted: climate change, nature and biodiversity, environment and health, and the management of natural resources and waste. Measures to achieve these priorities are outlined: improving the application of environmental legislation, working together with the market and citizens and ensuring that other Community policies take greater account of environmental considerations.

123. The range of environmental instruments available has expanded as environmental policy has developed. Not only has the Community adopted framework legislation providing for a high level of environmental protection while guaranteeing the operation of the internal market, but it has introduced a financial instrument (the LIFE programme) and technical instruments, such as eco-labelling, the Community system of environmental management and auditing, the system for assessment of the effects of public and private projects on the environment, and the criteria applicable to environmental inspections in the member states.

III. National Implementation

124. In this Section, two examples of national legislation will be reviewed. The first one is the 1992 Namibian Sea Fisheries Act, which contains quotas for fisheries. These quotas can have a limiting effect on free trade, but are in favour of conserving the environment. The second refers to Brazilian competition regulations; however, the environment is not specifically named in this regulation.

125. The Namibian Sea Fisheries Act, adopted in 1992, provides for regulations for the conservation of the marine ecology and the manageable exploitation, conservation, protection and promotion of certain marine resources and for that purpose to provide for the exercise of control over sea fisheries.

126. The Act establishes a Sea Fishery Advisory Council (Section 8). According to Sections 15 and 16, the Minister shall, in collaboration with the Sea Fishery Advisory Council, determine the total allowable catch of certain species, which shall be available for the allocation of quotas. Before a person can get a quota, one has to turn to the Minister for a right of exploitation. When this right has been received, one can apply to the Minister for an allocation of a quota.

127. Furthermore the Namibian Sea Fisheries Act provides in Section 26 for the licensing of factories and vessels, and Section 27 provides the Minister with the opportunity to grant fishing permits to foreign vessels on the basis of an agreement with the state to which the vessel belongs.

128. The Sea Fisheries Act of Namibia is a good example of a provision with the objective to protect the environment but which has an effect on free trade.

129. The Brazilian Congress approved a new antitrust law in 1994. This law simplified the regulatory framework and strengthened the mechanisms of enforcement of the antitrust laws. The law defines when there is a violation of the economic order, in other words, when the competition is being threatened. Harming the competition, dominating the relevant market of goods and services,

increasing the prices in an arbitrary manner, or abusing a dominant position in the market are not allowed.

130. The antitrust law also states that, among others, one of the following acts can constitute liability of violating the antitrust provisions: creating obstacles to the formation or development of competing business, erecting barriers to the entry of ompetitors, or hoarding or impeding access by competitors to patents and technology.

131. The antitrust law provides rules that regulate trade. It tries to create a sound economic environment for the consumers. Furthermore, the antitrust law promotes free trade, as it prohibits the creation of

trade barriers for new businesses to enter the market. This rule is not only applicable to Brazilian companies, but also to international companies. If a Brazilian company has the right to access the market without being barred, article III of the GATT demands the same treatment for international companies.

Prof. Gerhard Loibl, Chair of International Law and European Union Law, Diplomatische Akademie, Vienna

Barbara Ruis, Legal Officer, Division of Policy and Development and Law, UNEP

Resources

Internet Materials

ASSOCIATION OF SOUTHEAST ASIAN NATIONS available at http://www.aseansec.org/home.htm

DEVELOPMENT GATEWAY available at http://home.developmentgateway.org/

ECONOMIC COMMUNITY OF WEST AFRICAN STATES available at http://www.ecowas.int

EUROPEAN COMMISSION; TRADE DIRECTORATE GENERAL available at http://europa.eu.int/comm/dgs/trade/index_en.htm

FREE TRADE AREA OF THE AMERICAS available at http://www.ftaa-alca.org

INTERNATIONAL CENTRE FOR TRADE AND SUSTAINABLE DEVELOPMENT ON TRADE AND ENVIRONMENT available at http://www.trade-environment.org

INTERNATIONAL TRADE CENTRE UNCTAD/WTO available at http://www.intracen.org

INTERNATIONAL TRADE INSTRUMENTS, TREATIES, CONVENTIONS, MODEL LAWS AND RULES available at http://www.jus.uio.no/lm/treaties.and.organisations/lm.chronological.html

MERCOSUR (in Spanish and Portuguese only) available at http://www.mercosur.org.uy/

NORTH AMERICAN AGREEMENT ON ENVIRONMENTAL COOPERATION available at http://www.cec.org/pubs_info_resources/law_treat_agree/naaec/index.cfm?varlan=english

OECD; TRADE DIRECTORATE available at http://www.oecd.org/ech

REVISED GUIDE TO INTERNATIONAL TRADE LAW SOURCES ON THE INTERNET available at http://www.llrx.com/features/trade3.htm

S.D. MYERS VS CANADA available at http://www.appletonlaw.com/4b2myers.htm

TRADE AND DEVELOPMENT CENTRE WORLD BANK/WTO available at http://www.itd.org

TRADE AND ENVIRONMENT DATABASE available at http://gurukul.ucc.american.edu/ted/ted.htm

UN COMMISSION ON INTERNATIONAL TRADE LAW available at http://www.uncitral.org

UN CONFERENCE ON TRADE AND DEVELOPMENT available at http://www.unctad.org

UNEP-ECONOMICS AND TRADE BRANCH available at http://www.unep.ch/etu

WORLD TRADE ORGANIZATION available at http://www.wto.org

Text Resources

D.G. Craig, N.A. Robinson & K. Kheng-Lian (Eds.), CAPACITY BUILDING FOR ENVIRONMENTAL LAW IN THE ASIAN AND PACIFIC REGION APPROACHES AND RESOURCES VOLUME II, (Asian Development Bank, 2002).

D. Hunter, J. Salzman & D. Zaelke, INTERNATIONAL ENVIRONMENTAL LAW AND POLICY, (New York Foundation Press, Second Edition 2002).

E. Brown Weiss & J.H. Jackson (Eds.), RECONCILING ENVIRONMENT AND TRADE, (Transnational Publishers Inc., 2001).

G. Loibl, INTERNATIONAL ECONOMIC LAW IN INTERNATIONAL LAW, (Oxford University Press, 2003).

J.H. Jackson, THE JURISPRUDENCE OF GATT AND THE WTO: INSIGHT ON TREATY LAW AND ECONOMIC RELATIONS, (Cambridge University Press, First edition, reprinted 2002).

M. Stillwell, Environment, Trade and Sustainable Development: An Overview of Key Issues Arising From the World Summit on Sustainable Development and the WTO Doha Work Programme, in a BACKGROUND PAPER FOR THE MARCH 2003 UNEP CAPACITY BUILDING MEETING ON ENVIRONMENT TRADE AND SUSTAINABLE DEVELOPMENT FOR THE LATIN AMERICAN AND CARIBBEAN REGION, (2003).

P.M. Johnson & A. Beaulieu, THE ENVIRONMENT AND NAFTA: UNDERSTANDING AND IMPLEMETNING THE NEW CONTINENTAL LAW, (Washington D.C., First edition 1996).

Richard W. Emory, Jr., Probing the Protection in the Rotterdam Convention on Prior Informed Consent & Transposing to Enforceable National Laws the Obligations of the PIC and POPs Conventions for Imports and Exports, in COLORADO JOURNAL OF INTERNATIONAL ENVIRONMENTAL LAW AND POLICY, [2000 & 2001 Yearbooks].

R. Housman, Reconciling Trade and the Environment: Lessons from the North American Free Trade Agreement, in ENVIRONMENT AND TRADE 3, (UNEP 1994).

R.L. Revesz, P. Sands & R.B. Stewart (Eds.), ENVIRONMENTAL LAW, THE ECONOMY AND SUSTAINABLE DEVELOPMENT, THE UNITED STATES, THE EUROPEAN UNION AND THE INTERNATIONAL COMMUNITY, (Cambridge University Press, First edition 2000).

R. Twum-Barima & L.B. Campbell, Protecting the Ozone Layer through Trade Measures: Reconciling the Trad Provisions of the Montreal Protocol and the Rules of GATT, in ENVIRONMENT AND TRADE 6 (UNEP 1994).

S. Panitchpakdi, Achieving win-win-win, in Our Planet, Globalization, Poverty, IN TRADE AND ENVIRONMENT VOLUME 13, No. 4, (UNEP 2002).

Sungjoon Cho, Breaking the Barrier Between Regionalism and Multilateralism: A New Perspective on Trade Regionalism, in HARVARD INTERNATIONAL LAW JOURNAL, VOLUME 42, NUMBER 2, (Summer 2001).

25. ENERGY, RENEWABLE ENERGY AND NUCLEAR ENERGY

I. Introduction

1. Challenges of Sustainable Energy

1. Over the last two centuries, industrial evolution resulted in many innovations for human civilization. Today, the ready availability of plentiful, if only affordable energy would allow many people to enjoy unprecedented comfort, mobility and productivity. However, access to and use of energy varies widely among countries. Two billion people, representing one third of the world population, are deprived from taking advantage of this commericial form of technology. Most importantly for this Chapter, current energy generation and use are accompanied by environmental impact at local, regional and global levels.

2. Sustainable energy can be defined as energy produced and used in ways that support human development over the long term, in all its social, economic and environmental dimensions. However, as noted in the Agenda 21, much of the world's energy is currently produced and consumed in ways that could not be sustained if technology were to remain constant and overall quantities were to increase substantially. Aspects of the unsustainability of the current system include:

- Commercial fuels including electricity are not universally accessible,
- The current energy system is not sufficiently reliable or affordable to support widespread economic growth, and
- Negative local, regional and global environmental impacts of energy production and use threaten the health and well being of current and future generations.

3. Since the 1970s, serious warnings about the "limits to growth" sounded alarm around the world with little effect. Resource exploitation and wasteful consumption habits diminished non-renewable energy resources at an accelerated pace. Still, the amounts of energy needed are increasing. Unless policies change, energy demand will continue to grow steadily, whereby fossil fuels will continue to dominate the energy mix and most of the growth in demand will come from developing countries. Energy use by developing countries has increased three to four times as quickly as that by the Organization for Economic Cooperation and Development ("OECD") countries. This is a result of lifestyle changes due to rising incomes and higher population growth. Consequently, the share of developing countries in global commercial energy use increased from 13% in 1970 to 30% in 1998.

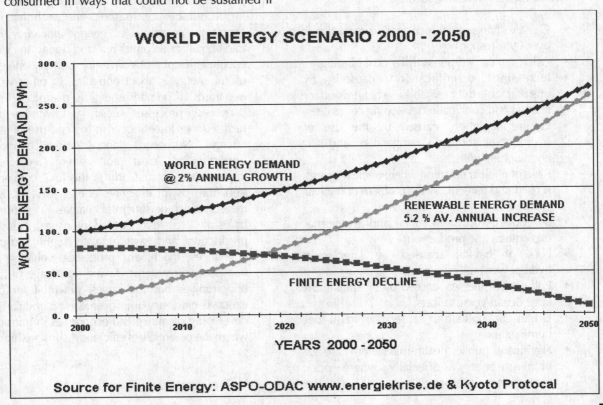

4. One of the most serious consequences of the fossil fuel age is the unbalancing of the biosphere and climate to a degree that is irreversibly affecting our life base. Growing deserts and acid rains spoil fertile lands. Rivers, lakes and ground waters are poisoned, which spoils badly needed drinking water for a growing world population. Increasingly frequent weather disasters, retracting glaciers, melting ice caps, landslides, more violent storms, and flooding of highly populated coastal areas and islands endanger people and species. All this to a certain extent is linked to the incessantly growing fossil fuel emissions, which cause global warming.

5. The Brundtland Report not only introduced the concept of sustainability but also placed strong emphasis on the importance of energy generation and use as part of this crucial concept. The Brundtland Report considered energy to be a major feature of sustainability, and identified the following key elements:

   • Sufficient growth of energy supplies to meet the needs of humanity (including an allowance for development in non-developed countries);
   • Energy efficiency and conservation measures;
   • Public health, recognizing the safety risks posed by use of certain energy types; and
   • Protection of the biosphere and elimination of local pollution problems.

6. The current unsustainable practices in energy use and production have led to most pressing environmental problems, such as:

   • Climate change, for which energy production is over 60% responsible;
   • Acid rain, caused primarily by coal burning;
   • Increasing desertification, caused by unsustainable but inevitable use of firewood for heating and cooking in developing countries;
   • Ozone depletion, caused by the use of hydrofluorocarbons in refrigerators and air-conditioning units;
   • Risks of nuclear radiation where nuclear energy is used and particularly the problem of nuclear waste;
   • Soil pollution, caused by oil and geothermal exploration and production;
   • Loss of habitat, caused by large-scale hydropower projects;
   • Pollution of the sea, caused by oil spills from large ocean-going tankers;
   • Urban air pollution, caused by fossil-fuel burning; and
   • Significant public health risks from use of biomass energy (especially where poor ventilation is widespread).

7. Some of these problems have already been, to some extent, tackled by the introduction of national legislation and/or international conventions. In Europe, acid rain is controlled by the 1979 Convention on Long-Range Transboundary Air Pollution together with its Protocols. Oil spills and oil pollution at sea are regulated by the International Convention for the Prevention of Pollution from Ships ("1973 MARPOL") and the 1982 Uinted Nations Convention on the Law of the Sea. Ozone depletion is being tackled by the 1985 Vienna Convention on the Protection of the Ozone Layer and its 1987 Montreal Protocol on substances that deplete the Ozone Layer. A Climate Change regime has been introduced through the 1992 United Nations Framework Convention on Climate Change and reinforced by the 1997 Kyoto Protocol. Also, the 1994 Convention on Desertification touches upon the issue of climate change and thus energy. The instruments regulating nuclear safety issues will be discussed later in this Chapter. However, notwithstanding the number of agreements that touch upon different aspects of energy generation and consumption, energy as an issue, has not, of its own been comprehensively addressed by an international convention up to now.

2. Energy Efficiency and Renewable Energies

8. The Brundtland Report stated that energy efficiency "should be at the cutting edge of national energy policies for sustainable development." However, for a number of reasons, the technical and economic potentials of energy efficiency have traditionally been under-realized. Today, the global energy efficiency of converting primary energy to useful energy is about one-third. In other words, two-thirds of primary energy is dissipated in the conversion processes, mostly as low-temperature heat. Further losses occur in the end-use of useful energy. Numerous and varied economic opportunities exist for energy efficiency improvement, particularly in this final conversion step from useful energy-to-energy services. Such measures include structural changes in economies by shifts to less energy-intensive industrial production and switching to highly efficient appliances, machinery, processes, vehicles, and transportation systems. Taking advantage of these opportunities has the largest potential for cost-effective efficiency improvements, particularly in developing countries and economies in transition, where the potentials of efficiency gains are highest.

9. The Brundtland Report further emphasized the need to shift the current energy mix more towards renewable energy resources. Such resources include solar energy (space and water heating and photovoltaics), wind energy, biomass, geothermal, small-scale hydropower, wave and tidal power. However, many political issues and vested interests are at stake and do not allow for radical change. Many oil-producing and oil-dependent nations are reluctant to accept the need to reduce their heavy reliance on fossil fuels fearing economic detriments. It is, therefore, no wonder that despite best intentions on the part of the international community, energy issues were neither specifically included as a specific chapter in Agenda 21, nor elaborated as a key aspect in the Millennium Development Goals of the United Nations.

10. Environmental law is traditionally focused on the environmental harm caused by energy use and production, rather than on energy itself. In relation to energy efficiency and renewable energies, promotion thereof is stipulated in various agreements, such as article 2 of the 1997 Kyoto Protocol. However, even though a strong factual interrelationship exists, international agreements adopted on climate change do not comprehensively address the energy side of the equation; and the link between desertification and energy has not even been officially recognized. This is particularly unfortunate, since scientific and technological advances in the energy sector have proceeded apace over the past decade. In terms of renewable energies, the efficiency of photovoltaic cells has increased dramatically, enabling the cells to be cost-effective in many regions of the world. New efficient designs of wind generators have been developed to enable the establishment of offshore wind generators. As far as energy efficiency and conservation is concerned, new super-efficient motors have been manufactured, enabling substantial energy savings in a wide range of industrial and domestic products possible. Also, much progress has been made in the development of alternatives to petroleum for motor fuels, such as ethanol, methanol and hydrogen.

11. The WSSD Plan of Implementation adopted at the World Summit of Sustainable Development ("WSSD Plan") in Johannesburg in 2002, makes references to energy efficiency and renewable energy. However, the WSSD Plan does not contain any binding national commitments in relation to energy, and the move to impose a mandatory percentage increase in the use of renewable energy resources was rejected. Nevertheless, it is part of the environmental instruments referred to as non-legally binding, which traditionally has played an important role in paving the way to stronger legal commitments. The WSSD Plan introduced a number of provisions relating to energy in its chapter II on "poverty reduction" (clause 9) and chapter III on "production and consumption" (clause 20). The WSSD Plan calls upon governments to:

- Take joint efforts to improve access to reliable and affordable energy services,
- Promote sustainable use of biomass, and
- Support the transition to cleaner use of fossil fuels. Some of the commitments made by the countries with regard to sustainable energy are to:
  - Promote the internalization of environmental costs and the use of economic instruments,
  - Establish domestic programme of energy efficiency,
  - Accelerate the development, dissemination and employment of affordable and cleaner energy efficiency and energy conservation technologies,
  - Recommend that international financial institutions' and other agencies' policies support countries to establish policy and regulatory frameworks that create a level playing field,
  - Support efforts to improve the functioning, transparency and information about energy markets with respect to both supply and demand,
  - Strengthen and facilitate, as appropriate, regional cooperation arrangements for promoting cross-border energy trade,
  - Implement transport strategies for sustainable development, and
  - Promote investment and partnerships for the development of sustainable energy efficiency, and multi-modal transportation systems.

12. As seen above, most of the issues resulting from unsustainable use and production of energy are implicitly dealt with in other areas of environmental law and thus in other chapters of this Training Manual. With regards to renewable energies, no comprehensive international regime is yet in place. This, however, does not derogate from the great importance to be attached in this source of energy particularly to the developing world. For the purposes of this Manual, this chapter will consequently mainly deal with nuclear energy safety and introduce the Energy Charter Treaty, which is the only legally binding instrument

providing for inter-governmental cooperation in the energy sector. In the second part, examples of national legislation in the fields of renewable energies and energy efficiency will be discussed.

3. Nuclear Energy

Safety Risks Posed by Energy Use and Production

13. As seen above, the Brundtland Report identified public health and safety of energy use and production as one of the key elements of sustainability. This touches upon the issue of nuclear energy and nuclear safety.

> On 26 April 1986, as a result of a combination of factors, a sudden, uncontrollable surge in power took place at Unit 4 of the Chernobyl nuclear power plant, resulting in the destruction of the reactor and a fire in the graphite moderator. This caused a prolonged release of radioactive materials into the environment and was followed by further releases, associated with the high temperatures reached in the core, between day seven and ten after the initial event.
>
> Radioactive contamination affected the territories of 19 subjects of the Russian Federation, with a total population of over 30 million people. The area of these territories contaminated was more than 56 thousand square kilometres. Approximately 3 million people live in the contamination zone.
>
> Over an area of 3,000 hectares which received high doses, 25% to 40% of pine forests died, and 90% to 95% of the trees showed some damage to reproductive functions. Direct deposition from the Chernobyl plume occurred in rivers, lakes and seas. Livestock and farm animals in this exclusion zone were destroyed and buried. In the resettlement zone, where contamination levels are lower, it has still been necessary to suspend most agricultural activities.

14. The accident at the Chernobyl nuclear power plant was a major humanitarian catastrophe of the twentieth century. However, it was not the first such accident. In 1979, a malfunction in the cooling system at the Three Mile Island Nuclear Generating Station (Pennsylvania, USA) led to the most serious commercial nuclear accident in American history and paved the way for reforms in the way nuclear power plants are operated and regulated. As these accidents show, modern nuclear technology creates unavoidable risks for all states, whether or not they choose to use this form of energy. Nuclear installations are potentially hazardous undertakings whose risk to health, safety and the environment is best met by regulation.

Since the consequences of failure may cause injury or pollution damage to other states and the global environment, international regulation, the setting of common standards, supervised by international institutions, offers the best means of ensuring a generally accepted minimum level of environmental protection.

15. The International Atomic Energy Agency ("IAEA") was established in 1956, in response to the deep-rooted fears and great expectations resulting from the discovery of nuclear energy. Originally, IAEA's main task was to encourage and facilitate the development and dissemination of nuclear power, ensuring that nuclear power is used for peaceful purposes only. To set standards for health and safety in collaboration with other international agencies was a secondary responsibility. The Chernobyl accident, however, resulted in a significant alternation of the IAEA's priorities. The IAEA provided the main forum for consideration of measures made necessary by the accident. The IAEA thus should promote better exchanges of information among states on safety and accident experience, develop additional safety guidelines and enhance its capacity to perform safety evaluation and inspections on request.

II. International Framework

1. International Legal Regimes: Nuclear

a) Convention on Early Notification of a Nuclear Accident

16. The Convention on Early Notification of a Nuclear Accident ("1986 Nuclear Accident Convention") was adopted and entered into force in 1986, following the Chernobyl nuclear plant accident. It establishes a notification system for nuclear accidents that may potentially be of radiological safety significance for another state. The 1986 Nuclear Accident Convention requires states to report the accident's time, location, radiation releases, and other data essential for assessing the situation. Notification is to be made to affected states directly or through the IAEA, and to the IAEA itself. Reporting is mandatory for any nuclear accident involving facilities and activities listed in article 1. Pursuant to article 3, states may notify other accidents as well. The five nuclear-weapon States (China, France, Russia, the United Kingdom, and the United States) have all declared their intent to also report accidents involving nuclear weapons and nuclear weapons tests.

b) Convention on Assistance in the Case of a Nuclear Accident Emergency or a Radiological Emergency

17. The Convention on Assistance in the Case of a Nuclear Accident Emergency or Radiological Emergency ("1986 Nuclear Emergency Convention") was also adopted following the Chernobyl nuclear plant accident and entered into force in 1987. The 1986 Nuclear Emergency Convention sets out an international framework for cooperation among states parties and with the IAEA to facilitate prompt assistance and support in the event of nuclear accidents or radiological emergencies. The Convention requires states to notify the IAEA of their available experts, equipment, and other materials for providing assistance. In case of a request, each state party decides whether it can render the requested assistance as well as its scope and terms. Assistance may be offered without costs taking into account, *inter alia*, the needs of developing countries and the particular needs of countries without nuclear facilities. The IAEA serves as the focal point for such cooperation by channeling information, supporting efforts, and providing its available services.

c) Convention on the Physical Protection of Nuclear Material

18. The Convention on the Physical Protection of Nuclear Material ("1979 Nuclear Material Convention") entered into force in 1987. The 1979 Nuclear Material Convention obliges Contracting states to ensure during international nuclear transport the protection of nuclear material within their territory or on board their ships or aircraft. At the first Review Conference in 1992 the parties considered, in particular, that the 1980 Nuclear Material Convention provides an appropriate framework for international cooperation in protection, recovery and return of stolen nuclear material and in the application of criminal sanctions against persons who commit criminal acts involving nuclear material.

d) Joint Convention on the Safety of Spent Fuel Management and on the Safety of Radioactive Waste Management

19. The Joint Convention on the Safety of Spent Fuel Management and on the Safety of Radioactive Waste Management ("1997 Joint Safety Convention") was adopted in 1997, and entered into force in June 2001. The 1997 Joint Safety Convention is the first international instrument that deals with the safety of management and storage of radioactive waste and spent fuel in countries with and without nuclear programme. The Convention also considerably elaborates on the existing IAEA nuclear safety regime and promotes international standards in the area. The 1997 Joint Safety Convention is aimed at achieving and maintaining a high level of safety in spent fuel and radioactive waste management, ensuring that there are effective defenses against potential hazards during all stages of management of such materials, and preventing accidents with radiological consequences. The Convention covers the safety of spent fuel and radioactive waste management from civilian applications. It also applies to the management of military or defense-originated spent fuel and radioactive waste if and when such materials are transferred permanently to and managed within exclusively civilian programme.

20. The 1997 Joint Safety Convention calls upon the contracting parties to review safety requirements and conduct environmental assessments, both at existing and proposed spent fuel and radioactive waste management facilities. It provides for the establishment and maintenance of a legislative and regulatory framework to govern the safety of spent fuel and radioactive waste management. The 1997 Joint Safety Convention establishes rules and conditions for the transboundary movement of spent fuel and radioactive waste that, *inter alia*, require a state of destination to have adequate administrative and technical capacity and regulatory structure to manage spent fuel or radioactive waste in a manner consistent with the Convention. It obligates a state of origin to take appropriate steps to permit re-entry into its territory of such material if a transboundary movement cannot be completed in conformity with the Convention.

21. The 1997 Joint Safety Convention provides for a binding reporting system that will address the measures taken to implement obligations under the Convention, including reporting on national inventories of radioactive waste and spent fuel. Each contracting party shall take, within the framework of its national law, the legislative, regulatory, and administrative measures and other steps necessary to implement its obligations under the 1997 Joint Safety Convention. In the event of a disagreement between two or more contracting parties concerning the interpretation or application of the Convention, the contracting parties shall consult within the framework of a Meeting of the Parties ("MOP") with a view to resolving the

disagreement. In the event that the consultations prove unproductive, recourse can be made to the mediation, conciliation and arbitration mechanisms provided for in international law, including the rules and practices prevailing within the IAEA.

e) The Convention on Nuclear Safety

22. The Convention on Nuclear Safety ("1994 Nuclear Safety Convention") entered into force in 1996. The 1994 Nuclear Safety Convention's aim is to legally commit participating states operating land-based nuclear power plants to maintain a high level of safety by setting international benchmarks to which states would subscribe, and to maintain a high level of nuclear safety in civil nuclear power plants and related facilities to protect individuals, society and the environment from harmful radiation and to prevent or mitigate accidents.

23. The 1994 Nuclear Safety Convention reaffirms that responsibility for nuclear safety rests with the state having jurisdiction over a nuclear installation. The Convention requires each party to establish and maintain a national legislative and regulatory framework for the safety of nuclear installations, which includes a system of licensing. The Preamble calls for a "commitment to the application of fundamental safety principles for nuclear installations rather than of detailed safety standards."

24. The obligations of the parties are based, to a large extent, on the principles contained in the IAEA Safety Fundamentals document "The Safety of Nuclear Installations." These obligations cover, for example, siting, design, construction, operation, the availability of adequate financial and human resources, the assessment and verification of safety, quality assurance and emergency preparedness.

25. Parties are also required to take 'appropriated steps' to ensure that

  - Safety at nuclear plants is given due priority,
  - Levels of trained staff are adequate;
  - Quality assurance programmes are established;
  - Comprehensive and systematic safety assessments are carried out periodically;
  - Radiation exposure is as low as reasonable achievable; and
  - Emergency plans are prepared.

26. The 1994 Nuclear Safety Convention is an incentive instrument. It is not designed to ensure fulfillment of obligations by parties through control and sanction but is based on their common interest to achieve higher levels of safety, which will be developed and promoted through regular Meetings of the Parties ("MOP"). The Convention obliges parties to submit reports on the implementation of their obligations for "peer review" at MOPs to be held at the IAEA. This mechanism is the main innovative and dynamic element of the 1994 Nuclear Safety Convention.

2. International Cooperation on Energy

a) The Energy Charter Treaty

27. After the nuclear catastrophe at Chernobyl and in the presence of other unsafe nuclear power plants in the former Soviet Union and other central and Eastern European states, Western countries in Europe have become strongly interested in the development of energy and nuclear energy in Eastern Europe. Furthermore, the competing interests of the necessity to import fossil fuels and the need to remain independent from foreign powers stimulated East/West interstate cooperation in Europe.

28. The 1994 Energy Charter Treaty was adopted in 1994, and entered into force in 1998. As of November 2005 the 1994 Energy Charter Treaty has 46 parties. The Treaty was developed on the basis of the European Energy Charter of 1991. Its main purpose is the guaranteed delivery of fossil fuels from the East to the West by means of investment protection, liberal trade connections, transit facilities and dispute settlement. The fundamental aim of the 1994 Energy Charter Treaty is to strengthen the rule of law on energy issues, thus minimizing the risks associated with energy related investments and trade. The 1994 Energy Charter Treaty is the only one legally binding multilateral instrument dealing specifically with inter-governmental cooperation in the energy sector. The treaty focuses on several areas:

  - Protection and promotion of foreign energy investments,
  - Free trade in energy materials,
  - Freedom for energy transit for pipelines and grids,
  - Reducing the negative impact of energy cycle through improving energy efficiency, and
  - The mechanisms for the resolution of State-to-State or Investor-to-State disputes.

29. Environmental issues, including energy efficiency, are limited to article 19, which reads in pertinent part:

**1994 Energy Charter Treaty
Article 19**

(1) In pursuit of sustainable development and taking into account its obligations under those international agreements concerning the environment to which it is party, each Contracting Party shall strive to minimize in an economically efficient manner harmful Environmental Impacts occurring either within or outside its Area from all operations within the Energy Cycle in its Area, taking proper account of safety. In doing so each Contracting Party shall act in a Cost-Effective manner. In its policies and actions each Contracting Party shall strive to take precautionary measures to prevent or minimize environmental degradation. The Contracting Parties agree that the polluter in the Areas of Contracting Parties, should, in principle, bear the cost of pollution, including transboundary pollution, with due regard to the public interest and without distorting Investment in the Energy Cycle or international trade. Contracting Parties shall accordingly:

"[...[

(d) have particular regard to Improving Energy Efficiency, to developing and using renewable energy sources, to promoting the use of cleaner fuels and to employing technologies and technological means that reduce pollution.
[...]"

---

30. Improving Energy Efficiency is defined in article 19(3)(c) as "...acting to maintain the same unit of output (of a good or service) without reducing the quality or performance of the output, while reducing the amount of energy required to produce that output."

Unfortunately, the wording of article 19 is phrased in a non-binding form. There is no possibility of international enforcement of any of these obligations and adherence by contracting parties can be regarded as discretionary. Furthermore, it is indicated that such environmental obligations are only secondary to economic considerations. Thus, each contracting party must strive to minimize harmful environmental impacts "in an economically efficient manner".

b) The Energy Charter Protocol on Energy Efficiency and Related Environmental Aspects ("PEEREA")

31. The Energy Charter Protocol on Energy Efficiency and Related Environmental Aspects ("1994 PEEREA") was added to the 1994 Energy Charter Treaty and was drawn up as a declaration of political intent to promote East-West energy cooperation. As of November 2005 it has 46 parties.

32. 1994 PEEREA requires its parties to formulate clear policy aims for improving energy efficiency and reducing the energy cycle's negative environmental impacts. These obligations are contained in articles 3, 5 and 8. Article 3 requires the parties to develop and implement energy efficiency policies, laws and regulations, while article 8 states that each party shall develop, implement and regularly update energy efficiency programmes best suited to its circumstances.

33. The major parts of article 3 read as follows:

"[...]
(2) Contracting Parties shall establish energy efficiency policies and appropriate legal and regulatory frameworks which promote, inter alia:
(a) efficient functioning of market mechanisms including market-oriented price formation and a fuller reflection of environmental costs and benefits;
(b) reduction of barriers to energy efficiency, thus stimulating investments;
(c) mechanisms for financing energy efficiency initiatives;
(d) education and awareness;
(e) dissemination and transfer of technologies;
(f) transparency of legal and regulatory frameworks.
[…]
(3) Contracting Parties shall strive to achieve the full benefit of energy efficiency throughout the Energy Cycle. To this end they shall, to the best of their competence, formulate and implement energy efficiency policies and cooperative or coordinated actions based on Cost-Effectiveness and economic efficiency, taking due account of environmental aspects.
[...]"

---

34. Through the implementation of 1994 PEEREA, the 1994 Energy Charter Treaty provides economies in transition with a menu of good practices and a form in which to share experiences and policy advice on energy efficiency issues with leading OECD states. Within this form, particular attention is paid to certain aspects of national energy efficiency strategy, such as taxation, pricing policy in the energy sector, environmentally related subsidies and other mechanisms for financing energy efficiency objectives.

35. The development of 1994 PEEREA is currently focused on a series of in depth energy efficiency reviews, designed to produce concrete recommendations for individual governments concerning ways of improving their national energy efficiency strategies. To date, such reviews have been conducted in Slovakia, Lithuania, Poland, Hungary, Bulgaria and Romania.

III. National Implementation

1. Republic of Korea

36. Over the past 30 years, the Republic of Korea has sustained rapid economic growth, which has transformed the country from an agrarian society into the industrialized middle-income nation it is today. As the Republic of Korea has no significant energy sources, it has had to import almost all energies from abroad to fuel the growing economy. Therefore, energy efficiency and conservation, together with a stable supply of energy, has had the utmost priority in the Republic's energy policies. In the wake of the second world oil shock, Republic of Korea established the Ministry of Energy and Resources in 1978 (now incorporated into Ministry of Trade, Industry and Energy ("MOTIE")), to administer the planning and enforcement of national energy policies. The Republic of Korea also promulgated the Rational Energy Utilization Act ("REUA") in December 1979, to ensure energy security in an emergency and promote energy efficiency and conservation.

37. The Republic of Korea's energy conservation programmes and activities as introduced below are based on the REUA. They have been put into action by the Republic of Korea Energy Management Corporation ("KEMCO"), established in 1980. KEMCO acts as the national energy efficiency center and is responsible for the implementation of national energy efficiency and conservation programmes.

a) Energy Conservation Policy

38. Every five years, the Minister of MOTIE drafts the Basic National Energy Plan and the Basic Plan for Rational Use of Energy. The latter is reviewed and assessed by the National Energy Conservation Promotion Committee, which is comprised of not more than 25 members and headed by the prime minister. On the basis of these national plans, the heads of the authorities concerned and city/province governors draft the Action Plan for Rational Use of Energy.

b) Policy Objectives

39. Based on the 1997 Basic Plan for Rational Use of Energy, the Republic of Korea's energy conservation policy objectives and directions are to:

- Improve trade deficit by reducing energy imports;
- Strengthen industrial competitiveness by

reducing production costs resulting from reduced energy use;
- Contribute to global environment protection by minimizing CO_2 emissions;
- Enhance efficiency in the whole energy flows of production, distribution and consumption to develop an energy-efficient socio-economic structure;
- Strengthen Demand-Side Management ("DSM") in power sector;
- Best use market mechanism to encourage energy efficiency investments;
- Intensify regulations to an appropriate level in key areas (including energy efficiency standards of the energy equipment and appliances);
- Foster an energy and resource-saving lifestyle by raising energy conservation awareness, adjusting energy price levels properly, and the like; and
- Strengthen international cooperation.

c) Major Energy Efficiency and Conservation Programmes

40. Over the past 20 years, the government of the Republic of Korea has made concentrated efforts to foster energy-intensive industries such as iron and steel, petrochemicals and machinery. This has led the industrial sector to account for more than half the nation's total energy consumption. The government has extensive energy efficiency programmes particularly aimed at these energy-intensive industries.

41. Article 25 authorizes the Minister of MOTIE to designate some heavy energy users as Energy Management-Required Users who must report to the government their annual production, energy facilities, equipment, annual energy use, and corporate energy conservation plan along with the results of implementing the previous year's plan. Two hundred specially identified companies account for approximately 50 % of the total industrial energy use. The specially identified companies are required to set up and implement their own 5-year Corporate Energy Conservation Plan. The Minister of MOTIE may announce Energy Management Guidelines to be adopted by heavy energy users.

d) Energy Audits and Technical Support

42. Article 30 states that the Minister of MOTIE may order the energy users to have an energy audit by the designated institution if a need is established by the Korean government's energy management guidance. Energy audits have been conducted mainly by KEMCO since 1980. KEMCO offers a fee-based detailed audit called a technical service

audit for large companies and a free audit for small and medium companies. Identified energy-saving measures are recommended coupled with technical assistance.

43. Article 35 instructs energy users to try to recover and utilize waste heat produced in their workplace or to help other third companies utilize it. The Korean government furthermore supports energy service companies by providing them with relevant information on new commercializable energy efficiency technologies, financial and taxation incentives and by holding relevant seminars in an attempt to induce investments in energy efficiency and conservation through third party financing.

e) Financial and Taxation Assistance to Energy Efficiency Investments

44. Since 1980, the government of the Republic of Korea has provided long term and low interest rate loans for energy efficiency and conservation through the Fund for Rational Use of Energy. Every fiscal year, a given amount is allotted to the eligible loan applicants. Loans are provided among others for research and development, installation of energy conservation facilities. The Korean government also offers tax credit for energy efficiency. Replacement of inefficient industrial furnaces and kilns, installation of cogeneration facilities, alternative fuel-using facilities and other facilities that are assessed to achieve more than 10% of energy saving are all qualified for a 5% income tax deduction both for domestic and foreign products.

f) Regional Energy Planning

45. Every five years, all local governments are required to make and implement their own regional energy plan suitable for the geographical and socio-economic needs and conditions of their respective regions and in tune with the Basic National Energy Plan. KEMCO provides training and education to the local governmental and produces a guidebook on the fundamentals of regional energy.

g) Energy Impacts Assessment on Energy-intensive Projects

46. Articles 8, 9, 10 and 11 provide for a reporting and consultation system of large-scale, energy-intensive projects. If a governmental or public institution desires to carry out a high energy-consuming project such as urban development projects, energy resources development projects, industrial

site or complex preparation projects, port and railroad construction projects, airport complex construction projects or tourist complex development projects, the institution should set up an energy use plan and ask MOTIE for consultation before execution of the project. If a private organization desires to execute projects that are estimated to consume energy in excess of a certain scale, the organisation should prepare an energy use plan and report it to KEMCO before it initiates the projects.

h) Demand-side Management

47. Because of growing difficulties in securing suitable sites and the huge investment capital for constructing new power supply facilities in the Republic of Korea today, DSM is progressively pursued. In July 1995, the government, through a revision of REUA in 1995, made it mandatory for all utilities to establish and implement a DSM investment plan on an annual basis and to report the plan and its implementation to the Korean government.

i) Management and Publication of Energy Statistics

48. The Minister of MOTIE should gather, analyze and manage domestic and foreign energy statistics and publish them, in order to use the information in establishing and implementing effectively the National Energy Basic Plan and related policy measures.

j) Public Awareness Programmes

49. On behalf of the Korean government, KEMCO engages in public campaigns. It produces and distributes films and leaflets and uses mass media such as television, radio, newspapers and to communicate its messages. KEMCO carries out joint activities with businesses and Non-Governmental Organizations to boost people's awareness and participation on a voluntary basis. KEMCO also organizes exhibitions and diverse cultural events on a regional basis to showcase successful energy conservation activities and projects.

k) Energy Equipment Efficiency Management: Standards and Labelling

50. Target Energy Performance Standards ("TEPS") and Minimum Energy Performance Standards ("MEPS") are currently applied to six items: electric refrigerators, air-conditioners, fluorescent lamps, lamp ballast, incandescent bulbs and passenger

cars. MEPS aim at expelling inefficient designs from the market, while TEPS are designed to encourage manufacturers to produce more energy-efficient goods.

51. Article 48 prescribes the labelling duty of the heat-using equipment manufacturers/importers. The label must contain specifications, performance and other features of the product. In addition, the Rating Labelling Programme provides the consumer with a relative ranking of the energy use of equipment and appliances. Product models are classed into one of five different grades, thus providing consumers with better information for decision making. Rating labelling is applied to electric refrigerators, electric air-conditioners, incandescent lamps, fluorescent lamps and fluorescent lamp ballast.

l) Inspection of Heat-using Equipment

52. Some kinds of heat-using equipment are to be inspected by the city/province governor during their manufacture, installation, re-installation, modification or replacement. Currently, six items (steel boiler, cast iron boiler, water heating boiler, pressure vessels group I, and metal heating furnace) in three categories of the heat-using equipment are subject to inspection.

m) Promotion of Research and Development of Energy Technologies

53. The government leads Research and Development ("R&D") activities in collaboration with industry, universities and research institutes. Priority projects are financed by the government budget and energy-related funds from the government and industry.

54. The Research and Development Center for Energy and Resources ("RACER") was founded as an affiliate of KEMCO in 1992, to take charge of managing the whole R&D process. At present, a 10-Year Energy Technology Development Plan is being implemented. This Plan focuses on the following three categories of energy conservation technologies:
- Core technologies such as photovoltaic, solar thermal, fuel-cell and IGCC;
- General technologies such as waste, bio, wind power and coal utilization technology; and
- Basic technologies such as small hydro, ocean, hydrogen and geothermal.

55. Renewable Energy Technologies are regulated by the 1987 Alternative Energy Development Promotion Act. Under this Act, a Basic Plan for the Development of New and Renewable Energy Technologies was established in 1988. The Basic Plan sets out four phases for enhancing new and renewable sources of energy. Upon completion of the fourth phase by 2006, new and renewable sources of energy are planned to contribute 2% of total energy demand.

56. Currently, eight energy sources (solar, bio, waste, small hydro, wind, hydrogen, ocean and geothermal) and two related technologies (fuel cell and coal utilization technologies) are defined by the Alternative Energy Development Promotion Act as target technologies. RACER is responsible for managing R&D for new and renewable energy sources through selection, support, operation, evaluation and management of the research and development projects. RACER receives applications for research projects for the following year, selects the appropriate research projects and provides full funding to universities and research centers and a portion of the funding to private companies.

2. Germany

57. Worldwatch Institute stated in the 2003 edition of its "State of the World" report:

> When the 1990s began, Germany had virtually no renewable energy industry, and in the view of most Germans the country was unlikely ever to be in the forefront of these alternative energy sources. ... Yet by the end of the 1990s, Germany had been transformed into a renewable energy leader. With a fraction as much potential in wind and solar power as the United States, Germany has almost three times as much installed wind capacity (more than one third of total global capacity) and is a world leader in solar photovoltaics as well. In the space of a decade, Germany created a new, multibillion-dollar industry and tens of thousands of new jobs. This metamorphosis provides helpful lessons for the scores of countries that have not yet determined how to unleash the potential of their own indigenous renewable energy sources.

58. The promotion of renewable energies started in 1998, with the promulgation of Germany's Renewable Energy Act. The Act has quadrupled the amount of electricity produced and fed into the public grid from regenerative sources. It has

resulted in the saving of some 56 million tonnes of carbon dioxide a year (2002) and has turned regenerative energy production into big business (one with annual revenues of Euro 9 billion and employing 130,000 persons). The Renewable Energy Act also has spawned similar undertakings in Spain, France, Austria, the Czech Republic and other countries.

59. In a second phase, the Renewable Energy Sources Act has been introduced. It obliges electricity grid operators to give priority to the purchase of electricity from solar energy, hydropower, wind power, geothermal power and biomass, and to pay a specified price for it. These changes, which shall take effect in 2004, will encourage the setting up of offshore wind parks and the further development of their successful counterparts on land. The level of compensation is based on the production costs. As investors know with certainty that they can sell their electricity at a fixed rate for 20 years, the banks will give the credits needed. This has resulted in the desired boom in the construction of new installations.

60. The revised Renewable Energy Sources Act will also encourage the modernization of small-sized hydraulic facilities and the building of Germany's first geothermal energy stations. Finally, the Act will provide home-based producers of photovoltaic power with long-term security of support.

61. Not only the climate benefits from the boom in renewable energy sources, which means an average of about 50 million tonnes of reduced greenhouse gases per year. The labor market also feels the boost through this growing industry: Today, there are about 130,000 jobs in Germany that are directly or indirectly linked to the expansion of renewable energies.

62. The German government aims at doubling the share of renewable energy sources in the energy supply sector by 2010, compared to 2000 levels. The aim is to increase gross electricity consumption from 6.3% in 2000 to 12.5%, and the share in primary energy consumption from 2.1% in 2000 to 4.2% in 2010. The German government has launched an offensive in favor of renewable energy sources by setting this objective. The fast paced developments in recent years have shown that the ambitious 2010 target of doubling the share can be met. Furthermore, the federal government is striving to provide half of the German consumption of primary energy from regenerative sources by the middle of the 21st century.

3. Australia

a) Regulatory Framework for Promotion of Energy Conservation and Energy Efficiency

63. Australia was established by its Constitution, which dates from 1901, as a federal jurisdiction. The country is governed centrally by the Commonwealth legislature. In addition, there are six states and two territories. The power to enact energy conservation legislation is shared between the various Australian governments. The states and territories have the power to legislate pursuant to Section 51 of the Constitution. The Commonwealth has the power to legislate to implement the terms of any international obligation. Where the Commonwealth and state laws clash, pursuant to Section 109 of the Constitution, the Commonwealth laws will prevail.

64. Australia has signed the Energy Charter Treaty and the associated Protocol on Energy Efficiency and Related Matters ("Treaty" and "Protocol," respectively). By acceding to these legal conventions, the Australian government has committed itself to take wide-sweeping legislative measures in support of energy conservation.

65. In 1997, in the lead up to Kyoto, the greenhouse statement by the Prime Minister titled Safeguarding the Future, mapped out the Commonwealth Government's action plan to address Australia's contribution to global climate change. The most significant component of the package was the formation of a national agency on greenhouse matters, the Australian Greenhouse Office ("AGO"). Established in 1998, and bringing together proms from three Commonwealth departments, the AGO formed the world's first national government greenhouse agency. The AGO is responsible for the coordination of domestic climate change policy and the delivery of key greenhouse response programs.

b) Domestic Appliances and Equipment

66. Energy consumed by equipment and appliances is a major source of greenhouse gas emissions. Indeed, these emissions are responsible for more than a quarter of net greenhouse gas emissions in Australia (excluding land use change and forestry). Consequently, improved energy efficiency of appliances and equipment is a key objective for Australian governments.

67. The 1998 National Greenhouse Strategy sets out the governments' policy objectives in this area in the following terms: "Improvements in the energy efficiency of domestic appliances and commercial and industrial equipment will be promoted by extending and enhancing the effectiveness of existing labeling and minimum energy performance standards".

68. The AGO has given effect to this vision by adopting two main strategies, namely, mandatory programmes and voluntary programmes.

c) Mandatory programmes

69. The AGO coordinates the implementation of state-based regulations, which compel industry stakeholders to meet Minimum Energy Performance Standards ("MEPS") or to disclose the energy efficiency of selected products through Appliance Labeling.

70. MEPS programmes are made mandatory in Australia by state government legislation and regulations which give force to the relevant Australian Standards. Regulations specify the general requirements for MEPS for appliances, including offences and penalties if a party does not comply with the requirements. Technical requirements for MEPS are set out in the relevant appliance standard, which is referenced in state regulations.

71. Regulations specify the general requirements for the energy labeling of appliances, including offences and penalties if a party does not comply with the requirements. Technical requirements for energy labeling are set out in "Part 2" of the relevant appliance standard, which is referenced in state regulations.

72. It is currently mandatory for all of the following electrical products offered for sale in Australia to carry an approved energy label:

- refrigerators and freezers,
- clothes washers,
- clothes dryers,
- dishwashers, and
- room air conditioners (single phase mandatory, three phase voluntary).

73. The following products are also regulated on the basis of MEPs, meaning that they have regulated minimum energy efficiency levels:

- Refrigerators and freezers (from 1 October 1999, revision 1 January 2005);

- Electric storage water heaters (from 1 October 1999);
- Three phase electric motors (0.73kW to <185kW) (from 1 October 2001);
- Ssingle phase air conditioners (from 1 October 2004, revision 1 October 2007);
- Three phase air conditioners up to 65kW cooling capacity (from 1 October 2001, revision 1 October 2007);
- Ballasts for linear fluorescent lamps (from 1 March 2003) (Note that in addition to MEPS, ballasts also have to be marked with an energy efficiency index (EEI));
- Linear fluorescent lamps - from 550mm to 1500mm inclusive with a nominal lamp power >16W (from 1 October 2004);
- Distribution transformers - 11kV and 22kV with a rating from 10kA to 2.5MVA (from 1 October 2004); and
- Commercial refrigeration (self contained and remote systems) (from 1 October 2004).

d) Voluntary Programmes

74. The AGO works in partnership with stakeholder groups to introduce programs that encourage market transformation by promoting highly efficient equipment or by identifying selected energy efficient products through appliance labeling.

75. The AGO is currently working with its stakeholders to reduce standby power losses - the power used by an electrical appliance when not performing its central function.

e) Buildings

76. As would be expected from a scenario of cheap energy and a particularly mild climate, Australian buildings have traditionally been wasteful of energy and thermally inefficient. In a land of abundant and cheap energy, energy efficiency had not traditionally had a high profile. This has been confirmed by studies on the residential building sector and the commercial building sector by the AGO in 1999.

77. The Prime Minister's Statement "Safeguarding the Future" identified the building sector as a key industry in the reduction of greenhouse gas emissions. In March 1999, following wide consultation, the Federal Government and the building industry, represented by the Australian Building Energy Council, reached a landmark agreement on a comprehensive strategy aimed at making Australian buildings more energy efficient.

78. The strategy encompasses:

- Federal Government and building industry support to encourage voluntary best practices in building design, construction and operation, plus
- The elimination of worst energy performance practices by incorporating a single standard for minimum performance requirements into the Building Code of Australia.

79. In 2002, a national public lecture tour, titled "Sustainable Housing," was organized to promote the benefits and showcase cutting edge examples of energy efficient dwellings. Many of these programmes were also designed to prepare the building industry for mandatory energy performance requirements. Key programmes funded by the Commonwealth Government include the Housing Industry Association's Partnership Advancing the Housing Environment, the Window Energy Rating Scheme, Master Builders Australia's Building Environment Dividends Programme and the residential consumer and technical guide project titled Your Home.

80. Voluntary programmes have been developed to create awareness of the impact of industry members and their products on the environment. The AGO has funded the documentation and promotion of excellence in energy efficient design.

81. The Commonwealth Government and the AGO are managing programmes which set Minimum Energy Performance Standards ("MEPS") for buildings. A scoping study by AGO in 1999, concluded that the Building Code of Australia can be amended to set MEPS for new residential and non-residential buildings, if it takes place with consensus agreement from all key stakeholders. For residential buildings, an important historical landmark has been the development of the nation-wide House Energy Rating Scheme ("HERS"). The HERS system consists of a five-star graded rating system for all new residential dwellings. The HERS system is optional in most jurisdictions, but has been adopted into legislation in the Australian Capital Territory and Victoria. In both of these jurisdictions, residential dwellings must rate at least four stars out of a maximum of five stars. The intention of the Commonwealth Government is that energy efficiency requirements will eventually become mandatory across Australia.

f) Electricity Generation and Distribution

82. One of the key features in the Prime Minister's climate change statement are Efficiency Standards for Power Generation. Generator Efficiency Standards took effect on 1 July 2000. The objective of the Generator Efficiency Standards Programme (GES) is to:

- Achieve movements towards best practice in the efficiency of electricity generation using fossil fuels, and to
- Deliver reductions in the greenhouse gas intensity of energy supply.

83. The Commonwealth enters into legally binding agreements with businesses. Standards apply to new electricity generation, significant refurbishment and existing generation. Based on initial estimates from independent experts, the programme is projected to save about 4 million tonnes of carbon dioxide per annum. Annual reporting from businesses affected provides a clear picture of progress towards these greenhouse savings.

84. Guidelines for the implementation of the measure have been developed following extensive consultation with industry, electricity users and the wider community. The first in a set of two guidelines outlines the key parameters of GES. It is complemented by a second set of guidelines that deal with the more technical aspects of the programme.

g) Transport

85. The Australian transport sector accounts for 73.9 million tonnes of Australia's total net greenhouse gas emissions, representing just over 16.1 % of Australia's total emissions. About 90.2 % of these emissions come from road transport, including cars, trucks and buses.

86. A mandatory fuel consumption labeling scheme has been developed for new passenger cars up to 2.7 tonnes gross vehicle mass. Under this scheme, which came into effect on 1 January 2001, a fuel consumption label is required to be placed on the windscreen of all new cars sold in Australia. These model-specific labels will show the car's fuel consumption in litres/100 km, based on tests set out in Australian Standard 2877.

87. As part of Australia's response to climate change the Commonwealth Government's alternative fuels programmes are designed to reduce greenhouse gases and other vehicular emissions from Australia's road transport sector. The aim of the programmes is to increase the use of alternative fuels, especially Compressed Natural Gas ("CNG") and Liquefied Petroleum Gas ("LPG"), in medium to heavy road vehicles.

88. The Government is currently negotiating with industry to set National Average Fuel Consumption ("NAFC") targets for new passenger vehicles for 2005 and 2010. In the November 1997 Prime Minister's greenhouse policy statement, Safeguarding the Future, the Government specified that it was seeking a commitment to a NAFC target in 2010, which is 15% below business-as-usual outcomes.

Prof. Adrian J. Bradbrook, Bonython Professor of Law, Law School, University of Adelaide

Eva Maria Duer, Associate Legal Expert, Division of Policy Development and Law, UNEP

Resources

Internet Materials

AUSTRALIAN GREENHOUSE OFFICE available at http://www.greenhouse.gov.au

BIOMASS ASIA (CHINA) available at http://www.platts.com/features/biomass/asia.shtml

CHERNOBYL CENTER available at http://www.chornobyl.net/eng

CHERNOBYL, TEN YEARS ON - RADIOLOGICAL AND HEALTH IMPACT, AN ASSESSMENT BY THE NEA COMMITTEE ON RADIATION PROTECTION AND PUBLIC HEALTH, OECD NUCLEAR ENERGY AGENCY, NOVEMBER 1995 available at http://www.geocities.com/Heartland/Pines/3459/Histree/allchernobyl.html

COMPENDIUM OF ENERGY CONSERVATION LEGISLATION IN COUNTRIES OF THE ASIA AND PACIFIC REGION available at www.unescap.org/esd/energy/efficiency

EEG GERMANY (English version) available at http://www.iwr.de/re/iwr/info0005e.html

ENERGY CHARTER TREATY available at http://www.encharter.org/

INTERNATIONAL ATOMIC ENERGY AGENCY available at http://www.iaea.org/worldatom/

INTERNATIONAL SUSTAINABLE ENERGY ORGANIZATION FOR RENEWABLE ENERGY AND ENERGY EFFICIENCY available at http://www.uniseo.org

LEGISLATION OF UKRAINE, ON STATE REGULATION OF NUCLEAR AND RADIATION SAFETY available at http://www.snrcu.gov.ua/eng/laws/pr000512.html

ORGANISATION FOR ECONOMIC CO-OPERATION AND DEVELOPMENT, ENERGY PAGE available at http://www.oecd.org/topic/0,2686,en_2649_37459_1_1_1_1_37459,00.html

PACE LAW SCHOOL ENERGY PROJECT available at http://law.pace.edu/energy/index.html

THE ENERGY AND RESOURCES INSTITUTE available at http://www.teriin.org/

THE WIND OF CHANGE BLOWS THROUGH GERMANY available at http://www.dw-world.de/english/0,3367,1446_A_763430,00.html

UNFCCC ENERGY TOPICS available at http://search.unfccc.int/query.html?col=fccc&qt=energy

UNITES STATES ENVIRONMENT PROTECTION AGENCY ENERGY INDUSTRY PAGE available at http://www.epa.gov/ebtpages/induindustenergyindustry.html

Text Materials

Adrian Bradbrook, REGULATORY FRAMWORK FOR PROMOTION OF ENERGY CONSERVATION AND ENERGY EFFICIENCY IN AUSTRALIA.

Adrian Bradbrook, Rosemary Lyster, Richard Ottinger, THE LAW OF ENERGY FOR SUSTAINABLE DEVELOPMENT, (Cambridge University Press, 2005).

Attilio Bisio & Sharon Boots, ENCYCLOPEDIA OF ENERGY TECHNOLOGY AND THE ENVIRONMENT, (Wiley, 1995).

Chris P. Neilsen & Peter Lydon (Eds.), ENERGIZING CHINA: RECONCILING ENVIRONMENTAL AND ECONOMIC GROWTH, (Harvard University Committee on Environment: Harvard University Press, 1998).
Earl Finbar Murphy, ENERGY AND ENVIRONMENTAL BALANCE, (Pergamon Press, 1980).

Eric R.A.N. Smith, ENERGY, THE ENVIRONMENT AND THE PUBLIC OPINION, (Rowman & Littlefield Pubs., 2002).

Fred P. Bosselman, ENERGY, ECONOMICS AND THE ENVIRONMENT: CASES AND MATERIALS, (Foundation Press, 2000).

Helen Cothran (Ed.), ENERGY ALTERNATIVES: OPPOSING VIEWPOINTS, (Greenhaven Press, 2002).

Janos Pasztor, BIOENERGY AND THE ENVIRONMENT, (Westview Press, 1990).

Leigh Hancher, EC ELECTRICITY LAW, (Chancery Law Pub., 1992).

Mapping the Energy Future: Energy Modelling and Climate Change Policy, in INTERNATIONAL ENERGY AGENCY (Paris 1998).

Patricia Birnie & Alan Boyle, INTERNATIONAL LAW AND THE ENVIRONMENT, (Oxford University Press).

Patricia D. Park, ENERGY LAW AND THE ENVIRONMENT, (Taylor & Francis, 2002).

Regina S. Axelrod, CONFLICT BETWEEN ENERGY AND URBAN ENVIRONMENT: CONSOLIDATED EDISON VERSUS THE CITY OF NEW YORK, (University Press of America, 1982).

Stephen Berry, Dr. Tony Marker & Mr. Philip Harrington, AUSTRALIA'S APPROACH TO ENERGY EFFICIENCY AND THE BUILDING CODE, Australian Greenhouse Office.

THE ENVIRONMENTAL IMPACTS OF PRODUCTION AND USE OF ENERGY, United Nations Environment Programme (Nairobi 1980).

WORLD ENERGY ASSESSMENT: ENERGY AND THE CHALLENGE OF SUSTAINABILITY, UNDP, UNDESA & the World Energy Council (2000).

26. CORPORATIONS AND THE ENVIRONMENT

I. Introduction

1. All economies depend on the success of business to manufacture much-needed commodities, process products, provide services and undertake a variety of economic activities either in their home market for export and import, or as foreign investors in other countries. In the process, businesses provide employment, and are a source of livelihood for many people across the globe. Despite these benefits, business also contributes greatly to environmental damage through contamination of environmental media (soil, water and air) and depletion of natural resources.

2. As business activities widen in scope and geographical range with the opening up of markets and investment opportunities through global trade initiatives, their potential for damage to the environment increase as well. As a result, laws, rules and regulations have been created specifically to control business activities in order to prevent harm to human health and the environment, and to reduce historic adverse impacts. Alongside these laws and regulations, there are increasing requirements on business to act in a transparent manner both to aid investment decisions and to keep the public informed of the impacts of business, whether locally or globally.

3. Law exists at three levels. At the international level, law exists in the form of binding rules and regulations that have been established in international treaties and agreements and customary practices. In regional legal orders, such as the European Union and the North American Free Trade Agreement, both legal instruments and voluntary codes of conduct help regulate environmental impacts, if only to produce level playing fields amongst competitors in these regions. At the national level, many countries have created domestic laws to regulate businesses. Some of the national laws have been created to transpose rules stipulated at the international level. In addition, there are rules and regulations created by businesses themselves for self-regulation in the business community, and voluntary regulations by individual companies. These exist in the form of business charters, codes of conduct, codes of ethics, corporations' best environmental practices, and in other forms. Some of the rules and regulations have been initiated by, or developed

with assistance from environmental organizations such as the United Nations Environment Programme.

4. This Chapter provides an overview of binding and non-binding international environmental agreements and other instruments establishing binding and non-binding rules to govern businesses. It also gives examples of implementation of the rules to illustrate their applicability. An overview of business self-regulation is also provided. The discussion includes environmental regulations created by business organizations and rules created by individual businesses for self-regulation. There are examples of voluntary compliance by industry with environmental self-regulation to show the significance of voluntary business regulations as instruments for health and environmental protection by limiting the adverse impacts of business activities. Further, this chapter provides three examples of regional approaches to environmental agreement and shows that there is sometimes greater symmetry of interstate regional level allowing more to be achieved. It also provides examples of national laws, rules and standards intended to regulate business. Some of the national legislation implements rules and standards established at the international level. Implementation and enforcement of the national laws are also considered as they are crucial to the prevention and reduction of adverse impacts of business activities on the environment.

5. Private businesses and other forms of industrial enterprise exist in every country of the world. While some operate within the country of their establishment, others have invested outside of their domestic base. As such, these businesses and enterprises have the capacity to relocate business operations from one country to another, and are commonly referred to as transnational corporations. Such businesses have played a crucial role in the social and economic development of many countries. They manufacture cars, chemicals of many different kinds, refrigerators, air conditioners and many other products that people need. In addition, they also process agricultural and other products, make clothes and other essential items, and trade nationally and internationally in a wide variety of products. In the process of doing these things, private business support the livelihoods of many people by providing vital sources of food and employment; they also contribute towards their professional development, thereby transforming social systems by providing major opportunities for

trading. The magnitude of wealth possessed by businesses indicates that they are capable of contributing significantly to the development of many nations.

6. In this way, private business plays a pivotal role in development. Many countries in Africa, Latin America, Asia, and Eastern Europe have chosen foreign direct investment as the key to their economic development. Foreign investment allows many foreign businesses to bring their capital and start business operations in the jurisdiction in question. However, while business activities make significant contributions to life and economic health in many areas, they may consume natural resources, produce goods that might pose environmental problems and contribute to unacceptable human health and environmental deficits.

7. Many developing countries have liberalized their economies and relaxed their laws, especially concerning labour and the environment in the hope of encouraging more foreign investors to bring in capital that will foster economic growth. In many cases, the rapid economic growth envisaged through such foreign investment militates against notions of sustainable development in the host countries. Absence of regulations for business, deregulatory programmes, weak or relaxed regulation, waiver of the applicable standards and lack of enforcement, as

well as problems of corruption have contributed to the destruction and degradation of the environment and its resources in many jurisdictions.

8. In many countries around the world, business activities have contributed to contaminatation of air, water and soil by for example generating (hazardous) wastes that are inadequately disposed of such and are sometimes discharged by manufacturing industries directly into the ground, polluting nearby water resources. Businesses also produce and market products that are harmful to human health and the environment. In some cases, businesses do so without informing consumers of the dangers of such products, or with false assurances to consumers that such products are safe.

9. Moreover, in the quest for raw materials to meet their business needs, industries and other businesses have destroyed forests and forest water catchment areas through logging and changing the entire nature of the landscape and land use. In many places, businesses have also over-extracted fish, minerals, oil and other natural resources. For example, reports indicate that activities of multinational oil corporations in the oil rich areas of the Niger Delta have not only over-extracted oil and gas resources, but have also heavily polluted the environment through poor and dangerous extraction and disposal operations, partly due to the relaxation, and lack of effective enforcement of

---

Example
Impacts of Poor Oil Extraction Practices: The Niger Delta Crisis

There is a long and terrible record of environmental destruction and human rights violations in the oil-producing regions of Nigeria. The gross level of environmental degradation caused by oil exploration and extraction in the Niger Delta has gone unchecked for the past 30 years. Evidence shows that the oil companies operating in Nigeria have not only disregarded their responsibility towards the environment but have acted in complicity with the military's repression of Nigerian citizens...

* **Gas flaring:** Testimonies to wasteful oil industry operations, gas flares are a distinctive feature of the Niger Delta landscape. Most of these flares burn 24 hours a day...gas does not have to be flared off, and in many countries there is little flaring...Yet companies in the Delta opt for flaring because...it is by far cheaper than the alternatives...the impact of gas flares on the local ecology and climate, as well as people's health and property, is evident. The extremely high levels of CO_2 and methane gases that are released to the atmosphere also impact climate patterns beyond the local level...Yet, the oil industry seems blatantly oblivious to the consequences of this wasteful practice...

* **Pipeline leaks**: ...On-site oil leaks and ruptured pipelines are a serious problem in the Niger Delta...On average, three major oil spills in the Niger Delta are recorded each month. In the first quarter of 1997 alone, Shell recorded 35 incidents of oil spills in its operations...Under Nigerian law, companies are not obliged to clean up or compensate for the effects of spills caused by sabotage...

* **Health:** ...serious respiratory problems witnessed in many communities can be linked to environmental pollution. Respiratory problems, coughing up blood, skin rashes, tumours, gastrointestinal problems, different forms of cancer, and malnourishment, were commonly reported ailments in many communities...Another problem facing the people of the Niger Delta is the illicit use of land by oil companies. In the community of Umuebulu, Rivers State, hardly 50 meters away from its perimeter, there is an unlined chemical waste pit. The company reportedly acquired this land under the pretence of building a "life camp"— an employee housing complex...The wall keeps people out but doesn't serve as a protection against the noxious fumes coming from the site. Some members of our delegation ...immediately recognised the smell of industrial waste...

> *** Environment, loss of biodiversity:** The Niger Delta has the third largest mangrove forest in the world, and the largest in Africa. Mangrove forests are important for sustaining local communities because of the ecological functions they perform and the many essential resources they provide including soil stability, medicines, healthy fisheries, wood for fuel and shelter, tannins and dyes, and critical wildlife habitats. Oil spills are contaminating, degrading, and destroying mangrove forests…Endangered species—including the Delta elephant, the white-crested monkey, the river hippopotamus…are increasingly threatened by oil exploitation…Destruction of habitats...The construction of infrastructure for oil facilities is done with little or no regard for environmental considerations. To facilitate road construction, waterways are frequently diverted, to the detriment of fish populations."
> *A US Non-Governmental Delegation Trip Report, Oil for Nothing: Multinational Corporations, Environmental Destruction and Impunity in the Niger, Delta*

applicable environmental regulations. This has led to severe contamination of the soil, water and other environments in the Delta region, leading to the deaths of fish and other aquatic resources that provided food and supported the livelihoods in the area. The poor practices have also made fishing and farming impossible, caused many kinds of health ailments and threatened to render whole populations destitute.

10. One of the problems that is highlighted in the Delegation Trip Report above is the lack of effective regulation of multinational corporations in developing countries. Businesses, especially foreign investors, continue to engage in practices that degrade the environment. This degradation calls for regulatory measures at all levels to supplement weak domestic efforts. As a result of the accelerated rate of business activities world wide and as a result of scientific advance, there has been increasing awareness and concern about harm to human health and environmental damage caused by private business activities. These problems make it necessary for business and industry to be regulated at all levels, and for the principle of sustainable development to be established in international and national environmental laws to ensure that foreign investment and other business activities lead to development that is sustainable in nature.

II. International Framework

1. The International Legal Regime

11. Laws that are intended to impose binding rules on business have been set out in many global, regional and bilateral agreements. A few examples of such agreements will suffice to explain the nature of such rules and how they can apply to regulate business activities. For the most part, the provisions covered here are to be found in greater detail elsewhere in the Manual. In the following Section, five examples that pursue slightly different objectives are highlighted. The examples include very specific regulation of a particular industry (tobacco) in order to minimize its impact; an

instrument that addresses the prevention of diffuse global damage by industry (climate change); another that tackles cross-border pollution (hazardous waste) and finally one that seeks to impose civil liability for environment damage (oil spillage).

a) United Nations Convention on the Law of Sea and the Fish Stocks Agreement

12. The United Nations Convention on the Law of the Sea ("UNCLOS") is a global agreement containing binding rules that apply to parties to the agreement with respect to the marine environment, and matters regulated by the treaty. It has been considered in greater detail in other chapters of this Manual. In this Chapter, an examination of its provisions is limited to those relevant to regulation of business in the marine environment. The objectives of UNCLOS include protection of marine mammals, plants and other organisms and their habitat from harm resulting from pollution and other human activities such as sea transportation and fisheries activities. Such activities are conducted by businesses and industries operating within and outside the marine environment, whose operations threaten the marine environment. Shipping and fisheries industries provide good examples. UNCLOS and its Agreement relating to the Conservation and Management of Straddling Fish Stocks and Highly Migratory Fish Species ("1995 Fish Stocks Agreement") aim to control the activities in order to meet the set objectives.

13. For the fisheries industries, article 61 of UNCLOS and article 6 of the 1995 Fish Stocks Agreement require coastal states that are parties to the agreements, and other parties whose nationals operate fisheries in the marine environment, to set limits on the amount of fish and other marine organisms that can be harvested over a period of time, or within a given area. The requirement is intended to avoid over-fishing that can, and has, in many cases, resulted in depletion of fish stocks and in the extinction of fish and other species in coastal areas and in the high seas.

14. Further, article 61(3) of UNCLOS and article 18 of the 1995 Fish Stocks Agreement require fishing vessels to use proper fishing gear that do not allow smaller fish to be caught or destroy other marine organisms that fishermen do not require. The articles also require fisheries industries to comply with any existing requirements and measures intended to conserve fish and other marine organisms. Such measures include those taken to restore populations of harvested species to maximum sustainable levels, in conformity with any national laws created by parties to regulate fisheries. Article 18 of the Fish Stocks Agreement expressly prohibits fishing vessels from engaging in any activity that undermines the effectiveness of conservation measures set out in UNCLOS or other agreements. For example, fishing vessels are prohibited from carrying out their activities, such as processing of fish in the high seas, in a way that can result in pollution of the waters. In addition, article 10(c) of the Fish Stocks Agreement requires fisheries industries to adopt international standards for responsible conduct during fishing operations to supplement UNCLOS requirements and to ensure that fisheries activities do not harm marine living resources and the marine environment. Such standards have been established, for example, in article 8 of the Food and Agriculture Organization's Code of Conduct for Responsible Fisheries.

15. There are also requirements upon parties to UNCLOS and to the 1995 Fish Stocks Agreement to control fisheries industries. Article 18(3) of the 1995 Fish Stocks Agreement requires parties to create national laws to implement licensing requirements for all fishing vessels authorised to carry out fisheries activities in their territorial waters, and for all vessels to fly their national flags while undertaking fisheries operations in coastal waters and in the high seas. Parties are also required to prohibit vessels that do not have fishing licences from undertaking fishing activities and to specify conditions for conservation that businesses engaging in fisheries must meet when issuing licences. Parties are also required to place conditions in fisheries licences that will ensure that fisheries activities are properly conducted to avoid adverse consequences to fish stocks, other marine organisms, or the marine environment. For example, parties may issue a licence on condition that a particular vessel harvests only a specified fish stock.

b) Framework Convention on Tobacco Control

16. The World Health Organisation's ("WHO") Framework Convention on Tobacco Control ("2003 FCTC") is a global agreement negotiated over a period of years under the auspices of the WHO. The agreement was unanimously adopted by representatives from 191 countries at the 56th World Health Assembly on 21 May 2003. The 2003 FCTC is specifically intended to regulate the tobacco industry and related businesses involved in the manufacturing, packaging, selling, advertising, and otherwise dealing with tobacco and tobacco products. The rules set out will be binding upon such tobacco businesses in and between countries that are parties to the Agreement. 2003 FCTC entered into force on 27 February 2005, and has currently (January 2006) 117 parties.

17. The Preamble to 2003 FCTC states that one of the objectives of controlling tobacco businesses is to prevent and reduce adverse human health and environmental impacts and consequences of tobacco, tobacco consumption, and exposure to tobacco smoke. To accomplish these objectives, when issuing licences article 4(5) requires parties to develop rules within their countries that would make tobacco businesses liable for any damage caused as a result of smoking and using other tobacco products. In its introductory parts, the 2003 FCTC notes the fatal and other human health impacts of tobacco toxicity. Tobacco businesses will be held liable for such deaths, even in countries that did not have such liability laws prior to the 2003 FCTC.

18. Article 5(2(b)) requires parties to create, maintain and enforce national rules and regulations that will reduce tobacco consumption. In the interest of safeguarding the environment and human health, governments have agreed to take measures that will reduce tobacco sales and that might, eventually drive some of the industries out of business, without incurring liability under international trading agreements, such as the General Agreement of Tariff and Trade ("GATT"). Further, articles 9, 13, and 21 require parties to create national laws requiring businesses to disclose the exact contents of tobacco and undertake a comprehensive ban of all tobacco advertising, promotion and sponsorship. This will also have a direct impact on the tobacco industry, especially by curbing the marketing of cigarette smoking as safe.

c) Ozone regime

19. The Vienna Convention for the Protection of the Ozone Layer ("1985 Vienna Convention") and the Montreal Protocol of 1987 ("1987 Montreal

Protocol") provide excellent examples of how international agreements might change the face of a whole industrial sector. These agreements arise out of concerns for the global atmosphere and, more particularly, concerns relating to the depletion of the ozone layer that would otherwise screen ultraviolet rays. For a fuller discussion of the two Conventions, see chapter 9 above. The 1985 Vienna Convention proved difficult to negotiate because of concerns from developing countries regarding the impact of controlling the substances that depleted the ozone on emerging industries, and resistance from developed countries on the basis that the phenomenon of ozone depletion was unproven. Consequently, the 1985 Vienna Convention was simply a framework demanding further assessment of and exchange of information about ozone depletion. Nonetheless, the 1985 Vienna Convention is significant for a number of reasons, namely because it addressed a global problem of diffuse pollution created by certain industrial sectors and opened a debate about precautionary action.

20. Following the 1985 Vienna Convention, the 1987 Montreal Protocol set clear targets for the reduction of substances that deplete the ozone layer, such as chlorofluorocarbons ("CFCs"), which were subject to a programme of phased reduction until the agreed limits. The 1987 Montreal Protocol was made possible by the interim work conducted by scientists under the auspices of UNEP allowing agreement both on the reality of ozone depletion and the timing of necessary action. Since the beginning of 1989, when the Protocol entered into force, there have been five major revisions of the Montreal Protocol's schedules for phasing out depleting substances.

21. The 1985 Vienna Convention and 1987 Montreal Protocol offer many lessons. Precautionary action proved not merely possible but also necessary and successful. The role of industry was vital. The chemical industry in the United States helped to lead the way through its recognition of the problem and its willingness to seek replacement substances. The 1987 Montreal Protocol is well recognized as one of the most successful ventures of international environmental law because stakeholders and their experts were involved in the design of the programme. Moreover, in a good example of differentiated responsibility, it was recognized that developed nations bore more responsibility for the creation of the problem and this is reflected in the longer period of adaptation allowed for developing countries in the Convention and in the Protocol. Finally, working in this way, and with carefully

prepared targets and pre-planning, industry has found it possible to move to alternative technologies without massive dislocation in the market for refrigerants and other goods. (See example in box titled 'Best Environmental Practices of Technology Industries below). The pity is that the success of the 1987 Montreal Protocol is proving much more difficult to repeat in the context of global warming caused by concentrations of greenhouse gases.

Example
Best Environmental Practices of Technology Industries

A number of companies that operate globally, including Honda, Trane, Aviation Partners, Energy Star and Seiko Epson have been able to use cutting-edge technology to protect the climate and/or the ozone layer from harmful substances, which demonstrates the contributions these companies are making to environmental protection. For example, Epson Corporation started using chlorofluorocarbons in its manufacturing processes in 1970. At the time, adverse impacts of CFCs on the environment were not known. CFCs are colourless, odourless, energy-efficient and seemed also perfect in almost every way for the manufacture of refrigerants, air conditioners and many other products until 1974, when research revealed that the chemicals were not only toxic but were also depleting the ozone layer that protects life on earth from the harmful effects of the sun.

Once the adverse effects of CFCs became known and negotiations for the Convention on Climate Change began, Epson's managers understood that as a matter of good business practice, since the company had contributed to the introduction of CFCs in the atmosphere, it was the duty of the company to take action to protect the ozone layer by eliminating CFCs. Using technological innovations, Epson's efforts began in 1988 after the company's president declared that it was the company's policy to eliminate CFCs. At a time when the Montreal Protocol only envisaged a fifty percent reduction in CFCs, Epson pledged to eliminate the use of CFCs in its Japanese companies within five years. The company later accelerated its goal to four years, and still managed to phase out CFCs by October 1992, more than three years before the time called for by the final Montreal Protocol phase-out schedule. Through technological innovation, Epson has been able to replace CFCs with substances that do not deplete ozone.

---

d) Basel Convention

22. The Basel Convention on the Control of Transboundary Movements of Hazardous Waste and their Disposal ("1989 Basel Convention") offers more lessons. Many manufacturing industries produce harmful wastes as a result of the processes of production. Following an outcry over industrial

practices in exporting harmful wastes in the 1980s, and interim moves by the European Commission, the Organization for Economic Cooperation and Development and the United Nations ("UN"), the 1989 Basel Convention sought to regulate international trade in such wastes. This was no easy matter since industries in developed nations were reluctant to narrow their disposal options for problematic waste streams, but the pace of change was forced by the urgent insistence of African nations that international trade in wastes should be banned. The 1989 Basel Convention operates on the basis of prior informed consent. Wastes cannot be trans-shipped from one state to another without the exporting state first informing and receiving the approval of the recipient state. This promotes a respect for national sovereignty in that any legislation in that recipient state banning or restricting the importation of waste must be honoured. Moreover, whether or not such measures are in place parties to the 1989 Basel Convention should not allow their industries to export waste unless they believe that the wastes will be treated in an environmentally sound manner. This will involve some consideration of the capacity and facilities of the receiving state. Where trans-shipment does take place under prior notification, there are rules on packaging, labelling and transportation to ensure the proper management of the waste. Importing states can insist on insurance or other financial guarantee.

23. There are a number of issues to note. The first is that the 1989 Basel Convention sits alongside other international agreements, particularly the Lomé Convention banning export from the EC to Afro-Caribbean-Pacific States, and the Bamako Convention prohibiting importation of waste into Africa from non-contracting states. In a sense, the latter convention is anone example of a number of regional agreements in this area that key into (though alter) the Basel Convention. The European Union has regulation pre and post dating the 1989 Basel Convention. All exports for disposal are prohibited, and from 1998, in line with a decision under the Basel Convention, all shipments for recovery from non-industrialized countries are prohibited. The pre-notification system under the Mexico-United States Hazardous Waste Agreement dates back to the mid-1980s. A second issue is that the mechanisms under the convention are cumbersome. Determining which goods are wastes and which are economic goods can be difficult, requiring elaborate listings of hazardous waste products. Pre-notification, even though it can involve advanced notification of regular shipments of waste of a similar description, places onerous obligations on industry and require a good

deal of regulatory supervision. As originally drafted, the Basel Convention had no agreement of liability for breach of the rules, and although this has improved a little by the adoption of a protocol on compensation for injury and economic loss caused by hazardous waste, this has yet to be ratified by, for example, the European Community.

24. On the other hand, the 1989 Basel Convention has done much to promote waste minimization by industry, better local waste recovery and environmentally sound waste practices. Moreover, the prior consent procedure again provided a working model for other international agreements, through which states seek to control industrial exports that might have damaging environmental effects. For example, the Cartagena Protocol to the Biodiversity Convention seeks to protect biological diversity from the potential risks posed by biotechnology through a process of advanced informed agreement. Again, this is a procedure for ensuring that countries are provided with the information necessary to make informed decisions before agreeing to the potentially damaging imports into their territory.

e) Liability for oil pollution

25. The international regimes for the compensation of oil pollution damage provide further insight. International civil liability refers to liability of legal or natural persons under the rules of national law where these are adopted in line with an international treaty obligation demanding harmonized minimum standards. Such schemes have been increasingly debated over the last decade as a means of managing environmental harm. Although a number of international civil liability regimes have been negotiated, few are in force and only one, the oil pollution regime has any practical experience of compensating victims of environmental harm. The regime was in response to the recognition that increasing sea-borne transportation of oil constituted a growing pollution risk as well as a threat to the seas and the oceans.

26. The regime consists of the Convention on Oil Pollution Damage ("1969 Oil Pollution Convention") and the 1971 International Fund Convention, which were updated and replaced in 1992 through new protocols. They were updated again in 2000. The liability regime for oil pollution is based on strict liability. Under the 1969 Oil Pollution Convention, the ship owner is strictly liable for pollution damage resulting from spills of persistent oils suffered in the territory (including territorial sea) of a state party to the convention.

Ship owners only are placed under an obligation to maintain insurance specifically to cover pollution damage. Under the regime, liability is limited and under article 6(a), impairment of the environment other than loss of profit from such impairment is limited to costs of reasonable measurement of reinstatement actually undertaken or to be undertaken. The 1971 International Fund Convention provides additional funds, where the limit of compensation available under the 1969 Oil Pollution Convention is exceeded. Payments are financed by levies on oil importers.

27. The limits of liability are criticized for being too low and every time there is a new incident, which show that the limits are insufficient, they are amended and increased. Further, limits on liability could be contrary to the polluter-pays principle, which requires that a polluter should be responsible for the full cost of the damage they may cause. There is further criticism to the extent of article 6(a), which in a strict sense excludes compensation for ecological damage as the fund only compensates economically quantifiable losses. The EC argues for a stronger regime based on a stricter application of the polluter-pays principle and that the limits of liability of the ship owner should not be unbreakable. In 1969, a strict liability regime with compulsory insurance may have been revolutionary, however, with the requirement to increase liability with every new pollution incident, the regime has been criticized for providing better protection to industry than to the victim. Despite this, it is still the only international civil liability regime what has actively required business to compensate victims.

2. International Non-Legally Binding Instruments

28. There exists a body of international agreements, declarations, codes of conduct, and other non-binding instruments setting forth non-legally binding rules that are specifically intended to influence businesses. Although they are not legally-enforceable, many of the regulations, known also as rules, standards, guidelines, codes of practice or ethical codes, have been widely accepted and applied in many countries to prevent environmental harm, reduce adverse health impacts, and serve several other purposes. A few examples will demonstrate the applicability of such regulations.

a) Agenda 21 and the Rio Declaration

29. Agenda 21 is a non-legally binding instrument for environmental protection and susatainable developement. With regard to businesses, Agenda 21 establishes a duty to disclose toxic emissions data. It requires industries to provide responsible governmental authorities, international bodies and other interested parties with data of substances that they produce in order to allow an assessment of risks and hazards that they pose to human health and the environment. This would allow measures to be taken to prevent, for example, industrial accidents such as the Bhopal and Seveso tragedies. The rule is backed by Principle 13 of the 1992 Rio Declaration on Environment and Development, which provides:

> **Rio Declaration**
> **Principle 13**
>
> "States shall develop national law regarding liability and compensation for the victims of pollution and other environmental damage. States shall also cooperate in an expeditious and more determined manner to develop further international law regarding liability and compensation for adverse effects of environmental damage caused by activities within their jurisdiction or control to areas beyond their jurisdiction."

30. Chapter 30 of Agenda 21 contains a framework for corporate environmental responsibility. The chapter entitled, "Strengthening the Role of Business and Industry," exhorts corporations to recognize environmental management as among the highest corporate priorities. How corporations operate and the policies they follow can play a major role in reducing impacts on resource use and the environment. In recognition of this, Chapter 30 puts forward two programme areas to further the role of business and industry. The first relates to "promoting cleaner production," which focuses on efficient resource utilization, reporting and codes of conduct on best environmental practices. The second programme highlights "promoting responsible entrepreneurship," which requires the implementation of sustainable development policies and responsible and ethical management of products and processes.

31. Chapter 30 has been considered by some to be the most important chapter within Agenda 21; when the chapter was published, it took an unprecedented approach to the role of business and the environment. It clearly identified that corporations were necessary for achieving sustainable development. In addition, chapter 30 highlighted the role of mixed policy initiatives from economic instruments, regulation and voluntary practices to encourage and persuade corporations to achieve improved environmental performance, whilst also achieving economic development.

b) Pesticides Code

32. The International Code of Conduct on the Distribution and Use of Pesticides ("Pesticides Code") is the worldwide guidance document on pesticide management for all public and private entities engaged in, or associated with, the distribution and use of pesticides, including governmental authorities and the pesticide industry. The Pesticides Code was adopted in 1985 and is designed to provide standards of conduct and to serve as a point of reference in relation to sound pesticide management practices.

33. The Pesticides Code sets out standards of conduct for businesses engaged in distribution, marketing, international trade and other activities involving pesticides. It was developed by the Food and Aricultural Organization ("FAO") in response to the health and environmental concerns about activities involving pesticides both in the country of manufacture and in countries to which they were exported, particularly developing countries. Some of the problems that the FAO identified were the export of banned pesticides to developing countries which caused chemical burns and other health problems, long persistence of pesticides in the environment, environmental contamination and other negative environmental impacts in destination countries, and the presence of residues of banned and restricted pesticides in imported agricultural commodities. Some of the developed countries expressing concerns are those whose businesses export the pesticides abroad, a problem known as "cycle of poison".

34. The FAO also noted that developing countries lacked necessary pesticide laws. Moreover, they had little capacity to determine whether pesticides whose uses are banned or restricted in the country of origin could be safely used in their importing countries. They lacked expertise to conduct scientific evaluations of pesticides to be able to effect appropriate regulations on domestic pesticide businesses. The FAO Pesticides Code provides some basic guidance on some of these issues. Article 4.1 of the Pesticides Code requires pesticide industries to carry out tests on pesticides to fully evaluate their hazard and risks to human health and the environment, taking into account the various conditions in regions or countries in which they are used. Pesticide industries are also required to share with governmental authorities, and with others carrying on pesticide trade, any information that they hold about the dangers and risks of pesticides.

35. Further, article 4 of the Pesticides Code requires industry engaged in manufacturing, distribution and use of pesticides to train their employees in the safe handling of pesticides to avoid causing harm to health and the environment. In addition, articles 6 through 10 of the Pesticides Code require pesticide manufacturers and others engaged in pesticide businesses to properly label all pesticides with correct information on their proper uses, hazardous nature, and precautionary measures. Pesticide manufactuers are also required to ensure that any unwanted pesticides or pesticide residues are disposed of in a proper way to avoid harm to human health and environmental contamination.

36. With regard to the export and import of banned and restricted pesticides, the FAO introduced a procedure for exchange of information between exporting and importing countries that adhere to the Pesticides Code. An important aspect of this procedure is the requirement under article 9 that developing countries make an informed decision on whether or not they will import pesticides that have been banned or restricted in exporting countries, and to give prior consent to every import of such pesticides. Once they do so, the Pesticides Code requires that they pass this information to the FAO, which then notifies other countries of measures to prohibit or restrict pesticide imports. On the other hand, the Pesticides Code also requires exporting countries to inform destination countries of any intended exports of banned or restricted pesticides. Countries that adhere to the Pesticides Code are required to establish national authorities or focal points to facilitate information exchange between the countries.

37. Although the application of the Pesticides Code has been voluntary, it has served as a useful point of reference, especially to countries that did not have laws to regulate pesticides. Its significance is also reflected in the binding international agreements that have been subsequently created to regulate pesticides, such as the Basel, Bamako and Prior Informed Consent Conventions. In these and other international agreements, the prior informed consent procedure and other aspects of the Pesticides Code have been incorporated and have become legally-binding on states that are parties to those agreements.

38. Further, although implementation of the Pesticides Code has been voluntary, a number of industries and industry associations have adopted and applied it. For example, CropLife America has actively supported implementation of the Pesticides Code among its members. CropLife

America is the national trade association representing the developers, manufacturers, formulators and distributors of plant science solutions for agriculture and pest management in the United States. Its member companies develop, produce, sell and distribute virtually all the crop protection and biotechnology products used by American farmers. The mission of CropLife is to foster the interests of the general public and CropLife member companies, which it does by promoting innovation and the environmentally sound discovery, manufacture, distribution and use of crop protection products. CropLife has found the Pesticides Code useful in accomplishing this mission. On the basis of the Pesticides Code, it encourages members to adopt environmentally sound production methods, and to comply with relevant laws for environmental and health protection.

c) Fisheries Code

39. The FAO has also developed a Code of Conduct for Responsible Fisheries ("Fisheries Code"), which has been substantively discussed in chapter 17 of this Manual. In article 6(6) and in other provisions, the Fisheries Code sets out rules and standards specifically for the fisheries industry and requires, for example, that those engaged in fisheries activities select environmentally safe fishing gear and adopt fishing practices that will not lead to depletion of fish stocks.

40. Although it is voluntary and has no enforcement mechanisms, the Fisheries Code has been adopted and applied by fisheries industries in a number of countries. In Australia, for example, the Fisheries Code has been used to develop a Code of Conduct for a Responsible Seafood Industry by the Australian Seafood Council ("Australian Code"). The Australian Code sets out principles and standards of behaviour for responsible practices to ensure that those engaged in the seafood industry carry out their activities in an ecologically sustainable manner. The principles and standards set out are intended to ensure the effective conservation, management and development of living aquatic resources, with due respect to ecosystem and biodiversity. For example, it requires those engaged in the seafood industry to minimize the catch of non-target species, minimize the incidental catch of non-utilized species including marine mammals, reptiles and seabirds and to avoid causing adverse impacts on associated or dependent species. To meet these requirements, it recommends limitation of the sizes of fishing nets and other gear, modification of

fishing gear where necessary and effecting closed areas or closed fishing seasons to allow fish stocks to increase.

d) OECD Guidelines

41. The OECD is an economic organization whose thirty member countries include, *inter alia*, the United Kingdom, United States, Japan, Australia, Belgium, Canada, Greece, Mexico and Finland. The OECD's guidelines are a set of standards and rules to govern multinational corporations and other businesses from or operating within their countries that were developed in constructive dialogue with the business community, labour representatives and Non-Governmental Organizations in member countries. The guidelines are intended to be applied by the businesses to domestic and overseas activities on a voluntary basis and as part of OECD's policy efforts to achieve the highest attainable economic growth in member countries and to promote the economic development of countries in which OECD multinationals carry out business. The OECD's guidelines supplement applicable national and international laws governing business activities and have been applied worldwide, even by businesses other than those originating in OECD countries. The OECD seeks to accomplish its objectives through the guidelines by, among other things, addressing health and environmental problems that might result from business activities. Therefore, the guidelines cover a broad range of issues, including consumer interests, such as health, safety and the environment.

42. The section of the OECD's guidelines on environment encourages multinational enterprises to raise environmental performance through improved internal environmental management. This requires, for example, that businesses originating in OECD countries make efforts to develop technologies that reduce emissions of hazardous substances and gases into the atmosphere. The guidelines also require multinational corporations to have good contingency plans to avoid adverse environmental impacts. Amongst other things, multinational corporations must maintain contingency plans for preventing and mitigating the consequences of industrial accidents and emergencies.

43. Further, multinational corporations are required to conduct assessments of the potential impacts of their planned business activities. The essence of this is that where assessment shows that high and unacceptable levels of environmental harm are

likely to result, planned activities should be abandoned. Assessments are also to be conducted in the course of conducting business activities and the guidelines require multinational corporations to take cost-effective measures to deal with actual and potential impacts on health and the environment revealed by assessments. Corporations are required to develop and provide products or services that have no undue environmental impacts, are safe in their intended use, are efficient in their consumption of energy and natural resources, and can be reused, recycled, or disposed of safely. Corporations are also required to adhere to and to respect laws, regulations and administrative practices, including international agreements that affect their businesses in the countries in which they operate.

44. There is no mechanism for enforcing these standards, but governments that are members of the OECD are expected to encourage companies in their countries to observe this code of conduct. Each member country is supposed to set up a national contact point- a government office or body that includes representatives of government agencies, industries and other interested parties to facilitate application of the guidelines. Under the OECD scheme, any interested party can file a complaint regarding alleged violations of the OECD Guidelines with the national contact points. Although no legal enforcement of the guidelines, even by the national contact points is envisaged, efforts by governments to implement the guidelines have led to their acceptance and application in many business activities.

e) International Standards - ISO

45. The International Standards Organization ("ISO") is a network comprising national standards institutes of 156 countries, on the basis of one member per country. It is a Non-Governmental Organization and its national delegates represent all the economic stakeholders concerned including private businesses, consumers, government regulators and other interest groups. Thus, ISO is able to act as a bridging organization in which a consensus can be reached on solutions that meet the requirements of all interested parties. The ISO, which officially began operations on 23 February 1947, has a Central Secretariat in Geneva, Switzerland, that coordinates its work.

46. The ISO's specific role is to facilitate the international coordination and unification of industrial standards. In its work to achieve this purpose, ISO has developed uniform standards for a wide variety of products, services, business processes, operations and coding of products and other items. ISO sets standards, for example, by specifying what quality standard a certain item must meet, to be generally acceptable in that business sector. It may also specify that to be of a particular acceptable quality, a product must have certain components or appear in a certain shape and colour. In construction, ISO might specify, for example, that a building intended for manufacturing pesticides must have ventilation and other engineering requirements. The specifications become the world standards that product qualities, engineering designs, manufacturing processes, safety operations, business activities and services must meet to be acceptable, or to be suitable for use internationally. These then become the rules with respect to products, services and designs that are applicable internationally.

47. Between 1947 and today, ISO has developed more than 13,700 international standards for a wide spectrum of products, activities, services, technologies and the like. For example, standards for screw threads help keep the frames of children's bicycles and aircraft together, and solve the repair and maintenance problems that could be caused by lack of standardization. ISO standards such as these allow international consensus on terminology, quality, quantity and other aspects of products and processes, thus making technology transfer easier.

48. In addition, ISO has developed specific standards that relate directly to public health and environmental protection. The first is ISO 9000, which is a series of product quality management standards or requirements that can help all business organizations, including industry, to manufacture products, adopt production processes in the manufacture of the products and provide services that meet customer satisfaction and requirements, and are recognized throughout the world. Included in the ISO 9000 requirements is a description of production practices that a company follows to ensure that its products and services met customer satisfaction. The ISO 9000 series of standards of requirements can achieve public health and environmental objectives, for example, by ensuring that manufactured products and services rendered are of such qualities that do not harm health and the environment.

49. Unlike ISO 9000, whose major system requirements are defined by customers and other stakeholders, ISO 14000 lays out standards for

environmental management, including standards for Environmental Management Systems ("EMS") under ISO 14001. ISO 14000 is primarily concerned with what a business organization does to manage the impacts of its activities on the environment and the system includes methods of evaluating environmental impacts and for responding to emergencies. For example, if a business is engaged in manufacturing, ISO will specify what the business needs to do to avoid environmental contamination. Whatever ISO specifies is achievable by similar manufacturing activities anywhere in the world to meet the same ends of environmental protection- minimizing harmful effects on the environment caused by its activities, and enabling businesses to continually improve their environmental performance. The ISO 14000 series of standards emerged primarily as a result of two major events with potentially conflicting goals, namely the Uruguay Round of negotiations of the GATT, which began in 1986, and the Rio Conference on Environment and Development held in 1992. While the GATT talks addressed the need to avoid or remove non-tariff barriers to trade, the Rio Earth Summit established an international commitment for protection of the global environment. With careful implementation, ISO 14000 standards should unite both trade and environmental concerns, more so because it has the potential to promote world trade while at the same time encouraging and assisting industries to be more environmentally responsible.

50. ISO standards are voluntary. As a Non-Governmental Organization, ISO has no legal authority to enforce the implementation of its standards. However, the standards have been widely applied in many countries by manufacturers and other businesses and by governments. In many countries, the standards have been incorporated into national legislation for control of businesses and have legal market requirements. For example, ISO's specifications of dimensions of freight containers and bank cards have been adopted world wide. In addition, the environmental standards, for example, ISO 9000, are currently implemented by more than half a million organizations in more sixty countries. The environmental standards provide the organisations with a framework for quality management throughout the processes of producing and delivering products and services for the customer that ensures health and environmental safety and protection. The fact that the standards are developed in response to market demand, and are based on consensus among the interested parties, ensures their widespread applicability. It is important to note that the supply chain promotes

ISO standards, for example, by a business demanding that its suppliers meet ISO standards.

f) Other instruments

51. In addition to the non-binding international instruments, there exists a large body of rules, regulations, codes of practice, conduct and guidelines developed by businesses themselves for their own self-regulation, on a voluntary basis. Many of these are developed by business organisations, and are specific to particular sectors. For example, in the tourism and travel sector, there exists a Charter of Ethics for Tourism and the Environment, among others. Some are specific to particular industries, such as agro-chemicals and engineering, for which there are the Vancouver Communiqué and Code of Best Agricultural Practices to Optimize Fertilizer Use and the Code of Environmental Ethics for Engineers, respectively. There are also codes that apply across sectors, such as the Business Charter for Sustainable Development that was initiated by the International Chamber of Commerce. Many of the codes and other industry regulations are applicable internationally. There are also individual businesses that have developed rules for their own application.

52. For example, the Business Charter for Sustainable Development ("Business Charter"), which was formally launched in April 1991, sets out sixteen principles on environmental management to guide businesses in their investment ventures and business activities. The Business Charter directs businesses that before starting an activity or enterprise, they should conduct an assessment of the project's environmental impacts. Similarly, they should conduct an assessment of the impacts of historic activities before decommissioning a facility or leaving a site.

53. Further, as a matter of priority, corporate entities should establish and implement policies, programmes and practices for conducting their operations in an environmentally sound manner. Once this is done, corporate entities should integrate these policies, programmes and practices fully into each business as an essential element of managing all of its functions. As an essential component of environmental measures, they should also educate, train, and motivate employees to conduct their activities in an environmentally responsible manner. The guidelines provided by the Business Charter are vital for sustainable development.

54. Although the application of the provisions of the Business Charter and other regulations in this category is voluntary, the provisions are often adhered to by businesses for a variety of reasons. For some, adherence is due to pressure from consumer groups and non-governmental organizations to maintain clean and safe products and production processes. For others, adherence is a matter of business decisions to maintain good reputation and good standing with governments, consumers and other stakeholders, or to cut the cost of environmentally damaging ways of doing business. For example, members of European Fertilizer Manufacturers Association ("EFMA") subscribe to the principles contained in the Business Charter and promote them within their organisations while undertaking programmes under Responsible Care, their self-regulation guideline. Industries that are members of EFMA have embraced the environmental principles set out in the Business Charter in their operations.

55. Within Europe, the European Chemical Industry Council, of which EFMA is an affiliated member, coordinates the development and implementation of principles, programmes and activities under Responsible Care and the Business Charter. The EFMA has developed best available techniques booklets covering the production processes for all the main fertilizer products for use by the authorities in the process of developing European best available fertilizer technologies that would prevent harm to human health and the environment.

56. Private business has the potential for good and bad. Further, there is an increasing awareness of the potential of business activities to cause negative health and environmental impacts that are likely to increase with accelerated rates of business activity especially cross-border activity. Existing international controls over businesses, including multinational corporations, are mostly non-legally binding and the examples provided show that there is an increase in the emphasis given to this form of regulation. In relation to self-regulation and voluntary codes, there have been a number of catalysts, including stakeholder or company-to-company pressure, the influence of investors in the form of large shareholders and insurers, and company reporting which increasingly includes environmental reporting.

57. Among its many benefits, non-legally binding agreements can be more practical and effective in controlling business conduct, especially where it crosses boundaries. Non-legally binding documents are also driven by market forces and can deliver greater benefits where businesses are prepared to go beyond what the law requires in order to gain competitive advantage. Non-legally binding agreements are also seen to be cheaper than the cost of regulation to the state in enforcing and to business in complying, which is increasingly becoming unacceptable. Moreover, they are perceived as quicker to develop and more flexible than legislation. Where a non-legally binding agreement is developed with full participation by all interests involved thus genuinely representing a consensus on what action is best, they can work in a more satisfactory manner.

58. Where non-legally binding agreements are lacking, or where there is scepticism about non-legally binding documents because of inadequate self-regulatory schemes which appear merely cosmetic, stringent regulation may be preferred because they carry sanctions for breaches and may be preferred as better guarantees of effectiveness. There are also specific areas where most consumers and consumer organizations would not accept non-legally binding agreements as an approach to regulation, especially on matters of fraud, risk to life and/or health, where unfair advantage is taken of people vulnerable for a variety of reasons, where competition alone cannot deliver essential services to consumers who are not of commercial interest to suppliers, and where strict regulation is needed to make competition work. Society in general has an interest in the outcome of regulation in these areas beyond the collective interest of individual consumers, which non-legally binding agreements alone cannot guarantee.

3. Regional Agreements

a) North American Free Trade Agreement

59. The North American Agreement on Environmental Cooperation Between the Governments of Canada, The Government of the United Mexican States and the Government of the United States of America ("NAAEC") is a regional agreement between the governments of Canada, Mexico and the United States that was adopted on 10 September 1993, and currently is in force. The agreement came as a supplement to the North American Free Trade Agreement ("NAFTA") that was created the same year and came into force on 1 January 2004. NAFTA was intended to promote free trade between the three parties but it was realised, shortly after its conclusion, that free trade between the countries might adversely affect environmental

conditions in the countries. This realisation prompted the creation of the side environmental agreement.

60. The three parties to the environmental agreement were convinced of the importance of conservation, protection, and enhancement of the environment in their territories in achieving sustainable development for the well-being of present and future generations. It was felt that real benefits of trade between the parties could only be realised if trade did not result in environmental deficits. Among other rules affecting private businesses in the countries, article 1(d-f) of NAAEC requires parties to promote the use of economic instruments for the efficient achievement of environmental goals. This means, for example, that parties could tax manufacturers for emitting pollutants into the atmosphere to persuade them to adopt cleaner methods of production.

61. Further, article 2 of NAAEC requires parties to regulate imports and exports of products by businesses in the relevant countries. Specifically, businesses are prohibited from exporting to any one of the three countries substances that are prohibited in their country and parties have the responsibility to ensure that the prohibition is complied with. For example, if the use of a particular chemical is banned in the United States because of its potential to cause adverse health and environmental impacts, businesses in Canada and Mexico are prohibited from exporting that chemical to the United States. Similarly, businesses in the United States will be prohibited from importing that chemical from Canada or Mexico, and any other country. Enforcement of the regulation is through machinery established at the national and regional levels to ensure adherence to the agreement.

62. In order to achieve high levels of environmental protection and compliance with environmental laws and regulations established in the agreement and in the national legislation of parties, each party is required by articles 2(a)- (f) and 37 of NAAEC to effectively enforce its environmental laws and regulations through appropriate governmental action. This may include conducting inspections of manufacturing and other business premises and the adoption of licensing and permitting requirements to control discharges of pollutants and mitigate other kinds of environmental harm. Further, in addition to national offices and authorities, parties are required to create inter-governmental commissions and bodies through which cross-border activities likely to cause environmental harm can be controlled. In view of accelerated rate

of trade between parties that NAFTA would encourage, effective implementation is demanded to prevent and reduce pollution and other harmful environmental effects that businesses could cause within the countries.

b) Association of South East Asian Nations

63. Unlike the constitutional basis of the European Union, the Association of South East Asian Nations ("ASEAN"), established in 1967, is based more upon mutual agreements and common goals rather than upon legislative acts. ASEAN is comprised of ten member states, including Indonesia, Malaysia, Philippines, Singapore, Thailand, Brunei Darussalam, Vietnam, Laos, Myanmar and Cambodia, with a population of about 500 million. Business and industry play a crucial role in the social and economic development of the region and the abundance of natural resources to be found in the member states contribute to the regions economic growth. ASEAN is faced with the challenge of balancing environmental concerns with the imperatives of development. ASEAN has recognised that the protection of the environment and the sustainable management of natural resources are essential to the long-term economic growth of the region.

64. A main goal of ASEAN is the harmonisation of environmental laws and standards throughout the region. However, a prime motive for the creation of the Association was to achieve peaceful co-operation amongst the members, whilst maintaining mutual respect for each other's independence and sovereignty. As such, agreements negotiated at ASEAN must be ratified and implemented into national laws. Most environmental agreements are still not in force, for example, the 1985 Agreement on Conservation of Nature and Natural Resources. This Agreement is one of the only environmental agreements to specifically contain provisions relating to business. Article 10(b) requires the development of sound industrial processes and products and article 10(d) holds the originator of any environmental degradation responsible for its prevention, reduction and wherever possible, for rehabilitation and remediation.

65. One agreement that has entered into force, in November 2003, is the ASEAN Agreement on Transboundary Haze Pollution. See chapter 8 above. It is the first such regional arrangement in the world that binds a group of contiguous states to tackle transboundary haze pollution resulting from land and forest fires. Members accepted that small farmers or large plantation companies, to clear

land at a minimum cost, had often deliberately set fires. ASEAN recognised not only the environmental degradation caused by the fires but also highlighted the negative impact on the region's economy. A zero burn policy has been implemented and a number of plantation companies have been investigated and prosecuted for illegal burning. Part of the zero burn policy includes dialogue with plantation companies to raise awareness of zero burn practices and techniques and has developed a best practice policy on zero and controlled burning for companies within the region. This may be an indicator to businesses that were the environment and the economy are intrinsically linked, countries within this region may be more willing to act.

c) European Union

66. As discussed above, international agreements on the liability of business for environmental damage are not easy to achieve, but at a regional level more may be possible. In 2004, the European Union introduced the European Union Directive on Environmental Liability, a legal measure committing all member states to introduce liability rules where industrial operators cause serious damage to natural resources (land, water, species and habitats). If activity in the course of a business or undertaking causes such damage then liability will result. For operational activities scheduled in the law (basically, industries regulated under European environmental law) liability will be strict (i.e., it is necessary only to show causation). Other operators can be liable but only if fault is proven.

67. Imminent threats can be curtailed by demanding preventive action. Where damage does occur, immediate clean-up and control will be necessary, but there will also be liability to ensure the longer term restoration of the site. If this takes time then interim damages for biodiversity loss can be ordered. This will generally take the form of some additional compensatory remediation or perhaps at another habitat. Such liability for biodiversity damage (e.g., to a species not in the ownership of any natural or legal person) is unusual, and non-governmental organizations have the right to request action. This is thought to be necessary to prompt intervention on behalf of the environment. Member states within Europe have the option of allowing a defence to the operator where it can show that the operation met the requirements of an environmental permit, or where the operator was working according to the state of scientific or technical knowledge at the time of the damage.

68. It remains to be seen how effective these provisions will prove to be as they have yet to come into force. However, combined with the greater transparency demanded of industry in relation to environmental performance, and easier access to information on the state of the environment, held by public bodies, there could be early requests by NGOs for legal action, to which the competent authorities will then be mandated to respond. The stumbling blocks may prove the difficulties in proving causation in relation to, for example, the deterioration of habitats, the lack of background data on the state of habitats, and the costing of remedial measures where these are not simply a question of restoration cost.

III. National Implementation:
National Legislation Governing Private Businesses

69. National legislation strengthens compliance with international environmental agreements and other instruments. National legislation also represents national policy on why, how and which businesses and industries must be controlled to protect health and the environment from adverse impacts. This part of the chapter is intended to provide examples of national legislation, including the implementation of business regulations established at the international level and laws that incorporate various industrial and other business codes. It also provides examples of how the legislation has been implemented and its applicability to the prevention of harm to health and to the environment from business activities based in two developed and two developing countries.

1. The Oil Pollution Act of the United States of America

70. The Oil Pollution Act of 1990 ("OPA") and the federal rules made under it in Title 33 of the Codes of Federal Regulations, parts 155 and 157 of 1996, are the United States' federal laws that regulates oil production, transportation and distribution industries. One of the specific matters regulated by OPA is the construction and size of oil vessels. Section 5225 of OPA provides that a tank vessel shall have or be constructed with a "double hull," but it does not define what amounts to a double hull. To fill the gap, the United States Coast Guard promulgated regulations, which were published on 10 March 1996, stating that a double hull construction shall have dimensions consistent with standards established by the International Maritime Organisation ("IMO"), an established United Nations agency with the responsibility of setting standards and adopting regulations that apply to all

vessels that operate internationally. The United States had adopted its standards for vessel construction earlier the same year.

71. A sample provision of OPA is as follows:

> **Rules for the Protection of the Marine Environment Relating to Tank Vessels Carrying Oil in Bulk Title 33—chapter I, part 157**
>
> (a) With the exceptions stated in Sec. 157.08(n), this section applies to a tank vessel-- (1) For which the building contract is awarded after June 30, 1990; (2) That is delivered after December 31, 1993; (3) That undergoes a major conversion for which; (I) The contract is awarded after June 30, 1990; or (ii) Conversion is completed after December 31, 1993; or (4) That is otherwise required to have a double hull by 46 U.S.C.
> (b) Each vessel to which this section applies must be fitted with: (1) A double hull in accordance with this section; and (2) If Sec.157.10 applies, segregated ballast tanks and a crude oil washing system in accordance with that section.
> (c) Except on a vessel to which Sec. 157(10d) (d) applies, tanks within the cargo tank length that carry any oil must be protected by double sides and a double bottom as follows: (1) Double sides must extend for the full depth of the vessel's side or from the uppermost deck, disregarding a rounded gunwale where fitted, to the top of the double bottom..." Subpart B--Design, Equipment, and Installation." (Sec. 157.10d, Double hulls on tank vessels).

72. The laws concerning double hull requirements for oil tankers have been applied in many court cases filed by persons engaged in the shipping industry in the United States. For example, in the case of Ray vs. Atlantic Richfield Company, the United States Supreme Court struck down the laws of one of the states that attempted to set out tanker construction regulations conflicting with the double hull federal requirements. This means that the federal government of the United States has overriding powers to regulate matters concerning tanker construction and design and can apply rules acceptable internationally for this purpose. This position was reaffirmed by Court in another 1996 case, International Association of Independent Tanker Owners vs. Lowery.

73. In a similar case, Maritrans Inc. vs. United States, a domestic tank operator sued the United States in the United States Supreme Court, alleging that the premature retirement of its single-hull tank vessels (that failed to meet double hull requirements by the date stipulated) was unconstitutional because it amounted to taking of its property without compensation. The Supreme Court applied the double hull laws and the authority of the federal government to enforce the laws and ruled that in fact retiring the complainant's vessels was lawful.

2. Philippine Fisheries Code of 1998

74. The preamble to the Philippines Fisheries Code ("Philippines Code") states that the code is the Philippine's law for the development, management and conservation of fisheries and aquatic resources. The Philippines Code incorporates many of the principles set out in the FAO Code of Conduct for Responsible Fisheries, as well as the fisheries regulations established under UNCLOS and its Agreement on Straddling Fish Stocks and Highly Migratory Fish Species. The Philippines is one of the parties to UNCLOS. Section 4(1) of the Philippines Code states that Code applies to The Philippines fisheries sectors, including firms or companies that supply, construct and maintain fishing vessels and nets. In relation to these matters, the Philippines Code makes provisions that echo the language of UNCLOS and the FAO Code.

75. The Philippines Code strictly regulates fisheries activities and, among other things, places a limit on the amount of fish catch that is allowed for particular businesses operating in Philippine waters under Sections 4(7) and 8. This is intended to guard against over-fishing that might lead to loss of species of fish. Section 4(4) of the Philippines Code also prohibits pollution of the waters forming part of the territory of the Philippines and requires those engaged in fishing and related activities to take all reasonable steps, measures and actions to avoid polluting the waters in the course of their activities. Further, Section 9 of the Philippines Code provides for closed seasons during which fishing may not take place in all or parts of its waters to allow increase in fish stocks and prevent depletion of fish species. Under Section 12, the Code requires environmental impact assessment of the waters to be conducted to determine whether and to what extent fisheries activities are causing pollution and other adverse impacts. This would allow appropriate measures to be taken to deal with such problems. In addition, Sections 30 and 51 provide for licensing of fishing vessels, including commercial boats. Conditions may be placed on licences to ensure proper fishing practices that would avoid damage to fish and other marine living organisms, and to the marine environment.

76. A sample provision of the Philippines Code is as follows:

**The Philippine Fisheries Code of 1998
Republic Act No. 8550, Section 12**

"The Secretary may prescribe limitations or quota on the total quantity of fish captured, for a specified period of time and specified area based on the best available evidence. Such a catch ceiling may be imposed per species of fish whenever necessary and practicable: Provided, however, that in municipal waters and fishery management areas, and waters under the jurisdiction of special agencies, catch ceilings may be established upon the concurrence and approval or recommendation of such special agency and the concerned. (Section 8)

All government agencies as well as private corporations, firms and entities who intend to undertake activities or projects which will affect the quality of the environment shall be required to prepare a detailed Environmental Impact Statement (EIS) prior to undertaking such development activity. The preparation of the EIS shall form an integral part of the entire planning process pursuant to the provisions of Presidential Decree No. 1586 as well as its implementing rules and regulations."

---

77. The Philippine's Department of Environment and Natural Resources is the governmental authority charged with the responsibility of implementing the Philippines Code. In collaboration with the country's League of Municipalities of the Philippines, the department has undertaken a number of coastal resources management conservation activities under the Philippines Code. These comprise actions, steps and programmes that achieve sustainable use and management of economically and ecologically valuable resources in the coastal areas, including the training of coastal communities on the use of proper fishing gear and proper waste disposal methods to avoid pollution of the waters. This earned the department and collaborating organisations a Best Coastal Management Programs Award in 1998.

3. National Pollutant Inventory of Australia

78. Increasingly, businesses are being required to provide information on the environmental impacts of their operational activities. Individuals, communities, and non-government organizations seek information on what emissions businesses release into air, land and water. The concept of the community right to know as an element of "environmental democracy" allows all those affected by the outcome of environmental issues, not just governments and industry, to have access to environmental information, which allows community members to be a part of any decision-making process. In essence, it is an instrument to make business operation more transparent and more accountable to the wider community. In return, people gain information on potential risks and hazards to the environment and to human health.

79. In a commitment to community right to know, the Federal Government of Australia introduced the National Pollutant Inventory ("NPI") which, was adopted as the first National Environmental Protection Measure in 1998. NPI is an Internet database designed to provide community, industry and government with information on the types and amounts of substances emitted into the environment from business facilities. NPI requires large industrial facilities, within certain identified industrial sectors, to report the emission of selected pollutants over a specified threshold on an annual basis. Estimates are based on self-reporting of discharges, which are prepared as a condition of an emission licence. The purpose of the database is not only to provide publicly accessible and available information on emissions to the environment, but also to provide information to enhance and facilitate policy formulation and decision-making. The system is dependent upon the self-reporting of those businesses required to participate.

80. However, Australian industries are required to report on only ninety substances, in contrast, American industries must report on nearly 600 substances in the Toxic Release Inventory. The extent of the NPI does not extend to information on storage, transportation or to the disposal of chemicals. A further criticism of NPI is that it is restricted to only a few facilities and therefore only provides selective information. To encourage candid reporting, clause 26 of the NPI states that information supplied will not be used as evidence in any legal proceedings. The intention is to encourage businesses to be open and honest about their activities, thereby providing accurate data.

81. As a Federal Government instrument of community right to know, the NPI fails. Exemptions, compliance and enforcement of the system are the responsibility of each individual Australian state. As a result, there are a number of inequalities in the practice and procedure of the system. For example, only New South Wales' Protection of the Environment Operations Act of 1997 permits third party enforcement, a central

principle of a successful community right to know system. Businesses within different states in Australia, therefore, experience different legislative requirements. However, the NPI can be used by businesses as a benchmark for their emissions and case studies on eco-efficiency are available for different industrial sectors providing details on cleaner production techniques and therefore means of reducing emissions.

4. Kenya and the Standards Act (Chapter 496)

82. The process of Kenya's development of standards for industry is very closely linked to standards setting activities of the ISO. To promote development, adoption and application of standards for products and services, the Kenyan government created the Kenya Bureau of Standards ("KBS") through the Standards Act, Chapter 496. The KBS is a member of the ISO, and has, through the years, participated in ISO's standard setting and standard specification activities that have been discussed previously within this Chapter.

83. In Kenya, the KBS is the governmental body charged with the statutory responsibility for setting industry standards for products and services. In this respect, activities of the KBS include actual development and specification of acceptable ingredients, qualities, and uses of products, among other standards. For example, KBS has set standards for the pesticide, diazinon, which specifies that diazinon must have a technical grade material and emulsifiable concentrates of a particular kind. The standards for diazinon also specify that in Kenya, diazinon refers to the acceptable common name by the ISO for diethyl (isoprophyl-6-methyl-4pyrimidyl) phosphorothiate.

84. Under Section 4 of the Standards Act, activities of the KBS also include: promoting adoption; development and application of standards in industry and commerce; assisting the government, industry and businesses with preparation of suitable codes of practice; controlling products that are marketed in the country, both locally manufactured and imports. To be able to perform these functions efficiently and to ensure that standards established are uniform to those of the ISO, the KBS collaborates very closely with the ISO. It has participated in ISO training and other capacity-building activities and has adopted many of ISO's standards for application in Kenya.

85. Sample provisions of the Standards Act are as follows:

**Kenya Standards Act
Section 9(4)**

An Act of Parliament to promote the standardisation of the specification of commodities, and to provide for the standardisation of commodities and codes of practice; to establish a Kenya Bureau of Standards, to define its functions and provide for its management and control; and for matters incidental to, and connected with, the foregoing. (Preamble.)

Where a Kenya standard has been declared under subsection (1), the Minister, on the advice of the council, shall, by order in the Gazette, prescribe a date after which no person shall manufacture or sell any commodity, method or procedure to which the relevant specification or code of practice relates unless it complies with that specification or code of practice. (Section 9(2).)

Where any person manufactures, or intends to manufacture, any commodity in respect of which a standardisation mark has been specified under paragraph (b) of subsection (1), he may notify the Bureau of his intention to comply with the approved specification and his wish to apply the relevant standardisation mark, and the Bureau, if it is satisfied that he is capable of manufacturing the commodity in accordance with the relevant specification, shall issue him with a permit to use that standardisation mark.

---

86. The KBS also has the statutory mandate to participate in the enforcement of established standards and is involved in the implementation of Chapter 496 to ensure that goods and items sold in Kenya, including imports, meet standards and specification that are acceptable in the country. To make this possible, the KBS has established, under its statutory authority, testing facilities in Nairobi where products are tested to determine whether they meet acceptable standards. The KBS carries out regular inspections of manufacturing and other premises, especially where complaints are made that particular products are causing health or environmental harm. In such cases, the KBS takes samples of the products, tests them at its facilities and if found to fall short of established standards, it has authority to confiscate them for safe disposal.

87. Further, by Legal Notice Number 227 of 1995, the Kenya Government expanded the functions of KBS and gave it authority to inspect imported products, including chemicals, to determine whether the products meet national standards before they are released into the Kenyan market. For this purpose, the KBS has set up offices at major entry points to

the country, including Mombasa and Busia. In the course of inspection, if KBS finds that imports do not meet specified standards, or that they can be harmful to health and the environment, the practice has been to take legal action to send them back to their country of origin.

88. These examples of national legislation show that appreciable efforts have been made to implement international instruments to regulate business and industry at domestic levels. However, there is still a lot of room at the national level for all players, including governments, environmental organizations and other parties to increase efforts to cause business and industry to adopt and implement voluntary and legally binding measures to ensure that business activities are conducted in a

manner that reduces and/or prevents adverse impacts on health and the environment. In particular, developing countries should be encouraged to incorporate the concept of sustainable development into their policies and regulatory mechanisms to allow consideration of the costs and benefits of business activity as a means to achieve development.

Prof. Robert Lee, Co-director ESRC Research Centre for Business Relationships, Accountability, Sustainability and Society (BRASS)/ Cardiff Law School, Cardiff University

Dr. Jane Dwasi, UNEP Consultant, University of Nairobi

Resources

Internet Materials

A US Non-Governmental Delegation Trip Report, Oil for Nothing: Multinational Corporations, Environmental Destruction and Impunity in the Niger, Delta available at www.essentialaction.org/shell/Final_Report.pdf

Environmental Compliance and Audits home page available at http://www.businesslaws.com/envtl.htm

Organisation for Economic Co-operation and Development, Corporate Governance available at http://www.oecd.org/topic/0,2686,en_2649_37439_1_1_1_1_37439,00.html

Overview of the Environmental Laws of Mexico available at http://www.natlaw.com/pubs/spmxen13.htm

Silicon Valley/San Jose Business Journal, Europe's Environmental Laws Impact U.S. High Tech available at http://www.bizjournals.com/sanjose/stories/2003/04/28/daily16.html

Transnational Corporations and Environmental Damage: Is Tort Law the Answer, Michael Anderson available at http://washburnlaw.edu/wlj/41-3/articles/ande.pdf

United Nations Environment Programme, UNEP Activities in Business and Industry available at http://www.unep.org/themes/business/

United Nations, The Global Impact available at http://www.unglobalcompact.org/Portal/Default.asp

United States Environmental Law search page available at http://www.business.com/search/rslt_default.asp?r4=t&query=us+environmental+laws

The World Health Organisation's Framework Convention on Tobacco Control available at www.fctc.org

World Environment Laws available at http://www.hg.org/environ.html

Text Materials

Aaron Gershonowitz, How The Environmental Regulatory System Works: A Business Primer (2nd ed.) (Government Institutes, 1993).

Daniel R. Mandelker, ENVIRONMENT AND EQUITY: A REGULATORY CHALLENGE (McGraw-Hill, 1981).

Dave Frohnmayer, ENVIRONMENT AND BUSINESS: COMPLEMENTS NOT OPPOSITES IN A NEW ERA, 11 J. Envtl. L. & Litig. 1 (1996).

DIANE S. CALENDINE, INVESTIGATING THE EXXON VALDEZ RESTORATION EFFORT: IS RESOURCE ACQUISITION REALLY RESTORATION?, 9 Dick J. Env. L. Pol. 341 (Fall 2000).

Elizabeth Glass Geltman, ENVIRONMENTAL LAW AND BUSINESS: CASES AND MATERIALS, (Michie Co., 1994).

Engaging Stakeholders: The Benchmark Survey: THE THIRD INTERNATIONAL PROGRESS REPORT ON COMPANY ENVIRONMENTAL REPORTING, S.1.: Sustainability: UNEP (1997).

Eric B. Rothberg, Sara B. Alyea & Courtney A. Smith, ENVIRONMENTAL ISSUES IN BUSINESS TRANSACTIONS UNDER U.S. LAW, 5 Wis. Envtl. L. J. 121 (Summer 1998).

Geoffrey Thomas, Moira L. Mc Connell & Lynne B. Huestis, ENVIRONMENTAL LAW AND BUSINESS IN CANADA, (Canada Law Book, 1993).

Gerard A. Caron, SEC DISCLOSURE REQUIREMENTS FOR CONTINGENT ENVIRONMENTAL LIABILITY, 14 B.C. Envtl. Aff. L. Rev. 729 (Summer 1987).
Jay D. Hair, BUSINESS AND ENVIRONMENT: THE EXPANDING DIALOGUE, 15 Envtl. L. 745 (Summer 1985).

Jeffery H. Leonard, ARE ENVIRONMENTAL REGULATIONS DRIVING U.S. INDUSTRY OVERSEAS, (Conservation Foundation, 1984).

Jochen Jesinghaus & Richard Janssen, ECOLOGICAL TAX REFROM: A POLICY PROPOSAL FOR SUSTAINABLE DEVELOPMENT, (Zed Books, 1992).

John R. Salter, CORPORATE ENVIRONMENTAL RESPONSIBILITY: LAW AND PRACTISE, (Butterworth Legal Pubs., 1992).

Joseph F. DiMento, ENVIRONMENTAL LAW AND AMERICAN BUSINESS: DILEMMAS OF COMPLIANCE, (Plenum Press, 1986).

Kerry R. Turner, ENVIRONMENTAL ECONOMICS: AN ELEMENTARY INTRODUCTION, (John Hopkins University Press, 1993).

Klaus North, ENVIRONMENTAL BUSINESS MANAGEMENT: AN INTRODUCTION, (International Labor Organization Office, 1992).

Linda S. Spedding et al, ECO-MANAGEMENT AND ECO-AUDITING: ENVIRONMENTAL ISSUES IN BUSINESS, (Chancery Law Pub., 1993).

Lisa K. Seilheimer, Supreme Court Review: October 1997 Term: United States v. Bestfoods, in 5 ENVTL. LAW. 303 (September 1998).

L.R. Jones, CORPORATE ENVIRONMENTAL POLICY AND GOVERNMENT REGULATION, (1994).

Marisa Yee, The Future of Environmental Regulation After Article 1110 of NAFTA: A Look at the Methanex and Metalclad Cases, in 9 HASTINGS W.-N.W. J. ENV. L. & POL'Y 85 (Fall 2002).

Mark Brealey (Ed.), ENVIRONMENTAL LIABILITIES AND REGULATION IN EUROPE, (International Business Pub., 1993).

Michael Ray Harris, An Examination of the Debate over Legal Protection for Environmental Audits, in 23 ECOLOGY L. Q. 663 (1996).

Michael S. Baram & Daniel G. Partan, CORPORATE DISCLOSURE OF ENVIRONMENTAL RISKS: U.S. AND EUROPEAN LAW, (Butterworth Legal Pubs., 1989).

Robert J. Fowler, International Environmental Standards for Transnational Corporations, in 25 ENVTL. L. 1 (Winter 1995).

Terra Pfund, Corporate Environmental Accountability, Expanding SEC Disclosures to Promote Market-Based Environmentalism, 11 MO. ENVTL. L. & POL'Y REV. 118 (2004).

Valerie Ann Zondorak, A New Face in Corporate Environmental Responsibility: The Valdez Principles, in 18 B.C. ENVTL. AFF. L. REV. 457 (Spring 1991).

Virginia Haufler, A PUBLIC ROLE FOR THE PRIVATE SECTOR: INDUSTRY SELF-REGULATION IN A GLOBAL ECONOMY, (2001).

William Hancock (Ed.), CORPORATE COUNCEL'S GUIDE TO ENVIRONMENTAL LAW, (Business Laws, Inc., 1989).